Belgium & Luxembourg

written and researched by

Martin Dunford and Phil Lee

with additional contributions by

Gavin Thomas and Michael Jackson

ROUGH GUIDES

www.roughguides.com

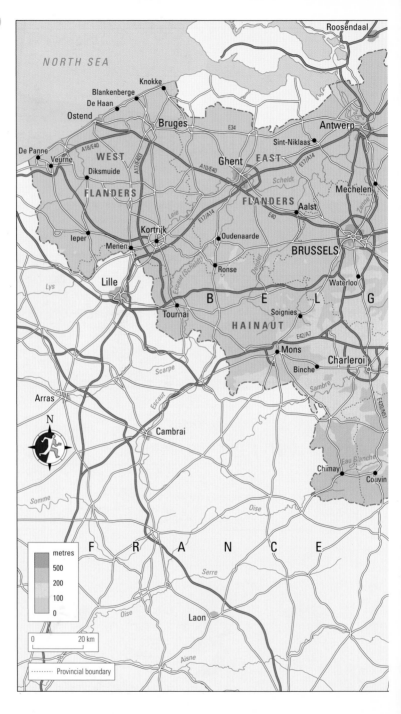

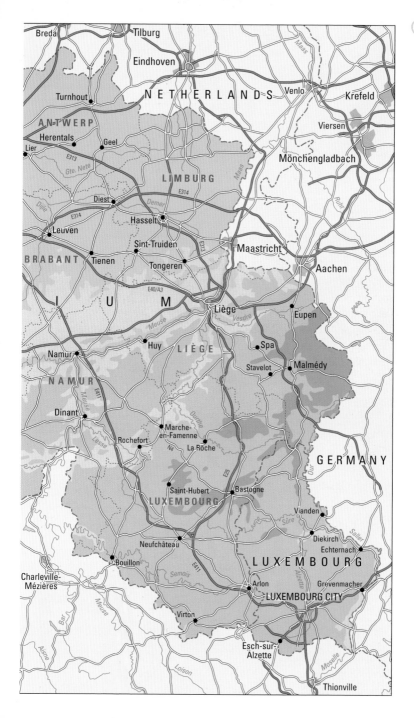

Introduction to

Belgium & Luxembourg

There isn't a country on earth quite like Belgium. It's one of the smallest nations in Europe, yet it has three official languages and an intense regional rivalry between the Flemish-speaking north and the French-speaking south. Its historic cities – most famously Bruges and Ghent – are the equal of any, as is its cuisine, with a host of regional specialities, alongside a marvellous range of beers and sumptuous chocolate. Neighbouring Luxembourg, commonly regarded as a refuge of bankers and diplomats, has surprises in store too: its capital, Luxembourg City, has a handsome setting, its tiny centre perched on a plateau above deep green gorges, and the rest of the country – diminutive though it is – boasts steep wooded hills and plunging valleys aplenty.

Many outsiders view Belgium and Luxembourg as good weekend-break material – but not much else, which is a pity, as this is historically one of the most complex and intriguing parts of Europe. Squeezed in between France, Germany and the Netherlands,

v

Fact file

● **Belgium** has a population of around 10 million. Of these, around 5.5 million live in Flemish-speaking Flanders, while 3.5 million dwell in French-speaking Wallonia; there's also a small German-speaking community in the east. The tenacity of regional (and linguistic) feeling is such that Belgium is a **federal state**: both Flanders and Wallonia have their own regional administrations, as does the capital, Brussels, which is officially bilingual and has a population of around 1 million. A **constitutional monarchy**, Belgium has a bicameral parliament, comprising the Senate and Chamber of Deputies.

● The tiny **Grand Duchy of Luxembourg** has a population of around 430,000, a fifth of which lives in the capital, Luxembourg City. Luxembourgers switch comfortably between French, German and their own official spoken language, **Lëtzeburgesch** (Luxembourgish), a dialect of German – all without so much as an intercommunal ripple. French and German are the official languages for all written purposes except governmental administration, which is conducted in French. The Duchy is a **constitutional monarchy** governed by the Chamber of Deputies, working in tandem with the Council of State. The vast majority of Belgians and Luxembourgers classify themselves as **Roman Catholics**.

Belgium and Luxembourg occupy a spot that has often decided the European balance of power. It was here that the Romans shared an important border with the Germanic tribes to the north; here that the Spanish Habsburgs finally met their match in the Protestant rebels of the Netherlands; here that Napoleon was finally defeated at the Battle of Waterloo; and – most famously – here, too, that the British and Belgians slugged it out with the Germans in

Food

The thing about Belgian food is the quality: there are, of course, exceptions, but almost everywhere the care and attention lavished on everything from a sandwich through to a restaurant meal is outstanding. Every province, and often a particular town, prides itself on its specialities, from the hearty fish or chicken stews of the north to the wild boar, hare, venison and pheasant of the south, via mussels and beef served every which way. The sheer creativity of the country's chefs fair takes the breath away – it's hard to imagine any other place where the humble white leaves of the chicory plant – endives – can spawn no less than fifty popular recipes. To help you munch your way across the country, we've given café and restaurant recommendations throughout our guide.

World War I. Indeed so many powers have had an interest in this region that it was only in 1830 that Belgium and Luxembourg became separate, independent states, free from foreign rule.

Where to go

Belgium divides between the Flemish (Dutch-speaking) north of the country, known as **Flanders**, and French-speaking **Wallonia** in the south. There's more to this divide than just language, though: the north and south of the country are visually very different. The **north**, made up of the provinces of West and East Flanders, Antwerp, Limburg and the top half of Brabant, is mainly flat, with a landscape and architecture not unlike the Netherlands. **Antwerp** is the largest city here, a sprawling, bustling old port with doses of high fashion and high art in roughly equal measure. Further west, in **Flanders**, are the great Belgian medieval cloth towns of **Bruges** and **Ghent**, with a stunning concentration of Flemish art and architecture. Bruges in particular is the country's biggest tourist pull, and although this inevitably means it gets very crowded, you shouldn't miss it on any account. Beyond lies the **Belgian coast**, which makes valiant attempts to compete with the seaside resorts of the rest of Europe but is ultimately let down by the coldness of the North Sea. Nonetheless, there are a couple of appealing seaside resorts, most notably **De Haan**, and the beaches and duney interludes along the coast are delightful. But you might be better off spending time in some of the other inland Flanders towns, not least **Ieper**, formerly and better known as Ypres, where every year visitors come to reflect on the stark sights of the nearby World War I

The Ardennes is an area of deep, wooded valleys and heathy plateaux, often very wild and excellent for hiking, cycling and canoeing

Beer

No other country on earth produces more beers than Belgium – around 700 and counting. There are strong, dark brews from a handful of Trappist monasteries, light wheat beers perfect for a hot summer's day, fruit beers bottled and corked like champagne, and strange and unusual concoctions that date back to medieval times and beyond. Every good Belgian bar has a beer menu, some of which run to several hundred brews, though mostly you'll be faced with a choice of twenty or thirty. To get you started, we've listed a top twenty of Belgian beers (see p.42) and if this whets your appetite – and curiosity – there's a more detailed appreciation of the country's various brews on pp.429–438.

battlefields and vast, sad acreages of cemeteries.

Marking the meeting of the Flemish and Walloon parts of Belgium, **Brussels**, the capital, is more exciting and varied than its reputation as a bland Euro-capital would suggest. Central enough to be pretty much unavoidable, it's moreover useful as a base for day-trips, especially given that Belgium isn't a large country and has an excellent public transport system. Bruges and Ghent are easily accessible from here, as is the old university city of **Leuven** to the east, and the cathedral city of **Mechelen**, halfway to Antwerp.

Flemish Brabant encircles Brussels, but to the south of the capital it narrows into a slender corridor beyond which lies Wallonian Brabant, distinguished by the splendid church at **Nivelles** and the elegaic abbey ruins at nearby **Villers-la-Ville**. West of here, the Walloon province of Hainaut is mostly agricultural country, dotted with industrial centres like **Charleroi** and the more appealing **Mons**, but also home to the handsome old town of **Tournai**. East of here lies Belgium's most scenically rewarding region, the **Ardennes**, spread across the three provinces of **Namur**, **Liège** and **Luxembourg**. This is an area of deep, wooded valleys and heathy plateaux, often very wild and excellent for hiking, cycling and canoeing. Use

> **Brussels is more exciting and varied than its reputation as a bland Euro-capital would suggest**

Chocolate

Belgians get through a lot of chocolate – several kilograms for each one of them every year – but there again, considering how good the chocolates are, it's a wonder it isn't more. The Belgians picked up their love of chocolate via the most circuitous of historical routes. The Aztecs of Mexico were drinking chocolate, which they believed gave them wisdom and power, when Hernando Cortéz's Spanish conquistadors turned up in 1519. Cortéz took a liking to the stuff and, after butchering the locals, brought cocoa beans back to Spain as a novelty gift for the Emperor Charles V in 1528. Within a few years its consumption had spread across Charles's empire, including today's Belgium and Luxembourg. At first the making of chocolate was confined to a few Spanish monasteries, but eventually Belgians got into the act and they now produce what are generally regarded as the best chocolates in the world. Every Belgian town and city has at least a couple of specialist chocolate shops and the more popular tourist spots – Brussels, Bruges, Ghent and so forth – have dozens; for more on this salivating subject, see p.41.

either Namur or Luxembourg City as a jumping-off point for the heart of the region, at **St-Hubert**, **Bouillon** or **La Roche-en-Ardenne**.

The Ardennes reaches across the Belgian border into the northern part of the **Grand Duchy of Luxembourg**, a green landscape of high hills and wooded ravines topped with crumbling castles overlooking rushing rivers. The two best centres for touring the countryside are the quiet little towns of **Vianden** and **Echternach**, featuring an extravagantly picturesque castle and a splendid abbey respectively. Indeed, despite its feeble reputation, the Duchy – or rather its northern reaches – packs more scenic highlights into its tight borders than many other more renowned holiday spots, and is perfect for hiking and, at a pinch, mountain-biking. The Ardennes fizzles

Surrealists

The French may have started it, but the Belgians had as much to say in the Surrealist movement that swept parts of Europe in the 1920s and 1930s, and was revisited thirty years later in the posters of a million student bedrooms. Of all the Surrealists, it's Belgium's own René Magritte who still has the power to disconcert, his scrupulously detailed canvases illuminated by all sorts of strange juxtapositions, most famously the bowler-hatted man without a face. Less well known are the ice-cool nudes and ruined cities of Paul Delvaux, who was born in the province of Liège; and Ostend's James Ensor, not a Surrealist per se, but a seminal artist whose gruesome and macabre paintings of masks – and people wearing masks – did much to set the Surrealist scene.

out as you reach the plainer scenery of the south, where the rolling agricultural terrain of the **Gutland** is a pleasant preamble to **Luxembourg City**, whose bastions and bulwarks recall the days when this was one of the strongest fortresses in Europe.

When to go

Belgium enjoys a fairly standard temperate **climate**, with warm, if mild, summers and moderately cold winters. Generally speaking, temperatures rise the further south you go, with Wallonia a couple of degrees warmer than Flanders for most of the year, though in the east this is offset by the more severe climate of continental Europe, and emphasized by the increase in altitude of the Ardennes. Luxembourg, too, has more extreme temperatures and harsher winters, often accompanied by snow. In both countries rain is always a possibility, and you can expect a greater degree of precipitation in the Ardennes and upland regions than on the northern plains.

The cities of Belgium and Luxembourg are all-year tourist destinations, though you might think twice about visiting Bruges, the region's most popular spot, during August, when things get mighty crowded. Flanders as a whole is best visited any time between early spring and late autumn, though winter time has its advantages too – iced canals and hoarfrost polders – if you don't mind the short hours of daylight. Wallonia,

Average daily temperatures (°C) and monthly rainfall (mm)

	Jan	Feb	Mar	Apr	May	June	July	Aug	Sept	Oct	Nov	Dec
Brussels												
daily max (C°)	4	7	10	14	18	22	23	22	21	15	9	6
daily min (C°)	-1	0	2	5	8	11	12	12	11	7	3	0
monthly rainfall (mm)	66	61	53	60	55	76	95	80	63	83	75	88
Luxembourg City												
daily max (C°)	3	4	10	14	18	21	23	22	19	13	7	4
daily min (C°)	-1	-1	1	4	8	11	13	12	10	6	3	0
monthly rainfall (mm)	61	65	42	47	64	64	60	84	72	53	67	81

especially the Ardennes, is more seasonal, with many things closing down in the winter, so try to visit between April and October.

things not to miss

It's not possible to see everything that Belgium and Luxembourg have to offer in one trip – and we don't suggest you try. What follows is a selective and subjective taste of the two countries' highlights, from wonderful food and striking Gothic architecture to handsome forested hills. They're all arranged in five colour-coded categories to help you find the very best things to see, do and experience. All entries have a page reference to take you straight into the guide, where you can find out more.

01 **Comic strips** Page **84** • Hergé's bequiffed Tintin and his mate Captain Haddock pop up and out at Brussels' excellent Comic Strip Centre.

03 Bruges Page **163** • With its canals, museums and gorgeous medieval and Renaissance architecture, Bruges is without question one of Europe's most beguiling cities.

02 Brussels' Art Nouveau Page **104** • The capital's middle class took to this style of architecture like ducks to water; Victor Horta is the name to conjure with.

04 Cycling Page **190** • Pancake-flat northern Belgium is perfect for this; cycle paths are legion, the prettiest of which run alongside the poplar-lined canals near Bruges.

05 **Luxembourg City** Page **377** • The mighty bastions and stern ramparts of the Old Town offer commanding views of the valleys below.

06 **Bastogne** Page **345** • The Ardennes saw determined American resistance during the Battle of the Bulge, Hitler's last, desperate throw of the military dice in the winter of 1944; Bastogne has the key sights.

07 **Carnival** Page **48** • Nowhere else in Europe, perhaps, celebrates carnival with the vim and gusto of Belgium. For originality, the pick of the carnival crop is at Binche, Aalst, Eupen and Stavelot.

08 **Vianden** Page **395** • This pretty little town, in the middle of wild, wooded country-side, possesses the most impressive of Luxembourg's many hilltop castles.

09 **Ghent's St Baafskathedraal** Page **197** • Home to Jan van Eyck's *Adoration of the Mystic Lamb*, quite simply one of the medieval world's most astonishing paintings.

10 **Place du Jeu de Balle** Page **121** • Fleamarket-mania overtakes Brussels on a Sunday morning and this is the place to head for, in the gritty Marolles district.

11 **Tyne Cot** Page **154** • World War I was decided on the plain of Flanders, a point hammered home by the interminable gravestones at this enormous cemetery near Ieper.

12 **Schueberfouer** Page **388** Held in Luxembourg City in September, this lays claim to being the biggest mobile funfair in the world.

13 **Trésor du Prieuré d'Oignies** Page **318** • A fabulous horde of exquisitely crafted, jewel-encrusted metalwork dating from the early thirteenth century is displayed here in Namur.

14 **Kayaking and hiking in the Ardennes** Page **313** • A real treat, especially around La Roche, Bouillon or Echternach – you don't have to be a zealous athlete to enjoy it either.

15 **Grand-Place, Brussels** Page **77** • There are beautiful, delicately carved guildhouses in many Belgian towns, but none quite reach the heights of those in the capital's main square.

16 **Café society** Page **39** • In every town square in Belgium and Luxembourg, locals sip coffee and nibble at cakes and biscuits by day, moving on to the beer and wine in the evening. Nothing could be more hospitable.

17 **Museés Royaux des Beaux Arts** Page **91** • You'd have to go an awfully long way to beat Belgium's best art museum, with superb collections ranging from Jan van Eyck, Bosch and Bruegel to Ensor and Magritte.

18 **Antwerp's Cathedral** Page **229** • Perhaps the most beautiful Gothic structure in Belgium and, even better, it's graced by four fine paintings by Rubens.

19 **Het Zwin** Page **140** • This nature reserve on the Belgian coast offers a pristine coastal landscape of polders and dykes, marshes and salt flats, attracting a rich birdlife.

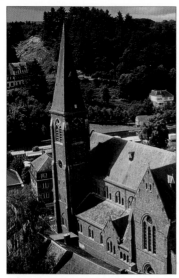

21 **The Heintz Hotel** Page **397** • In Luxembourg's Vianden, this has oodles of character, from the cosy, wood-panelled bar to the infinitely comfortable bedrooms.

20 **La Roche-en-Ardenne** Page **346** • Nestling among wooded hills and beneath the craggy ruins of a castle is one of the prettiest resorts in the Ardennes, busy in summer with campers, walkers and kayakers.

22 **Luxembourg's vineyards** Page **390** • Many of the duchy's vineyards, strung along the River Moselle, offer tours and tastings of their deliciously fruity wines.

23 **The Hautes Fagnes**. Page **368** A high plateau in the Ardennes region, providing some fabulous hiking amid a wild and windswept expanse of wood and moorland.

24 **Procession of the Holy Blood, Bruges** Page **175** • Once a sombre religious ceremony, though these days it's as much a (rather classy) historical pageant.

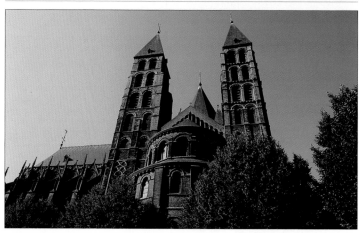

25 **Tournai** Page **282** • Not nearly as well known among English-speaking visitors as it should be, this absorbing town boasts a superb Romanesque cathedral.

26 **Beer** Page **41** • With over 700 different Belgian beers to choose from, you've got to start somewhere; the brews of the Trappist monks – Chimay, Orval and so forth – will do very nicely.

27 **Moules frites** Page **41** Belgian cuisine is second to none, but it's not all about rich sauces and fancy preparation – the national dish, mussels and fries, proves the point.

Contents

Using the Rough Guide

We've tried to make this Rough Guide a good read and easy to use. The book is divided into six main sections, and you should be able to find whatever you want in one of them.

colour section

The front colour section offers a quick tour of Belgium and Luxembourg. The **introduction** aims to give you a feel for the two places, with suggestions on where to go. We also tell you what the weather is like and include a basic country fact file. Next, our authors round up their favourite aspects of the two countries in the **things not to miss** section – whether it's a glorious cathedral, a stunning art gallery or fabulous cuisine. Right after this comes a full **contents** list.

basics

The Basics section covers all the **pre-departure** nitty-gritty to help you plan your trip. This is where to find out which airlines fly to your destination, what paperwork you'll need, what to do about money and insurance, about internet access, food, security, public transport, car rental – in fact just about every piece of **general practical information** you might need.

guide

This is the heart of the Rough Guide, divided into user-friendly chapters, each of which covers a specific region. Every chapter starts with a list of **highlights** and an **introduction** that helps you to decide where to go, depending on your time and budget. Likewise, introductions to the various towns and smaller regions within each chapter should help you plan your

itinerary. We start most town accounts with information on arrival and accommodation, followed by a tour of the sights, and finally reviews of places to eat and drink, and details of nightlife. Longer accounts also have a directory of practical listings. Each chapter concludes with **public transport** details for that region.

contexts

Read Contexts to get a deeper understanding of what makes Belgium and Luxembourg tick. We include a brief **history**, articles about art and Belgian beer, and a detailed further-reading section that reviews dozens of **books** relating to the two countries.

language

The **language** section gives useful guidance for speaking Flemish and French and pulls together all the vocabulary you might need on your trip, including a comprehensive menu reader. Here you'll also find a glossary of words and terms peculiar to the two countries.

index + small print

Apart from a **full index**, which includes maps as well as places, this section covers publishing information, credits and acknowledgements, and also has our contact details in case you want to send in updates and corrections to the book – or suggestions as to how we might improve it.

Chapter list and map

- Colour section
- Contents
- Basics

1. Brussels
2. Flanders
3. Antwerp and the northeast

4. Hainaut and the Wallonian Brabant
5. The Ardennes
6. Luxembourg

- Contexts
- Language
- Index

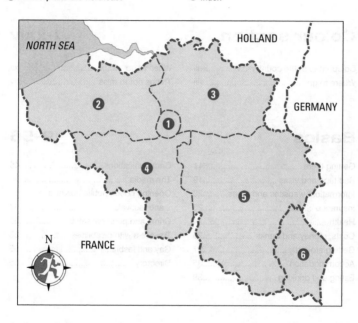

Contents

Contexts

Language

Index + small print

Map symbols

maps are listed in the full index using coloured text

-----	Chapter division boundary		☉	Statue
--·--·	International boundary		🏛	Memorial/monument
--·--	Regional boundary		🏠	Abbey
▬▬▬	Motorway		♦	Museum
═══	Road		🅿	Parking
▬▬▬	Pedestrianized street		Ⓜ	Metro station
▥▥▥	Steps		✈	Airport
------	Footpath		★	Bus/tram stop
▬─▬─	Railway		ⓘ	Information office
— —	Ferry route		✉	Post office
═══	River		@	Internet access
♦	Point of interest		▬	Building
▲	Mountain peak		✛	Church
ᵤᴺᴴᴴᴛᵤᴺ	Cliffs		▦	Park
♜	Castle		⊞	Cemetery
——	Wall		▦	Beach
⊠ ⊠	Gate			

Basics

Basics

Getting there

BASICS | Getting there

UK travellers are spoilt for choice when it comes to deciding how to get to Belgium. There are flights to Brussels from London and a string of regional airports; Eurostar trains from London to Brussels; ferries from Dover and Hull to Zeebrugge, near Bruges; Eurotunnel services from Folkestone to Calais, a short drive from the Belgian coast; and a number of international buses to, among several destinations, Brussels, Antwerp, Bruges and Ghent. Buses are usually the least expensive means of transportation, but Eurostar is faster and often not that much more expensive, and there all sorts of great deals on flights too. Luxembourg is also easy to get to: there are flights from London and a couple of regional airports, long-distance buses and, perhaps most tempting of all, it's just two and a half hours from Brussels to Luxembourg City by train.

North American travellers can, of course, only fly to Europe, the main decision here being whether to fly direct to Brussels – though the options are limited – or fly via another European city, probably London. **Australians** and **New Zealanders** have to fly via another city – there are no nonstop flights. If you're intending to see Belgium and Luxembourg as part of a wider journey around Europe by train, note that some **train passes** have to be bought before you leave home (see p.30).

Airfares from North America, Australia and New Zealand to Belgium depend on the **season**, with the highest prices applying from around late June to early September, the peak tourist season; you'll get the best prices during the low season, mid-November through to April (excluding Christmas and New Year when prices are hiked up and seats are at a premium). Note also that flying on the weekend is generally more expensive and that all sorts of other factors may affect prices dramatically too, most notably seat availability. If you're flying from the UK or Ireland, the same general strictures apply except on the London–Brussels route, where competition is so intense that flights can cost almost nothing – the budget airline Ryanair has been known to offer return flights from London Stansted to Belgium for £3.50.

Special deals aside, you can often cut airfare costs by going through a **specialist flight agent** rather than an airline. These agents come in two main forms: there are

consolidators, who buy up blocks of tickets from the airlines and sell them at a discount, and **discount agents**, who in addition to dealing with discounted flights may also offer special student and youth fares and a range of other travel-related services such as travel insurance, rail passes, car rentals and the like. Some agents specialize in **charter flights**, which may be cheaper than anything available on a scheduled flight – and are the only means of flying direct/nonstop from Canada to Brussels – though be aware that departure dates are fixed and withdrawal penalties are high.

A further possibility from North America is to see if you can arrange a **courier flight**, although you'll need a flexible schedule, and preferably be travelling alone with very little luggage. In return for shepherding a parcel through customs, you can expect to get a deeply discounted ticket, though you'll probably be restricted in the duration of your stay.

Package deals from **tour operators** are rarely going to save you money on a trip to Belgium and Luxembourg, but several of the best firms provide special-interest tours that will put you in touch with other like-minded souls, from cyclists to canal lovers.

Booking flights online

Good deals can often be found through **websites** run by airlines and specialist flight agents, offering you the opportunity to book tickets online. You may also turn up a good fare through discount or auction sites.

11

Online booking agents and general travel sites

ⓦ www.cheapflights.com Bookings from the UK and Ireland only. Flight deals, travel agents, plus links to other travel sites.

ⓦ www.cheaptickets.com Discount flight specialists.

ⓦ www.etn.nl/discount.htm A website of consolidator and discount agent links, maintained by the non-profit European Travel Network.

ⓦ www.expedia.com Discount airfares, all-airline search engine and daily deals.

ⓦ www.flyaow.com Online air travel info and reservations site.

ⓦ www.hotwire.com Bookings from the US only. Last-minute savings of up to forty percent on regular published fares. Travellers must be at least 18 and there are no refunds, transfers or changes allowed.

ⓦ www.lastminute.com UK-based firm offering good last-minute holiday package and flight-only deals.

ⓦ www.priceline.com Name-your-own-price website that has deals at around forty percent off standard fares.

ⓦ www.skyauction.com Bookings from the US only. Auctions tickets and travel packages using a "second bid" scheme. The best strategy is to bid the maximum you're willing to pay, since if you win you then pay only just enough to beat the runner-up regardless of your original bid.

ⓦ www.travelocity.com Destination guides, hot web fares and best deals for car hire, accommodation and lodging as well as fares. Provides access to the travel agent system SABRE, the most comprehensive central reservations system in the US.

ⓦ www.travelshop.com.au Australian website offering discounted flights, packages, insurance, online bookings.

Flights from the UK and Ireland

From the UK, Belgium and Luxembourg's two major airports – Brussels and Luxembourg City – are readily reached from London and a number of regional airports. There's also Brussels-Charleroi airport, whose name is a tad deceptive – it's actually on the edge of Charleroi, an industrial town about 60km south of the capital. Flying times are insignificant: London and Newcastle to Brussels take a little over an hour, London to Luxembourg one hour and twenty minutes.

Fierce competition keeps **prices** down,

especially on the London–Brussels route, though the least expensive tickets are usually hedged with restrictions, commonly requiring the booking to be made seven days in advance, and obliging you to spend one Saturday night abroad. A standard, fully flexible return with British Airways from London to Brussels costs around £360, £440 from Manchester, whereas their least expensive tickets from either airport cost just £90. Alternatively, the budget airline Ryanair charges between £20 and £109 for a single flight from London Stansted to Brussels-Charleroi, fares comparable to those of another budget operator, Virgin Express. British Airways' Gatwick–Luxembourg service comes in at £450 for a standard return, £150 with restrictions.

Flying from Ireland, there's much less choice, but Ryanair charges a very reasonable €60–120 for a single fare from Dublin to Brussels-Charleroi.

Airlines

Air Canada UK ☎0870/524 7226, Republic of Ireland ☎01/679 3958, ⓦ www.cdnair.ca. Heathrow to Brussels.

Air France UK ☎0845/084 5111, Republic of Ireland ☎01/605 0383, ⓦ www.airfrance.co.uk. Birmingham, Edinburgh and Newcastle to Brussels.

Aer Lingus UK ☎0845/973 7747, Republic of Ireland ☎0818/365 000, ⓦ www.aerlingus.ie. Dublin to Brussels.

Air New Zealand UK ☎020/8741 2299, ⓦ www.airnz.co.uk. Heathrow to Brussels.

Bmi British Midland UK ☎0870/607 0555, Republic of Ireland ☎01/407 3036, ⓦ www.flybmi.com. Heathrow, East Midlands, Leeds and Edinburgh to Brussels.

British Airways UK ☎0845/773 3377, Republic of Ireland ☎1800/626 747, ⓦ www.britishairways.com. Birmingham, Cardiff, Gatwick, Heathrow, Manchester and Southampton to Brussels; Gatwick to Luxembourg.

British European UK ☎0870/567 6676, Republic of Ireland ☎1890/925 532, ⓦ www.flybe.com. Birmingham, Edinburgh and Newcastle to Brussels.

Delta UK ☎0800/414 767, Republic of Ireland ☎01/407 3165, ⓦ www.delta.com. Newcastle to Brussels.

Luxair (Luxembourg Airlines) UK ☎01293/596633, ⓦ www.luxair.lu. Dublin, Heathrow, Stansted, London City and Manchester to Luxembourg.

Ryanair UK ☎0871/246 0000, Republic of Ireland

☏01/609 7800, ⓦwww.ryanair.com. Budget scheduled airline, flying from Dublin, Glasgow, Liverpool, Stansted and Shannon to Brussels-Charleroi.

SN Brussels Airlines (Formerly Sabena) UK ☏0870/735 2345, ⓦwww.brussels-airlines.com. Birmingham, Bristol, Heathrow, London City, Manchester and Newcastle to Brussels.

United Airlines UK ☏0845/844 4777, ⓦwww.ual.com. Heathrow to Brussels.

Virgin Express ☏0800/891199, ⓦwww.virgin -express.com. London Heathrow to Brussels.

VLM Airlines ☏020/7476 6677, ⓦwww.vlm -airlines.com. Belgian carrier geared up for the business travel market; flies from London City Airport to Brussels (Mon–Fri 5 daily, Sun 1 daily) and from Manchester to Antwerp via Rotterdam (Mon–Fri 2 daily).

Specialist flight agents

UK

Co-op Travel Care ☏028/9047 1717, ⓦwww.travelcareonline.com. Flights and holidays, including city breaks.

Flightbookers ☏0870/010 7000, ⓦwww.ebookers.com. Low fares on an extensive selection of scheduled flights.

North South Travel ☏ & ⓕ01245/608 291, ⓦwww.northsouthtravel.co.uk. Travel agency offering discounted fares; profits are used to support projects in the developing world, especially the promotion of sustainable tourism.

STA Travel ☏0870/1600 599, ⓦwww.statravel.co.uk. Specialists in low-cost flights and tours for students and under-26s, though other customers welcome.

Top Deck UK ☏020/7370 4555, ⓦwww.topdecktravel.co.uk. Long-established agent dealing in discount flights.

Republic of Ireland

CIE Tours International ☏01/703 1888, ⓦwww.cietours.ie. General flight and tour agent.

Go Holidays ☏01/874 4126, ⓦwww.goholidays.ie. Package-tour specialists.

Joe Walsh Tours ☏01/676 0991, ⓦwww.joewalshtours.ie. General budget fares agent.

Lee Travel ☏021/277 111, ⓦwww.leetravel.ie. Flights and holidays.

McCarthy's Travel ☏021/427 0127, ⓦwww.mccarthystravel.ie. General flight agent.

Neenan Travel ☏01/607 9900, ⓦwww.neenantrav.ie. Specialists in European city breaks.

Student & Group Travel ☏01/677 7834. Student and group specialists, mostly to Europe.

usit NOW ☏01/602 1600, ⓦwww.usitnow.ie. Student and youth specialists for flights and trains.

Tour operators

In both the UK and Ireland, high-street travel agents will have the details of the many large-scale **tour operators** who include Belgian city breaks – primarily to Antwerp, Bruges and Brussels – in their programmes. Specialist tour operators are thin on the ground, but there are one or two who venture out from the cities into less familiar territory – the Ardennes and the Flemish battlefields for example.

Belgian Travel Service ☏0870/191 7120, ⓦwww.belgiantravel.co.uk. The leading tour operator to Belgium. Reasonably priced city breaks to a long list of Belgian cities by rail, coach, Hoverspeed and/or car. Belgian coast, Flemish battlefields and Ardennes excursions too.

British Airways Holidays ☏0870/242 4245, ⓦwww.baholidays.co.uk. Using British Airways and other quality international airlines, they offer an exhaustive range of package and tailor-made holidays around the world – including Brussels and Bruges.

Osprey City Holidays ☏0870 560 5605, wwww.osprey-holidays.co.uk. Edinburgh travel agency that does a good line in city breaks, including trips to Bruges and Brussels.

Thomas Cook ☏0870/5666 222, ⓦwww.thomascook.co.uk. Long-established one-stop 24hr travel agency for package holidays or scheduled flights, with city breaks available in Brussels, Antwerp, Bruges and Ghent. Also offer traveller's cheques, travel insurance and car rental.

Travelscene ☏0870/777 9987, ⓦwww.travelscene.co.uk. City breaks in Antwerp, Bruges, Brussels, Ghent and Luxembourg City – plus self-drive holidays, including hotel accommodation, across all the prettiest parts of Belgium.

Flights from the US and Canada

Considering that **Brussels** is the effective capital of the European Union and its airport the only major flight gateway into Belgium, there are surprisingly few direct, scheduled flights there **from the US**. Nonstop flights to

Brussels are limited to a handful of carriers: American Airlines, Continental, Delta, United and VG Airlines. **Fares** vary enormously, the key criteria being seat availability and the time of year you want to travel. The least expensive tickets are usually non-refundable, have to booked a specified period ahead of time and require a minimum stay. As a sample price, Delta's lowest summer fare from New York is around US$600, $400 in winter. Add another US$300 or so for the least expensive flights from Washington and Atlanta, US$400 from the West Coast.

Going to Brussels **via London**, you'll often be able to undercut the price of a non-stop US–Brussels routing by a good margin. Dozens of airlines fly from New York and lots of other US cities to London and many airlines will include the onward flight at no extra cost. The best low-season fares from New York to London hover around $360 return, $390 from Washington, $440 from Houston and $860 from the West Coast; add $150–250 for high-season flights.

With regard to **Canada**, there are no direct scheduled services to Brussels at all, though charter flights do fill in some of the gaps during the summer. You'll usually get the best deals flying **via London**. A return from Toronto to Brussels via London costs in the region of CDN$1200 in low season, CDN$1700 high. Add a couple of hundred dollars more for west Canadian cities, such as Vancouver and Calgary.

Figure on seven and a half hours' **flying time** from New York to Brussels, though note that the prevailing headwinds usually make the return journey half-an-hour to an hour longer. New York to London takes around six and a half hours, London to Brussels just over an hour. Most eastbound flights cross the Atlantic overnight, depositing you at your destination the next morning without much sleep, but if you can manage to stay awake until the early evening, you should be over the worst of the jet lag by the next morning. Some Transatlantic flights arrive late in the evening, but this lands you in Europe just as many things are closing down – a recipe for disorientation if ever there was one.

As you might expect, there are currently no direct/nonstop scheduled flights from North America to **Luxembourg**. The best

bet is to fly to London, from where there are lots of flights onto Luxembourg.

Airlines

Air Canada ☏1-888/247-2262, ⓦwww.aircanada.ca. Calgary, Halifax, Montréal, Ottawa, Toronto and Vancouver to Brussels, via London.
American Airlines ☏1-800/433-7300, ⓦwww.aa.com. Chicago to Brussels; also flies from Chicago, Dallas/Fort Worth, Los Angeles, Miami, New York and Raleigh to London.
British Airways ☏1-800/247-9297, ⓦwww.british-airways.com. Flights from numerous North American cities to London, with onward connections to Brussels and Luxembourg.
Continental Airlines ☏1-800/231-0856, ⓦwww.continental.com. Newark to Brussels; Cleveland, Houston and Newark to London.
Delta Air Lines ☏1-800/241-4141, ⓦwww.delta.com. Atlanta and New York (JFK) to Brussels. Atlanta and Cincinnati to London.
United Airlines ☏1-800/538-2929, ⓦwww.ual.com. Washington DC to Brussels. Chicago, Los Angeles, Newark, New York, San Diego, San Francisco and Washington DC to London.
VG Air Belgium ☏+32/3 303 00 00, ⓦwww.vgair.be. Belgian carrier operating nonstop flights from Boston & New York (JFK) to Brussels.
Virgin Atlantic Airways ☏1-800/862-8621, ⓦwww.virgin-atlantic.com. Boston, Chicago, Los Angeles, Miami, Newark, New York, Orlando, San Francisco and Washington DC to London.

Specialist flight agents

Council Travel ☏1-800/226-8624, Ⓕ617/528-2091, ⓦwww.counciltravel.com. Nationwide organization that specializes in student/budget travel. Flights from the US to destinations worldwide.
Educational Travel Center ☏1-800/747-5551 or 608/256-5551, ⓦwww.edtrav.com. Student/youth discount agent.
New Frontiers/Nouvelles Frontières ☏1-800/677-0720, ⓦwww.newfrontiers.com. French-owned discount-travel firm specializing in flights from the US to Europe.
Skylink US ☏1-800/247-6659 or 212/573-8980, Canada ☏1-800/759-5465, ⓦwww.skylinkus.com. Consolidator.
STA Travel ☏1-800/777-0112 or 1-800/781-4040, ⓦwww.sta-travel.com. Worldwide specialists in independent travel; also student IDs, travel insurance, car rental, rail passes etc.

Student Flights ☎ 1-800/255-8000 or 480/951-1177, ⊛ www.isecard.com. Student/youth fares, student IDs.

TFI Tours International ☎ 1-800/745-8000 or 212/736-1140, ⊛ www.lowestairprice.com. Consolidator.

Travac ☎ 1-800/872-8800, ⊛ www.thetravelsite.com. Consolidator and charter broker with offices in New York City and Orlando.

Travel Avenue ☎ 1-800/333-3335, ⊛ www.travelavenue.com. Full-service travel agent that offers discounts in the form of rebates.

Travel Cuts Canada ☎ 1-800/667-2887, US ☎ 1-866/246-9762, ⊛ www.travelcuts.com. Canadian student-travel organization.

Courier flights

Air Courier Association ☎ 1-800/282-1202, ⊛ www.aircourier.org or www.cheaptrips.com. Courier flight broker. Membership (1yr $39, 3yr $59, 5yr $89, lifetime $99) also entitles you to twenty percent discount on travel insurance and name-your-own-price non-courier flights.

Now Voyager ☎ 212/459-1616, ⊛ www.nowvoyagertravel.com. Courier flight broker and consolidator.

International Association of Air Travel Couriers ☎ 352/475-1584, ⊛ www.courier.org. Courier flight broker with membership fee of $45 a year or $80 for two years.

Package-tour operators

In North America, Belgium and Luxembourg are not major tourist destinations, a fact reflected in the lack of specialist **package-tour companies** dealing with either country. Where they appear at all, Belgium and Luxembourg are mostly slotted into a more general zip round Europe.

Abercrombie & Kent ☎ 1-800/323-7308 or 630/954-2944, ⊛ www.abercrombiekent.com. Luxury six-night river and canal cruising tours in Belgium and southern Holland.

AESU Travel ☎ 1-800/638-7640, ⊛ www.aesu.com. Reasonably priced tours, independent city stays, and discount airfares for the 18–35s. Brussels turns up on many itineraries.

CBT Bicycle Tours ☎ 1-800/736-2453, ⊛ www.cbttours.com. Affordable cycling tours in Belgium and Luxembourg.

Euro-Bike & Walking Tours ☎ 1-800/321-6060, ⊛ www.eurobike.com. Upscale, fourteen-day cycling tours and "bicycling and barging" tours in Belgium and Luxembourg.

Flights from Australia and New Zealand

There are **no direct flights** to Belgium and Luxembourg from either Australia or New Zealand. Consequently, most travellers opt to fly into one of Europe's major airports – London, Paris, Milan etc – and catch an onward flight from there. In many instances, this onward flight is thrown in for free. Flights from Australia and New Zealand to London take about twenty hours.

From Australia, the Southeast Asia–London routing provides the most competitive fares as a general rule, starting at around A$1500/NZ$2000, though a more likely figure is about A$1800/NZ$2275. Fares from Australia's eastern cities are common-rated. The most direct route **from New Zealand** is via North America, with fares starting at around NZ$2200 in the low season, NZ$3400 in the high season.

Airlines

Air New Zealand Australia ☎ 13 24 76, New Zealand ☎ 0800/737 000, ⊛ www.airnz.com. Daily flights to London from Brisbane, Melbourne and Sydney via Asia, and from New Zealand via Los Angeles.

Alitalia Australia ☎ 02/9262 3925, ⊛ www.alitalia.com. Three flights weekly to Milan from Brisbane, Sydney and Melbourne, with onward connections to Brussels.

British Airways Australia ☎ 02/8904 8800, New Zealand ☎ 0800/274 847, ⊛ www.britishairways.com. Daily direct flights to London from Brisbane, Melbourne, Perth and Sydney; also daily from Auckland via Los Angeles. Code share with Qantas from other major Australian cities. Onward connections to Brussels and Luxembourg.

KLM Australia ☎ 1300/303 747, New Zealand ☎ 09/309 1782, ⊛ www.klm.com. Twice weekly flights from Sydney to Amsterdam and London via Singapore. From Amsterdam, it's a short onward flight to Brussels, and there are frequent trains to Luxembourg and various Belgian cities.

Qantas Australia ☎ 13 13 13, New Zealand ☎ 09/357 8900, ⊛ www.qantas.com.au. Daily flights from Adelaide, Auckland, Brisbane, Christchurch, Darwin, Melbourne, Perth, Sydney and Wellington to London via Bangkok or Singapore.

Singapore Airlines Australia ☎13 10 11, New Zealand ☎09/303 2129,
ⓦwww.singaporeair.com. Daily flights from Auckland, Brisbane, Christchurch, Melbourne, Perth, and Sydney and several weekly from Adelaide and Cairns to Singapore, with three weekly onward flights to Brussels.

Thai Airways Australia ☎1300/651 960, New Zealand ☎09/377 3886, ⓦwww.thaiair.com. Several flights a week from Auckland, Brisbane, Melbourne, Perth and Sydney to Bangkok; three weekly flights from there to Brussels via Frankfurt.

United Airlines Australia ☎13 17 77, New Zealand ☎09/379 3800 or 0800/508 648, ⓦwww.ual.com. Daily flights from Auckland to London.

Specialist flight agents

Budget Travel New Zealand ☎09/366 0061 or 0800/808 040, ⓦwww.budgettravel.co.nz.
Destinations Unlimited New Zealand ☎09/373 4033.
Flight Centres Australia ☎13 31 33 or 02/9235 3522, New Zealand ☎09/358 4310, ⓦwww.flightcentre.com.au.
Northern Gateway Australia ☎08/8941 1394, ⓦwww.northerngateway.com.au.
STA Travel Australia ☎1300/733 035, ⓦwww.statravel.com.au; New Zealand ☎0508/782 872, ⓦwww.statravel.co.nz.
Student Uni Travel Australia ☎02/9232 8444, ⓦwww.usitbeyond.co.au; New Zealand ☎09/300 8266, ⓦwww.usitbeyond.co.nz
Trailfinders Australia ☎02/9247 7666, ⓦwww.trailfinders.com.au.

Package-tour operators

Belgium and Luxembourg do not have high profiles as tourist destinations in either Australia or New Zealand. As a consequence, there are no specialist **package-tour companies** dealing with either country, though one or two do slot Belgium and Luxembourg into longer European itineraries.

Contiki Holidays Australia ☎02/9511 0200, New Zealand ☎09/305 8824, ⓦwww.contiki.com. Packages tailored to 18- to 35-years-olds.
Explore Holidays Australia ☎02/9857 6200 or 1300/731 000, ⓦwww.exploreholidays.com.au. Accommodation and sightseeing package tours to Europe, including Brussels.

By rail from the UK and Ireland

Eurostar trains running through the Channel Tunnel put Belgium within easy striking distance of London's Waterloo and Kent's Ashford train stations. Indeed, considering the time it takes to check into any of London's airports, Eurostar is often faster than a flight. The same cannot be said if you're heading off to Belgium with Eurostar from much of the rest of the UK, but at least it's possible to keep costs down by through-ticketing from your home station. Alternatively, you can get the train to either Hull or Rosyth, from where there are direct car ferries to Zeebrugge, or Dover, served by car ferries to Zeebrugge and catamarans to Ostend; see opposite for more details. Travelling to Belgium by train **from Ireland** means going via England – a time-consuming journey that is barely worth considering.

Eurostar

There are normally seven or eight Eurostar departures from London Waterloo to **Brussels** every day (arriving at Bruxelles-Midi station; 2hr 50min). En route, most trains stop at Ashford in Kent; all services stop at Lille in France. From Bruxelles-Midi, Belgian Railways operates an hourly service to Luxembourg City, the journey taking three hours. For further information on Belgian Railways, see p.27.

Fares are set to compete with the airlines: full, unrestricted (and fully refundable) second-class returns go for about £300, a standard but non-refundable youth (under-26) fare for around £80. Special deals and bargains are commonplace, especially in the low season, and you can also reduce costs by accepting certain ticketing restrictions. At time of writing, the least expensive fare allows no refunds, involves an enforced stay of at least two nights – or just a Saturday night – and has to be booked at least fourteen days in advance.

Inter-Rail pass and Eurail **pass holders** qualify for Eurostar discounts, but remember that Eurail passes have to be purchased before arrival in Europe; for more on rail passes, see "Getting Around" (p.27).

UK rail contacts

Belgian Railways ☎020/7593 2332, ⓦwww.b-rail.be.

Eurostar ☎0870/160 6600,
🖰www.eurostar.com.
International Rail ☎01962/773 646. Agents for Dutch and Belgian railways.
Rail Europe ☎0870/584 8848,
🖰www.raileurope.co.uk. Sells tickets and passes for European rail travel; agents for SNCF French Railways.

By ferry and catamaran from the UK and Ireland

Some people still prefer to go to Belgium **from England by ferry**, feeling that it's a more leisurely and enjoyable journey. It's also well worth considering if you're travelling with your own vehicle, even though the Channel Tunnel – and the operations of Eurotunnel (see p.18) – have provided what is invariably a faster alternative.

Another nautical option, also faster than the ferries, is Hoverspeed's **Seacat catamaran** service from **Dover to Ostend**. The trip takes two hours and there are up to two sailings daily; a five-day excursion fare for a car and up to five passengers costs between £185 and £240. Hoverspeed also operates a Dover–Calais service with up to fifteen sailings daily and a journey time of just forty minutes.

Ferries

At time of writing, there are two **direct car ferries** from **England to Belgium**, P&O Stena Line's service from Dover and P&O North Sea Ferries sailings from Hull both going to Zeebrugge, which is just a few kilometres from Bruges. (Note, however, that the restructuring of P&O's operations may well mean the closure of the Dover–Zeebrugge route by/in 2004.) Another ferry route that might appeal is the P&O North Sea Ferries' service from Hull to Rotterdam; this leaves you just an hour or so's drive from northern Belgium. The quickest **Channel ferries** – with Sea France and/or P&O Stena Line – link Dover with Calais, from where it's about 50km north along the coast to the Belgian border near De Panne. **From Scotland**, there's just one car ferry to Belgium, Superfast Ferries' service from Rosyth.

Tariffs on these ferries are very complicated. Prices vary with the month, day and even hour that you're travelling, how long you're staying, and the size of your car. That said, discounted weekend or short-period excursion fares are commonplace, as are special deals for children and very competitively priced package tours. As a sample fare, P&O Stena Line charge from £120 to transport a car and four passengers from Dover to Zeebrugge. For the latest details, the best bet is to contact the ferry companies direct – see below for details.

Booking ahead is strongly recommended for motorists – indeed it's essential in high season. **Foot passengers** should reserve too and, in the case of Zeebrugge, ensure that the ferry company will provide onward bus transport from the harbour to Zeebrugge train station, a couple of kilometres away.

There are no direct **ferries from Ireland** to the Belgian coast, leaving travellers with two main options: they can either cross over the Irish Sea by ferry and then head for an English port, or travel with Irish Ferries from Ireland to France and then drive onto Belgium from there.

Ferry and catamaran operators

Hoverspeed UK ☎0870/240 8282,
🖰www.hoverspeed.com. Catamaran services from Dover to Calais (8–15 daily; 40min) and Ostend (Easter & mid-May to Dec 1 or 2 daily; 2hr).
Irish Ferries UK ☎0870/517 1717, Republic of Ireland ☎01/661 0511, 🖰www.irishferries.com. Dublin to Holyhead; Rosslare to Cherbourg and Roscoff. Continental services March to end Sept.
P&O Irish Sea UK ☎0870/242 4777, Republic of Ireland ☎1800/409 049, 🖰www.poirishsea.com. Larne to Cairnryan and to Fleetwood; Dublin to Liverpool.
P&O Stena Line UK ☎0870/600 0600,
🖰www.posl.com. Dover to Calais (30–35 daily; 1hr 15min) and Zeebrugge (April–Dec 3 or 4 daily; 4hr 30min). It costs £120–165 to transport a car (up to 6m long) and four passengers to Zeebrugge; charges are substantially greater on the Calais route, with prices in the £170–300 range.
P&O North Sea Ferries UK ☎0870/129 6002,
🖰www.mycruiseferries.com. Hull to Zeebrugge (Feb–Dec 1 daily; 13hr) and Rotterdam (Feb–Dec 1 daily; 10hr). Charges between £290 and £535 to carry a car and four passengers from Hull to Zeebrugge, including cabin accommodation (which is compulsory on both this and the Hull–Rotterdam route).
Sea France ☎0870/571 1711,
🖰www.seafrance.com. Dover to Calais.
Superfast Ferries ☎0800/068 1676,
🖰www.superfast.com. Rosyth to Zeebrugge (1

daily; 17hr 30min). Charges range from £52 in low season (£79 high) for a passenger return fare and a seat, up to £290 (£474) with a cabin; cars cost from £65 (£90).

By bus from the UK and Ireland

Given the low cost of airfares, travelling by long-distance bus **from the UK** to Belgium may not seem too attractive a proposition, but it is still likely to be the cheapest way of getting there, more so if you're heading straight for Luxembourg, not a bargain-airfare destination. The same cannot be said for travelling to either country by bus **from Ireland** – which is, given the time it takes, effectively not an option at all.

Eurolines, a division of the National Express bus company, offers several reliable services to both Belgium and Luxembourg. They have four daily departures from London's Victoria coach station to **Brussels** with a journey time of between eight and nine hours. Return tickets, valid for six months, cost in the region of £40–50 for adults and £25 for children aged 4–12. In addition, there are modest discounts for seniors (aged 60 or over), students and young people (aged 13–25). There are other types of ticket too, notably open-jaw returns, which allow passengers to arrive and depart from different cities. The same ticket and fare structure applies on all their UK–Belgium/Luxembourg routes. Other Belgium-bound Eurolines buses from London's Victoria coach station travel to **Antwerp** (2 or 3 daily; 8hr); **Ghent** (3 daily; 7hr); **Kortrijk** (1 daily; 7hr); and **Bruges** (1 daily; 7hr). The fares are as for Brussels, give or take the odd pound. All these buses are routed via Dover.

If you're travelling to Belgium from the Midlands, Wales, the North or Scotland, you will be routed via London's Victoria coach station (and Dover). Eurolines also operates a once-daily London to **Luxembourg City** service from Victoria coach station, via Dover, Brussels, Leuven and Liège, taking 13 hours; an adult return ticket on this, valid for six months, costs around £80. Eurolines offers a variety of **bus passes** for European travel – see their website for further details.

Bus operators

Via Eurotunnel

In addition to the car ferries detailed above, drivers, motorcyclists as well as bicyclists heading for mainland Europe from the UK have the option of using **Eurotunnel** (UK ☎0870/535 3535, ⓦwww.eurotunnel.com), which operates vehicle-carrying shuttle trains through the **Channel Tunnel**. These trains run 24 hours a day between Folkestone and Coquelles, near Calais, with up to four departures per hour (only 1 hourly midnight–6am) and take around 35 minutes, though you must arrive at least half an hour before the train you want to catch leaves. Advance booking is advisable, though it is possible to turn up and buy your **ticket** at the toll booths (after exiting the M20 at junction 11a). From Calais, it's about 50km north along the coast to the Belgian border near De Panne.

Rates depend on the time of year, time of day and length of stay (the cheapest ticket is for a day-trip, followed by a five-day return); it's cheaper to travel between 10pm and 6am, while the highest fares are reserved for weekend departures and returns in July and August. For example, a five-day fully flexible return for a car and its passengers travelling off-peak costs £180, £215 in high season. Travelling between 10pm and 6am brings the price down to £145. Motorcycles are charged as cars. There's a charge for **bicycles** (£31 single; £32 return on excursion fares) but these can only go on certain departures, with reservation by phone needed at least 24 hours in advance.

Overland from neighbouring countries

Belgium and Luxembourg have borders with France, Germany and the Netherlands. A veritable raft of **rail lines** runs into Belgium from its neighbours – and Luxembourg has good international connections too. Ordinary trains service many cities and towns and there are also the express trains of **Thalys**, a combined project of the Belgian, Dutch, French and German railways. The hub of the Thalys network is Brussels, from where there are trains to – among many destinations – Rotterdam, Amsterdam, Paris and Cologne.

Mainland Europe rail contacts

French Railways (SNCF) France ☎08 36 35 35 35, ⊛www.sncf.fr.
German Rail UK ☎0870/243 5363, Germany ☎01805 996633, ⊛www.bahn.de.

Holland Rail UK ☎01962/773 646, Holland ☎0900 9296, ⊛www.hollandrail.com.
Thalys ⊛www.thalys.com. Runs express trains linking various cities in France, Germany and the Netherlands with nine Belgian cities, including Antwerp and Brussels.

Red tape and visas

Citizens of the UK and Ireland and other EU countries, Canada, the USA, Australia and New Zealand, need only a valid passport to stay ninety days in Belgium or Luxembourg. For stays of over ninety days, EU nationals need to apply for a residence permit; the local police grant these and will take details (and often fingerprints) before issuing a renewable, three-month residence card. After six months, EU nationals can apply for an identity card, which is valid for five years.

Likewise, **non-EU nationals** require residence permits for visits of over ninety days, though things are much more difficult: applications must be made from their registered country of residence (an application made in London by an Australian temporarily living there would, for instance, not be processed). These residence permits are issued for various lengths of time – a one-year permit is the most common – upon proof of income from sources other than employment in the country receiving the application, and sometimes not even then.

Work permits for non-EU nationals are even harder to get: your prospective employer must apply locally (and prove that no other EU national can do the job) while you simultaneously apply at home; both parties must await its issuance (by no means automatic) before proceeding.

Belgian embassies and consulates

Australia Embassy: 19 Arkana St, Yarralumla, Canberra, ACT 2600 ☎02/62 73 25 01, ⓔCanberra@diplobel.org. Consulate in Sydney. Honorary Consulates in Adelaide, Brisbane, Darwin, Hobart, Melbourne, Perth.
Canada Embassy: 80 Elgin St, 4th Floor, Ottawa, Ontario, K1P 1B7 ☎613/236 72 67,

ⓔOttawa@diplobel.org. Consulates in Montréal and Toronto. Honorary Consulates in Edmonton, Halifax, Québec, Vancouver, Winnipeg.
Denmark Embassy: Øster Allé 7, 2100 Copenhagen Ø ☎35 25 02 00, ⓔCopenhagen@diplobel.org. Honorary Consulates in Esberg, Haderslev, Odense.
Ireland Embassy: 2 Shrewsbury Rd, Ballsbridge, Dublin 4 ☎01/269 2082, ⓔDublin@diplobel.org. Honorary Consulates in Cork and Limerick.
Luxembourg Embassy: Résidence Champagne, rue des Girondins 4, 1626 Luxembourg ☎44 27 46, ⓔLuxembourg@diplobel.org.
Netherlands Embassy: Alexanderveld 97, 2585 DB Den Haag ☎070/312 3456, ⓔTheHague@diplobel.org. Honorary Consulates in Amsterdam, Breda, Groningen, Maastricht, Nijmegen, Rotterdam and Vlissingen.
New Zealand Embassy: Axon House, 12th Floor, 1 Willeston St, PB 3379 Wellington ☎04/91 70 237, ⓔWellington@diplobel.org. Honorary Consulates in Auckland and Christchurch.
Sweden Embassy: Villagatan 13A, 100-41 Stockholm ☎08/534 80 200; ⓔStockholm@diplobel.org.
UK Embassy: 103 Eaton Square, London SW1W 9AB ☎020/7470 3700, ⓔLondon@diplobel.org. Honorary Consulates in Belfast, Birmingham, Cardiff, Dover, Edinburgh, Kingston-upon-Hull, Manchester, Newcastle, Plymouth, Saint Helier, Southampton.

USA Embassy: 3330 Garfield St NW, Washington DC 20008 ☎202/333 6900, ©Washington@diplobel.org. Consulates in Atlanta, Chicago, Los Angeles and New York. Honorary consulates in 28 other cities nationwide.

Luxembourg embassies

Belgium Embassy: avenue de Cortenbergh 75, B-1000 Brussels ☎02 737 57 00.
Denmark Embassy: Fridtjof Nansens Plads 5, DK-2100 Copenhagen ☎35 26 82 00.
Netherlands Embassy: Nassaulaan 8, 2514 JS The Hague ☎070/360 7516.
UK Embassy: 27 Wilton Crescent, London SW1X 8SD ☎020/7235 6961.
USA Embassy: 2200 Massachusetts Ave NW, Washington DC 20008 ☎202/265 4171.

Duty-free restrictions

Every adult **EU citizen** has a **traveller's allowance**, whereby items bought in one EU country and brought back directly to another do not incur import/export taxes as long as they are deemed as being for personal use. The maximum levels per adult are generous: 800 cigarettes (or 1kg of tobacco), 10 litres of strong spirit or 20 litres of fortified wine, 90 litres of table wine and 110 litres of beer. If you keep within these limits and within the EU, you don't need to make a declaration to customs at your place of entry.

On arrival, **non-EU residents** have a tax- or duty-free import allowance of 200 cigarettes (or 250g of tobacco), one litre of spirits or two litres of fortified wine, and two litres of table wine. Returning home, the limits are generally the same, but check with the carrier if you're uncertain. There are also restrictions as to the value of goods you can take home without paying tax – again ask the carrier if you're unsure. Remember that the importing of fresh food, plants or animals back into Britain, Ireland, the USA, Canada, Australia or New Zealand is severely restricted.

Information, websites and maps

Both Belgium and Luxembourg have branches of their national tourist offices in several of their key markets and, if you've the time and the diligence, you can pick up a wide range of information from them before you leave home. Another obvious source of advance information is the internet, where Belgium and Luxembourg are very well represented – almost all their towns and cities have their own websites. We've listed lots of websites in the guide and a few of the more general are given here. If you don't get round to any of this, rest assured that information is easy to get hold of after you've arrived: all the major towns and most of the larger villages in both countries have well-equipped and efficient tourist information offices.

The **maps** provided in the guide should be sufficient for most purposes, but drivers will need to buy a good road map and prospective hikers will need specialist hiking maps.

Websites

See also the list of tourist-office websites opposite.
Artsite Belgium ⓦwww.artsite.be. A comprehensive list of the country's main art galleries with links to their often impressive websites. Also provides links to private galleries and antique dealers.
Belgian Travel Network ⓦwww.trabel.com. General advice and information, plus useful links to the country's regional tourist offices.
Confederation of Belgian Breweries ⓦwww.beerparadise.be. One of a large number of sites extolling the virtues of Belgian beer, providing

details of brewers, brewery tours and beer generally.

Famous Belgians ⓦ www.famousbelgians.net. Irritated by all the dreary jokes about Belgium, an expatriate Belgian has compiled a list of over two hundred famous Belgians, along with potted biographies.

Neuhaus Chocolates ⓦ www.neuhaus.be. A real palate-whetter of a site from arguably the best of Belgium's chocolate chains, illustrating their full range of confections and explaining how chocolate of this quality is made.

Tintin.com ⓦ www.tintin.be. The official – and most comprehensive – Hergé and Tintin site; there are lots of quirky/peculiar unofficial ones too.

Tourist offices

The **Belgian Tourist Office** – or its Flanders–Brussels and Wallonia–Bruxelles incarnations – offers a particularly efficient service, stocking a range of glossy, free booklets of both a general and specific nature. There are usually at least three versions of all the more important booklets – one for Wallonia, another for the Flemish-speaking regions (aka Flanders) and a separate one for the capital, though information on Brussels often appears in the Wallonian/Flemish publications too. One of the most useful brochures is the **hotel guide**, which provides comprehensive and classified listings and comes in four versions – one each for Brussels, Wallonia, the Belgian coast and Flanders minus the coast. The equally useful **campsite guide** follows the same pattern, but here there are only three versions as there isn't a separate one for Brussels. There are also publications tailored to meet specific interests, most notably a comprehensive *Events in Flanders* brochure and a *Belsud Holiday Accommodation* booklet, with details of dozens of Wallonian gîtes. The Belgian Tourist Office (or Flanders–Brussels) is also good for material on the popular tourist destinations of Antwerp, Bruges and Ghent. In addition, they issue a free map of the country and stock simplified train timetables.

In Belgium itself, **tourist offices** are ten-a-penny. In the smaller towns and larger villages, you can pretty much guarantee they'll dole out a free map and a list of local sights and hotels, as in the larger towns, where most of the tourist offices offer all sorts of supplementary services – from money exchange to co-ordinating guided tours. All but the smallest tourist office will book hotel accommodation on your behalf at no cost, though you'll need to stump up a refundable deposit, which is deducted from your final bill; in the larger cities the tourist office often has a separate accommodation booking facility. Many tourist offices also book B&B accommodation, either from a published list (as in Bruges) or from a list kept by themselves (as in Kortrijk). For further details, see "Accommodation" on p.35. **Opening hours** vary considerably, but the larger tourist offices are open all year, often every day of the week. We've specified individual opening hours in the guide.

If anything, the **Luxembourg Tourist Office** is even more efficient and its free publications are certainly first rate. Highlights include a booklet of hotel and restaurant listings, with reliable prices and gradings, a comprehensive camping guide, and another on farm and rural holidays. They also supply free maps, issue glossy guides to particular districts and produce an excellent *Sights and Attractions* booklet, which details everything from the opening hours of the country's major tourist sights to where to go ballooning. All this countrywide material is available at both the Luxembourg Tourist Offices detailed below and at their office at Luxembourg City train station, which also operates a hotel booking service. In addition, most of Luxembourg's towns and larger villages have their own **tourist office**, though these concentrate on local matters and do not always have supplies of the national publications. We've given their opening times in the guide.

Tourist-office websites

Belgian Tourist Office for North America
ⓦ www.visitbelgium.com. Provides standard tourist information with an American slant.

Tourism Flanders–Brussels
ⓦ www.visitflanders.com. Detailed multilingual guide covering accommodation and sights through to events and practicalities. Competent but a little dull.

Wallonia–Bruxelles tourist office
ⓦ www.belgium-tourism.net. Portal site with lots of useful links.

Luxembourg City Tourist Information
ⓦ www.luxembourg-city.lu. A well-structured site, containing everything you'd want or need to know about the city.

National Luxembourg Tourist Information
ⓦwww.ont.lu. A first-rate and comprehensive guide to the duchy's tourist attractions, with special interest links, as well as practical information.

Belgian tourist offices abroad

One bureaucratic oddity is that in some countries, like the UK, the Belgian tourist office is divided into two – Flanders–Brussels and Wallonia–Bruxelles – but in others, such as the USA, one office covers the whole of the country.

Canada Belgian Tourist Office, PO Box 760, Succursale NDG, Montréal, Québec H4A 3S2 ☎514/484 3594, Ⓕ489 8965, ⓦwww.visitbelgium.com.

Denmark Tourism Flanders-Brussels, Vester Farimagsgade 1, DK-1606 Copenhagen ☎033/93 01 30, Ⓕ93 48 08, ⓦwww.belgien.dk.

Netherlands Tourism Flanders-Brussels, Koninginnegracht 86, 2514 AJ Den Haag ☎070/416 81 10, Ⓕ416 81 20, ⓦwww.toerismevlaanderen.be.

Netherlands Wallonia–Brussels Tourist Office, Postbus 2324, 2002 CH Haarlem ☎023/534 09 78, Ⓕ534 20 50, ⓦwww.belgie-toerisme.net.

UK Tourism Flanders–Brussels, 31 Pepper St, London E14 9RW ☎0800/954 5245 Ⓕ020/7458 0045, ⓦwww.visitflanders.co.uk.

Wallonia–Bruxelles Tourist Office, 225 Marsh Wall, London E14 9FW ☎0800/954 5245 for free brochures, ☎0906/302 0245 live operator (premium-rate line), Ⓕ020/7531 0393, ⓦwww.belgiumtheplaceto.be.

USA Belgian Tourist Office, 780 3rd Ave, Suite 1501, New York, NY 10017 ☎212/758 8130, Ⓕ355 7675, ⓦwww.visitbelgium.com.

Luxembourg tourist offices abroad

Belgium avenue Louise 104, B-1050 Brussels ☎02 646 03 70, Ⓕ02 648 61 00.

Denmark Vester Farimagsgade 1, DK-1606 Copenhagen ☎033/91 61 91, Ⓕ91 63 91.

UK 122 Regent St, London W1B 5SA ☎020/7434 2800, Ⓕ7734 1205, ⓦwww.luxembourg.co.uk.

USA 17 Beekman Place, New York, NY 10022 ☎212/935 8888, Ⓕ935 5896, ⓦwww.visitluxembourg.com.

Maps

The Belgian Tourist Office gives out a decent **free map** of the country that indicates the most important highways as well as provin-

cial and international boundaries, though it doesn't mark in the railways or have an index. The Luxembourg Tourist Office produces a comparable free map. Otherwise, the best-value general road map is the clear and easy-to-use Baedeker & AA *Belgium and Luxembourg* (1:250,000) map, though again this doesn't have an index. An alternative is the 1:350,000 Michelin *Belgium and Luxembourg* map, which has the advantage of an index, but isn't quite as clear as the AA/Baedeker version. Michelin does, however, publish the best map of Luxembourg (1:150,000), with an index and marking the most scenic roads.

As for **regional maps**, several Michelin maps in their 1:200,000 series cover parts of Belgium and Luxembourg, but these tend to be too crowded for easy use and there's no index. Much better – and clearer at 1:100,000 – are the provincial maps produced by Geocart, with an index. Geocart also produces a very good map of Wallonia at the 1:190,000 scale, again with an index and including several more detailed city insets. They also turn out a number of excellent **city maps** – for example Ghent and Bruges, both at 1:15,000 and with an index – as well as several tourist-orientated, city-centre maps, for example Antwerp, at 1:10,000.

Belgium's Institut Géographique National/Nationaal Geografisch Instituut (IGN/NGI) publishes authoritative **hiking maps** (1:25,000) of all of the country. Luxembourg is covered by two series of Ordnance Survey maps, one at 1:50,000 (2 sheets), the other at 1:20,000 (30 sheets).

All of the maps mentioned above – except possibly the AA/Baedeker – are widely available at better bookshops in Belgium and Luxembourg for €5–7, and the map outlet places listed below shouldn't have much difficulty in getting hold of most of these maps. Inevitably, though, local maps – especially city maps – are easier to get hold of locally, as are Luxembourg's Ordnance Survey maps.

Map outlets

UK and Ireland

Blackwell's Map and Travel Shop 50 Broad St, Oxford OX1 3BQ ☎01865/793 550, ⓦmaps.blackwell.co.uk/index.html.
Easons Bookshop 40 O'Connell St, Dublin 1 ☎01/873 3811, ⓦwww.eason.ie.

Heffers Map and Travel 20 Trinity St, Cambridge CB2 1TJ ☎01865/333 536, ⓦwww.heffers.co.uk.

Hodges Figgis Bookshop 56–58 Dawson St, Dublin 2 ☎01/677 4754, ⓦwww.hodgesfiggis.com.

The Map Shop 30a Belvoir St, Leicester LE1 6QH ☎0116/247 1400, ⓦwww.mapshopleicester.co.uk.

National Map Centre 22–24 Caxton St, London SW1H 0QU ☎020/7222 2466, ⓦwww.mapsnmc.co.uk.

Newcastle Map Centre 55 Grey St, Newcastle-upon-Tyne, NE1 6EF ☎0191/261 5622.

Stanfords 12–14 Long Acre, WC2E 9LP ☎020/7836 1321, ⓦwww.stanfords.co.uk.

The Travel Bookshop 13–15 Blenheim Crescent, London W11 2EE ☎020/7229 5260, ⓦwww.thetravelbookshop.co.uk.

US and Canada

Adventurous Traveler Bookstore 102 Lake Street, Burlington, VT 05401 ☎1-800/282-3963, ⓦwww.adventuroustraveler.com.

Book Passage 51 Tamal Vista Blvd, Corte Madera, CA 94925 ☎1-800/999-7909, ⓦwww.bookpassage.com.

Distant Lands 56 S Raymond Ave, Pasadena, CA 91105 ☎1-800/310-3220, ⓦwww.distantlands.com.

Elliot Bay Book Company 101 S Main St, Seattle, WA 98104 ☎1-800/962-5311, ⓦwww.elliotbaybook.com.

Forsyth Travel Library 226 Westchester Ave, White Plains, NY 10604 ☎1-800/367-7984, ⓦwww.forsyth.com.

Globe Corner Bookstore 28 Church St, Cambridge, MA 02138 ☎1-800/358-6013, ⓦwww.globercorner.com.

GORP Travel ☎1-877/440-4677, ⓦwww.gorp.com/gorp/books/main.htm.

Rand McNally ☎1-800/333-0136, ⓦwww.randmcnally.com. Around thirty stores across the US; dial ext 2111 or check the website for the nearest location.

The Travel Bug Bookstore 2667 W Broadway, Vancouver V6K 2G2 ☎604/737-1122, ⓦwww.swifty.com/tbug.

World of Maps 1235 Wellington St, Ottawa, Ontario K1Y 3A3 ☎1-800/214-8524, ⓦwww.worldofmaps.com.

Australia and New Zealand

Mapland 372 Little Bourke St, Melbourne, Victoria 3000 ☎03/9670 4383, ⓦwww.mapland.com.au.

Map Shop 6–10 Peel St, Adelaide, SA 5000 ☎08/8231 2033, ⓦwww.mapshop.net.au.

MapWorld 173 Gloucester St, Christchurch, New Zealand ☎0800/627 967 or 03/374 5399, ⓦwww.mapworld.co.nz.

Perth Map Centre 1/884 Hay St, Perth, WA 6000 ☎08/9322 5733, ⓦwww.perthmap.com.au.

Specialty Maps 46 Albert St, Auckland 1001 ☎09/307 2217, ⓦwwww.ubdonline.co.nz/maps.

Insurance

Prior to travelling, you'd do well to take out an insurance policy to cover against theft, loss and illness or injury. Before paying for a new policy, however, it's worth checking whether you already have some degree of cover: EU health care privileges apply in both Belgium and Luxembourg (see p.24), some all-risks home insurance policies may cover your possessions when overseas, and many private medical schemes include cover when abroad. In Canada, provincial health plans usually provide partial cover for medical mishaps overseas, while holders of official student/teacher/youth cards in Canada and the US are entitled to meagre accident coverage and hospital in-patient benefits. Students will often find that their student health coverage extends during the vacations and for one term beyond the date of last enrolment.

After exhausting the possibilities above, you might want to contact a specialist travel insurance company. A typical travel insurance policy usually provides cover for the loss of baggage, tickets and – up to a certain limit – cash or cheques, as well as cancellation or curtailment of your journey. Most of them exclude so-called **dangerous sports** – climbing, rafting and windsurfing and so forth – unless an extra premium is paid. Many policies can be chopped and changed to exclude coverage you don't need – for example, sickness and accident benefits can often be excluded or included at will. If you do take medical coverage, ascertain whether benefits will be paid as treatment proceeds or only after your return home, and whether there is a 24-hour medical emergency number. When securing baggage cover, make sure that the per-article limit – typically under £500 – will cover your most valuable possession. If you need to make a claim, you should keep receipts for medicines and medical treatment, and in the event you have anything stolen, you must obtain a crime report statement or number.

Rough Guides travel insurance

Rough Guides offers its own travel insurance, customized for our readers by a leading UK broker and backed by a Lloyd's underwriter. It's available for anyone, of any nationality and any age, travelling anywhere in the world.

There are two main Rough Guide insurance plans: **Essential**, for basic, no-frills cover; and **Premier** – with more generous and extensive benefits. Alternatively, you can take out **annual multi-trip insurance**, which covers you for any number of trips throughout the year (with a maximum of 60 days for any one trip). Unlike many policies, the Rough Guides schemes are calculated by the day, so if you're travelling for 27 days rather than a month, that's all you pay for. If you intend to be away for the whole year, the **Adventurer policy** will cover you for 365 days. Each plan can be supplemented with a "Hazardous Activities Premium" if you plan to indulge in sports considered dangerous, such as climbing, scuba-diving or trekking.

For a policy quote, call the Rough Guide Insurance Line on UK freefone ℡0800/015 0906; US toll-free ℡1-866/220 5588, or, if you're calling from elsewhere, ℡+44 1243/621 046. Alternatively, get an online quote or buy online at ⊛www.roughguidesinsurance.com.

Health

Under reciprocal health arrangements involving members of the European Union (EU), nationals of EU countries are entitled to free or discounted medical treatment within the respective public health care systems. Non-EU nationals should take out their own medical insurance to travel in Belgium and Luxembourg. Indeed this can be handy for EU citizens as well, as it will cover the cost of items not within the EU's scheme, such as dental treatment and repatriation on medical grounds. That said, most private insurance policies don't cover prescription charges – their "excesses" are usually greater than the cost of the medicines. The more worthwhile policies promise to sort matters out before you pay (rather than after) in the case of major expense; if you do, however, have to pay upfront, get and keep the receipts. For more on insurance, see p.22.

If you're an EU national, you should **complete form E111** before you travel, as it provides proof of your entitlement to treatment under EU arrangements. The form is available from most post offices in the UK and from health boards in the Republic of Ireland. If you don't have an E111 form with you on your travels, you will have to pay upfront for any medical treatment you need; in this eventuality, ensure that you get a receipt so that you can claim against your insurance policy or your local health authority back home.

Pharmacies

Minor ailments can be remedied at **pharmacies** (French *pharmacie*, Flemish *apotheek*), which supply non-prescription drugs as well as toiletries, tampons, condoms and the like. Most are open Monday to Friday 9am to 6pm or 7pm, some on Saturdays too, and in the cities a rota system keeps at least one open 24 hours a day. The rota should be displayed in the window of every pharmacy, and tourist offices also have details as do some of the better hotels. Outside the cities, you'll find a pharmacy in every town and most of the larger villages, but the smaller the place, the less likelihood there is of late-night opening.

Seeking medical treatment

Your local pharmacy, tourist office or hotel should be able to provide the address of an **English-speaking doctor** or **dentist** if you need one. If you're seeking treatment under EU health agreements, double-check that the doctor is working within (and seeing you as) a patient of the public health care system. This being the case, you'll need to pay upfront for treatment and medicines; you'll then be able to reclaim a proportion of the cost (around 75 percent in Belgium) by applying to the local Sickness Fund Office (ask the doctor for details) with your E111 form.

You can anticipate that some **hospital** staff will speak English in Flemish Belgium and in Brussels and Luxembourg, though in parts of Wallonia you'll be struggling unless you have some rudimentary grasp of French. If you know you're going to be admitted to hospital and you're an EU national, try to contact the Sickness Office in advance, producing your E111 form and asking them where to obtain the cheapest treatment. They will give you a certificate confirming they will pay part of the cost of treatment in Belgium, or usually all of the cost in Luxembourg excluding a non-refundable daily charge. In medical **emergencies**, you can reach the ambulance service by calling ☏100 in Belgium or ☏112 in Luxembourg, and you should produce your E111 form when you're admitted to hospital.

Costs, money and banks

By western European standards, Belgium and Luxembourg are moderately expensive when it comes to accommodation and food, though this is partly offset by the low cost of public transport. More precise costs for places to stay and eat are given in the guide, and you should consult p.35 for general guidelines on accommodation prices.

ATMs are routine in all the big cities and are the easiest way to get cash, but currency-exchange facilities are widespread too.

Average costs

If you're prepared to buy your own picnic lunch, stay in youth hostels, and stick to the less expensive bars and restaurants, you could get by on around **£30/US$50 a day**. Staying in two-star hotels, eating out in medium-range restaurants most nights and drinking in bars, you'll get through at least **£65/$95 a day** – in Luxembourg it might be more – with the main variable being the cost of your room. On **£100/$150 a day** and upwards, you'll be limited only by your energy reserves – though if you're planning to stay in a five-star hotel and to have a big night out, this still won't be enough. As always, if you're travelling alone you'll spend much more on accommodation than you would in a group of two or more: most hotels do have single rooms, but they're fixed at about 75 percent of the price of a double.

Restaurants don't come cheap, but costs remain manageable if you avoid the extras and concentrate on the main courses, for which around £10/$14 will normally suffice – twice that with a drink, starter and dessert. You can, of course, pay a lot more – a top restaurant in Brussels can be twice as expensive again, and then some.

Currency

On January 1, 2002, Belgium and Luxembourg (along with Austria, Finland, France, Germany, Greece, Ireland, Italy, Portugal, Spain and the Netherlands) replaced their existing currencies with a common currency, the **euro** (€). The euro is split into 100 cents. There are seven euro **notes** – in denominations of €500, €200, €100, €50, €20, €10 and €5, each a different colour and size – and eight different **coins**, including €2 and €1, then 50, 20, 10, 5, 2 and 1 cents. Euro coins feature a common EU design on one face, but different country-specific designs on the other. All euro notes and coins can be used in any of the twelve "euro-zone" states.

Traveller's cheques

The main advantage of buying **traveller's cheques** is that they are a safe way of carrying funds. The usual fee for their purchase is one or two percent of face value, though this fee is often waived if you buy the cheques through a bank where you have an account.

It pays to get a selection of denominations, and to make sure that the purchase agreement and a record of cheque serial numbers are kept safe and separate from the cheques themselves. In the event that cheques are lost or stolen, the issuing company will expect you to report the loss immediately. Consequently, when you buy your traveller's cheques, ensure you have the details of the company's emergency contact numbers or the addresses of their local offices. Most companies claim to replace lost or stolen cheques within 24 hours.

Both Euro and US dollar traveller's cheques are commonly accepted as form of payment in both Belgium and Luxembourg. American Express cheques, sold through most North American, Australasian and European banks, are particularly widely accepted in the two countries. That said, both countries are so familiar with exchanging currency that any well-known brand of traveller's cheque in any major currency will do. When you **cash your cheques**, you'll find that almost all banks make a percentage charge per transaction on top of a basic minimum charge.

ATMS and credit cards

ATMs are commonplace in both Belgium and Luxembourg, especially in the cities. Using ATMs is undoubtedly the quickest and easiest way of getting money, especially as most of them give instructions in a variety of languages. They accept a host of **debit cards**, including all those bearing the Cirrus mark. If in doubt, check with your bank to find out if the card you wish to use will be accepted – and if you need a new (international) PIN. You'll rarely be charged a transaction fee as the banks make their profits from applying different exchange rates. **Credit cards** can be used in ATMs too, but in this case transactions are treated as loans, with interest accruing daily from the date of withdrawal. All major credit cards, including American Express, Visa and Mastercard, are widely accepted in both Belgium and Luxembourg.

Banks and exchange

Banking hours in Belgium are generally from Monday to Friday 9am to 4pm, sometimes with a one-hour lunch break occuring between noon and 2pm. In Luxembourg normal banking hours are Monday to Friday 9am to 4.30pm, again with a one-hour lunch break between noon and 2pm; in cities some banks are open on Saturday mornings. For **changing currency**, almost every bank takes a commission of between one and two percent with a minimum charge of about €5; if commission is waived, double-check the exchange rate to ensure that it hasn't been lowered to compensate the bank.

Outside banking hours, most major hotels, many travel agents and some hostels, tourist offices and campsites will change money at less generous rates and with variable commissions, as will the **foreign exchange kiosks** (*bureaux de change/wisselkantoren*) to be found in the bigger cities, usually at the main train station.

Wiring money

Having **money wired** from home using one of the companies listed below is never convenient or cheap, and should only be considered as a last resort. One variation on the theme is to have **your own bank** send the money through. For that, you need to nominate a receiving bank in Belgium or Luxembourg; any local branch will do, but

those in the bigger cities will probably be more familiar with the process. Naturally you need to confirm the co-operation of the local bank before you set the wheels in motion back home. The sending bank's fees are geared to the amount being transferred and the urgency of the service you require – the fastest transfers, taking two or three days, start at around £25/\$40 for the first £300–400/\$450–600.

Money-wiring companies

Moneygram UK & Republic of Ireland ☏ +800/6663 9472, US & Canada ☏ 1-800/926-9400, Australia ☏ 1800/230 100, New Zealand ☏ 09/379 8243 or 0800/262 263; ⓦ www.moneygram.com.

Thomas Cook UK ☏ 01733/318 922, Republic of Ireland ☏ 01/677 1721, US ☏ 1-800/287-7362, Canada ☏ 1-888/823-4732; ⓦ www.us.thomascook.com.

Western Union UK ☏ 0800/833 833, Republic of Ireland ☏ 1800/395 395, US and Canada ☏ 1-800/325-6000, Australia ☏ 1800/649 565, New Zealand ☏ 09/270 0050; ⓦ www.westernunion.com.

Getting around

Travelling around Belgium is almost always easy: it's a small country, and there's an extremely well-organized – and reasonably priced – public transport system in which an extensive train network is supplemented by (and tied in with) a plethora of local bus services. Luxembourg is, of course, even smaller, but here matters are not so straightforward: the train network is limited, and the public transport system is largely based around buses, whose timetables often demand careful scrutiny if you're doing much independent travelling.

Travel **between Belgium and Luxembourg** by train is a seamless affair – with no border controls and with routine through-ticketing. Two main rail lines link the two countries – one from Brussels to Luxembourg City via Namur and Arlon; the other from Liège to Luxembourg City. Journey times are insignificant – Brussels to Luxembourg City takes three hours – and services are frequent.

Trains

The best way of getting around **Belgium** is by train. Run by the Société Nationale des Chemins de Fer Belges/Belgische Spoorwegen (**Belgian Railways**), denoted by a simple "B" in an oval, the system is comprehensive and efficient, and fares are relatively low. For example, a **standard, second-class ticket** (*billet ordinaire/gewone bil-*

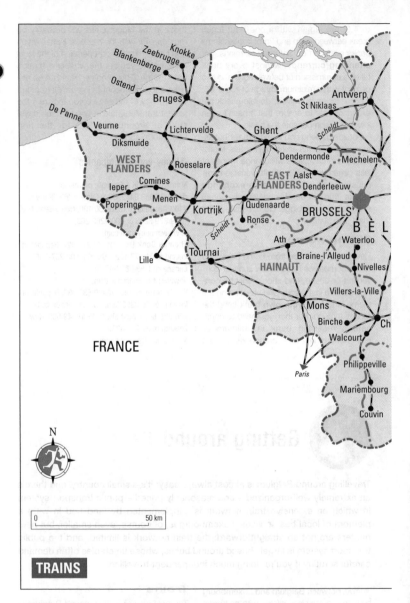

TRAINS

jet) from Brussels to Leuven, 40km away, is €3.80, while Brussels to Arlon, at 200km one of the longest domestic train journeys you can make, costs just €15.40 one way. Standard return tickets are twice the cost of a single and first-class tickets are about fifty percent more expensive. Children under the age of 12 travel free up to a maximum of four per adult, except during the weekday rush-hour (Mon–Fri before 9am). Seniors (65+) are charged a flat-rate of €2.50 for one day-return journey anywhere in Belgium outside the rush-hour. In addition, a variety of **special deals** on specific routes at certain times can cut the cost of a standard fare by around forty percent: there are weekend tickets, special return tariffs and bargain deals on day returns, with a day-trip from Brussels and other inland towns to the seaside being one particularly popular option.

If you're going to be doing a lot of travelling, consider investing in a **rail pass**. The Belgian Tourrail pass (B-Tourrail) gives entitlement to five days' unlimited rail travel within a month-long period for €58 (€90 first class). There is also the **fixed-price reduction card** (Carte de réduction à prix fixe; Reductiekaart tegen vaste prijs), which for €16.30 allows you to purchase first- and second-class tickets at half-price during the period of a month, and the **Go Pass**, for travellers aged between 12 and 25, which is valid for ten second-class journeys between two specified stations within six months – price €3.90.

Belgian Railways has an excellent **English-language website** (ⓦwww.b-rail.be), which covers every aspect of the network and has an online ticket booking facility. Furthermore, they publish lots of information including a comprehensive **national timetable** (*Indicateur Intérieur/Spoorboekje Binnenland*; €5), sold at major train stations.

Luxembourg trains

In Luxembourg the trains are run by the Société Nationale des Chemins de Fer Luxembourgeois – **CFL** – and are not nearly as wide-reaching as those in Belgium. The **network** comprises just a handful of lines, with the principal route cutting north–south down the middle of the country from Belgium's Liège to Luxembourg City via Clervaux and Ettelbruck. The other lines radiate out from Luxembourg City: one heads northwest to Belgium's Arlon and Brussels,

another travels east to Trier in Germany and the remainder service the industrial southwest corner of the country. The **timetable** is simplicity itself, with trains travelling to and from every station hourly at the same time past the hour between 8am and 8pm. A free diagrammatic plan of the country's bus and train network is available at most train stations, as are individual train and bus timetables, or you can purchase a countrywide bus and train timetable from train stations and major newsagents at minimal cost.

Tickets are very reasonably priced and cover both trains and buses. They come in two types: short-distance tickets, valid for one hour, cost €1.10 each (€8.80 for 10), while a **one-day national pass** (the Oeko-Pass) costs €4.40, €17.60 for a pack of five. These are valid from the first time you use them (you must punch them in the machines provided to record the time) until 8am the following day. Another option, available between Easter and October, is the **Luxembourg Card**, allowing free travel on the country's buses and trains. It also provides free or discounted admission to many tourist attractions (a booklet giving details comes with the Card). It can be bought for one-, two- or three-day periods, and costs €9, €16, €22 respectively per person, or €18, €32 or €44 for a family card covering up to five people. The Card is widely available at hotels, hostels and tourist offices.

CFL has its own French-language **website** ⓦwww.cfl.lu; a general guide is provided in English at ⓦwww.luxembourg.co.uk/pubtrans.html.

Rail passes

In addition to the country-specific passes mentioned above, a bewildering variety of **rail passes** is on offer, covering whole parts of Europe. Some have to be bought outside Europe, while others can only be bought in specific countries within Europe. **Rail Europe** is the umbrella company for all national and international rail purchases, and its comprehensive website (ⓦwww.raileurope.com) is the most useful source of information on which rail passes are available; it also gives current prices.

Eurail

A **Eurail Pass** is not going to pay for itself if you're planning to stick to Belgium and

Luxembourg, but is an economic option if you're planning a grander itinerary. The pass, which must be purchased before arrival in Europe, allows unlimited free first-class train travel in 17 countries including Belgium and Luxembourg. It's available in increments of 15 days, 21 days, 1 month, 2 months and 3 months. If you're under 26, you can save money with a **Eurail Youthpass**, which is valid for second-class travel or, if you're travelling with up to four companions, a joint **Eurail Saverpass**, both of which are available in the same increments as the Eurail Pass. Another option is a **Eurail Flexipass**, which is good for 10 or 15 days' travel within a two-month period. This, too, comes in first-class, under-26/second-class (**Eurorail Youth Flexipass**) and group (**Eurail Saver Flexipass**) versions.

A scaled-down version of the Flexipass, the **Europass**, is also available; it allows first-class and youth (second-class) travel in France, Germany, Italy, Spain and Switzerland for a specified number of days within a two-month period, with up to four "associate" countries (including Belgium and Luxembourg) included for an additional fee. The **Europass Saverpass** is a version of the Europass for people travelling in groups of two or more that offers a saving of fifteen percent per person on the regular fare.

Inter-Rail and Euro Domino passes

The **Inter-Rail pass** is only available to residents of European countries, and you will be asked to provide proof of residency before being allowed to purchase one. They come in over-26 and (cheaper) under-26 versions, and cover 28 European countries grouped together in zones: **Zone E** covers France, Belgium, the Netherlands and Luxembourg. The passes are available for 22 days (one zone only) or 1 month; you can purchase a pass covering up to 3 zones or a global pass including all zones.

Also available only to European residents, the **Euro Domino pass** is an individual country pass that provides unlimited travel in 28 European and North African countries – including Belgium and Luxembourg. The passes are available for between three and eight days' travel within a one-month period. There is a discounted youth price for those under 26, and a half-price child (age 4–11) fare.

Benelux Tourrail Pass

Another rail pass worth considering is the **Benelux Tourrail Pass**, costing €116 (first class €174). It's valid for any five days' travel within a month on the Belgian, Dutch and Luxembourg national rail networks; it also entitles bearers to discounts on Eurostar from London to Brussels. The under-26 version, the Benelux Tourrail Junior Pass (second class only) costs €87.

Buses

As so much of the country is covered by the rail network, **Belgian buses** are mainly of use for travelling short distances, and wherever there's a choice of transportation the train is quicker and not that much more expensive. Indeed, in much of Belgium buses essentially supplement the trains, with services radiating out from the train station and/or connecting different rail lines. That said, local buses are very useful for travelling around and into the environs of major towns and cities, and invaluable in some parts of rural Belgium, like the Botte de Hainaut and the Ardennes, where the train network fizzles out. Three **bus companies** provide nation-wide coverage: De Lijn (Ⓦwww.delijn.be) in the Flemish-speaking areas, STIB (Ⓦwww.stib.irisnet.be) in Brussels, and TEC in Wallonia.

As regards **Luxembourg's buses**, the reverse is true: because of the sparseness of the rail system, buses are much more important, though again bus and train services are fully integrated. A free diagrammatic plan of the country's bus and train network is available at major bus and train stations, as are individual bus timetables; alternatively, for a few euros, you can purchase a countrywide bus and train timetable from train stations and major newsagents. For details of tickets and fares, see "Luxembourg trains" above.

Driving and car rental

Both Belgium and Luxembourg possess a first-rate road network, which includes toll-free motorways, though driving in Belgium is not without its difficulties: the country is so crowded – and the distances between places often so small – that navigation can require lightning reflexes and an intuitive sense of direction. Another issue is **big-city driving**, where congestion and one-way systems are often time-consuming and difficult in equal measure – never mind on-street

French and Flemish place names

The list below provides the French and Flemish names of some of the more important towns in Belgium where the difference may cause confusion. The official name comes first, the alternative afterwards, except in the case of Brussels where both languages are of equal standing.

French–Flemish
Bruxelles – Brussel
Ath – Aat
Liège – Luik
Mons – Bergen
Namur – Namen
Nivelles – Nijvel
Soignies – Zinnik
Tournai – Doornik

Flemish–French
Antwerpen – Anvers
Brugge – Bruges
De Haan – Le Coq

Gent – Gand
Ieper – Ypres
Kortrijk – Courtrai
Leuven – Louvain
Mechelen – Malines
Oostende – Ostende
Oudenaarde – Audenarde
Ronse – Renaix
Sint Truiden – St Trond
Tienen – Tirlemont
Tongeren – Tongres
Veurne – Furnes
Zoutleeuw – Léau

parking, which can be well-nigh impossible, and the fact that drivers in Belgium, and especially Brussels, are generally considered to be some of the most pugnacious in Europe.

Belgian place names can be confusing, though in most cases the French and Flemish names are similar – or at least mutually recognizable (see box above, for some of the trickier examples). In Brussels and its environs, all the road signs are bilingual, but this is not the case in the rest of the Belgium. This situation presents no problems until you cross the language divide, when the name you've been following on the road signs can simply disappear, with, for example, "Liège" suddenly transformed into "Luik". Whatever you do, make sure you've got a good road map (see p.22).

Petrol stations are plentiful and most accept major credit cards. Fuel costs are broadly the same as the UK, much higher than those in the US – reckon on about €1.10 per litre for four-star fuel (96-octane).

Foreign licences and breakdown cover

Many foreign **driving licences** are honoured in Belgium and Luxembourg – including all EU, US, Australian, New Zealand and Canadian ones – but an **International Driver's Licence** (available at minimum cost from your home motoring organization, is an easy way to set your mind at rest. Provisional licences are, however, not acceptable. If you're bringing your own car, you must have adequate insurance or a green card, a first-aid kit and a warning triangle. Extra insurance coverage for unforeseen legal costs is also well worth having, as is an appropriate **breakdown policy** from your home motoring organization. In the case of the latter, be sure there is an appropriate emergency contact number. In Britain, as an example, the RAC and AA charge members and non-members about £100 for a month's Europe-wide breakdown cover, with all the appropriate documentation, including green card, provided. Note, however, that rates vary depending on the age of the vehicle and increase if you're towing anything.

Motoring organizations

UK and Ireland

RAC UK ☎0800/55 00 55, ⊛www.rac.co.uk.
AA UK ☎0800/44 45 00, ⊛www.theaa.co.uk;
Republic of Ireland ☎01/617 9988,
⊛www.aaireland.ie.

US and Canada

American Automobile Association (AAA) Each state has its own club – check the phone book for local address and phone number (or call ☎1-800/222-4357 or check ⊛www.aaa.com).

Canadian Automobile Association (CAA) Each province has its own club – check the phone book for local address and phone number (or call ☎613/247-0117 or check ⓦwww.caa.com).

Australia and New Zealand

Australian Automobile Association ☎02/6247 7311, ⓦwww.aaa.asn.au.
New Zealand Automobile Association ☎09/377 4660, ⓦwww.aa.co.nz.

Rules of the road

Throughout both countries **speed limits** are widely posted: it's 50kph in all built-up areas, 90kph on main roads and 120kph on motorways. If you're stopped for any violation, the police can (and usually will) levy a stiff fine anywhere between €25 and €150 depending on the seriousness of the offence. Most **driving rules** and regulations are pretty standard: seat belts are compulsory, penalties for drunken driving are severe – more than a glass of wine and you'll be pushing the limit – and you drive on the right. Remember also that trams have right of way over any other vehicle, and that, unless indicated otherwise, motorists must give way to traffic merging from the right. Finally, drivers are supposed to stop at zebra crossings, but they rarely do – so if you intend to stop, try to make sure the vehicle on your tail has advance warning.

Car rental

To rent a car, you'll have to be 21 or over (and have been driving for at least a year), and you'll need a credit card. Rental **charges** are high, beginning at around €350 per week for unlimited mileage in the smallest vehicle, but include collision damage waiver and vehicle (but not personal) insurance. To cut costs, watch for the special deals offered by the bigger companies (a Friday to Monday weekend rental might, for example, cost as little as €100). Alternatively, you could go to a smaller, local company, though you should, in this case, proceed with care: check the policy for the excess applied to claims, and ensure that the policy includes collision damage waiver (applicable if an accident is your fault), and, in general, adequate levels of financial cover. Note that it's almost always less expensive to rent your car before you leave home than after arrival.

Car rental agencies

All the major international **car rental** companies are represented in Belgium and Luxembourg. Addresses for them are given in the "Listings" sections of city accounts in the guide; many tourist offices have lists of local car rental companies.

UK

Avis ☎0870/606 0100, ⓦwww.avisworld.co.uk.
Budget ☎0800/181 181, ⓦwww.budget.co.uk.
Europcar ☎0845/722 2525, ⓦwww.europcar.co.uk.
Hertz ☎0870/844 8844, ⓦwww.hertz.co.uk.
Holiday Autos ☎0870/400 0099, ⓦwww.holidayautos.co.uk.
National ☎0870/536 5365, ⓦwww.nationalcar.com.
Thrifty ☎01494/751 600, ⓦwww.thrifty.co.uk.

Republic of Ireland

Avis ☎01/605 7500, ⓦwww.avis.co.ie.
Budget ☎0903/27711, ⓦwww.budgetcarrental.ie.
Europcar ☎01/614 2800, ⓦwww.europcar.ie.
Hertz ☎01/676 7476, ⓦwww.hertz.ie.
Holiday Autos Republic of Ireland ☎01/872 9366, ⓦwww.holidayautos.ie.

US and Canada

Avis US ☎1-800/331-1084, Canada ☎1-800/272-5871, ⓦwww.avis.com.
Budget US ☎1-800/527-0700, ⓦwww.budgetrentacar.com.
Dollar US ☎1-800/800-4000, ⓦwww.dollar.com.
Hertz US ☎1-800/654-3001, Canada ☎1-800/263-0600, ⓦwww.hertz.com.
National ☎1-800/227-7368, ⓦwww.nationalcar.com.
Thrifty ☎1-800/367-2277, ⓦwww.thrifty.com.

Australia

Avis ☎13 63 33, ⓦwww.avis.com.
Budget ☎1300/362 848, ⓦwww.budget.com.
Dollar ☎02/9223 1444 or 1800/358 008, ⓦwww.dollarcar.com.au.
Hertz ☎13 30 39, ⓦwww.hertz.com.
National ☎13 10 45, ⓦwww.nationalcar.com.au.
Thrifty ☎1300/367 227, ⓦwww.thrifty.com.au.

New Zealand

Avis ☎0800 655 111 or 09/526 2847, ⓦwww.avis.co.nz.
Budget ☎0800/652 227 or 09/976 2222, ⓦwww.budget.co.nz.

Hertz ℡0800/654 321, ⓦwww.hertz.co.nz.
National ℡0800/800 115 or 03/366 5574,
ⓦwww.nationalcar.co.nz.
Thrifty ℡09/309 0111, ⓦwww.thrifty.co.nz.

Cycling

Cycling is something of a national passion in **Belgium**, and it's also – given the short distances and largely flat terrain – a viable and fairly effortless way of getting around. That said, you do have to be selective: cycling in most of the big cities and on the majority of trunk roads – where separate cycle lanes are a rarity – is precarious, verging on the suicidal. On the other hand, once you've reached the countryside, there are dozens of clearly signposted cycle routes to follow – and local tourist offices will invariably have maps and route descriptions, which you can supplement with the relevant IGN (NGI) map (see p.22). The logic of all this means that most Belgian cyclists – from Eddy Merckx lookalikes to families on an afternoon's pedal – carry their bikes to their chosen cycling location by car or train (though not by bus – it's not allowed). Belgian Railways transports bicycles for a flat rate of €4.10 per single journey, €6.90 for a day-return if you buy the ticket before you board the train; if you pay on the train, it costs half as much again.

If you haven't brought your own bicycle, you can **rent** seven-gear touring bikes from 35 train stations nationwide and 21-gear mountain bikes from four Ardennes stations, most notably Spa. Prices start at around €8.50 per day. There's also the **Train & Bike** (Train & Vélo/Trein & Fiets) package, in which the price of a day-long excursion includes both a return train ticket and cycle hire. Prices are based on the distance between the departure station and the bike rental station. The shortest excursions cost €9.30 for the train ticket and the hire of a seven-gear bike, €17.35 for the twenty-one gear version; the longest excursions cost €17.23 and €23.30 respectively. A refundable deposit of €13 is payable for the seven-gear bike, €37 for the mountain bike. In all cases, bikes have to be returned to the issuing station office, so you should check opening hours before you set off, though most are open from April to September daily from 7am to 8pm. For a full list of stations offering this service, either consult ⓦwww.b-rail.be or pick up Belgian Railways' *Train & Bike* leaflet, available for free from major Belgian train stations. It's a good idea to **reserve** your bike ahead of time during the summer.

Luxembourg

The Grand Duchy is popular with cyclists and has over 500km of cycle tracks, many of them following old railway lines. The Luxembourg Tourist Office has all the information and helped produce the most detailed booklet on the subject, *40 Cycle Tours*, published by Guy Binsfeld and available at newsagents and bookshops in the Grand Duchy. You can **rent bikes** at an assortment of campsites, hostels, hotels and tourist offices for around €10 a day (€20 for a mountain bike); local tourist offices have details of locations where they're not mentioned in the guide. Bear in mind also that you can take your bike on trains (but not buses) anywhere in the country for €1.10.

Accommodation

Inevitably, hotel accommodation is one of the major expenses you'll incur on a trip to Belgium and Luxembourg – indeed, if you're after a degree of comfort, it's going to be the costliest item by far. There are, however, budget alternatives, beginning with the no-frills end of the hotel market and B&Bs – though note these are effectively rented rooms in private houses rather than the British-style bed-and-breakfast. Even cheaper are student rooms – courtesy of a few of the larger universities – and both Hostelling International-registered and "unofficial" youth hostels. Handily, most of the latter are located in the larger cities and/or main tourist spots.

In summer you'd be well advised to **reserve** rooms in advance, especially in the more popular destinations such as Bruges, Antwerp and the Ardennes. You can do this by phoning, faxing or emailing direct – we've given contact details throughout the guide – or by using the free **Belgian Tourist Reservations service** (BTR), bd Anspach 111 B4, 1000 Brussels (☏02 513 74 84, ℗02 513 92 77, ℗www.horeca.be), through which you can book hotel rooms nationwide. Reservations can also be made through most tourist offices on arrival, again for free – the modest deposit they levy is deducted from your final bill.

Hotels

Across Belgium and Luxembourg (and the Netherlands), a common **Benelux standard** is used to classify all hotels, guesthouses (*auberges/gasthofs*) and motels that are recognized and licensed by the appropriate government agency. In Belgium, there are three such licensing agencies – one each for Brussels and the French- and Flemish-speaking regions; Luxembourg has just one. The Benelux standard grades establishments within general categories – from one-star to five-star – and the appropriate number of stars is displayed outside all licensed premises on a **blue permit shield**; places that fail to obtain a licence are not allowed a shield. The classification system is, by necessity, measured against easily identifiable criteria – lifts, toilets, room service etc – rather than aesthetics, specific location or even cost. Consequently, they only provide a general guide to both quality and prices: a poky room in a three-star hotel in a mediocre part of Bruges may, for instance, cost more than a comfortable room in a four-star hotel in the

centre of a less popular town. That said, one- and two-star places are frequently rudimentary (incidentally, hotel foyers can be deceptively plush compared with the rooms beyond) and, in general, you only begin to hit the real comfort zone at three stars.

For a full **list of approved hotels** throughout Belgium, with details of prices and facilities, pick up copies of the *Hotel Guide Flanders – Flemish Countryside* and *Hotel Guide Flanders – Belgian Coast*, which together cover the Flemish-speaking regions; Wallonia has *Hôtels Wallonie* and the capital has *Brussels Hotels*. All three publications are available free at major tourist offices both in Belgium and abroad (see p.22 for their addresses outside Belgium). Note that in tourist material the designation "Flanders" often covers all Flemish-speaking areas, and "Wallonia" the French zone. In Luxembourg, the tourist office publishes a *Luxembourg Hotels* booklet detailing all the country's approved hotels, with prices and facilities. It's available free at any major Luxembourg tourist office, both inside the country and abroad (for overseas addresses, see p.22).

Hotel **prices** range from an absolute minimum of around €30–40 for a double room in the least expensive, one-star establishment, through €70–120 for a double in a middle-range, three-star hotel, and on up to around €140 and more in the big city luxury hotels. That said, watch out for summer discounts and weekend specials that can reduce costs by up to 35 percent, especially at the top end of the market. Almost all hotels offer **breakfast** (usually included in the rate), ranging from a roll and coffee at the less expensive places through to full-scale banquets at top-range hotels.

Accommodation price codes

All the **accommodation** we've listed in Belgium and Luxembourg has been categorized according to the price codes detailed below. These represent how much you can expect to pay for the **least expensive double room** in that establishment during high season; they do not take into account special or weekend discounts. Our categories are simply a guide to prices and do not give an indication of the facilities you might expect, other than the broad outlines we provide below; as such they differ from the star-system applied by the tourist authorities. Where dormitory beds are available, their prices are listed in euros – they usually come in at €12–15 per night.

❶ **Up to €30** Most hostels have some private accommodation in the form of single-, double- and triple-bedded rooms, and this price code applies to the cheaper doubles. These rooms are normally without any kind of private facilities beyond a washbasin, or, sometimes, a shower. Expect decor, etc, to be fairly grim, particularly in big-city locations.

❷ **€30–40** This category covers the majority of the doubles provided at many hostels – both HI and "unofficial".

❸ **€40–60** Comprises mainly two-star, one-star or un-starred hotels, sporting a mixture of adequate, functional rooms with no private facilities and a selection of slightly more upscale choices with basic private facilities. Again, expect the decor to be frugal-cum-dour. Also covers most B&Bs.

❹ **€60–80** This grade, basically two- merging into three-star hotels, comes up frequently in the guide. It's a little more comfortable than the previous grouping, and the emphasis is on rooms with en-suite facilities.

❺ **€80–100** Standard three-star hotel accommodation, where facilities will almost always be private and you will often have the use of a phone and TV. At this price, you can expect the room to be small and the decor neat and trim but

fairly uninspired – though there are exceptions. This category also covers the best of the B&Bs, many of which are really very classy.

❻ **€100–120** Top-of-the-range three-star and many four-star hotels, whose rooms are always en suite and mostly come equipped with phone, TV, perhaps a mini-bar, and occasionally room service. Many of the better chain hotels aim for this price range and you can expect rooms to be smart and neat, if hardly inspirational, though there are some notable (and delightful) exceptions.

❼ **€120–150** Some three-star, but mostly four-star, hotels with all the attendant facilities you would expect – private bathroom, mini-bar, phone and TV, room service, and perhaps even a gym, swimming pool or sauna.

❽ **€150–180** Top quality, often attractively located four- and occasional five-star hotels with all amenities – frequently a gym, swimming pool and sauna too. Some really superb places here.

❾ **€180 and over** This category takes in four- and five-star establishments where service and facilities are second-to-none, along with establishments of special distinction – notable either for their location, architecture, or perhaps their history.

B&Bs

In recent years, the number of Belgian **B&Bs** (*chambres d'hôtes/gastenkamers*) has increased rapidly, though "B&B" is perhaps something of a misnomer as guests rarely have much contact with their hosts – it's more like a rented room in a private house. The average B&B in both Belgium and Luxembourg works out at about €40–60 per double per night, €80 in Brussels and

Bruges. The only common snag is that many B&Bs are inconveniently situated far from the respective town or city centre – be sure to check out the location before you accept a room.

In most places, the tourist office has a list of local B&Bs, which it will issue to visitors, but in the more popular destinations – especially Bruges – B&Bs are publicized alongside hotels. Another permutation is the **B&B guild**, which registers and lists a locality's B&Bs in conjunction with the tourist office; Antwerp B&Bs are organized like this. In Luxembourg, B&Bs are less of a feature, though again local tourist offices have the details. Wherever the arrangements are more formalized – eg Bruges – the B&B premises are inspected and awarded stars in accordance with the Benelux standard (see under "Hotels", p.35).

Hostels and student rooms

Belgium has around twenty-five **HI-registered youth hostels** (*auberges de jeunesse/jeugdherbergen*) run by two separate organizations, one for the Flemish regions and one for Wallonia, with both operating hostels in Brussels. There's very little difference between the two groups, though the Flemish ones tend to be more geared up for school parties than those in Wallonia, which are perhaps a tad less regimented. In both regions, there are hostels in most of the major tourist towns, but many are situated in out-of-the-way places or less-visited towns. We've detailed all the key hostels in the guide; for a complete list, contact either your home hostelling organization or the Vlaamse Jeugdherbergcentrale, Van Stralenstraat 40, B-2060 Antwerp (☎03 232 72 18, ℗03 231 81 26, ⓦwww.vjh.be) or Les Auberges de Jeunesse de Wallonie, rue de la Sablonnière 28, B-1000 Brussels (☎02 219 56 76, ℗02 219 14 51, ⓦwww.laj.be).

For HI members, Belgium's HI hostels **charge** a flat rate per person of between €12.50 and €14.50 for a bed in a dormitory, including breakfast, though one or two of the smarter hostels – like those in Ostend and Ghent – cost a few euros more. Bed linen is often included in the overnight rate, but where it isn't you can expect to pay an extra €3–4. Many Belgian hostels also offer lunch at around €5, and dinner at around €7 or so. Non-HI members pay a surcharge of around ten to fifteen percent on the overnight rate.

In addition to the HI hostels, some of the larger Belgian cities – primarily Antwerp, Bruges and Brussels – have a number of **"unofficial"** (i.e. non-HI) **youth hostels**, usually referred to as *logements pour jeunes/jeugdlogies*). These normally charge €12–15 for a dormitory bed and are often just as comfortable and a good deal more intimate – though the quality varies enormously and some are real dives. In Belgium, you'll also find some universities offering **student rooms** for rent during the summer holidays – Ghent being a good example. The rooms are frugal, but rates are very reasonable – reckon on about €15 per person per night.

Luxembourg

Luxembourg has eleven **youth hostels**, all members of the Centrale des Auberges de Jeunesse Luxembourgeoises (AJL), place de la Gare 24, L-1616 Luxembourg (☎26 29 35 00, ℗26 29 35 03, ⓦwww.youthhostels.lu). Rates for HI members are €14–16 per person for a dorm bed, with breakfast and bed linen included. Some places also serve meals – reckon on €6–7 for lunch or dinner. From November to February, most of the hostels are exclusively for use by groups (school parties and so forth); if you're to be in with a chance of staying at this time you'll probably need to be in a group of ten or more.

Youth hostelling associations

If you're planning on staying at a lot of hostels, it makes sense to join your home youth hostelling organization before you leave, in order to avoid the surcharges that non-HI members pay.

Australia Youth Hostels Association, 422 Kent St, Sydney ☎02/9261 1111, ⓦwww.yha.com.au.
Canada Hostelling International/Canadian Hostelling Association, Room 400, 205 Catherine St, Ottawa, ON K2P 1C3 ☎1-800/663 5777, ⓦwww.hostellingintl.ca.
England and Wales Youth Hostel Association (YHA), Trevelyan House, 8 St Stephen's Hill, St Albans, Herts AL1 2DY ☎0870/870 8808, ⓦwww.yha.org.uk & ⓦwww.iyhf.org.
New Zealand Youth Hostels Association 173 Gloucester St, Christchurch ☎03/379 9970, ⓦwww.yha.co.nz.

Belgian campsite classification

Belgian campsites are graded within the following general categories. They provide a guide as to facilities, but not necessarily to cost.

1-star Must comply with minimum camping regulations by having drinking water facilities, cold showers, flush toilets, washbasins and power points.

2-star As for previous grade, but must have daytime supervision and more electrical facilities.

3-star Must have hot showers, sports facilities and a shop.

4-star As for previous grade, but must also possess a restaurant, children's playing area and electrical fixtures throughout the site.

5-star As for previous grade, but more facilities per person and a high level of supervision.

Northern Ireland Hostelling International Northern Ireland 22–32 Donegall Rd, Belfast BT12 5JN ☎ 028/9032 4733, ⓦ www.hini.org.uk.

Republic of Ireland An Óige, 61 Mountjoy St, Dublin 7 ☎ 01/830 4555, ⓦ www.irelandyha.org.

Scotland Scottish Youth Hostel Association, 7 Glebe Crescent, Stirling, FK8 2JA ☎ 0870/155 3255, ⓦ www.syha.org.uk.

USA Hostelling International-American Youth Hostels (HI-AYH) 733 15th St NW, Suite 840, PO Box 37613, Washington, DC 20005 ☎ 202/783-6161, ⓦ www.hiayh.org.

Camping

Camping is a popular pastime in both Belgium and Luxembourg. In **Belgium**, there are literally hundreds of campsites to choose from, anything from a field with a few tent pitches through to extensive complexes with all mod cons. As with the hotels, the country's campsites are regulated by three governmental agencies – one for Flanders, one for Wallonia and one for Brussels – and each produces its own **camping booklet(s)**. Currently, the Wallonian booklet details around 250 campsites, the Flemish (ⓦ www.camping.be) about the same, divided between the *Flemish Countryside* and the *Belgian Coast* publications. Note also that many Belgian campsites are situated with the motorist in mind and consequently a substantial proportion occupy key locations beside main roads.

All three governmental agencies apply the same **grading system**, classifying campsites on a one- to five-star matrix (see box, above). The majority are one- and two-star establishments, for which a family of two adults, two children, a car and a tent can expect to pay between €12 and €18 per night. Surprisingly, most four-star sites don't

cost much (if any) more – add about €2.50 – though the rate for the occasional five-star campsite can reach around €30.

Luxembourg has around ninety registered campsites, all detailed in the free booklet available from the national tourist board. They are **classified** into three broad bands. The majority are in Category 1, the best-equipped and most expensive classification, where each site must have, for example, one hot shower per one hundred and one washstand per twenty guests, playgrounds, electric connections for camping installations, and 24-hour staffing. Simpler Category 3 sites must, among several requirements, have a washstand for every thirty guests and a camp leader on site or in the vicinity. Prices vary even within each category, but are usually €3–5 per person, plus €3–7 for a site.

During peak season it can, in both countries, be a good idea to **reserve ahead** if you have a car and large tent or trailer. Phone numbers for campsites are listed in this guide and in the free camping booklets; In Luxembourg, the national tourist office operates a peak-season camping information and reservation line on ☎ 42 82 82 20.

Farm and rural holidays

In both Belgium and Luxembourg, the tourist authorities have developed an imaginative and extensive programme of short-break holidays – anything from cycling tours and gastronomic excursions through to beer and antique-buying weekends. In Wallonia and Luxembourg, they also co-ordinate farm and rural holidays, ranging from "*en famille*" accommodation in a **farmhouse**, to the renting of rural apartments and country dwellings (gîtes ruraux). There are also **gîtes d'étapes** – dormitory-style lodgings situated in relatively remote parts of the country – which can house anywhere between ten and one hundred people per establishment. You can often choose to rent just part of the gîte d'étape or stay on a bed-and-breakfast basis. Some of the larger gîtes d'étapes (or gîtes de groupes) cater for large groups only, accepting bookings for a minimum of 25 people.

In all cases, advance booking is essential and prices, naturally enough, vary widely depending on the quality of accommodation, the length of stay and the season. As examples, a high season (mid-June to Aug), week-long booking of a pleasantly situated and comfortable farmhouse for four adults and three children might cost you in the region of €300, whereas a ten-person gîte d'étape might cost €250, €25 less in winter. On the other hand, one night's bed and breakfast costs around €12 – sometimes less if you're under 26 – and about €5 for children under 6 years old. For further details, contact the Wallonian and Luxembourg tourist offices, each of which produces a detailed, specialist brochure, respectively *Belsud Holiday Accommodation* and *Luxembourg: Holiday Apartments, Farm and Rural Holidays*.

Eating and drinking

Belgian cuisine, particularly that of Brussels and Wallonia, is held in high regard worldwide, and in most of Europe is seen as second only to French in quality – indeed many feel it's of equal standing. For such a small country, there's a surprising amount of provincial diversity, but it's generally true to say that pork, beef, game, fish and seafood, especially mussels, are staple items, often cooked with butter, cream and herbs, or sometimes beer – which is, after all, the Belgian national drink. Soup is also common, a hearty stew-like affair offered in a huge tureen from which you can help yourself – a satisfying and reasonably priced meal in itself. The better Belgian chefs are often eclectic, dipping into many other cuisines, especially those of the Mediterranean, and also borrowing freely from across their own country's cultural/linguistic divide.

Luxembourg cuisine doesn't rise to quite such giddy heights, though it's still of an excellent standard. The food here borrows extensively from the Ardennes, but, as you might expect, it has more Germanic influences, with sausages and sauerkraut featuring on menus, as well as pork, game and river fish.

As for **drink**, beer is one of the real delights of Belgium, and Luxembourg produces some very drinkable white wines along its bank of the River Moselle.

Food

The least expensive places to eat are **cafés** and **bars** – though the distinction between the two is often blurred. A number of these establishments flank every main square in every small and medium-sized town, offering basic dishes, such as omelettes, soups, croque monsieur (a toasted ham and cheese sandwich with salad) and chicken or steak with chips. Prices are usually very reasonable – reckon on about €6 for the more modest dishes, €10 for the more substantial – though of course you will often pay more in the most popular tourist destinations. In general, and especially in Wallonia, the quality of these dishes will regularly be excellent and portions characteristically substantial. In

For glossaries of French and Flemish terms for food and drink, see p.450.

the big cities, these cafés and bars play second fiddle to more specialist – and equally inexpensive – places, primarily pasta and pizza joints, cafés that cater for the shopper – and specialize in cakes and pastries – and ethnic café-restaurants, noodle houses and so forth.

Though there's often a thin dividing line between the café and the **restaurant**, the latter are mostly a little more formal and, not surprisingly, rather more expensive. Even in the cheapest restaurant a main course will rarely cost under €10, with a more usual figure being between €12 and €18. Restaurants are usually open at lunch time (noon–2pm), but the main focus is in the evening. In addition, many restaurants close one day a week, usually Monday or Tuesday, and in the smaller towns kitchens start to wind down around 9.30pm.

Throughout the guide, we've given **phone numbers** for restaurants where it's advisable to make reservations. One final point is that many bars, cafés and restaurants offer a good-value *plat du jour/dagschotel*, usually for around €10, and frequently including a drink.

Wallonian cuisine

Wallonian cuisine is broadly similar to French, based upon a fondness for rich sauces and the freshest of ingredients. From the Walloons come *truite à l'Ardennaise*, trout cooked in a wine sauce; *chicorées gratinés au four*, chicory with ham and cheese; *fricassée Liègeois*, basically, fried eggs, bacon and sausage or blood pudding; *fricadelles à la bière*, meatballs in beer; and *carbonnades de porc Bruxelloise*, pork with a tarragon and tomato sauce.

The Ardennes, in particular, is well known for its cured ham (similar to Italian Parma ham) and, of course, its pâté, made from pork, beef, liver and kidney – though it often takes a particular name from an additional ingredient, for example *pâté de faisan* (pheasant) or *pâté de lièvre* (hare). Unsurprisingly, game (*gibiers*) features heavily on most Ardennes menus. Among the many salads you'll find are *salade de Liège*, made from beans and potatoes, and *salade wallonie*, a warm salad of lettuce, fried potatoes and bits of bacon.

Flemish cuisine

In **Flanders**, the food is more akin to that of Holland, characteristically plainer and sim-

pler. Indeed, for decades traditional Flemish cuisine was regarded with much disdain as crude and unsubtle, but in recent years there's been a dramatic **revival** of its fortunes, and nowadays Flemish dishes appear on most menus in the north and there are dozens of speciality Flemish restaurants too.

Commonplace dishes include *waterzooi*, a soup-cum-stew consisting of chicken or fish boiled with fresh vegetables; *konijn met pruimen*, an old Flemish standby of rabbit with prunes; *paling in 't groen*, eel braised in a green (spinach) sauce with herbs; *karbonaden*, cubes of beef marinated in beer and cooked with herbs and onions; *stoemp*, mashed potato mixed with vegetable and/or meat purée; and *hutsepot*, literally hotchpotch, a mixed stew of mutton, beef and pork.

Luxembourg cuisine

Favourite dishes in Luxembourg include smoked pork with beans; liver dumplings with sauerkraut and potatoes; *tripe à la Luxembourgeoise*; *boudin*, black pudding served with apple sauce and mashed potatoes; and *judd mat gardeboenen*, cooked ham served with sauté potatoes and broad beans in a cream sauce. On the Moselle many restaurants serve *friture de la Moselle* – small fried fish. At many annual celebrations and fairs restaurants serve *fesch* – whole fish fried in batter.

Vegetarian fare

Traditional Belgian and Luxembourg food is fairly meat-based, which means vegetarians are in for a difficult time, especially if they want to sample the local specialities – though this is considerably easier if seafood is acceptable. Most of the larger towns have one or two **vegetarian cafés** or restaurants, but that's all – and even these are mostly part-time places, open for lunch and a couple of evenings only. The main exceptions are Brussels and Antwerp, where vegetarian menu options are more common and there's a reasonable selection of specifically vegetarian restaurants too.

Foreign cuisines

The quality and diversity of Belgium's native cuisine means that the vast majority of restaurants stick to it, though many supplement their menus with **Italian** and **French** offerings. Indeed, among foreign cuisines, it's the Italian and French restaurants which dominate, both in the major cities and the smaller towns, and the food they offer is almost invariably of good, if not excellent, quality. Other, less commonplace cuisines are to be found in Brussels in abundance, less so in the other conurbations, though Antwerp, in particular, is catching up. Among them, **Chinese** and **Vietnamese** restaurants are fairly widespread, while **Turkish** and **Greek** restaurants are especially good in Brussels. **Balkan** restaurants crop up here and there and Luxembourg's sizeable Portuguese community has spawned a reasonable supply of **Portuguese** places. In Brussels especially there are also a handful of **African** (mostly Congolese) and a goodly selection of **North African** (Moroccan and Tunisian) restaurants – worth sampling, and often very good bargains.

Breakfast and snacks

In most parts of Belgium and Luxembourg you'll **breakfast** in routine fashion with a cup of coffee and a roll or croissant, though the more expensive hotels usually offer sumptuous banquet-like breakfasts with cereals, fruit, hams and cheeses. Everywhere, **coffee** is almost always first-rate – aromatic and strong, but rarely bitter; in Brussels and the south it's often accompanied by hot milk (*café au lait*), but throughout Belgium there's a tendency to serve it in the Dutch fashion, with a small tub of evaporated rather than fresh milk.

Later in the day, the most common **snack** is *frites* (chips) – served everywhere in Belgium from *friture/frituur* stands or parked vans, with salt or mayonnaise, or more exotic dressings. **Mussels** – *moules/mosselen* – cooked in a variety of ways and served with chips, is akin to Belgium's national dish, and makes a good fast lunch in cafeterias. Rather more wholesome are the filled **baguettes** (*broodjes*) that many bakeries and cafés prepare on the spot – imaginative, tasty creations that make a meal in themselves. Many fish shops, especially on the coast, also do an appetizing line in seafood baguettes, while street vendors in the north sell various sorts of toxic-looking **sausage** (*worst*), especially black pudding (*bloedworst*).

Everywhere there are stands selling **waffles** (*gaufres/wafels*), served up steaming hot with jam and honey. There are two main types of waffle – the more common Liège waffle, sweet, caramelized and with the corners squared off; and the Brussels waffle, larger, fluffier and needing a topping to give added flavour.

Cakes, pastries and chocolate

Belgium heaves with patisseries, where you can pick up freshly baked bread and choose from a mouth-watering range of **cakes** and **pastries** – from mousse slices through to raspberry tarts and beyond.

Belgium is also famous for its **chocolate**; each Belgian eats 12.5kg of the stuff annually on average, and chocolates are the favoured gift when visiting friends. The biggest Belgian chocolatiers, Godiva and Leonidas, have stores in all the main towns and cities, and their **pralines**, filled with cream, liqueurs or *ganache* (a fine dark chocolate); and **truffles**, made of chocolate, butter, cream and sugar, are delicious, if somewhat sugar-sticky for some tastes. Reckon on spending around €10 for 500g of their chocolates – though you can pay much more for what many feel is a far superior, less sugary chocolate at one of the small, independent chocolate makers you'll find in all the bigger cities. Arguably the best of the chains is Neuhaus, much smaller than Godiva and Leonidas but with outlets in all the major cities.

Apart from chocolate, look out for *speculaas* or *speculoos*, a speciality of the northern part of the country. A rich and hard cinnamon-flavoured biscuit, it was originally baked in the form of saints and religious figures, though it now comes in all shapes and sizes.

Drink

No trip to Belgium would be complete without sampling its beer, which is always good, almost always reasonably priced and comes in a bewildering variety of brews. There's a **bar** on almost every corner and most serve at least twenty types of beer; in some the

Although it's unlikely that any one establishment will have all the brews we've listed, all of them will (or should) have at least a couple. For a more detailed approach to the subject, see "Belgium's Great Beers" in Contexts, p.429.

Brugse Straffe Hendrik (Blond 6.5%, Bruin 8.5%)
Huisbrouwerij De Halve Mann, a small brewery located in the centre of Bruges, produces zippy, refreshing ales. Their Blond is a light and tangy pale ale, whereas the Bruin is a classic brown ale with a full body.

Bush Beer (7.5% and 12%)
A Walloon speciality. It's claimed that the original version is – at 12% – the strongest beer in Belgium, but it's actually more like a barley wine, and has a lovely golden colour and an earthy aroma. The 7.5% Bush is a tasty pale ale with a zip of coriander.

Chimay (red top 7%, blue top 9%)
Made by the Trappist monks of Forges-les-Chimay, in southern Belgium, Chimay beers are widely regarded as being amongst the best in the world. Of the several brews they produce, these two are the most readily available, fruity and strong, deep in body, and somewhat spicy with a hint of nutmeg and thyme.

La Chouffe (8%)
Produced in the Ardennes, this distinctive beer is instantly recognisable by the red-hooded gnome (*chouffe*) which adorns its label. It's a refreshing pale ale with a hint of coriander and it leaves a peachy aftertaste.

Corsendonk Pater Noster (5.6%)
The creation of the brewmaster Jef Keersmaekers, this bottled beer is easily the pick of the many Corsendonk brews. It is known for its Burgundy-brown colour and smoky bouquet.

De Koninck (5%)
Antwerp's leading brewery, De Koninck, is something of a Flemish institution – for some a way of life. Its standard beer, De Koninck, is a smooth, yellowish pale ale that's very drinkable, with a sharp aftertaste; better on draft than in the bottle.

Delirium Tremens (9%)
Great name for this spicy amber ale that is the leading product of Ghent's Huyghe brewery.

Gouden Carolus (8%)
Named after – and allegedly the favourite tipple of – the Habsburg emperor Charles V, Gouden Carolus is a full-bodied dark brown ale with a sour and slightly fruity aftertaste. Brewed in the Flemish town of Mechelen.

Gueuze (Cantillon Gueuze Lambic 5%)
A type of beer rather than an individual brew, gueuze is made by blending old and new lambic (see opposite) to fuel re-fermentation with the end result being bottled. This process makes gueuze a little sweeter and fuller bodied than lambic. Traditional gueuze – like the brand mentioned – can, however, be hard to track down and you may have to settle for the sweeter, more commercial brands, notably Belle Vue Gueuze (5.2%), Timmermans Gueuze (5.5%) and the exemplary Lindemans Gueuze (5.2%).

Hoegaarden (5%)
The role model of all Belgian wheat beers, Hoegaarden – named after a small town east of Leuven – is light and extremely refreshing, despite its cloudy appearance. The ideal drink for a hot summer's day, it's brewed from equal parts of wheat and malted barley. The history of wheat beers is curious: in the late 1950s, they were unloved and unsung and facing extinction, but within twenty years they had been taken up by a new generation of drinkers and are now massively popular.

Kriek (Cantillon Kriek Lambic 5%, Belle Vue Kriek 5.2%, Mort Subite Kriek 4.3%)
A type of beer rather than a particular brew, Kriek is made from a base beer to which are added cherries or, in the case of the more commercial brands, cherry juice and perhaps even sugar.

Other fruit beers are available too, but Kriek is perhaps the happiest, and the better examples – including the three mentioned above – are not too sweet and taste simply wonderful. Kriek is decanted from a bottle with a cork – like a sparkling wine.

Kwak (8%)

This Flemish beer, the main product of the family-run Bosteels brewery, is not all that special – it's an amber ale sweetened by a little sugar – but it's served in dramatic style with its distinctive hourglass placed in a wooden stand.

Lambic beers (Cantillon Lambik 5%, Lindemans Lambik 4%)

Representing one of the world's oldest styles of beer manufacture, lambic beers are tart because they are brewed with at least thirty percent raw wheat as well as the more usual malted barley. The key feature is, however, the use of wild yeast in their production, a process of spontaneous fermentation in which the yeasts of the atmosphere gravitate down into open wooden casks over a period of between two and three years. This balance of wild yeasts is specific to the Brussels area. Draught lambic is extremely rare, but the bottled varieties are more commonplace, even though most are modified in production. Cantillon Lambik is entirely authentic, an excellent drink with a lemony zip. Lindemans Lambik is similar and a tad more available.

Leffe (Leffe Brune 6.5%, Leffe Blond 6.6%)

Brewed in Leuven, Leffe is strong and malty and comes in two main varieties: Leffe Blond, bright, fragrant and with a slight orangey flavour; and Leffe Brune, dark, aromatic and full of body. Very popular, but a little gassy for some tastes.

Orval (6.2%)

One of the world's most distinctive malt beers, Orval is made in the Ardennes at the Abbaye d'Orval, founded in the twelfth century by Benedictine monks from Calabria. The beer is a lovely amber colour, refreshingly bitter and makes a great aperitif.

Rochefort (Rochefort 6 7.5%, Rochefort 8 9.2%, Rochefort 10 11.3%)

Produced at a Trappist monastery in the Ardennes, Rochefort beers are typically dark and sweet and come in three main versions: Rochefort 6, Rochefort 8 and the extremely popular Rochefort 10, which has a deep reddish-brown colour and a delicious fruity palate.

Rodenbach (Rodenbach 5% and Rodenbach Grand Cru 6.5%)

Located in the Flemish town of Roeselare, the Rodenbach brewery produces a reddish-brown ale in several different formats with the best brews aged in oak containers. Their widely available Rodenbach (5%) is a tangy brown ale with a hint of sourness. The much fuller – and sourer – Rodenbach Grand Cru is far more difficult to get hold of, but is particularly delicious.

Verboden Vrucht (Forbidden Fruit 9%)

Forbidden Fruit is worth buying just for the label, which depicts a fig-leaf clad Adam offering a strategically covered Eve a glass of beer in the garden of Eden. The actual drink is dark, strong and has a spicy aroma. Produced by Hoegaarden, it has something of a cult following in Flanders.

Westmalle (Westmalle Dubbel 7%, Tripel 9%)

The Trappist monks of Westmalle, just north of Antwerp, claim their beers not only cure loss of appetite and insomnia, but reduce stress by half. Whatever the truth, the prescription certainly tastes good. Their most famous beer, the Westmalle Tripel, is deliciously creamy and aromatic, while the popular Westmalle Dubbel is dark and supremely malty.

Westvleteren (Special 6° 6.2%, Extra 8° 8%).

Made at the abbey of St Sixtus in West Flanders, Westvleteren beers come in several varieties. These two are the most common, dark and full-bodied, sour with an almost chocolate-like taste.

beer list runs into the hundreds. Traditionally, Belgian bars are cosy, unpretentious places, the walls stained brown by years of tobacco smoke. However, in recent years many have been decorated in anything from a sort of potty medievalism (wooden beams etc) through to Art Nouveau and a frugal post-modernist style, which is especially fashionable in the big cities. Many bars serve simple food too, while a significant percentage pride themselves on first-rate dishes from small but well-conceived menus.

Luxembourg has a good supply of bars too, with imported Belgian beers commonplace alongside the fairly modest lagers of the country's three dominant breweries and the white wines of the west bank of the River Moselle.

Beer

Beer has been a passion in Belgium since the early Middle Ages, when monks did much of the brewing. Later, brewers established themselves in all the larger towns, associating themselves in guilds, which became among the most influential of the country's institutions. Today, there are up to seven hundred different kinds of beer in Belgium, many brewed by small family breweries and some still produced by monasteries. Most of these are of the lager – or Pilsner – type, but there are other tasty/tastier types too.

In both Belgium and Luxembourg, ask for a *bière/bier* in a **bar** and you can expect to be served a 250ml glass of whatever the bar has on tap. The most common beers you'll see in Belgium are the Leuven-based Stella Artois, Jupiler from Liège (the country's biggest-selling beer) and Maes. In Luxembourg the most widespread brands are Diekirch (the largest domestic brewer), Mousel and Bofferding.

Inevitably, bar **prices** vary considerably, largely depending on the quality of the brew. Run-of-the-mill lagers start at around €0.90, but add a touch more quality and you're soon heading off towards €1.50. For speciality bottled beers like Chimay (see p.42) you'll pay somewhere between €2 and €3.50. All the better bars have a **beer menu**.

Wines and spirits

In Belgium, beer very much overshadows **wine**, but the latter is widely available at about €10 a bottle or so and upwards in a café or restaurant. French wines are the most popular. **Luxembourg wines** are pleasant whites, fruitier and drier than the average French wine, being more akin to the vintages of Germany. A Luxembourg speciality is its sparkling, *méthode champenoise* wine – very palatable and reasonably priced: try the St Martin brand, which is excellent and dry. To guarantee quality, all the premium Luxembourg wines are marked with the appellation "Marque Nationale".

There's no one national Belgian **spirit**, but the Flemings have a penchant – like their Dutch neighbours – for **jenever**, which is similar to gin, made from grain spirit and flavoured by juniper berries. It's available in most ordinary as well as specialist bars, the latter selling as many as several hundred varieties. Broadly speaking, jenever comes in two types, young (*jonge*) and old (*oude*), the latter characteristically pale yellow and smoother than the former; both are served ice-cold. In Luxembourg, you'll come across locally produced bottles of **eau de vie** – distilled from various fruits and around fifty percent alcohol by volume. Finally, all the usual spirits – gin, whisky etc – are widely available.

Communications

Belgium and Luxembourg have competent and comprehensive postal systems, with post boxes and post offices liberally distributed right across the region. The telephone network is comparable – and public telephone boxes are ubiquitous. There are internet cafés in all the major towns of Belgium and Luxembourg – see the guide for details.

Mail

Post offices in Belgium and Luxembourg are usually open Monday to Friday 9am to noon and 2 to 5pm. Some urban post offices open much longer hours (broadly 7am–7pm) and a handful open Saturday (sometimes in the morning only) as well. Mail to the US takes seven days or so, within Europe two to three days. **Mail boxes** are painted red in Belgium and yellow in Luxembourg.

You can **receive letters** at any main city post office by having them addressed "Poste Restante" followed by your surname (preferably underlined and in capitals), then the name of the town and country. To collect your mail, take along your passport or identity card and – if you're expecting post and your initial enquiry produces nothing – ask the clerk to check under all of your names and initials, as letters sometimes get misfiled.

Telephones

You can make domestic and international **telephone calls** with equal ease from public (and private) phones in both Belgium and Luxembourg. Phone booths are plentiful, and most have English instructions displayed inside. The vast majority of hotel rooms have phones, but note that there is almost always an exorbitant surcharge for their use. To make a **reverse-charge** or collect call, phone the International operator (they almost all speak English).

Public telephones are of the usual European kind, where you deposit the money before you make your call, though coin-operated public phones are being phased out in favour of those that only take credit cards and **telecards**. The latter can be purchased at newsstands, post offices, major train stations and some supermarkets in several denominations, beginning at €5.

Useful telephone numbers and codes

For emergency services, see p.56.

International calls

To call Belgium and Luxembourg **from abroad**, dial your local international access code, then ☎32 for Belgium or ☎352 for Luxembourg, followed by the number you require, omitting the initial zero if dialling Belgium.

To call abroad **from Belgium and Luxembourg**, begin with the dialling codes below, then dial the number you want, omitting the initial zero if present.

Australia	☎0061	UK	☎0044
New Zealand	☎0064	USA and Canada	☎001
Republic of Ireland	☎00353		

Operator numbers

	Belgium	Luxembourg
Domestic directory enquiries	☎1405	☎017
International directory enquiries	☎1405	☎016
International operator assistance	☎1324/1224	☎010

There are **no area codes** in either Belgium or Luxembourg (though note that Belgian numbers begin with a zero, a relic of former area codes which have been incorporated into the numbers themselves). Calls anywhere in Belgium are **charged** at the same rate – €0.05 at peak times (Mon–Fri 8am–7pm), half that at other times. At phone booths, telephone calls cost a minimum of €1, while €2 is enough to start an international telephone call, but not much more. Charges in Luxembourg are comparable.

Telephone charge cards and credit-card calls

One of the most convenient ways of phoning home from abroad is via a **telephone charge card** from your phone company back home. Using a local access number and a PIN, you can make calls from most hotel, public and private phones that will be charged to your phone bill back home. Since most major charge cards are free to obtain, it's certainly worth getting one at least for emergencies; enquire first though whether Belgium and Luxembourg are covered, and bear in mind that rates aren't necessarily cheaper than calling from a public phone.

Some international phone providers – such as AT&T (Ⓦ www.att.com/traveler) – allow you to route calls from Belgium and Luxembourg over their network. This means dialling a local access number before the number you wish to call; the cost of the call is charged to your credit card. Though convenient, this can be much more expensive than simply using coins or a telecard, so before going down this route you'll need to check the charges and local access numbers with the company whose network you wish to use.

Mobile phones

In both Belgium and Luxembourg, mobile phone access is routine in all the major cities and in most of the countryside. If you want to use a mobile phone bought **at home**, you'll need to check cellular access with your phone provider before you set out. In particular, note that phones bought in North America need to be of the **triband** variety to access the cellular network in Europe. Note also that you are likely to be charged extra for incoming calls when abroad, as the people calling you will be paying the usual rate. The same often applies to text messages, though in many cases these can now be received with the greatest of ease – no fiddly codes and so forth – and at ordinary rates.

The media

British newspapers and magazines are easy to get hold of in both Belgium and Luxembourg and neither is there much difficulty in getting hold of American publications. Two of Britain's leading TV channels – BBC1 and BBC2 – are picked up by most hotel TVs in Flanders.

The press

The major newspapers in **Wallonia** are the influential, independent *Le Soir*; the right-wing, very Catholic *La Libre Belgique*; and *La Dernière Heure*, which is noted for its sports coverage. In **Flanders** you'll see the leftish *De Morgen*, traditionally the favourite of socialists and trade unionists; the right-

leaning *De Standaard*; and the populist, vaguely liberal *Het Laatste Nieuws*. In **Luxembourg**, the biggest circulation newspaper is the politically middle-of-the-road *Luxemburger Wort*.

In Brussels, there's also an excellent **English-language weekly**, the *Bulletin*, a magazine catering primarily for the sizeable expat community resident in the capital. Its news articles are interesting and diverse, picking up on key Belgian themes and issues, and its listings section is first-rate. It also carries a fair-sized classified section – useful if you've just arrived for an extended stay and are looking for an apartment or even work.

In the cities and larger towns of both countries and in the resorts of the Belgian coast, **British newspapers** – from tabloid through to broadsheet – as well as the more popular **English-language magazines** are widely available either on the day of publication or the day after. Internationally distributed **American newspapers** – principally the *Wall Street Journal*, *USA Today* and the *International Herald Tribune* – are also easy to get hold of, though distribution is extensive only in the larger cities. Train-station bookstands are usually the best bet for English-language newspapers and magazines.

TV and radio

British radio stations can be picked up in much of Belgium and Luxembourg: you'll find BBC Radio 4 on 198kHz (1515m) long wave, Radio 5 Live on 909kHz and 693 kHz (330m & 432m) medium wave, and the World Service on 648kHz (463m) medium wave. Shortwave frequencies and schedules for BBC World Service (@www.bbc.co.uk/worldservice), Radio Canada (@www.rcinet.ca) and Voice of America (@www.voa.gov) are listed on their respective websites.

As far as **British TV** is concerned, BBC1 and BBC2 television channels are on most hotel-room TVs in Belgium, and on some in Luxembourg too. Many bars and many hotels are geared up for (at least a couple of) the big pan-European **cable and satellite** channels: MTV, CNN, Eurosport and so forth. In most parts of both countries, you can also pick up all the Dutch and German stations, and often those from France and Italy too. **Domestic TV** is largely uninspiring, though the Flemish-language TV1 and Kanaal 2 usually run English-language films with subtitles, whereas the main Wallonian channels – RTBF 1 and ARTE – mostly dub.

Opening hours, public holidays and festivals

Opening hours for shops, businesses and tourist attractions remain fairly traditional, although there's recently been some movement towards greater flexibility. In both Belgium and Luxembourg, travel plans can be disrupted on public holidays when most things close down (though not, of course, restaurants, bars and hotels) and public transport is reduced to a limited (Sunday) timetable. At a local level, the same applies during festivals and major events.

Opening hours

Business hours (ie office hours) normally run from Monday to Friday 10am to 5pm. Normal **shopping hours** are Monday through Saturday 10am to 6pm, though many smaller shops open late on Monday morning and/or close a tad earlier on Saturdays. In addition, in some of the smaller towns and villages many places close at lunchtime (noon–2pm) and for the half-day on Wednesdays or Thursdays. At the other extreme, larger establishments – primarily supermarkets and department stores – are increasingly likely to have extended hours, often on Fridays when many remain open till 8pm or 9pm. In the big cities a smattering of convenience stores (*magasins de nuit/avondwinkels*) stay open either all night or until 1am or 2am daily; other than these, only die-hard money makers – including some souvenir shops – are open late or on Sunday. Most towns also have a **market day**, usually midweek (and sometimes Saturday morning); this is often the liveliest time to visit, particularly when the stalls fill the central square (Grand-Place or Grote Markt).

Almost all Belgian towns and most of the larger villages have a **museum** of some description, and the same applies in Luxembourg. Most museums are open Tuesday to Saturday from 9.30am or 10am to 4.30pm or 5pm, and frequently on Sunday, with many of the smaller concerns closing for lunch, sometime between noon and 2pm. Opening hours are often more restrictive outside the April–September period – when, indeed, many less important and/or less popular museums simply close down.

The most important and frequently visited **churches** are normally open Monday to Saturday from around 9am to 5pm, with more restrictive opening hours on Sunday. However, visiting many of the less distinguished but still significant churches can be problematic, particularly those which are rarely, if ever, open for worship. In these cases gaining access is really hit or miss – even the local tourist office may be unaware of their opening times. As a general rule of thumb, try around 5 or 6pm when the priest and the occasional worthy might drop by.

Wallonia and Luxembourg have an abundance of **castles**, ranging from stern medieval strongholds to dignified, stately chateaux. Many have passed into state ownership and these have opening hours akin to those of the major museums. Privately owned castles are characteristically open for just a couple of days (or afternoons) a week, often only between April and September.

Public holidays and festivals

In **Belgium**, there are ten national public holidays per year, most of which are keenly observed. With two exceptions, **Luxem-**bourg has the same national public holidays. Both countries are big on **festivals** and annual events, everything from religious processions – which are among the most intriguing events you're likely to come across in the whole of the EU – to carnivals to more contemporary-based jazz binges and the like. These are spread right throughout the year, though, as you might expect, most tourist-oriented events take place in the summer.

Belgian festivals

Belgium's annual **carnivals** (*carnaval*), held in February and early March, are original, colourful and boisterous in equal measure. One of the most renowned is held in February at **Binche**, in Hainaut, when there's a procession involving some 1500 extravagantly dressed dancers called Gilles. There are also carnivals in Ostend and Aalst, and in **Eupen**, where the action lasts over the weekend before Shrove Tuesday and culminates with Rosenmontag on the Monday – a pageant of costumed groups and floats parading through the town centre. And, most uniquely, there is **Stavelot**'s carnival where the so-called Blancs Moussis, townsfolk clothed in white hooded costumes and equipped with long red noses, take to the streets.

Nominally commemorating the arrival by boat of a miraculous statue of the Virgin Mary from Antwerp in the fourteenth century, the Brussels **Ommegang** is the best known of the festivals with a religious inspiration; a largely secular event these days, it's held on the first Tuesday and Thursday of July. If you want to see anything on the Grand-Place, however, where most of the action is, you have to reserve seats months in advance. You might be better off visiting the town of **Veurne** in Flanders for its annual Boetprocessie (Processions of the Penitents), on the last Sunday in July; here,

Public holidays in Belgium And Luxembourg

New Year's Day	Belgium National Day (July 21)
Easter Monday	Assumption (mid-August)
Labour Day (May 1)	All Saints' Day (November 1)
Ascension Day (forty days after Easter)	Armistice Day – Belgium only
Whit Monday	(November 11)
Luxembourg National Day (June 23)	Christmas Day

(Note that if any one of the above falls on a Sunday, the next day becomes a holiday.)

cross-bearers dressed in the brown cowls of the Capuchins process through the town – a truly macabre sight. Among the other religious events perhaps the most notable is the Heilig-Bloedprocessie (Procession of the Holy Blood) held in **Bruges** on Ascension Day, when the shrine encasing the medieval phial which supposedly contains the blood of Christ is carried solemnly through the streets.

Among any number of folkloric events and fairs, one of the biggest is **Brussels'** *Plantation du Meiboom*, in which a maypole is paraded round the streets before being ceremonially planted on August 9. Also good fun is the *Gentse Feesten*, a big nine-day knees-up held in **Ghent** in late July, with all sorts of events from music and theatre through to fireworks and fairs.

Festivals in Luxembourg

Carnival is a big thing in Luxembourg too, with most communities having some kind of celebration – if nothing else, almost every patisserie sells small doughnut-like cakes, *knudd*, during the days beforehand. On Ash Wednesday, a great straw doll is set alight and then dropped off the Moselle bridge in Remich with much whooping-it-up, while on the first Sunday after carnival bonfires are lit on hilltops all over the country on Buurgbrennen. **Mid-Lent Sunday** sees Bretzelsonndeg (Pretzel Sunday), when pretzels are sold in all the duchy's bakeries and there are lots of processions. At **Easter**, no church bells are rung in the whole of the country between Maundy Thursday and Easter Saturday – folklore asserts that the bells fly off to Rome for confession. Their place is taken by children, who walk the streets with rattles announcing the Masses from about 6am onwards. On Easter Monday morning, with the bells "back", the children call on every house to collect their reward – brightly coloured Easter eggs. From the third to fifth Sunday after Easter, the Octave pilgrimage is held, when the duchy's more devout Catholics go on a pilgrimage to Luxembourg City's cathedral, a tradition since 1628.

Every village in Luxembourg has an annual **fair** – *kermess* – which varies in scale and duration according to the size of the village, ranging from a stand selling fries and hot dogs, to a full-scale funfair. The **Schueberfouer** in Luxembourg City – over the first three weeks of September – is one of the biggest mobile fairs in Europe, held since

1340 (it started life as a sheep market) and traditionally opened by the royal family. On the middle Sunday, in the Hammelsmarsch, shepherds bring their sheep to town, accompanied by a band, and work their way round the bars.

Luxembourg's **National Day** is on June 23, and on the previous evening, at 11 pm or so, there is an enormous fireworks display off the Pont Adolphe in the capital and all the bars and cafés are open through most of the night. On June 23 itself there are parades and celebrations across most of the country.

A festival calendar

Information lines and websites have been listed for certain festivals below, and you can also contact the national tourist offices at home, and tourist offices within Belgium and Luxembourg, for details of the exact dates of events each year. For further information on some of the more important events themselves, see the relevant town accounts in the guide.

January

Last two weeks The **Brussels Film Festival** is a good opportunity to see European – especially Belgian – film premieres. Films are screened at various locations around the city. Information: ℡02 513 89 40, ⊛www.brusselsfilmfest.be.

February

Shrove Tuesday and the preceding four or five days Eupen Carnaval kicks off with the appearance of His Madness the Prince and climaxes with the Rosenmontag (Rose Monday) procession. On the Sunday in Malmédy – where carnival is called **Cwarmê** – roving groups of Haguètes, masked figures in red robes and plumed hats, wander around seizing passersby with wooden pincers
Sunday preceding Shrove Tuesday Carnival parades take place in several Luxembourg towns, including Diekirch and Remich.
Shrove Tuesday and the preceding two days Binche Carnaval builds up to the parade of the Gilles, locals dressed in fancy gear, complete with ostrich-feather hats. **Aalst Carnaval** begins on the Sunday with a parade of the giants – locals on stilts hidden by elaborate costumes – and floats, often with a contemporary/satirical theme. There are more parades on the following two days.

March

First Saturday Held in the casino, Ostend's **Bal Rat Mort** (Dead Rat Ball) is a lavish, fancy-dress

carnival ball with a different theme each year.
Information: ☎059 70 51 11, ⓦwww.ramort.be.
Early March *(first Sun after Carnival)*
Buurgbrennen (Bonfire Day) all over
Luxembourg.
Refreshment Sunday *(fourth Sun in Lent)*
Stavelot Carnaval with the famous parade of the
Blancs Moussis, all hoods and long red noses.

April

Late April Bloesemfeesten (Blossom festival).
Blessing of the blossoms in Sint Truiden, at the
heart of the Haspengouw fruit-growing region.
Information: ☎011 70 18 18.

May

May to November The **Festival van
Vlaanderen** (Festival of Flanders) comprises more
than 120 classical concerts staged in churches,
castles and other stylish venues in over sixty
Flemish towns. Information: ☎02 548 95 95,
ⓦwww.festival-van-vlaanderen.be.
Early to late May Brussels' **Concours Musical
International** is a world-famous classical music
competition founded fifty years ago by Belgium's
violin-playing Queen Elisabeth. The categories
change annually, rotating piano, voice and violin.
The venues include the splendid Palais des Beaux
Arts and the Conservatoire Royal de Musique, and
the winners perform live in the Grand-Place in
July. Tickets for the competition can be difficult to
get hold of and can cost as much as €50.
Information: ☎02 513 00 99, ⓦwww.concours-
reine-elisabeth.be.
**From the third to fifth Sunday after Easter
Octave pilgrimage** in Luxembourg, culminating
in a procession through the capital to the
cathedral. Information ☎46 20 23.
**Sunday before Ascension Day
Hanswijkprocessie** (Procession of our Lady of
Hanswijck) is a large and ancient religious
procession held in the centre of Mechelen.
Traditionally focused on the veneration of the
Virgin Mary, but more a historical pageant today.
Information: ☎015 42 01 40.
Ascension Day *(forty days after Easter)* The **Heilig
Bloedprocessie** (Procession of The Holy Blood) in
Bruges involves carrying one of Christendom's
holiest relics, the phial of the Holy Blood – believed
to contain a few drops of the blood of Christ –
through the centre of Bruges. See p.175 for more.
Whit Tuesday In Echternach, Luxembourg, the
Sprangprozessioun is an ancient and really
rather eccentric dancing procession
commemorating the eighth-century English
missionary St Willibrord.

Trinity Sunday (late May or early June) The
Fiertel pilgrimage sees the reliquary of St
Hermes carried along a 32.6km route through the
hills around Ronse.

June

**Second Saturday & Sunday Les journées des
quatre cortèges** (Days of the Four Processions)
in Tournai is a lively carnival mixing modern and
traditional themes. Features include fifteen folkloric
giants representing historic figures with local
connections, such as Louis XIV and the
Merovingian king Childeric, plus flower-decked
floats and military bands.
June 23 Luxembourg National Day. Fireworks
in the capital and celebrations – including much
flag-waving – all over the Grand Duchy.
Late June to late July Knokke-Heist's
Internationaal Cartoonfestival, established in
the 1960s, showcases several hundred world-
class cartoons selected from around the globe.
Information: ☎050 63 04 30.
Last weekend House Torhout in Torhout, West
Flanders. Three tents showcase top dance music
at this three-day festival including special drum 'n'
bass and techno tents. Information:
ⓦwww.housetorhout.be.
Last weekend Rock Werchter is Belgium's
most famous open-air rock event, held just outside
Leuven. Information: ⓦwww.werchter.nl.

July

First Tuesday & Thursday One of Brussels's
best-known annual events, the **Ommegang**, a
procession from Grand Sablon to the Grand-Place,
has people in period costumes and the
descendants of nobles playing the roles of their
ancestors. It all finishes up with a traditional dance
on the Grand-Place. Further information: ☎02 512
19 61, ⓦwww.ommegang-brussels.be.
**Two days over the first or second weekend
Axion Beach Rock**, one of Belgium's best rock
festivals, is held on the beach at Ostend.
Information: ⓦwww.axionbeachrock.be.
Three days over the second weekend Going
strong for over twenty years, Bruges'
Cactusfestival is something of a classic, pushing
against the musical mainstream with rock, reggae,
rap, roots and R&B all rolling along together.
Information: ☎050 33 20 14,
ⓦwww.cactusfestival.be.
Mid- to late July For ten days every July, Ghent
gets stuck into partying in a big way as local
bands perform free open-air gigs right across town
and street performers turn up all over the place
too – fire-eaters, buskers, comedians, actors,

puppeteers and so forth. Information: ☎09 239 42 67, ⓦwww.gentsefeesten.be.

Last Sunday in July Veurne's **Boetprocessie** (Penitents' Procession) is morbid and fascinating in equal measure, made up of around three hundred participants dressed in the brown cowls of the Capuchins and dragging heavy crosses behind them. Information: ☎058 31 26 61.

Last weekend Sfinks is Belgium's best world music festival, held in the suburb of Boechout, about 10km from downtown Antwerp. Information: ☎03 455 69 44, ⓦwww.sfinks.be.

Last week of July and first week of August Bruges' **Musica Antiqua** is a well-established, well-regarded festival of medieval music at a variety of historic venues – churches, chapels and the like. The evening concerts are built around themes, while lunchtime performances tend to be one-offs. Tickets go on sale in February at Bruges tourist office and are snapped up fast.

August

Aug 9 Brussels' **Plantation du Meiboom** (Planting of the Maypole) sees the Maypole paraded round the streets and then planted at the corner of rue des Sables and rue du Marais.

Mid-Aug Leuven's lively **Marktrock** ("Market Square Rock") is a three-day, city-centre event showcasing local rock groups with a handful of foreign acts thrown in for good measure. Information: ☎016 29 08 23, ⓦwww.marktrock.be.

Mid-Aug to mid-Sept Sand sculpture competitions and festivals are popular along the Belgian coast throughout the summer – and Zeebrugge's is one of the best. Amazing creations – everything from the bizarre to the surreal and beyond. Information: ⓦwww.zandsculptuur.com.

Fourth Sunday Ath's **Ducasse**, dating back to the thirteenth century, focuses on an exuberant parade in which giant figures– or goliaths – represent historical and folkloric characters.

Last Thursday Dendermonde's **Traditionele Reuzenommegang** has several hundred locals in fancy dress jigging away around three giants as they parade through town. Information: ☎052 21 39 56.

Last weekend Hasselt's *Pukkelpop* is a progressive music festival running the gamut from indie through R&B to house. Information: ☎011 40 22 67, ⓦwww.pukkelpop.be.

September

First three weeks Luxembourg's **Schueberfouer**, a former shepherds' market, is now the capital's largest funfair.

Second Sun In Tournai, the **Grande Procession**

Historique is part secular shindig in historic costume, part religious ceremony involving the carrying of the reliquary of St Eleuthère through the streets.

Last Sun in Sept or first Sun in Oct Beginning in the centre of Nivelle, the **Tour de Sainte Gertrude** is a religious procession in which the reliquary of St Gertrude is escorted on a circular, 12km route out through the surrounding countryside. Townsfolk dressed in historic gear and several goliaths join the last leg of the procession when the jollity gets going.

October

Twelve days from early Oct The **Flanders International Film Festival** in Ghent has developed into one of Europe's foremost cinematic events, offering around two hundred feature films and a hundred shorts from all over the world. In particular, the festival presents the best of world and Belgian cinema well before it hits the public circuit. There is also a special focus on music in film. Information: ☎09 242 80 60, ⓦwww.filmfestival.be.

Mid- to late October Hasselt's **Hasseltse Jeneverfeesten** is a two-day celebration of jenever, a gin-like spirit produced in this part of Belgium. It's all a bit silly, but good fun all the same; events range from the "fastest-running waiter" competition to the *borrelmanneke* (little jenever man) who toddles round town dispensing free shots of the stuff. Information: ☎011 24 11 44, ⓦwww.hasselt.be.

November

Sunday after All Saints' Day The basilica at Scherpenheuvel, near Diest, is the site of Belgium's most important annual pilgrimage – the **Kaarskensprocessie** – in honour of the Virgin Mary. The main event is a candlelight procession that takes place in the afternoon and is accompanied by the offering of *ex voto*s.

Mid-Nov In Vianden, Luxembourg, **Miertchen** ("St Martin's Fire") is a celebration of the end of the harvest (and formerly the payment of the levy to the feudal lord), with bonfires and a big open-air market. Information: ☎83 42 57.

Last Sun in Nov or first Sunday in Dec Bouillon's **Fête de Saint Eloi** begins with an early morning procession in which stretcher-loads of cakes are carried round town. Mass is then celebrated and the cakes are given out.

December

Dec 6 The **Arrival of St Nicholas** is celebrated by processions and the giving of sweets to children right across Belgium and Luxembourg. In Luxembourg, he's accompanied by "Père Fouettard" (the bogey-man) dressed in black and carrying a whip to punish naughty children.

Crime and personal safety

There's little reason why you should ever come into contact with the police forces of Belgium or Luxembourg. For one thing, it's statistically unlikely you'll be a victim of crime; for another, the police generally keep a low profile, though they do blitz areas – especially big-city train stations – when they feel things are getting out of hand. As far as personal safety goes, it's generally possible to walk around the larger cities without fear of harassment or assault. However, both Antwerp and Brussels have their shady areas and everywhere it's better to err on the side of caution late at night, when – for instance – badly lit or empty streets should be avoided.

The police

In Belgium, there are two main types of police. The **Gendarmerie Nationale** (Flemish: Rijkswacht) who wear blue uniforms with red stripes on their trousers, patrol the motorways and deal with major crime; the municipal **Police** (Politie), in their dark blue uniforms, cover everything else. Many officers in Belgium's Flemish-speaking regions, Brussels and Luxembourg City **speak English**, as do many members of Luxembourg's own police force, but in Wallonia and rural Luxembourg you'll mostly be struggling to make yourself understood if you don't have a modicum of French.

Petty crime

Almost all the problems tourists encounter in Belgium and Luxembourg are to do with **petty crime** – pick-pocketing and bag-snatching – rather than more serious physical confrontations. If you're **robbed**, you need to go to the police to report it, not least because your insurance company will require a police report, so remember to make a note of the report number – or, better still, ask for a copy of the statement itself. Don't expect a great deal of concern if your loss is relatively small – and don't be surprised if the process of completing forms and formalities takes ages. In the unlikely event that you're **mugged** or otherwise threatened, never resist, and try to reduce your contact with the robber to a minimum. Either just hand over what's wanted, or throw money in one direction and take off in the other. Afterwards, go straight to the police, who will be much more sympathetic and helpful on these occasions – especially in tourist centres like Bruges.

It's as well to be on your guard and know where your possessions are at all times. Sensible **precautions** include: carrying bags slung across your neck and not over your shoulder; not carrying anything in pockets that are easy to dip into; having photocopies of your passport, airline ticket and driving licence; leaving passports and tickets in the hotel safe; and noting down traveller's-cheque and credit-card numbers. When you're looking for a **hotel room**, never leave your bags unattended.

If you have a car, don't leave anything in view when you park. Vehicle theft is still fairly uncommon, but luggage and valuables left in cars do make a tempting target. If you're on a **bicycle**, make sure it is well locked up – bike theft and resale is a big deal in urban Belgium.

At **night**, you'd be well advised to avoid walking round the tougher, rougher parts of any of the larger cities, particularly Antwerp (just to the north of the centre) and Brussels (round Gare du Midi). Also, as general precautions, don't go out brimming with valuables, and try not to appear hopelessly lost – doubly so if you're travelling alone. Using public transport, even late at night, isn't usually a problem, but if in doubt – take a taxi.

Thieves often work in pairs and, although

theft is far from rife, you should be aware of certain **ploys**, such as: the "helpful" person pointing out "birdshit" (actually shaving cream or similar) on your coat, while someone else relieves you of your money; the card or paper you're invited to read on the street to distract your attention; the move by someone in a café for your drink with one hand while the other is in your bag as you react to save your drink; and if you're in a crowd of tourists, watch out for people moving in unusually close.

Minor offences

You ought to be aware of a couple of **offences** that you might commit unwittingly. In theory you're supposed to carry some kind of official **identification** at all times, and the police can stop you in the streets and demand to see it. If you can't produce identification or otherwise prove your identity, you can be held at a police station even if this is your only "crime". Citizens of Luxembourg and Belgium carry identity cards (*carte d'identité/identiteitskaart*) as do most EU nationals, but for others a passport will suffice. In practice, however, it's extremely unlikely that you'll be stopped unless there's a particular reason – for example involvement in a road accident.

In Belgium and Luxembourg the laws on the possession of illegal substances (ie **drugs**) are fairly strict, though their use is often very visible in the big cities. Travellers arriving from Holland, where it is effectively legal to possess small amounts of cannabis for personal use, are sometimes blissfully unaware of the differences between the Benelux countries in this regard, which can mean a major hassle. If you're carrying dope, you'd be well advised to leave it at the Dutch border.

Should you be **arrested** on any charge, you have the right to contact your **consulate** – see "Listings" at the end of the big-city accounts in the guide for local addresses. Unfortunately, consular officials are notoriously reluctant to get involved, though most are required to assist you to some degree if you have your passport stolen or lose all your money. If you've been detained for a drugs offence, don't expect any sympathy or help.

Sexual harassment

In the normal course of events, **women travellers** are unlikely to feel threatened and intimidated or attract unwanted attention in almost any part of Belgium and Luxembourg. The main exception is in the seedier areas of the big cities, where the atmosphere may feel frightening especially late at night – but with common sense and circumspection you shouldn't have anything to worry about. The men who hang around nightclubs and bars pose no greater or lesser threat than similar operators at home, though the language barrier (where it exists) makes it harder to know whom to trust.

Travellers with disabilities

Neither Belgium nor Luxembourg is particularly well equipped to accommodate travellers with disabilities. Lifts and ramps are few, steep steps and rough sidewalks are common – and even when an effort has been made, obstacles are frequent. That said, attitudes have changed: new buildings are required by law to be fully accessible and the number of existing premises geared up for the disabled traveller has increased dramatically in the last few years. Today, all the big cities and most of the larger towns have at least one hotel with wheelchair access and other appropriate facilities, while a goodly sample of restaurants and cafés are beginning to get into the act too. In addition, many of the region's campsites have at least a degree of accessibility, as do over half of Belgium's youth hostels. In Luxembourg, only the Eisenborn hostel is listed as being suitable for wheelchair users.

The smoothest part of your journey may well be the trip across the North Sea; P&O have installed wheelchair-accessible toilets and cabins as well as lifts in their ferries, and the airlines flying into Belgium and Luxembourg also cater for (or will assist) travellers to some degree. Thereafter, **transport** in Belgium and Luxembourg is problematic, as buses, trains and train stations are not equipped for disabled travellers – instead you have the rigmarole of contacting the station master so that special arrangements can be made. On a more positive note, drivers will find that most motorway service stations are wheelchair-accessible.

Contacts for travellers with disabilities

UK and Ireland

Access Travel 6 The Hillock, Astley, Lancashire M29 7GW ☎01942/888 844, ⓦwww.access-travel.co.uk. Tour operator which can arrange flights, transfers and accommodation, personally checking out places before recommendation.

Holiday Care 2nd floor, Imperial Building, Victoria Rd, Horley, Surrey RH6 7PZ ☎01293/774 535, Minicom ☎01293/776 943, ⓦwww.holidaycare.org.uk. Provides free lists of accessible accommodation abroad. Information on financial help for holidays available.

Irish Wheelchair Association Blackheath Drive, Clontarf, Dublin 3 ☎01/833 8241, ⑤833 3873, ⓔiwa@iol.ie. Useful information provided about travelling abroad with a wheelchair.

RADAR (Royal Association for Disability and Rehabilitation) 12 City Forum, 250 City Rd, London EC1V 8AF ☎020/7250 3222, Minicom ☎020/7250 4119, ⓦwww.radar.org.uk. A good source of advice on holidays and travel. They produce an annual holiday guide to Europe for £11. Their website is useful and well organized.

Tripscope Alexandra House, Albany Rd, Brentford, Middlesex TW8 0NE ☎0845/758 5641, ⓦwww.justmobility.co.uk/tripscope. This registered charity provides a national telephone information service offering free advice on transport for those with a mobility problem.

US and Canada

Access-Able ⓦwww.access-able.com. Online resource for travellers with disabilities.

Directions Unlimited 123 Green Lane, Bedford Hills, NY 10507 ☎1-800/533-5343 or 914/241-1700. Specializes in custom tours for people with disabilities.

Mobility International USA 451 Broadway, Eugene, OR 97401 ☎541/343-1284, ⓦwww.miusa.org. Information and referral services, access guides, tours and exchange programmes.

Travel Information Service ☎215/456-9600. Telephone-only information and referral service.

Wheels Up! ☎1-888/389-4335, ⓦwww.wheelsup.com. Provides discounted airfare, tour and cruise prices for disabled travellers; also publishes a free monthly newsletter and has a comprehensive website.

Australia and New Zealand

ACROD (Australian Council for Rehabilitation of the Disabled) PO Box 60, Curtin ACT 2605 ☎02/6282 4333, ⓦwww.acrod.org.au. Provides lists of travel agencies and tour operators for people with disabilities.

Disabled Persons Assembly 4/173–175 Victoria St, Wellington, New Zealand ☎04/801 9100. Resource centre with lists of travel agencies and tour operators for people with disabilities.

Gay and lesbian life

Gay and lesbian life in Belgium and Luxembourg isn't nearly so upfront as in the Netherlands just to the north. Brussels and Antwerp are the main centres, but both sit very firmly in Amsterdam's shadow – and most gay and lesbian travellers overlook what is, by and large, a far less "international" scene. That said, there are gay bars and clubs in every major town, a number of gay-orientated hotels in the larger cities and a light scattering of lesbian café-clubs, again in the cities.

In both countries the gay/lesbian scene is left largely unmolested by the rest of society, a pragmatic tolerance – or intolerance soaked in indifference – that has, in the case of Belgium, provided opportunities for legislative change. In 1998, the Belgians passed a law granting certain rights to cohabiting couples irrespective of their sex. The legal age of consent for gay men is 16 in both Belgium and Luxembourg.

Contacts for gay and lesbian travellers

There are several local gay and lesbian organizations offering information, help and support. Of particular note is Brussels' **Tels Quels**, rue du Marché au Charbon 81 (℡02 512 45 87, ⓦwww.telsquels.be), a long-established, Francophone organization whose wide range of services includes a gay and lesbian library and a café-bar/meeting point (Mon, Tues & Thurs 5pm–2am, Wed 2pm–2am, Fri & Sat 2pm–4am). It also publishes a monthly magazine which includes political reports and news of up-and-coming events. A comparable set of services is on offer in Antwerp at **Het Roze Huis**, on the Draakplaats (℡03 288 00 84, ⓦwww.het-rozehuis.be).

Directory

ADDRESSES In the French-speaking part of Belgium and in Luxembourg, addresses are usually written to a standard format. The first line begins with the category of the street or thoroughfare (rue, boulevard etc), followed by the name and then the number; the second line gives the area – or zip – code, followed by the town or area. Common abbrevations include *bld* or *bd* for boulevard, *av* for avenue, *pl* for place (square) and *ch* for chaussée. An exception is the hyphenated Grand-Place (main square), written in full. In the Flemish-speaking areas, the first line gives the name of the street which is followed by (and joined to) its category – hence Krakeelplein is Krakeel square, Krakeelstraat is Krakeel street; the number comes next. The second line gives the area – or zip – code followed by the town or area. Consequently, Flemish abbreviations occur at the end of words: thus *Hofstr* for Hofstraat. An exception is *Grote Markt* (main square), which is not abbreviated. Common categories include *plein* for square, *plaats* for place, *laan* or *weg* for avenue, *kaai* for quay, and *straat* for street. In bilingual Brussels, all signs give both the French and Flemish versions. In many cases, this is fairly straightforward as they are either the same or similar, but sometimes it's extremely confusing, most notoriously in the name of one of the three principal train stations – in French, *Bruxelles-Midi*; in Flemish *Brussel-Zuid*.

CHILDREN Most hotels welcome children and many offer rooms with three or four beds – or will

55

readily add an extra foldaway bed or cot. Certain hotels, particularly the better ones on the coast, offer a babysitting service, and some resorts organize a municipal service of registered babysitters too. Belgium has many attractions designed with children in mind – amusement parks and the like – and all the big cities have indoor swimming pools. Restaurants and cafés readily accept children, but they expect them to be well behaved – shouting and running around is definitely unacceptable. Disposable nappies and other basic supplies are widely available.

ELECTRICITY The current is 220 volts AC, with standard European-style two-pin plugs. Brits will need an adaptor to connect their appliances, North Americans both an adaptor and a transformer.

EMERGENCIES In Belgium, call ☎ 100 for an ambulance or the fire brigade, ☎ 101 for the police. In Luxembourg, call ☎ 112 for an ambulance or the fire brigade, ☎ 113 for the police.

LEFT LUGGAGE Major train stations have luggage offices (normally open daily 6am–midnight) and many smaller stations have them too, though opening hours are more restricted (often Mon–Fri 9am–5pm). Most train stations also have coin-operated lockers.

SMOKING Smoking is forbidden in many public places from theatres through to town halls. Most train compartments are no-smoking and so are the confined spaces of train stations, but you can light up on open-air platforms. No-smoking hotel rooms are a rarity (though they are catching on at the top end of the market) and remarkably few restaurants have no-smoking areas.

TIME One hour ahead of Britain; normally six hours ahead of Eastern Standard Time, nine hours ahead of Pacific Standard Time.

TIPPING There's no necessity to tip, though a ten to fifteen percent tip is expected by taxi drivers and anticipated by many restaurant waiters.

TOILETS Public toilets remain comparatively rare, but many cafés and bars in Brussels operate what amounts to an ablutionary side-line with a €10 fee to use the toilets; you'll spot the plate for the money as you enter.

Guide

Guide

Brussels

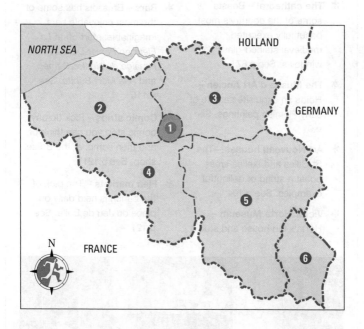

CHAPTER 1

Highlights

✳ **The Grand-Place** – One of Europe's most perfectly preserved Gothic-Baroque squares and still the focus of the city. See p.77

✳ **The Fondation internationale Jacques Brel** – For devotees of *chanson*. See p.85

✳ **The cathedral** – Boasts some of the country's most beautifully executed medieval stained-glass windows. See p.87

✳ **The Musée d'Art Ancien** – Holds an exquisite sample of early Flemish paintings. See p.91

✳ **Art Nouveau houses** – The St Gilles and Ixelles areas boast a string of delightful examples. See p.104

✳ **Victor Horta Museum** – Horta's old house and studio are now a fascinating museum of the work of this leading exponent of Art Nouveau. See p.104

✳ **Seafood** – The fare served up at the restaurants clustering place Ste Catherine is hard to beat. See p.113

✳ **Bars** – Brussels has some of the most enjoyable bars imaginable: start off at *La Fleur en Papier Doré, À l'Imaige de Nostre-Dame* and *À la Mort Subite*. See p.115

✳ **Comic strips** – Pick up any comic strip you can think of, and then some, at the Brüsel shop. See p.121

✳ **Flea markets** – The pick of the bunch is held daily on place du Jeu de Balle. See p.121

1

Brussels

Wherever else you go in Belgium, allow at least a little time for **BRUSSELS**, which is by any standard one of Europe's premier cities. Certainly, don't let Brussels' unjustified reputation as a dull, faceless centre of EU bureaucracy deter you: in postwar years, the city has become a thriving, cosmopolitan metropolis, with top-flight architecture and museums, not to mention a well-preserved late seventeenth-century centre, a superb restaurant scene and an energetic nightlife. Moreover, most of the key attractions are crowded into a centre that is small enough to be absorbed over a few long days, its boundaries largely defined by a ring of boulevards – the "**petit ring**".

First-time visitors to Brussels are often surprised by the raw vitality of the **city centre**. It isn't neat and tidy, and many of the old tenement houses are shabby and ill-used, but there's a buzz about the place that's hard to resist. The city centre is itself divided into two main areas. The larger westerly portion comprises the **Lower Town**, fanning out from the marvellous **Grand-Place**, with its exquisite guildhouses and town hall, while up above to the east lies the much smaller **Upper Town**, home to the finest art collection in the country in the Musées Royaux des Beaux Arts.

Since the eleventh century, monarchs, aristocrats and the well-heeled have lived in the Upper Town, keeping a beady eye on the workers and shopkeepers below – a state of affairs which is still in part true. This fundamental class division, so obvious in the layout of the centre, has in recent decades been further complicated by discord between Belgium's two main linguistic groups, the Walloons (the French-speakers) and the Flemings (the Dutch-speakers). To add to these communal complexities, the Walloons and the Flemings now share their city with many other groups, with EU civil servants, diplomats, and immigrants from North and Central Africa, Turkey and the Mediterranean currently constituting a quarter of the population. Each of these communities tends to live a very separate, distinct existence; there's a sharp contrast between, say, the internationalism of the centre and EU zone, to the east of the city centre – beyond the "petit ring" – and the sharp trendiness of the district round Ste Catherine or Turkish St Josse. The city's compact nature heightens the contrasts: in five minutes you can walk from a designer shopping mall into an African bazaar, or from a depressed slum quarter to a resplendent square of antique shops and exclusive cafés. This is something which only increases the city's allure, not least in the number and variety of affordable ethnic **restaurants**. But, even without these, Brussels would still be a wonderful place to eat: its gastronomic reputation rivals that of Paris, and though traditional meals in homegrown restaurants are rarely cheap, there is great-value food to be had in

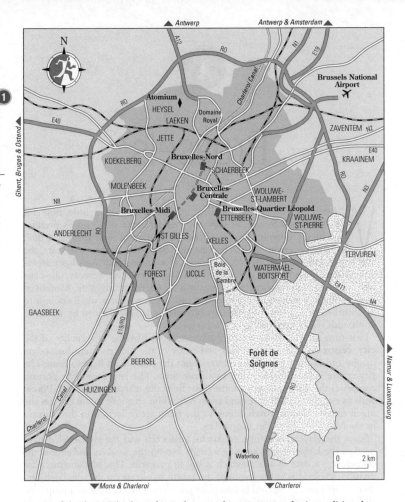

many of the **bars**. The bars themselves can be sumptuous, basic, traditional or very fashionable – and are one of the city's real delights.

The city's **specialist shops** are another pleasure. Everyone knows about Belgian chocolates, but here in the capital there are also huge, sprawling markets, contemporary art galleries, and establishments devoted to anything from comic books to costume jewellery and clubland fashion. Belgium is such a small country, and the rail network so fast and efficient, that Brussels also makes the perfect base for a wide range of day-trips. An obvious target is the battlefield of **Waterloo**, one of the region's most visited attractions.

Some history

Brussels takes its name from Broekzele, or "village of the marsh", the community which grew up beside the wide and shallow River Senne in the sixth century, allegedly around a chapel built here by St Géry. A tiny and insignificant part of Charlemagne's empire at the end of the eighth century, it was subsequently inherited by the dukes of **Lower Lorraine** (or Lotharingia – roughly Wallonia and northeast France), who constructed a fortress here in 979. Protected, the village benefited from its position on the trade route between Cologne and the burgeoning towns of Bruges and Ghent to become a significant trading centre in its own right. The surrounding marshes were drained to allow for further expansion, and in 1229 the city was granted its first charter by the **dukes of Brabant**, the new feudal overlords who controlled things here, on and off, for around two hundred years. In the early fifteenth century, marriage merged the interests of the Duchy of Brabant with that of Burgundy, whose territories passed to the **Habsburgs** in 1482, when Mary, the last of the Burgundian line, died; she was succeeded by her husband, Maximilian I, who was anointed Holy Roman Emperor in 1494.

The first Habsburg rulers had close ties with Brussels, and the **Emperor Charles V** (1519–55) ran his vast kingdom from the city for over a decade, making it wealthy and politically important in equal measure. By contrast, his successor **Philip II** lived in Spain and ruled through a governor (for the whole of the Low Countries) resident in Brussels. It could have been a perfectly reasonable arrangement, but Philip's fanatical Catholicism soon unpicked the equilibrium of Charles's reign. He imposed a series of anti-Protestant edicts which provoked extensive rioting across the Low Countries, and in response he dispatched a hardline reactionary, the Duke of Albe, to Brussels with an army of ten thousand men. Albe quickly restored order and then, with the help of the Inquisition, set about the rioters with gusto, his Commission of Civil Unrest soon nicknamed the "**Council of Blood**" after its habit of executing those it examined. Goaded into rebellion by Albe's brutality, Brussels, along with much of the Low Countries, exploded in revolt, and, in 1577, the one-time protégé of the Habsburgs, **William the Silent**, made a triumphant entry into the city and installed a Calvinist government. Protestant control lasted for just eight years, before Philip's armies recaptured the city. The Protestants left in their hundreds and the economy slumped, though complete catastrophe was averted by the conspicuous consumption of the (Brussels-based) Habsburg elite, whose high spending kept hundreds of workers in employment. Brussels also benefited from the digging of the Willebroek Canal, which linked it to the sea for the first time in its history.

By the 1580s, the Habsburgs had lost control of the northern part of the Low Countries (now the Netherlands) and Brussels was confirmed as the capital of the remainder, the **Spanish Netherlands** (broadly modern Belgium). Brussels prospered more than the rest of the country, but it was always prey to the dynastic squabbling between France and Spain; in 1695, **Louis XIV** bombarded Brussels for 36 hours merely to teach his rivals a lesson. (The guilds rapidly rebuilt their devastated city, and it's this version of the Grand-Place that survives today.)

In 1700 Charles II, the last of the Spanish Habsburgs, died without issue. The ensuing **War of the Spanish Succession** dragged on for over a decade, but eventually the Spanish Netherlands were passed to the Austrian Habsburgs,

Language

As a cumbersome compromise between Belgium's French- and Flemish-speaking communities, Brussels is the country's only officially **bilingual** region. This means that every instance of the written word, from road signs and street names to the Yellow Pages, has by law to appear in both languages. For simplicity we've used the French version of street names, sights, etc throughout this chapter.

who ruled – as had their predecessors – through a governor based in Brussels. It was during this period as capital of the **Austrian Netherlands** (1713–94) that most of the monumental buildings of the Upper Town were constructed and the Neoclassical avenues and boulevards were laid out – grand extravagance in the context of an increasingly industrialized city crammed with a desperately poor working class.

The **French Revolutionary army** brushed the Austrians aside at the Battle of Fleurus in 1794 and the Austrian Netherlands promptly became a *département* of France. This lasted until the defeat of Napoleon when, under the terms of the Congress of Vienna which ended hostilities, the great powers decided to absorb the country into the new **Kingdom of the Netherlands**, ruled by the Dutch King William I. Brussels took turns with The Hague as the capital, but the experiment was short-lived, and in 1830 a Brussels-led rebellion removed the Dutch and led to the creation of an independent Belgian state with Brussels as capital.

The nineteenth century was a period of modernization and expansion, during which the city achieved all the attributes of a modern European capital under the guidance of Burgomaster Anspach and **King Léopold II**. New boulevards were built; the free university was founded; the Senne – which by then had become an open sewer – was covered over in the city centre; many slum areas were cleared; and a series of grand buildings were erected. The whole enterprise culminated in the golden jubilee exhibition celebrating the founding of the Belgian state in the newly inaugurated Parc de Cinquantenaire.

Since the German occupation of Belgium in World War II, the modernization of Brussels has proceeded inexorably, with many major development projects – not least the new métro system – refashioning the city and reflecting its elevated status as the headquarters of both NATO and the EU.

Orientation, arrival and information

The **centre** of Brussels sits neatly within the rough pentagon of boulevards that enclose it, a "**petit ring**" which follows the course of the fourteenth-century city walls, running from place Rogier in the north round to Porte de Hal in the south. The city centre divides into two. The **Lower Town**, built for the working and lower-middle classes, is now the commercial centre of Brussels, a bustling quarter that's home to most of the city's best restaurants, shops and hotels. It fans out from the **Grand-Place**, north, south and west to the boulevards of the petit ring, and east as far as the foot of the slope which marks the start of the smaller **Upper Town**, the traditional home of the Francophile upper classes, and the site of the city's finest art museum. The boundary between the two zones broadly follows the boulevard which cuts through the centre under several names – Berlaimont, L'Impératrice and L'Empereur.

Brussels has the country's only major international airport and is on the main routes heading inland from the Channel ports via the Flemish towns. Trains arrive here direct from London via the Channel Tunnel and, in addition, it's a convenient stop on the railway line between France and Holland. Brussels itself has an excellent public transport system which puts the main **points of arrival** – its airport, train and bus stations – within easy reach of the city centre, where there are two **tourist offices**, one for the city, the other for the rest of the country.

By air

Most flights to Brussels land at the city's **international airport** in Zaventem, 13km northeast of the city centre. There are two **tourist information desks** in the arrivals hall. One, Info Tourisme (daily 6am–9pm), has a reasonable range of information on Brussels and its surroundings, and shares its space with Espace Wallonie, representing OPT, the Wallonian tourist board; the other is Destination Belgium (daily 6am–10pm), where the emphasis is on the Flemish-speaking regions. Destination Belgium (but not Info Tourisme) will make hotel reservations on your behalf anywhere in Belgium, a service that is provided free – you just pay a percentage of the room rate as a deposit, which is subtracted from your final hotel bill. In addition, the arrivals hall has all the facilities you would expect of a major airport, notably bureaux de change, a bank, a post office and ATMs.

From the airport, trains run every fifteen or twenty minutes to the city's main stations. The journey time to Bruxelles-Centrale (the nearest station to the Grand-Place) is about twenty minutes and costs €2.40 one-way. Tickets can be bought from the ticket office in the train station that is part of the airport complex (you can also pay the ticket inspector on the train, but there's a small surcharge). Trains run from around 5am until midnight, after which you'll need to take a **taxi** into the city centre – reckon on paying around €35 for the trip. Finally, there's an hourly **bus** service from the airport complex through the city's northeastern suburbs to the Gare du Nord; the journey takes about 45 minutes – much longer during rush hour.

Ryanair flights from the UK and Ireland land 55km south of the capital at **Brussels-Charleroi airport**, from where there are connecting buses to Bruxelles-Midi train station.

By train

Brussels has three main **train stations** – Bruxelles-Nord, Bruxelles-Centrale and Bruxelles-Midi. Almost all **domestic** trains stop at all three, but the majority of **international** services only stop at Bruxelles-Midi, including Eurostar trains from London and Thalys express trains from Amsterdam, Paris, Cologne and Aachen.

Bruxelles-Centrale is, as its name suggests, the most central of the stations, a five-minute walk from the Grand-Place; **Bruxelles-Nord** lies among the bristling tower blocks of the business area just north of the main ring road; and **Bruxelles-Midi** is located in a depressed area to the south of the city centre. Note that on bus timetables and on maps of the city transit system, Bruxelles-Nord appears as "Gare du Nord", Bruxelles-Centrale as "Gare Centrale" and Bruxelles-Midi as "Gare du Midi", after the names of their respective métro stops. If you arrive late at night, it's best to take a taxi to your hotel or hostel – and you should certainly avoid the streets around Bruxelles-Midi.

If you need to transfer from one of the three main train stations to another, simply jump on the next available mainline train; there are services between the three stations every ten minutes or so, the journey only takes minutes and all you'll have to do (at most) is swap platforms. In addition, Bruxelles-Midi and Bruxelles-Nord are linked by underground tram – the **prémétro** – with several services shuttling underneath the city centre between these two stations. Thus there are two ways to reach the Grand-Place from either Bruxelles-Nord or Bruxelles-Midi: take either a mainline train to Bruxelles-Centrale, or the prémétro to the Bourse station; from either it's a brief walk to the Grand-Place.

By bus

Most **international bus** services to Brussels, including those from Britain, are operated by Eurolines, whose terminal is in the Bruxelles-Nord station

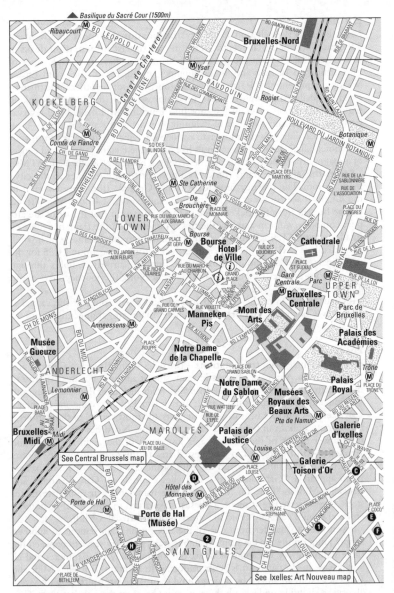

▲ *Basilique du Sacré Cœur (1500m)*

complex. Belgium's comprehensive rail network means that it's unlikely that you'll arrive in the city by long-distance domestic bus, but if you do, Bruxelles-Nord is the main terminal for these services too.

Information

Aside from the offices at the airport, there are two **tourist information offices** in the city, both located right in the centre. The main one is the **BI-**

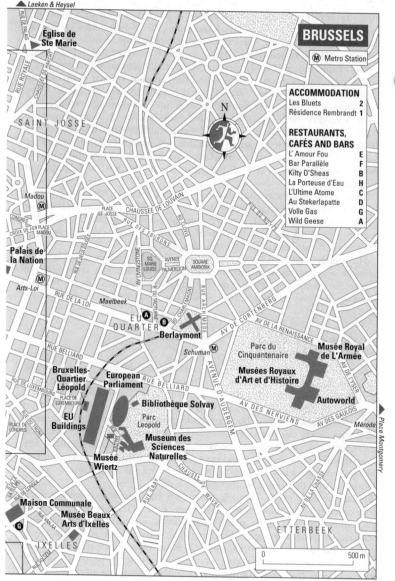

TC, in the Hôtel de Ville on the Grand-Place (Mon–Sat 9am–6pm, plus Sun: May–Sept 9am–6pm & Oct–Dec 10am–2pm; ☎02 513 89 40, ℉02 513 83 20, ⓦwww.tib.be), which handles information on the city only. It stocks a wide range of handouts, including free city maps, has details of up-and-coming events and concerts, and sells a variety of general- and specialist-interest guides, the most useful of which is the detailed *Brussels Guide and Map* (€2). In addition, the BI-TC issues a list of all the city's (recognized) hotels and can make hotel **reservations** for free – the deposit is subtracted from your final hotel bill. It can help with public transport too, selling the 24-hour *carte d'un jour* pass (see below) and handing out free public transport maps. Finally, the BI-TC offers several **packaged deals**, combining public transport and admission into certain sights, though frankly these aren't especially economical or enticing.

The city centre's second tourist office, the **Belgian tourist information centre**, footsteps from the Grand-Place at rue Marché aux Herbes 63 (May, June, Sept & Oct Mon–Fri 9am–6pm, Sat & Sun 9am–1pm & 2–6pm; July & Aug Mon–Fri 9am–7pm, Sat & Sun 9am–1pm & 2–7pm; Nov–April Mon–Fri 9am–6pm, Sat 9am–1pm & 2–6pm, Sun 9am–1pm; ☎02 504 03 90, ℱ02 504 02 70; ⓦwww.belgique-tourisme.net), provides information on the whole of Belgium, leaving Brussels largely to the BI-TC. They also operate a hotel room reservation service, but again it's for the rest of Belgium, not Brussels.

If you need a large city **map**, buy the *Girault Gilbert* (1:10,000) map, which comes complete with an index; it's available at most city-centre newsagents and bookshops for about €5. For wider coverage – including the city's outlying suburbs – stick to the *Falkplan* map of Brussels (1:12,500-31,500), which is available at better bookshops and again has an index.

The weekly *Bulletin* (€2.50), the city's main English-language magazine, contains an excellent **entertainment listings** section, detailing what's on and where; the magazine is on sale at most downtown newsagents. The BI-TC provides the *Bulletin*'s listings section – *What's On* – for free.

City transport

The easiest way to get around the city centre, within the petit ring, is to **walk**. To get from one side of the centre to the other, or to reach some of the more widely dispersed attractions, you will, however, need to use **public transport**. Operated by STIB (information line ☎02 515 20 00), the urban system runs on an integrated mixture of bus, tram, underground tram (prémétro) and métro lines that covers the city comprehensively. It's a user-friendly network, with every métro station carrying métro system diagrams, **route maps** available free from the BI-TC tourist office and from most major métro stations, and timetables posted at most bus and tram stops. Furthermore, the STIB has information kiosks at Porte de Namur, Rogier and Midi métro stations.

Tickets are fairly cheap – a single ticket costs €1.40, a strip of five €6, and a strip of ten €9 – and can be used on any part of the STIB system. They're available either from tram or bus drivers, métro kiosks, automatic machines at métro stations, or from newsagents displaying the STIB sign. A go-as-you-please **carte d'un jour**, for €3.60, allows for 24 hours of city-wide travel on public transport; on the weekend, it covers two passengers. At the beginning of each journey, you're trusted to **stamp tickets** yourself, using one of the machines on every métro station concourse or inside every tram and bus. After that, the ticket is valid for an hour, during which you can get on and off as many trams, métros and buses as you like (note that **doors** on métros, trams and buses mostly have to be opened manually). The system can seem open to abuse, as ticket controls at the métro stations are almost non-existent and you can get on at the back of any tram without ever showing a ticket. Bear in mind, however, that there are roving inspectors who impose heavy on-the-spot fines for anyone caught without a valid ticket.

Guided tours

Guided tours are big business in Brussels; on offer are everything from a quick stroll or bus ride round the city centre to themed visits. The BI-TC has the details of – and takes bookings for – about twenty operators. As a general rule, the more predictable tours can be booked on the day, while the more exotic tours need to be booked ahead of time, the BI-TC normally requiring at least two weeks' advance notice. Among the many more straightforward options, **De Boeck**, rue de la Colline 8 (☏02 513 77 44, www.brussels-city-tours.com), operate a breathless, three-hour bus tour round the city and its major sights for €20 between twice and four times daily. They also run the rather more agreeable *Visit Brussels Line*, a hop-on, hop-off bus service which loops round the city, visiting twelve of its principal sights (daily 10am–6pm; tickets, valid for 24hr, cost €12.15).

More promising still, **Chatterbus**, rue des Thuyas 12 (☏02 673 18 35, ⓔchatterbus@skynet.be), runs well-regarded walking tours throughout the summer, with their first-rate "Brussels through the Ages" tour lasting about three hours and costing €7.50. Chatterbus also operates (French-only) excursions devoted to a particular theme, for example Baroque Brussels or Belgian beers. Another recommendation is **ARAU** (Atelier de Recherche et d'Action Urbaines), boulevard Adolphe Max 55 (☏02 219 33 45), a heritage action group which provides tours exploring the city's architectural history – with particular emphasis on Art Nouveau – from March through to December, at about €15 per person.

Cyclists are catered for by **Pro Vélo**, rue de Londres 15 (☏02 502 73 55, ☏02 502 86 41, ⓔprovelo@skynet.be); they operate several half-day cycle tours round the city and its environs and also offer an evening city-centre excursion. The charge is €7.50 per tour, with bike hire costing an extra €5.

Métro and trams

The **métro** system consists of two underground lines – #1 and #2. Line #1 runs west–east through the centre, and splits into two branches (#1A and #1B) at either end to serve the city's suburbs. Line #2 circles the centre, its route roughly following that of the petit ring up above. Brussels also has a substantial **tram** system serving the city centre and the suburbs. These trams are at their speediest when they go underground to form what is sometimes called the **prémétro**, that part of the system which runs underneath the heart of the city from Bruxelles-Nord, through De Brouckère and Bourse, to Bruxelles-Midi, Porte de Hal and on underneath St Gilles.

Times of operation and frequency vary considerably among the multitude of routes, but key parts of the system operate from 6am until midnight. Lone travellers should avoid the métro late at night.

Buses, local trains and taxis

STIB **buses** supplement the trams and métro. In particular, they provide a limited and sporadic **night bus** service on major routes. In addition, De Lijn (☏02 526 28 28) runs **buses** from the city to the Flemish-speaking communities that surround the capital, while TEC (☏010 230 53 53) operates services to the French-speaking areas. Most of these buses run from – or at least call in at – the Gare du Nord complex. Both companies also run services to other Belgian cities, but they can take up to four times longer than the train.

Supplementing the STIB network are **local trains**, run by Belgian Railways, which shuttle in and out of the city's four smaller train stations and connect different parts of the inner city and the outskirts; unless you're living and working in the city, you're unlikely to need to use them.

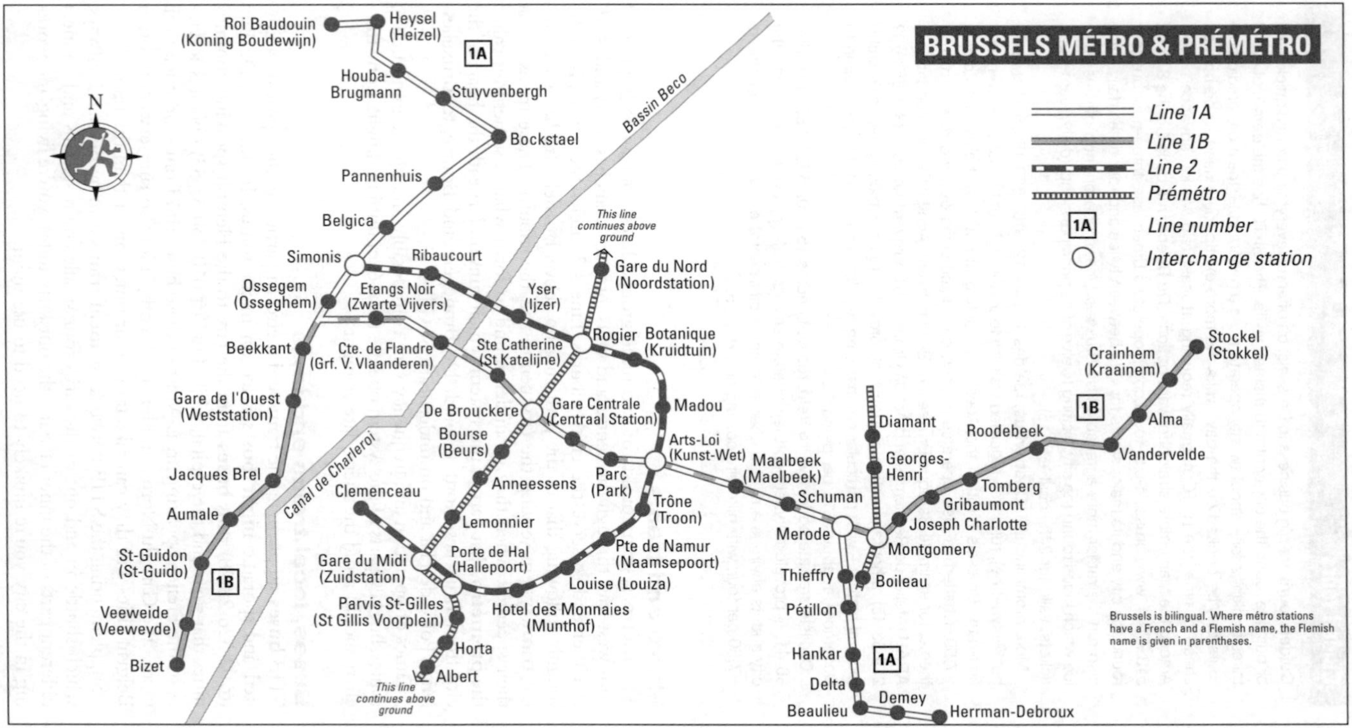

BRUSSELS MÉTRO & PRÉMÉTRO

Line 1A
Line 1B
Line 2
Prémétro
1A Line number
◯ Interchange station

Brussels is bilingual. Where metro stations have a French and a Flemish name, the Flemish name is given in parentheses.

Taxis don't cruise the streets but can be picked up at stands spread around the city – notably on Bourse, De Brouckère and Porte de Namur, at train stations and outside the smarter hotels. There is a fixed **tariff** consisting of two main elements – a fixed charge of €2.40 (€4.25 at night) and the price per km (€1 inside the city). If you can't find a taxi, phone Taxis Verts (℡02 349 49 49), Taxis Orange (℡02 349 43 43), or Autolux (℡02 411 12 21).

Accommodation

With over fifty hotels and several hostels dotted within its central ring of boulevards, Brussels has no shortage of **places to stay**. Some of the most opulent – as well as some of the most basic – places are scattered around the narrow lanes near the **Grand-Place**, and staying here is an attractive option which obviously puts you at the centre of the action. The fashionable neighbourhood of **Ste Catherine**, a five- to ten-minute walk northwest of the Grand-Place, is well worth considering too, its cobbled squares and sidestreets sprinkled with a reasonably good selection of both budget and moderately priced hotels. There's another cluster of hotels just beyond the southern edge of the centre in one of the older, more prosperous residential areas around **avenue Louise**, and another trailing north from the Bourse along dreary **boulevard Adolphe Max** to **place Rogier**. The places to stay reviewed below are marked on the Central Brussels map (see pp.72–73) or else on the map of the Lower Town (p.76) or greater Brussels (pp.66–67).

Despite the number of hotels in Brussels, accommodation can still run short anytime from spring to autumn, so to be sure of a bed it's prudent to **reserve** at least for your first night. The simplest approach is to telephone or fax the hotel direct – language is rarely a problem as most hotel receptionists speak at least some English. Alternatively, **BTR** (Belgium Tourist Reservation; ℡02 513 74 84; ℉02/513 92 77, Ⓔ btr@horeca.be) will make a hotel reservation on your behalf at no charge, as will the tourist office in the Grand-Place (see p.66). At the pricier hotels, **weekend discounts** are commonplace, with the average discount being about fifteen percent, though some places may knock down prices by up to fifty percent. Almost everywhere, breakfast is included in the overnight rate; where this isn't the case, reckon on paying an extra €6.

Hotels

Expensive (over €150)

Amigo rue de l'Amigo 1–3 ℡02 547 47 47, ℉02 513 52 77, Ⓦ www.roccofortehotels.com. Right in the middle of the old city centre, around the corner from the Grand-Place, this delightful hotel occupies an attractive 1950s building designed in the style of an eighteenth-century mansion. The hotel has bags of atmosphere, an amiable informality that's quintessentially Belgian, and the rooms are cosy and intimate, with furnishings to match. The rack rate is €350 for a double, but comes down to a bargain €160 or so on the weekend. Prémétro Bourse. ❾
Atlas rue du Vieux Marché-aux-Grains 30 ℡02 502 60 06, ℉02 502 69 35, Ⓦ www.atlas.be. Comfortable if somewhat bland modern hotel in a

refurbished town house in the fashionable Ste Catherine district, a five- to ten-minute walk northwest of the Grand-Place. Métro Ste Catherine. ❽
Le Dixseptième rue de la Madeleine 25 ℡02 502 17 17, ℉02 502 64 24, Ⓦ www.ledixseptieme.be. Arguably the most charming small hotel in Brussels, located in a tastefully renovated seventeenth-century mansion a couple of minutes' walk from the Grand-Place. Parquet flooring, crystal chandeliers and pastel-painted woodwork all add to the flavour. Doubles begin at €190, but there's usually a hefty discount at the weekend. Métro Gare Centrale. ❾
Jolly Hotel du Grand Sablon rue Bodenbroeck 2, place du Grand Sablon ℡02 518 11 00, ℉02 512

CENTRAL BRUSSELS

ACCOMMODATION

Le Centre Vincent van Gogh	2
Comfort Art Hotel Siru	1
George V	6
Jacques Brel	3
Jolly Hotel du Grand Sablon	7
Sabina	5
La Tasse d'Argent	4

**RESTAURANTS,
CAFÉS AND BARS**

Bla Bla & Gallery	H
Les Brigittines aux	C
Marchés de la Chapelle	
La Grande Porte	E
In 't Spinnekopke	B
Le Pain Quotidien	F
Le Perroquet	G
Les Petits Oignons	D
De Skievers Architeck	I
De Ulteme Hallucinatie	A

Bruxelles-Nord (100ml)

Le Botanique

Parc du Jardin Botanique

Centre Rogier

Centre Belge de la Bande Dessinée

Colonne du Congrès

Cirque Royal

Palais de la Nation

Cathédrale

Théâtre Flamand

Hospice Pacheco

St Jean Baptiste au Béguinage

Théâtre Royal de la Monnaie

Galeries St. Hubert

St.Nicolas

Centre Monnaie

Ste Catherine

Bourse

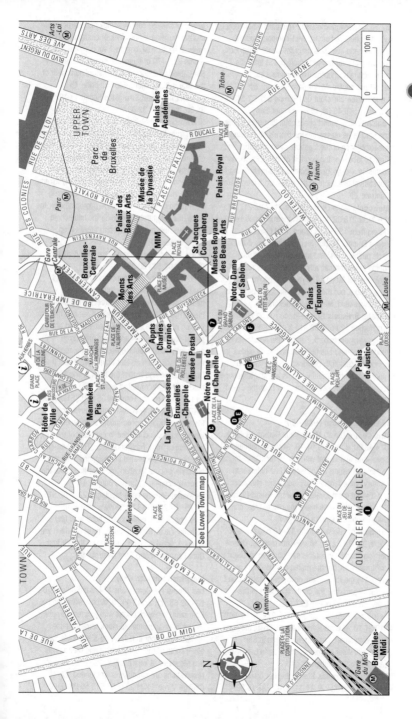

67 66, Ⓦ www.jollyhotels.it. This plush chain hotel, with two hundred smart, well-equipped rooms, doesn't quite live up to its great location overlooking the place du Grand Sablon, but at least it's architecturally unobtrusive. Rack rate starts at €260 per double. Métro Gare Centrale. ❾

Le Meridien carrefour de l'Europe 3 ℡ 02 548 42 11, ℻ 02 548 40 80, Ⓦ www.lemeridien -brussels.com. Smart chain hotel that tries a little too hard to be classy, though there's no denying the excellence of the location – just near the Grand-Place – or the comfort of its briskly modern rooms. In a large, good-looking modern building. Substantial discounts at the weekend. Métro Gare Centrale. ❼

Métropole place De Brouckère 31 ℡ 02 217 23 00, ℻ 02 218 02 20, Ⓦ www.metropolehotel.com. Dating from 1895, this grand hotel boasts gorgeous Empire, Art Nouveau and Art Deco flourishes in its public areas, and although some of the rooms are comparatively routine, others retain their original fittings. The rack rate begins at €325 for a double, but there are usually large discounts at the weekend. Métro de Brouckère. ❾

Novotel Brussels Grand-Place rue du Marché aux Herbes 120 5 ℡ 02 514 33 33, ℻ 02 511 77 23, Ⓦ www.accor.com. Smart chain hotel with all mod cons – and one hundred and thirty rooms. In a modern, tastefully designed and very stylish block that blends prettily into its architectural surroundings. Great location too, just near the Grand-Place. ❽

Moderately priced (€80–150)

Aris Centre rue du Marché aux Herbes 78 ℡ 02 514 43 00, ℻ 02 514 01 19, Ⓦ www.arishotel.be. Spick-and-span hotel with smart, functional rooms to match. Despite the attractive late nineteenth-century stone facade, the place lacks character, but it's in a great location near the Grand-Place. Significant discounts make the place a real snip on the weekend. Prémétro Bourse. ❻

Arlequin rue de la Fourche 17–19 ℡ 02 514 16 15, ℻ 02 514 22 02, Ⓦ www.arlequin.be. There's nothing homely about this straightforward, slightly unkempt hotel, but the rooms are adequate and it is right in the thick of the downtown action. Don't be too deterred by the grotty approach to the hotel. Prémétro Bourse. ❻

Astrid place du Samedi 11 ℡ 02 219 31 19, ℻ 02 219 31 70, Ⓦ www.astridhotel.be. Crisp, modern hotel with smart, comfortable rooms in Ste Catherine. Weekend discounts of up to twenty percent. Métro Ste Catherine. ❺

Citadines Bruxelles Ste Catherine quai au Bois à Brûler 51 ℡ 02 221 14 11, ℻ 02 221 15 99,

Ⓦ www.citadines.com. A somewhat characterless modern building, whose lack of charm is partly relieved by its neat, compact, modern en-suite rooms – all 170 of them. It's located in the lively Ste Catherine district, a 10min stroll northwest of the Grand-Place. Métro Ste Catherine. ❺

Comfort Art Hotel Siru place Rogier 1 ℡ 02 203 35 80, ℻ 02 203 33 03, Ⓦ www.comforthotelsiru.com. It may not look like much from the outside – just another skyrise overlooking place Rogier – but the interior is the most original in town: each room was individually decorated by an art student in a broadly modernistic style, and all manner of figurines, mini-polystyrene effigies, murals and cartoon strips – everything from Tintin to Marilyn Monroe – pop up all over the place. It's delightful – providing the hotel chain that have now purchased it don't mess it up. Métro Rogier. ❻

Floris Grand-Place rue des Harengs 6 ℡ 02 514 07 60, ℻ 02 548 90 39, Ⓔ floris.grandplace@grouptorus.com. Unusual chain hotel in a pair of adjoining old terrace houses down a narrow sidestreet off the Grand-Place. The interior has been kitted out in a modern version of antique style – all stained wood and pastel-painted walls – and there are eleven pleasantly comfortable, en-suite rooms; rooms at the back are much quieter than those at the front. One disadvantage is that the hotel is short of natural light. Métro Gare Centrale. ❺

La Légende rue du Lombard 35 ℡ 02 512 82 90, ℻ 02 512 34 93, Ⓦ www.hotellalegende.com. Pleasant, if frugal, accommodation in an old building set around a courtyard in the heart of the city, just metres from the Grand-Place. The 26 en-suite bedrooms are decorated in undistinguished modern style, but the location and the price make this a popular choice. Prémétro Bourse. ❺

La Madeleine rue de la Montagne 22 ℡ 02 513 29 73, ℻ 02 502 13 50, Ⓦ www.madeleine -hotel.be. A competent budget hotel with fifty, squeaky-clean, modern rooms, most of which are en suite. Great location – just down the hill from Gare Centrale. Métro Gare Centrale. ❺

Inexpensive (under €80)

Les Bluets rue Berckmans 124, Saint Gilles ℡ 02 534 39 83, ℻ 02 543 09 70, Ⓔ bluets@swing.be. Charming, family-run hotel with just ten en-suite rooms in a handsome old stone terrace house. Immaculate decor in rich fin-de-siècle style. One block south of the "petit ring" – and Métro Hôtel des Monnaies. A very popular choice, so advance reservations are strongly recommended. ❸

George V rue 't Kint 23 ℡ 02 513 50 93, ℻ 02

513 44 93, @www.george5.com. A 5–10min walk west of the Grand-Place. A ramshackle old hotel in an atmospheric, though somewhat down-at-heel, neighbourhood of big, fin-de-siècle, balconied and grilled tenement blocks. The rooms are plain and modern, and feature well-appointed bathrooms. Prémétro Bourse. ❹

Mirabeau place Fontainas 18 ☎02 511 19 72, ⒻF02 511 00 36, ©hotel.mirabeau@skynet.be. Overlooking a busy square bordering bld Anspach, this welcoming, medium-sized hotel has thirty neat and trim, en-suite rooms decorated in modern style. Occupies a good-looking, early twentieth-century, seven-storey block, complete with long, slender windows and wrought-iron grilles. Prémétro Anneessens. ❹

Résidence Rembrandt rue de la Concorde 42, Ixelles ☎02 512 71 39, ⒻF02 511 71 36, ©rembrandt@brutele.be. Located on a dispiriting side-street off avenue Louise, near place Stéphanie. Popular and pleasant pension-style hotel with a pink exterior, thirteen clean and comfortable rooms – six en suite – and kitsch bygones in the foyer. Trams #93 and #94 run along ave Louise. ❹

Sabina rue du Nord 78 ☎02 218 26 37, ⒻF02 219 32 39, @www.hotelsabina.com. Reasonably priced, medium-sized hotel with twenty-four, workaday, en-suite rooms in a late nineteenth-century terrace town house. In an appealing residential area that was once a favourite haunt of the city's Victorian bourgeoisie. Métro Madou. ❹

Saint-Michel Grand-Place 15 ☎02 511 09 56, ⒻF02 511 46 00, ©hotelsaintmichel@hotmail.com. One of the city's most distinctive hotels and the only one to look out over the Grand-Place. It occupies an old guildhouse on the east side of the square, but the grandness of the facade isn't universally matched by the rooms inside – which range from the basic and small at the back of the building to more elegant period rooms at the front (for the latter, you'll almost certainly need to make an advance booking). Still, the hotel represents a real bargain – though if you're a light sleeper, revellers on the Grand-Place may well disturb your slumbers. Prémétro Bourse. ❹

La Tasse d'Argent rue du Congrès 48 ☎ & ⒻF02

218 83 75. One-star, popular family-run hotel in a good-looking, early twentieth-century mansion, about 5min walk north of the cathedral. There are just eight modest, modern rooms, so advance booking is advised. Métro Madou. ❹

Hostels

Bruegel rue du Saint Esprit 2 ☎02 511 04 36, ⒻF02 512 07 11, @www.vjh.be. Housed in a smart, modern building, this HI hostel has 135 beds. A basic breakfast is included in the overnight fee – €17.50 per person in a double room, €14.50 in a room for four, €12.50 in a room for 6–12. It's fairly central too, located beside the church of Notre Dame de la Chapelle, close to the Upper Town and just 300m south of Gare Centrale. Check-in 7am–1pm; 1am curfew. Métro Gare Centrale. ❷

Le Centre Vincent van Gogh – CHAB (Centre de Hébergement de l'Agglomeration de Bruxelles) rue Traversière 8 ☎02 217 01 58, ⒻF02 219 79 95, @www.ping.be/chab. A rambling, spacious hostel with a good reputation and slightly lower prices than the official youth hostels, though it can seem chaotic. Sinks in all rooms, but showers and toilets are shared. No curfew. Breakfast is included in the cost of an overnight stay – singles €21, doubles €15.50 per person, quads €13. Sheet rental €3.50. Métro Botanique. ❷

Jacques Brel rue de la Sablonnière 30 ☎02 218 01 87, ⒻF02 217 20 05, @www.planet.be/aubjeun. A modern, comfortable HI hostel, with a hotel-like atmosphere. Facilities include bar, restaurant and meeting room, and there's a shower in every bedroom. Beds in 4- to 12-bedded dorms cost around €12.50 each; prices include breakfast and sheets. No curfew. Métro Madou or Botanique. ❷

New Sleep Well rue du Damier 23 ☎02 218 50 50, ⒻF02 218 13 13, @www.sleepwell.be. Bright and breezy hostel in a recently refurbished building, a 5min walk from place Rogier. Hotel-style facilities including a bar, and there's good disabled access. Singles €18; doubles €15 per person; triples or quads €13. Bed sheets – at an extra €3.50 – are compulsory on the first night. Advance booking well-nigh essential. Métro Rogier. ❷

The Lower Town

One of Europe's most beautiful squares, the **Grand-Place** is the unquestionable centre of Brussels, a focus for tourists and residents alike, who come to admire its magnificent guildhouses and Gothic town hall. It's also the focus of

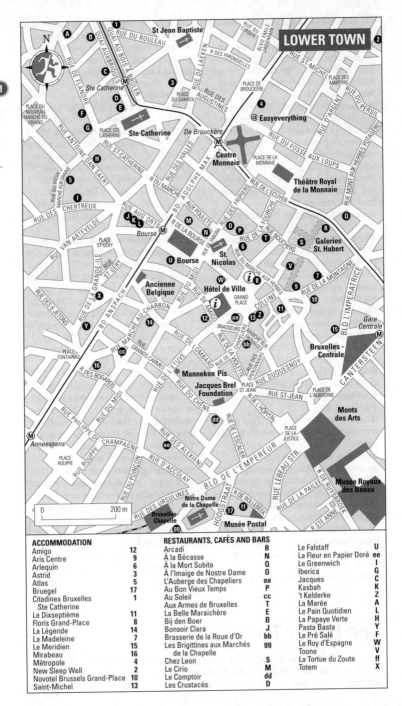

LOWER TOWN

ACCOMMODATION

Amigo	12
Aris Centre	9
Arlequin	6
Astrid	3
Atlas	5
Bruegel	17
Citadines Bruxelles	
Ste Catherine	1
Le Dixseptième	11
Floris Grand-Place	8
La Légende	14
La Madeleine	
Le Meridien	7
Mirabeau	16
Métropole	4
New Sleep Well	2
Novotel Brussels Grand-Place	10
Saint-Michel	13

RESTAURANTS, CAFÉS AND BARS

Arcadi	R	Le Falstaff	U
À la Bécasse	N	La Fleur en Papier Doré	ee
À la Mort Subite	Q	Le Greenwich	I
À l'Imaige de Nostre Dame	O	Iberica	G
L'Auberge des Chapeliers	aa	Jacques	C
Au Bon Vieux Temps	P	Kasbah	K
Au Soleil	cc	't Kelderke	Z
Aux Armes de Bruxelles	T	La Marée	A
La Belle Maraichère	E	Le Pain Quotidien	L
Bij den Boer	B	La Papaye Verte	H
Bonsoir Clara	J	Pasta Basta	Y
Brasserie de la Roue d'Or	bb	Le Pré Salé	F
Les Brigittines aux Marchés		Le Roy d'Espagne	W
de la Chapelle	S	Toone	V
Chez Leon	M	La Tortue du Zoute	ff
Le Cirio	M	Totem	X
Le Comptoir	dd		
Les Crustacés	D		

the **Lower Town**, whose cramped and populous quarters spread out in all directions, bisected by one major north–south boulevard, variously named Adolphe Max, Anspach and Lemonnier. Setting aside the boulevard – which was ploughed through in the nineteenth century – the **layout** of the Lower Town remains essentially medieval, a cobweb of narrow, cobbled lanes and alleys in which almost every street is crimped by tall and angular town houses. There's nothing neat and tidy about all of this, but that's what gives it its appeal – dilapidated terraces stand next to prestigious mansions and the whole district is dotted with superb buildings, everything from beautiful Baroque churches through to Art Nouveau department stores.

The Lower Town is at its most beguiling to the **northwest** of the Grand-Place, where the churches of Ste Catherine and St Jean Baptiste au Béguinage stand amid a cobweb of quaint, narrow lanes and tiny squares. By comparison the streets to the **north and northeast** of the Grand-Place are of less immediate appeal, with dreary rue Neuve, a pedestrianized main street that's home to the city's mainstream shops and department stores, leading up to the clumping skyscrapers that surround the place Rogier and the Gare du Nord. This is an uninviting part of the city, but relief is at hand in the precise if bedraggled Habsburg symmetries of the place des Martyrs and at the Belgian Comic Strip Centre, the Centre Belge de la Bande Dessinée. To the **south** of the Grand-Place lie the old working-class streets of the Marolles district, then the depressed, predominantly immigrant area in the vicinity of the Gare du Midi.

The Grand-Place

The obvious place to begin any tour of Brussels is the **Grand-Place**, which sits among a labyrinth of narrow, cobbled lanes and alleys at the heart of the Lower Town. Here, the Gothic extravagance of the Hôtel de Ville (town hall) presides over the gilded facades of a full set of late seventeenth-century guildhouses, whose columns, scrolled gables and dainty sculptures encapsulate Baroque ideals of balance and harmony. Inevitably, such an outstanding attraction draws tourists and expats in their droves, but the square is still stunning; indeed, there's no better place to get a taste of Brussels' past and Eurocapital present – though the paltry flower market that occupies the square every day except Monday is a pale reflection of earlier markets.

Originally marshland, the Grand-Place was drained in the twelfth century, and by 1350 covered markets for bread, meat and cloth had been erected, born of an economic boom that was underpinned by a flourishing cloth industry. Later, the Grand-Place's role as the commercial hub of the emergent city was cemented when the city's guilds built their headquarters on the square, and, in the fifteenth century, it also assumed a civic and political function with the construction of the Hôtel de Ville. The ruling dukes visited the square to meet the people or show off in tournaments, official decrees and pronouncements were proclaimed here, and justice was meted out with public executions, drawing large, excited crowds.

During the religious wars of the sixteenth century, the Grand-Place became as much a place of public execution as trade, but thereafter the square resumed its former role as a market place. Of the square's medieval buildings, however, only parts of the Hôtel de Ville and one or two guildhouses have survived, the consequence of an early example of the precepts of total war, a 36-hour **French artillery bombardment** which pretty much razed Brussels to the ground in 1695; the commander of the French artillery gloated, "I have never yet seen such a great fire nor so much desolation." After the French withdrew, the city's guildsmen dusted themselves down and speedily had their headquarters rebuilt, adopting the distinctive and flamboyant Baroque style that characterizes the square today.

The Hôtel de Ville

From the south side of the Grand-Place, the newly scrubbed and polished **Hôtel de Ville** (Town Hall) dominates the proceedings, its 96-metre spire soaring above two long series of robust windows, whose straight lines are mitigated by fancy tracery, striking gargoyles and an arcaded gallery. The edifice dates from the beginning of the fifteenth century, when the town council decided to build itself a mansion that adequately reflected its wealth and power. The first part to be completed was the **east wing** – the original entrance is marked by the twin lions of the Lion Staircase, though the animals were only added in 1770. Work started on the **west wing** in 1444 and continued until 1480. Despite the gap, the wings are of very similar style, and you have to look hard to notice that the later wing is slightly shorter than its neighbour, allegedly at the insistence of Charles the Bold who – for some unknown reason – refused to have the adjacent rue de la Tête d'Or narrowed. The niches were left empty and the statues seen today, which represent leading figures from the city's past, were added as part of a heavy-handed nineteenth-century refurbishment.

By any standard, the **tower** of the Hôtel de Ville is quite extraordinary, its remarkably slender appearance the work of Jan van Ruysbroeck, the leading spire specialist of the day who also played a leading role in the building of the cathedral (see p.87) and Sts Pierre et Guido in Anderlecht (see p.109). Ruysbroeck had the lower section built square to support the weight above, choosing a design that blended seamlessly with the elaborately carved facade on either side – or almost: look carefully and you'll see that the main entrance is slightly out of kilter. Ruysbroeck used the old belfry porch as the base for the new tower, hence the misalignment, a deliberate decision rather than the miscalculation which, according to legend, prompted the architect's suicide. Above the cornice protrudes an octagonal extension where the basic design of narrow windows flanked by pencil-thin columns and pinnacles is repeated up as far as the pyramid-shaped **spire**, a delicate affair surmounted by a gilded figure of **St Michael**, protector of Christians in general and of soldiers in particular. The tower is off-limits, and **guided tours** in English (April–Sept Tues 3.15pm, Wed 3.15pm & Sun 12.15pm; Oct–March Tues 3.15pm only; €2.50) are confined to a string of lavish official rooms used for receptions and town council meetings. The most dazzling of these is the sixteenth-century **Council Chamber**, decorated with gilt moulding, faded tapestries and an oak floor inlaid with ebony. Tours begin at the reception desk off the interior quadrangle; be prepared for the guides' overly reverential script.

The west side of the square

Flanking and facing the Hôtel de Ville are the **guildhouses** that give the Grand-Place its character, their slender, gilded facades swirling with exuberant, self-publicizing carvings and sculptures. Each guildhouse has a name, usually derived from one of the statues, symbols or architectural quirks decorating its facade. On the west side of the Grand-Place, at the end of the row, stands **no. 1**: **Roi d'Espagne**, a particularly fine building which was once the headquarters of the guild of bakers; it's named after the bust of King Charles II of Spain on the upper storey, flanked by a Moorish and a Native American prisoner, symbolic trophies of war. Balanced on the balustrade are allegorical statues of Energy, Fire, Water, Wind, Wheat and Prudence, presumably meant to represent the elements necessary for baking the ideal loaf. The guildhouse now holds the most famous of the square's bars, *Le Roy d'Espagne*, a surreal (but somewhat dingy) affair with animal bladders and marionettes hanging from the ceiling – and repro halberds in the toilets. More appealing is the café next door, *La Brouette*, in **nos. 2–3**: **La Maison de la Brouette**, once the tallow makers' guildhouse, though it takes its name from the wheelbarrows etched into the cartouches. The figure at the top is St Gilles, the guild's patron saint. Next door, the three lower storeys of the **Maison du Sac**, at **no. 4**, escaped the French bombardment of 1695. The building was constructed for the carpenters and coopers, with the upper storeys being appropriately designed by a cabinet-maker, and featuring pilasters and caryatids which resemble the ornate legs of Baroque furniture.

The adjacent **Maison de la Louve**, at **no. 5**, also survived the French artillery, and was originally home to the influential archers' guild. The pilastered facade is studded with sanctimonious representations of concepts like Peace and Discord, and the medallions just beneath the pediment carry the likenesses of four Roman emperors set above allegorical motifs indicating their particular attributes. Thus, Trajan is shown above the Sun, a symbol of Truth; Tiberius with a net and cage for Falsehood; Augustus with the globe of Peace; and Julius Caesar with a bleeding heart for Disunity. Above the door, there's a charming bas-relief of the Roman she-wolf suckling Romulus and Remus, while the pediment holds a relief of Apollo firing at a python; right on top, the Phoenix rises from the ashes.

At **no. 6**, the **Maison du Cornet** was the headquarters of the boatmen's guild and is a fanciful creation of 1697, sporting a top storey resembling the stern of a ship. Charles II makes another appearance here too – it's his head in the medallion, flanked by representations of the four winds and of a pair of sailors.

The house of the haberdashers' guild, **Maison du Renard** at **no. 7**, displays animated cherubs in bas-relief playing at haberdashery on the ground floor, while a scrawny, gilded fox – after which the house is named – squats above the door. Up on the third storey a statue of Justice, flanked by figures symbolizing the four continents, suggests the guild's designs on world markets – an aim to which St Nicholas, patron saint of merchants, glinting above, clearly gives his blessing.

The south side of the square

Beside the Hôtel de Ville, the arcaded **Maison de l'Étoile**, at **no. 8**, is a nineteenth-century rebuilding of the medieval home of the city magistrate. In the arcaded gallery, the exploits of one Everard 't Serclaes are commemorated: in 1356 the Francophile Count of Flanders attempted to seize power from the Duke of Brabant, occupying the magistrate's house and flying his standard from the roof. 'T Serclaes scaled the building, replaced Flanders' standard with that of the Duke of Brabant, and went on to lead the recapturing of the city, events represented in bas-relief above a reclining statue of 't Serclaes. His effigy is polished smooth from the long-standing superstition that good luck will come to those who stroke it – surprising really, as 't Serclaes was hunted down and hacked to death by the count's men in 1388.

Next door, the mansion that takes its name from the ostentatious swan on the facade, **Maison du Cygne** at **no. 9**, once housed a bar where Karl Marx regularly met up with Engels during his exile in Belgium. It was in Brussels in February 1848 that they wrote the *Communist Manifesto*, only to be deported as political undesirables the following month. Appropriately enough, the Belgian Workers' Party was founded here in 1885, though nowadays the building shelters one of the city's more exclusive restaurants.

The adjacent **Maison de l'Arbre d'Or**, at **no. 10**, is the only house on the Grand-Place still to be owned by a guild – the brewers' – not that the equestrian figure stuck on top gives any clues: the original effigy (of one of the city's Habsburg governors) dropped off, and the present statue, picturing the eighteenth-century aristocrat Charles of Lorraine, was moved here simply to fill the gap. Inside, the small and mundane **Musée de la Brasserie** (daily 10am–5pm; €2.50) has various bits of brewing paraphernalia; a beer is included in the price of admission.

The east side of the square

The seven guildhouses (**nos. 13–19**) that fill out the east side of the Grand-Place have been subsumed within one grand facade, whose slender symmetries are set off by a curved pediment and narrow pilasters, sporting nineteen busts of the dukes of Brabant. Perhaps more than any other building on the Grand-Place, the **Maison des Ducs de Brabant** has the flavour of the aristocracy – as distinct from the bourgeoisie – and, needless to say, it was much admired by the city's Habsburg governors. There's another museum here too – the uninformative **Musée du Cacao et du Chocolat**, at no. 13 (Tues–Sun 10am–5pm; €5).

The north side of the square

The guildhouses and private mansions (**nos. 20–39**) running along the north side of the Grand-Place are not as distinguished as their neighbours, though the **Maison du Pigeon** (**nos. 26–27**), the painters' guildhouse, is of interest as the house where Victor Hugo spent some time during his exile from France – he was expelled for his support of the French insurrection of 1848. The house also bears four unusual masks in the manner of the "green man" of Romano-Celtic folklore. The adjacent **Maison des Tailleurs** (**nos. 24–25**) is appealing too, the old headquarters of the tailors' guild, adorned by a pious bust of St Barbara, their patron saint.

Maison du Roi

Much of the northern side of the Grand-Place is taken up by the late nineteenth-century **Maison du Roi**, a fairly faithful reconstruction of the palatial Gothic structure commissioned by Charles V in 1515. The emperor had a point to make: the Hôtel de Ville was an assertion of municipal independence, and Charles wanted to emphasize imperial power by erecting his own building directly opposite. Despite its name, no sovereign ever lived here permanently, though this is where the Habsburgs installed their tax men and law courts, and held their more important prisoners – the counts of Egmont and Hoorn (see p.410) spent their last night in the Maison du Roi before being beheaded just outside. The building now holds the **Musée de la Ville de Bruxelles** (Tues–Fri 10am–5pm, Sat & Sun 10am–1pm; €2.50), a wide-ranging but patchy collection whose best sections feature medieval fine and applied art – not that you'll glean much from the scanty (French and Flemish) labelling.

The first of the rooms to the right of the entrance boasts superb **altarpieces** – or retables; from the end of the fourteenth century until the economic slump of the 1640s, the city produced hundreds of them, in a manner similar to a production line, with panel- and cabinet-makers, wood carvers, painters and goldsmiths (who did the gilding) working on several altarpieces at any one time. The standard format was to create a series of mini-tableaux illustrating Biblical scenes, with the characters wearing medieval gear in a medieval landscape. It's the extraordinary detail – a Brussels speciality – that impresses: look closely at the niche carvings on the whopping **Saluzzo** altarpiece (aka *The Life of the Virgin and the Infant Christ*) of 1505 and you'll spy the candle-sticks, embroidered pillowcase and carefully draped coverlet of Mary's bedroom in the *Annunciation* scene. Up above, in a swirling, phantasmagorical landscape (of what look like climbing toadstools), is the *Shepherds Hear the Good News*. Also in this room is Pieter Bruegel the Elder's *Wedding Procession*, a good-natured scene with country folk walking to church to the accompaniment of bagpipes.

The second room to the right is devoted to four large-scale **tapestries** from the sixteenth and seventeenth centuries. The earliest of the four – from 1516 – relates the legend of *Notre Dame du Sablon*, the tedious tale of the transfer of a much revered statue of the Virgin from Antwerp to Brussels (see p.98) – though fortunately the tapestry is much better than the story. Easily the most striking tapestry is the Solemn Funeral of the Roman Consul Decius Mus, based on drawings by Rubens. This is an extraordinary work, crowded with classical figures of muscular men and fleshy women surrounding the consul, who won a decisive victory against the Samnites, securing Roman control of Italy in the third century BC. Decius is laid out on a chaise-longue and even inanimate objects join in the general mourning – with the lion head of the chaise-longue, for instance, glancing sorrowfully at the onlooker.

The museum's upper floors are less diverting; the first floor has scale models of the city and various sections on aspects of its development, the second continuing in the same vein. On the second floor also is a goodly sample of the **Manneken Pis'** (see below) vast wardrobe, around one hundred sickeningly saccharine costumes ranging from Mickey Mouse to a maharajah, all of them gifts from various visiting dignitaries.

Around the Grand-Place – the Manneken Pis

In the 1890s, burgomaster **Charles Buls** spearheaded a campaign to preserve the city's ancient buildings. One of his rewards was to have a street named after him, running south from the Grand-Place. It was on the corner of **rue des Brasseurs** – the first street on the left – where, in 1873, the French Symbolist poet Paul Verlaine shot his fellow poet and lover Arthur Rimbaud, a rash act that earned him a two-year prison sentence – and all because Rimbaud had dashed from Paris to dissuade him from joining the Spanish army. The second turn on the left is rue de la Violette, and here at no. 6, the **Musée de Costume et de la Dentelle** (Mon–Fri 10am–12.30pm & 1.30–5pm, Sat & Sun 2–4.30pm; €2.50) has many examples of antique and contemporary lace mixed in with various temporary displays on costume.

From the foot of rue de la Violette, rue de l'Étuve runs south to the **Manneken Pis**, a diminutive statue of a pissing urchin stuck high up in a shrine-like affair, protected from the hordes of tourists by an iron fence. There are all sorts of folkloric tales about the origins of the lad, from lost aristocratic children recovered when they were taking a pee, to peasant lads putting out dangerous fires and – least likely of the lot – boys slashing on the city's enemies from the trees and putting them to flight. However, it's reputed that Jerome Duquesnoy, who cast the original bronze statue in the 1600s, intended the Manneken to embody the "irreverent spirit" of the city; its popularity blossomed during the sombre, priest-dominated years following the Thirty Years' War. Though it's possible his bronze replaced an earlier stone version of ancient provenance, it's more likely that it was Duquesnoy himself who invented the Manneken Pis. As a talisman, it has certainly attracted the attention of thieves, notably in 1817 when a French ex-convict swiped it before breaking it into pieces. The thief and the smashed Manneken were apprehended, the former publicly branded on the Grand-Place and sentenced to a life of forced labour, while the fragments of the latter were used to create the mould in which the present-day Manneken was cast. It's long been the custom for visiting VIPs to donate a costume, and the little chap is regularly kitted out in different tackle – often military or folkloric gear.

Northwest of the Grand-Place

Along rue au Beurre, the pint-sized church of **St Nicolas** (Mon–Fri 8am–6.30pm, Sat 9am–6pm & Sun 9am–7.30pm; free) dates from the twelfth century, though it's been heavily restored on several occasions, most recently in the 1950s when parts of the outer shell were reconstructed in a plain Gothic style. The church is dedicated to St Nicholas of Bari in his capacity as the patron saint of sailors, or as he's better known, Santa Claus. The church is unusual in so far as the three aisles of the nave were built at an angle to the chancel, in order to avoid a stream. Otherwise, the gloomy church hardly sets the pulse racing, although – among a scattering of *objets d'art* – there's a handsome reliquary shrine near the entrance. Of gilded copper, the shrine was made in Germany in the nineteenth century to honour a group of Catholics martyred by Protestants in the Netherlands in 1572. More cheerfully, **Maison Dandoy**, across the street at rue au Beurre 31, is a long-established confectioners whose tasty specialities are macaroons and *spekuloos*, a sugary brown, cinnamon-flavoured biscuit that's prepared in a variety of intricate traditional moulds.

Opposite the church rises the grandiose **Bourse**, formerly the home of the city's stock exchange, a Neoclassical structure of 1873 caked with fruit, fronds, languishing nudes and frolicking putti. This breezily self-confident structure sports a host of allegorical figures (Industry, Navigation, Asia, Africa etc) which both reflect the preoccupations of the nineteenth-century Belgian bourgeoisie and, in their easy self-satisfaction, imply that wealth and pleasure are synonymous. The Bourse is flanked by good-looking though dilapidated town houses, the setting for two of the city's more famous cafés, the Art Nouveau *Falstaff*, on the south side at rue Henri Maus 17–23, and the fin-de-siècle *Le Cirio*, on the other side at rue de la Bourse 18.

The square in front of the Bourse – **place de la Bourse** – is little more than an unsightly, heavily trafficked pause along boulevard Anspach, but the streets on the other side of the boulevard have more appeal, with tiny **place St Géry** crowded by high-sided tenements, whose stone balconies and wrought-iron grilles hark back to the days of bustles and parasols. The square is thought to occupy the site of the sixth-century chapel from which the medieval city grew, but this is a matter of conjecture – no archaeological evidence has ever been unearthed. Place St Géry has one specific attraction in the recently refurbished, late nineteenth-century covered market, the **Halles St Géry**, an airy glass, brick and iron edifice.

Rue Antoine Dansaert and place Ste Catherine

From place St Géry, it's a couple of minutes' stroll north to **rue Antoine Dansaert**, where the most innovative and stylish of the city's **fashion designers** have set up shop amongst the dilapidated old houses that stretch up to place du Nouveau Marché aux Grains. Among several outstanding boutiques, three of the best are Nicole Cadine, at no. 28; Oliver Strelli, at no. 46; and Via Della Spiga, at no. 44, which sells everything from locally designed gear to Westwood, McQueen and Paul Smith. Stijl, at no. 74, showcases a bevy of big-name designers too, and there's strikingly original furniture at Max, whose two shops face each other across the street at nos. 90 and 103.

Take a right turn off rue Antoine Dansaert along rue du Vieux Marché aux Grains for **place Ste Catherine** which, despite its dishevelled appearance, lies at the heart of one of the city's most fashionable districts, not least because of its excellent seafood restaurants. Presiding over the square is the **church of Ste Catherine** (daily 8.30am–5.30pm; free) a battered nineteenth-century replacement for the Baroque original, of which the creamy, curvy belfry is the solitary survivor. Venture inside the church and you'll spy – behind the glass screen that closes off most of the nave – a fourteenth-century Black Madonna and Child, a sensually carved stone statuette that was chucked into the Senne by Protestants, but fished out while floating on a fortuitous clod of peat.

Quai aux Briques

Quai aux Briques and the parallel quai aux Bois à Brûler extend northwest from place Ste Catherine on either side of a wide and open area that was – until it was filled in – the most central part of the city's main **dock**. Strolling along this open area, you'll pass a motley assortment of nineteenth-century warehouses, shops and bars which maintain an appealing canalside feel – an impression heightened in the early morning when the streets are choked with lorries bearing trays of fish for local restaurants. The fanciful **Anspach water fountain** at the end of the old quays, with its lizards and dolphins, honours Burgomaster Anspach, a driving force in the move to modernize the city during the 1880s.

St Jean Baptiste au Béguinage

Just north of place Ste Catherine, place du Samedi and then rue du Cyprès squeeze through to **place du Béguinage**, an attractive piazza dominated by **St Jean Baptiste au Béguinage** (normally July & Aug Tues–Sat 11am–5pm, Sun 10am–5pm; Sept–June Tues–Fri 10am–5pm, but closed at time of writing by fire damage; free). A supple, billowing structure dating from the second half of the seventeenth century, this beautiful church is the only building left from the Béguine convent founded here in the thirteenth century. The convent once crowded in on the church and only since its demolition – and the creation of the star-shaped place du Béguinage in 1855 – has it been possible to view the exterior with any degree of ease. There's a sense of movement in each and every feature, a dynamism of design culminating in three soaring gables where the upper portion of the central tower is decorated with pinnacles that echo those of the Hôtel de Ville.

The church's light, spacious interior is lavishly decorated, the white stone columns and arches dripping with solemn-faced cherubs intent on reminding the congregation of their mortality. The nave and aisles are wide and open, offering unobstructed views of the high altar, but you can't fail to notice the enormous wooden **pulpit** featuring St Dominic preaching against heresy – and trampling a heretic under foot for good measure.

North and northeast of the Grand-Place

Just to the north of the Grand-Place, the quarter hinging on the pedestrianized **rue des Bouchers** is the city centre's restaurant ghetto, the narrow cobblestone streets transformed at night into fairy-lit tunnels where establishments vie for custom with elaborate displays of dull-eyed fish and glistening seafood. Things are certainly more subdued in the nearby **Galeries St**

Hubert, whose trio of glass-vaulted galleries – du Roi, de la Reine and the smaller des Princes – cut across rue des Bouchers. Opened by Léopold I in 1847, these galleries were one of Europe's earliest shopping arcades, and the pastel-painted walls, classical columns and cameo sculptures still retain an aura of genteel sophistication.

At the north end of the Galerie du Roi, it's a brief walk down rue de l'Écuyer to **place de la Monnaie**, the drab and dreary modern square that's over-shadowed by the huge **centre Monnaie**, housing offices, shops and the main post office. The only building of interest here is the **Théâtre de la Monnaie**, Brussels' opera house, a Neoclassical structure built in 1819 and with an inte-rior added in 1856 to a design by Poelaert, the architect of the Palais de Justice (see p.98). The theatre's real claim to fame, however, is as the starting-point of the revolution against the Dutch in 1830: a nationalistic libretto in Auber's *The Mute Girl of Portici* sent the audience wild, and they poured out into the streets to raise the flag of Brabant, signalling the start of the rebellion. The opera told the tale of an Italian uprising against the Spanish, with such lines as "To my country I owe my life, to me it will owe its liberty"; as a furious King William I pointed out, one of the Dutch censors – of whom there were many – should really have seen what was coming.

From place de la Monnaie, **rue Neuve** forges north, a workaday pedestrian-ized shopping street that is home to the big chain stores and the City 2 shop-ping mall. About halfway up, turn east along rue St Michel for the **place des Martyrs**, a cool, rational square imposed on the city by the Habsburgs in the 1770s. Long neglected, the square is very much the worse for wear – work has at last started on a thoroughgoing refurbishment – but there's still no mistak-ing the architectural elegance of the ensemble, completed in the last years of Austrian control. The only stylistic blip is the nineteenth-century centrepiece, a clumsy representation of the Fatherland Crowned rising from an arcaded gallery inscribed with the names of those 445 rebels who died in the Belgian revolution of 1830.

The Grand Magasin Waucquez and the Belgian Comic Strip Centre

East of place des Martyrs, it's a dreary five-minute walk through run-down offices and warehouses to rue des Sables, where at no. 20 you come to the city's only surviving Horta-designed department store, the **Grand Magasin Waucquez**. Recently restored after lying empty for many years, it's a wonder-fully airy, summery construction, with light flooding through the stained glass that encloses the expansive entrance hall. It was completed in 1906, built for a textile tycoon, and exhibits all the classic features of Victor Horta's work (see p.105) – from the soft lines of the ornamentation to the metal grilles, exposed girders and balustrades.

Maypole planting

Every year, on August 9, the corner of rue des Sables and rue du Marais is the site for the **Plantation du Meiboom** (Planting of the Maypole) – following a procession that involves much boozing, food and general partying. The story goes that in 1213 a wedding party was celebrating outside the city gates when a street gang from Leuven attacked it. The marauders were beaten off (with the help of a group of archers, who just happened to be passing by), and in thanks, the local duke gave them permission to plant a maypole on the eve of their patron saints' feast day.

Around the entrance hall is the café, reference library, bookshop and ticket office of the **Centre Belge de la Bande Dessinée** (Belgian Comic Strip Centre; Tues–Sun 10am–6pm; €6.20. Library Tues–Thurs noon–5pm, Fri noon–6pm & Sat 10am–6pm; no extra charge). The centre's displays track the stylistic evolution of the Belgian comic strip, with special features on the most familiar characters – there's an especially interesting section on that national hero, **Tintin**.

Le Botanique

Heading north from the Centre Belge de la Bande Dessinée along **rue du Marais**, you'll soon hit the petit ring and, on the other side, an attractive **park**, whose carefully manicured woods, lawns and borders are decorated by statues and a tiny lake. The park slopes up to **Le Botanique**, an appealingly grandiose greenhouse dating from 1826. The building once housed the city's botanical gardens, but these were moved out long ago and the place has been turned into a Francophone cultural centre. Despite the proximity of the traffic-congested boulevards of the ring road, it's a pleasant spot, though be warned that dodgy characters haunt its precincts in the evening. From the park, it's a quick walk west to place Rogier, from where glistening new office blocks march up rue du Progrès to the recently revamped **Gare du Nord**.

South of the Grand-Place

The labyrinth of cobbled lanes immediately to the **southwest of the Grand-Place** make for an enjoyable stroll, but inevitably you'll soon stumble across the two uninteresting, dead straight boulevards that run down from the Bourse to the **Gare du Midi**, which lies just beyond the petit ring. The area round the station is home to the city's many North African immigrants, a severely depressed and at times seedy quarter with an uneasy undertow by day and sometimes overtly threatening at night. The only good time to visit is on a Sunday morning, when a vibrant souk-like **market** is held under the station's rail arches and along boulevard du Midi.

Far better to avoid the Midi and instead walk **south** from the Grand-Place down rue de l'Étuve and then – a block before the Mannekin Pis (see p.81) – turn left up rue du Lombard for **place Saint Jean**, where the memorial in the middle of the square commemorates the remarkable **Gabrielle Petit**. Equipped with a formidable – some say photographic – memory, Petit played a leading role in the Resistance movement during the German occupation of World War I. Caught, she refused to appeal even though (as a woman) she would almost certainly have had her sentence commuted; instead she declared that she would show the Germans how a Belgian woman could die. And that is precisely what she did: the Germans executed her by firing squad in 1916.

Just to the south of the square, place de la Vieille-Halle aux Blés holds the **Fondation internationale Jacques Brel** (Tues–Sat 11am–6pm; €5), a small but inventive museum celebrating the life and times of the Belgian singer Jacques Brel (1933–78), who became famous in the 1960s as a singer of mournful *chansons* about death and love. The museum begins with a false lift that actually doesn't move at all, despite the sounds. Beyond, a sequence of life-size tableaux give the impression that you have just missed Brel – a cigarette still burns in the replica bar, and you can hear him pouring out his feelings on a mock-up stage. It's all good fun (if you like this type of music), though the labelling of the exhibits is only in French and Dutch.

Notre Dame de la Chapelle

From the square, it's a short walk south to **boulevard de l'Empereur**, a busy carriageway that disfigures this part of the centre. Across the boulevard, you'll spy the crumbling brickwork of **La Tour Anneessens**, a chunky remnant of the medieval city wall, while to the south gleams the recently restored **Notre Dame de la Chapelle** (June–Sept Mon–Sat 9am–5pm & Sun 11.30–4.30pm; Oct–May daily 12.30–4.30pm; free). The city's oldest church, founded in 1134, it's a sprawling, broadly Gothic structure that boasts an attractive if somewhat incongruous Baroque bell tower added after the French artillery bombardment of 1695 had damaged the original. Inside, the well-proportioned **nave** is supported by heavyweight columns with curly-kale capitals and bathed in light from the huge clerestory windows. The **pulpit** is an extraordinary affair, a flashy, intricately carved hunk featuring Eli in the desert beneath the palm trees. The prophet looks mightily fed up, but then he hasn't realised that there's an angel beside him with a loaf of bread (manna). Also of note is the statue of **Our Lady of Solitude**, in the second chapel of the north aisle – to the left of the entrance. It was the Spaniards who first dressed their statues in finery (the Flemings were accustomed to religious statues whose clothing formed part of the original carving), and this is an example, gifted to the church by the Spanish Infanta in the 1570s. Yet the church's main claim to fame is the memorial plaque to Pieter Bruegel the Elder, made by his son Jan and located in the fourth chapel off the south aisle; Pieter is supposed to have lived and died just down the street at rue Haute 132.

South of Notre Dame de la Chapelle, the Quartier Marolles, stacked on the slopes below the Palais de Justice, is an earthy neighbourhood of run-down housing and cheap, basic restaurants, shops and bars. Frankly, there isn't too much reason to press on here; a better bet is to backtrack to La Tour Anneessens, round the corner from which is **rue de Rollebeek**, a pleasant pedestrianized lane, dotted with cafés and restaurants, that climbs up to the place du Grand Sablon in the Upper Town (see p.98).

The Quartier Marolles

Rue Blaes, together with the less appealing **rue Haute**, form the double spine of the **Quartier Marolles**, which grew up in the seventeenth century as a centre for artisans working on the nearby mansions of the Sablon. Industrialized in the eighteenth century, it remained a thriving working-class district until the 1870s, when the paving-over of the Senne led to the riverside factories closing down and moving to the suburbs. The workers and their families followed, abandoning Marolles to the old and poor. Today, gentrification is creeping into the district, but **place du Jeu de Balle**, the heart of Marolles, is relatively unchanged, a shabby square surrounded by rough-edged bars that is the scene of the city's best **flea market** (daily 7am–2pm). The market is at its most hectic on Sunday mornings, when the square and the surrounding streets are completely taken over by pile after pile of rusty junk alongside muddles of eccentric bric-à-brac – everything from a chipped buddha or a rococo angel to horn-rimmed glasses or a stuffed bear.

The neighbourhood is one of the few places in the city where you can still hear older people using the traditional dialect, **Brusselse Sproek** or Marollien, a brand of Flemish which is now in danger of dying out. The locals, who have set up an academy to preserve it, propose – to add to the capital's linguistic complexities – that all newcomers to Brussels should learn one hundred words of this colourful, ribald language. You could make a start with *dikenek*, "big mouth"; *schieve lavabo*, "idiot" (literally "a twisted toilet"); or *fieu* – "son of a bitch".

The Upper Town

From the heights of the **Upper Town**, the Francophile ruling class long kept a beady eye on the proletarians down the hill, and it was here they built their palaces and mansions, churches and parks. Political power is no longer concentrated hereabouts, but the wide avenues and grand architecture of this aristocratic quarter – the bulk of which dates from the late eighteenth and nineteenth centuries – has survived pretty much intact, lending a stately, dignified feel that's markedly different from the bustle of the Lower Town below.

The Lower Town ends and the Upper Town begins at the foot of the sharp slope which runs north to south from one end of the city centre to the other, its course marked – in general terms at least – by a traffic-choked boulevard that's variously named Berlaimont, L'Impératrice and L'Empereur. This slope is home to the city's recently restored **cathedral**, but otherwise is little more than an obstacle to be climbed by a series of stairways. Among the latter, the most frequently used are the covered walkway running through the **Galerie Ravenstein** shopping arcade behind the **Gare Centrale**, and the open-air stairway that climbs up through the stodgy, modern buildings of the so-called **Mont des Arts**. Léopold II gave the area its name in anticipation of a fine art museum he intended to build, but the project was never completed, and the land was only properly built upon in the 1950s.

Above the rigorous layout of the Mont des Arts lie the **rue Royale** and **rue de la Régence**, which together make up the Upper Town's spine, a suitably smart location for the outstanding **Musées Royaux des Beaux Arts**, probably the best of Belgium's many fine art collections, and the surprisingly low-key **Palais Royal**. Further south, rue de la Régence soon leads to the well-heeled **Sablon** neighbourhood, whose antique shops and chic bars and cafés fan out from the medieval church of **Notre Dame du Sablon**. Beyond this is the monstrous **Palais de Justice**, traditionally one of the city's most disliked buildings.

The Cathedral

It only takes a couple of minutes to walk from the Grand-Place to the east end of rue d'Arenberg, where a short slope climbs up to the **Cathedral** (daily 8am–6pm; free), a splendid Gothic edifice whose commanding position has been sorely compromised by a rash of modern office blocks. Begun in 1215, and three hundred years in the making, the cathedral is dedicated jointly to the patron and patroness of Brussels, respectively St Michael the Archangel and St Gudule, the latter a vague seventh-century figure whose reputation was based on her gentle determination: despite all sorts of shenanigans, the devil could never make her think an uncharitable thought.

The cathedral sports a striking, twin-towered, white stone **facade**, with the central double doorway trimmed by fanciful tracery as well as statues of the Apostles and – on the central column – the Three Wise Men. The facade was erected in the fifteenth century in High Gothic style, but the intensity of the decoration fades away inside with the airy triple-aisled nave, completed a century before. Other parts of the interior illustrate several phases of Gothic design, the chancel being the oldest part of the church, built in stages between 1215 and 1280 in the Early Gothic style.

The interior is short on furnishings and fittings, reflecting the combined efforts of the Protestants, who ransacked the church (and stole the shrine of St Gudule) in the middle of the seventeenth century, and the French Republican army, who wrecked the place a century later. Unfortunately, neither of them dismantled the ponderous sculptures that are attached to the columns of the nave – clumsy seventeenth-century representations of the Apostles, which only serve to dent the nave's soaring lines. Much more appealing – and another survivor – is the massive oak **pulpit**, an extravagant chunk of frippery by the Antwerp sculptor Hendrik Verbruggen. Among several vignettes, the pulpit features Adam and Eve, dressed in rustic gear, being chased from the Garden of Eden, while up above the Virgin Mary stamps on the head of the serpent.

The cathedral also boasts some superb sixteenth-century **stained-glass windows**, beginning above the main doors with the hurly-burly of the Last Judgement. Look closely and you'll spy the donor in the lower foreground with an angel on one side and a woman with long blonde hair (symbolizing Faith) on the other. Each of the main colours has a symbolic meaning, green representing hope, yellow eternal glory and light blue heaven.

There's more remarkable work in the **transepts**, where the stained glass is distinguished by the extraordinary clarity of the blue backgrounds. These windows are eulogies to the Habsburgs – in the north transept, Charles V kneels alongside his wife beneath a vast triumphal arch as their patron saints present them to God the Father, and in the south transept Charles V's sister, Marie, and her husband, King Louis of Hungary, play out a similar scenario. Both windows were designed by Bernard van Orley (1490–1541), long-time favourite of the royal family and the leading Brussels artist of his day.

Chapelle du Saint Sacrement de Miracle and the crypt

Just beyond the north transept, flanking the choir, the cathedral treasury is displayed in the Flamboyant Gothic **Chapelle du Saint Sacrement de Miracle**, named after a shameful anti-Semitic legend whose key components were repeated again and again across medieval Christendom. Dating back to the 1360s, this particular version begins with a Jew from a small Flemish town stealing the consecrated Host from his local church. Shortly afterwards, he is murdered in a brawl and his wife moves to Brussels, taking the Host with her. The woman then presents the Host at the synagogue on Good Friday and her fellow Jews stab it with daggers, whereupon it starts to bleed. Terrified, the Jews disperse and the woman tries to save her soul by giving the Host to the city's cathedral – hence this chapel which was built to display the retrieved Host in the 1530s. The four stained-glass **windows** of the chapel retell the tale, a strip cartoon that unfolds above representations of the aristocrats who paid for the windows. The workmanship is delightful – based on designs by van Orley and his one-time apprentice Michiel van Coxie (1499–1592) – but the effects of this unsavoury legend on the congregation are not hard to imagine. The **treasury** (*Le trésor*; Mon–Fri 10am–12.30pm & 2–5pm, Sat 10am–12.30pm & 2–3.30pm, Sun 2–5pm; €2.50) itself holds a fairly predictable collection of monstrances and reliquaries, but there is a splendid Anglo-Saxon reliquary of the True Cross (Item 5) and a flowing altar painting, *The Legend of Ste Gudule*, by Michiel van Coxie (Item 3). He was arguably a better engraver than a painter, so it was something of a surprise when Philip II asked him to make a copy of van Eyck's *Adoration of the Mystic Lamb* (see p.199) for his personal collection – but then again it was better than the king just taking it.

Finally, a stairway in the north side-aisle leads down to the Romanesque **crypt** (Tues–Thurs 10am–noon & 2–5pm; €1.25) which gives an inkling as to the layout of the first church built on this site in the eleventh century.

Galerie Ravenstein and the Musée du Cinéma

Just to the south of the cathedral, along boulevard de l'Impératrice, the carrefour de l'Europe roundabout is dominated by the *Le Meridien Hotel*, with the **Gare Centrale** opposite, a bleak and somewhat surly Art Deco creation seemingly dug deep into the slope. Behind the station, on the far side of rue Cantersteen, the **Galerie Ravenstein** shopping arcade is traversed by a covered walkway that clambers up to rue Ravenstein, where the **Palais des Beaux Arts** is a severe, low-lying edifice designed by Victor Horta during the 1920s. The building holds a theatre and concert hall and hosts numerous temporary exhibitions, mostly of modern and contemporary art. Part of the complex – it also has its own entrance a few metres up the stairway at the side – accommodates the **Musée du Cinéma** (daily 5.30–10.30pm; €2.50), which has displays on the pioneering days of cinema and shows old movies every evening. One projection room presents two silent films with piano accompaniment every night, the other shows three early "talkies".

From the cinema museum, you can either climb the steps up to rue Royale and the Musées Royaux des Beaux Arts (see p.91), or stroll south along rue Ravenstein to the top of Mont des Arts and the Musée des Instruments de Musique (the Musical Instruments Museum).

Mont des Arts and the place du Musée

The wide stone stairway that cuts up through the **Mont des Arts** begins on **place de l'Albertine**, where the figure of Queen Elizabeth, bouquet in hand, stands opposite a statue honouring her husband, **Albert I**, who is depicted in military gear on his favourite horse. Easily the most popular king Belgium has ever had,

△ Mont des Arts

Albert became a national hero for his determined resistance to the Germans in World War I; he died in a climbing accident near Namur, in southern Belgium, in 1934. Flanked by severe 1940s and 1950s government buildings, the stairway leads to a piazza, equipped with water fountains and gravel footpaths, and then carries on up to rue Ravenstein, from where there are wide views over the Lower Town.

At the top of the stairway, on the right, a short flight of steps leads up to the **place du Musée**, a handsome cobbled square edged by a crisp architectural ensemble of sober symmetry, subtly adorned by Neoclassical sculptures – urns, cherubs and so forth. On the north side of the square are the **Appartements de Charles de Lorraine**, five elegant salons which are all that remain of the lavish palace built for Charles de Lorraine, the Austrian governor-general from 1749 to 1780. Recently restored, and scheduled to be open to the public in the next couple of years, the salons feature attractive marble floors and a plethora of Rococo decoration, Greek gods and cherubs scattered everywhere.

Charles built his own private chapel next door – he was well known as a rake, so presumably it was handy for confession – and he decorated it in suitably ornate style, dripping with delicate stucco work and glitzy chandeliers. After his death, no one knew quite what to do with it, but in 1804 the chapel was turned over to the city's Protestants, becoming the **Église Protestante de Bruxelles**.

The Musée des Instruments de Musique

Across from the place du Musée, at rue Montagne de la Cour 2, the **Old England building** is a whimsical Art Nouveau confection, all glass and wrought-iron, that started life as a store, taking its name from the British company who had the place built as their Brussels headquarters in 1899. It has recently been refurbished to house **Le Musée des Instruments de Musique** (MIM; Tues, Wed & Fri 9.30am–5pm, Thurs 9.30am–8pm, Sat & Sun 10am–5pm; €4), a very glitzy, prestige development focussing on no fewer than ninety musical themes – and 1500 instruments – displayed over four floors. The infrared headphones allow visitors to listen to scores of musical extracts from ancient Greece to the present day. There's a concert hall too – with regular performances on Thursday evenings – and the café on the top floor offers a great view over the city.

Place Royale

Composed and self-assured, **place Royale** forms a fitting climax to rue Royale, the dead straight backbone of the Upper Town, which runs the 2km north to the Turkish inner-city suburb of St Josse. Precisely symmetrical, the square is framed by late eighteenth-century mansions, each an exercise in architectural restraint, though there's no mistaking their size or the probable cost of their construction. Pushing into this understated opulence is the facade of the church of **St Jacques sur Coudenberg** (Sat 10am–6pm, Sun 10–11am; free), a fanciful, 1780s version of a Roman temple with a colourfully frescoed pediment representing Our Lady as Comforter of the Depressed. Indeed, the building was so secular in appearance that the French Revolutionary army had no hesitation in renaming it a Temple of Reason. The French also destroyed the statue of a Habsburg governor that once stood in front of the church; its replacement – a dashing equestrian representation of **Godfrey de Bouillon**, one of the leaders of the first Crusade – dates from the 1840s.

The Musées Royaux des Beaux Arts

A few metres from place Royale, at the start of rue de la Régence, the **Musées Royaux des Beaux Arts** comprise two museums (Tues–Sun 10am–5pm; €5 combined ticket), one displaying modern art, the other older works. Together they make up Belgium's most satisfying all-round collection of fine art, with marvellous collections of work by – among many – Pieter Bruegel the Elder, Rubens and the surrealists Paul Delvaux and René Magritte.

Both museums are large, and to do them justice you should see them in separate visits. Finding your way around is made easy by the detailed English-language **museum plan** on sale at the entrance. The older paintings – up to the beginning of the nineteenth century – are well presented, if not exactly well organized, in the **Musée d'Art Ancien**, which is saved from confusion by its colour-coded zones. The **blue** area shows paintings of the fifteenth and sixteenth centuries, including the Bruegels, and the **brown** area concentrates on paintings of the seventeenth and eighteenth centuries, with the collection of Rubens (for which the museum is internationally famous) as the highlight. The **orange** area comprises the small and undistinguished Gallery of Sculptures. The **Musée d'Art Moderne** has a **yellow** area devoted to nineteeth-century works, notably the canvases of Ostend-born James Ensor, and a **green** area whose eight subterranean levels cover the twentieth century.

The Musée d'Art Ancien also hosts, in the **red** area, a prestigious programme of **temporary exhibitions** for which a supplementary admission fee is usually required. For the most popular you'll need to buy a ticket ahead of time; the ticket may specify the time of admission. The larger exhibitions may cause some disruption to the permanent collection, so treat with a little caution the room numbers we give below. Inevitably, the account below scratches the surface; the museum's **bookshop** sells a well-illustrated guide to the collections (€15) plus a wide range of other detailed texts.

Musée d'Art Ancien

By any standard the **Musée d'Art Ancien** holds a superb collection, but its speciality – and for this it is world-renowed – is its **Flemish primitives**, exhibited in the blue zone.

Rogier van der Weyden and Dieric Bouts

Rooms 11 and **12** hold several paintings by **Rogier van der Weyden** (1399–1464), the one-time official city painter to Brussels. When it came to portraiture, his favourite technique was to highlight the features of his subject – and tokens of rank – against a black background. His *Portrait of the Grand Bâtard de Bourgogne* is a good example, with Anthony, the illegitimate son of Philip the Good, casting a haughty, tight-lipped stare to his right while wearing the chain of the Order of the Golden Fleece and clasping an arrow, the emblem of the guild of archers.

In **Room 13**, the two panels of the *Justice of the Emperor Otto* are the work of Weyden's contemporary, the Leuven-based **Dieric Bouts** (1410–75). The story was well known: in revenge for refusing her advances, the empress accuses a nobleman of attempting to seduce her. He is executed, but the man's wife remains convinced of his innocence and subsequently proves her point by means of an ordeal by fire, in which she holds a red-hot iron bar.

Hans Memling and the Master of the Legends of St Lucy

Room 14 has some fine portraits by **Hans Memling** (1430–94) as well as his softly hued *Martyrdom of St Sebastian*. Legend asserts that Sebastian was an officer in Diocletian's bodyguard until his Christian faith was discovered, at which point he was sentenced to be shot to death by the imperial archers. Left for dead by the bowmen, Sebastian recovered and Diocletian had to send a bunch of assassins to finish him off with cudgels. The tale made Sebastian popular with archers across Western Europe, and Memling's picture – showing the trussed-up saint serenely indifferent to the arrows of the firing squad – was commissioned by the guild of archers in Bruges around 1470. In the same room, the **Master of the Legend of St Lucy** weighs in with a finely detailed, richly allegorical *Madonna with Saints* where, with the city of Bruges in the background, the Madonna presents the infant Jesus for the adoration of eleven holy women. Decked out in elaborate medieval attire, the women have blank, almost expressionless faces, but each bears a token of her sainthood, which would have been easily recognized by a medieval congregation. St Lucy, whose assistance was sought by those with sight problems, holds two eyes in a dish.

The Master of the Legend of St Barbara

In **Room 15**, there's more early Flemish art in the shape of the *Scenes from the Life of St Barbara*, one panel from an original pair by the **Master of the Legend of St Barbara**. One of the most popular of medieval saints, Barbara – so the story goes – was a woman of great beauty, whose father, Dioscurus, locked her in a tower away from her admirers. The imprisoned Barbara became a Christian, whereupon Dioscurus tried to kill her, only to be thwarted by a miracle that placed her out of his reach – a part of the tale that's ingeniously depicted in this painting. Naturally, no self-respecting saint could escape so easily, so later parts of the story have Barbara handed over to the local prince, who tortures her for her faith. Barbara resists and the prince orders Dioscurus to kill her himself, which he does, only to be immediately incinerated by a bolt of lightning.

School of Hieronymus Bosch

Room 17 boasts a copy of the **Hieronymus Bosch** *Temptations of St Anthony* that's in the Museu Nacional in Lisbon. No one is quite sure who painted this triptych – it may or may not have been one of Bosch's apprentices – but it was certainly produced in Holland in the late fifteenth or early sixteenth century. The painting refers to St Anthony, a third-century nobleman who withdrew into the desert, where he endured fifteen years of temptation before settling down into his long stint as a hermit. It was the temptations that interested Bosch – rather than the ascetic steeliness of Anthony – and the central panel has an inconspicuous saint sticking desperately to his prayers surrounded by all manner of fiendish phantoms. The side panels develop the theme – to the right Anthony is tempted by lust and greed, and on the left Anthony's companions help him back to his shelter after he's been transported through the skies by weird-looking demons.

Cranach, Gerard David and Matsys

Next door, **Room 18** holds works by Martin Luther's friend, the Bavarian artist **Lucas Cranach** (1472–1553), whose *Adam and Eve* presents a stylized, Renaissance view of the Garden of Eden, with an earnest-looking Adam on the other side of the Tree of Knowledge from a coquettish Eve, painted with legs entwined and her teeth marks visible on the apple. Room 21 displays a couple of panels by **Gerard David** (1460–1523), a Bruges-based artist whose draughtsmanship may not be of the highest order, but whose paintings do display a tender serenity, as exhibited here in his *Adoration of the Magi* and *Virgin and Child*.

In **Room 22**, **Quentin Matsys** (1465–1530) is well represented by the *Triptych of the Holy Kindred*. Matsys' work illustrates a turning point in the development of Flemish painting, and in this triptych, completed in 1509, Matsys abandons the realistic interiors and landscapes of his Flemish predecessors in favour of the grand columns and porticoes of the Renaissance. Each scene is rigorously structured, its characters – all relations of Jesus – assuming lofty, idealized poses.

The Bruegels

The museum's collection of works by the Bruegel family, notably **Pieter the Elder** (1527–69), is focused on Room 31. Although he is often regarded as the finest Netherlandish painter of the sixteenth century, little is known of Pieter the Elder's life, but it's likely he was apprenticed in Antwerp, and he certainly moved to Brussels in the early 1560s. He also made at least one long trip to Italy, but judging by his oeuvre, he was – unlike most of his "Belgian" contemporaries – decidedly unimpressed by Italian art. He preferred instead to paint in the Netherlandish tradition and his works often depict crowded Flemish scenes in which are embedded religious or mythical stories. This sympathetic portrayal of everyday life revelled in the seasons and was worked in muted browns, greys and bluey greens with red or yellow highlights. Typifying this approach, and on display here, are two particularly absorbing works, the *Adoration of the Magi* and the *Census at Bethlehem* – a scene that Pieter (1564–1638), his son, repeated on several occasions – in which the traditionally momentous events happen, almost incidentally, among the bustle of everyday life. The versatile Pieter also dabbled with the lurid imagery of Bosch, whose influence is seen most clearly in the *Fall of the Rebel Angels*, a frantic panel painting which had actually been attributed to Bosch until Bruegel's signature was discovered hidden under the frame. The *Fall of Icarus* is, however, his most haunting work, its mood perfectly captured by Auden in his poem "Musée des Beaux Arts":

In Bruegel's Icarus, for instance: how everything turns away
Quite leisurely from the disaster; the ploughman may
Have heard the splash, the forsaken cry,
But for him it was not an important failure; the sun shone
As it had to on the white legs disappearing into the green
Water; and the expensive delicate ship that must have seen
Something amazing, a boy falling out of the sky,
Had somewhere to get to and sailed calmly on.

Rubens and his contemporaries

Apprenticed in Antwerp, **Rubens** (1577–1640) spent eight years in Italy studying the Renaissance masters before returning home, where he quickly completed a stunning series of paintings for Antwerp Cathedral (see p.229). His fame spread far and wide, and for the rest of his days Rubens was inundated with work, receiving commissions from all over Europe. In **Room 52**, the popular misconception that Rubens painted nothing but chubby nude women and muscular men is dispelled with a sequence of fine portraits, each aristocratic head drawn with great care and attention to detail – in particular, note the exquisite ruffs adorning the Archduke Albert and Isabella. *Studies of a Negro's Head* is likewise wonderfully observed, a preparation for the black magus in the *Adoration of the Magi*, a luminous work that's one of several huge canvases next door in **Room 62**. Here you'll also find the *Ascent to Calvary*, an intensely physical painting, capturing the confusion, agony and strain as Christ struggles on hands and knees under the weight of the cross. There's also the bloodcurdling *Martyrdom of St Lieven*, whose cruel torture – his tongue has just been ripped out and fed to a dog – is watched from on high by cherubs and angels.

Two of Rubens' pupils, **Anthony van Dyck** (1599–1641) and **Jacob Jordaens** (1593–1678), also feature in this part of the museum, with the studied portraits of the former dotted along the length of **Room 53** and the big and brassy canvases of Jordaens dominating **Room 57**. Like Rubens, Jordaens had a bulging order-book, and for years he and his apprentices churned out paintings by the cart load. His best work is generally agreed to have been completed early on – between about 1620 and 1640 – and there's evidence here in the two versions of the *Satyr and the Peasant*, the earlier work clever and inventive, the second a hastily cobbled together piece that verges on buffoonery.

Close by, in **Room 60**, is a modest sample of Dutch painting, including a couple of sombre and carefully composed **Rembrandt**s (1606–69). One of them – the self-assured *Portrait of Nicolaas van Bambeeck* – was completed in 1641, when the artist was finishing off his famous *Night Watch*, now exhibited in Amsterdam's Rijksmuseum. Rembrandt's pupils are displayed in the same room, principally **Nicolaes Maes** (1634–93), who is well represented by the delicate *Dreaming Old Woman*. In this room also are several canvases by Rembrandt's talented contemporary, **Frans Hals** (1580–1666), notably his charming *Three Children and a Cart drawn by a Goat*.

Musée d'Art Moderne

To reach the **Musée d'Art Moderne**, you'll need to use the underground passageway which leads from the main museum entrance to Level -2 of the **yellow** area, whose nineteenth-century, mostly Belgian, paintings are spread over five small floors – two underground and three above. Another stairway, on this same Level -2, leads down to the six subterranean half-floors that constitute the **green** area of twentieth-century works. The green area is comparatively small and has an international flavour, with the work of Belgian artists – including René Magritte and Paul Delvaux – supplemented by the likes of Dalí, Picasso, Chagall, Henry Moore, Miró, Matisse and Francis Bacon.

Social Realists

Level -2 features the work of the **Social Realists**, whose paintings and sculptures championed the working class. One of the early figures in this movement was **Charles de Groux** (1825–70), whose paternalistic *Poor People's Pew* and *Benediction* are typical of his work. Much more talented was **Constantin Meunier** (1831–1905; see p.107), who is well represented here by two particularly forceful bronzes, *Firedamp* and the *Iron Worker*. Look out also for the stirring canvases of their mutual friend **Eugene Laermans** (1864–1940), who shifted from the Realist style into more Expressionistic works, as in the overtly political *Red Flag* and *The Corpse*, a sorrowful vision which is perhaps Laermans' most successful painting.

Jacques-Louis David and his contemporaries

The obvious highlight of Level +1 is **Jacques-Louis David**'s famous *Death of Marat*, a propagandist piece of 1793 showing Jean-Paul Marat, the French revolutionary hero, dying in his bath after being stabbed by Charlotte Corday. David (1748–1825) has given Marat a perfectly proportioned, classical torso and a face which, with its large hooded eyes, looks almost Christ-like, the effect heightened by the flatness of the composition and the emptiness of the background. The dead man clasps a quill in one hand and the letter given him by

Corday in the other, inscribed "my deepest grief is all it takes to be entitled to your benevolence". There's another note, on the wooden chest, written by Marat and beginning, "You will give this warrant to that mother with the five children, whose husband died for his country". This was David's paean to a fellow revolutionary for, like Marat, he was a Jacobin – the deadly rivals of the Girondins, who were supported by Corday – and had voted for the execution of Louis XVI. He was also a leading light of the Neoclassical movement and became the new regime's Superintendent of the Fine Arts. He did well under Napoleon, too, but after Waterloo David, along with all the other regicides, was exiled, ending his days in Brussels.

Symbolism and James Ensor

The Symbolists are clustered on Level +2 and among them are the disconcerting canvases of **Fernand Khnopff** (1858–1921), who painted his sister, Marguerite, again and again, using her refined, almost plastic, beauty to stir a vague sense of passion – for she's desirable and utterly unobtainable in equal measure. His haunting *Memories of Lawn Tennis* is typical of his oeuvre, a work without narrative, a dream-like scene with each of the seven women bearing the likeness of Marguerite. In *Caresses* Marguerite pops up once more, this time with the body of a cheetah pawing sensually at an androgynous youth. **Antoine Wiertz**, who has a museum all to himself near the EU Parliament building (see p.101), pops up too, his *La Belle Rosme*, a typically disagreeable painting in which the woman concerned faces a skeleton.

In a separate section on Level -2 is a superb sample of the work of **James Ensor** (1860–1949). Ensor, the son of a Flemish mother and an English father, spent nearly all of his long life working in Ostend, his home town (see p.136). His first paintings were demure portraits and landscapes, but in the early 1880s he switched to a more Impressionistic style, delicately picking out his colours as in *The Lady in Blue*. It is, however, Ensor's use of masks which sets his work apart – ambiguous carnival masks with the sniff of death or perversity. His *Scandalized Masks* of 1883 was his first mask painting, a typically unnerving canvas that works on several levels, while his *Skeletons Quarrelling for a Kipper* (1891) is one of the most savage and macabre paintings you're ever likely to see.

Impressionism and Post-Impressionism

Level +3 has a sprinkling of French Impressionists and Post-Impressionists – Monet, Seurat, Gauguin – alongside the studied pointillism of **Théo van Rysselberghe** (1862–1926), a versatile Brussels artist and founder member of Les XX (see p.427). **Henry van de Velde** (1863–1957), another member of Les XX, changed his painting style as often as Rysselberghe, but in the late 1880s he was under the influence of Seurat – hence *The Mender*.

Cubists, Expressionists and Fauvists

A stairway leads down from yellow-coded Level -2 to the green area, whose six subterranean half-floors (Levels -3 to -8) hold a diverse collection of modern art and sculpture. It's a challenging collection of international dimensions that starts as it means to continue – at the entrance to Level -3/4 – with a lumpy, uncompromising Henry Moore and an eerie Francis Bacon, *The Pope with Owls*. Beyond lies an assortment of works by Picasso, Braque and Matisse, a Dufy *Port of Marseilles*, and two fanciful paintings by Chagall, one of which is the endearingly eccentric *The Frog that Wanted to Make Itself as Big as a Bull*. Another highlight is **Léon Spilliaert**'s evocations of intense loneliness, from monochromatic beaches to empty rooms and train cars. Spilliaert (1881–1946) lived in Ostend, the setting for much of his work, including the piercing *Woman on the Dyke*. Another noteworthy Belgian is **Constant Permeke** (1886–1952), whose grim, gritty Expressionism is best illustrated here by *The Potato Eater* (1935).

Surrealism – Delvaux and Magritte

Level -5/6 is given over to the Surrealists. There's a fine **Dalí**, *The Temptation of St Anthony*, a hallucinatory work in which spindly legged elephants tempt the saint with fleshy women, and a couple of haunting **de Chirico** paintings of dressmakers' dummies. Among the Belgian Surrealists, **Paul Delvaux** (1897–1994; see p.142) is represented by his trademark themes of ice-cool nudes set against a disintegrating backdrop as well as by trains and stations – see the *Evening Train* and the *Public Voice*. Even more elusive is the gallery's collection of paintings by **René Magritte** (1898–1967; see p.111), perplexing works whose weird, almost photographically realized images and bizarre juxtapositions aim to disconcert. Magritte was the prime mover in Belgian surrealism, developing – by the time he was 30 – an individualistic style that remained fairly constant throughout his entire career. It was not, however, a style that brought him much initial success and, surprising as it may seem today, he remained relatively unknown until the 1950s. The museum has a substantial sample of his work, among which two of the more intriguing pieces are the baffling *Secret Player* and the subtly discordant *Empire of Lights*.

Contemporary art

Down on Level -7/8, there's some pretty incomprehensible modern stuff, featuring an international range of artists with the displays – and installations – regularly rotated. All the same, you're likely to spot the tongue-in-cheek work of **Marcel Broodthaers** (1924–76), famously his *Red Mussels Casserole*, and the swirling abstracts of Brussels-born and Paris-based Pierre Alechinsky (b. 1927). A painter and graphic artist, Alechinsky was briefly a member of the CoBrA group, but left in 1951. Thereafter, his work picked up on all sorts of international themes and movements, from Japanese calligraphy through to Nordic Expressionism, with a good dose of Surrealism (and Ensor) thrown in.

The Palais Royal – and the Musée de la Dynastie

Around the corner from place Royale, the long and low **Palais Royal** (late July to Sept Tues–Sun 10.30am–4.30pm; free) is something of an anticlimax, a sombre nineteenth-century conversion of some late eighteenth-century town houses, begun by King William I, the Dutch royal who ruled both Belgium and the Netherlands from 1815 to 1830. The Belgian rebellion of 1830 polished off the joint kingdom, and since then the kings of independent Belgium haven't spent much money on the palace. Indeed, although it remains their official residence, the royals have lived elsewhere (in Laeken, see p.111) for decades and it's hardly surprising, therefore, that the **palace interior** is formal and unwelcoming. It consists of little more than a predictable sequence of opulent rooms – all gilt trimmings, parquet floors, and endless royal portraits, though the tapestries designed by Goya and the magnificent chandeliers of the Throne Room make a visit (just about) worthwhile.

One of the mansions that makes up the Palais Royal, the **Hôtel Bellevue**, at the corner of place des Palais and rue Royale, has been turned into **Musée de la Dynastie** (Tues–Sun 10am–6pm; museum €6.20, Coudenberg Palace €5;

combined ticket €7.50), which tracks through the brief history of the Belgian royal family. It's all very professionally done, comprising a brisk chronological trawl juiced up by a wide range of personal artefacts – clothes, shoes, letters and the like – donated by the royals, with separate sections on each of the country's monarchs. There is a particularly detailed section on the recently deceased King Baudouin, who seems to have been a kind and gentle soul, but the museum almost always dodges the controversies that have surrounded several of its kings. It is particularly shameless in its treatment of Léopold II: apparently, he loved to travel and was quite an adventurer, attributes which his colonial (Congolese) victims – of whom there is scarcely a mention – would have been hard pressed to appreciate.

The museum also gives access to the labyrinth of caves that are all that remain of the **Coudenberg Palace** (Tues–Sun 10am–6pm), which once occupied the top of the hill on what is now place Royale. A castle was built here in the eleventh century and enlarged on several subsequent occasions, but it was badly damaged by fire in 1731 and the site was cleared in 1775. The foundations were, however, left untouched and have recently been cleared of debris. Further restorative work is planned, but at the moment visitors can wander round these dusty foundations, the most notable feature of which is the massive **Magna Aula**, or great hall, built by Philip the Good in the 1450s. A map of the layout of the palace is provided at reception, but you still need a vivid imagination to get much out of a visit.

Parc de Bruxelles and place du Trône

Opposite the Palais Royal, the **Parc de Bruxelles** is the most central of the city's larger parks, along whose tree-shaded footpaths civil servants and office workers stroll at lunchtime, or race to catch the métro in the evenings. They might well wish the greenery was a bit more interesting. Laid out in the formal French style in 1780, the park undoubtedly suited the courtly – and courting – rituals of the times, but today the straight footpaths and long lines of trees merely seem tedious, though the classical statues dotted hither and thither do cheer things up a bit.

From the east side of the royal palace, rue Ducale leads to **place du Trône**. The pompous equestrian statue of Léopold II here was the work of Thomas Vinçotte, whose skills were much used by the king – look out for Vinçotte's chariot on top of the Parc du Cinquantenaire's triumphal arch (see p.102). Place du Trône is a short walk from the EU Parliament building and the EU Quarter – see p.99.

Sablon and place Louise

Anchoring the southern end of the Upper Town, the Sablon neighbourhood is centred on **place du Petit Sablon**, a small rectangular area which was laid out as a public garden in 1890 after previous use as a horse market. The wrought-iron fence surrounding the garden is decorated with 48 statuettes representing the medieval guilds while inside, near the top of the slope, are ten – slightly larger – statues honouring some of the country's leading sixteenth-century figures. The ten are hardly household names in Belgium, never mind anywhere else, but one or two may ring a few bells – Mercator, the geographer and cartographer responsible for Mercator's projection of the earth's surface; and William the Silent, the founder of the Netherlands (see p.410). Here also, on top of the fountain, are the figures of the counts **Egmont and Hoorn**, beheaded on the Grand-Place for their opposition to the Habsburgs in 1568 (see p.410).

Count Egmont is further remembered by the **Palais d'Egmont** (no entry) at the back of the square. An elegant structure that has been remodelled on several occasions, it was originally built in 1534 for Françoise of Luxembourg, mother of the executed count.

Notre Dame du Sablon and the place du Grand Sablon

Opposite the foot of the park, the fifteenth-century church of **Notre Dame du Sablon** (Mon–Fri 9am–5pm, Sat 10am–5pm & Sun 1–5pm; free) began life as a chapel for.the guild of archers in 1304. Its fortunes were, however, transformed when a statue of Mary, thought to have healing powers, was brought here from Antwerp in 1348. The chapel became a centre of pilgrimage and a proper church – in high Gothic style – was built to accommodate its visitors. Though it did endure some inappropriate tinkering at the end of the nineteenth century, it's a handsome, honey-colour structure, with arching buttresses, slender parapets, screeching gargoyles and delicate pinnacles, and it has greatly benefited from its recent refurbishment. The **interior** no longer holds the statue of Mary – the Protestants chopped it up in 1565 – but two carvings of a boat and its passengers, one in the nave, the other above the inside of the rue de la Régence entrance, recall the story; the woman in the boat is one Béatrice Sodkens, the pious creature whose visions prompted her to procure the statue and bring it here. The occasion of its arrival in Brussels is still celebrated annually in July by the **Ommegang** procession (see below).

Behind the church, the **place du Grand Sablon** is one of Brussels' most charming squares, a sloping wedge of cobblestones flanked by tall, slender town houses plus the occasional Art Nouveau facade. The square serves as the centre of one of the city's wealthiest districts, and is busiest at weekends, when there's an **antiques market** here. Many of the shops on Sablon and the surrounding streets are devoted to antiques and art, and you could easily spend an hour or so browsing – or you can soak up the atmosphere in one of Sablon's cafés.

Palais de Justice and place Louise

From place du Grand Sablon, rue Ernest Allard leads up the hill to **place Poelaert**, named after the architect who designed the immense **Palais de Justice**, a monstrous Greco-Roman wedding cake of a building, dwarfing the square and everything around it. It's possible to wander into the building's sepulchral main hall, but it's the size alone that impresses – not that it pleased the several thousand townsfolk who were forcibly evicted so that the place could be built. Poelaert became one of the most hated men in the capital and, when he went insane and died in 1879, it was widely believed a *steekes* (witch) from the Marolles had been sticking pins into an effigy of him.

The Ommegang

Brussels has several first-rate festivals, of which the **Ommegang** (literally "walkabout"; more info on ☏ 02 512 19 61 or ⊛ www.ommegang-brussels.be) is the best known. A grand procession from Grand Sablon to the Grand-Place, it began in the fourteenth century as a religious event, celebrating the arrival by boat of a statue of the Virgin from Antwerp. The celebration became increasingly secular – an excuse for the nobility, guilds and civic bigwigs to parade their finery – and was witnessed by no less than the Emperor Charles V in 1549. Today's Ommegang, which finishes up with a dance on the Grand-Place, is so popular that it is now held twice each year, on the first Tuesday and Thursday of July. If you want a **ticket** for the finale, you'll need to reserve (at the tourist office) at least six months ahead.

A stone's throw from the Palais de Justice, **place Louise**, part square, part traffic junction, heralds the start of the city's most exclusive shopping district. Here and in the immediate vicinity you'll find designer boutiques, jewellers and glossy shopping malls. The glitz spreads east along boulevard de Waterloo and south down the first part of avenue Louise, which is described on p.107.

Outside the petit ring

Brussels by no means ends with the **petit ring**. Léopold II pushed the city limits out beyond the course of the old walls, grabbing land from the surrounding *communes* to create the irregular boundaries that survive today. To the **east**, he sequestered a rough rectangle of land across which he ploughed two wide boulevards to link the city centre with **Le Cinquantenaire**, a self-glorifying and over-sized monument erected to celebrate Belgium's golden jubilee, and now housing three sprawling museums. There's no disputing the grandness of Léopold's design, but in recent decades it has been overlaid with the uncompromising office blocks of the EU. These high-rises coalesce hereabouts to form the loosely defined **EU quarter**, not a particularly enjoyable area to explore, though the strikingly flashy European Parliament building is of passing interest (and just footsteps from the fascinating paintings of the Musée Antoine Wiertz). If, however, you've an insatiable appetite for the monuments of Léopold, then you should venture further east to **Tervuren**, where the king built the grandiose Musée Royal de L'Afrique Centrale on the edge of the Forêt de Soignes.

Léopold's hand doesn't lie so heavily on the *communes* to the **south** of the city centre. Here, **St Gilles** is an animated and cosmopolitan district, though the immigrant areas around the Gare du Midi are scarred by poverty, while neighbouring **Ixelles** has become the trendiest part of Brussels, its old, well-worn streets much favoured by artists, intellectuals and students. These two *communes* also boast the best of the city's **Art Nouveau** architecture, including the sinuous virtuosity of the one-time house and studio of Victor Horta. Ixelles is cut into two by **avenue Louise**, a prosperous corridor that is actually part of the city – a territorial anomaly inherited from Léopold II – and one which merits a visit for the Musée Constantin Meunier.

West of the city centre, the partly industrialized suburb of **Anderlecht** is famous for its soccer team, but it's an ancient *commune* that possesses the fascinating Maison d'Erasme, where the polyglot scholar and church reformer Desiderius Erasmus lodged in 1521, and the Musée Bruxellois de la Gueuze, a museum in an operational brewery. Finally, **north** of the city centre, beyond the tough districts of St Josse and Schaerbeek, are the suburbs of **Jette**, home to the René Magritte Museum; **Laeken**, city residence of the Belgian royal family; and **Heysel**, with its trademark Atomium, a clumsy leftover from the 1958 World's Fair.

The EU quarter, Parc Léopold and Le Cinquantenaire

To enjoy a visit to this part of the city, you'll need to follow a clear itinerary, one which avoids the worst of the EU area, where the streets groan with traffic and a vast building programme has turned whole blocks into dusty construction sites. Essentially, this means dodging – as far as possible – rues de la Loi and Belliard, the two wide boulevards that serve as the area's main thoroughfares. The best place to start is in the vicinity of **Parc Léopold**, where – just a few minutes stroll from the petit ring – you'll find the intriguing **Musée Wiertz**, exhibiting the huge and eccentric paintings of the eponymous artist, and the **European Parliament building**. From here, it's a ten-minute walk to **Le Cinquantenaire**, one of Léopold's most excessive extravagances, a triumphal arch built to celebrate the golden jubilee of Belgian independence and containing three museums, the pick of which is the wide-ranging **Musées Royaux d'Art et d'Histoire**.

Place du Trône to the European Parliament building

Part of the petit ring and on the métro line, **place du Trône** is distinguished by its double lion gates and life-size statue of Léopold II, perched on his horse. From here, **rue du Luxembourg** heads east to bisect a small park whose northern half contains a modest memorial to **Julien Dillens**, a popular nineteenth-century sculptor responsible for the effigy of Everard 't Serclaes on the Grand-Place (see p.79). Just along the street, the **place du Luxembourg** has had varying fortunes, but now it's on the up, fashionable cafés moving in as the three-storey, stone-trimmed houses are refurbished.

On the far side of the square, follow the signs (to rue Wiertz) through the tatty Gare du Quartier Léopold train station, and you'll quickly reach a gigantic, new EU office block, whose undulating lines sweep way down to rue Belliard. Fortunately, there's a breach in this edifice dead ahead, and just beyond it – through the passageway and down the steps – is the equally new

---

The EU in Brussels

The **European Union** is operated by three main institutions, each of which does most of its work in Brussels.

The **European Parliament** – the only EU institution to meet and debate in public – sits in Strasbourg, but meets in Brussels for around six, two-day plenary sessions per year. During sessions, Members of the European Parliament (MEPs) – there are currently just over six hundred – sit in political blocs and not in national delegations. The Parliament has a President and fourteen Vice-Presidents, each of whom is elected for two and a half years by Parliament itself. The President (or a Vice-President) meets with the leaders of the political groups to plan future parliamentary business. Supporting and advising this political edifice is a complex network of committees, mostly based in Brussels.

The **Council of Ministers** consists of the heads of government of each of the member states and the President of the European Commission; they meet regularly in the much-publicized "European Summits". Most Council meetings are not, however, attended by the heads of government themselves, but by a delegated minister. There are complex rules regarding decision-making: some subjects require only a simple majority, others need unanimous support. This political structure is underpinned by scores of Brussels-based committees and working parties, made up of both civil servants and political appointees.

Headquartered in Brussels, the **European Commission** has over ten thousand civil servants, and acts as the EU's executive arm and board of control, managing funds and monitoring all manner of agreements. The twenty Commissioners are nominated by their home country but responsible to the European Parliament once they're in office. The president of the Commission is elected for a three-year period of office.

European Union Parliament building, another glass, stone and steel behemoth equipped with a curved glass roof that rises to a height of 70m. Completed in 1997, the building contains a large, semicircular assembly room as well as the offices of the President of the Parliament and their General Secretariat. The building has its admirers, but is known locally as the "*caprice des dieux*". You can usually (subject to what's happening in the Parliament) take a free, thirty-minute audio-guided tour of the building (Sept–July Mon–Thurs at 10am & 5pm, Fri 10am; also mid-April to mid-Oct Sat 10am, 11.30am & 2.30pm).

Musée Wiertz

Behind the European Parliament building at rue Vautier 62 – head right from the entrance, then swing left up the slope – the **Musée Wiertz** (Tues–Fri 10am–noon & 1–5pm; alternate weekends 10am–noon & 1–5pm; free; ☎02 648 17 18) is devoted to the works of one of the city's most distinctive, if disagreeable, nineteenth-century artists. Once immensely popular (so much so that in *Tess of the d'Urbervilles* Thomas Hardy could write of "the staring and ghastly attitudes of a Wiertz museum"), Antoine-Joseph Wiertz (1806–65) painted religious and mythological canvases, featuring gory hells and strapping nudes, as well as fearsome scenes of human madness and suffering.

The core of the museum is housed in his **studio**, a large, airy space that was built for him by the Belgian state on the understanding that he bequeathed his oeuvre to the nation. Pictures include *The Burnt Child, The Thoughts and Visions of a Severed Head* and a small but especially gruesome *Suicide* – not for the squeamish. There are also a number of smaller, quite elegantly painted quasi-erotic pieces featuring coy nudes and a colossal *Triumph of Christ*, a melodramatic painting of which Wiertz was inordinately proud. Three adjoining **rooms** contain further macabre works, such as *Premature Burial* and (the most appalling of them all) his *Hunger, Folly, Crime* – in which a madwoman is pictured shortly after hacking off her child's leg and throwing it into the cooking pot. Mercifully, there is some more restrained stuff here too, including several portraits and more saucy girls in various states of undress. Wiertz eventually came to believe that he was a better painter than his artistic forebears, Rubens and Michelangelo; judge for yourself.

Muséum des Sciences Naturelles

The **Muséum des Sciences Naturelles** (Tues–Fri 9.30am–4.45pm, Sat & Sun 10am–6pm; €4), just along the street from the Musée Wiertz, at rue Vautier 29, holds the city's natural history collection. It's a large, sprawling museum divided into fifteen clearly signed areas, each of which focuses on a particular aspect of the natural world, and several of which try to be child-friendly – robotic dinosaurs and suchlike. The dinosaur section is, indeed, the most impressive, featuring **iguanodons** whose skeletons parade across the ground floor; a whole group of them was discovered in the coal mines of Hainaut in the late nineteenth century. Other highlights include a first-rate collection of tropical shells, an insect room, a section comparing the Arctic and Antarctic, and a whale gallery featuring eighteen skeletons, including the enormous remains of a blue whale.

Parc Léopold

On rue Vautier, almost opposite the Musée Wiertz, a scruffy back entrance leads into the rear of **Parc Léopold**, a hilly, leafy enclave landscaped around a lake. The park is pleasant enough, but its open spaces were encroached upon years ago when the industrialist Ernest Solvay began constructing the educational and research facilities of a prototype science centre here. The end result is a string of big, old buildings that spreads along the park's western periphery. The most interesting is the first you'll come to, the newly refurbished **Bibliothèque Solvay** (no set opening times), a splendid barrel-vaulted structure with magnificent mahogany panelling. Down below the library and the other buildings, at the bottom of the slope, is the main entrance to Parc Léopold, where a set of stumpy stone gates bear the legend "Jardin royal de zoologie" – Léopold wanted the park to be a zoo, but for once his plans went awry.

To Parc du Cinquantenaire

From the front entrance to the Parc Léopold, it takes a little less than ten minutes to walk east along **rue Belliard** to Parc du Cinquantenaire. Both **this street** and the parallel **rue de la Loi**, originally built by Léopold II to connect the park with the city centre, are thronged by the office blocks of the EU, whose penchant for modernistic, state-of-the-art high-rises is not only depressing but also surprising, given the difficulties the EU has had with its best-known construction, the **Centre Berlaymont**. A huge office building on rue de la Loi beside Métro Schuman, the Berlaymont was widely praised for its ground-breaking design when it was opened in 1967, but in 1991 it was abandoned – the building was riddled with asbestos and work still continues on its refurbishment.

Within the **Parc du Cinquantenaire**, wide and largely featureless lawns slope up towards a gargantuan **triumphal arch** surmounted by a huge and bombastic bronze entitled *Brabant Raising the National Flag*. The arch, along with the two heavyweight stone buildings it connects, comprise **Le Cinquantenaire**, placed here by Léopold II for an exhibition to mark the golden jubilee of the Belgian state in 1880. By all accounts the exhibition of all things made in Belgium and its colonies was a great success, and the park continues to host shows and trade fairs of various kinds, while the buildings themselves – which are a brief walk from the Métro Merode – contain extensive collections of art and applied art, weapons and cars, displayed in three separate museums.

Musées Royaux d'Art et d'Histoire

The **Musées Royaux d'Art et d'Histoire** (Tues–Fri 9.30am–5pm, Sat & Sun 10am–5pm; €4), on the south side of the south wing of the complex, are made up of a maddening (and badly labelled) maze of pottery, carvings, furniture, tapestries, glassware and lacework from all over the world. There is almost too much to absorb in even a couple of visits, and your best bet is to pick up the plan and index at reception and select the areas which interest you most. There are enormous galleries of mostly run-of-the-mill Greek, Egyptian and Roman artefacts, complete with mummies of a jackal, crocodile and falcon. Elsewhere, another part of the collection has an assortment of Near and Far Eastern gods, porcelain, jewellery and textiles, and there are pre-Columbian Native American carvings and effigies too.

The **European decorative arts** sections, located on Level 1 (rooms 45–75) and Level 2 (rooms 89–105), have the most immediacy. They are divided into over twenty distinct collections, featuring everything from Delft ceramics, altarpieces, porcelain and silverware through to tapestries, Art Deco and Art Nouveau furnishings. It's all a little bewildering, with little to link one set of artefacts to another, but the sub-section entitled **The Middle Ages to Baroque** (Level 1, rooms 53–70) is outstanding and comparatively easy to absorb.

Finally, don't leave without poking your nose round the **Art Nouveau** sections, especially Room 50. The display cases here, designed by Victor Horta for a firm of jewellers, now accommodate the celebrated *Mysterious Sphinx*, a ceramic bust of archetypal Art Nouveau design, the work of Charles van der Stappen in 1897.

Autoworld

Housed in a vast hangar-like building in the south wing of Le Cinquantenaire, **Autoworld** (daily: April–Sept 10am–6pm, Oct–March 10am–5pm; €5) is a chronological stroll through the short history of the automobile, with a huge display of vintage vehicles, beginning with early turn-of-the-century motorized cycles and Model Ts. Perhaps inevitably, European varieties predominate: there are lots of vehicles from Peugeot, Renault and Benz, and homegrown examples too, including a Minerva from 1925 which once belonged to the Belgian royals. American makes include early Cadillacs, a Lincoln from 1965 that was also owned by the Belgian king, and some great gangster-style Oldsmobiles. The museum's major drawback is its lack of contemporary vehicles – few cars date from after the mid-1970s. That said, there's good English labelling, at least on the downstairs exhibits, and a decent museum shop, with lots of automobile-related matter, including a great selection of model cars.

Musée Royal de l'Armée et d'Histoire Militaire

In the north wing of Le Cinquantenaire, on the other side of the triumphal arch from the other two museums, the **Musée Royal de l'Armée et d'Histoire Militaire** (Tues–Sun 9am–noon & 1–4.30pm; free) displays collections tracing the history of the Belgian army from independence to the present day, by means of weapons, uniforms and paintings. There are also modest sections dealing with "Belgian" regiments in the Austrian and Napoleonic armies and, more interestingly, the volunteers who formed the nucleus of the 1830 revolution. Other galleries are devoted to armoured cars, artillery and military aircraft, though they're far from required viewing. One surprise is that from the top floor you can get out onto the triumphal arch and enjoy extensive views over the city.

Tervuren's Musée Royal de L'Afrique Centrale

The ten-kilometre-long **avenue de Tervuren** leads east from the Parc du Cinquantenaire to the suburb of **Tervuren**, lined with embassies and mansions in its upper reaches and then delving through the wooded peripheries of the Forêt de Soignes. It's a pleasant journey and one that is best completed on **tram** #44 from place (and Métro) Montgomery. Tervuren's only notable attraction is the **Musée Royal de L'Afrique Centrale** (Tues–Fri 10am–5pm, Sat & Sun 10am–6pm; €2), a short walk from the tram terminal, and housed in a pompous custom-built pile constructed on the orders of King Léopold II early in the twentieth century.

Personally presented with the vast Congo River basin by a conference of the European Powers in 1885, Léopold became one of the country's richest men as a result. His initial attempts to secure control of the area were abetted by the explorer – and ex-Confederate soldier – Henry Stanley, who went to the Congo on a five-year fact-finding mission in 1879, just a few years after he had famously found the missionary David Livingstone. Even by the standards of the colonial powers, Léopold's regime was too chaotic and too extraordinarily cruel to stomach, and in 1908, one year before the museum opened, the Belgian government took over the territory, installing a marginally more liberal state bureaucracy. The country gained independence as the Republic of Congo in 1960, and its subsequent history (as Zaire from the 1970s until quite recently) has been one of the most bloodstained in Africa.

The museum was Léopold's own idea, a blatantly colonialist and racist enterprise, which treats the Africans as a naive and primitive people and the Belgians as their paternalistic benefactors. Nevertheless, the **collection** is undeniably rich if a little old-fashioned, and sometimes positively eccentric: one room is entirely devoted to examples of different sorts of timber. Surprisingly there is little about Léopold's administration or its savagery. The most interesting displays cover many aspects of Congolese life, from masks, idols and musical instruments to weapons and an impressive array of dope pipes, and there's a superb 22-metre dugout canoe. The museum's grounds are also worth a stroll, the formal gardens set around a series of geometric lakes, flanked by wanderable woods.

St Gilles, avenue Louise and Ixelles

Cobwebbed by tiny squares and twisting streets, home to a plethora of local bars and some of the capital's finest Art Nouveau houses, the neighbouring areas of St Gilles and Ixelles, just south of the petit ring, make a great escape from the hustle and bustle of the city centre. This is Brussels without the razzmatazz, and tourists are few and far between, especially in **St Gilles**, the smaller of the two *communes*, which is often regarded as little more than an example of inner city decay. Frankly, this is true enough of its most westerly section, comprising the depressing immigrant quarters of Gare du Midi and the downtrodden streets of Porte de Hal, but St Gilles gets more beautiful the further east it spreads, its run-down streets left behind for refined avenues interspersed with dignified squares.

Ixelles, for its part, is one of the capital's most attractive and exciting outer areas, with a diverse street-life and café scene. Historically something of a cultural crossroads, Ixelles has long drawn artists, writers and intellectuals – Karl Marx, Auguste Rodin and Alexandre Dumas all lived here – and today it retains an arty, sometimes Bohemian feel. Ixelles is divided into two portions by **avenue Louise**, home to the haute bourgeoisie ever since Léopold II had the avenue laid out in the 1840s. It's here you'll find some of the city's most expensive shops and hotels, pricey jewellers, slick office blocks and the interesting **Musée Constantin Meunier**, sited in the sculptor's old house.

More than anything else, however, it's the superb range of **Art Nouveau** buildings clustering the streets of St Gilles and Ixelles which really grab the attention. Many of the finest examples are concentrated on and around the boundary between the two communes – in between chaussée de Charleroi and avenue Louise. In particular, there's Horta's own house, now the glorious **Musée Horta**, one of the few Art Nouveau buildings in the country fully open to the public, as well as examples of the work of Paul Hankar. Access to most of the city's Art Nouveau buildings is restricted, so you can either settle for the view from outside, or enrol on one of ARAU's specialist tours (see p.69).

Musée Victor Horta

The best place to start a visit to St Gilles is the delightful **Musée Victor Horta** (Tues–Sun 2–5.30pm; €5), just off the chaussée de Charleroi at rue Américaine 23 and 25, and reachable by tram #91 or #92 from place Louise. The museum occupies the two houses Horta designed as his home and studio at the end of the nineteenth century, and was where he lived until 1919. From the outside the building is quite modest, a dark, narrow terraced structure with a fluid facade and almost casually knotted and twisted ironwork. It's for his interiors that Horta is famous, though, and inside is a sunny, sensuous dwelling exhibiting all the architect's favourite flourishes – wrought iron, stained glass, ornate furniture and panelling made from several different types of timber. The main feature is the **staircase**, a dainty spiralling affair which runs through the centre of the house up to the skylight, ensuring the house gets as much light as possible. Decorated with painted motifs and surrounded by mirrors, it remains one of Horta's most magnificent and ingenious creations, giving access to a sequence of wide, bright rooms. Also of interest is the modest but enjoyable selection of paintings, many of which were given to Horta by friends and colleagues, including works by Félicien Rops and Joseph Heymans.

Victor Horta

The son of a shoemaker, **Victor Horta** (1861–1947) was born in Ghent, where he failed in his first career, being unceremoniously expelled from the city's music conservatory for indiscipline. He promptly moved to Paris to study architecture, returning to Belgium in 1880 to complete his internship in Brussels with Alphonse Balat, the architect to King Léopold II. Balat was a traditionalist, partly responsible for the classical facades of the Palais Royal – among many other prestigious projects – and Horta looked elsewhere for inspiration. He found it in the work of William Morris, the leading figure of the English Arts and Crafts movement, whose designs were key to the development of **Art Nouveau**. Taking its name from the Maison de l'Art Nouveau, a Parisian shop which sold items of modern design, Art Nouveau rejected the imitative architectures which were popular at the time – Neoclassical and neo-Gothic – in favour of an innovatory style characterized by sinuous, flowing lines. In England, Morris and his colleagues had focused on book illustrations and furnishings, but in Belgium Horta extrapolated the new style into architecture, experimenting with new building materials – steel and concrete – as well as traditional stone, glass and wood.

In 1893, Horta completed the curvaceous **Hôtel Tassel**, Brussels' first Art Nouveau building ("hôtel" meaning town house). Inevitably, there were howls of protest from the traditionalists, but no matter what his opponents said, Horta never lacked work again. The following years – roughly 1893 to 1905 – were Horta's most inventive and prolific. He designed over forty buildings, including the **Hôtel Solvay** and his own beautifully decorated house and studio, now the **Musée Victor Horta**. The delight Horta took in his work is obvious, especially when employed on private houses, and his enthusiasm was all-encompassing – he almost always designed everything from the blueprints to the wallpaper and carpets. He never kept a straight line or sharp angle where he could deploy a curve, and his use of light was revolutionary, often filtering through from above, with skylights and as many windows as possible.

Completed in 1906, the **Grand Magasin Waucquez** (see p.84) department store was a transitional building signalling the end of Horta's Art Nouveau period. His later works were more Modernist constructions, whose understated lines were a far cry from the ornateness of his earlier work. In Brussels, the best example of his later work is the **Palais des Beaux Arts** of 1928 (see p.89).

Horta felt that the architect was as much an artist as the painter or sculptor, and so he insisted on complete stylistic freedom; curiously, he also believed that originality was born of frustration, so he deliberately created architectural difficulties, pushing himself to find harmonious solutions. It was part of a well-thought-out value system that allied him with both Les XX (see p.427) and the Left; as he wrote, "My friends and I were reds, without however having thought about Marx or his theories."

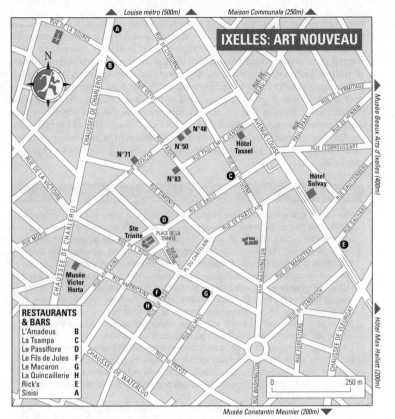

Louise métro (500m) ▲   Maison Communale (250m) ▲

IXELLES: ART NOUVEAU

N

Musée Beaux Arts d'Ixelles (400m) ▶

RUE DE LA SOURCE
RUE DE L'ERMITAGE
RUE DE L'IVOIRNE
RUE DE BEAULIEU
RUE DE HENNIN
CHAUSSÉE DE CHARLEROI
RUE VEYDT
AVENUE LOUISE
RUE PAUL SPAAK
RUE LESBROUSSART
N°48
N°50
Hôtel Tassel
RUE PAUL ÉMILE JANSON
N°71
RUE DEFACQZ
RUE FAIDER
Hôtel Solvay
RUE DE LA VICTOIRE
N°83
RUE DAUTZENBERG
RUE SIMONIS
RUE DE L'IVOIRNE
RUE SACHARD
RUE DU BAILLI
RUE DE CHÂTELAIN
Ste Trinité
RUE MORIS
PLACE DE LA TRINITÉ
CHAUSSÉE DE CHARLEROI
RUE DE L'AQUEDUC
RUE DE CHÂTELAIN
RUE DU MAGISTRAT
RUE AFRICAINE
P. DU CHÂTELAIN
RUE DE TENBOSCH
Musée Victor Horta
RUE AMERICAINE
RUE WASHINGTON
RUE DU PAGE
CHAUSSÉE DE VLEURGAT
Hôtel Max Hallett (200m) ▶

RESTAURANTS & BARS

L'Amadeus	B
La Tsampa	C
Le Passiflore	D
Le Fils de Jules	F
Le Macaron	G
La Quincaillerie	H
Rick's	E
Sisisi	A

CHAUSSÉE DE WATERLOO
RUE DU MAIL
RUE FORESTIÈRE
RUE DU PRÉVOT
RUE WASHINGTON

0   250 m

Musée Constantin Meunier (200m) ▼

Art Nouveau buildings

From the Musée Victor Horta, it's a five-minute walk north to **rue De facqz**, the site of several charming Art Nouveau houses. Three were designed by **Paul Hankar** (1859–1901), a classically trained architect and contemporary of Horta, who developed a real penchant for sgraffiti – akin to frescoes – and multicoloured brickwork. Hankar was regarded as one of the most distinguished exponents of Art Nouveau and his old home, at **no. 71**, is marked by its skeletal metalwork, handsome bay windows and four sgraffiti beneath the cornice – one each for morning, afternoon, evening and night. Hankar designed his home in the early 1890s, making it one of the city's earliest Art Nouveau buildings. **Number 50** is a Hankar creation too, built for the painter René Janssens in 1898 and noteworthy for its fanciful brickwork; so was the adjacent **no. 48**, which sports a fine, flowing facade, decorated with sgraffiti representing the Ages of Man.

There are more Art Nouveau treats in store on neighbouring **rue Faider**, where **no. 83** boasts a splendidly flamboyant facade with ironwork foliage round the windows and frescoes of languishing pre-Raphaelite women, all to a design by **Armand Van Waesberghe**. Directly opposite is **rue Paul Émile Janson**, at the bottom of which, at no. 6, is the celebrated **Hôtel Tassel** (no public access), the building that made Horta's reputation. The supple facade is appealing enough, with clawed columns, stained glass and spiralling ironwork, but it was with the interior that Horta really made a splash, an uncompromising fantasy featuring a fanciful wrought-iron staircase and walls covered with linear decoration.

At the end of rue Paul Emile Janson you hit **avenue Louise**, where a right turn will take you – in a couple of hundred metres – to the **Hôtel Solvay** (no public access), at no. 224 – another Horta extravagance which, like the Musée Horta, contains most of the original furnishings and fittings. The 33-year-old Horta was given complete freedom and unlimited funds by the Solvay family (they made a fortune in soft drinks) to design this opulent town house, whose facade is graced by bow windows, delicate metalwork and contrasting types of stone. Also on avenue Louise, five minutes further along at no. 346, is Horta's **Hôtel Max Hallet** (no public access), a comparatively plain structure of 1904 where the straight, slender facade is decorated with elegant doors and windows plus an elongated stone balcony with a wrought-iron balustrade. Just beyond, the modern **sculpture** stranded in the middle of the traffic island, named *Phénix 44*, looks like a pair of elephant tusks, but is in fact a representation by Olivier Strebelle of the "V" for Victory sign of World War II.

From the Max Hallet residence, it's a quick tram ride north to the smart commercialism of place Louise, or a five- to ten-minute stroll south to the Musée Constantin Meunier (see below).

Avenue Louise

Named after the eldest daughter of its creator, Léopold II, **avenue Louise** slices southeast from the petit ring, its beginnings lined by some of the city's most expensive shops and boutiques. Trams #93 and #94 clatter up and down its length, passing by Victor Horta's Hôtel Max Hallet (see above) to reach – about 500m further on – the foot of the rue de l'Abbaye, where the **Musée Constantin Meunier** is at no. 59 (Tues–Fri & alternate weekends 10am–noon & 1–5pm; free; ☎02 648 44 49). The museum is housed in the unassuming home and studio of Brussels-born Constantin Meunier (1831–1905), who lived here from 1899 until his death at the age of 74. Meunier began as a painter, but it's as a sculptor that he's best remembered, and the museum has an extensive collection of his dark, brooding bronzes. The biggest and most important pieces are in the room at the back, where a series of muscular men with purposeful faces stand around looking heroic – *The Reaper* and *The Sower* are typical. There are oil paintings in this room too, gritty industrial scenes like the coalfield of *Black Country Borinage* and the gloomy dockside of *The Port*, one of Meunier's most forceful works.

Meunier was angered by the harsh living conditions of Belgium's workers, particularly (like Van Gogh before him) the harsh life of the coal miners of the Borinage. This anger fuelled his art, which asserted the dignity of the working class in a style that was to be copied by the Social Realists of his and later generations. According to Hobsbawm's *Age of Empire*, "Meunier invented the international stereotype of the sculptured proletarian".

Abbaye de la Cambre

In a lovely little wooded dell on the other side of avenue Louise from the Meunier Museum – and readily approached via rue de l'Aurore – lies the **Abbaye de la Cambre**. Of medieval foundation, the abbey was suppressed by the French Revolutionary army, but its attractive eighteenth-century brick buildings survived; surrounding a pretty little courtyard, they're now used by several government departments. On the courtyard is the main entrance to the abbey **church** (Mon–Fri 9am–noon & 3–6pm free), an amalgamation of styles, incorporating both Gothic and Classical features – its nave, with its barrel vaulting, is an exercise in simplicity. The church holds one marvellous painting, Albert Bouts' *The Mocking of Christ*, an early sixteenth-century work showing a mournful, blood-spattered Jesus. Behind the abbey's buildings are the walled and terraced **gardens**, an oasis of peace away from the hubbub of avenue Louise.

Beyond the abbey, at the end of avenue Louise, the **Bois de la Cambre** is unpleasantly crisscrossed by the main commuter access roads in its upper reaches, but a good deal more agreeable around the lake that lies further to the south. It's Brussels' most popular park, bustling with joggers, dog-walkers, families and lovers at weekends, and is the northerly finger of the large **Forêt de Soignes**, whose once mighty forests are chopped up by a clutch of dual carriageways, and, more promisingly, scores of quiet footpaths.

The chaussée d'Ixelles to place Fernand Cocq

To the east of avenue Louise, the more fashionable part of **Ixelles** radiates out from the petit ring, its busy streets lined by the workaday shops and stores of the **chaussée d'Ixelles**. The district may be modish, but there are few specific sights, with nothing in particular to stop for on the chaussée d'Ixelles until you reach **place Fernand Cocq**. This small, refreshingly leafy square is named after a one-time Ixelles burgomaster, and lined by a good selection of bars. The square's centrepiece is the **Maison communale**, a sturdy Neoclassical building erected in 1833 for the opera singer Maria Malibran, née Garcia (1808–36), and her lover, the Belgian violinist Charles de Bériot. Her father, one Manuel Garcia, trained her and organized her tours, and she became one of the great stars of her day, but he also pushed her into a most unfortunate marriage in New York. Mr Malibran turned out to be a bankrupt and Maria pluckily left husband and father behind, returning to Europe to pick up her career. After her death, the house lay uninhabited until it was bought by the Ixelles *commune* in 1849; the gardens in which Maria once practised have been reduced to the small park which now edges the house.

Musée des Beaux-Arts d'Ixelles

The excellent **Musée des Beaux-Arts d'Ixelles** (Tues–Fri 1–6.30pm, Sat & Sun 10am–5pm; free, but admission charged for temporary exhibitions), rue Jean van Volsem 71, is located about ten minutes' walk southeast of place Fernand Cocq – via rue du Collège. Established in an old slaughterhouse in 1892, the museum was enlarged and refurbished a few years back, and since then it has built up an excellent reputation for the quality of its temporary exhibitions. The permanent collection is mainly nineteenth- and early twentieth-century French and Belgian material, but there's a small sample of earlier paintings in the first wing, including *Tobie and the Angel* by **Rembrandt** (1606–69) and a sketch, *The Stork*, by **Albrecht Dürer** (1471–1528). In the same wing, **Jacques-Louis David** (1748–1825), one-time revolutionary and the leading light among France's Neoclassical painters, is well represented by *The Man at the Gallows*. There's also a wonderful collection of haunting works by **Charles Herman**, one of a group of Belgian realists who struggled to get their work exhibited in the capital's salons: until the late 1870s the salons would contemplate only Romantic and Neoclassical works. Also, look out for the large collection of posters featuring the work of **Toulouse-Lautrec** (1864–1901) – thirty of his total output of thirty-two are displayed here.

The museum's two other wings hold an enjoyable sample of the work of the country's leading modern artists, from well-known figures such as the surrealists **Magritte** (1898–1967; see p.111) and **Paul Delvaux** (1897–1994; see p.142) to less familiar artists like **Edgar Tytgat** (1879–1957), **Rik Wouters** (1882–1916) and **Constant Permeke** (1886–1952). There's a smattering of sculptures, too, with the main event being **Rodin**'s (1840–1917) *La Lorraine* and *J.B. Willems*. Rodin used to have a studio nearby at rue Sans Souci 111, in the heart of Ixelles, and this was where he designed his first major work, *The Age of Bronze*. When it was exhibited in 1878, there was outrage: Rodin's naturalistic treatment of the naked body broke with convention and created something of a scandal – he was even accused of casting his sculptures round live models.

Anderlecht and Koekelberg

It's small surprise that the gritty suburbs to the immediate west of the petit ring – principally Anderlecht and Koekelberg – are little visited by tourists. For the most part, the area is distinctly short on charm, though it is home to one of Europe's premier football teams – Anderlecht – as well as a smattering of sights. **Anderlecht** easily outshines its neighbours, containing the fascinating Maison d'Erasme, where Erasmus holed up for a few months in 1521, and the Musée Gueuze, devoted to the production of the eponymous brew, whereas **Koekelberg** can only compete with the enormous Basilique du Sacré Coeur.

Anderlecht

No one could say **Anderlecht** was beautiful, but it has its attractive nooks and crannies, particularly in the vicinity of **Métro St Guidon** on line 1B. Come out of the station, turn left and it's a few metres down the slope to place de la Vaillance, a pleasant triangular plaza flanked by little cafés and the whitestone tower and facade of the church of **Sts Pierre et Guidon** (Mon–Fri 2–5pm; free). The facade, which mostly dates from the fifteenth century, is unusually long and slender, its stonework graced by delicate flourishes and a fine set of gargoyles. Inside, the church has a surprisingly low and poorly lit nave, in a corner of which is a vaulted chapel dedicated to **St Guido**, otherwise known as St Guy. A local eleventh-century figure of peasant origins, Guido entered the priesthood but was sacked after he invested all of his church's money in an enterprise that went bust. He spent the next seven years as a pilgrim, a sackcloth-and-ashes extravaganza that ultimately earned him a sainthood – as the patron saint of peasants and horses. The chapel contains a breezy *Miracle of St Guido* by Gaspard de Crayer, a local, seventeenth-century artist who made a tidy income from religious paintings in the style of Rubens.

Maison d'Erasme

From Sts Pierre et Guidon, it's just a couple of minutes' walk to the **Maison d'Erasme** (Tues–Sun 10am–5pm; €1.25), at rue du Chapitre 31 – walk east along the front of the church onto rue d'Aumale and it's on the right behind the distinctive red-brick wall. Dating from 1468, the house, with its pretty dormer windows and sturdy symmetrical lines, was built to accommodate important visitors to the church. Easily the most celebrated of these was the theologian – and accidental stirrer of the Reformation – **Desiderius Erasmus** (1466–1536), who lodged here in 1521. The house contains none of Erasmus' actual belongings, but features a host of contemporaneous artefacts, all squeezed into half a dozen, clearly signed rooms. The Cabinet de Travail (study) holds original portraits of Erasmus by Holbein, Dürer and others, as well as a mould of his skull, but the best paintings are concentrated in the Salle du Chapitre (chapterhouse). Here, there's a charmingly inquisitive *Adoration of the Magi* by Hieronymous Bosch, a gentle *Nativity* from Gerard David, and a hallucinatory *Temptation of St Anthony* by Pieter Huys. The Salle Blanche (white room) contains a good sample of first editions of Erasmus's work, alongside an intriguing cabinet of altered and amended texts: some show scrawled comments made by irate readers, others are the work of the Inquisition and assorted clerical censors.

Musée Bruxellois de la Gueuze

The **Musée Bruxellois de la Gueuze** (Mon–Fri 9am–5pm; Sat 10am–5pm; €3), rue Gheude 56, is located ten minutes' walk north of Métro Gare du Midi, via avenue Paul Henri Spaak and rue Limnander; to get there direct from Maison d'Erasme, take tram #56 from Métro St Guidon and get off – or ask to be put off – at place Bara, at the foot of rue Limnander. Founded in 1879, the museum is home to the Cantillon Brewery, the last surviving **gueuze** brewery in Brussels. The museum gives fairly dry explanation of how gueuze is still brewed here according to traditional methods: the beer, made only of wheat, malted barley, hops and water, is allowed to ferment naturally, reacting with the yeasts that are peculiar to the Brussels air, and is bottled for two years before it is ready to drink.

In the mustily evocative brewery, you can see the huge vats the ingredients are boiled in before they're placed in the large oak barrels where the fermentation process begins. The result is unique, as you can find out at the tasting at the end of a visit.

Koekelberg – Basilique du Sacré Coeur

From Métro Simonis, tram #19 rattles west round the edge of the lawns leading up to the ugliest church in the capital, the **Basilique du Sacré Coeur** (Church daily: Easter–Oct 8am–6pm; Nov–Easter 8am–5pm; free; dome daily: Easter–Oct 9am–5pm; Nov–Easter 10am–4pm; €2.50), a huge structure – 140m long with a ninety-metre-tall dome – which dominates the commune of **Koekelberg**. Begun in 1905 on the orders of Léopold II but never completed to the original design, the basilica was conceived as a neo-Gothic extravagance in imitation of the basilica to the Sacré Coeur in Montmartre, Paris – a structure which had made the Belgian king green with envy. The construction costs proved colossal and the plans had to be modified; the result is a vaguely ludicrous amalgamation of the original neo-Gothic design with Art Deco features added in the 1920s. While you're here, it's worth climbing up to the top of the **dome** for a panoramic view of the city.

Jette, Laeken and Heysel

To the north, Koekelberg quickly fades into the well-heeled suburb of **Jette**, where the main event is the **Musée René Magritte**, which contains a plethora of the surrealist's paraphernalia, as well as a modest collection of his early paintings and sketches. East of here is leafy **Laeken**, marked by the presence of the Belgian royal family, who have long used it as their main residence; next door again is **Heysel**, with its trademark Atomium, a hand-me-down from the 1958 World's Fair.

Jette – Musée René Magritte

From 1930 until 1954, Magritte lived with his wife Georgette on the ground floor of what is now the **Musée René Magritte**, at rue Esseghem 135 (Wed–Sun 10am–6pm; €6), building a studio – which he named Dongo – in

René Magritte

René Magritte (1898–1967) is easily the most famous of Belgium's modern artists, his disconcerting, strangely haunting images a familiar part of popular culture. Born in a small town just outside Charleroi, he entered the Royal Academy of Fine Arts in Brussels in 1915, and was a student there until 1920. His appearances were, however, few and far between as he preferred the company of a group of artists and friends fascinated with the **Surrealist movement** of the 1920s. Their antics were supposed to incorporate a serious intent – the undermining of bourgeois convention – but the surviving home movies of Magritte and his chums fooling around don't appear very revolutionary today.

Initially, Magritte worked in a broadly Cubist manner, but in 1925, influenced by Giorgio de Chirico, he switched over to Surrealism and almost immediately stumbled upon the themes and images that would preoccupy him for decades to come. The **hallmarks** of his work were striking, incorporating startling comparisons between the ordinary and the extraordinary, with the occasional erotic element. Favourite images included men in bowler hats, metamorphic figures, enormous rocks floating in the sky, tubas, fishes with human legs, bilboquets (the cup and ball game), and juxtapositions of night and day – one part of the canvas lit by artificial light, the other basking in full sunlight. He also dabbled in word paintings, mislabelling familiar forms to illustrate (or expose) the arbitrariness of linguistic signs. His canvases were devoid of emotion, deadpan images that were easy to recognize but perplexing because of their setting – perhaps most famously, the man in the suit with a bowler hat and an apple for a face.

He broke with this characteristic style on two occasions, once during the War – in despair over the Nazi occupation – and again in 1948, to revenge long years of neglect by the French artistic establishment. Hundreds had turned up to see Magritte's first **Paris exhibition**, but were confronted with crass and crude paintings of childlike simplicity. These so-called Vache paintings created a furore, and Magritte beat a hasty artistic retreat behind a smokescreen of self-justification. These two experiments alienated Magritte from most of the other Surrealists but in the event this was of little consequence as Magritte was picked up and popularized by an American art dealer, Alexander Iolas, who made Magritte very rich and very famous.

---

the garden. In this studio, he produced his bread-and-butter work such as graphics and posters, whereas his dining-room studio was set aside for the creation of the paintings that were his real passion. The dining room, along with the rest of the ground floor, has been restored to its appearance in the early 1950s, and is also where the only work of art by another artist that Magritte owned is displayed, a photo by Man Ray. Up above, the **first and second floors** are taken up by letters, photos, telegrams, lithographs, posters and sketches, all displayed in chronological order. Among them are two fine posters announcing the world film and fine arts festivals which took place in Brussels in 1947 and 1949, as well as Magritte's first painting, a naive landscape which he produced at the tender age of 12. Finally, a number of Magritte's personal objects are displayed in the **attic**, including his last easel. The museum is a ten-minute walk northwest of Métro Pannenhuis, on Line 1A, via rue Pannenhuis.

Laeken

Beginning some 5km north of the Grand-Place, **Laeken** is the royal suburb of Brussels, home of the Belgian royal family, who occupy a large out-of-bounds estate and have colonized the surrounding parkland with their memorials. From the city centre, Laeken is best approached on tram #52 (from the Gare du Nord among other locations). Get off at the Araucaria tram stop, which is just off avenue des Croix du Feu – and just behind the **Pavillon Chinois** (Tues–Sun 10am–4.30pm; €2; joint ticket with Tour Japonaise, €3), an elegant and attractive replica of a Chinese pavilion, built here by Léopold II after he had seen one at the World Fair in Paris in 1900. The king intended his creation to be a fancy restaurant, but this never materialized and the pavilion now houses a first-rate collection of Chinese porcelain. Across the road – and reached by a tunnel from beside the pavilion – is the matching **Tour Japonaise** (same times as Pavillon Chinois; €2), another of Léopold's follies. This one is a copy of a Buddhist pagoda with parts made in Paris, Brussels and Yokohama, and now in use as a venue for temporary exhibitions of Japanese art (admission extra).

Around the corner behind the railings, along the congested avenue du Parc Royal, lie the **Serres Royales**, enormous greenhouses built for Léopold II. They shelter a mind-boggling variety of tropical and Mediterranean flora, but are only open to the public during April and May (times from the tourist office) and the queues to see them can be daunting. Just beyond the greenhouses is the sedate **Palais Royal** (no entry), the main royal palace. Built in 1790, its most famous occupant was Napoleon, who stayed here on a number of occasions and signed the declaration of war on Russia here in 1812.

Opposite the front of the royal palace, a wide footpath leads up to the fanciful neo-Gothic monument erected in honour of Léopold I. It's the focal point of the pretty **Parc de Laeken**, whose lawns and wooded thickets extend west for a couple of kilometres to Heysel.

Heysel

Heysel, a two-square-kilometre estate bequeathed to the city by Léopold II in 1909, is best described as a theme park without a theme. Its most famous attraction is the **Atomium** (daily: April–Aug 9am–7.30pm; Sept–March 10am–5.30pm; €5.45), a curious model of a molecule expanded 165 billion times, which was built for the 1958 World Fair. Poking its knobbly – and very distinctive – head into the sky, the structure has become something of a symbol of the city, but its interior can only muster up an unremarkable exhibition on the construction of – and the concepts behind – itself. Indeed, the only real interest is the feeling of disorientation when travelling from sphere to sphere by escalator.

The Atomium borders a large trade fair area – the **Parc des Expositions** – and the **Stade du Roi Baudouin**, formerly the Heysel football stadium, in which 39 mainly Italian supporters were crushed to death when a sector wall collapsed in 1985. The **Bruparck** leisure complex is also close by, its child-oriented attractions including Océade, a water funpark; a gigantic cinema complex called Kinepolis; and Mini-Europe, where you can see scaled-down models of selected European buildings. Fortunately, the proximity of the métro makes an early exit easy.

Eating and drinking

Brussels has an international reputation for the quality of its cuisine, and it's richly deserved. Even at the dowdiest snack bar, you'll almost always find that the food is well prepared and generously seasoned – and then there are the city's **restaurants**, many of which equal anywhere in Europe, although those in the much-vaunted restaurant area of Rue des Bouchers get very mixed reviews. Traditional Bruxellois dishes feature on many restaurant menus, canny amalgamations of Walloon and Flemish ingredients and cooking styles – whether it be rabbit cooked in beer, steamed pigs' feet or *waterzooi* (see p.40 for more on Belgian specialities). The city is also among Europe's best for sampling a wide range of different cuisines – from ubiquitous Italian places and the Turkish restaurants of St Josse, at the north end of rue Royale, through to Spanish, Vietnamese, Japanese and vegetarian restaurants. You can also eat magnificent fish and seafood, especially in and around the fashionable district of Ste Catherine.

For the most part, eating out is rarely inexpensive, but the **prices** are almost universally justified by the quality. As a general rule, the less formal the restaurant, the less expensive the meal; indeed it's hard to distinguish between the less expensive restaurants and the city's **cafés**, many of which provide some of the tastiest food in town.

For **fast food**, aside from the multinational burger and pizza chains, there are plenty of *frites* stands and kebab places around the Grand-Place, notably on rue du Marché aux Fromages and near the beginning of rue des Bouchers. Pitta is also popular, stuffed with a wide range of fillings – though vegetarian ones are rare – along with the more substantial thin Turkish pizzas, or *pide*, topped with combinations of cheese, ground meat or even a fried egg, sold at any number of cafés along rue du Méridien and chaussée de Haecht in St Josse.

Drinking in Brussels, as in the rest of the country, is a joy. The city boasts an enormous variety of **bars**: sumptuous Art Nouveau establishments, traditional bars with ceilings stained brown by a century's smoke, bars whose walls are plastered with sepia photographs and ancient beer ads, speciality beer bars with literally hundreds of different varieties of ale, and, of course, more modern hangouts. Many of the more distinctive bars are handily located within a few minutes' walk of the Grand-Place, but there are smashing places all over the city. In addition, many bars also serve food, often just spaghetti, sandwiches and croque-monsieurs, though many offer a much more ambitious spread.

Restaurants

Restaurant **opening times** are pretty standard – a couple of hours at lunch, usually noon to 2pm or 2.30pm and again in the evening from 7pm to around 10pm; where they are noticeably different, and where restaurants close one day a week, we have given details in the reviews below. Phone numbers are provided where advance reservations are recommended.

Within the petit-ring
On and around the Grand-Place
L'Auberge des Chapeliers rue des Chapeliers 1–3 ☏ 02 513 73 18. Sited just south of the Grand-Place, this well-established restaurant serves excellent Belgian cuisine such as salmon steak in white beer, *stoemp*, and *waterzooi*. It also specializes in mussels prepared in a variety of ways, *provençales*, *gratinées* and *marinières*. Main courses at around €20.
Aux Armes de Bruxelles rue des Bouchers 13 ☏ 02 511 55 50. Right in the centre of the restaurant district near the Grand-Place, this polished and fairly expensive spot divides into two – a formal restaurant popular with the pearls-and-blue-

rinse brigade, and a bistro with wooden benches. Both serve traditional Belgian cuisine to a very high standard. Great *moules*. Closed Mon.
Brasserie de la Roue d'Or rue des Chapeliers 26 ☏ 02 514 25 54. Just south of the Grand-Place. This eminently appealing old brasserie, with wood panelling, stained glass and brass fittings, serves generous portions of Belgian regional specialities, such as *poulet à la Bruxelles*, and a mouthwatering selection of seafood. Also recommended are the delicious lamb with mustard and the endive salad with salmon.
Chez Léon rue des Bouchers 18–22. Something of an institution, this well-known bistro-style restaurant has been serving Belgian specialities,

mainly mussels, for over a century. It attracts tourists by the bus load and consequently the food is characteristically bland; the decor matches the fare. Daily noon–11pm.

't Kelderke Grand-Place 15 ℡ 02 513 73 44. Busy cellar restaurant specializing in traditional Bruxellois dishes. Serves an excellent *lapin à la gueuze* (rabbit cooked in *gueuze*) and a superb *carbonnades flamandes à la bière* (beef in beer). Daily noon–2am.

On and around place Ste Catherine

La Belle Maraichère place Ste Catherine 11 ℡ 02 512 97 59. Smart bistro-style restaurant with superbly prepared Belgian cuisine and oodles of wood panelling. The seafood is a treat. Main courses average €20–25. Closed Wed & Thurs.

Bonsoir Clara rue Antoine Dansaert 22 ℡ 02 502 09 90. One of the capital's trendiest restaurants, on arguably the hippest street in Brussels. Moody, atmospheric lighting, 1970s geometrically mirrored walls and zinc-topped tables set the tone. Expect to find a menu full of Mediterranean, French and Belgian classics, all excellent, though expensive, and make sure you reserve. Mon–Fri noon–2.30pm & 7–11.30pm, Sat & Sun 7–11.30pm.

Les Crustacés quai aux Briques 8 ℡ 02 511 56 44. Long-established, smart seafood restaurant in the Ste Catherine district. Lobster – cooked many different ways – is the house speciality.

Iberica rue de Flandre 8 ℡ 02 511 79 36. At the place Ste Catherine end of the street. Agreeable Spanish restaurant offering all the classics – sardines, Parma ham and so forth – plus a delicious paella. Tapas cost around €6, main courses €16. The only drawback is the decor, which is more than a tad gauche. Closed Wed.

Jacques quai aux Briques 44 ℡ 02 513 27 62. A long-established and extremely popular fish restaurant in pleasant, wood-panelled premises. Expect a sedate, middle-aged clientele at lunchtime, and a younger, international crowd in the evenings. The *cabillaud de poche* (poached cod) is highly recommended. Main courses from around €16. Closed Sun.

Kasbah rue Antoine Dansaert 20. Popular with a youthful, groovy crowd, this vibrant Moroccan establishment is famous for serving enormous portions of couscous and other North African specialities. It's run by the same people as the equally hip *Bonsoir Clara* next door, though the lantern-lit decor makes it seem slightly less fashion-conscious and more welcoming. Set menus from €18.

La Marée rue du Flandre 99 ℡ 02 511 00 40. Outstanding, pocket-sized restaurant near Ste Catherine – and not to be confused with its namesake on rue au Beurre. The speciality is seafood, always fresh and always prepared in a simple, direct manner. The frugal decor somehow manages to feel quite cosy. Main courses average €10–15. Closed all day Mon & Sun evening.

La Papaye Verte rue Antoine Dansaert 53. First-rate Vietnamese food at bargain prices, with a good range of vegetarian options and a smart, authentically Vietnamese interior.

Le Pré Salé rue de Flandre 16 ℡ 02 513 43 23. Friendly, old-fashioned, very Bruxellois neighbourhood restaurant, just off place Ste Catherine, providing a nice alternative to the swankier restaurants of the district. Great mussels, fish dishes and Belgian specialities. Daily specials and a fixed-price menu from around €25. Closed Mon.

On and near place du Grand Sablon

Bla Bla & Gallery rue des Capucins ℡ 02 503 59 18. Below the Palais de Justice, in the Marolles. The latest Brussels restaurant to take a stab at the suave interior/*nouvelle cuisine* combo, with excellent results. Sit back in the leather bench seats amid the bare brick walls and tuck into delicious mozzarella, artichoke and pancetta ravioli, or duck carpaccio. Live piano music during the week. Main courses at around €15. Daily 7–11pm, Sat & Sun buffet-brunch 10.30am–4pm.

Les Brigittines aux Marchés de la Chapelle Behind the church of Notre Dame de la Chapelle, place de la Chapelle 5 ℡ 02 512 68 91. Excellent bistro-style restaurant with *belle époque* flourishes that manages to be smart and informal at the same time. The menu is fairly short, but the food is superb – the *cabillaud danois poché aux poireaux* (Danish cod poached with pears) is particularly exquisite. Closed Sun.

La Grande Porte rue Notre Seigneur 9 ℡ 02 512 89 98. Just south of Notre Dame de la Chapelle. Long, narrow and cosy old restaurant, whose walls are plastered with ancient posters and photos. The food is good, hearty and traditional, and you're quite free to go just for a drink. Be warned, though, that it can get very crowded and the service is patchy. Closed Sat lunch & all day Sun.

Les Petits Oignons rue Notre Seigneur 13 ℡ 02 512 47 38. Just south of Notre Dame de la Chapelle. First-rate, popular restaurant serving Belgian cuisine with flair in intimate premises. Fish and meat dishes from €12–20.

La Tortue du Zoute rue de Rollebeek 31 ℡ 02 513 10 62. Metres from the place du Grand Sablon. Swish little restaurant with an imaginative menu in the French style. Main courses hover at around €15, though lobster – the house speciality – costs a chunk more. Closed all day Tues & Sun evening.

Elsewhere inside the petit ring

Au Stekerlapatte rue des Prêtres 4 ☎02 512 86 81. Situated on the far (southern) side of the Palais de Justice, this is a wonderful old brasserie that comes complete with most of its original, early twentieth-century furnishings and fittings. Offers a wide-ranging menu featuring the best of traditional Bruxellois cuisine – everything from eel through to pigs' feet. Main courses at around €18. Popular with a youngish crowd and usually very busy. A great atmosphere. Tues–Sun 7pm–1am.

In 't Spinnekope place du Jardin aux Fleurs 1 ☎02 511 86 95. Just west of place St Géry. Ancient restaurant and bar that serves many traditional Bruxellois dishes cooked in beer – the owner has published a book of beer recipes. It's also one of the few places to serve beers from the Cantillon brewery in Anderlecht. Closed Sun.

Pasta Basta rue de la Grande Île 34. Off boulevard Anspach, 5–10min walk south of Prémétro Bourse. Popular with a young crowd, this pasta-lovers' favourite serves up all the staples – cannelloni with spinach and ricotta etc – plus special feature dishes every Fri & Sat night. Inexpensive. Daily 7pm–midnight.

Totem rue de la Grande Île 42. Tucked away down a sidestreet off boulevard Anspach, this fashionable restaurant is a hit with Brussels-based veggies, who come here for the friendly atmosphere and wholesome food – organic soups, fresh salads, tofu, and a delicious selection of cakes and pastries. Has a good choice of organic wines and serves meat dishes too. Main courses at around €13; no credit cards. Closed Mon.

Outside the petit ring

L'Amadeus rue Veydt 13, Ixelles ☎02 538 34 27. Not far from place Stéphanie, just off chaussée de Charleroi. Fashionable restaurant and wine bar in the former studio of Auguste Rodin. Top-drawer Belgian dishes – reckon on about €20 – and an all-you-can-eat Sunday brunch (10am–2pm) for €18. Closed Mon.

Le Fils de Jules rue du Page 37, Ixelles ☎02 534 00 57. In the swankiest part of Ixelles, close to the Musée Victor Horta. First-class Basque cuisine is the speciality of this excellent bistro-style restaurant. Main courses from around €20. Mon–Thurs noon–2pm & 7–11pm, Fri & Sat 7–11pm.

Le Macaron rue du Mail 1, Ixelles. Charming restaurant just off place du Châtelain on the corner of rue de Mail. The convivial ambience, homely surroundings and cheap fish, meat and pasta dishes – main courses under €9 – mean the place is often packed to bursting, even on weekdays. The spaghetti bolognese is superlative. Tues–Sun 6.30pm–1am.

La Quincaillerie rue du Page 45, Ixelles ☎02 538 25 53. Mouth-watering Belgian and French cuisine in this delightful restaurant, occupying an imaginatively converted old hardware shop with all sorts of splendid Art Nouveau flourishes. Especially good for fish and fowl, often cooked up in imaginative ways. There's normally a *plat du jour* at a very reasonable €10, but the à la carte is much pricier, with main courses kicking off at about €25. Mon–Fri noon–2pm & 7pm–midnight, Sat & Sun 7pm–midnight.

Sahbaz chaussée de Haecht 102, Schaerbeek ☎02 217 02 77. Without much doubt, the best Turkish restaurant in the capital. The food is cheap – main courses at around €8 – and delicious, the staff friendly and attentive, and there are cheerful crowds most of the week. It is, however, a good way from the centre, just beyond the northern edge of St Josse in Schaerbeek, and it's in a very insalubrious area – two good reasons for taking a taxi, though trams #92, #93 pass by. Daily 11.30am–3pm & 6pm–midnight.

Shanti ave Adolphe Buyl 68, Ixelles ☎02 649 40 96. First-class vegetarian restaurant – popular with meat-eaters too – with a lovely neo-oriental interior filled with plants. Dishes include fish tandoori and tofu and crab combinations. Main courses at around €10. A bio and natural products store occupies the ground floor. The only problem is in its location – far from the centre, in southern Ixelles; tram #93 or #94 come here from Porte de Namur. Tues–Sat noon–2pm & 6.30pm–10pm. Closed mid-July to mid-Aug.

La Tsampa rue de Livourne 109, Ixelles ☎02 647 03 67. Congenial vegetarian restaurant one block west of avenue Louise, with main courses averaging around €10. Mon–Sat noon–2pm & 7–9.30pm.

Bars and cafés

Belgians make little – or no – distinction between their bars and cafés – both serve alcohol, many stay open till late (until 2am or even 3am) and most sell food. **Opening hours** are fairly elastic, but most bars and cafés are open by 11am or noon and few are closed much before 1am.

Within the petit-ring
On and around the Grand-Place

Arcadi rue de L'Ecuyer 99. At the north end of the Galeries St Hubert, this rabbit warren of a café is a pleasant spot for lunch, with a great selection of home-made quiches – their speciality – as well as salads and cakes. Gets very hot in the summer. Mon–Sat 9am–6pm.

À la Bécasse rue de Tabora 11. Just to the northwest of the Grand-Place – and metres from St Nicolas. Old-fashioned bar with neo-baronial decor; has long wooden benches, ancient blue and white tiles on the walls and serves beer in earthenware jugs. The beer menu is excellent – this is one of the few places in the country you can drink authentic lambic and gueuze.

Au Bon Vieux Temps rue du Marché aux Herbes 12. Cosy place dating back to 1695, tucked down an alley just a minute's walk from the Grand-Place. The building boasts tile-inlaid tables and a handsome seventeenth-century chimney piece; the stained-glass window depicting the Virgin Mary and St Michael was originally in the local parish church. Popular with British servicemen just after the end of World War II, the bar still has comforting old-fashioned signs advertising Mackenzies' Port and Bass pale ale. A great place for a quiet drink.

La Fleur en Papier Doré rue des Alexiens 53. Just south of the Grand-Place. Cluttered, cosy locals' bar, with walls covered with doodles and poems, that was once (one of) the chosen drinking places of René Magritte. The novelist Hugo Claus (see p.000) apparently held his second wedding reception here.

À l'Imaige de Nostre-Dame rue du Marché aux Herbes 6. A welcoming, quirky little bar, decorated like an old Dutch kitchen, and situated at the end of a long, narrow alley. Good range of speciality beers.

À la Mort Subite rue Montagne aux Herbes Potagères 7. Just northeast of the Grand-Place, opposite the far end of the Galeries St Hubert. A 1920s bar that loaned its name to a widely available bottled beer. In a long, narrow room with nicotine-stained walls and mirrors, a dissolute-arty clientèle and an animated atmosphere. Snacks served, or just order a plate of cheese cubes to accompany your beer.

Le Roy d'Espagne Grand-Place 1. Supremely touristy café-bar in a seventeenth-century guild-house with a collection of marionettes and inflated animal bladders suspended from the ceiling, and naff pikes in the boys' toilet. You get a fine view of the Grand-Place from the rooms upstairs, as well as from the pavement-terrace, and the

drinks aren't too expensive. Daily 10am–midnight.

Au Soleil rue Marché au Charbon 86. Southwest of the Grand-Place, at corner of rue des Grands Carmes. Popular bar with a wide choice of beers, crowded every night until late with a young, self-consciously trendy crowd.

Toone Impasse Schuddeveld 6, off Petite rue des Bouchers. Largely undiscovered bar belonging to the Toone puppet theatre, just north of the Grand-Place. Two small rooms with old posters on rough plaster walls, a reasonably priced beer list, a modest selection of snacks, and a classical and jazz soundtrack, make it one of the centre's more congenial watering-holes.

On and around the Bourse and place Ste Catherine

Bij den Boer quai aux Briques 60 ☎02 512 61 22. There's nothing pretentious in this good old neighbourhood café-bar with its tiled floor and bygones on the wall. A great place for a drink or a meal, though the service can be slow. The seafood is delicious and reasonably priced. Closed Sun.

Café Métropole place De Brouckère 31. Sumptuously ritzy fin-de-siècle café, belonging to an equally opulent hotel. Astonishingly, many people prefer to sit outside, for a view of flashing ads and zipping traffic. If you've got cash to spare, indulge in a brunch of smoked salmon or caviar.

Le Cirio rue de la Bourse 18. On the north side of the Bourse. One of Brussels' oldest bars, sumptuously decorated in fin-de-siècle style, though now somewhat frayed round the edges. Once frequented, they say, by Jacques Brel.

Le Falstaff rue Henri Maus 17–23. Art Nouveau café next to – and on the south side of – the Bourse, attracting a mixed bag of tourists, gays, Eurocrats and bourgeois Bruxellois. Full of atmosphere, and so crowded in the evenings that you're unlikely to find a seat. Inexpensive beer and sandwiches, plus pastries that will make you go weak at the knees.

Le Greenwich rue des Chartreux 7. A short walk west of the Bourse. Brussels' traditional chess café, with a lovely old wood-panelled and mirrored interior. Laid-back atmosphere.

Elsewhere inside the petit ring

De Ultieme Hallucinatie rue Royale 316. North of Métro Botanique, just south of the rue Royale/Dupont intersection. Well-known and fancifully ornate Art Nouveau bar done up like an old 1920s train car. The youngish crowd sinks a good choice of beers, reasonably priced drinks and food

– omelettes, lasagne etc. There's also a sumptuous restaurant in the front. Occasional live music too. It's a chancy neighborhood – so be careful at night. Mon–Fri 11am–2am, Sat & Sun 5pm–3am.

De Skievers Architeck place du Jeu de Balle 50. The smartest café-bar on the square at the heart of the Marolles quarter. Serves a wide range of inexpensive but tasty meals and snacks, has newspapers to browse, and offers a good beer menu, yet it can't but seem a little tame when compared with the rough-and-ready bars flanking the rest of the square. Daily 6am–1am.

Le Pain Quotidien rue des Sablon 11. One of an extremely successful chain of bakery-cafés, this agreeable place comes decked out with long wooden tables, and offers wholesome salads, various types of brown bread, soup, cakes, pastries and snacks at very reasonable prices. Also at rue Antoine Dansaert 22. Mon–Fri 7.30am–7pm, Sat & Sun 8am–7pm.

Le Perroquet rue Watteeu 31. Busy semi-circular café-bar occupying attractive Art Nouveau premises close to the place du Grand Sablon. Imaginative range of stuffed pitta and salads and other tasty snacks – though you'll find it difficult to get a seat Fri or Sat night. Excellent beer menu.

St Gilles and Ixelles

L'Amour Fou chaussée d'Ixelles 185, Ixelles. Popular, upbeat café off place Fernand Cocq, where you can drink a delicious selection of vodkas, mezcal and tequila while checking your emails. Eccentric modern art on the walls matches the offbeat furnishings and fittings. Food too, nothing fancy – mushrooms on toast and so forth – but inexpensive. Daily till 2am or 3am.

Bar Parallèle place Fernand Cocq 25. The third tip of the drinking-and-eating triangle that includes *Volle Gas* and *L'Amour Fou*. A nifty outdoor terrace and large, spartan interior help create a relaxed atmosphere. Attracts a bouncy young crowd on the weekends.

Le Passiflore rue du Bailli 97, Ixelles. Overlooking the church of Ste Trinité, this trendy but relaxing café serves light lunches, including home-made salmon and spinach quiche, crêpes and a variety of salads, all for under €8. The *croque-monsieurs* are the finest in the capital. Mon–Fri 8am–7pm,

Sat & Sun 9am–7pm.

La Porteuse d'Eau ave Jean Volders 48a, St Gilles. Refurbished Art Nouveau café on the corner of rue Vanderschrick, near the Porte de Hal. One of the few signs of gentrification in this rundown section of St Gilles. The food isn't good, but the ornate interior is well worth the price of a beer.

Rick's ave Louise 344. Situated in a smart part of the city towards the southern end of avenue Louise, this bar-restaurant has been a gathering-place of resident English-speakers for close on thirty years. The bar can get lively, and there's a full menu available, though it's most famous for its ribs.

SiSiSi chaussée de Charleroi 174, in the eastern, more prosperous part of St Gilles, a 5–10min walk north of the Musée Victor Horta, close to place Paul Janson. Youthful, laid-back bar offering a tempting range of salads and stuffed pittas. Especially popular at lunchtimes. Very economical. Daily 10am–2am, Sat & Sun from noon; food served noon–3pm & 6–11pm.

L'Ultime Atome rue St Boniface 14, Ixelles. Near the Porte de Namur, in between the chaussées d'Ixelles and de Wavre. Congenial café-bar with a good range of beers and a youngish clientele. Food – at lunchtime & 7pm–12.30am – ranges from pasta and elaborate salads to more exotic fare, such as ravioli with artichokes and *osso bucco*.

Volle Gas place Fernand Cocq 21. Traditional bar-brasserie offering a good range of beers plus classic Belgian cuisine in a friendly, family atmosphere. The Brussels specialities on offer include the delicious *carbonnades de boeuf à la gueuze*. Occasional live jazz too.

The EU Quarter

Kitty O'Shea's bld Charlemagne 42. Large and busy expat bar right opposite the Centre Berlaymont. Serves Irish food plus draught Guinness. Late 20s clientèle.

Wild Geese ave Livingstone 2–4, off rue de la Loi, beside Métro Maelbeek. This enormous Irish theme pub is the preferred watering hole of the EU crowd, especially Thurs nights when the Euro-youth strut their stuff en masse. It also serves good-value bar food, including large baked potatoes with salads and fillings for under €5. Occasional live music.

Nightlife and entertainment

As far as **nightlife** goes, it's likely you'll be happy to while away the evenings in one of the city's bars – there are plenty in which you can drink until sunrise. After a slow start, **club** culture has made some headway in the city and, although it's hardly cutting-edge stuff, the centre now boasts several really good spots. As a general rule, clubs **open** Thursday to Saturday from 11pm to 5/6am and entry **prices** seldom exceed €10; many of the smaller clubs have no cover charge at all, though you do have to tip the bouncer a nominal fee (€2 or so) on the way out.

Brussels is also a reasonably good place to catch **live bands**, although it doesn't have as lively a scene as some European capitals. Along with Antwerp, the city is a regular stop on the European tours of major artists, though admittedly the indigenous rock scene is pretty thin; rather better is the **jazz**, with several bars playing host to local and international acts.

The **classical musical scene** is, by comparison, rather more impressive. The Orchestre National de Belgique fully deserves its international reputation, and the city showcases a number of excellent classical music festivals. Pick of the bunch are the Ars Musica festival of contemporary music held in March (ⓦ www.arsmusica.be), and May's prestigious Concours Musical Reine Elisabeth (ⓦ www.concours-reine-elisabeth.be), a competition for piano, violin and voice which numbers among its prize-winners Vladimir Ashkenazy, David Oistrakh and Gidon Kremer.

As for **theatre**, Brussels is home to a new generation of young and talented playwrights like Philippe Blasband and Jean-Marie Piemme. Obviously almost all productions are staged in French or Flemish, but the city is regularly visited by big-name touring troupes who perform in their own language. There's also the **Théâtre Royal de Toone**, which puts on puppet plays in the Bruxellois dialect and has become one of the city's major tourist pulls.

About half the **films** shown in Brussels are in English with French and Flemish subtitles (coded "VO", *version originale*). Most screens are devoted to the big US box-office hits, but there are several more adventurous cinemas showing an eclectic mix of foreign films. There's also the annual, two-week **Brussels Film Festival** in January (ⓦ www.brusselsfestival.be), the highlight of which is the "Tremplin" – or "Springboard" – section, which features international films favoured by critics but not yet taken on by Belgian distributors.

For **listings** of concerts and events, check the *What's On* section of the weekly *Bulletin*, the city's well-regarded English-language magazine. **Tickets** for most things are available from Fnac in the City 2 complex, rue Neuve (ⓣ 02 209 22 11).

Clubs

Le Bazaar rue des Capucins 63, in the Marolles, off rue Haute – and below the Palais de Justice. Split-level club with a very competent restaurant upstairs and a dance-floor down below, offering funk, soul, rock and indie. Tues–Thurs & Sun 7pm–1am, Fri & Sat 7.30pm–5am.

Cartagena rue du Marché au Charbon 70. Enjoyable downtown club offering arguably the best and certainly the widest range of South American and Latin sounds in town. Attracts late-20-somethings. Entry €5. Fri & Sat 11pm–4am.

The Fuse rue Blaes 208, Marolles. Near the junction with rue Pieremans. Large, young and vibrant techno, jungle and house club with chill-out rooms and visuals, where big-name, international DJs are a regular feature. Sat 10pm–7am. Métro Porte de Hal.

Le Pacha rue de l'Écuyer 41. Near the Grand-Place. Much vaunted Ibiza import. Spectacular stuff, with all the fury and action you'd expect from a crowd that includes Brussels' finest clubbers and skin-barers. Fridays are dedicated to "Flower Power", which includes funk, Sixties and Seventies rock, soul and house, while Sat is house-music night, with several dance acts thrown in for free. Fri–Sun 11pm–late.

Pitt's Bar rue des Minimes 53. Near the Palais de Justice. Techno, garage, bhangra and house; popular with students. Tues–Sun 8pm–3am.

Who's Who Land rue du Poinçon 17, a short walk east of Prémétro Annessens. One of the capital's runaway success stories, this trendy house club (with occasional foam parties) is always packed. Legions of young latex-wearing revellers pile through the doors and make a beeline for the main dance area, where classic techno and house anthems are blasted out until the early hours. Entrance around €10. Sat 10pm–7am.

Live music bars

L'Archiduc rue Antoine Dansaert 6 ☎ 02 512 06 52. Small, tasteful bar with regular live jazz on the weekend.

Le Cercle rue Ste Anne 20 ☎ 02 514 03 53. Just off place du Grand Sablon. Small, unremarkable venue in itself, but the live music is a real attraction – everything from jazz and latin through to *chanson française* three or four times a week.

Magazin 4 rue du Magasin 4 ☎ 02 223 34 74. In an old warehouse off bld d'Anvers, this is a favourite venue for up-and-coming Belgian indie bands. Only open when there's a gig. Métro Yser.

Sounds rue de la Tulipe 28, Ixelles ☎ 02 512 92 50. Off place Ferdinand Cocq. Atmospheric café which has showcased both local and internationally acclaimed jazz acts for over twenty years. Live music most nights, but the biggies usually appear Sat. Closed Sun.

VK rue de l'Ecole 76 ☎ 02 414 29 07. Regularly features top-class hip-hop, ragga, rock and indie acts and occasionally puts on the odd punk band too – it's probably the best cutting-edge "alternative" venue in the capital. Entrance €7.50–10. You could use Métro Comte de Flandre, but consider taking a taxi there and back as the area has a bad reputation.

Concert halls and large performance venues

AB (Ancienne Belgique) bld Anspach 110 ☎ 02 548 24 24. The capital's leading rock and indie venue; artistes perform either in the main auditorium or the smaller space on the 1st floor. Usually around four gigs a week. Closed July & Aug.

Cirque Royal rue de l'Enseignement 81 ☎ 02 218 20 15. Some big names in international rock, dance and classical music have appeared here, in a venue that was formerly an indoor circus.

Forest National ave du Globe 36 ☎ 0900 00 991. Brussels' main arena for big-name international concerts – Michael Jackson, B.B. King and so forth – holding around 11,000 people. Tram #18 from various stops in the city centre, including the Gare du Midi.

Palais des Beaux Arts rue Ravenstein 23 ☎ 02 507 82 00. Home of the Orchestre National de Belgique, the Palais also hosts visiting orchestras and is a prime venue for French-language theatre, plus modern dance and classical ballet.

Théâtre Royal de la Monnaie place de la Monnaie ☎ 02 229 12 11. Belgium's premier opera house, consistently earning itself glowing reviews and renowned for its adventurous repertoire. It has a policy of nurturing promising singers rather than casting the more established stars, so it's a good place to spot up-and-coming talent. Book in advance as tickets are often difficult to come by.

Theatres

Théâtre National Centre Rogier, place Rogier ☎ 02 203 53 03. This French-only theatre offers high-quality productions ranging from Molière to Brecht. It's also popular with a wide range of visiting theatre companies who perform in their native language, including the RSC, the Parisian Théâtre Odeon and the Berlin-based Berliner Scubuhne.

Théâtre Royal de Toone (Puppet Theatre) Impasse de Schuddeveld 6, off Petite rue des Bouchers ☎ 02 511 71 37. A short walk from the Grand-Place. Excellent puppet plays in the Bruxellois dialect, plus occasional English renditions. Tickets (at €10) are available at the box office half an hour before the performance, but advance booking is advised. Performances Tues–Sat 8.30pm.

Cinemas

Actors Studio petite rue des Bouchers 16 ☎ 02 512 16 96. Probably the best place in the city centre to catch art-house or independent films, this small cinema is also one of the leading venues for the Brussels Film Festival.

Arenberg Galleries Galerie de la Reine 26, close to the Grand-Place, in Galeries St Hubert ☎ 02 512 80 63. Best known for its "Sneak Previews" held every Thurs evening. Also screens an adventurous variety of world films.

Musée du Cinéma In the Palais des Beaux Arts, rue Baron Horta 9 ☎ 02 507 83 70. This small museum-cum-cinema (see p.87 for more) is popular with film buffs, who come to watch an excellent selection of old silent movies with piano accompaniment.

UGC de Brouckère place De Brouckère 38 ☎ 0900 10 440. A ten-screen cinema showing the usual Hollywood films. On Sun morning you get a coffee and croissant included in the price of the ticket.

Vendôme chaussée de Wavre 18 ☎02 502 37 00. A trendy five-screen cinema well known for showing a wide selection of arty films – *The Ice Storm*, *Kundrun* – as well as more mainstream flicks. They usually have at least two English-language films showing at the same time. Métro Porte de Namur.

Gay and lesbian scene

For the latest information on the **lesbian and gay** scene, including events, clubs and restaurants, either pick up a copy of the widely available freebie paper *Queensize*, or contact Tels Quels, a social centre (with a political slant) that welcomes both lesbians and gay men, at rue du Marché au Charbon 81 (Mon–Thurs & Sun 5pm–2am, Fri & Sat 5pm–4am; ☎02 512 45 87). Something of a city institution, Tels Quels has had a great influence on the development of the city's gay and lesbian scene over the years, one of the more obvious results being the concentration of **gay bars** nearby. Despite its battered decor, *Le Belgica*, at no. 32 (Thurs–Sat 10pm–3am), is the most fashionable of these – though the smarter *Le Comptoir*, a restaurant-bar near Gare Centrale at place de la Vieille Halle aux Blés 24 (daily 7pm–3am), would dispute that. In terms of **clubs**, the biggest event for gay men is the weekly shindig *La Démence*, held at the *The Fuse* club (currently Sun 11pm–7am; see p.118). The music is pretty down to earth – mainstream rave, house and garage anthems – and the crowd very mixed.

There is less of a **lesbian** scene, but there are two popular spots, *Le Sapho*, rue St Géry 1 (Fri & Sat 10pm–late), where the atmosphere is friendly, and members of the opposite sex are not made to feel unwelcome; and *Pussy Galore*, which also takes place at *The Fuse* (currently second Fri of the month).

Shopping

Like every other EU capital city, Brussels is swimming with **shops**. The main central shopping street, home to most of the leading chains, is **rue Neuve**, which runs from place de la Monnaie to place Rogier. Towards the top end of rue Neuve, **City 2** is the ultimate in sanitized shopping malls, with cinemas, restaurants, department stores, clothes shops and a large supermarket. More distinctive are the city's covered shopping "streets", or **galeries**, principally the cloistered elegance of the Galeries St Hubert near the Grand-Place. There are also the African shops of the **Galerie d'Ixelles**, off chaussée d'Ixelles near Porte de Namur, and, just opposite, the deluxe designer shops of the **Galerie de la Toison d'Or**. But visitors to Brussels mostly go hunting for two commodities – **chocolate** and **lace** – while some track down **comic strips** and the city's **markets**.

Generally speaking, shops and stores are **open** from 10am to 6pm or 7pm Monday through Saturday. On Fridays, most department stores stay open till 8pm, and some tourist-oriented shops open on Sundays too. Opening times are given below where they differ noticeably from the norm.

Chocolates

Léonidas bld Anspach 46. Léonidas remains one of the most popular and widespread outlets for Belgian chocolates and pralines. Like *Godiva* – another mainstream chocolate chain – the chocolates are straight off the production line, and the prices are very competitive. Léonidas chocs are perhaps rather sickly-sweet in comparison with other brands, but then they (probably) won't mind back home. Branches all over the city – this one is open daily 9am–7pm.

Mary's rue Royale 73, close to the junction with rue du Congrès. A very exclusive, pricey shop, with beautiful period decor and a fine line in handmade chocolates – you can easily taste the difference between theirs and those of the chains.

Tues–Fri & Sun 9am–6pm, Sat 9am–12.30pm & 2–7pm. Métro Botanique.

Neuhaus Grand-Place 27. A chocoholic's paradise, this expensive outlet is part of a chain, but still stocks some of the best chocolates in town. Check out their specialities – the hand-made Caprices, which are pralines stuffed with crispy nougat, fresh cream and soft-centered chocolate. Also sample the delicious Manons, stuffed white chocolates which come in fresh cream, vanilla and coffee fillings. They have branches all over the town; the other centrally located shop is in the Galerie de la Reine.

Wittamer place du Grand Sablon 6. Brussels' most famous patisserie and chocolate shop, established in 1910 and still run by the Wittamer family, who sell gorgeous, if expensive, light pastries, cakes, mousses – and chocolates. They serve speciality teas and coffees in their tearoom along the street at no. 12.

Lace

Manufacture Belge de Dentelle Galerie de la Reine 6–8, in the Galeries St Hubert. The city's largest lace merchant, in business since 1810, sells a wide variety of modern and antique lace at fairly reasonable prices. The service is helpfully old-fashioned.

F. Rubbrecht Grand-Place 23. Traditional lace shop, not as tacky as some of the tourist traps around the Manneken Pis, specializing in authentic hand-made Brussels lace. They do wholesale and retail, and also valuing and buying. Mon–Sat 9am–7pm, Sunday 10am–6pm.

Comic strips

Brüsel bld Anspach 100. This well-known comic shop stocks more than eight thousand new issues and specializes in French underground editions – *Association*, *Amok* and *Bill* to name but three. You'll also find the complete works of the Belgian comic book artist Schuiten, most popularly known for his controversial comic *Brüsel*, which depicts the architectural destruction of a city (guess which

one) in the 1960s. Mega Tintin collection too. Prémétro Bourse.

Centre Belge de la Bande Dessinée rue des Sables 20. The museum bookstore is definitely worth a visit for its wide range of new comics. Tues–Sun 10am–6pm.

Espace Tintin rue de la Colline 13. Just off the Grand-Place. Set up, no doubt, by someone with an unhealthy obsession with Hergé's quiffed hero. Expect to find anything and everything to do with Tintin – comic books, postcards, stationery, figurines, T-shirts, sweaters, and all Hergé's other cartoon creations, such as Quick & Flupke. Mon 11am–6pm, Tues–Sat 10am–6pm, Sun 11am–5pm.

Markets

Gare du Midi Brussels' largest, most colourful food market is held here every Sun at a bazaar-like affair, with traders crammed under the railway bridge and spilling out into the surrounding streets. Among the vegetables and cheap clothes, stands sell pitta, olives, North African raï tapes, spices, herbs and pulses. Sun 6am–1.30pm.

Grand-Place A small flower market is held here Tues–Sun 8am–6pm, and there's a bird market Sun 9am–1pm.

Place du Châtelain. A food and general market takes place here weekly, when this busy Ixelles square is packed with stalls selling fresh vegetables, cheeses, cakes and pastries, as well as plants and flowers, and home-made wines. Wed 2–7pm.

Place du Grand Sablon The swankiest antiques and collectibles market in town. Pricey antique shops in the surrounding streets too. Sat 9am–6pm, Sun 9am–2pm.

Place du Jeu de Balle In the Marolles quarter. The sprawling flea market does business every morning, but it's at its biggest on the weekend, when an eccentric muddle of colonial spoils, quirky odds and ends and domestic and ecclesiastical bric-a-brac give an impression of a century's fads and fashions. Daily 7am–2pm.

Listings

Airlines Aer Lingus, rue du Trône 98 ☎02 548 98 48; Air Canada ☎02 513 91 50; American Airlines ☎02 711 99 77; British Airways, rue du Trône 98 ☎02 548 21 22; British Midland, ave des Pléiades ☎02 713 12 84; Canada 3000 ☎02 502 99 92; Continental ☎02 643 39 39; Delta ☎02 711 97 99; KLM ☎02 717 20 70; SN Brussels ☎07 035

11 11; United ☎02 713 36 00; VG ☎02 303 00 00; Virgin Express ☎02 752 05 05; VLM ☎02 287 80 80.

Airport information For flight information at Brussels' international airport, call ☎0900 70 000 or go to ⊛www.brusselsairport.be.

Banks and exchange There are ATMs dotted

right across the city centre, and most banks will change currency without any problems.

Additionally, there are bureaux de change with extended opening hours at Gare du Nord (daily 8am–8.30pm), Gare du Midi (daily 6.45am–10pm) and Gare Centrale (daily 8am–9pm).

Books and magazines There are two major English-language bookshops in the city centre: Waterstones, bld Adolphe Max 71–75; and Sterling Books, rue du Fossé aux Loups 38, off pl de la Monnaie. Alternatively, Standaard Boekhandel, pl de la Monnaie 4, has a good English-language book section, including a reasonable range of travel guides and hiking maps, as has Fnac, in the City 2 shopping centre on rue Neuve. There's an excellent range of English second-hand books at Pêle-Mêle, bld Maurice Lemonnier 55, by Prémétro Annessens. A wide selection of English-language magazines is available from Waterstones and Sterling Books as well as from leading city newsagents. Among the latter, two of the best are L'Agora, near the Gare Centrale at rue de la Madeleine 21; and Librairie de Rome, ave Louise 50.

Bus enquiries Within the city, STIB ☎02 515 20 00; for the Walloon communities south of the city, TEC ☎010 23 53 53; for the Flemish communities north of the city, De Lijn ☎02 526 28 28.

Car rental Avis, rue Américaine 145 ☎02 537 12 80, and at the airport ☎02 720 09 44; Budget, at the airport ☎02 753 21 70; Europcar, rue du Page 29 ☎02 538 25 91, and at the airport ☎02 721 05 92; Hertz, at the airport ☎02 720 60 44.

Credit-card companies American Express, boulevard du Souverain 100 ☎02 676 21 11; Visa, bld du Roi Albert II 9 ☎02 205 85 85.

Dentists Standby municipal dentist ☎02 426 10 26.

Doctors Standby municipal doctor ☎02 479 18 18.

Embassies Australia, rue Guimard 6–8 ☎02 286 05 00; Canada, ave de Tervuren 2 ☎02 741 06 11; Ireland, rue Froissart 89 ☎02 230 53 37; New Zealand, bld du Régent 47–48 ☎02 512 10 40; UK, rue d'Arlon 85 ☎02 287 62 11; USA, bld du Régent 27 ☎02 508 21 11.

Emergencies Police ☎101; ambulance/fire brigade ☎100.

Football Brussels has several soccer teams, of which Royal Sporting Club (RSC) Anderlecht are by far the best known and most consistent, regularly among the contenders for the Belgian league championship (the season is Aug–April). Their stadium is the Stade Constant Vanden Stock, at ave Théo Verbeeck 2 (☎02 522 15 39), within comfortable walking distance of Métro St Guidon.

Internet access easyInternetCafé provides internet and email facilities at its large premises at place De Brouckère 9 (daily 8am–11.30pm).

Left luggage There are coin-operated lockers at all three main train stations, plus left-luggage offices (daily 6am–midnight).

Lost property For the métro, buses and trams, the lost property office is at ave de la Toison d'Or 15 (☎02 515 23 94); for items lost on the train, inquire at the terminus of the service you were using or on ☎02 224 51 11.

Mail The main central post office is on the first floor of the Centre Monnaie, pl de la Monnaie (Mon–Fri 8am–7pm & Sat 10am–3pm).

Pharmacies One of the largest and most central is Multipharma, rue du Marché aux Poulets 37, near the Grand-Place (Mon–Fri 8.30am–6.30pm, Sat 9.30am–6.30pm). On Sat, Sun & holidays, and outside normal working hours, details of duty pharmacies are usually posted on the front door of all other pharmacies. Details of 24hr chemists are available from the tourist office.

Police Brussels Central Police Station, rue du Marché au Charbon 30 ☎02 517 96 11.

Train enquiries Belgian Rail ☎02 555 25 25; Eurostar, TGV and Thalys information ☎0900 10 366, reservations ☎0900 10 177.

Women's organizations Amazone, rue du Méridien 10 (☎02 229 38 00, ☎02 229 38 01, ⓦwww.amazone.be), is a women's centre that houses the headquarters of many different women's groups from both the French- and Flemish-speaking communities, as well as a café/meeting point.

Around Brussels: Waterloo

Brussels lies at the centre of **Brabant**, one of Belgium's nine provinces. The lion's share of Brabant is claimed by the Flemings, whose portion actually encircles the capital, incorporating the narrow corridor of Flemish-speaking communities that runs round the southern limits of the city. The highlights of the province – most notably Leuven (see p.262) and Zoutleeuw (see p.275) – are covered in other chapters, but the **battlefield of Waterloo**, one of Belgium's most popular attractions, is best seen on a day-trip from the capital.

Waterloo

A run-of-the-mill suburb about 18km south of the centre of Brussels, **Waterloo** has a resonance far beyond its size. It was here on June 18, 1815, at this small crossroads town on what was once the main route into Brussels from France, that Wellington masterminded the battle which put an end to the imperial ambitions of Napoleon. Indeed, the battle actually had far more significance than even its generals realized, for not only was this the last throw of the dice for the formidable army born of the French Revolution, but it also marked the final end of France's prolonged attempts to dominate Europe militarily.

The historic importance of Waterloo has not, however, saved the **battlefield** from interference – a motorway cuts right across it – and if you do visit you'll need a lively imagination to picture what happened and where, unless, that is, you're around to see the large-scale re-enactment of the battle which takes place every five years in June; the next one is scheduled for 2005. Scattered round the battlefield are several monuments and memorials, the most satisfying of which is the **Butte de Lion**, a huge earth mound that's part viewpoint and part commemoration. The battlefield is 3.5km north of the centre of Waterloo, where the **Musée Wellington** is the pick of the district's museums.

Practicalities

The most effective way to visit Waterloo and its scattering of sights is to make a **loop** by train, bus and train. Begin by catching the **train** direct to Waterloo from any of Brussels' three main stations (Mon–Fri 3 hourly, Sat & Sun 1 hourly; 25min). From Waterloo train station, it's an easy fifteen minutes' **walk** – turn right outside the station building and then first left along inconsequential rue de la Station – to Waterloo tourist office and the Musée Wellington (see below). After you've finished at the museum, walk across the street – the chaussée de Bruxelles – to the bus stop, catch **bus #W** (every 30min) and ask to be put off at the Butte de Lion (see p.125). The bus stops about 600m from the Butte de Lion – which you can't miss. After visiting the Butte, return to the same bus stop and catch bus #W onto **Braine-l'Alleud train station**, from where there is a fast and frequent service back to Brussels' three main train stations (Mon–Fri every 15min, Sat & Sun every 30min; 15min).

Waterloo **tourist office**, the Syndicat d'Initiative et de Tourisme, is handily located in the centre of town, next door to the Musée Wellington at chaussée de Bruxelles 149 (daily: April–Sept 9.30am–6.30pm; Oct–March 10.30am–5pm; ☎02 354 99 10, ✉tourisme.waterloo@advalvas.be). They provide free town maps and have several booklets recounting the story of the battle, the most competent of which is titled *The Battlefield of Waterloo Step by Step* (€4.50). The tourist office also sells a combined ticket for all the battle-related attractions (€10), though if you're at all selective (and you should be) this won't work out as a saving at all.

There's no real reason to stay the night, but Waterloo tourist office does have the details of several **hotels**, among which the comfortable *Hotel Le 1815* has the advantage of being near the Butte de Lion at route du Lion 367 (☎02 387 00 60, ☏02 387 12 92; ❺). For **food**, *La Brioche* is a pleasant café serving up a good line in sandwiches and cakes; it's located just up from the tourist office at chaussée de Bruxelles 161.

The Musée Wellington and the church of St Joseph

The best starting point for a visit to Waterloo is next door to the tourist office in the old inn, at chaussée de Bruxelles 147, where Wellington slept the night before the battle, and Alexander Gordon, Wellington's principal aide-de-camp,

The Battle of Waterloo

Escaping from imprisonment on the island of **Elba** on February 26, 1815, **Napoleon** landed in Cannes three days later and moved swiftly north, entering Paris on March 20 just as his unpopular replacement – the slothful King Louis XVIII – high-tailed it to Ghent (see p.206). Thousands of Frenchmen rushed to Napoleon's colours and, as soon as possible, Napoleon marched northeast to crush the two armies, both in Belgium, that threatened his future. One, an assortment of British, Dutch and German soldiers, was commanded by the Duke of Wellington; the other was a Prussian army led by Marshal Blücher.

At the start of the campaign, Napoleon's army was about 130,000 strong, larger than each of the opposing armies but not big enough to fight them both at the same time. Napoleon's strategy was, therefore, quite straightforward – he had to stop Wellington and Blücher from joining together – and to this end he crossed the Belgian frontier near Charleroi to launch a quick attack. On June 16, the French hit the Prussians hard, forcing them to retreat and giving Napoleon the opportunity he was looking for. Napoleon detached a force of 30,000 soldiers to harry the retreating Prussians, while he concentrated his main army against Wellington, hoping to deliver a knock-out blow. Meanwhile, Wellington had assembled his troops at Waterloo, on the main road to Brussels.

At dawn on Sunday June 18, the two armies faced each other. Wellington had some 68,000 men, about one third of whom were British, and Napoleon around 5,000 more. The armies were deployed just 1500m apart, with Wellington on the ridge north of – and uphill from – the enemy. It had rained heavily during the night, so Napoleon delayed his first attack to give the ground a chance to dry. At 11.30am, the battle began when the French assaulted the fortified farm of **Hougoumont**, which was crucial for the defence of Wellington's right. The assault failed, and at approximately 1pm there was more bad news for Napoleon when he heard that the Prussians had eluded their pursuers and were closing fast. To gain time he sent 14,000 troops off to impede their progress; at 2pm he tried to regain the initiative by launching a large-scale infantry attack against Wellington's left. This second French attack also proved inconclusive, so two hours later Napoleon's cavalry charged Wellington's centre, where the British infantry formed into squares and just managed to keep the French at bay – a desperate engagement that cost hundreds of lives. By 5.30pm, the Prussians had begun to reach the battlefield in numbers to the right of the French lines and, at 7.30pm, with the odds getting longer and longer, Napoleon made a final bid to break Wellington's centre, sending in his best soldiers, the Imperial Guard. But, slowed down by the mud churned up by their own cavalry, they proved easy targets for the British infantry, and were beaten back with great loss. At 8.15pm, Wellington, who knew victory was within his grasp, rode down the ranks to encourage his soldiers before ordering the large-scale counterattack that proved decisive.

The French were vanquished and Napoleon subsequently **abdicated**, ending his days in exile on St Helena, where he died in 1821. Popular memory, however, refused to vilify him as the aggressor, not only in France, as you would expect, but right across Europe, where the emperor's bust was a common feature of the nineteenth-century drawing room. In part, this was to do with Napoleon's obvious all-round brilliance, but more crucially he soon became a symbol of opportunity: in him the emergent middle classes saw a common man becoming greater than the crowned heads of Europe, an almost unique event at the time.

was brought to die. The inn has been turned into the enjoyable **Musée Wellington** (daily: April–Sept 9.30am–6.30pm; Oct–March 10.30am–5pm; €3), whose displays detail the events of the battle with plans and models, alongside the assorted personal effects of Wellington, Gordon and Napoleon. In Wellington's bedroom, there are also copies of the messages Wellington sent to his commanders during the course of the battle, curiously formal epistles laced with phrases like "Could you be so kind as . . ." and "We ought to . . .", as well as the artificial leg of Lord Uxbridge: "I say, I've lost my leg," Uxbridge is reported to have said during the battle, to which Wellington replied, "By God, sir, so you have!" After the battle, Uxbridge's leg was buried here in Waterloo, but it was returned to London when he died to join the rest of his body; as a consolation his artificial leg was donated to the museum. Such insouciance was not uncommon among the British ruling class – another of Wellington's ADCs, Lord Fitzroy, had his arm smashed by a musket ball and did not even murmur when it was amputated, only calling out when the surgeon tossed it away: "Hey, bring my arm back. There's a ring my wife gave me on the finger." And neither were the bits and pieces of dead soldiers considered sacrosanct: tooth dealers roamed the battlefields of the Napoleonic Wars pulling out teeth which were then stuck on two pieces of board with a spring at the back – primitive dentures known in England as "Waterloos".

Across the street, the church of **Saint Joseph** is an unusual affair, its domed, circular **portico** of 1689 built as part of a larger chapel on the orders of the Habsburg governor in the hope that it would encourage God to grant King Charles II of Spain an heir. It didn't happen, but the plea to God survives in the Latin inscription on the pediment. The chapel behind the portico was demolished in the nineteenth century and its clumsy replacement is only noteworthy for its assorted **memorial plaques** to the British soldiers who died at Waterloo.

The battlefield – the Butte de Lion

From outside the church of Saint Joseph, pick up bus #W for the quick four-kilometre journey to the **battlefield** – an undulating landscape where the rolling farmland is punctuated by the whitewashed walls of the occasional farmstead and the odd copse. A motley assortment of attractions is clustered on the ridge where Wellington once marshalled his army. Avoid the **Centre du Visiteur** (daily: March 10am–5pm; April–Sept 9.30am–6.30pm; Oct 9.30am–5.30pm; Nov–Feb 10.30am–4pm; €5), which features a dire audio-visual display on the battle, and instead walk up the adjacent hundred-metre-high **Butte de Lion** (same hours; €1). Built by local women with soil from the battlefield, the butte marks the spot where Holland's Prince William of Orange – one of Wellington's commanders and later King William II of the Netherlands – was wounded. It was only a nick, so goodness knows how high the mound would have been if William had been seriously wounded, but even as it is, it's a commanding monument, topped by a regal 28-tonne lion atop a stout column. From the viewing platform, there's a panoramic view over the battlefield, and a diagrammatic plan identifies which army was where.

There are two more modest attractions at the base of the butte, beginning with an awful wax museum, the **Musée de Cires** (April–Sept daily 9.30am–7pm, till 6pm in October; Nov–March Sat & Sun 10am–5pm; €2). The second is the **Panorama de la Bataille** (daily: March 10am–5pm; April–Sept 9.30am–6.30pm; Oct 9.30am–5.30pm; Nov–Feb 10.30am–4pm; €3 or €7.50 with Centre du Visiteur & Butte de Lion), where a naturalistic painting of the battle is displayed in a purpose-built, rotunda-like gallery. A circular canvas no less than 110m in circumference, it was completed in 1913, the work of the French artist Louis Demoulin.

Le Caillou

Napoleon spent the eve of the battle at **Le Caillou** (April–Oct daily 10am–6.30pm; Nov–March daily 1–5pm; €2), a two-storey brick farmhouse about 4km south from the Butte de Lion on the chaussée de Bruxelles. The museum's mementoes, including Napoleon's army cot and death mask, are a memorial to the emperor and his army, but it's hardly riveting stuff. Getting there without your own transport is a pain: you're reliant on bus #365A from opposite the Musée Wellington (every 2hr).

Travel details

Trains

Trains stop at all three of the capital's principal train stations – Bruxelles-Nord, Bruxelles-Centrale, and Bruxelles-Midi – unless otherwise indicated.

Brussels (by Belgian Rail) to: Amsterdam (1 hourly; 3hr); Antwerp (3 hourly; 40min); Bruges (2 hourly; 1hr); Charleroi (2 hourly; 50min);

Ghent (2 hourly; 40min); Liège (1 hourly; 1hr 20min); Leuven (every 30 min; 25min); Luxembourg (1 hourly; 3hr); Maastricht (1 hourly; 2hr); Mons (2 hourly; 55min); Namur (1 hourly; 1hr); Ostend (2 hourly; 1hr 15min); Rotterdam (1 hourly; 1hr 45min).

Brussels (by Thalys trains from Bruxelles-Midi) to: Amsterdam (5 daily; 2hr 30min); Cologne (every 2hr; 2hr 30min); Paris (every 2hr; 1hr 30min).

Flanders

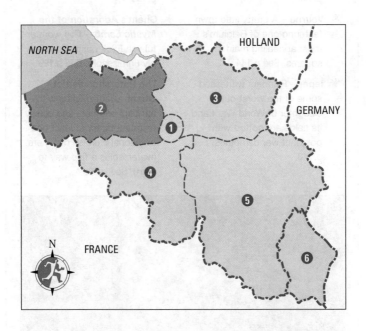

CHAPTER 2 # Highlights

✳ **The beach** – The Belgian coast boasts a first-rate sandy beach for almost its entire length. See p.131

✳ **Het Zwin** – The polders and dykes of this nature reserve in Knokke-Heist make for perfect coastal cycling. See p.140

✳ **Veurne** – A pretty little town featuring one of Belgium's most appealing main squares. See p.144

✳ **Ieper** – Flanders witnessed some of the worst of the slaughter of World War I and its fields are dotted with poignant war cemetries. See p.148

✳ **Flemish tapestries** – Some of the most richly decorated examples can be seen in pleasantly old-fashioned Oudenaarde. See p.159

✳ **Bruges** – Its antique centre, latticed with canals, is one of the prettiest in Europe. See p.163

✳ **Ghent's *Adoration of the Mystic Lamb*** – This wonderful van Eyck painting is simply unmissable. See p.199

✳ **The Patershol district, Ghent** – Jam-packed with atmospheric bars and classy restaurants; try at least one traditional Flemish dish here (*waterzooi* is a fine way to start). See p.203

2

Flanders

T he Flemish-speaking provinces of **East Flanders** and **West Flanders** (Oost Vlaanderen and West Vlaanderen) roll east from the North Sea coast, stretching out to the peripheries of Brussels and Antwerp. As early as the thirteenth century, Flanders was one of the most prosperous areas of Europe, with an advanced, integrated economy dependent on the cloth trade. But by the sixteenth century the region was in decline as trade slipped north towards Holland, and England's cloth manufacturers began to undermine its economic base. The speed of the collapse was accelerated by religious conflict, for though the great Flemish towns were by inclination Protestant, their kings and queens were Catholic. Indeed, once the Habsburgs had seen off the Protestant challenge, thousands of Flemish weavers, merchants and skilled artisans poured north to escape religious persecution. The ultimate economic price was the closure of the River Scheldt, the main waterway to the North Sea, at the insistence of the Dutch in 1648. Thereafter, Flanders sank into poverty and decay, a static, priest-ridden and traditional society where nearly every aspect of life was controlled by decree, and only three percent of the population could read or write. As Voltaire quipped:

In this sad place wherein I stay,
Ignorance, torpidity,
And boredom hold their lasting sway,
With unconcerned stupidity;
A land where old obedience sits,
Well filled with faith, devoid of wits.

With precious little say in the matter, the Flemish peasantry of the seventeenth and eighteenth centuries saw their lands crossed and re-crossed by the armies of the Great Powers, for it was here that the relative fortunes of dynasties and nations were decided. Only with Belgian independence did the situation begin to change: the towns started to industrialize, tariffs protected the cloth industry, Zeebrugge was built and Ostend was modernized, all in a flurry of activity that shook the land from its centuries-old torpor. This steady progress was severely interrupted by the German occupations of both World Wars, but Flanders has emerged prosperous, its citizens maintaining a distinctive cultural and linguistic identity – though often in sharp opposition to their Walloon (French-speaking) neighbours.

With the exception of the range of low hills around Ronse and the sea dunes along the coast, Flanders is unrelentingly flat, a somewhat dreary landscape at its best in its quieter recesses, where poplar trees and whitewashed farmhouses still decorate sluggish canals. More remarkably, there are many reminders of

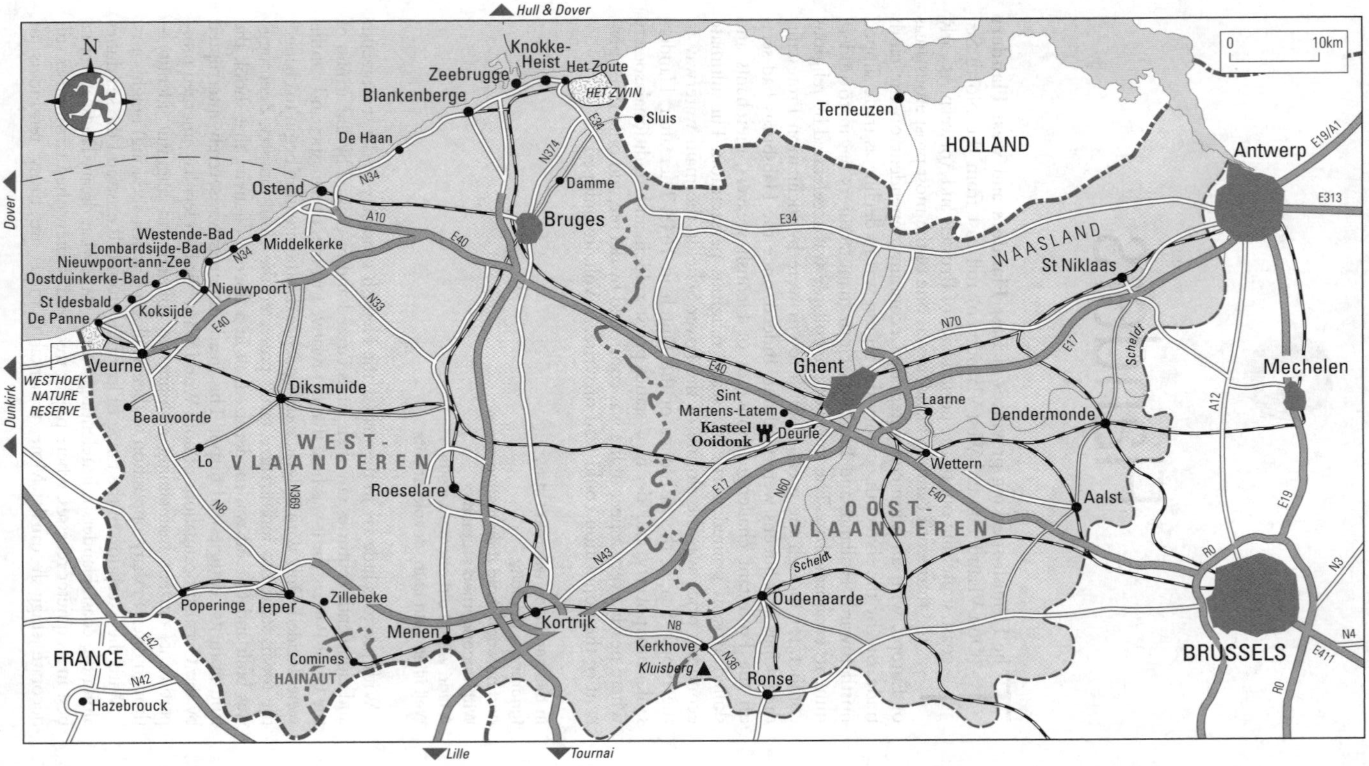

N

10km

0

Hull & Dover ▲

Dover ▼

Dunkirk ▼

Lille ▼

Tournai ▼

Antwerp

E313

E19/A1

Mechelen

N3

N4

E411

BRUSSELS

R0

A12

E19

E17

St Niklaas

WAASLAND

HOLLAND

Terneuzen

Scheldt

Dendermonde

Aalst

N70

Laarne

Wettem

E40

OOST-

VLAANDEREN

Ghent

E34

Sint Martens-Latem

Kasteel Ooidonk

Deurle

Oudenaarde

N60

N36

Scheldt

Ronse

N8

Kerkhove

Kluisberg

E40

E40

E17

Sluis

HET ZWIN

Knokke-Heist Het Zoute

Damme

N374

Bruges

Zeebrugge

Blankenberge

De Haan

A10

N34

N33

N43

Kortrijk

Ostend

Middelkerke

Nieuwpoort

E40

Roeselare

Menen

Lille ▼

Westende-Bad

Lombardsijde-Bad

Nieuwpoort-ann-Zee

Oostduinkerke-Bad

Koksijde

St Idesbald

De Panne

Veurne

Beauvoorde

Diksmuide

N369

N8

Lo

WEST-

VLAANDEREN

Zillebeke

Ieper

Poperinge

Comines

HAINAUT

WESTHOEK NATURE RESERVE

France

Hazebrouck

N42

E42

N43

Flanders' medieval greatness, beginning with the ancient and fascinating cloth cities of **Bruges** and **Ghent**, both of which hold marvellous collections of early Flemish art. Less familiar are a clutch of intriguing smaller towns, most memorably **Oudenaarde**, which has a delightful town hall and is famed for its tapestries; **Kortrijk**, with its classic small-town charms and fine old churches; and **Veurne**, whose main square is framed by a beguiling medley of fine old buildings. There is also, of course, the legacy of **World War I**. The trenches extended from the North Sea coast, close to Nieuwpoort, as far as Switzerland, cutting across West Flanders via Diksmuide and Ieper, and many of the key engagements of the war were fought here. Every year hundreds of visitors head for **Ieper** (formerly Ypres) to see the numerous cemeteries and monuments around the town – sad reminders of what proved to be a desperately futile conflict.

Not far from the battlefields, the Belgian coast is **beach** territory, an almost continuous stretch of golden sand that is filled by thousands of tourists every summer. An excellent **tram** service connects all the major resorts, and although a lot of the development has been crass, cosy **De Haan** has kept much of its turn-of-the-century charm, and **Knokke** has all the pretensions of a sophisticated resort. The largest town on the coast is **Ostend**, a lively, working seaport and resort crammed with popular bars and restaurants.

Aside from the trams that shuttle up and down the coast, **trains** link all the major inland towns at least once an hour. Where the trains fizzle out, **buses** run by De Lijn take over.

The coast

Some 70km from tip to toe, much of the Belgian **coast** groans under an ugly covering of apartment blocks and bungalow settlements, a veritable carpet of concrete that largely – but no means entirely – obscures a landscape that lay pretty much untouched until the nineteenth century. Before the developers, the beach backed onto an empty line of sand dunes on which nothing grew except rushes and stunted Lombardy poplars. Behind lay a narrow strip of undulating ground ("Ter Streep"), seldom more than a kilometre or so in width and covered with moss and bushes, separating the sand dunes from the farms of the Flemish plain. The dunes were always an inadequate protection against the sea, and the inhabitants hereabouts were building dykes as early as the tenth century, an arrangement formalized two hundred years later when Count Baldwin IX of Flanders appointed guardians charged with the duty of constructing defensive works. Despite these efforts, life on the coast remained precarious, and most people chose to live inland; indeed, when Belgium achieved independence in 1830, there were only two coastal settlements of any size – Ostend, a small fortified town with an antiquated harbour, and Nieuwpoort, in a state of what was thought to be terminal decay.

It was **Léopold I**, the first king of the Belgians, who began the transformation of the coast, assisted by the development of the country's rail system. In 1834 he chose Ostend as a royal residence, had the town modernized and connected it by train to Brussels. Fashionable by royal approval and now easy to reach, the coast was soon dotted with resorts, and the number of seaside visitors rose meteorically. The next king – **Léopold II** – carried on the work of his father, building a light railway along the shore and completing the long chain of massive sea walls that still punctuate the coastline. Barring the extraordinary, the Belgian coast was safe at last.

The coastal tram

Fast and efficient **trams** travel the length of the Belgian coast from Knokke-Heist in the east to De Panne in the west, putting all the Belgian resorts within easy striking distance of each other. There are numerous tram stops and one tram station, in Ostend beside the train station. Services in both directions depart every ten or fifteen minutes in summer, every half-hour in winter. **Tickets** can be bought from the driver or the ticket office at Ostend tram station; fares are relatively inexpensive – Ostend to either Knokke-Heist or De Panne, for instance, costs €4.20. You can also buy tickets for unlimited tram travel, valid for either one day (€8.20) or three days (€13.90).

Popular ever since as a **holiday destination**, the coast has long been thronged by dozens of hotels, though nowadays these rarely offer sea views as the prime sites are almost exclusively occupied by apartment blocks. Bear in mind also that, although there are scores of campsites, many are no more than a few caravans on a field – and surprisingly few are listed by the tourist authorities. Another distinctive feature is the long lines of tiny wooden huts that cut a dash across the more popular beaches. Owned by the local municipalities, each is rented out for the season and, if you're planning to glue yourself to the beach, some are available by the week at reasonable rates – check with the local tourist office. If you're after a quick burst of sun, sea and sand, **Ostend** is as pleasant a spot as anywhere, and it also boasts several interesting sights plus a handful of very recommendable restaurants and hotels. For a longer beach holiday, the pick of the resorts is **De Haan**, a charming little place with easy access to a slender slice of pristine coastline.

Ostend

The 1900 *Baedeker* distinguished **OSTEND** as "One of the most fashionable and cosmopolitan watering places in Europe". The gloss may be long gone, and the town's aristocratic visitors have moved on to more exotic climes, but Ostend remains a likeable, liveable seaport with lots of first-rate seafood restaurants, a couple of enjoyable art museums and – easily the most popular of the lot – a long slice of sandy **beach**. Ostend is also the focal point of the region's public transport system, including the fast, frequent and efficient trams that run behind the beach to Knokke-Heist in the east and De Panne in the west. In addition, Hoverspeed operates a regular catamaran service to and from Dover.

The old fishing village of Ostend was given a town charter in the thirteenth century, in recognition of its growing importance as a port for trade across the Channel. Flanked by an empty expanse of sand dune, it remained the only important harbour along this stretch of the coast until the construction of Zeebrugge in the nineteenth century. Like so many other towns in the Spanish Netherlands, it was attacked and besieged time and again, winning the admiration of Protestant Europe in resisting the Spaniards during a desperate siege that lasted from 1601 to 1604. Later, convinced of the wholesome qualities of sea air and determined to impress other European rulers with their sophistication, Belgium's first kings, Léopold I and II, turned Ostend into a chi-chi resort, demolishing the town walls and dotting the outskirts with prestigious buildings and parks. Several of these have survived, but others were destroyed during World War II, when the town's docks made it a prime bombing target.

Subsequently, Ostend resumed its role as a major cross-channel port until the completion of the Channel Tunnel undermined its position. Since then, Ostend has had to re-invent itself, at least in part, and is attempting to emphasize its charms as a seaside resort and centre of culture. There's a long way to go, perhaps – and parts of the centre remain resolutely miserable – but there's no denying the town is on the up.

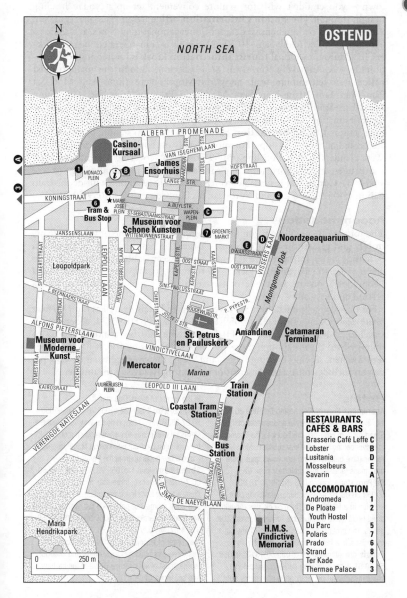

OSTEND

NORTH SEA

ALBERT I PROMENADE

Casino-Kursaal

James Ensorhuis

MONACO-PLEIN

KONINGSTRAAT

Tram & Bus Stop

MARIE JOSE PLEIN

Museum voor Schone Kunsten

JANSSENSLAAN

Leopoldpark

WITTENONNENSTRAAT

GROENTE-MARKT

Noordzeeaquarium

Montgomery Dok

Museum voor Moderne Kunst

Mercator

Marina

St. Petrus en Pauluskerk

Amandine

Catamaran Terminal

Maria Hendrikapark

Train Station

Coastal Tram Station

Bus Station

H.M.S. Vindictive Memorial

0   250 m

RESTAURANTS, CAFÉS & BARS

Brasserie Café Leffe	C
Lobster	B
Lusitania	D
Mosselbeurs	E
Savarin	A

ACCOMODATION

Andromeda	1
De Ploate Youth Hostel	2
Du Parc	5
Polaris	7
Prado	6
Strand	8
Ter Kade	4
Thermae Palace	3

133

Curiously enough it was here in Ostend that **Marvin Gaye** hunkered down with friends in 1981 until, the following year, family and musical ties pulled him back to the US – and his untimely demise two years later.

Arrival, information and transport

With regular services from Dover (March–Dec), Ostend's **catamaran terminal** is next to the **train station**, a couple of minutes' walk from the centre of town – you couldn't wish for a more convenient set-up if you're heading straight through. The **station's information office** (Mon–Sat 8am–7pm, Sun 9am–5pm) has comprehensive details of international train times, and there's a left luggage office (daily 5am–10.30pm) as well as coin-operated luggage lockers. In addition, a seasonal **tourist information kiosk** is located inside the station (July & Aug daily 9am–1pm & 4–7.30pm), though the main **tourist office** is a ten-minute walk away on Monacoplein (June–Aug Mon–Sat 9am–7pm, Sun 10am–7pm; Sept–May Mon–Fri 9am–6pm, Sat 10am–6pm, Sun 10am–5pm; ☎059 70 11 99, ⓦ www.oostende.be).

For destinations along the coast, **trams** leave from the tram station beside the train station. Ostend **bus station** backs on to the tram station; bus timetables are posted at most bus stops. For more details on bus journeys, call De Lijn's West Flanders information line (☎059 56 53 53), covering Ostend, the coast and Bruges, or the information line for East Flanders, including Ghent (☎092 10 94 91). **Car rental** is available from Avis, who have an office inside the train station (☎059 23 36 22) and Europcar, Archimedesstraat 7 (☎059 70 01 01).

Accommodation

The tourist office will help you find accommodation in one of Ostend's many **hotels** and **guesthouses** at no extra charge. The best option is to head for a beachside hotel, but these are few and far between – most of the seashore is given over to apartment blocks. Alternatively, plump for the area round Léopoldpark on the west side of the centre – it's a pleasant district with a relaxed and easy air.

For those on a budget, there are several bargain hotels, as well as the *De Ploate Youth Hostel*, Langestraat 82 (☎059 80 52 97, ⓕ059 80 92 74, ⓔdeploate@travel.to), a neat, well-cared-for HI **hostel** with 120 beds, mostly in six- to nine-bedded dorms, though there are some family rooms too. It has a competent kitchen, serving evening meals, and a bar; the overnight fee of €15 per person includes breakfast. Reservations are strongly advised in summer.

Hotels

Andromeda Kursaal Westhelling 5 ☎059 80 66 11, ⓕ059 80 66 29, ⓦ www.andromedahotel.be. Smart modern high-rise next door to the Casino, and overlooking the town's best beach. Most rooms have balconies and sea views, plus there are fitness facilities and an indoor pool. ❺

Du Parc Marie Joséplein 3 ☎059 70 16 80, ⓕ059 80 08 79, ⓦ www.duparcoostende.com. Located in a fetching Art Deco block, this medium-sized hotel offers comfortable rooms at reasonable prices. The ground-floor café, with its Tiffany glass trimmings, is a favourite with locals. ❹

Polaris Groentemarkt 19 ☎059 50 16 02, ⓕ059 51 40 01. A good-looking *belle époque* exterior hides modest but perfectly adequate rooms right in the centre of town. One star. ❸

Prado Léopold II-laan 22 ☎059 70 53 06, ⓕ059 80 87 35, ⓦ www.hotelprado.be. Very likeable three-star hotel with neatly furnished modern rooms. Ask for a room on the front overlooking Marie Joséplein – and a few floors up from the traffic. ❸

Strand Visserskaai 1 ☎059 70 33 83, ⓕ059 80 36 78. No-nonsense, three-star, modern hotel a stone's throw from the train station. Twenty spick-and-span rooms, but perhaps a tad over-priced. ❺

Ter Kade Visserskaai 49 ☎059 50 09 15, ⓕ059 51 04 87, ⓦ www.terkade.com. A high-rise near the corner of Visserskaai and Albert I Promenade, this three-star hotel has forty bright and cheerful rooms, most of which have views of the harbour and seashore. ❹

Thermae Palace Koningin Astridlaan 7 ☎059 80 66 44, ⓕ059 80 52 74, ⓦwww.adsleisure.com. Much hyped, this hotel enjoys the reputation of being Ostend's best. The building is certainly striking – an Art Deco extravagance with expan- sive public rooms and spacious bedrooms offering sea views – but the place can't but help seem a little sorry for itself – there's so much to keep in good working order. A 10min walk west of the centre. ❼

The Town

There's precious little left of medieval Ostend, and today's **town centre**, which fans out from beside the train station, is a largely modern affair, whose narrow, straight streets are lined by clunky postwar apartment blocks and a scattering of older – and much more appealing – stone mansions. Roughly square in shape, the town centre is bounded by the beach to the north, harbours to the east, the marina to the south, and Leopold II-laan to the west; it takes between ten and fifteen minutes to walk from one end to the other.

In front of the train station, the first specific sight is the **Amandine** (Mon 2–7pm, Tues–Sun 10am–7pm; €2.50), a former Ostend-based, deep-sea fish- ing boat of unremarkable modern design that was decommissioned in 1995 – and then parked here. The boat's interior has been turned into a museum with displays on fishing, nautical dioramas and so forth, plus simulated fishy smells. Straight ahead from the boat rises the whopping **St Petrus en Pauluskerk**, which looks old but in fact dates from the early twentieth century. Behind the church, the last remnant of its predecessor is a massive sixteenth-century brick **tower** with a canopied, rather morbid shrine of the Crucifixion at its base. Nearby, pedestrianized **Kapellestraat**, the principal shopping street, leads north into the main square, **Wapenplein**, a pleasant open space that zeroes in on an old-fashioned bandstand. The south side of the square is dominated by the Feest-en Kultuurpaleis (Festival and Culture Hall), a big bruiser of a build- ing that dates from the 1950s.

Museum voor Schone Kunsten

The third floor of the Feest-en Kultuurpaleis is occupied by the **Museum voor Schone Kunsten** (Fine Art Museum; daily except Tues 10am–noon & 2–5pm; €1.25), which offers a lively programme of temporary exhibitions as well as a small but enjoyable permanent collection. Highlights of the latter include the harsh surrealism of **Paul Delvaux**'s (1897–1994) *The Izjzer Time* and several piercing canvases by **Leon Spilliaert** (1881–1946), a native of Ostend whose works combine both Expressionist and Symbolist elements. Spilliaert was smitten by the land and seascapes of Ostend, using them in his work time and again – as in *The Gust of Wind*, with its dark, forbidding colours and screaming woman, and the comparable *Fit of Giddiness*. There's also an excellent sample of the work of **James Ensor** (1860–1949), who was born in Ostend, the son of an English father and Flemish mother. Barely noticed until the 1920s, Ensor spent nearly all his 89 years working in his home town, and is nowadays considered a pioneer of Expressionism. His first paintings were rather sombre portraits and landscapes, but in the early 1880s he switched to brilliantly contrasting colours, most familiar in his *Self-portrait with Flowered Hat*, a deliberate variation on Rubens' famous self-portraits. Less well known is *The Artist's Mother in Death*, a fine, penetrating example of his preoccupation with the grim and macabre. Look out also for portraits of Ensor by his con- temporaries, particularly those by the talented **Henry de Groux**, and – as a curiosity – **Charles Louis Verboeckhoven**'s *The Visit of Queen Victoria to Ostend in 1843*: the painting is pretty dire, but it celebrates one of the royal events that put the resort firmly on the international map.

The James Ensorhuis and the PMMK

A couple of minutes' walk north of the Wapenplein, the **James Ensorhuis**, Vlaanderenstraat 27 (June–Sept Wed–Mon 10am–noon & 2–5pm; Oct–May Sat & Sun only 2–5pm; €4), is of some specialist interest as the artist's home for the last thirty years of his life. On the ground floor there's a passable recreation of the old shop where his aunt and uncle sold shells and souvenirs, while up above the painter's living room and studio have been returned to something like their appearance at the time of his death, though the works on display aren't originals. From here, it's a brief stroll west to the **Casino-Kursaal** (gaming daily from 3pm), an unlovely structure built in 1953 as a successor to the first casino of 1852. On the first Saturday of every March, the Casino hosts the *Bal Rat Mort* (Dead Rat Ball; ℡059 70 51 11, ⓦwww.ramort.be), a lavish, fancy-dress carnival ball with a different theme each year. From here, it's another short stretch to the little lakes, mini-bridges and artificial grottoes of **Leopoldpark**.

Just beyond the south side of the park, at Romestraat 11, is the **PMMK – Museum voor Moderne Kunst** (Modern Art Museum; Tues–Sun 10am–6pm; €3; ⓦwww.pmmk.be), where a wide selection of modern Belgian paintings, sculptures and ceramics are exhibited in rotation – everything from the Expressionists of the St Martens-Latem group (see p.212) through to Pop and Conceptual art. Artists represented in the permanent collection include Delvaux, Spilliaert, Constant Permeke and the versatile **Jean Brusselmans** (1884–1953), who tried his hand at several different styles. The museum also puts on an imaginative range of temporary exhibitions (when the entry fee is usually increased).

The seafront and the marina

To the **west of the Casino** is Ostend's main attraction, its sandy **beach**, which extends west as far as the eye can see. On summer days thousands drive into the town to soak up the sun, swim and amble along the seafront **promenade**, which runs along the top of the sea wall. Part sea defence and part royal ostentation, the promenade was once the main route from the town centre to the Wellington racecourse 2km to the west. It was – and remains – an intentionally grand walkway designed to pander to Léopold II, whose imperial statue, with fawning Belgians and Congolese at its base, still stands in the middle of a long line of stone columns that now adjoin the **Thermae Palace Hotel**. Built in the 1930s, this is similarly regal, although it spoils the lines of the original walkway.

Leading east from the Casino, Albert I Promenade runs along the seashore into the Visserskaai. Here the **Noordzeeaquarium** (April–Sept daily 10am–12.30pm & 2–6pm; €2), housed in the former shrimp market on the east side of the street, holds a series of displays on North Sea fish, crustacea, flora and fauna. The Visserskaai leads back down to the train station and the **marina**, where the sailing ship **Mercator** (April–June & Sept daily 10am–1pm & 2–6pm; July & Aug daily 10am–7pm; Oct–March Sat & Sun 11am–1pm & 2–5pm; €2), the old training vessel of the Belgian merchant navy, has been converted into a marine museum holding a hotch-potch of items accumulated during her world voyages.

Finally, a five- to ten-minute walk south of the train station, in a sunken garden beside one of the old city docks, stands the prow of the **HMS Vindictive**. On the night of May 9, 1918, the British made a desperate attempt to block Ostend's harbour. The sacrificial ships were crewed by volunteers, and one of these vessels, the *Vindictive*, was successfully sunk at the port entrance. After the war the bow was retrieved and kept as a memorial to the sailors who lost their lives. This was one of the most audacious operations of the war, but tragically it was based on false intelligence: German submarines hardly ever used the harbour.

Eating and drinking

The sheer variety of places to eat in Ostend is almost daunting. Along Visserskaai (where in summer there's also a long line of seafood stalls) and through the central city streets are innumerable **cafés**, **café-bars** and **restaurants**. Many of them serve some pretty mediocre stuff, but there are lots of good spots too, and everywhere there are plates of fresh North Sea mussels and french fries.

Brasserie Café Leffe Wapenplein 110. Pleasant café-bar in the main square, serving Leffe on draught.

Café du Parc Marie Joséplein 3. Sociable, old-fashioned café-bar, part of the *Hotel du Parc*, with Art Deco bits and pieces close to the Casino.

Lobster Van Iseghemlaan 64. Smart restaurant close to the tourist office which specializes in (you guessed it) lobster. Main courses hover around €20. Closed Tues.

Lusitania Visserskaai 35 ⌕059 70 17 65.

Excellent and long-established restaurant serving great seafood, especially lobster. Main courses from €21 as well as set menus.

Mosselbeurs Dwarsstraat 10. One of the liveliest restaurants in town with cheerfully naff nautical fittings and top-notch fishy dishes, especially eels and mussels. Reasonable prices.

Savarin Albert I Promenade 75 ⌕059 51 31 71, a 5min walk west of the Casino. Classic Franco–Belgian cuisine with the emphasis on seafood. Expensive, but then it's one of the best restaurants in town.

East from Ostend

Clearing Ostend's suburbs, the coastal tram shoots through a series of routine tourist developments on its way to **DE HAAN**, probably the prettiest and definitely the most distinctive resort on the coast. Established at the end of the nineteenth century, De Haan was carefully conceived as an exclusive seaside village in a rustic Gothic Revival style, called *style Normand*. The building plots were irregularly dispersed between the tram station and the sea, around a pattern of winding streets reminiscent of – and influenced by – contemporaneous English suburbs such as Liverpool's Sefton Park. The only formality was provided by a central circus around a casino (demolished in 1929). The casino apart, De Haan has survived pretty much intact, a welcome relief from the surrounding high-rise development, and, flanked by empty sand dunes, it's become a popular family resort, with an excellent **beach** and pleasant seafront cafés.

De Haan **tourist office** is next to De Haan Aan Zee tram stop, five minutes' walk from the beach along Leopoldlaan (April–Oct daily 9am–noon & 2–5/6pm; Nov–March Mon–Fri 10am–noon & 2–5pm; ⌕059 23 44 38, ⓔtourism@dehaan.be). They issue a useful English-language leaflet describing walking and cycling routes in the vicinity of De Haan; one pleasant option is the 43-kilometre Oude Dijken (Old Dykes) cycle route, which threads along several canals and passes a number of country pubs. **Cycle hire** is available at several outlets, including André at Leopoldlaan 9 (⌕059 23 37 89).

The tourist office has a small cache of **B&Bs** (❷–❹); in addition there are no fewer than 25 **hotels** in or near the village centre, including a couple of reasonably priced places in Gothic Revival piles a few steps from the tram stop. These are the one-star *Des Brasseurs*, Koninklijk Plein 1 (⌕059 23 52 94, Ⓕ059 23 65 96; ❸), which offers sixteen plain but pleasant, en suite rooms, and the rather more enticing and considerably larger, three-star *Belle Vue*, at Koninklijk Plein 5 (⌕059 23 34 39, Ⓕ059 23 75 22; ❺). However, easily the pick of the hotels is the first-rate *Auberge des Rois*, Zeedijk 1 (⌕059 23 30 18, Ⓕ059 23 60 78, ⓌWww.beachhotel.be; ❺), a smart, modern, medium-sized hotel overlooking the beach and adjacent to an undeveloped tract of sand dune; ask for a room with a sea view. Needless to say, it's popular – reservations are advised.

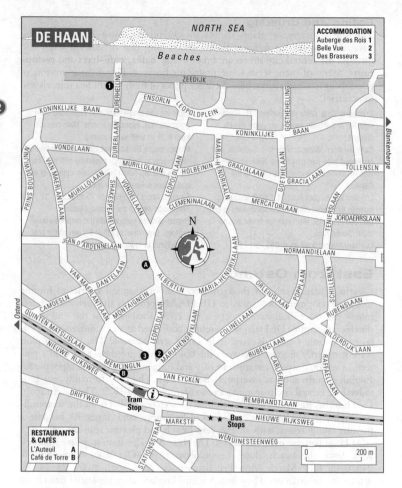

DE HAAN

NORTH SEA

Beaches

ACCOMMODATION	
Auberge des Rois	1
Belle Vue	2
Des Brasseurs	3

Café-restaurants line up along the seafront, and your best bet is to stroll along until you find somewhere you fancy. Alternatively, *L'Auteuil*, on the central circus at Leopoldlaan 18, serves particularly good mussels, while the *Café de Torre* (closed Mon & Tues out of season), across from the De Haan Aan Zee tram stop, has a great range of beers, good music and filling snacks.

Blankenberge

Nine kilometres east of De Haan, **BLANKENBERGE** is one of the busiest places on the coast, but there's precious little to recommend it. Hopelessly overcrowded during the summer, it's the archetypal seaside town, with a 1930s pier, a tiled, seafront Art Deco casino, dozens of cheap hotels – and fast-food bars pumping out high-energy singalongs. The **tourist office** is on Koning Léopold III plein (daily: April–June & Sept 9am–12.30pm & 2–6pm; July & Aug 9am–8pm; Oct–March Mon–Sat 9am–noon & 1.30–5pm, Sun 10am–1pm; ☎050 41 22 27), next to the train station and the Blankenberge

Station tram stop, and five minutes' walk from the beach along the main pedestrianized street, **Kerkstraat**.

Zeebrugge

In 1895 work began on a brand new seaport and harbour next to the tiny village of **ZEEBRUGGE**, some 5km beyond Blankenberge. Connected to the rail and canal systems, the harbour was an ambitious attempt to improve Belgium's coastal facilities and provide easy access to the sea from Bruges via the Leopoldkanaal. The key to the project was a crescent-shaped mole some 2.5km long and 100m wide that was built up from the shore, protecting incoming and outgoing shipping from the vagaries of the North Sea. Completed in 1907, the harbour was a great commercial success, although two world wars badly damaged its prospects. During World War I, the Allies were convinced that Zeebrugge was a German submarine base, and, in conjunction with the assault on Ostend (see p.136), attempted to obstruct Zeebrugge's harbour in April 1918. Block ships, crewed by volunteers, were taken to strategic positions and sunk, resulting in heavy casualties and only partial success. There's a **monument** to the dead sailors and a map of the action at the base of the mole, restored after it was destroyed during the German occupation. World War II saw the same job done rather more proficiently, but it didn't stop further bombing raids and the demolition of the port by the retreating Germans in 1944. The last of the block ships (the *Thetis*) was finally cleared and the harbour reopened in 1957, since when business has boomed and the port has continued to expand.

Practicalities

Spreading out along the coast among the series of giant docks, present-day Zeebrugge divides into sections, each with its own tram stop. On the west side, a couple of minutes' walk from **Zeebrugge Strandwijk tram stop**, is the small **beach resort**. There's nothing much to see, but, pushed up against the base of the original mole to the east and edged by sand dunes to the west, it's a surprisingly pleasant place to stay particularly if you've got a ferry to catch. There's one good **hotel** here too, the four-star *Maritime*, Zeedijk 6 (☎050 54 40 66, ℻050 54 66 08; ❹), a well-kept, six-storey concrete and glass high-rise whose rooms offer wide sea views. Also on the seafront of the beach resort is a good café-bar, the *'t Zandlopertje*, which has a decent range of beers, and a **tourist information kiosk** (July & Aug daily 10am–1pm & 2–6pm; ☎050 54 50 42). They can provide up-to-date details of the irregular **bus** service to Bruges train station (#791; July & Aug 3–4 daily; Sept–June Mon–Sat 2 daily; 30min) and of **ferries** to England; P&O North Sea Ferries has sailings to Hull and P&O runs to Dover. At present the former takes foot passengers and provides transport from Zeebrugge train station to the **ferry terminal**, out on one of the moles; the latter only takes motorists.

From the beach resort, it's a twenty-minute walk east along the main road – or a couple of minutes by tram to the Zeebrugge Vaart tram stop – to Zeebrugge **train station**, which is surrounded by several blocks of terraced houses originally built for harbour workers at the beginning of the twentieth century. Trains leave here for Bruges every hour. A further 1km to the east, the oldest part of Zeebrugge fans out north from the tram line to the original fishing harbour, now part of the general dock complex.

Knokke-Heist

Generally regarded as Belgium's most sophisticated resort, **KNOKKE-HEIST** is the collective name for five villages whose individual identities have disappeared in a sprawling development, jam-packed in summer, that stretches for some 7km along the coast almost to the Dutch frontier. The sophistication is hidden by the confusion of high-rise apartment blocks that string along the beach, but reveals itself if you wander the leafy avenues of expensive holiday homes hidden away on the resort's eastern peripheries.

To attract the crowds, a lot of effort goes into planning Knokke-Heist's varied special events programme, which includes an annual sandcastle-building competition and the **International Cartoon Festival**, with eight hundred entries selected by an international panel and shown in the **Cultureel Centrum Scharpoord** exhibition centre, at Meerlaan 32 (℡050 63 04 30), during the second half of June and most of July. The Cultural Centre is a five- to ten-minute walk northwest of Knokke tram terminus and nearby train station. Up-to-date details of all events are available from Knokke tourist office (see below).

Knokke and Albertstrand

The most agreeable part of this elongated resort is at the east end around **KNOKKE**, a resolutely bourgeois holiday town with a splendid beach, an excellent range of sporting facilities and a clutch of private art galleries where many of the big names of contemporary Belgian and Dutch art come to exhibit and sell. The centre of all this conspicuous consumption is the sumptuous **casino** (gambling daily from 3pm; ⓦwww.casinoknokke.be), which is located in adjacent **ALBERTSTRAND**, a ten-minute walk west of Knokke along the seafront. To emphasize its ritzy credentials, the casino is decorated with canvases by Paul Delvaux in the lobby and René Magritte's *Le Domaine Enchanté* in the gaming room.

Het Zoute

To the east of Knokke is **HET ZOUTE**, whose well-heeled villas stretch along and behind the seashore for a couple of kilometres before fading into the narrow band of polder, dyke, salt marsh and mud flat that extends east across the Dutch border. Strange as it seems today, this undeveloped slice of coast was once one of the busiest waterways in the world, connecting Bruges with the North Sea until the River Zwin silted up in the sixteenth century. In 1340, it was also the site of one of the largest naval engagements of the century, when Edward III of England sailed up the estuary with his Flemish allies to destroy a French fleet gathered for a projected invasion of England. Nowadays, this tranquil area holds some unusual flora and fauna nourished by a combination of the river and occasional sea flooding. The best way to see it is by bike; Knokke train station rents bikes out for €8 per day. You'll also need a detailed map, available from the Knokke tourist office. Part of the area has been incorporated into the **Het Zwin Natuurreservat**, very popular with noisy school parties.

Practicalities

Knokke is well connected to Ostend by **tram** and to Bruges by **train** (every 30min; 15min). Knokke's tram terminus, train and bus stations are grouped together at the south end of the long and featureless main street, Lippenslaan, an inconvenient 2km south of the seafront. Knokke **tourist office** is on the seafront at Zeedijk 660 – just to the east of Van Bunenplein, at the end of Lippenslaan (daily: May–Sept 9am–12.30pm & 1.30–6pm; Oct–April Mon–Fri 9am–noon & 1.30–5.30pm, Sat & Sun 9am–12.30pm & 1.30–6pm; ℡050 63 03 80, ⓦwww.knokke-heist.be). They have a useful range of local leaflets and will phone around to make a booking in any local **hotel**. There are plenty to choose from, though only a handful of them are actually on the seafront. Easily the pick of these is *Des Nations*, Zeedijk Het Zoute 704 (☎050 61 99 11, ⓕ61 99 99; ❼), a swanky, modern high-rise five minutes' walk east of the tourist office. More affordable – if really rather routine – are the two medium-sized hotels of Lippenslaan: the *Prince's Hotel*, above the shops at no. 171 (☎050 60 11 11, ⓕ050 62 46 24; ❹), offering run-of-the mill but reasonably comfortable rooms, and the similar three-star *Prins Boudewijn*, at no. 35 (☎050 60 10 16, ⓕ050 62 35 46, ⓔinfo@prinsboudewijn.be; ❹), which provides a bit more space and comfort. The nearest listed **campsites**, *De Vuurtoren* (☎050 51 17 82, ⓔkampvuurtoren@attglobal.net; mid-March to mid-Oct) and *De Zilvermeeuw* (☎050 51 27 26, ⓦwww.camping-zilvermeeuw.com; March to early Nov), are at the west end of Knokke-Heist in Heist, at Heistlaan 168 and 166.

West from Ostend

West of Ostend, the tram skirts the sand dunes of a long and almost entirely undeveloped stretch of coast dotted with the occasional remains – gun emplacements, bunkers and so forth – left behind from the German occupation of World War II. Thereafter, the tram scoots into **Middelkerke**, the first of a sequence of undistinguished seaside resorts whose apartments and villas crimp the coast as far as **Westende-Bad** and **Lombardsijde-Bad**.

Nieuwpoort

After Lombardsijde-Bad, the tram line cuts inland to round the estuary of the River Ijzer (Yser) at the small town of **NIEUWPOORT** (tram stop Nieuwpoort Stad) – not to be confused with the unenticing high-rise development of Nieuwpoort-aan-Zee just up the road (and further along the tram line from Ostend). Nieuwpoort hasn't had much luck. Founded in the twelfth century, it was besieged nine times in the following six hundred years, but this was nothing compared to its misfortune in World War I. In 1914, the first German campaign reached the Ijzer, prompting the Belgians to open the sluices along the Noordvaart canal, just to the east of the town centre. The water stopped the invaders in their tracks and permanently separated the armies, but it also put Nieuwpoort on the front line, where it remained for the rest of the war. Every day volunteers had to abandon the safety of their bunkers to operate the ring of sluice gates, without which the water would either have drained away or risen to flood the Belgian trenches. Beside the bridge near the Nieuwpoort Stad tram stop, you can still see – and walk round – the ring of **sluice gates**, dotted with memorials to the hundreds who died. The largest monument consists of a sombre rotunda with King Albert I at the centre.

Four years of shelling reduced the town to a ruin, and what there is now is the result of a meticulous restoration that lasted well into the 1920s. A series of parallel sidestreets, flanked by neat brick terraces, lead south from the tram line to the **Marktplein**, the good-looking main square, which is overseen by a row of replica medieval buildings – the **Onze Lieve Vrouwekerk** church, the neo-Renaissance **Stadhuis** and the **Halle**. It's all very pleasant – in a low-key sort of way – and, if you decide to stay, the **tourist office**, in the Stadhuis at Marktplein 7 (Mon–Fri 8am–noon & 1.30–5.30pm; ☎058 22 44 44), has a small stock of inexpensive **B&Bs** (❷–❸). There's also one town-centre **hotel**, the three-star *Clarenhof*, a spick-and-span little place in a former convent just one block west of Marktplein at Hoogstraat 4 (☎058 22 48 00, ⓕ058 22 48 01, ⓦwww.restofun.com; ❹). The nearest **campsite**, *IC-Camping*, Brugsesteenweg 49 (☎058 23 60 37, ⓦwww.ic-camping.be; Easter to early Nov), is a sizeable, well-equipped affair beside the River Ijzer about 2km southeast of town.

For somewhere to **eat**, there are a couple of competent, reasonably priced café-restaurants on the Marktplein – the *Brasserie Nieuwpoort* is the best – but the *Mondial*, close to the Nieuwpoort Stad tram stop at Kaai 15 (closed Tues), offers more interesting food in relaxed, informal surroundings; the speciality here is seafood, especially mussels. Part of the catch from Nieuwpoort's own small fishing fleet is sold at Vishandel Tracy (℡058 23 82 60), one of the province's finest **fish shops**, just along from the tram stop at Kaai 23; people drive here from all over Flanders to either carry the fish off or eat it on the spot – the shop does an excellent line in seafood baguettes.

St Idesbald

Heading on from Nieuwpoort, trams scuttle back to the coast at **Nieuwpoort-aan-Zee** and then push on west through **Oostduinkerke-Bad**, which merges seamlessly into **Koksijde-Bad**. Next up is **ST IDES-BALD**, a modest, mostly modern seaside town and resort. It would be of no particular interest were it not for the artist Paul Delvaux (1897–1994), who stumbled across what was then an empty stretch of coast at the end of World War II and stayed here – despite the development that went on all around him – for the rest of his life. His old home and studio have been turned into the **Paul Delvaux Museum**, Delvauxlaan 42 (April–Sept Tues–Sun 10.30am–5.30pm; Oct–Dec Thurs–Sun 10.30am–5.30pm; €4.71; Ⓦwww.pauldelvaux.be), with the addition of a large subterranean extension – to avoid disfiguring the house above. The museum holds a comprehensive collection of Delvaux's work, following his development from early Expressionist days through to the Surrealism which defined his oeuvre from the 1930s. Two of his pet motifs are train stations, in one guise or another, and nude or semi-nude women set against some sort of classical backdrop. The intention is to usher the viewer into the unconscious with dream-like images where every perspective is exact, but, despite the impeccable craftsmanship, there's something very cold about his vision. At their best, his paintings achieve an almost palpable sense of foreboding, good examples being *The Garden* of 1971 and *The Procession* dated to 1963, while *The Station in the Forest* of 1960 has the most wonderful trees. A full catalogue of the collection is available at reception.

Finding the museum is a bit tricky. From the St Idesbald tram stop, walk back towards Ostend and turn right (away from the coast) down the resort's main street, Strandlaan. Keep going until you reach Delvauxlaan, a turning on the right; the walk takes fifteen to twenty minutes.

De Panne

Three kilometres or so further west, sitting close to the French frontier, **DE PANNE** is now one of the largest settlements on the Belgian coast, though as late as the 1880s it was a tiny fishing village of low white cottages, nestling in a slight wooded hollow (*panne*) from which it takes its name. Most of the villagers of the time had their own fishing boats and a plot of land surrounded by trees and hedges. The peace and quiet ended with the arrival of surveyors and architects, who reinforced the sea dyke and laid out paths and roads in preparation for the rapid construction of lines of villas and holiday homes. However, with the exception of the buildings on the seafront, the contours of the land were respected, and the houses of much of today's resort perch prettily among the dunes to the south of the beach.

The peripheries of De Panne may be appealing, but the town centre is unprepossessing, its humdrum modern buildings jostling a seafront that becomes decidedly overcrowded in the summer. That said, the beach is excellent and De

Panne comes equipped with all the amenities of a seaside resort, including land sailing. There's one specific sight too, the rather grand **monument** at the west end of Zeedijk, marking the spot where King Léopold I first set foot on Belgian soil in 1831. Otherwise, the town achieved ephemeral fame in World War I, when it was part of the tiny triangle of Belgian territory that the German army failed to occupy, becoming the home of King Albert's government from 1914 to 1918. A generation later, the retreating British army managed to reach the sand dunes between De Panne and Dunkirk, 15km to the west, just in time for their miraculous evacuation back to England. In eight days, an armada of vessels of all sizes and shapes rescued over 300,000 Allied soldiers, a deliverance that prompted Churchill to his most famous speech: ". . . we shall fight on the beaches . . . we shall fight in the fields and in the streets, we shall fight in the hills; we shall never surrender".

De Westhoek Staatsnatuurreservaat

On the western edge of De Panne, a small segment of these same sand dunes has been protected by the creation of **De Westhoek Staatsnatuurreservaat**, an open-access, three-square kilometre expanse of wild, unspoiled coastline, mainly consisting of dunes and dune valleys, crisscrossed by six marked footpaths. Rabbits thrive here and birdlife finds shelter in the patches of woodland and scrub, in particular, songbirds such as common stonechats, nightingales, willow warblers and turtledoves. Occasionally there are guided walks – ask at the tourist office for information. The main access point is about 2km west of the town centre: follow Duinkerkelaan, the main east–west street, to the traffic island, turn right down Dynastielaan and keep going as far as the T-junction at the end, where you make a left turn along Schuilhavenlaan. The walk is a bore, but the tram does go part of the way; even better, **bikes** can be rented at several central locations including Roger, Zeedijk 46 (☎058 41 21 46).

Practicalities

Trams travel the length of De Panne's main street, Nieuwpoortlaan/ Duinkerkelaan, which cuts through the centre of the resort running parallel to, and one block south of, the beach. The west end of Duinkerkelaan curves inland to terminate at the Dynastielaan traffic island. It is shadowed by the trams, which then proceed south to the **train station**. For the beach and the town centre, get off at De Panne Centrum tram stop, which is also close to the **tourist information kiosk** on Koning Albertplein (mid-June to mid-Sept daily 10am–noon & 2–6pm; ☎058 42 18 19). The **main tourist office** is in the Gemeentehuis (City Hall; July & Aug Mon–Sat 9am–noon & 1–6pm; Sept–June Mon–Fri 9am–noon & 1–5pm; ☎058 42 18 18, ⓦwww.depanne.be), a ten-minute walk south from the seafront at no. 21, Zeelaan, the principal north–south axis, which begins a few metres to the east of Koning Albertplein.

Both tourist offices have lists of **B&Bs** (❷–❹) and will phone around to find vacancies, providing they aren't too busy. Alternatively, about half of De Panne's thirty-odd **hotels** are clustered near where Zeelaan meets the main street. Options here include the *Terlinck*, Zeelaan 175 (☎058 42 01 08, ⓕ058 42 05 86; ❹), a pleasant three-star hotel right on the seafront, and the *Artevelde*, Sloepenlaan 24 (☎058 41 10 51, ⓕ058 42 14 44; ❸), an unassuming family two-star hotel in an attractive Art Deco building. Alternatively, there are several perfectly adequate hotels just to the west of the centre along Duinkerkelaan – and a (longish) stone's throw from the beach: try the three-star *Ambassador*, at no 43 (☎058 41 16 12, ⓕ058 42 18 84; ❸) or, even better, the comfortable four-star *Iris*, at no. 41 (☎058 41 51 41, ⓕ058 42 11 77; ❹), both brisk, modern medium-sized hotels.

There are literally dozens of places to **eat**; the best bet is to walk along the seashore promenade until you find somewhere that takes your fancy.

❷ Veurne and around

Rural Flanders at its prettiest, **VEURNE** is a charming market town, situated just 6km inland by road and rail from De Panne. Founded in the ninth century, it was originally one of a chain of fortresses built to defend the region from the raids of the Vikings, without much success. The town failed to flourish and two centuries later it was small, poor and insignificant. All that changed when Robert II of Flanders returned from the Crusades in 1099 with a piece of the True Cross. His ship was caught in a gale, and in desperation he vowed to offer the relic to the first church he saw if he survived. The church was St Walburga at Veurne, and the annual procession that commemorated the gift made the town an important centre of medieval pilgrimage for some three hundred years. These days Veurne is one of the more popular day-trip destinations in West Flanders, a neat and dreamy backwater whose one real attraction is its Grote Markt, one of the best-preserved town squares in Belgium.

The Town

All the main sights are on or around the **Grote Markt**, beginning in the northwest corner with the **Stadhuis**, an engaging mix of Gothic and Renaissance styles built between 1596 and 1612 and with a fine blue and gold decorated stone loggia projecting from the original brick facade. Inside, a **museum** (April–Sept 4 daily guided tours, Oct–March 2 daily except Sun; €2) displays items of unexceptional interest, the best of which is a set of leather

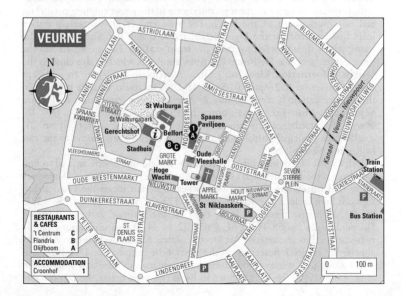

The Penitents' Procession

In 1650 a young soldier named Mannaert was on garrison duty in Veurne when he was persuaded by his best friend to commit a mortal sin. After receiving the conse-crated wafer during Communion, he took it out of his mouth, wrapped it in a cloth, and returned to his lodgings where he charred it over a fire, under the delusion that by reducing it to powder he would make himself invulnerable to injury. The news got out, and he was later arrested, tried and executed, his friend suffering the same fate a few weeks later. Fearful of the consequences of this sacrilege in their town, the people of Veurne resolved that something must be done, deciding on a procession to commemorate the Passion of Christ. This survives as the **Penitents' Procession** (Boetprocessie), held on the **last Sunday in July** – an odd and distinctly macabre reminder of a remote past. Trailing through the streets, the leading figures dress in the brown cowls of the Capuchins and carry wooden crosses that weigh anything up to 50kg.

wall coverings made in Cordoba. The Stadhuis connects with the more austere classicism of the **Gerechtshof** (Law Courts), whose symmetrical pillars and long, rectangular windows now hold the tourist office, but once sheltered the Inquisition as it set about the Flemish peasantry with gusto. The attached tiered and balconied **Belfort** (no public access) was completed in 1628, its Gothic lines culminating in a dainty Baroque tower, from where **carillon concerts** ring out over the town (Wed 10.30–11.30am, plus July & Aug Sun 8–9pm; for more on the instrument, see p.257). The Belfort is, however, dwarfed by the adjacent **St Walburga** (June–Sept daily 10am–noon & 3–6pm; free), the objec-tive of the medieval pilgrims, an enormous buttressed and gargoyled affair with weather-beaten brick walls dating from the thirteenth century. It's actually the second church to be built on the spot; the original version – which in turn replaced a pagan temple dedicated to Wotan – was razed by the Vikings. The hangar-like interior has one virtue, the lavishly carved Flemish Renaissance choir stalls.

Moving on to the northeast corner of the Grote Markt, the **Spaans Paviljoen** (Spanish Pavilion), at the end of Ooststraat, was built as the town hall in the middle of the fifteenth century, but takes its name from its later adaptation as the officers' quarters of the Habsburg garrison. It's a self-confi-dent building, the initial square brick tower, with its castellated parapet, extend-ed by a facade of long, slender windows and flowing stone tracery in the true Gothic manner – an obvious contrast to the Flemish shutters and gables of the **Oude Vleeshalle** (Old Meat Hall) standing directly opposite. Crossing over to the southeast side of the square, the **Hoge Wacht**, which originally served as the quarters of the town watch, displays a fetching amalgam of styles, its brick gable cheered up by a small arcaded gallery. The east side of this building edges the Appelmarkt, home to the clumping medieval mass of **St Niklaaskerk**, whose detached **tower** gives spectacular views over the surrounding country-side (mid-June to mid-Sept 10am–11.45 & 2–5.15pm; €1.50).

Practicalities

Hourly **trains** connect Veurne with the seaside resort of De Panne to the west, as well as with Diksmuide and Ghent to the east. Regular **buses** also link the town with Ieper, some 25km to the south; for bus timetable details, call the De Lijn bus company on ☎059 56 53 53. Veurne's **train and bus stations** are adja-cent to each other, a ten-minute stroll from the town centre. The **tourist office**, at Grote Markt 29 (April–Sept daily 10am–noon & 1.30–5.30pm; Oct to mid-Nov daily 10am–noon & 2–4pm; mid-Nov to March Mon–Sat 10am–noon & 2–4pm; ☎058 33 05 31; ⓦwww.veurne.be), issues a useful and free town brochure, which includes an events' calendar and accommodation listings.

Accommodation and eating

Accommodation in Veurne is thin on the ground, but the tourist office does have a small cache of **B&Bs** (❸), and there are two central **hotels**. Easily the better of the two is the three-star *Croonhof* (☎058 31 31 28, ⓕ058 31 56 81, ⓔcroonhof@online.be; ❺), a smart, well-cared-for little place in an attractively converted old house with spotless rooms, just off the Grote Markt at Noordstraat 9. It's a popular spot, so be sure to call ahead in summer to make certain of a bed.

The Grote Markt is lined with **cafés** and **bars**. One of the more popular places is *'t Centrum*, Grote Markt 33 (Sept–June closed Mon), which offers reasonably priced snacks and meals from a straightforward Flemish menu; pancakes are a house speciality. Another option is the comparable *Flandria*, a cosy spot next door to the tourist office at Grote Markt 30 (closed Thurs); snacks here average about €7 and are best washed down with the local Trappist ale, Westvleteren. The *Croonhof* has an excellent **restaurant** featuring Flemish regional cuisine (closed all day Mon & Sun eve, plus mid- to end Sept), main dishes hovering between €16–20. Next door, the *Olijfboom* (☎058 31 70 77; closed Mon & Sun) is similarly chic, a smart little restaurant which specializes in lobster.

Around Veurne: Beauvoorde, Lo and Diksmuide

Veurne is the capital of the **Veurne-Ambacht**, a pancake-flat agricultural region of quiet villages and narrow country lanes which stretches south of the town, encircled by the French border and the River Ijzer. Of all the villages, **Lo** is the prettiest – and a good base for further explorations – though there's also a sprinkling of World War I sights along the line of the River Ijzer, which formed the front line for most of the war; the most interesting of these are in the vicinity of the small town of **Diksmuide**.

The best way to see the district is by **bike** – cycles can be rented at Veurne train station and maps of cycle routes are available from Veurne tourist office. In addition, De Lijn operates a reasonably good **bus** service to most of the villages from Veurne (and Ieper); their information line is ☎059 56 53 53.

Beauvoorde

About 8km south of Veurne, the first obvious target is the demure early-seventeenth-century chateau of **Beauvoorde** (guided tours only: June & Sept Tues & Thurs 3pm, Sun 2.30pm & 4pm; July & Aug Tues–Thurs & Sat 3pm, Sun 2.30pm & 4pm; €3), whose angular crow-stepped gables and unadorned brick walls sit prettily behind a narrow moat amid the woods of a small park. The castle's interior has been remodelled on several occasions and now holds a mildly diverting collection of ceramics, silverware, paintings and glass. Another refurbishment is planned, so check times of tours at Veurne tourist office. Around the castle, the woods make for a pleasant stroll, after which you can pop across to the church and spend a few minutes exploring the trail of low stone cottages that make up the village of **Wulveringem** (Beauvoorde being the name of the castle and the district).

By car, the quickest way to get to the château from Veurne is to take the main Ieper road, the N8, for about 5km and then watch for the signed turning on the right, from where it's a further 2km.

Lo

The agreeable little hamlet of **LO**, off the N8 some 15km southeast of Veurne, has one claim to fame. It was here that Julius Caesar tethered his horse to a yew on his way across Gaul, an event recalled by a plaque and a battered old tree by what is now the **Westpoort**, whose twin turrets and gateway are all that remain of the medieval ramparts. Less apocryphally, the village once prospered under the patronage of its Augustinian abbey, founded in the twelfth century and suppressed by the French at the time of the Revolution. Of the abbey, only the **dovecote** survives, hidden away beside the *Hotel Oude Abidj*, which is itself tucked in behind the present **church**, a sterling edifice graced by a soaring crocketed spire. Lo's old stone houses fan out from the church and the adjacent main square – nothing remarkable, but it's the peace and quiet that appeals most.

The best way to reach Lo is by bike from Veurne along byroads and country lanes, but the village is also on the Veurne–Ieper **bus** route (Mon–Fri 5 daily, Sat 4 daily, Sun 2 daily; 30min). On the main square, Lo has its own seasonal **tourist office** (T058 28 91 66), useful for local maps and cycle routes, and details of a couple of local **B&Bs** (❹). There are two central **hotels**, the more expensive of which, the *Oude Abdij*, Noordstraat 3 (T058 28 82 65, F058 28 94 07; ❹), is a somewhat glum, three-star affair with a garden and modern rooms. The rival two-star *Stadhuis*, Markt 1 (T058 28 80 16, F058 28 89 05; ❸), is more engaging, with five clean, simple, en-suite rooms. It occupies part of the old Stadhuis, a much-modified sixteenth-century structure made appealing by a slender, arcaded tower. The ground floor **restaurant-bar** serves up standard Flemish food.

Diksmuide

The western approaches to **DIKSMUIDE**, 11km northeast of Lo and 15km southeast of Veurne, are dominated by the Ijzertoren, a massive war memorial bearing the letters AVV-VVK – Alles voor Vlaanderen ("All for Flanders") and Vlaanderen voor Kristus ("Flanders for Christ"). At 84m high, this domineering tower recalls the sufferings of Diksmuide during World War I when it was so extensively shelled that, by 1918, its location could only be identified from a map. The obliteration was a consequence of its position immediately east of the River Ijzer, which formed the front line from October 1914.

The careful reconstruction of the town works best round the **Grote Markt**, a pleasant, spacious square flanked by brick gables in the traditional Flemish style. There's nothing spectacular to see, but it's an enjoyable spot to nurse a coffee, and you could drop by the enormous church of **St Niklaaskerk**, built to the original Gothic design, complete with a splendid spire. Otherwise, for a fine view across the plain of Flanders, it's a fifteen-minute walk from the Grote Markt along Reuzemolenstraat and then Ijzerlaan to the looming **Ijzertoren** (daily: mid-Jan to March & Oct–Dec 10am–5pm, April–Sept until 6pm; €6). The present structure, a broody affair, dates from the 1950s – the original tower, built in 1930, was blown up in mysterious circumstances in 1946, probably by Fascist sympathizers – and now holds an international peace museum chronicling the gruesome events of World War I. There's another reminder of the war about 2km to the north along the west bank of the Ijzer in the **Dodengang** (April–Sept daily 9am–noon & 1.30–5pm; €1.50), an especially dangerous slice of trench which was held by the Belgians throughout the war.

Around 300m of trench are viewable, but the preservation has been heavy-handed: twisting lines of concrete "sand bags" – and that's pretty much all there is – convey little, and the orientation table-cum-viewpoint needs an overhaul.

Practicalities

Diksmuide is easy to reach by **bus** from Lo and Ieper, and by **train** from Veurne and Ghent. From the town's bus and train stations, it's a five- to ten-minute walk west along Stationsstraat to the Grote Markt. The **tourist office**, on Beerstblotestraat (mid-Jan to March, Oct & Nov Tues–Fri 10am–5pm, Sat & Sun 10am–6pm; April–Sept Mon–Fri 10am–6pm, Sat & Sun 10am–5pm; ☏051 51 94 19), is located another ten-minute walk to the west in Westoria, in old flour mills that have been converted into a visitor centre, with interactive shenanigans about the life of a grain of corn. Diksmuide has two comfortable **hotels** among the Flemish-style buildings on the Grote Markt – the two-star *Polderbloem*, at no. 8 (☏051 50 29 05, ℱ051 50 29 06, ⓦwww.polderbloem.be; ❸), and the larger, slightly more expensive three-star *De Vrede*, at no. 35 (☏051 50 00 38, ℱ051 51 06 21; ❸).

Ieper

At heart, **IEPER**, about 30km south of Veurne, is a pleasant, middling sort of place, a typical Flemish small town with a bright and breezy main square, which is overlooked by the haughty reminders of its medieval heyday as a centre of the cloth trade. Initial appearances are, however, deceptive, for all the old buildings of the town centre were built from scratch after World War I, when Ieper – or **Ypres** as it was then known – was literally shelled to smithereens.

Ieper's long and troubled history dates back to the tenth century, when it was founded at the point where the Bruges–Paris trade route crossed the River Ieperlee. Success came quickly and the town became a major player in the cloth trade, its thirteenth-century population of two hundred thousand sharing economic control of the region with rivals Ghent and Bruges. The most precariously sited of the great Flemish cities, Ypres was too near the French frontier for comfort, and too strategically important to be ignored by any of the armies whose campaigns crisscrossed the town's surroundings with depressing frequency. The city governors kept disaster at bay by reinforcing their defences and switching alliances whenever necessary, fighting against the French at the Battle of the Golden Spurs in 1302 (see p.158), and with them forty years later at Roosebeke. The first major misjudgement came in 1383 when Henry Spencer, bishop of Norwich, landed at Calais under the pretext of supporting the armies of Pope Urban VI, who occupied the Vatican, against his rival Clement VII, who was installed in Avignon. The burghers of Ghent and Bruges flocked to Spencer's standard, and the allies had little difficulty in agreeing on an attack against Ypres, which had decided to champion Clement and trust the French for support. The ensuing siege lasted two months before a French army appeared to save the day, and all of Ypres celebrated the victory. In fact, the town was ruined, its trade never recovered and, unable to challenge its two main competitors again, many of the weavers migrated. The process of depopulation proved irreversible, and by the sixteenth century the town had shrunk to a mere five thousand inhabitants.

In **World War I**, the first German thrust of 1914 left a bulge in the Allied line to the immediate east of Ypres. This **Salient** (see p.154) preoccupied the generals of both sides; during the next four years a series of futile offensives attempted to use it to break through the enemy's front line, with disastrous consequences for Ypres, which served as the Allied communications centre. Comfortably within the range of German artillery, Ypres was soon reduced to rubble and its inhabitants had to be evacuated in 1915. After the war, the returning population determined to rebuild their town, a twenty-year project in which the most prominent medieval buildings – the Lakenhalle and cathedral – were meticulously reconstructed. The end result must once have seemed strangely antiseptic – old-style edifices with no signs of decay or erosion – but now, after seventy-odd years, the brickwork has mellowed and the centre looks authentically antique. Nonetheless, the main reason to visit is the mementos of World War I that speckle both the town and its environs.

Arrival, information and accommodation

Ieper is readily accessible by train from Kortrijk, and by bus from Veurne and Diksmuide. The town's **train** and **bus stations** stand on the western edge of the centre, a ten-minute walk from the Grote Markt, straight down Gustave de Stuersstraat. The **tourist office**, in the Lakenhalle on the Grote Markt

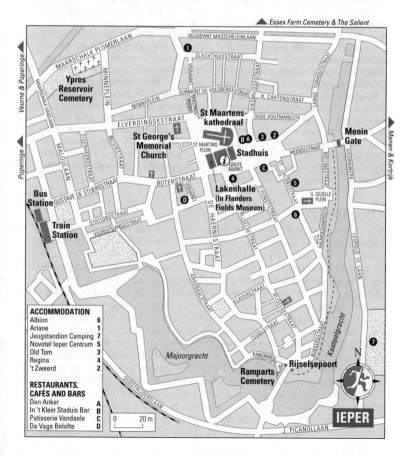

(April–Sept Mon–Sat 9am–6pm, Sun 10am–6pm; Oct–March until 5pm; ☎057 22 85 84, ⓦwww.ieper.be), has good town maps, details of suggested car and cycle routes around the Salient and a reasonable range of books on World War I. Bike rental is available at the train station at standard rates.

Accommodation

Ieper tourist office has the details of around a dozen **B&Bs** (❸), though most are inconveniently situated on the periphery of town. In addition, there are half a dozen **hotels**, reviewed below; they're located on or very near the Grote Markt, and are generally quite reasonably priced. There's also a small and central municipal **campsite**, *Jeugstadion Camping*, at Léopold III-laan 16 just east of the old moat (☎057 21 72 82, ⓕ057 21 61 21; mid-March to Oct); with just eleven pitches, plus hook-ups, toilets and showers; it's fifteen minutes' walk from the train station.

Albion Hotel Sint Jacobsstraat 28 ☎057 20 02 20, ⓕ057 20 02 15, ⓦwww.albionhotel.be. A brief stroll from the Grote Markt. New and appealing three-star hotel with eighteen en-suite rooms decorated in crisp modern style, and excellent breakfasts. A good choice. ❺

Ariane Slachthuisstraat 58 ☎057 21 82 18, ⓕ057 21 87 99, ⓦwww.ariane.be. A prim and proper garden surrounds this ultra-modern four-star hotel, a 5min walk north of the Grote Markt along Boezingepoort. Presumably it was built with the passing business trade in mind, but somehow it doesn't quite work – it looks marooned rather than secluded. Nevertheless, the fifty en-suite rooms are very comfortable. ❻

Novotel Ieper Centrum Sint Jacobsstraat 79 ☎057 42 96 00, ⓕ057 42 96 01. Lovers of chain hotels will be pleased to find this here in Ieper. The building is a bit of a modern bruiser, but the 120 rooms are all comfortably modern in true

Novotel style, and there are fitness facilities and a sauna. ❻

Old Tom Grote Markt 8 ☎057 20 15 41, ⓕ057 21 91 20, ⓦwww.oldtom.be. Nine plain but pleasant en-suite rooms above a café-bar bang in the centre of town. Much favoured by English visitors. One star. ❸

Regina Grote Markt 45 ☎057 21 88 88, ⓕ057 21 90 20, ⓦwww.hotelregina.be. This four-star establishment, housed in a 1920s copy of a grand turn-of-the-century edifice, is the most expensive hotel on the Grote Markt. Perfectly adequate, though the bland, modern rooms aren't worth the extra; it often has vacancies when its competitors are full. ❹

't Zweerd Grote Markt 2 ☎057 20 04 75, ⓕ057 21 78 96, ⓦwww.tzweerd.be. Seventeen mundanely modern, en-suite rooms are on offer in this three-star affair, located above a café-bar. A little more expensive and a little less cheery than the rival *Old Tom*. ❹

The Town

A monument to the power and wealth of the medieval guilds, the replica **Lakenhalle**, on the Grote Markt, is a copy of the thirteenth-century original that stood beside the River Ieperlee, which now flows underground. Too long to be pretty and too square to be elegant, it is nonetheless an impressive edifice, one that was built with practical considerations uppermost: no fewer than 48 doors once gave access from the street to the old selling halls, while boats sailed in and out of the jetty on the west wing, under the watchful eyes of the mighty, turreted belfry. During winter, wool was stored on the upper floor and cats were brought in to keep the mice down. The cats may have had a good time in winter, but they couldn't have relished the prospect of spring when they were thrown out of the windows to a hostile crowd below as part of the **Kattestoet** or Cats' Festival, the slaughter intended to symbolize the killing of evil spirits. The festival ran right up until 1817, and was revived in 1938, when the cats were replaced by cloth imitations. Since then it's developed into Ieper's principal shindig, held every three years on the second Sunday in May – the next one is in 2003. The main event is the parade of cats, a large-scale celebration of all things feline, complete with processions, dancers and bands, and some of the biggest models and puppets imaginable.

The interior of the Lakenhalle holds the ambitious **In Flanders Fields Museum** (late Jan to March & Oct–Dec Tues–Sun 10am–5pm; April–Sept daily 10am–6pm; €7.50), which focuses on the experiences of those caught up in the war rather than the ebb and flow of the military campaigns. In part this is very successful – the section simulating a gas attack is most effective – but the interactive clutter (touch screens and the like) tends to get in the way, and there's not nearly enough about individuals – lots of personal artefacts but precious little about the men and women who owned them. That said, the museum is wide-ranging and thoughtful, and the (multilingual) quotations are well chosen. The photographs are particularly powerful – soldiers grimly digging trenches, the pathetic casualties of a gas attack, flyblown corpses in the mud and panoramas of a blasted landscape.

Back outside, the east end of the Lakenhalle is attached to the **Stadhuis**, whose fancy Renaissance facade rises above an elegant arcaded gallery; round the back is **St Maartenskathedraal**, built in 1930 as a copy of the thirteenth-century Gothic original. The church's cavernous nave is a formal, rather bland affair, but the rose window above the south transept door is a fine tribute to King Albert I, its yellow, green, red and blue stained glass the gift of the British armed forces. Just to the northwest, near the end of Elverdingestraat, stands **St George's Memorial Church** (daily 9.30am–4pm, often longer; free), a modest brick building finished in 1929. The interior is crowded with brass plaques honouring the dead of many British regiments, and the chairs carry individual and regimental tributes. It's hard not to be moved, for there's nothing vainglorious in this public space, so consumed as it is with private grief. From here, it's a brief walk north up the Minneplein to one of two British Commonwealth graveyards in the town centre, the **Ypres Reservoir Cemetery**.

Heading back towards the Grote Markt via Boterstraat, take a look at the fancy Baroque portal heralding the **Vismarkt** (Fish Market), another 1920s reconstruction, complete with a dinky little toll house and canopied stone stalls.

The Menin Gate and the Ramparts Cemetery

Beyond the east side of the Grote Markt, the **Menin Gate** war memorial was built on the site of the old Menenpoort, which served as the main route for British soldiers heading for the front. It's a simple, brooding monument, towering over the edge of the town, its walls covered with the names of those fifty thousand British and Commonwealth troops who died in the Ypres Salient but have no grave. The simple inscription above the lists of the dead has none of the arrogance of the victor but rather a sense of great loss. The self-justifying formality of the memorial did, however, offend many veterans and prompted a bitter verse from Siegfried Sassoon:

Was ever an immolation so belied
As these intolerably nameless names?
Well might the Dead who struggled in slime
Rise and deride this sepulchre of crime.

The **Last Post** is sounded beneath the gate every evening at 8pm. Oddly enough, the seventeenth-century brick and earthen **ramparts** on either side of the Menin Gate were well enough constructed to survive World War I intact – the vaults even served as some of the safest bunkers on the front. These massive ramparts and their protective moat still extend right round the east and south of the town centre, and there's a pleasant footpath along the top. The stroll takes you past the **Ramparts Cemetery**, a British Commonwealth War

Cemetery beside the old Lille Gate – the present Rijselsepoort – from where it takes about ten minutes to get back to the Grote Markt.

Eating and drinking

With one or two exceptions, Ieper's **cafés** and **restaurants**, most of which are dotted round the Grote Markt, aren't a particularly distinguished bunch, but the meals on offer are usually substantial and reasonably priced. Almost all of Ieper's **bars** are on the main square too, and though the action could hardly be described as frenetic, there's enough to keep most visitors happy.

Den Anker Grote Markt 29. Competent restaurant that's strong on mussels, cooked in all sorts of ways, and seafood. Main courses from around €15, though the full set menu will set you back much more.

In 't Klein Stadhuis Bar Adjacent to the Stadhuis on the Grote Markt. The nearest thing Ieper has to a hot spot, this lively bar stays open till late.

Old Tom Grote Markt 8. Straightforward restaurant offering good-quality Flemish cuisine at affordable price – eel €18, omelettes from €5 – and a promising selection of Belgian beers to wash it down.

Patisserie Vandaele Grote Markt 9. With its Art Nouveau flourishes, this is perhaps the most appealing of the cafés on the main square. The patisserie is at the front, the café at the back.

De Vage Belofte Vismarkt 3. Amenable, laid-back bar in pleasant surroundings, with a good range of brews.

Around Ieper: Poperinge

Some 12km west of Ieper, at the centre of a hop-growing area, **POPERINGE** was a posting station for soldiers heading in and out of the Ypres Salient. It was here that the Reverend Philip Clayton opened the Everyman's Club at Talbot House, Gasthuisstraat 43, where everyone, regardless of rank, was able to come and rest or seek spiritual help. Clayton went on to found **Toc H**, the worldwide Christian fellowship that took its name from the army signallers' code for Talbot House – after Gilbert Talbot, the son of the Bishop of Winchester, who was killed in battle in the Salient in 1915. The original building – though little remains to remind you of its history – is still run as a charity, is open for visitors (daily 10am–noon & 2–5pm; €3) and offers simple hostel-style **accommodation** (℡057 33 32 28, ℻057 33 21 83, ✉talbot.house@skynet.be; dorm beds €18, ❷).

The Ypres Salient

The **Ypres Salient** occupies a basin-shaped parcel of land about 25km long, and never more than 15km deep immediately to the east of Ieper. For the generals of World War I, the area's key feature was the long and low sequence of ridges which sweep south from the hamlet of Langemark to the French border. These gave the occupants a clear view of Ieper and its surroundings, and consequently the British and Germans spent the war trying to capture and keep them. The dips and sloping ridges that were then so vitally important are still much in evidence, but today the tranquillity of the landscape makes it difficult to imagine what the war was actually like.

In fact it's surprisingly difficult to find anything which gives any real impression of the scale and nature of the conflict. The most resonant reminders of the blood-letting are the 160 or so **British Commonwealth War Cemeteries**, immaculately maintained by the Commonwealth War Graves Commission. Each cemetery has a **Cross of Sacrifice** in white Portland stone, and the larger ones also have a sarcophagus-like **Stone of Remembrance** bearing the legend "Their Name Liveth For Ever More", a quotation selected by Rudyard Kipling from Ecclesiasticus. The graves line up at precisely spaced intervals and, wherever possible, headstones bears the individual's name, rank, serial number, age, date of death, and the badge of the military unit, or a national emblem, plus an appropriate religious symbol and, at the base, an inscription chosen by relatives. Thousands of gravestones do not, however, carry any or all of these tags as the bodies were buried without ever being properly identified.

To navigate round the scores of sites and to understand the various battles in detail, you'll need *Major & Mrs Holt's Field Guide to the Ypres Salient*, which describes several manageable itineraries and comes complete with a map; it's on sale at Ieper tourist office. Alternatively, the tourist office produces several brochures describing other possible routes, the pick of which is the eighty-kilometre-long *In Flanders Fields Route*, though you do have to be very interested to find this enjoyable. Locally, **guided tours** from Ypres are provided by **Flanders Battlefield Tours** (advance reservations required; ☎057 36 04 60, ⊛www.ypres-fbt.be), who offer both a four-hour Grand Tour (all year; €22) and a two-and-a-half hour Standard Tour (mid-March to mid-Nov; €16). In addition, **Quasimodo** operates excellent all-inclusive battlefield tours from Bruges (see box on p.168).

A tour of the Salient

A detailed exploration of the **Salient** could take weeks; below we've outlined an abbreviated itinerary that can be completed comfortably **by car** in half a day. Beginning and ending in Ieper, the route focuses on the Salient's central – and most revealing – section.

Ieper's one-way system initially makes things confusing, but leave the town to the north along the **N369**, the road to Diksmuide. After about 3km, just beyond the flyover, watch for **Essex Farm Cemetery** on the right, where the

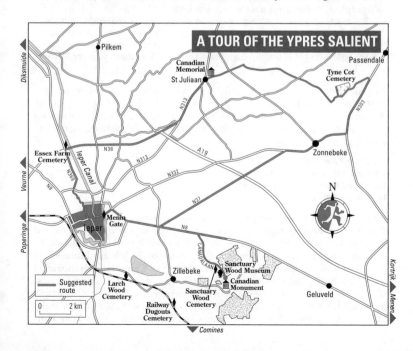

The Ypres Salient

The creation of the Ypres Salient was entirely **accidental**. When the German army launched the war in the west by invading Belgium, they were following the principles – if not the details – laid down by a chief of the German General Staff, Alfred von Schlieffen, who had died eight years earlier. The idea was simple: to avoid fighting a war on two fronts, the German army would outflank the French and capture Paris by attacking through Belgium, well before the Russians had assembled on the eastern frontier. It didn't work, with the result that as the initial German offensive ground to a halt, so two lines of opposing **trenches** were dug, which soon stretched from the North Sea down to Switzerland.

No one knew quite what to do next, but attention focused on the two main bulges – or **salients** – in the line, one at Ieper, the other at Verdun, on the Franco–German frontier just to the south of Luxembourg. To the Allied generals, the bulge at Ieper – the Ypres Salient – was a good place to break through the German lines and roll up their front; to the Germans it represented an ideal opportunity to break the deadlock by attacking key enemy positions from several sides at the same time. Contemporary **military doctrine** on both sides held that the way to win a war was to destroy the enemy's strongest forces first. In retrospect this may seem strange, but the generals of the day were schooled in cavalry tactics, where a charge that broke the enemy's key formations was guaranteed to spread disorder and confusion among the rest, paving the way for victory. The consequence of this tactical similitude was that the salients attracted armies like magnets. However, technological changes had shifted the balance of war in favour of defence: machine guns had become more efficient, barbed wire more effective, and, most important of all, the railways could shift defensive reserves far faster than an advancing army could march. Another issue was **supply**. Great efforts had been made to raise vast armies but they couldn't be fed off the land, and once they advanced much beyond the reach of the railways, the supply problems were enormous. As the historian A.J.P. Taylor put it, "Defence was mechanized; attack was not."

Seemingly incapable of rethinking their strategy, the generals had no answer to the stalemate save for an amazing profligacy with people's lives. Their tactical innovations were limited, and two of the new techniques – gas attack and a heavy preliminary bombardment – actually made matters worse. The **shells** forewarned the

wounded and dead from the battlefield across the adjacent canal were brought. In the bank behind (and to the left of) the cemetery's Cross of Sacrifice are the remains of several British bunkers, part of a combined forward position and first-aid post where the Canadian John McCrae wrote arguably the war's best-known poem, *In Flanders Fields*:

. . . We are the Dead. Short days ago
We lived, felt dawn, saw sunsets glow,
Loved and were loved, and now we lie
In Flanders fields . . .

Retracing your route briefly back along the N369 from Essex Farm, take the **N38** east by turning right onto the flyover from its southern side (signed Brugge). The N38 leads straight – and under a major road – into the **N313** and, after 6.5km, you pass through the village of St Juliaan. Immediately beyond the village is Vancouver Corner, where the **Canadian Memorial**, a ten-metre-high granite statue topped by the bust of a Canadian soldier, was raised in honour of those who endured the first German chlorine gas attacks in April 1915. On this side of the memorial, turn right and then first left at the little roadside shrine to follow the country lane leading 4km east to **Tyne Cot**.

enemy of an offensive and churned the trenches into a muddy maelstrom where men, horses and machinery were simply engulfed; the **gas** was as dangerous to the advancing soldiers as it was to the retreating enemy. **Tanks** could have broken the impasse, but their development was never prioritized.

Naturally enough, soldiers of all armies involved lost confidence in their generals, and by 1917, despite court martials and firing squads, the sheer futility of the endless round of failed offensives made **desertion** commonplace and threatened to bring mass mutiny to the western front. However, although it is undeniably true that few of the military commanders of the day showed much understanding of how to break the **deadlock** – and they have been savagely criticized for their failures – some of the blame must be apportioned to the politicians. They demanded assault rather than defence, and continued to call for a general "victory" even after it had become obvious that this was beyond reach and that each attack cost thousands of lives. Every government concerned had believed that a clear victor would emerge by Christmas 1914, and none of them was able to adjust to the **military impasse**. There were no moves toward a negotiated settlement, because no one was quite sure what they would settle for – a lack of clarity that contrasted starkly with the jingoistic sentiments stirred up to help sustain the conflict, which demanded victory or at least military success. In this context, how could a general recommend a defensive strategy or a politician propose a compromise? Those who did were dismissed.

This was the background to the four years of war that raged in and around the Ypres Salient, the scene of **four major battles**. The first, in October and November of 1914, settled the lines of the bulge as both armies tried to outflank each other; the second was a German attack the following spring, that moved the trenches a couple of kilometres west. The third, launched by British Empire soldiers in July 1917, was even more pointless, with thousands of men dying for an advance of only a few kilometres. It's frequently called the Battle of Passchendaele, but Lloyd George more accurately referred to it as the "battle of the mud", a disaster that cost 250,000 British lives. The fourth and final battle, in April 1918, was another German attack inspired by General Ludendorff's desire to break the British army. Instead it broke his own, and led to the **Armistice** of November 11.

This is the largest British Commonwealth war cemetery in the world, containing 11,956 graves and the Memorial to the Missing, a semicircular wall inscribed with the names of a further 35,000 men whose bodies were never recovered. The soldiers of a Northumbrian division gave the place its name, wryly observing, as they tried to fight their way up the ridge, that the German blockhouses on the horizon looked like Tyneside cottages.

The largest of these concrete bunkers was, at the suggestion of George V, incorporated within the mound beneath the Cross of Sacrifice; you can still see a piece of it where a slab of stone has been deliberately omitted. The scattered graves behind the cross were dug during the final weeks of the war and have remained in their original positions, adding a further poignancy to the seemingly endless lines of tombstones below. Strangely, the Memorial to the Missing at the back of the cemetery wasn't part of the original design: the intention was that these names be recorded on the Menin Gate, but there was not enough room.

Tyne Cot cemetery overlooks the shallow valley which gently climbs up to Passendale, known then as **Passchendaele**. This village was the British objective in the Third Battle of Ypres, but torrential rain and intensive shelling turned the valley into a giant quagmire. Men, horses and guns simply sank into the mud and disappeared without trace. The whole affair came to symbolize the futility of the war and the incompetence of its generals: when Field Marshall Haig's Chief of Staff ventured out of his HQ to inspect progress, he allegedly said, "Good God, did we really send men to fight in that?"

Follow the road round the back of Tyne Cot to the right and after about 600m you reach a wider road – the **N303** – which runs along the top of the Passendale ridge. Turn right onto it and shortly afterwards, after 800m, turn right again, down the N332 into **Zonnebeke**. At the far end of the village, fork left onto the **N37**, keep straight over the motorway and you'll soon reach the **N8**, the Ieper–Menen road, which cuts across the back of the Salient – crowded with marching armies at night and peppered by German shrapnel during the day. Go round the island onto the N8 heading east (in the direction of Menen), and after 1.2km turn right up Canadalaan for the 1.3-kilometre trip to **Sanctuary Wood Cemetery**, where Gilbert Talbot, who gave his name to Talbot House in Poperinge (see p.52), lies buried.

Just beyond, the **Sanctuary Wood Museum** holds a ragbag of shells, rifles, bayonets, billycans, and incidental artefacts (daily 9.30am–7pm or dusk; €4). Outside, things have been left much as they were the day the war ended, with some primitive zigzags of sand-bagged trench, shell craters and a few shattered trees that convey something of the desolateness of it all. The woods and the adjacent Hill 62 saw ferocious fighting, and there's a modest **Canadian monument** on the brow of the hill 300m up the road from the museum. From here, you can see Ieper, 5km away, across the rolling ridges of the countryside. The N8 leads back to the Menin Gate.

Comines and Menen

From Ieper, hourly trains to Comines slip south past a pair of spruce **war cemeteries** – Railway Dugouts and Larch Wood – just outside the village of **Zillebeke**, scene of some of the bloodiest fighting of World War I. Further along the tracks, the border town of **Comines** is French-speaking, a linguistic outpost in Flemish-speaking Flanders that has prompted a very Belgian administrative fudge – Comines is part of the province of Hainaut, even though it is separated from the rest of it by a chunk of France. From Comines, trains travel on to **Menen**, the terminus of the infamous "Menin" road from Ypres, on which Allied troops were cruelly exposed to German guns positioned on the higher ground to the east.

Kortrijk

Just 10km from both Menen and the French border, **KORTRIJK** (Courtrai in French) is the largest town and main rail junction in this part of West Flanders, tracing its origins to a Roman settlement named Cortracum. In the Middle Ages, its fortunes paralleled those of Ypres, but although it became an important centre of the cloth trade, it was far too near France for comfort; time and again Kortrijk was embroiled in the wars that swept across Flanders, right up to the two German occupations of the last century.

Kortrijk is quite different from its Flemish neighbours: it's very much a Francophile town, with a lively café scene and several ritzy hotels, which – together with its smattering of medieval buildings – makes for an enjoyable overnight stay.

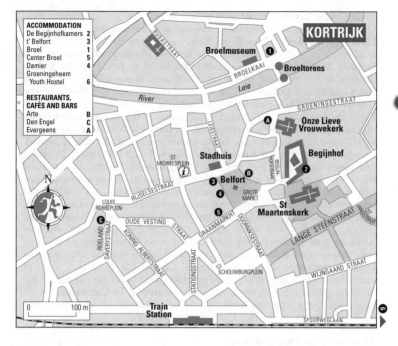

The Town

Heavily bombed during World War II, the **Grote Markt**, at the centre of Kortrijk, is a comely but architecturally incoherent mixture of bits of the old and a lot of the new, surrounding the forlorn, turreted **Belfort** – all that remains of the medieval cloth hall. The rather grand **war memorial** at its base is still tended with much care and attention. At the northwest corner of the Grote Markt, the **Stadhuis** (Mon–Fri 9am–noon & 2–5pm; free) is a sedate edifice with modern statues of the counts of Flanders on the facade, above and beside two lines of ugly windows. Inside, there are two fine sixteenth-century chimneypieces: one in the old Schepenzaal (Aldermen's Room) on the ground floor, a proud, intricate work decorated with municipal coats of arms and carvings of the Archdukes Albert and Isabella of Spain; the other, upstairs in the Raadzaal (Council Chamber), a more didactic affair, ornamented by three rows of precise statuettes, representing, from top to bottom, the virtues, the vices (to either side of the Emperor Charles V), and the torments of hell.

Opposite, off the southeast corner of the Grote Markt, the heavyweight tower of **St Maartenskerk** dates from the fifteenth century (Mon–Fri 8am–12.30pm & 2.30–5pm, Sat & Sun 10am–1pm & usually 5.30–7pm; free), its gleaming white-stone exterior recently cleaned of decades of grime. You can pop inside the church for a look at the gilded stone tabernacle (near the high altar), whose cluster of slender columns shelters a series of figurines, including a grumpy-looking Jesus with his cross, the work of Hendrik Maes in 1585. Immediately to the north, the **Begijnhof**, founded in 1238 by a certain Joanna of Constantinople, preserves the cosy informality of its seventeenth-century houses, and a small **museum** sheds a little light on the simple life of the Beguines (daily except Tues 2–5pm; €1).

The Onze Lieve Vrouwekerk

On the north side of the Begijnhof, pushing into Groeningestraat, is the **Onze Lieve Vrouwekerk** (Church of Our Lady; Mon–Fri 8.30am–noon & 2–6.30pm, Sat till 4pm, & Sun 9am–noon; free), a hulking grey structure that formerly doubled as part of the city's fortifications. In July 1302, the nave of the church was crammed with hundreds of spurs, ripped off the feet of dead and dying French knights at what has become known as the **Battle of the Golden Spurs**. These plundered spurs were the pathetic remains of the army Philip the Fair had sent to avenge the slaughter of the Bruges Matins earlier that year (see p.165). The two armies, Philip's heavily armoured cavalry and the lightly armed Flemish weavers, had met outside Kortrijk on marshy ground, strategic parts of which the Flemish had disguised with brushwood. Despising their lowly-born adversaries, the French knights made no reconnaissance and fell into the trap, milling around in the mud like cumbersome dinosaurs. They were massacred, marking the first time an amateur civilian army had defeated professional mail-clad knights. The spurs disappeared long ago and today much of the inside of the church is in a predictable Baroque style. However, the gloomy and truncated north transept does hold one splendid painting, **Anthony van Dyck**'s *Raising of the Cross*, a muscular, sweeping work with a pale, almost vague-looking Christ, completed just before the artist went to England. Across the church, the **Counts' Chapel** has an unusual series of somewhat crude, nineteenth-century portraits painted into the wall niches, but the highlight is a sensuous medieval alabaster **statue of St Catherine**, her left hand clutching a representation of the spiked wheel on which her enemies tried to break her (hence the "Catherine wheel" firework).

The rest of the centre

From opposite the Onze Lieve Vrouwekerk, an alley cuts through to the River Leie, where the squat and sturdy twin towers, the **Broeltorens**, are all that remain of the old town walls. On the far side of the bridge, the **Broelmuseum**, Broelkaai 6 (Tues–Sun 10am–noon & 2–5pm; free), houses a fine sample of Flemish tiles and porcelainware, an interesting collection of locally made damask, and several paintings by the sixteenth-century Flemish artist **Roelandt Savery** (1576–1639). Trained in Amsterdam, Savery worked for the Habsburgs in Prague and Vienna before returning to the Netherlands. To suit the tastes of his German patrons, he infused many of his landscapes with the romantic classicism that they preferred – the Garden of Eden and Orpheus were two favourite subjects – but the finely observed detail of his paintings was always in the true Flemish tradition. Among the works on display is the striking *Plundering of a Village*, where there's a palpable sense of outrage, in contrast to *The Drinking-Place*, depicting a romanticized, arboreal idyll.

Practicalities

The town's **train station** is a five-minute walk from the Grote Markt. The **tourist office** is a short walk west of the Grote Markt along Rijselsestraat at St Michielsplein 5 (mid-April to mid-Oct Mon–Fri 8.30am–5pm, Sat 10am–4pm; July & Aug also Sun 10am–4pm; mid-Oct to mid-April Mon–Fri 8.30am–5pm; ☎056 23 93 71). They issue free town brochures and will make room reservations on your behalf at no extra charge from a healthy supply of local accommodation, which includes a handful of inexpensive **B&Bs** (❸–❹) and a couple of especially enticing **hotels**. There's also a medium-sized HI **hostel**, *Groeningeheem*, Passionistenlaan 1a (☎056 20 14 42, ℻056 20 46 63; dorm beds €17.5, ❷), with 25 single or double rooms, plus a bar and café, serving snacks and meals. It's located on the edge of the town, an inconvenient twenty-minute walk east of the station.

Hotels and B&Bs

De Begijnhofkamers Begijnhof 23 ☎056 22 83 74, ℗056 52 02 66, ✉a.vanhauwere@belga-com.net. This tempting B&B occupies one of the old whitewashed cottages in the middle of the Begijnhof – a charming setting if ever there was one. Offers two neat and trim en-suite guest rooms. ❹

Hotel 't Belfort Grote Markt 53 ☎056 22 22 20, ℗056 20 13 06, ✉hotel.belfort@ping.be. A smart and comfortable, medium-sized modern hotel across the street from the Stadhuis. Three-star; thirty rooms. ❺

Hotel Broel Broelkaai 8, on the north bank of the River Leie ☎056 21 83 51, ℗056 20 03 02, ⓦwww.hotelbroel.be. The plain exterior is decep-tive, for the inside of the building, which was once a tobacco factory, has a mock-monastic theme, its tunnels and stone-trimmed arches entirely bogus but great fun. Each of the seventy en-suite rooms is spacious and relaxing, and decorated in tasteful modern style. Four-star. ❼

Hotel Center Broel Graanmarkt 6 ☎056 21 97 21, ℗056 20 03 66. Modern, standard-issue three-star hotel that's marginally less expensive than its rivals. ❻

Hotel Damier Grote Markt 41 ☎056 22 15 47, ℗056 22 86 31, ⓦwww.hoteldamier.be. A plush and classy, four-star establishment with fifty com-modious rooms decorated in brisk modern style. Set behind an imperious Neoclassical facade, complete with the old carriage archway. ❼

Eating and drinking

The best **restaurant** in town is *Evergreens*, opposite the church at Onze Lieve Vrouwestraat 48 (closed Thurs), a cosy, intimate and reasonably priced spot, whose adventurous, ever-changing menu features everything from reindeer to mussels. There's also *Den Engel*, Roelandt Saverystraat 6 (closed Sun), a laid-back café kitted out in a sort of bright Baroque style and offering affordable home-made specials – lasagne, moussaka and the like; it's situated to the west of the tourist office – along Rijselsestraat and left at Louis Robbeplein. Alternatively, you'll find a long line of **cafés** and **bars** on the Grote Markt; the *Arte*, at no. 3, serves up tasty salads and pasta from around €8.

Oudenaarde and around

Some 25km east across the Flanders plain from Kortrijk, the attractive and gently old-fashioned town of **OUDENAARDE**, literally "old landing place", hugs the banks of the River Scheldt as it twists its way north toward Ghent. The town has a long and chequered history. Granted a charter in 1193, it con-centrated on cloth manufacture until the early fifteenth century, when its weavers cleverly switched to **tapestry-making**, an industry that made its burghers rich and the town famous, with the best tapestries becoming the prized possessions of the kings of France and Spain. So far so good, but Oudenaarde became a key military objective during the religious and dynas-tic wars of the sixteenth to the eighteenth centuries, perhaps most famously in July 1708, when the Duke of Marlborough came to the rescue and won a spectacular victory here against the French in the War of the Spanish Succession. Attacked and besieged time and again, the town found it impos-sible to sustain municipal expansion, and the demise of the tapestry industry pauperized the town, rendering it an insignificant backwater in one of the poorest parts of Flanders. In the last few years, however, things have improved considerably due to its canny use of regional development funds, and today's town – with its clutch of fascinating old buildings – makes an interesting and pleasant day out.

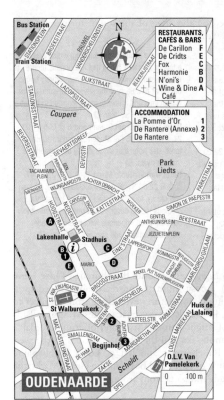

RESTAURANTS, CAFES & BARS
De Carillon   F
De Cridts   E
Fox   C
Harmonie   B
N'oni's   D
Wine & Dine   A
Café

ACCOMMODATION
La Pomme d'Or   1
De Rantere (Annexe) 2
De Rantere   3

OUDENAARDE

0   100 m

Arrival, information and accommodation

Linked by fast and frequent services with a number of towns and cities, including Ghent, Kortrijk and Brussels, Oudenaarde's modern **train station** has usurped its neo-Gothic predecessor, which stands forlorn and abandoned next door. From the station, it's a fifteen-minute walk to the town centre, where the **tourist office**, in the Stadhuis on the Markt (April–Oct Mon–Fri 9am–6pm, Sat & Sun 10am–6pm; Nov–March Mon–Fri 8.30am–noon & 1.30–4.30pm, Sat 2–5pm; ☎055 31 72 51, ⓦ www.oudenaarde.be), issues free town brochures, sells cycling maps of the surrounding district – the Vlaamse Ardennen (see p.163) – and has an accommodation list, though the options are limited. **Bike rental** is available at the train station.

Oudenaarde has just two recommendable **hotels**, the better of which is the enjoyable *De Rantere*, Jan Zonder Vreeslaan 8 (☎055 31 89 88, ⓕ055 33 01 11, ⓦwww.derantere.be; ⑥), a spruce and comfortable modern place overlooking the River Scheldt a brief walk to the south of the Markt. It has a less well-appointed annexe just a couple of minutes' walk away at Burg 18, also with pleasantly furnished rooms. The other option is *La Pomme d'Or*, Markt 62 (☎055 31 19 00, ⓕ055 30 08 44, ⓦwww.lapommedor.be; ⑤), which occupies a large old house on the main square and offers plain, but perfectly adequate, high-ceilinged rooms. The nearest **campsite**, *IC-Camping*, is part of the holiday complex *Vlaamse Ardennen* (☎055 31 54 73, ⓕ055 30 08 65, ⓔoudenaarde@ic-camping.be; April to mid-Nov), some 2km west of the Markt along Minderbroedersstraat, at Kortrijkstraat 342.

The Town

The middle of the **Tacambaroplein**, on the way into town at the southern end of Stationsstraat, is taken up by a romantic war memorial commemorating those who were daft or unscrupulous enough to volunteer to go to Mexico and fight for Maximilian, the Habsburg son-in-law of the Belgian king, Leopold I. Unwanted and unloved, Maximilian was imposed on the Mexicans by a French army provided by Napoleon III, who wanted to create his own western empire while the eyes of the US were averted by the American Civil War. It was, however, all too fanciful and the occupation rapidly turned into a fiasco. Maximilian paid for the adventure with his life in 1867, and few of his soldiers made the return trip. The reasons for this calamity seem to have been entirely lost on Maximilian, who declared, in front of the firing squad that was about to polish him off, "Men of my class and lineage are created by God to be the happiness of nations or their martyrs . . . Long live Mexico, long live independence".

The Markt

The wide open space of the **Markt** is edged by the **Stadhuis** (tours: April–Oct Mon–Thurs at 11am & 3pm, Fri 11am, Sat & Sun 2pm & 4pm; €4; times subject to change – ring the tourist office to confirm), one of the finest examples of Flamboyant Gothic in the country. An exquisite creation of around 1525, its

---

The Oudenaarde tapestry industry

Tapestry manufacture in Oudenaarde began in the middle of the fifteenth century, an embryonic industry that soon came to be based on a dual system of **workshop** and **outworker**, the one with paid employees, the other with workers paid on a piecework basis. From the beginning, the town authorities took a keen interest in the business, ensuring its success by a rigorous system of quality control that soon gave the town an international reputation for consistently well-made tapestries. The other side of this interventionist policy was less palatable: wages were kept down and the Guild of the Masters cunningly took over the running of the Guild of Weavers in 1501. To make matters worse, tapestries were by definition a luxury item, and workers were hardly ever able to accumulate enough capital to buy either their own looms or even raw materials.

The first great period of Oudenaarde tapestry-making lasted until the middle of the sixteenth century, when religious conflict overwhelmed the town and many of its Protestant-inclined weavers, who had come into direct conflict with their Catholic masters, migrated north to the rival workshops of Antwerp and Ghent. In 1582 Oudenaarde was finally incorporated into the Spanish Netherlands, precipitating a revival of tapestry production, fostered by the king and queen of Spain, who were keen to support the industry and passed draconian laws banning the movement of weavers. Later, however, French occupation and the shrinking of the Spanish market led to diminishing production, the industry finally fizzling out in the late eighteenth century.

There were only two significant types of tapestry: **decorative**, principally *verdures*, showing scenes of foliage in an almost abstract way (the Oudenaarde speciality), and **pictorial** – usually variations on the same basic themes, particularly rural life, knights, hunting parties and religious scenes. Over the centuries, changes in style were strictly limited, though the early part of the seventeenth century saw an increased use of elaborate woven borders, an appreciation of perspective and the use of a far brighter, more varied range of colours.

The **technique** of producing tapestries was a cross between embroidery and ordinary weaving. It consisted of interlacing a wool weft above and below the strings of a vertical linen "chain", a process similar to weaving; the appearance of a tapestry was entirely determined by the weft, the design being taken from a painting to which the weaver made constant reference. However, the weaver had to stop to change colour, requiring as many shuttles for the weft as he had colours, as in embroidery.

Standard-size Oudenaarde tapestries took six months to make and were produced exclusively for the very wealthy. The tapestries were normally in yellow, brown, pale blue and shades of green, with an occasional splash of red, though the most important clients would, on occasion, insist on the use of gold and silver thread. Some also insisted on the employment of the most famous **artists** of the day for the preparatory painting – Pieter Paul Rubens, Jacob Jordaens and David Teniers all completed tapestry commissions.

elegantly symmetrical facade spreads out on either side of the extravagant tiers, balconies and parapets of a slender central tower, which is topped by the gilded figure of a knight, *Hanske de Krijger* ("Little John the Warrior"). Underneath the knight, the cupola is in the shape of a crown, a theme reinforced by the two groups of cherubs on the dormer windows below, who lovingly clutch at the royal insignia. Inside, a magnificent oak **doorway** forms the entrance to the old Schepenzaal (Aldermen's Hall). A stylistically influential piece of 1531, by a certain Paulwel Vander Schelde, the doorway consists of an intricate sequence of carvings, surmounted by miniature cherubs who frolic above three coats of arms and a 28-panel door, each rectangle a masterpiece of precise execution; the design was copied in several other Flemish town halls. Of the paintings on display in the Stadhuis, the most distinguished are those by **Adriaen Brouwer**, a native of Oudenaarde, whose representations of the five senses are typical of his ogre-like, caricaturist's style.

To the rear of the Stadhuis sulks the dour and gloomy exterior of the adjoining Romanesque **Lakenhalle**, which dates from the thirteenth century. It contains a superb collection of **tapestries**, the first being the eighteenth-century *Nymphs in a Landscape*, a leafy romantic scene in which four nymphs pick and arrange flowers. The adjacent *Return from Market*, which also dates from the eighteenth century, features trees in shades of blue and green, edged by sky and bare earth – a composition reminiscent of Dutch landscape paintings. There are several excellent examples of the classical tapestries which were all the rage in the sixteenth century, beginning with *Hercules and the Stymphalian Birds*, a scene set among what appear to be cabbage leaves. Equally impressive is *Scipio and Hannibal*, in which the border is decorated with medallions depicting the Seven Wonders of the World – though the Hanging Gardens of Babylon appear twice to create the symmetry. Glamorized pastoral scenes were perennially popular: the seventeenth-century *Landscape with Two Pheasants* frames a distant castle with an intricate design of trees and plants, while *La Main Chaude* depicts a game of blind man's buff.

South of the Markt

Immediately southwest of the Markt, **St Walburgakerk** (Thurs 10–11am & July–Sept Tues & Sat 2.30–4.30pm) is a hulking mass of Gothic masonry, which was badly in need of the restoration work that is now well underway. The interior is cluttered with gaudy Baroque altarpieces, but of some interest are several locally manufactured tapestries and a monument to the four Catholic priests who were thrown into the Scheldt in 1572 from the windows of the town castle (since demolished). Across the road, opposite the church, a group of old mansions follows the bend in what was once the line of the town wall. These are also being repaired and refurbished – not before time. Close by, narrow Voorburg and then Kasteelstraat lead down to the river past a trim seventeenth-century **portal**, the entrance to the former Begijnhof.

If you're keen to discover more about tapestries, head for the municipal repair workshops, sited in a grand old mansion, the **Huis de Lalaing**, on the far side of the river at Bourgondiestraat 9 (Mon–Fri 9am–noon & 1.30–4.30pm; free). The workshops don't make a big thing out of showing visitors around, but everyone is quite friendly and you can poke around looking at the various restorative processes.

Eating and drinking

The Markt is lined with **cafés** and bars, one good option being *De Cridts,* at no. 58, an old-fashioned café-restaurant serving standard-issue Flemish dishes at very reasonable prices. Close by, at no. 63, the *Harmonie Restaurant* (Mon–Thurs & Sun 10am–9pm, Fri 6–9pm) is a tad more formal, but there's a wider choice, with snacks from €7 and tasty main courses for around €18. Better still is the *Wine & Dine Café*, Hoogstraat 34, a nattily decorated place that offers a short but wide-ranging and reasonably priced menu, fish and meat dishes averaging €15, salads €9–15.

As for **drinking**, the local Roman brewery rules the municipal roost, its most distinctive products being Tripel Ename, a strong blond beer, and Roman Dobbelen Bruinen, a snappy, filtered stout. These are usually available at the best bars in town: try *N'oni's*, a fashionable, pastel-decorated bar off the east side of the Grote Markt at Einestraat 3, or the *Fox*, a similarly lively and youthful spot directly opposite. A third option is *De Carillon*, a quieter place in the old brick-gabled building in the shadow of St Walburgakerk.

Ronse and the Flemish Ardennes

To the south of Oudenaarde, the flattened fields of the Flanders plain give way to a ridge of low hills that make up the southwest corner of the province of East Flanders. It's a pretty area, though the sobriquet **Vlaamse Ardennen** (Flemish Ardennes), used by local tourist offices, is desperately optimistic. The best scenery is actually beside the **N36**, the road from Kerkhove (and Kortrijk), which crosses the ridge from the west, passing near the hilltop vantage point of **Kluisberg** (Mont de l'Enclus).

In the middle of these hills, 12km south of Oudenaarde on the N60 (or by hourly train; 10min), lies the tiny textile town of **RONSE**, whose main claim to fame is **St Hermeskerk**, an imposing late Gothic edifice situated in the town centre, a ten-minute walk from the train station straight down Stationsstraat. The church takes its name from a Roman martyr, Hermes, who was recognized for his skills as an exorcist. His relics were presented to Ronse during the ninth century and became the object of pilgrimages, the "possessed" dragged here from all over the Low Countries in the hope of a miraculous cure. The chapel on the south side of the choir is dedicated to St Hermes: above the chapel altar, a kitsch marble statue portrays St Hermes on horseback, dragging a devil behind him, while the three rusted iron rings opposite recall the time when those considered insane were chained up waiting for exorcism. The church's other interesting feature is its capacious Romanesque **crypt** (April–Sept Tues–Fri 10am–noon & 1.30–5pm, Sat & Sun 10am–12.30pm & 2–6pm; €1), dating from 1089.

Known as the **Bruul**, the parcel of land immediately to the east of the church has been tidied and landscaped to house Ronse's other tourist attractions – primarily a textile museum – but these are of only limited interest, as is the adjacent Grote Markt, an ugly square whose obelisk was originally surmounted by a "W" in honour of William I, though this soon disappeared after the Revolution of 1830. In the unlikely event you decide to stay the night, Ronse **tourist office**, on the Bruul, has accommodation details as well as town maps (Mon–Fri 9am–noon & 12.30–4.30pm, mid-May to Sept also Sat & Sun 10am–noon & 2–5pm; ☎055 23 28 16).

Bruges

"Somewhere within the dingy casing lay the ancient city," wrote Graham Greene of **BRUGES**, "like a notorious jewel, too stared at, talked of, and trafficked over". And it's true that Bruges' reputation as one of the most perfectly preserved medieval cities in western Europe has made it the most popular tourist destination in Belgium, packed with visitors throughout the summer season. Inevitably, the crowds tend to overwhelm the town, but you'd be mad to come to Flanders and miss the place: its museums hold some of the country's finest collections of Flemish art, and its intimate, winding streets, woven around a skein of narrow canals and lined with gorgeous ancient buildings, live up to even the most inflated tourist hype. See it out of season, or in the early morning before the hordes have descended, and it can be memorable – though not so much on **Mondays**, when most of the sights are closed.

Some history

Bruges originated from a ninth-century fortress built by the warlike first count of Flanders, **Baldwin Iron Arm**, who was intent on defending the Flemish coast from Viking attack. The settlement prospered, and by the fourteenth century it shared effective control of the **cloth trade** with its two great rivals, Ghent and Ypres, turning high-quality English wool into clothing that was exported all over the known world. An immensely profitable business, it made the city a focus of international trade: at its height, the town was a key member of – and showcase for the products of – the **Hanseatic League**, the most powerful economic alliance in medieval Europe. Through the harbours and docks of Bruges, Flemish cloth and Hansa goods were exchanged for hogs from Denmark, spices from Venice, hides from Ireland, wax from Russia, gold and silver from Poland and furs from Bulgaria. The business of these foreign traders was protected by no fewer than 21 consulates, and the city developed a wide range of support services, including banking, money-changing, maritime insurance and an elementary shipping code, known as the *Roles de Damme*.

Despite (or perhaps because of) this lucrative state of affairs, Bruges was dogged by **war**. Its weavers and merchants were dependent on the goodwill of

△ Canal view, Bruges

the kings of England for the proper functioning of the wool trade, but their feudal overlords, the counts of Flanders, and their successors, the dukes of Burgundy (from 1384), were vassals of the rival king of France. Although some of the dukes and counts were strong enough to defy their king, most felt obliged to obey his orders and thus take his side against the English when the two countries were at war. This conflict of interests was compounded by the designs the French monarchy had on the independence of Bruges itself. Time and again, the French sought to assert control over the towns of West Flanders, but more often than not they encountered armed rebellion. In Bruges, the most famous insurrection was precipitated by **Philip the Fair** at the beginning of the fourteenth century. Philip and his wife, Joanna of Navarre, had held a grand reception in Bruges, but it had only served to feed their envy. In the face of the city's splendour, Joanna moaned, "I thought that I alone was Queen; but here in this place I have six hundred rivals." The opportunity to flex royal muscles came shortly afterwards when the town's guildsmen flatly refused to pay a new round of taxes. Enraged, Philip dispatched an army to restore order and garrison the town, but at dawn on Friday, May 18, 1302, a rebellious force of Flemings crept into the city and massacred Philip's sleepy army – an occasion later known as the **Bruges Matins**. Anyone who couldn't correctly pronounce the Flemish shibboleth *schild en vriend* ("shield and friend") was put to the sword.

The Habsburgs, who inherited Flanders – as well as the rest of present-day Belgium and Holland in 1482 – whittled away at the power of the Flemish cities, no one more so than **Charles V**, the ruler of a vast kingdom that included the Low Countries and Spain. As part of his policy, Charles favoured Antwerp at the expense of Flanders and, to make matters worse, the Flemish cloth industry began its long decline in the 1480s. Bruges was especially badly hit and, as a sign of its decline, failed to dredge the silted-up River Zwin, the city's trading lifeline to the North Sea. By the 1510s, the stretch of water between Sluis and Damme was only navigable by smaller ships, and by the 1530s the town's sea trade had collapsed completely. Bruges simply withered away, its houses deserted, its canals empty and its money spirited north with the merchants.

Some four centuries later, **Georges Rodenbach**'s novel *Bruges-la-Morte* alerted well-heeled Europeans to the town's aged, quiet charms, and Bruges – frozen in time – escaped damage in both world wars to emerge the perfect tourist attraction.

Arrival and information

Bruges **train station** adjoins the **bus station**, about 2km southwest of the town centre. Inside the train station, there's a **tourist office** (Mon–Sat 10am–6pm; ☎050 44 86 86) which concentrates on making hotel reservations at no charge, though they do require a small deposit which is deducted from the final bill. They carry a limited range of tourist information, leaving this task to the main tourist office in the town centre. Most of the **local buses** that leave from outside the train station head off to the Markt, with some services stopping on the square itself and others stopping on adjacent Wollestraat. All local buses have destination signs at the front, but if in doubt check with the driver. A **taxi** from the train station to the centre costs about €7.

Most **motorists** arrive in Bruges via the **E40**, which runs west from Brussels to Ostend and Veurne. Within Bruges' oval-shaped centre, which is encircled by the **R30** ring road, on-street **parking** is almost impossible to find, the city centre's handful of car parks being often filled to the gunnels. Easily the best option is to use the massive car park by the train station, particularly as the price – €2.50 per day – includes the cost of the bus ride into (and out of) the centre.

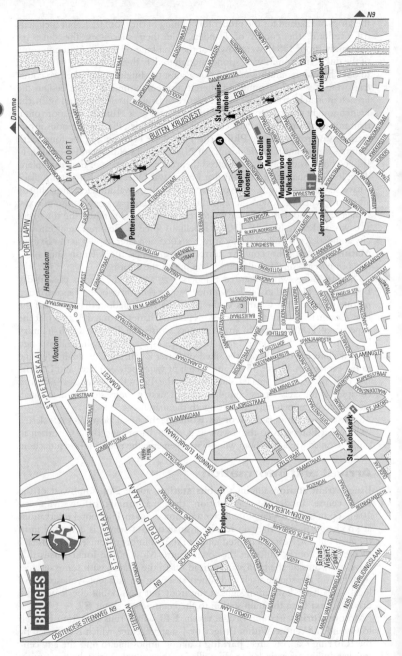

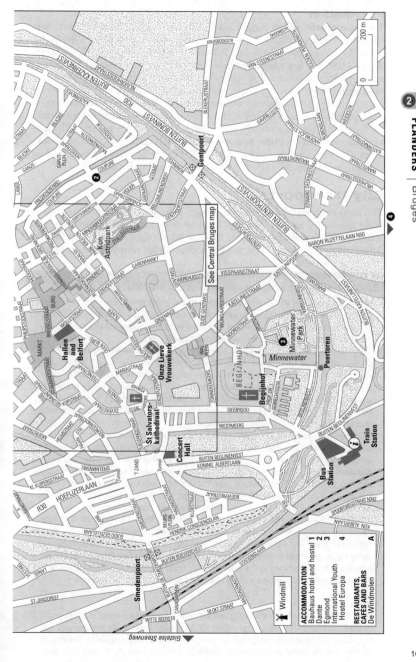

ACCOMMODATION
Bauhaus hotel and hostel 1
Dante   2
Egmond   3
International Youth
 Hostel Europa   4

RESTAURANTS,
CAFES AND BARS
De Windmolen   A

✈ Windmill

Hallen
and Belfort

Onze Lieve
Vrouwekerk

St Salvators-
kathedraal

Concert
Hall

Begijnhof

Minnewater
Park

Minnewater

Poertoren

Bus
Station

Train
Station

ⓘ

Kon.
Astridpark

Gentpoort

Smedenpoort

▲ Gistelse Steenweg

See Central Bruges map

0   200 m

Information

The main **tourist office** is right in the centre of town at Burg 11 (April–Sept Mon–Fri 9.30am–6.30pm, Sat & Sun 10am–noon & 2–6.30pm; Oct–March Mon–Fri 9.30am–5pm, Sat & Sun 9.30am–1pm & 2–5.30pm; ℡050 44 86 86, ℻050 44 86 00, ⓦwww.brugge.be). They offer an accommodation-booking service and, in addition, sell all manner of brochures about the city, one of the most useful being a general guide with suggested walking routes and museum opening times (€0.70). Among a variety of free leaflets, there's a comprehensive accommodation listings brochure and a bi-monthly, multilingual events booklet, though the latter isn't nearly as detailed as "**EXit**", a free monthly, Flemish-language newssheet available here and at many city-centre bars, cafés and bookshops. The tourist office also has currency-exchange facilities and local bus and train timetables, and sells tickets for many events and performances.

City transport

The most enjoyable way to explore Bruges is to **walk**, and the centre is certainly compact – and flat – enough to make this an easy proposition. The city is also ideal for **cycling**, with cycle lanes on many of the roads, and cycle racks dotted across the centre. There are half a dozen **bike rental** places in Bruges,

---

Guided tours and boat trips

The tourist office has all the details of **guided tours**, which are big business in Bruges; on offer are all sorts of ways of exploring the centre, from bus rides and walking tours to horse and carriage jaunts and boat trips, as well as excursions out into the Flemish countryside, most notably to the battlefields of World War I.

Sightseeing Line (℡050 35 50 24) operates fifty-minute **mini-coach tours** of the city centre, departing from the Markt, for €10 per adult (pay the driver); passengers are issued with individual headphones in the language of their choice. Rather more sociable are the guided **walking tours** organized by the tourist office (€5 per adult; advance booking required). Alternatively, **horse-drawn carriages** line up on the Markt offering a thirty-minute canter round town for €27.50. These are extremely popular, so expect to queue at the weekend.

Quasimodo Tours is the pick of the city's tour operators (℡050 37 04 70, ⓦwww.quasimodo.be), offering a first-rate programme of excursions both in and around Bruges and out into Flanders. Highly recommended is their laid-back **Flanders Fields** minibus tour of the World War I battlefields near Ieper (see p.000; mid-Feb to mid-Nov Tues, Thurs & Sun; 7hr 30min); tours cost €45 (under-26 €38) including picnic lunch. Reservations are required and hotel or train station pick-up can be arranged. Quasimodo also runs two **bike tours**, starting from the Burg. Their "Bruges by Bike" excursion (daily April–Sept at 10am; 3hr; €16, under-26 €14) zips round the main sights and then explores less visited parts of the city, while their "Border by Bike" tour (daily April–Sept at 1pm; 4hr; €16/14) is a 25-kilometre ride out along the poplar-lined canals to the north of Bruges, visiting Damme and Oostkerke with stops and stories along the way. Both are good fun and the price includes bottled water and mountain bike and rain-jacket hire; reservations are required.

Boat trips

Half-hour boat trips around the city's central **canals** leave from a number of jetties south of the Burg (March–Nov daily 10am–6pm; €5.20). Boats depart every few minutes, but long queues still build up during high season, with few visitors concerned by the clichéd commentary. In wintertime (Dec–Feb), there's a spasmodic service at weekends only. There are also boat excursions out to the attractive town of **Damme** (see p.189).

but Belgian Railways sets the benchmark, hiring out bikes at the railway station (☎050 30 23 29; €8.80 per day). Two other options are Christophe's, Dweersstraat 4 (☎050 33 86 04; €8.70 per day), and the Bauhaus International Youth Hotel, Langestraat 135 (☎050 34 10 93; €8.70 per day). The tourist office issues a free and useful leaflet detailing five **cycle routes** in the countryside around Bruges; logically enough it's called *5x By Bike Around Bruges*. Quasimodo Tours offers two guided cycling tours (see opposite).

Bruges has an excellent network of local **bus** services, shuttling round the centre and the suburbs from the main bus station. These are operated by De Lijn, who have an information kiosk at the bus station (Mon–Fri 7.30am–6pm, Sat 9am–6pm & Sun 10am–5pm) as well as a regional information line (☎059 56 53 53). Most local services are routed through the city centre. The standard single fare is €1, or a booklet of ten tickets costs €7.50; pay the driver. The information kiosk also sells a 24-hour city bus pass, the Dagpas, for €2.90.

Accommodation

Bruges has over one hundred hotels, dozens of bed-and-breakfasts and several unofficial youth hostels, but still can't accommodate all its visitors at the height of the season. If you're arriving in July or August, be sure to **book ahead** or, at a pinch, make sure you get here in the morning before all the rooms have gone. Given the crush, many visitors use the hotel and B&B **accommodation booking service** provided by the tourist office (see above) – it's efficient and can save you endless hassle. At other times of the year, things are usually much less pressing, though it's still a good idea to reserve ahead. Standards are generally high, with room tariffs primarily related to the hotel's facilities and the size of the room; note, however, that hoteliers are wont to deck out their foyers rather grandly, often in contrast to the spartan rooms beyond, while many places offer rooms of widely divergent size and comfort. Twenty-odd Bruges establishments are reviewed below (and marked either on the Bruges map on pp.166–167 or on the central Bruges map on p.172), but in addition the city's tourist office issues a free **accommodation booklet** providing comprehensive listings including hotel photographs, websites and a city map.

The centre is liberally sprinkled with **hotels**, many of which occupy quaint and/or elegant old buildings. There's a cluster immediately to the south of one of the two main squares, the Burg – though places here tend to be the most expensive – and another, more affordable group in the vicinity of the Spiegelrei canal, one of the prettiest and quieter parts of the centre. Most of the city's hotels are small – twenty rooms, often less – and few are owned by a chain.

B&Bs are generously distributed across the city centre too, and many offer an excellent standard of en-suite accommodation. A reasonable average price is €40–60 per double, but some of the more luxurious establishments charge in the region of €80. In addition, Bruges has a handful of unofficial **youth hostels**, offering dormitory beds at around €13 per person per night. Most of these places, as well as the official **HI youth hostel**, which is tucked away in the suburbs, also have a limited supply of smaller rooms, with doubles at about €30–40 per night.

Hotels

Over €80

Adornes St Annarei 26 ☎050 34 13 36, ℻050 34 20 85, ⊛www.proximedia.be. This tastefully converted old Flemish town house, with its plain, high-gabled facade, has none of the fussiness of many of its competitors – both the public areas and the comfortable bedrooms are decorated in bright whites and creams, which emphasize the antique charm of the place. Great location, too, at the junction of two canals near the east end of Spiegelrei. Three star. **❺**

Castillion Heilige-Geeststraat 1 ☎050 34 30 01, ℻050 33 94 75, ⊛www.castillion.be. Two old

Flemish houses, with high crow-stepped gables, have been transformed into this neat hotel across from the cathedral. There are just twenty bedrooms, small but comfortable, with spruce, modern furnishings. The public areas are done out in a repro antique style that can be a little overpowering. Four star. ❻

Dante Coupure 29 ☎ 050 34 01 94, ℻ 050 34 35 39, ⓦ www.hoteldante.be. A little off the beaten track but still within a 10min walk of the Markt, this is a well turned out, modern hotel built in traditional style with dormer windows and so forth. The twenty rooms are reasonably large, with crisp patterned furnishings and lots of wicker chairs. The hotel overlooks one of the city centre's wider canals, which is still used by heavy-laden barges. Three star. ❻

Die Swaene Steenhouwersdijk 1 ☎ 050 34 27 98, ℻ 050 33 66 74, ⓦ www.dieswaene-hotel.com. The unassuming brick exterior of this long-established, family-run hotel is deceptive, as the rooms beyond are luxuriously furnished in antique style. The location is perfect too, beside a particularly pretty section of canal a short walk from the Burg – which partly accounts for its reputation as one of the city's most "romantic" hotels. Pool and sauna. Four star. ❾

Egmond Minnewater 15 ☎ 050 34 14 45, ℻ 050 34 29 40, ⓦ www.egmond.be. There are only eight bedrooms in this rambling old house, standing in its own gardens just metres from the Minnewater on the southern edge of the city centre. The interior has wooden beamed ceilings and fine eighteenth-century chimneypieces, harking back to the days when it was a manor house. Attractive rooms in a quiet location at surprisingly affordable prices. Three star. ❻

Relais Oud Huis Amsterdam, Spiegelrei 3 ☎ 050 34 18 10, ℻ 050 33 88 91. Tastefully turned out hotel in a grand eighteenth-century mansion overlooking the Spiegelrei canal. Many of the furnishings and fittings are period, but more so in the public areas than in the 34 rooms. Four star. ❾

Ter Brughe Oost-Gistelhof 2 ☎ 050 34 03 24, ℻ 050 33 88 73, ⓦ www.hotelterbrughe.com. In an old and dignified merchant's house overlooking one of the prettiest canals in the city, this smart, four-star hotel has opted for a minimalist, modern refurbishment, with bare wood floors and pastel-painted walls. The 24 rooms are comfortable and well-appointed, though quite why the old English prints (of hunting etc) are doing on the walls is hard to fathom. Very pleasant. ❻

De Tuilerieën Dijver 7 ☎ 050 34 36 91, ℻ 050 34 04 00. Occupying a tastefully refurbished mansion close to the Burg, this delightful hotel, with 45 rooms, is one of the best in town. Some rooms overlook the Dijver canal. Breakfast is taken in a lovely neo-Baroque salon. Four star. ❾

Walburg Boomgaardstraat 13 ☎ 050 34 94 14, ℻ 050 33 68 84. Engaging hotel in an elegant nineteenth-century mansion – with splendidly large wooden doors – a short walk east of the Burg along Hoogstraat. The rooms are smart and comfortable, and there are capacious suites. ❽

Under €80

Bauhaus Hotel Langestraat 133 ☎ 050 34 10 93, ℻ 050 33 41 80, ⓦ www.bauhaus.be. Adjacent to the *Bauhaus Hostel*, this one-star hotel, popular with backpackers, offers 21 very spartan rooms, just one of which is en suite. Don't expect too much in the way of creature comforts, but the atmosphere is usually very agreeable, and the clientele are friendly. ❸

Cordoeanier Cordoeaniersstraat 18 ☎ 050 33 90 51, ℻ 050 34 61 11, ⓦ www.cordoeanier.be. Medium-sized, family-run hotel handily located in the narrow side-streets a couple of minutes north of the Burg. Mosquitoes can be a problem here, but the small rooms are clean and pleasant. Two star. ❹

Europ Augustijnenrei 18 ☎ 050 33 79 75, ℻ 050 34 52 66, ⓦ www.hoteleurop.com. This dignified late-nineteenth-century town house overlooks a canal about 5min walk north of the Burg. The public areas are somewhat frumpy and the modern bedrooms are a little too spartan, but it's a pleasant place to stay all the same. Two star. ❺

De Goezeput Goezeputstraat 29 ☎ 050 34 26 94, ℻ 050 34 20 13. Outstanding two-star hotel in an immaculately refurbished, eighteenth-century convent, complete with wooden beams and oodles of antiques. Charming location, on a quiet street near the cathedral. Fifteen en-suite rooms. Newly opened, so don't be surprised if prices go up once it's better known, but currently a snip. ❹

Jacobs Baliestraat 1 ☎ 050 33 98 31, ℻ 050 33 56 94, ⓦ www.hoteljacobs.be. Pleasant hotel in a creatively modernized old brick building complete with a precipitous crow-step gable. Occupies a quiet location in one of the more attractive parts of the centre, a 10min walk northeast of the Markt via Jan van Eyckplein. There are twenty-three rooms, decorated in brisk modern style, though some are really rather small. Three star. ❹

Passage Hotel Dweersstraat 28 ☎ 050 34 02 32, ℻ 050 34 01 40. Ten simple but well-maintained rooms – four en suite, and with some three-bed and four-bed rooms – a 10min stroll west of the Markt and next door to the *Passage Hostel*. It's a very popular spot, so advance reservations are

pretty much essential, and there's a busy bar that's a favourite with backpackers. A real steal. **②**
De Pauw St Gilliskerkhof 8 ☎050 33 71 18, ⓕ050 34 51 40, ⓦwww.hoteldepauw.be. A competent, two-star (if not particularly exciting) establishment occupying an unassuming brick building in a pleasant, quiet part of town, about 10min walk from the Markt. Has eight sparse but perfectly adequate rooms, six en suite. Closed Jan. **③**

Bed & breakfasts

Bistro Die Maene Markt 17 ☎050 33 39 59, ⓕ050 33 44 60, ⓦwww.huyzediemaene.be. Above a brasserie plum in the centre of town, with two well-appointed, en-suite rooms decked out in comfortable modern style. Credit cards accepted. **⑤**
Mr & Mrs Gheeraert Riddersstraat 9 ☎050 33 56 27, ⓕ050 34 52 01, ⓔpaul.gheeraert@skynet.be. Occupying the top floor of a creatively modernized old house a short walk east from the Burg, the three en-suite guest rooms here are immaculate, with TV and refrigerator. No credit cards. Closed Jan. **③**
Salvators Korte Vulderstraat 7 ☎050 33 19 21, ⓕ050 33 94 64, ⓦwww.hotelsalvators.be. Operated in tandem with the eponymous hotel, just round the corner on St Salvatorskerkhof, this smart guesthouse offers three rooms, two en suite. Occupies an attractive, well-maintained, three-storey brick house in a handy location, metres from the cathedral. **④**
Mr Van Nevel Carmersstraat 13 ☎050 34 68 60, ⓕ050 34 76 16, ⓔrobert.vannevel@advalvas.be. A few euros cheaper than many of its rivals, this B&B has two unassuming guest rooms with shared bathroom. Situated in an appealing part of town near the Spiegelrei canal. No credit cards. **③**

Hostels

Bauhaus International Youth Hotel Langestraat 135 ☎050 34 10 93, ⓕ050 33 41 80, ⓦwww.bauhaus.be. About 15min walk east of the Burg, next to the bargain-basement *Bauhaus Hotel* (see opposite). Laid-back hostel with several dormitories, sleeping up to eight apiece, and a mishmash of double and triple rooms. The popular downstairs bar serves filling portions of food, and there are facilities for bike hire and currency exchange, as well as coin-operated lockers. Dorm beds from €13, **①**
Charlie Rockets Hoogstraat 19 ☎050 33 06 60, ⓕ050 34 36 30, ⓦwww.charlierockets.com. New kid on the hostel block that steals a march on its rivals by being so much closer to the Markt. Has eleven rooms on two upper floors in a variety of shapes and sizes. Above a busy American-style bar. Dorm beds from €13, **③**
International Youth Hostel Europa Baron Ruzettelaan 143 ☎050 35 26 79, ⓕ050 35 37 32, ⓦwww.vjh.be. Local city bus #2 from the train station goes within 100m of the hostel. In its own grounds a dreary 2km south of the centre in the suburb of Assebroek, this modern HI-affiliated establishment has over two hundred beds in a mixture of rooms from singles through to six-bed dorms. Breakfast is included in the rate. Lockout 10am–1pm, till 5pm on Sunday. Closed Christmas to mid-Jan. Dorm beds €12.50, **①**
Passage Dweersstraat 26 ☎050 34 02 32, ⓕ050 34 01 40. The most agreeable hostel in Bruges, sleeping fifty people in ten comparatively comfortable dormitories, all with shared bathrooms. Located in an interesting old part of town, about 10min walk west of the Markt. The *Passage Hotel* next door is also a bargain (see opposite). Dorm beds from €14.

The City

Passing through Bruges in 1820, William Wordsworth declared that this was where he discovered "a deeper peace than in deserts found". He was neither the first nor the last Victorian to fall in love with the place; by the 1840s there was a substantial **British colony** here, its members enraptured by the city's medieval architecture and air of lost splendour. The expatriates were not slow to exercise their economic muscle, applying an architectural **Gothic Revival** brush to parts of the city that weren't "medieval" enough. Time and again, they intervened in municipal planning decisions, allying themselves to like-minded Flemings in a movement that changed, or at least modified, the face of the city – and ultimately paid out mega bucks with the arrival of mass tourism in the 1960s. Thus, Bruges is not the perfectly preserved medieval city of much tourist literature, but rather a clever, frequently seamless combination of medieval original and nineteenth- and sometimes twentieth-century addition.

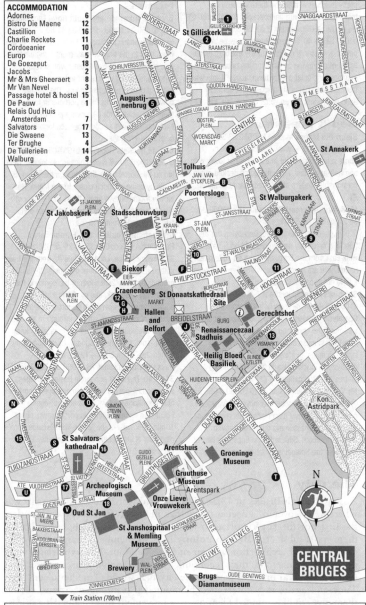

ACCOMMODATION

Adornes	6
Bistro Die Maene	12
Castillion	16
Charlie Rockets	11
Cordoeanier	10
Europ	5
De Goezeput	18
Jacobs	2
Mr & Mrs Gheeraert	8
Mr Van Nevel	3
Passage hotel & hostel	15
De Pauw	1
Relais Oud Huis Amsterdam	7
Salvators	17
Die Swaene	13
Ter Brughe	4
De Tuilerieën	14
Walburg	9

CENTRAL BRUGES

▼ Train Station (700m)

RESTAURANTS, CAFÉS & BARS

Den Amand	H	Cohiba	S	L'Intermède	N	De Verbeelding	P
De Bolero	T	Het Dagelijks Brood	F	Jan van Eyck	B	De Visscherie	K
Het Brugs Beertje	O	Het Dreupelhuisje	Q	Lokkedize	U	De Vlaamsche Pot	M
Cactus Club	D	Le Due Venezie	I	De Lotteburg	V	Du Vuurmolen	C
Cafedraal	S	Den Dyver	R	Oud Vlissinghe	A	Wijnbar Est	L
Café Craenenburg	G	De Garre	J	De Republiek	D	De Wittekop	E

The obvious place to start an exploration of the city is in the two principal squares: the **Markt**, overlooked by the mighty **belfry**, and the **Burg**, flanked by the city's most impressive architectural ensemble. Almost within shouting distance, along the Dijver, are the city's three main museums, among which the **Groeninge Museum** offers a wonderful sample of early Flemish art. Another short hop brings you to **St Janshospitaal** and the important paintings of the fifteenth-century artist **Hans Memling**, as well as Bruges' most satisfying churches, **Onze Lieve Vrouwekerk** and **Sint Salvatorskathedraal**.

Further afield, the gentle canals and maze-like cobbled streets of eastern Bruges – stretching out from **Jan van Eyckplein** – are extraordinarily pretty. The most characteristic architectural feature is the crow-step gable, popular from the fourteenth to the eighteenth century and revived by the restorers of the 1880s and later, but there are also expansive Georgian-style mansions and humble, homely cottages. There are one or two obvious targets here, principally the **Lace Centre**, where you can buy locally made lace and watch its manufacture, and the city's most unusual church, the adjacent **Jeruzalemkerk**. Above all, eastern Bruges excels in the detail, surprising the eye again and again with its sober and subtle variety, featuring everything from intimate arched doorways, bendy tiled roofs and wonky chimneys to a bevy of discrete shrines and miniature statues.

The Markt

At the heart of Bruges is the **Markt**, an airy open space edged on three sides by rows of gabled buildings and with horse-drawn buggies clattering over the cobbles. The burghers of nineteenth-century Bruges were keen to put something suitably civic in the middle of the square and the result was the conspicuous **monument** to the leaders of the Bruges Matins, Pieter de Coninck, of the guild of weavers, and Jan Breydel, dean of the guild of butchers. Standing close together, they clutch the hilt of the same sword, their faces turned to the south in slightly absurd poses of heroic determination.

The biscuit-tin buildings flanking most of the Markt are a charming ensemble, largely mellow ruddy-brown brick, each gable compatible with but slightly different from its neighbour. Most are late nineteenth- or even twentieth-century re-creations – or re-inventions – of older buildings, though the **post office**, which hogs the east side of the square, is a thunderous neo-Gothic edifice that refuses to camouflage its modern construction. The **Craenenburg Café**, on the corner of St Amandsstraat at Markt 16, occupies a modern building too, but it marks the site of the eponymous medieval mansion in which the guildsmen of Bruges imprisoned the Habsburg heir, Archduke Maximilian, for three months in 1488. The reason for their difference of opinion was the archduke's efforts to limit the city's privileges, but whatever the justice of their cause, the guildsmen made a big mistake. Maximilian made all sorts of promises to escape their clutches, but a few weeks after his release his dad, the Emperor Frederick III, turned up with an army to take imperial revenge. Maximilian became emperor in 1493 and he never forgave Bruges, doing his considerable best to push trade north to its great rival, Antwerp.

The Belfort

Filling out the south side of the Markt, the mighty **Belfort** (Tues–Sun 9.30am–5pm; €5) was built in the thirteenth century when the town was at its richest and most extravagant. A potent symbol of civic pride and municipal independence, its distinctive octagonal lantern is visible for miles across the surrounding polders.

Entry to the belfry is via the quadrangular **Hallen** at its base. Now used for temporary exhibitions, the Hallen is a much-restored edifice also dating from the thirteenth century, its style and structure modelled on the Lakenhalle at Ieper. In the middle, overlooked by a long line of galleries, is a rectangular courtyard, which originally served as the town's principal market, its cobblestones once crammed with merchants and their wares. On the north side of the courtyard, up a flight of steps, is the entrance to the belfry. Inside, the **belfry staircase** begins innocuously enough, but it gets steeper and much narrower as it nears the top. On the way up, it passes several mildly interesting chambers, beginning with the **Treasury Room**, where the town charters and money chest were locked for safe keeping. Further up is the **Carillon Room**, where you can observe the slow turning of the large spiked drum that controls the 47 bells of the municipal carillon (for more on the instrument, see p.257). The city still employs a full-time bell ringer – you're likely to see him fiddling around in the Carillon Room – who puts on regular **carillon concerts** (late June to Sept Mon, Wed & Sat 9–10pm plus Sun 2.15–3pm; Oct to mid-June Wed, Sat & Sun 2.15–3pm; free). A few stairs up from here and you emerge onto the belfry roof, which offers fabulous views over the city, especially in the late afternoon when the warm colours of the town are at their deepest.

The Burg

From the east side of the Markt, Breidelstraat leads through to the city's other main square, the **Burg**, named after the fortress built here by the first count of Flanders, Baldwin Iron Arm, in the ninth century. The fortress disappeared centuries ago, but the Burg long remained the centre of political and ecclesiastical power with the Stadhuis – which has survived – on one side, and **St Donaaskathedraal** (St Donatian's Cathedral) – razed by the French in 1799 – on the other. The modern *Crowne Plaza Hotel* marks the site of the cathedral, which was, by all accounts, a splendid structure, in which – emulating Charlemagne's Palatine Chapel in Aachen – the octagonal main building was flanked by a sixteen-sided ambulatory and an imposing tower. The foundations were uncovered in 1955, but they were promptly re-interred and although there have been vague plans to carry out another archeological dig, nothing has happened yet.

Heilig Bloed Basiliek

The southern half of the Burg is fringed by the city's finest group of buildings, beginning on the right with the **Heilig Bloed Basiliek** (Basilica of the Holy Blood; daily: April–Sept 9.30am–noon & 2–6pm; Oct–March Mon–Tues & Thurs–Sun 10am–noon & 2–4pm, Wed 10am–noon; free), named after the holy relic that found its way here in the Middle Ages. The church divides into two parts. Tucked away in the corner, the **lower chapel** is a shadowy, crypt-like affair, originally built at the beginning of the twelfth century to shelter another relic, that of St Basil, one of the great figures of the early Greek Church. The chapel's heavy, simple Romanesque lines are decorated with just one relief, which is carved above an interior doorway – a representation of the baptism of Basil in which a strange giant bird, depicting the Holy Spirit, plunges into a pool of water.

Next door, approached up a wide, low-vaulted curving staircase, the **upper chapel** was built a few years later, but has been renovated so frequently that it's impossible to make out the original structure. In addition, the interior has been spoiled by excessively rich nineteenth-century decoration. The building may be disappointing, but the rock-crystal phial that contains the Holy Blood is stored within a magnificent silver **tabernacle**, the gift of Albert and Isabella of

Spain in 1611. One of the holiest relics in medieval Europe, the phial purports to contain a few drops of blood and water washed from the body of Christ by Joseph of Arimathea. Local legend asserts that it was the gift of Diederik d'Alsace, a Flemish knight who distinguished himself by his bravery during the Second Crusade and was given the phial by a grateful patriarch of Jerusalem in 1150. It is, however, rather more likely that the relic was acquired during the sacking of Constantinople in 1204, when the Crusaders simply ignored their collective job description and robbed and slaughtered the Byzantines instead – hence the historical invention. Whatever the truth, after several weeks in Bruges, the relic was found to be dry, but thereafter it proceeded to liquefy every Friday at 6pm until 1325, a miracle attested to by all sorts of church dignitaries, including Pope Clement V.

The Holy Blood is still venerated and, despite modern scepticism, reverence for it remains strong, not least on Ascension Day (mid-May) when it is carried through the town in a colourful but solemn **procession**, the **Heilig-Bloedprocessie**. The procession starts on 't Zand – in front of the new Concertgebouw (Concert Hall) – at 3pm and then wends its way round the centre, taking in Steenstraat, Simon Stevinplein, Dyver, Wollestraat, the Markt, Geldmunstraat and Noordzandstraat, before returning to 't Zand at about 5.30pm. The reliquary that holds the phial when it's moved from the basilica during the procession is displayed in the tiny **treasury** (same times as basilica; €1.25), next to the upper chapel. Dating to 1617, it's a superb piece of work, the gold and silver superstructure encrusted with jewels and decorated with tiny religious scenes. The treasury also contains an incidental collection of vestments and lesser reliquaries plus a handful of old paintings. Look out also, above the treasury door, for the faded strands of a locally woven seventeenth-century tapestry depicting St Augustine's funeral, the sea of helmeted heads, torches and pikes that surround the monks and abbots very much a Catholic view of a muscular State supporting a holy Church.

The Stadhuis

Immediately to the left of the basilica, the **Stadhuis** (Tues–Sun 9.30am–5pm; €2.50 including the Renaissance Hall, see p.176) has a beautiful sandstone facade, a much-copied exterior that dates from 1376 – though its statues (of the counts and countesses of Flanders) are modern replacements of those destroyed by the occupying French army in 1792. Inside, a flight of stairs climbs up to the magnificent **Gothic Hall**, dating from 1400; it was the setting for the first meeting of the States General (parliamentary assembly) in 1464. The ceiling has been restored in a vibrant mixture of maroon, dark brown, black and gold, dripping pendant arches like decorated stalactites. The ribs of the arches converge in twelve circular **vault-keys**, picturing scenes from the New Testament. These are hard to see without binoculars, but down below – and much easier to view – are the sixteen gilded **corbels** which support them. They represent the months and the four elements, beginning in the left-hand corner beside the chimney with January and continuing in a clockwise direction right round the hall. The **frescoes** around the walls were commissioned in 1895 to illustrate the history of the town – or rather history as the council wanted to recall it. The largest scene, commemorating the victory over the French at the Battle of the Golden Spurs in 1302, has lots of noble knights hurrah-ing, though it's hard to take this seriously when you look at the dogs, one of which clearly has a mis-match between its body and head.

In the adjoining **historical room**, a display of miscellaneous artefacts includes navigational aids, the old, seven-lock municipal treasure chest, and a pair of antique city maps.

Renaissancezaal 't Brugse Vrije and the Gerechtshof

Next door to the Stadhuis, the bright and cheery **Oude Griffie** (no admission) was built to house the municipal records office in 1537, its elegant facade decorated with Renaissance columns and friezes superimposed on the Gothic lines of the gables below. The adjacent **Paleis van het Brugse Vrije** (Mansion of the Liberty of Bruges) is demure by comparison, but pop inside to look at the only room to have survived from the original fifteenth-century mansion, the Schepenkamer (Aldermen's Room) – now known as the **Renaissancezaal 't Brugse Vrije** (Renaissance Hall of the Liberty of Bruges; Tues–Sun 9.30am–12.30pm & 1.30–5pm; €2.50 including the Stadhuis) – which boasts an enormous marble and oak **chimneypiece**. A fine example of Renaissance carving, it was completed in 1531 under the direction of Lancelot Blondeel, to celebrate the defeat of the French at Pavia in 1525 and the advantageous Treaty of Cambrai that followed. A paean of praise to the Habsburgs, the work is dominated by figures of the Emperor Charles V and his Austrian and Spanish relatives, each person identified by both the free leaflet and the audio-guide, although it's the trio of bulbous codpieces that really catch the eye.

Adjoining the Bruges Vrije, the plodding courtyard complex of the **Gerechtshof** (Law Courts), dating from 1722, is now home to the main tourist office.

To the Dijver

From the arch beside the Oude Griffie, **Blinde Ezelstraat** (Blind Donkey Street) leads south across the canal to the plain and sombre eighteenth-century Doric colonnades of the fish market, the **Vismarkt**. There's not much marine action here today, and neither are there any tanners in the huddle of picturesque houses that crimp the **Huidenvettersplein**, the old tanners' quarter immediately to the west. Tourists converge on this pint-sized square in their droves, holing up in its bars and restaurants and snapping away at the postcard-perfect views of the belfry from the adjacent **Rozenhoedkaai**. From here, it's a short hop west to the Wollestraat bridge, which is overlooked by a statue of the patron saint of bridges, **St John Nepomuk**. The bridge marks the start of the **Dijver**, which tracks along the canal as far as Nieuwstraat, passing the path to the first of the city's main museums, the Groeninge.

The Groeninge Museum

The superb **Groeninge Museum** (Tues–Sun 9.30am–5pm), the city's finest art museum, is in a state of flux. In 2002, to celebrate the city's selection as a cultural capital of Europe, the museum hosted a prestigious exhibition on Jan van Eyck and his Netherlandish contemporaries. Afterwards, the museum was closed for an extensive refurbishment and will not reopen until 2003. The description below details some of the major works of the permanent collection, but it is impossible to say at this stage exactly what will be displayed and how. That said, it's unthinkable that the new, improved Groeninge will not showcase its wonderful sample of **early Flemish paintings**, one of the world's finest and the kernel of the permanent collection.

A **combined ticket** for five of Bruges' central museums – the Stadhuis, Renaissancezaal 't Brugse Vrije, Arentshuis, Gruuthuse and Memling – is available at any of them, as well as from the tourist office, for €15. The Groeninge Museum is closed until 2003, but when it reopens the combined ticket will no doubt be modified.

Jan van Eyck

Arguably the greatest of the early Flemish masters, **Jan van Eyck** (1385–1441) lived and worked in Bruges from 1430 until his death eleven years later. He was a key figure in the development of oil painting, modulating its tones to create paintings of extraordinary clarity and realism. The Groeninge has two gorgeous examples of his work in its permanent collection, beginning with the miniature portrait of his wife, *Margareta van Eyck*, painted in 1439 and bearing his motto, "als ich can" (the best I can do). The second van Eyck painting is the remarkable *Madonna and Child with Canon George van der Paele*, a glowing and richly analytical work with three figures surrounding the Madonna: the kneeling canon, St George (his patron saint) and St Donatian, to whom he is being presented.

Rogier van der Weyden and Hugo van der Goes

The Groeninge possesses two fine and roughly contemporaneous copies of paintings by **Rogier van der Weyden** (1399–1464), one-time official city painter to Brussels. The first is a tiny *Portrait of Philip the Good*, in which the pallor of the duke's aquiline features, along with the brightness of his hatpin and chain of office, are skilfully balanced by the sombre cloak and hat. The second, much larger painting is *St Luke Painting the Portrait of Our Lady*, a rendering of a popular if highly improbable legend, which claimed that Luke painted Mary – thereby becoming the patron saint of painters. The painting is notable for the detail of its Flemish background and the cheeky-chappie smile of the baby Christ.

One the most gifted of the early Flemish artists, **Hugo van der Goes** (d. 1482) is a shadowy figure, though it is known that he became master of the painters' guild in Ghent in 1467. Eight years later, he entered a Ghent priory as a lay-brother and this may be related to the prolonged bouts of acute depression which afflicted him. Few of his paintings have survived, but these exhibit a superb compositional balance and a keen observational eye – and his last work, the luminescent *Death of Our Lady*, is here at the Groeninge. Sticking to religious legend, the Apostles have been miraculously transported to Mary's deathbed, where, in a state of agitation, they surround the prostrate woman. Mary is dressed in blue, but there are no signs of luxury, reflecting der Goes' asceticism; he may well have been appalled by the church's love of glitter and gold.

The Master of the Ursula Legend

Another Groeninge highlight is the two matching panels of *The Legend of St Ursula*, the work of an unknown fifteenth-century artist known as the "**Master of the Ursula Legend**". The panels, each of which has five miniature scenes, were probably inspired by the twelfth-century discovery of the supposed bones of St Ursula and the women who were massacred with her in Cologne seven centuries before – a sensational find that would certainly have been common knowledge in Bruges. The original legend, which surfaced in the ninth century, described St Ursula as a British princess who avoided an unwanted marriage by going on a pilgrimage to Rome accompanied by eleven female companions, sometimes referred to as nuns or virgins. On their way back, a tempest blew their ship off course and they landed at Cologne, where the (pagan) Huns promptly slaughtered them. Somewhere along the line the eleven women became eleven thousand – possibly because the buckets of bones found in Cologne were from an old public burial ground and had nothing at all to do with Ursula and her chums.

Hans Memling, Gerard David and Hieronymus Bosch

Other early Flemish highlights include a pair of *Annunciation* panels from a triptych by **Hans Memling** (1430–94) – gentle, romantic representations of an angel and Mary, in contrasting shades of grey, a monochrome technique known as grisaille. Here also is Memling's *Moreel Triptych*, in which the formality of the design is offset by the warm colours and the gentleness of the detail. These two are, however, no more than a preamble to the work of Memling, whose finest paintings are exhibited in the city's outstanding Memling Museum (see p.182).

Born near Gouda, the Dutchman **Gerard David** (c. 1460–1523) moved to Bruges in his early 20s. Soon admitted into the local painters' guild, he quickly rose through the ranks, becoming the city's leading artistic light after the death of Memling. Official commissions rained in on David, mostly for religious paintings, which he approached in a formal manner but with a fine eye for detail. The Groeninge holds two excellent examples of his work, starting with the *Baptism of Christ Triptych* in which a boyish, lightly bearded Christ is depicted as part of the Holy Trinity in the central panel. The other work, the intriguing *Judgement of Cambyses*, is one of David's few secular ventures, based on a Persian legend related by Herodotus. The first panel's background shows the corrupt judge Sisamnes accepting a bribe, with the result – his arrest by grim-faced aldermen – filling out the rest of the panel. In the gruesome second panel the king's servants carry out the judgement, applying themselves to the task with clinical detachment. Behind, in the top right corner, the fable is completed with the judge's son dispensing justice from his father's old chair, which is now draped with the flayed skin. Completed in 1498, the painting was hung in the council chamber by the city burghers to encourage honesty amongst its magistrates and as a sort of public apology for the imprisonment of Archduke Maximilian in Bruges in 1488.

The Groeninge also has **Hieronymus Bosch**'s (1450–1516) *Last Judgement*, a trio of oak panels crammed with mysterious beasts, microscopic mutants and scenes of awful cruelty – men boiled in a pit or cut in half by a giant knife. It looks like unbridled fantasy, but in fact the scenes were read as parables, a sort of strip cartoon of legend, proverb and tradition. Indeed Bosch's religious orthodoxy is confirmed by the appeal his work had for that most Catholic of Spanish kings, Philip II.

Jan Provoost and Adriaen Isenbrant

There's more grim symbolism in **Jan Provoost**'s (1465–1529) crowded and melodramatic *Last Judgement*, painted for the Stadhuis in 1525, and his striking *The Miser and Death*, which portrays the merchant with his money in one panel, trying desperately to pass a promissory note to the grinning skeleton in the next. Provoost's career was typical of many of the Flemish artists of the early sixteenth century. Initially he worked in the Flemish manner, his style greatly influenced by Gerard David, but from about 1521 his work was reinvigorated by contact with the German painter and engraver Albrecht Dürer, who had himself been inspired by the artists of the early Italian Renaissance. Provoost moved around too, working in Valenciennes and Antwerp, before settling in Bruges in 1494. One of his Bruges contemporaries was **Adriaen Isenbrant** (d. 1551), whose speciality was small, precisely executed panels. Here, his technically proficient work is exemplified by the *Virgin and Child* triptych – while his sumptuous *Madonna of the Seven Sorrows* is displayed in Bruges' Onze Lieve Vrouwekerk (see p.181).

Pieter Pourbus and Jacob van Oost the Elder

The Groeninge's collection of late sixteenth- and seventeenth-century paintings isn't especially strong, but there's easily enough to discern the period's watering down of religious themes in favour of more secular preoccupations. In particular, **Pieter Pourbus** (1523–84) is well represented by a series of austere and often surprisingly unflattering portraits of the movers and shakers of his day. There's also his *Last Judgement*, a much larger but atypical work, crammed with muscular men and fleshy women; completed in 1551, its inspiration came from Michelangelo's Sistine Chapel.

Jacob van Oost the Elder (1603–71) was the city's most prominent artist during the Baroque period and the Groeninge has a substantial cache of his work. Frankly, however, his canvases are pretty meagre stuff, his *Portrait of a Theologian*, for example, being a stultifyingly formal and didactic affair only partly redeemed by its crisp draughtsmanship, while his *Portrait of a Bruges Family* drips with bourgeois sentimentality.

Jean Delville and Fernand Khnopff

Much more diverting are the Symbolists, among whom **Jean Delville** (1867–1953) takes pride of place with his enormous – and inordinately weird – *De Godmens*, a repulsive yet compelling picture of writhing bodies yearning for salvation. Delville was an ardent and prolific polemicist for modern art, constantly re-defining its aesthetic as he himself changed his style and technique. This particular piece, of 1903, was arguably the high point of his Symbolist period and accorded with his assertion, in *La Mission de L'Art*, that art should have a messianic ideal and a redemptive quality.

Delville distanced himself from Les XX art movement (see box, p.427), but his contemporary – and fellow Symbolist – **Fernand Khnopff** (1858–1921) was a founding member. Khnopff is represented by *Secret Reflections*, not one of his better paintings perhaps, but interesting in so far as its lower panel, showing Sint Janshospitaal (see p.182) reflected in a canal, confirms one of the Symbolists' favourite conceits – "Bruges the dead city" (Bruges la Morte). The upper panel is a play on appearance and desire, but it's pretty feeble, unlike Khnopff's later attempts, in which he painted his sister, Marguerite, again and again.

Twentieth-century art

The Groeninge's **twentieth-century paintings** are really rather pedestrian, though there is a healthy sample of the work of the talented **Constant Permeke** (1886–1952). Permeke's grim wartime experiences – he was wounded in World War I – helped him develop a distinctive Expressionist style in which his subjects – usually agricultural workers, fishermen and so forth – were monumental in form, but invested with sombre, sometimes threatening emotion. His charcoal drawing the *Angelus* is a typically dark and earthy representation of Belgian peasant life. In similar vein is **Gustave van de Woestijne**'s (1881–1947) enormous *Last Supper*, another excellent example of Belgian Expressionism with Jesus and the disciples, all elliptical eyes and restrained movement, trapped within prison-like walls.

In addition, there a couple of minor works by **James Ensor** (1860–1949), **Magritte**'s (1898–1967) characteristically unnerving *The Assault*, and the spookily stark surrealism of **Paul Delvaux**'s (1897–1994; & see p.142) *Serenity*.

The Arentspark and the Arentshuis

From the entrance to the Groeninge, a footpath leads west to the first of two gateways on either side of a narrow cobbled lane. The second gateway leads into tiny **Arentspark**, where the tiniest of humpbacked bridges – **St Bonifaciusbrug** – is framed against a tumble of antique brick houses. Altogether one of Bruges' most picturesque (and photographed) spots, the bridge looks like the epitome of everything medieval, but in fact it was only built in 1910.

The **Arentshuis**, the mansion in the north corner of the Arentspark at Dijver 16 (Tues–Sun 9.30am–5pm; €2.50), is divided into two separate sections. The ground floor is given over to temporary exhibitions, usually of fine art; upstairs is the **Brangwyn Museum**, which displays the moody etchings, lithographs, studies and paintings of the much-travelled artist **Frank Brangwyn** (1867–1956). Born in Bruges, of Welsh parents, Brangwyn donated this sample of his work to his native town in 1936. Apprenticed to William Morris in the early 1880s and an official UK war artist in World War I, Brangwyn was a versatile artist who turned his hand to several different mediums, though his drawings are much more appealing than his paintings, which often slide into sentimentality. In particular, look out for the sequence of line drawings exploring industrial themes – powerful, almost melodramatic scenes of shipbuilding, docks, construction and the like.

The Gruuthuse Museum

The **Gruuthuse Museum** (Tues–Sun 9.30am–5pm; €5), just along the street from the Arentshuis at Dijver 17, occupies a rambling mansion that dates from the fifteenth century. A fine example of civil Gothic architecture, the house takes its name from the owners' historical right to tax the *gruit*, the dried herb and flower mixture once added to barley during the beer-brewing process to improve the flavour. In the fourteenth century, the city's brewers abandoned the *gruit* in favour of hops, but the name of the house stuck.

Distributed among the mansion's many rooms is a baffling hotchpotch of Flemish fine, applied and decorative arts, mostly dating from the medieval and early modern period. The collection holds something for most tastes, from paintings and sculptures through to silverware, lace, ceramics and musical instruments, while antique furniture crops up just about everywhere. The museum's strongest suite is its superb collection of **tapestries**, mostly woven in Brussels or Bruges and dating from the sixteenth and seventeenth centuries. Audio-guides are available at reception at no extra charge and each room carries multilingual cards explaining the more important exhibits, but there are times when you wonder if the museum has been a dumping ground for artefacts that no one knows anything much about.

That said, the collection starts well, the first room holding a charming set of four, early seventeenth-century Bruges tapestries depicting scenes of rural merry-making – with lashings of sauciness thrown in. Room 2 boasts an acclaimed polychromatic terracotta **bust** of Charles V, a German carving of 1520 that reveals a young and disconcertingly thin-faced emperor. Upstairs, look out for a bold and richly coloured set of classical tapestries, produced in Bruges in 1675 and entitled *De Zeven Vrije Kunsten* (the "Seven Free Arts"). The arts concerned were those skills considered necessary for the rounded education of a gentleman – rhetoric, astrology and so forth.

Most intriguing of all, however, is the 1472 oak-panelled **oratory**, which juts out from the first floor of the museum to overlook the high altar of the cathedral next door. A curiously intimate room, it has a low, hooped ceiling partly decorated with simple floral tracery, and corbels cut in the form of tiny angels. The oratory allowed the lords of the *gruit* to worship without leaving home – a real social coup.

Onze Lieve Vrouwekerk

Next door to the Gruuthuse, the **Onze Lieve Vrouwekerk** (Church of Our Lady; Tues–Sat 9.30am–12.30pm & 1.30–5pm, Sun 1.30–5pm; free) is a rambling shambles of a building, a clamour of different dates and different styles, whose brick spire is – at 122m – one of the tallest in Belgium. Entered from the south, the **nave** was three hundred years in the making, an architecturally discordant affair, whose thirteenth-century, grey-stone central aisle, with its precise blind arcading, is the oldest part of the church. At the east end of the south aisle is the church's most celebrated objet d'art, a delicate marble *Madonna and Child* by **Michelangelo**. The only one of Michelangelo's works to leave Italy during the artist's lifetime, it had a significant influence on the painters then working in Bruges, though its present setting – beneath cold stone walls at the centre of an ugly eighteenth-century altar – is hardly inspiring. It's actually remarkable that the statue is here at all: the French stole it during their occupation of the city at the end of the eighteenth century and the Germans did the same in 1944, but on both occasions it managed to work its way back to Bruges.

The chancel

Michelangelo apart, the most interesting of the church's accumulated treasures are situated in the **chancel** (€2.50), which is marked off from the nave by a chunky, black and white marble rood screen. Here, the **mausoleums** of Charles the Bold and his daughter Mary of Burgundy are exquisite examples of Renaissance carving, their side panels decorated with coats of arms connected by the most intricate of floral designs. The royal figures are enhanced in the detail, from the helmet and gauntlets placed gracefully by Charles' side to the pair of watchful dogs nestled at Mary's feet. Both Mary and Charles died in unfortunate circumstances, she after a riding accident in 1482, when she was only 25, and Charles during the siege of Nancy in 1477. However, there is some argument as to whether Charles was ever interred in Bruges at all. Initially, Charles' battle-battered body was buried in Nancy, but seventy years later his great grandson, the Emperor Charles V, ordered it to be exhumed and moved to Bruges for a more suitable burial. This greatly irritated the French, who may well have sent a dud skeleton, specifically one of the knights who died in the same engagement. In the 1970s, archaeologists had a bash at solving the mystery when they dug up this part of the choir, but, among the assorted tombs, which had been buried here over several centuries, they failed to authoritatively identify either the body or the tomb of Charles. Mary proved more tractable, her skeleton confirming the known details of her hunting accident.

The hole the archaeologists dug in the choir beneath the mausoleums was never filled in, and mirrors now give sight of Mary's coffin along with the brick **burial vaults** of several unknown medieval dignitaries. In total, seventeen of these vaults were unearthed, three of which have been placed in the **Lanchals Chapel**, just across the ambulatory. Plastered with lime mortar, the inside walls of all the vaults sport brightly coloured **grave frescoes**, a specific art that flourished hereabouts from the late thirteenth to the middle of the fifteenth century.

The chancel holds several first-rate **paintings**, beginning with Bernard van Orley's bold, if somewhat sentimental, *Passion* triptych above the high altar. The finest work – exhibited on the railings directly opposite the Lanchals Chapel – is, however, Adriaen Isenbrant's finely executed *Madonna of the Seven Sorrows*, in which the Virgin, hands clasped in prayer, is surrounded by seven cameos depicting her tribulations – the Flight into Egypt, the Carrying of the Cross, the Crucifixion and so forth.

Sint Janshospitaal and the Hans Memling Museum

Opposite the entrance to Onze Lieve Vrouwekerk, across Mariastraat, is **Sint Janshospitaal** (Tues–Sun 9.30am–5pm; €7), a sprawling complex that was used as an infirmary until the nineteenth century. The oldest part of the hospital is at the front, behind two sombre stone gable ends. Dating from the twelfth century, it has recently been turned into a sleek and slick **museum** with one large section – in the former ward – exploring the historical background to the hospital by means of documents, paintings and religious objets d'art. The other, smaller – but much more alluring – section, sited in the old hospital chapel, is dedicated to the paintings of Hans Memling. In both, the labelling is minimal, but the audio-guide, issued free at reception, provides copious (if uninspiring) background information.

A passageway on the right-hand side of the museum leads from Mariastraat to the hospital's old **Apotheek** (dispensary), also part of the museum and complete with row upon row of antique porcelain jars. The passageway continues on to the elongated brick block added in the nineteenth century, now a (boringly modern) exhibition-cum-shopping centre called – rather confusingly – **Oud Sint-Jan**.

Sint Janshospitaal

Sint Janshospitaal had just one ward, a large open area broken up by a series of heavyweight stone arches. The creators of the museum have filled this with all manner of medieval paraphernalia – from paintings through to hospital ledgers – all of which have at least some connection with either medieval hospitals in general or this hospital in particular. By themselves, however, the artefacts give little indication as to what the hospital actually felt and looked like and, furthermore, many of the exhibits – of which there are over one hundred – are distinctly second rate. Nevertheless, there are a handful of highlights, most notably a stylish, intimately observed diptych by Jan Provoost (no. 38).

The Memling collection

Born near Frankfurt, **Hans Memling** (1433–94) spent most of his working life in Bruges, where he was taught by Rogier van der Weyden. He adopted much of his tutor's style and stuck to the detailed symbolism of his contemporaries, but his painterly manner was distinctly restrained, often pious and grave. Graceful and warmly coloured, his figures also had a velvet-like quality that greatly appealed to the city's burghers. Indeed, their enthusiasm made Memling a rich man – in 1480 he was listed among the town's major moneylenders.

Of the six works on display in the hospital **chapel**, *Reliquary of St Ursula* (1489) is the most unusual, a lovely piece of craftsmanship comprising a miniature wooden Gothic church painted with the story of St Ursula. His six panels show Ursula and her ten companions (unlike most of his contemporaries, Memling didn't believe there were ten thousand virgins accompanying her) on their way to Rome, only to be massacred by Huns as they passed through Germany. It is, however, the mass of incidental detail that makes the reliquary so enchanting – the tiny ships, figures and churches in the background effortlessly evoking the late medieval world.

The magnificent *Mystical Marriage of St Catherine* forms the middle panel of a large triptych painted for the **altar** of the hospital church between 1475 and 1479. Its symbolism was easily understood by the hospital's sisters, who were well versed in the stories of the saints: St Catherine, representing contemplation, receives a ring from the baby Jesus to seal their spiritual union, while the figure to the right is St Barbara, symbol of good deeds. The complementary side panels depict the beheading of St John the Baptist and a visionary St John writing the book of *Revelation* on the bare and rocky island of Patmos. Again, it's the detail that impresses most: between the inner and outer rainbows above St John, for instance, the prophets make music on tiny instruments – look closely and you'll spy a lute, a flute, a harp and a hurdy-gurdy.

In the adjoining **side chapel**, Memling's skill as a portraitist is demonstrated by his *Virgin and Martin van Nieuwenhove* diptych, in which the eponymous merchant has the flush of youth and, despite his prayerful position, a hint of arrogance. His lips pout, his hair cascades down to his shoulders and he is dressed in the most fashionable of doublets – by the middle of the 1480s, when the portrait was commissioned, no Bruges merchant wanted to appear too pious. There's more fine face-work in Memling's *Portrait of a Woman*, also in the side chapel, where the richly dressed subject stares dreamily into the middle distance, her hands – in a wonderful optical illusion typical of Memling's oeuvre – seeming to clasp the picture frame. The lighting is subtle and sensuous, with the woman set against a dark background, her gauze veil dappling the side of her face. A high forehead was then considered a sign of great feminine beauty, so her hair is pulled right back and was probably plucked – as are her eyebrows. There's no knowing who the woman was, but in the seventeenth century her fancy headgear convinced observers that she was one of the legendary Persian sibyls who predicted Christ's birth; so convinced were they that they added the cartouche in the top left hand corner, describing her as *Sibylla Sambetha* – and the painting is often referred to by this name.

St Salvatorskathedraal
From St Janshospitaal, it's a couple of minutes' walk north along Heilige-Geeststraat to **St Salvatorskathedraal** (Holy Saviour's Cathedral; Mon 2–5.45pm, Tues–Fri 9am–noon & 2–5.45pm, Sat 9am–noon & 2–3.30pm, Sun 9am–10.15 & 2–5.45pm; free), a bulky Gothic edifice that mostly dates from the late thirteenth century, though the Flamboyant Gothic ambulatory was added some two centuries later. A parish church for most of its history, it was only made a cathedral in 1834 following the destruction of St Donatian's (see p.174) by the French some thirty years before.

At the end of a long-term refurbishment, the cathedral's **nave** has recently emerged from centuries of accumulated grime, but it remains a cheerless, cavernous affair despite – or perhaps because of – the acres of browny-cream paint. The only item of any real interest is the set of eight **paintings** by Jan van Orley displayed in and around the transepts. Commissioned in the 1730s, the paintings were used for the manufacture of a matching set of **tapestries** from a Brussels workshop; remarkably enough, these too have survived and hang in sequence in the choir and transepts. Each of the eight scenes is a fluent, dramatic composition featuring a familiar episode from the life of Christ – from the Nativity to the Resurrection – complete with a handful of animals, including a remarkably determined Palm Sunday donkey. The tapestries are mirror images of the paintings as the weavers worked with the rear of the tapestries uppermost on their looms; the weavers also had sight of the tapestry paintings – or rather cartoon copies as the originals were too valuable to be kept beside the looms.

The **cathedral museum** (closed for long-term refurbishment), ranged around the neo-Gothic cloisters adjacent to the ambulatory, contains a motley assortment of ecclesiastical knick-knacks.

South to the Begijnhof and the Minnewater

South from St Janshospitaal, the second turning on the right – Walstraat – gives onto Walplein, where the brewery **Huisbrouwerij De Halve Mann**, at no. 26, offers guided visits for €3.70 per person, including a glass of beer (April–Sept frequent tours 11am–4pm; Oct–March at 11am & 3pm; 45min). From here, it's another short hop to **Wijngaardstraat**, whose antique terrace houses are crammed with souvenir shops, bars and restaurants. The street and its immediate surroundings heave with tourists, unpleasantly so in summer, one of the attractions being the mildly entertaining **Brugs Diamantmuseum** (Bruges Diamond Museum; daily 10.30am–5.30pm; €5), at Katelijnestraat 43, opposite the east end of Wijngaardstraat. Newly created, the museum tracks through the history of the city's diamond industry in a series of smartly presented displays, with daily demonstrations of diamond polishing.

Much more appealing – if just as over-visited – is the **Begijnhof** (daily 9am–6pm or sunset; free), immediately beyond the west end of Wijngaardstraat, where a rough circle of infinitely pretty, old whitewashed houses surrounds a central green. There were once *begijnhofs* all over Belgium (see p.407) and this is one of the few to have survived in good nick. Margaret, Countess of Flanders, founded Bruges' begijnhof in 1245 and, although most of the houses now standing date from the eighteenth century, the medieval layout has survived intact, retaining the impression of the begijnhof as a self-contained village with access controlled through two large gates. The houses are still in private hands, but, with the beguines long gone, they are now occupied by Benedictine nuns. Only one is open to the public – the **Begijnenhuisje** (March–Nov daily 10am–noon & 1.45–5/6pm; €2), a pint-sized celebration of the simple life of the beguines. The best time to visit is in spring, when a carpet of daffodils pushes up between the wispy elms, creating one of the most photographed scenes in Bruges.

It's a short walk from the begijnhof to the **Minnewater**, billed in much publicity hype as the "Lake of Love". The tag certainly gets the canoodlers going, but in fact the lake – more a large pond – started life as a city harbour. The distinctive stone lock house at the head of the Minnewater recalls its earlier function, though it's actually a very fanciful nineteenth-century reconstruction of the medieval original.

North and east of the Markt

Jan van Eyckplein, a five-minute walk north of the Markt, is one of the prettiest squares in Bruges, backdropped by the easy sweep of the Spiegelrei canal. The centrepiece of the square is an earnest **statue** of Van Eyck, erected in 1878, while on the north side is the **Tolhuis**, whose fancy Renaissance entrance is decorated with the coat of arms of the dukes of Luxembourg, who long levied tolls here. The Tolhuis dates from the late fifteenth century, but was extensively remodelled in medieval style in the 1870s, as was the **Poortersloge** (Merchants' Lodge), whose slender tower pokes up above the rooftops on the west side of the square.

Stretching east from Jan van Eyckplein, the **Spiegelrei canal** was once the heart of the foreign merchants' quarter, its frenetic quays overlooked by the trade missions of many of the city's trading partners. The medieval buildings were demolished long ago, but they have been replaced by an exquisite medley of architectural styles from expansive Georgian-style mansions to pirouetting crow-step gables.

The Kantcentrum and Jeruzalemkerk

Further afield, to the east, the complex of buildings that originally belonged to the wealthy Adornes family, who migrated here from Genoa in the thirteenth century, is located at the foot of Balstraat in the middle of an old working-class district of low, brick cottages. Inside the complex, the **Kantcentrum** (Lace Centre; Mon–Fri 10am–noon & 2–6pm, Sat 10am–noon & 2–5pm; €1.50), on the right-hand side of the entrance, has a couple of busy workshops and offers demonstrations of traditional lace-making in the afternoon.

Across the passageway is one of the city's real oddities, the **Jeruzalemkerk** (same times and ticket), built by the Adornes family in the fifteenth century as a copy of the church of the Holy Sepulchre in Jerusalem, after one of their number, Pieter, had returned from a pilgrimage to the Holy Land. The interior is on two levels: the lower level is dominated by a large and ghoulish altarpiece, decorated with skulls and ladders, in front of which is the black marble tomb of Anselm Adornes, the son of the church's founder, and his wife Margaretha. The pilgrimage didn't bring the Adornes family much luck: Anselm was murdered in gruesome circumstances in Scotland in 1483 while serving as Bruges' consul. There's more grisliness at the back of the church where the small vaulted chapel holds a replica of Christ's tomb – you can glimpse the imitation body down the tunnel behind the iron grating. To either side of the main altar, steps ascend to the choir, which is situated right below the eccentric, onion-domed lantern tower. Behind the church, the tiny **Lace Museum** (same times and ticket) is of passing interest for its samples of antique lace.

Museum voor Volkskunde, the windmills and Engels Klooster

A couple of minutes' walk away, at the north end of Balstraat, the **Museum voor Volkskunde** (Folklore Museum; Tues–Sun 9.30am–5pm; €2.50), at Rolweg 40, occupies a long line of low-ceilinged almshouses set beside a trim courtyard. It's a varied collection, comprising a string of period rooms and workshops with the emphasis on the nineteenth and early twentieth centuries. The labelling is, however, well nigh nonexistent, and what you'll find is only in Dutch, so to make much sense of the exhibits you'll need to pick up an English guidebook at reception (€2). Rooms 1–5 are to the right of the entrance, rooms 6–14 are dead ahead. Beside the entrance, in Room 15, *De Zwarte Kat* is a small tavern done out in traditional style and serving ales and snacks.

At the east end of Rolweg, a long and wide earthen bank marks the path of the old town walls. Perched on top today are a quartet of relocated **windmills** – two close by and two about 600m further to the north. You'd have to be something of a windmill fanatic to want to visit them all, but the nearest pair are mildly diverting – and the closest, **St Janshuismolen**, is in working order (Tues–Sun 9.30am–12.30pm & 1.30–5pm; €2).

Nearby is the enjoyable **Engels Klooster** at Carmersstraat 85 (English Cloister; Mon–Sat 2–3.45pm & 4.15–5.15pm; free). Founded in 1629, the convent was long a haven for English Catholic exiles, though – perhaps surprisingly – this didn't stop Queen Victoria from popping in during her visit to Belgium in 1843. Nowadays, the nuns provide an enthusiastic, twenty-minute guided tour of their lavishly decorated Baroque church, whose finest features are the handsome cupola and the altar, an extraordinarily flashy affair made of 23 different types of marble. It was the gift of the Nithsdales, English aristocrats whose loyalty to the Catholic faith got them in no end of scrapes.

Museum Onze-Lieve-Vrouw ter Potterie

From the English Convent, it's a ten-minute walk north to the canalside **Museum Onze-Lieve-Vrouw ter Potterie** Potterierei 79 (Museum of Our Lady of The Pottery; Tues–Sun 9.30am–12.30pm & 1.30–5pm; €2.50). The complex was founded as a hospital in the thirteenth century on the site of an earlier pottery, though "hospital" is a tad misleading as – and this was normal – the buildings were used as much to accommodate visitors as tend the sick; only later did the emphasis fall more heavily on medical treatment.

The hospital was remodelled on several occasions and the three brick gables that front the building today span three centuries. Inside, the museum occupies a handful of the old sick rooms and one of the two chapels. The old religious paintings on display are of no particular distinction, though there are several spectacularly unflattering portraits of Habsburg officials and a couple of pen and ink drawings reputedly by Jan van Eyck. The **chapel**, on the other hand, is delightful, distinguished by its splendid Baroque altarpieces and a sumptuous marble rood screen. From here, it's a ten-minute stroll along the canal back to Jan van Eyckplein.

Eating

There are scores of **restaurants** and **cafés** in Bruges, and very few establishments are owned by chains, with the result that the majority are small and cosy. Standards are very variable, though, with a whole slew of places churning out some pretty mediocre stuff to cater for the enormous number of day-trippers, who congregate in the Markt, the Burg and in the Begijnhof. There are, of course, lots of exceptions, including the places we recommend below. The city's special strength is its top-quality restaurants, among which are several prestigious establishments that are generally reckoned to be among the best in the whole of Belgium – no mean feat in such a gastronomic country.

Most waiters speak at least a modicum of English – many are fluent – and multilingual menus are commonplace. **Prices** run the gamut, but a filling main course in a café or cheaper restaurant should cost €7–12, in a mid-range restaurant €15–20. Note also that kitchens start to wind down at about 9pm, and most establishments close for one day a week.

Cafés

Het Dagelijks Brood Philipstockstraat 21. Very handy location, just off the Burg. Excellent bread shop which doubles as a wholefood café with one long wooden table (the enforced communalism can be good fun) and a few smaller side tables. Mouth-watering home-made soup and bread makes a meal in itself for just €7, or you can chomp away on a range of snacks and cakes. Mon & Wed–Sat 7am–6pm, Sun 8am–6pm.

Gran Kaffee de Passage Dweersstraat 26. This lively café is extremely popular with backpackers, many of whom have bunked down in the adjoining *Passage Hostel* (see p.171). Serves up a good and filling line in Flemish food with many dishes cooked in beer. Mussels are featured too, along with vegetarian options. Not much in the way of frills, but then main courses only cost about €10. Daily 6pm–midnight.

Lokkedize Korte Vuldersstraat 33. Sympathetic bar-café, all subdued lighting, fresh flowers and jazz music, serving up good Mediterranean food with main courses averaging around €9. Attracts a youthful crowd. Tues–Fri 7pm–2am, Fri & Sat 6pm–3am.

De Verbeelding Oude Burg 26. Low-key, amenable café-bar serving a reasonably satisfying range of salads, pastas and tapas. Few would say the food was brilliant, but it is inexpensive and – at its best – very tasty. Main courses around €10, half that for tapas. Handy for the Markt. Mon–Sat 11am–11pm.

De Windmolen Carmersstraat 135. Amiable neighbourhood joint in an old brick house at the east end of Carmersstraat. Dishes up a decent line in inexpensive snacks and light meals – croque monsieur, spaghetti, lasagne and so forth – and possesses a competent beer menu. Has a pleasant outside terrace and an interior dotted with folksy knick-knacks. Daily except Sat 10am–9pm.

Restaurants

Den Amand St Amandstraat 4 ☏050 34 01 22. Small, family-run restaurant beginning to establish a name for itself for its inventive cuisine, combining both French and Flemish traditions. Limited but well-chosen menu – swordfish, rack of lamb – with main courses averaging about €20. Decorated in pleasant modern style. Tues & Thurs–Sun noon–3pm & 6–10pm, Wed noon–3pm.

Cafedraal Zilverstraat 38 ☎050 34 08 45.
Fashionable and tremendously popular restaurant
decked out in ersatz medieval style. A lively menu
runs the gamut of French and Flemish dishes, but
it's hard to beat the North Sea bouillabaisse.
Shares its premises with the *Cohiba* bar (see
p.188). Tues–Sat 11.30am–2am, food served
11am–2pm & 6.30–11pm.

Le Due Venezie Kleine Sint Amandstraat 2. Long-
established Italian restaurant serving up all the
classics at reasonable prices with main courses in
the region of €12–18, though spaghetti costs as
little as €7, pizzas from €6. Occupying an attractive old house close to the Markt, it prides itself on
its rustic atmosphere – lit by candles and with
wine bottles hanging all over the place. Daily
except Tues noon–2.30pm & 6–10pm.

Den Dyver Dijver 5 (☎050 33 60 69). Top-flight
restaurant specializing in traditional Flemish dishes
cooked in beer – the quail and rabbit are magnificent, though the seafood runs them close. Mains
are around €25. Plush antique decor. Popular with
an older clientele. Mon, Tues & Fri–Sun noon–2pm
& 6.30–9pm, Wed & Thurs 6.30–9pm.

L'Intermède Wulfhagestraat 3 ☎050 33 16 74.
Tastefully decorated, very chic little restaurant
serving exquisite French cuisine with a Flemish
twist. Reasonable prices and away from the main
tourist zone. Tues–Sat noon–1.30pm &
7–9.30pm.

Jan van Eyck Restaurant-Tearoom Jan van
Eyckplein 12. This brightly decorated restaurant-
cum-tearoom does a tasty line in snacks and light
meals. Main courses work out at about €15–18,
though veggie dishes cost around €10. Also has a
good line in *stoemp* and serves thirteen sorts of
beer. Daily except Wed 11.30am–2pm &
6.30–10.30pm.

De Lotteburg Goezeputstraat 43 ☎050 33 75 35.
One of the best restaurants in town, this very
smart, formal little place has a superb seafood
menu. The key is its creativity, with imaginative,
carefully prepared dishes like shrimps and truffle
oil, sole and mushrooms. Set menus cost an arm
and a leg, but main courses average €30–35 –
expensive but well worth it. Lunches cost in the
region of €30. Don't miss the fish soup.
Reservations essential. Wed–Fri & Sun noon–2pm
& 7–9.30pm, Sat 7–9.30pm.

De Visscherie Vismarkt 8 ☎050 33 02 12.
Outstanding seafood restaurant that manages to
be smart and relaxed at the same time. The well-
presented, imaginative menu features such
delights as a spectacularly tasty fish soup for €15
and seafood *waterzooi* for €25. It occupies a spacious nineteenth-century mansion a short walk
south of the Burg, but the decor has some intriguing modern touches – small sculptures and so on
– and the chairs are supremely comfortable. Daily
except Tues noon–2pm & 7–10pm.

De Vlaamsche Pot Helmstraat 3–5. Informal and
friendly, this enjoyable little restaurant, with its
cosy furnishings and fittings – red check table
clothes and so forth – has quickly become popular.
The menu is confined to a few traditional Flemish
dishes, each competently prepared and excellent
value, with prices hovering around €16. Daily
noon–9pm.

Drinking, nightlife and entertainment

Few would say Bruges' **bars** are cutting edge, but neither are they staid and
dull – far from it if you know where to go. Indeed, drinking in the city can be
a real pleasure and one of the potential highlights of any visit. Here, as elsewhere in Belgium, the distinction between the city's cafés and bars is blurred,
with good beer bars often selling excellent food, and cafés frequently boasting
an extensive beer list. Nonetheless, the city's specialist bars – from traditional
haunts to sleek modern places – are generally more distinctive than the Euro-
style pavement cafés which litter the centre and flank the Markt. As for the
club scene, Bruges struggles to make a real fist of it, though its handful of
places are enjoyable enough. **Opening hours** are fairly elastic; although we've
given them for each of our recommendations, don't be amazed if the bar you're
in sails on past the supposed closing time.

Bruges boasts lots of **cultural** festivals. Three of the best are the Bruges Festival
of World Music (☎050 34 87 47), held over four days in the last week of February;
Cinema Novo (☎050 33 54 86, ⒲www.cinemanovo.be), a city-wide international film festival lasting ten days in March; and the three-day Cactusfestival of
rock, reggae, rap, roots and R&B (☎050 33 20 14, ⒲www.cactusfestival.be), that
takes place in the second weekend of July in the park beside the Minnewater.

Bars and clubs

De Bolero Garenmarkt 32 ☎050 33 81 11. A brief walk south of the Markt via Wollestraat. Currently the only gay and lesbian bar/club in town, but heteros are welcome too. There's no admission fee and the drinks are very reasonably priced, even the cocktails. Regular dance evenings with a wide range of sounds, from Abba to house. Daily except Thurs 9pm–4am.

Het Brugs Beertje Kemelstraat 5. Just a 5min walk southwest of the Markt, off Steenstraat. Small, friendly speciality beer bar that claims a stock of three hundred beers, which aficionados reckon is one of the best selections in Belgium. Daily except Wed 4pm–1am.

Cactus Club Sint-Jacobsstraat 36 ☎050 33 20 14, @info@cactusmusic.be. Scheduled to relocate in 2003. Trendiest club in town – groovy and alternative – featuring all sorts of contemporary and world music, both live and spun by well-known DJs. Especially popular at the weekend. Admission usually costs around €10. Open for concerts and performances only – see *Exit* magazine for details.

Café Craenenburg Markt 16. Unlike many of the café-restaurants lining the Markt, this old-fashioned place still attracts a loyal, local clientele. With its leather and wood panelling, wooden benches and stained glass, the *Craenenburg* has the flavour of old Flanders and although the daytime-only food is routine, it has a good range of beers, including the locally produced, tangy brown ale Brugse Tripel. Daily 10am till late.

Cohiba Zilverstraat 38. Idiosyncratic bar – attached to the smart ersatz-medieval *Cafedraal Restaurant* (see p.187) – whose sprightly, imaginative decor attracts a fashionable, 30-something crew. Fantastically popular; drinking garden/den too. Tues–Sat 11.30am till early in the morning.

Het Dreupelhuisje Kemelstraat 9. Tiny and eminently agreeable, laid-back bar specializing in jenevers and advocaats, of which it has an outstand-

ing range. Daily except Tues 6pm–2am.

De Garre De Garre 1. Down a narrow alley off Breidelstraat between the Markt and the Burg, this cramped but charming tavern (*estaminet*) has a great range of Belgian beers and tasty snacks. Classical music and magazines add to the relaxed air. Daily noon–1am.

Oud Vlissinghe Blekerstraat 2, a 5min walk from Jan van Eyckplein. With its wood panelling, antique paintings and long wooden tables, this is one of the oldest and most distinctive bars in Bruges, thought to date from 1515. The atmosphere is relaxed and easy-going, with the emphasis on quiet conversation – there are certainly no juke-boxes here. Garden terrace too. Wed–Sun 11am–midnight.

De Republiek Sint-Jacobsstraat 38. Arguably one of the most fashionable and certainly one of the most popular bars in town, with an arty, sometimes alternative crew. Basic-verging-on-grim decor. Does filling snacks, including vegetarian fare and pastas. Daily 11am–3am.

De Vuurmolen Kraanplein 5. Not far from the Markt, this crowded, youthful bar is a lively spot, with a reasonably wide range of beers and some of the best DJs in town playing a good mix of sounds – techno through house and beyond. Daily 10am–7am.

Wijnbar Est Noordzandstraat 34. The best wine bar in town, with an extensive cellar and over twenty different wines available by the glass every day. Especially strong on New World vintages. Also serves inexpensive, tasty lunches. Sedate atmosphere. Daily except Wed 5pm till late.

De Wittekop St-Jakobstraat 14. The oldest café-bar in town, the decor an appealing mixture of the tasteful and the kitsch. Small and intimate with classy background music – jazz and blues – plus good food, notably tasty stews. The narrow staircase leads up to an even cosier little room. A student favourite. Tues–Sat from 10am.

Listings

Bike rental There are half a dozen bike rental places in Bruges, all charging around €9 per day, including Belgian Railways at the railway station (☎050 30 23 29); Christophe's, Dweersstraat 4 (☎050 33 86 04); and the *Bauhaus International Youth Hotel*, Langestraat 135 (☎050 34 10 93).

Books A reasonable range of English titles and a good selection of Belgian walking maps are available at De Brugse Boekhandel, Dijver 2, beside the bridge at the bottom of Wollestraat.

Buses All local bus services are operated by De

Lijn. City bus information can be had from the De Lijn kiosk outside the train station (Mon–Fri 7.30am–6pm, Sat 9am–6pm, Sun 10am–5pm). De Lijn's local information line is ☎059 56 53 53. The tourist office on the Burg also has bus timetables.

Car rental Europcar, St Pieterskaai 48 (☎050 31 45 44); Luxauto, St Pieterskaai 59 (☎050 31 48 48).

Cinema The Lumière, St-Jacobsstraat 36 (☎050 34 34 65), is Bruges's premier venue for alternative, cult, foreign and art-house movies, with three screens.

Doctors A list of doctors is available from the tourist office; for weekend doctors (Fri 8pm–Mon 8am) call ☎ 050 81 38 99.

Football Founded in 1890, Club Bruges is currently Flanders' premier soccer club and a regular recent winner of the Belgian league and cup. They play in the Jan Breydel Stadium, a 10min drive southwest from the centre along Gistelse Steenweg; on match days there are special buses to the ground from the train station. Fixture details from the tourist office.

Internet access Cafés and coffee shops offering internet access are sprouting up all over central Bruges and computer facilities are now commonplace at the more expensive hotels. One particularly good and convenient spot is *The Coffee Link* (Mon–Fri 10am–9.30pm, Sat & Sun 10am–8.30pm; ☎ 050 34 99 73, ⓦ www.thecoffeelink.com), in the Oud St-Jan exhibition-cum-shopping centre off Mariastraat. Rates are around €0.07 per minute, €4 for one hour.

Left luggage Lockers at the train station: large lockers, €3.30 per 24hr, medium-sized €2.80, small €1.50. Also left luggage office – €2.50 per item.

Markets Not much to get excited about – the Saturday food and general goods market on 't Zand (7am–1pm) is the brightest and best.

Performing Arts Bruges does not have its own full-blown orchestra or opera company, but it does attract a slew of international performers from rock bands through to touring theatre companies. The principal venue is the Concertgebouw, a gleaming new, high spec Concert Hall on 't Zand (☎ 050 44 81 11, ⓦ www.concertgebouw-brugge.be).

Pharmacies Two central pharmacies can be found at 6 St-Jakobsstraat and 50 Katelijnestraat. Details of late-night pharmacies are available from the tourist office; also, duty rotas are usually displayed in pharmacists' windows.

Post office Markt 5 (Mon–Fri 9am–7pm, Sat 9.30am–12.30pm).

Taxis There's a taxi rank on the Markt (☎ 050 33 44 44) and outside the train station on Stationsplein (☎ 050 38 46 60).

Train enquiries Either in person at the train station (and the tourist office) or call ☎ 050 38 23 82 (daily 7am–9pm).

Damme

A popular day-trippers' destination, the quaint village of **DAMME**, 7km northeast of Bruges, was originally the city's main port and fortified outer harbour. It stood on the banks of the River Zwin, which gave Bruges direct access to the sea, but the river silted up in the late fifteenth century and Damme, whose population had reached ten thousand, slipped into a long decline. In its pomp, Damme hosted several important events, notably the grand wedding of Charles the Bold and Margaret of York, and it was also the scene of a famous naval engagement on June 24, 1340. In the summer of that year, a French fleet assembled in the estuary of the Zwin to prepare for an invasion of England. To combat the threat the English king, Edward III, sailed across the Channel and attacked at dawn. Although they were outnumbered three to one, Edward's fleet won an extraordinary victory, his bowmen causing chaos by showering the French ships with arrows at what was (for them) a safe distance – a foretaste of the Battle of Crécy. There was so little left of the French force that no one dared tell King Philip of France, until finally the court jester took matters into his own hands: "Oh! The English cowards! They had not the courage to jump into the sea as our noble Frenchmen did." Philip's reply is not recorded.

The Town

Damme sits beside the canal linking Bruges with tiny Sluis, over the border in Holland, though more importantly, 2km to the northeast of Damme, this waterway also intersects with the modern Leopoldkanaal which cuts down to the coast at the burgeoning container port of Zeebrugge (see p.139). At right angles to the Sluis canal, Damme's one main street, **Kerkstraat**, is edged by

Damme lies at the start of a pretty little parcel of land extending as far as the E34 motorway, about 6km away. Perfect **cycling country**, it's a rural backwater criss-crossed by drowsy canals and causeways, each of which is framed by long lines of trees and sprinkled with comely farmhouses. To explore the area in detail, you should buy the appropriate Nationaal geografisch instituut map (1:25000) in Bruges before you set out.

One especially delightful itinerary, taking in some of the most charming scenery, is a fifteen-kilometre round-trip that begins by leaving Damme to the northeast along the Brugge–Sluis canal; the route then crosses over the Leopoldkanaal and proceeds on to the hamlet of Hoeke. Here, just over the bridge, turn hard left for the narrow causeway – the Krinkeldijk – that wanders straight back in the direction of Damme, running to the north of the Brugge–Sluis canal. Just over 3km long, the dike drifts across a beguiling landscape of bright whitewashed farmhouses, deep green grassy fields and poplar-lined canals, and ultimately reaches an intersection where you turn left to regain the Brugge–Sluis waterway.

---

what remains of the medieval town. Funded by a special tax on barrels of herrings, the fifteenth-century **Stadhuis** is easily the best-looking building, its elegant, symmetrical facade balanced by the graceful lines of its exterior stairway. In one of the niches you'll spy Charles the Bold offering a wedding ring to Margaret, who stands in the next niche along. Just down the street, **St Janshospitaal** (April–Sept Mon & Fri 2–6pm, Tues–Thurs 11am–noon, Sat & Sun 2–4.30pm; Oct–March Sat & Sun only 2–4.30pm; €1) accommodates a small museum of five rooms and a dainty little chapel. A couple of curiously crude parchment-and-straw peasants' pictures of St Peter and St Paul can be found in Room 1, while in Rooms 2 and 3 there's some fine old furniture. Room 4, the main room, displays an enjoyable sample of Delftware and pewter, but it's the chimneypiece which grabs the attention, a Baroque extravagance with a cast-iron backplate depicting the penance of King David for the murder of Bathsheba's husband. Otherwise, the museum holds a mildly diverting assortment of liturgical objects, a potpourri of ceramicware and folksy votive offerings.

From here, it's a couple of minutes' walk further down Kerkstraat to the **Onze Lieve Vrouwekerk** (April–Sept daily 10.30am–noon & 2.30–5.30pm; free), a sturdy brick structure attached to a ruined segment of the original **nave** that speaks volumes about Damme's decline. The church was built in the thirteenth century, but part of the nave was abandoned when the population shrank; the remnants are now stuck between the present church and its clumpy **tower** (same times; €0.50). If you climb the tower you'll get panoramic views over the surrounding polders.

Practicalities

There are several ways to get to Damme **from Bruges**, the most rewarding being the 7km **cycle ride** out along the tree-lined Brugge–Sluis canal, which begins at the Dampoort, on the northeast edge of the centre of Bruges. You can also get there by **canal boat** from the Noorweegse Kaai, 2km north of Bruges' centre (Easter–Sept 5 daily; 40min; one-way €5, return €6.50). Connecting bus #4 runs to the Noorweegse Kaai from the Markt, except in July and August, when getting to the jetty means catching the Bruges–Damme **bus**, #799, from the Markt or the bus station. Using the #799 bus itself for a day-trip to Damme is only easy in July and August (6 daily each way; 15min); at other times of year, the bus runs less frequently – not at all on Sunday – and you'll be consigned to an overlong stay if, indeed, you can make the return journey at all.

Damme's **tourist office** (mid-April to mid-Oct Mon–Fri 9am–noon & 2–6pm, Sat & Sun 10am–noon & 2–6pm; mid-Oct to mid-April Mon–Fri 9am–noon & 2–5pm, Sat & Sun 2–5pm; ☎050 28 86 10), across from the Stadhuis, has a good range of local information. **Bike rental** is available in Damme at Tijl en Nele, round the corner from the Stadhuis at Jacob van Maerlantstraat 2 (reservations advised on ☎050 35 71 92; closed Wed; €9 per day).

Accommodation and eating

There's no strong reason to overnight here, but if you do decide to stay the tourist office can help you find a bed – Damme has a reasonable range of **B&Bs**. Alternatively, just wander along Kerkstraat and watch for the signs, though you'll be lucky to find a vacancy in the height of the season. One place to try is *Le Rêve Restaurant*, right by the canal at the top of Kerkstraat at Damse Vaart Zuid 12 (☎050 35 42 17; ❸). Above the restaurant there are a handful of rooms – nothing fancy but perfectly adequate – with en suite costing an extra €10. A good alternative are the slightly smarter rooms above *'t Trompetje Restaurant*, at Kerkstraat 30 (☎050 35 64 30, ☏050 67 80 91; ❸).

Damme's real forte is its **restaurants**, with a string of first-class places lining up along Kerkstraat. Pick of the bunch is the excellent *Bij Lamme Goedzak*, Kerkstraat 13 (☎050 35 20 03), which serves mouth-watering traditional Flemish dishes, often featuring wild game; main courses run at about €20. Similarly enticing is the French-inspired cuisine of *Le Rêve Restaurant*, by the canal at Damse Vaart Zuid 12 (☎050 35 42 17). If your budget won't stretch that far, head for *'t Uylenspieghel*, Kerkstraat 44, a café-tearoom which serves tasty snacks – croque monsieur through to pancakes – and a good range of beers, including a couple of local village brews.

Ghent

Though more sprawling and less immediately picturesque than Bruges, its great rival, **GHENT** still musters a string of fine Gothic buildings and many delightful, intimate streetscapes, with antique brick houses woven around a skein of narrow canals. The city's star turn is undoubtedly **St Baafskathedraal** – or at least its principal treasure, Jan van Eyck's remarkable *Adoration of the Mystic Lamb* – but it's well-supported by the likes of **St Niklaaskerk**, with its extraordinary soaring arches, and the forbidding castle of the Counts of Flanders, **Het Gravensteen**. Close by are exquisite medieval guildhouses and a clutch of enjoyable museums, not to mention a bevy of lively bars and first-class restaurants clustering the cobbled lanes of the **Patershol** district. These central attractions are supplemented by several out-lying sights, most notably **SMAK**, a prestigious Museum of Contemporary Art, and the **Museum voor Schone Kunsten** (Fine Art). Lastly, Ghent remains a quintessentially Flemish city with a tourist industry – rather than the other way round – and if you're put off by the tourists and tweeness of Bruges, this is the place to decamp.

Some history

The principal seat of the counts of Flanders and the largest town in western Europe during the thirteenth and fourteenth centuries, Ghent was once at the

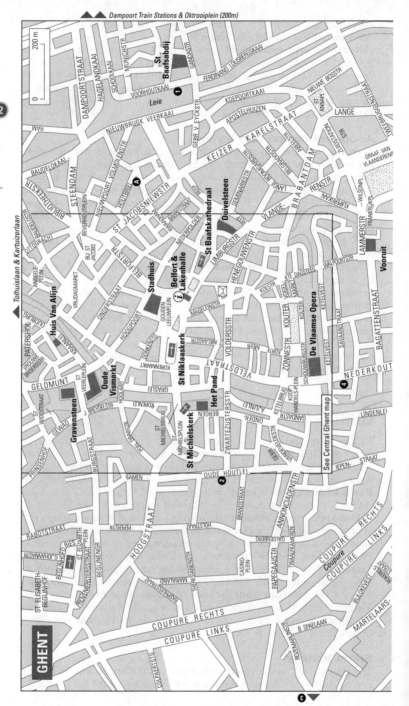

Dampoort Train Stations & Oktrooiplein (200m)

GHENT

200 m

St Baafsabdii

Leie

Dampoortstraat
Hagelandkaai
Schoolkaai
Munichstr
Gandastraat
Ferdinand Toussbergskaai

Voorhoutkaai

Nieuwbrug Veerkaai
Gebr. V. Eyckstr
Koepoortkaai
Apostelhuizen
St Annapl
Nieuwe Bosstr
Lange
Leeuwbrugenstraat

Ham

Baudelokaal
Steendam
Nieuwpoort Volmolenstr
St Jacobsnieuwstr
Keizer Karelstraat
Abeelstr
Bergstr
Lange Boomgaardstr
Brabantdam
Renstr
Zuistationstr
Graaf van Vlaanderenpl

Bibliotheekstr
Ottogracht
Beverhoutplein
Baliestraat
Nederpolder
Vlande-
Seminariestr
Duivelsteen
St Baafskathedraal
Limburgstr
Henegouwenstr
Wilsonpl
Klipkerskaai
Frankrijkpl

Anseele Plein
Bij St Jacobs
Vrijdagmarkt
Belfort & Lakenhalle
Stadhuis
Onderstraat
Hoogpoort
Gouden Leeuwplein
Magelemstr
St Niklastr
Kte Dagsteeg
Vogel Markt
Kte Meer
Kolestr
Koestr
Walpoortstr

Lammerstr
Vooruit
Bagattenstraat

Huis Van Alijn
Patershol
Oudburg
Kraanlei
Vrouwe Broersstr
Geldmunt
St Veerleplein
Holland
Breydelstr
Oude Vismarkt
Korenlei
Graslei
Korenmarkt
Koestr
St Niklaaskerk
Volderstr
Niklassstr
Meer
Kolte
Kolter
Schoumburgstr
De Vlaamse Opera
Ketelvest
Savaanstraat

Gravensteen
Prinsenhof
Gewad
Burgstraat
Wl Wilderstr
St Michielsplein
St Michielsbrug
Bergen
Zwartezustersstr
Onder-
A.Ijnlei
Ketelbrug
Koop Handelsplein
Ketelvest
Nederkout
Lindenlei

Het Pand
St Michielskerk
Onder Houtlei
Oude Houtlei
See Central Ghent map
Gandastr
Iepen-straat

Raboststraat
Hoogstraat
Ramen
Brandstraat
Holstraat
Annonciadenstr
Galgenberg
Casino-plein
Twaalfkameren
Coupure Rechts
Coupure Links

St Elisabeth-Begijnhof
Ries
St Elisabeth Plein
Begijnengr
Peperstr
Therziekenstr
Marialand
Baudeloostraat
Papegaaistr
Coupure
Bijlokevest
Rozemarijnstr
Prof J Johannstr
Prof Frederikstraat
G Johannstr
Begijnhof

Coupure Rechts
Coupure Links
B Spaelaan
Martelaars-

Tolhuislaan & Kartuizerlaan

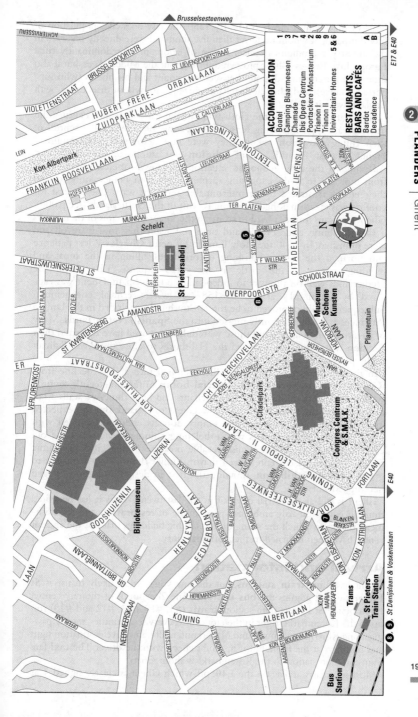

▲ *Brusselsesteenweg*

ACCOMMODATION
Boatel	1
Camping Blaarmeesen	3
Chamade	7
Ibis Opera Centrum	4
Poortackere Monasterium	2
Trianon I	8
Trianon II	9
Universitaire Homes	5 & 6

RESTAURANTS, BARS AND CAFÉS
Bardot	A
Decadence	B

Kon Albertpark

Scheldt

St Pietersabdij

Museum Schone Kunsten

Plantentuin

Citadelpark

Congres Centrum & S.M.A.K.

Bijlokemuseum

St Pieters Train Station

Trams

Bus Station

E17 & E40 ▶

▶ E40

▶ St Denijslaan & Voskenslaan

▶ ⑧, ⑨. St Denijslaan & Voskenslaan

heart of the Flemish **cloth trade**. By 1350, the city boasted a population of fifty thousand, of whom no fewer than five thousand were directly involved in the industry, a prodigious concentration of labour in a predominantly rural Europe. Like Bruges, Ghent prospered throughout the Middle Ages, but it also suffered from endemic disputes between the count and his nobles (who supported France) and the cloth-reliant citizens (to whom friendship with England was vital).

The relative decline of the cloth trade in the early sixteenth century did little to ease the underlying tension, the people of Ghent still resentful of their ruling class, from whom they were now separated by **language** – French against Flemish – and **religion** – Catholic against Protestant. Adapting to the new economic situation, the town's merchants switched from industry to trade, exporting surplus grain from France, only to find their efforts frustrated by an interminable series of wars. The catalyst for conflict was taxation: long before the Revolt of the Netherlands (see p.000), Ghent's artisans found it hard to stomach the financial dictates of their rulers – the Habsburgs after 1482 – and time and again they rose in revolt and were punished. In 1540 the Holy Roman Emperor **Charles V** lost patience and stormed the town, abolishing its privileges, filling in the moat and building a new secure castle at the city's expense. Later, with the Netherlands well on the way to independence from Spain, Ghent was captured by Philip II's armies in 1584. It was a crucial engagement. Subsequently, Ghent proved to be too far south to be included in the United Provinces and was reluctantly pressed into the **Spanish Netherlands**. Many of its citizens fled north, and those who didn't may well have regretted their decision when the Dutch forced the Habsburgs to close the River Scheldt as the price of peace in 1648.

In the centuries that followed, Ghent slipped into a slow decline from which it emerged during the **industrial boom** of the nineteenth century. In optimistic mood, the medieval merchants had built the city's walls a fair distance from the town centre to allow Ghent to expand. But the expected growth never took place, and the empty districts ended up choked with nineteenth-century factories whose belching chimneys encrusted the old city with soot and grime, a disagreeable measure of the city's economic revival. Indeed, its entrepreneurial mayor, Emille Braun, even managed to get the **Great Exhibition**, showing the best in design and goods, staged here in 1913.

Ghent is still an industrial city, but in the last twenty years it has benefited from an extraordinarily ambitious programme of **restoration** and refurbishment, thanks to which the string of fine Gothic buildings that dot the ancient centre have been returned to their original glory.

Arrival and information

Ghent has three **train stations**, but the one you're most likely to use is **St Pieters**, which adjoins the **bus station**, some 2km south of the city centre. From beside St Pieters train station, **trams** (#1, #10, #11, #12 and #13) run up to the Korenmarkt, right in the city centre, every few minutes, mostly passing along Kortrijksesteenweg and Nederkouter. All trams have destination signs and numbers at the front, but if in doubt check with the driver. The **taxi** fare from the train station to the Korenmarkt is about €6.

Most motorists arrive via the **E40**, off which Ghent is clearly signed. Car parks within the city centre – an oval encircled by the **R40** ring road – are often jam-packed; to help, the city has signed two **parking routes** (*parkeer-route*), one signed with yellow arrows, the other with green, both of which lead to – or past – the ten car parks that lie in or close to the centre. The green route is better for the central car parks and is a little less convoluted than the other; the 24-hour car park beneath the Vrijdagmarkt is one of the best placed.

Ghent's **tourist office** is right in the centre of the city, in the crypt of the Lakenhalle (daily: April–Oct 9.30am–6.30pm; Nov–March 9.30am–4.30pm; ☎09 226 52 32, ⊛www.gent.be). They have a wide range of city information, including a full list of local accommodation, along with prices. The tourist office will book hotel accommodation on your behalf – an especially useful service on busy summer weekends.

City transport

All **tram** and **bus** services are operated by De Lijn (information line ☎09 210 93 11). A standard one-way fare costs €1; tickets, valid for an hour, are bought direct from the driver, who will give change if required. A ten-journey Rittenkaart, costing €7.50, can be bought from selected shops and newsstands all over town, or at any of the De Lijn **kiosks** by the tram stops on the Korenmarkt (Mon–Fri 7am–7pm, Sat 10.30am–5.30pm) and at St Pieters train station (Mon–Fri 7am–7pm). The kiosks also sell a 24-hour city transport pass, the Dagpas, which represents good value at just €2.90, and issue free maps of the transport system (the Netplan). These tickets and passes are also valid on the city's one and only **trolley bus line** (#3), which cuts across the city from east and west.

Ghent is very flat and thus especially good for **cycling**, with cycle lanes on many of the roads and cycle racks dotted across the centre. There are a couple of **bike rental** outlets in Ghent, but Belgian Railways sets the benchmark, hiring out bikes at St Pieters railway station (☎09 241 22 24; daily 7am–8pm) for €8.80 per day.

Walking tours and boat trips

Guided walking tours are particularly popular in Ghent. The standard walking tour, organized by the tourist office, is a two-hour jaunt round the city centre (April Sat & Sun at 2.30pm, May–Oct daily at 2.30pm; €6); advance booking – is strongly recommended. Alternatively, **horse-drawn carriages** line up outside the Lakenhalle, on St Baafsplein, offering a thirty-minute canter round town for €23 (Easter to Oct daily 10am–6pm & most winter weekends).

Throughout the year, **boat trips** explore Ghent's inner **waterways**, departing from the Korenlei and Graslei quays, just near the Korenmarkt (March to early Nov daily 10am–6pm, mid-Nov to Feb Sat & Sun 11am–4pm; €4.50). Trips last forty minutes and leave roughly every fifteen minutes, though the wait can be longer as boats often only leave when reasonably full. Other, longer nautical excursions leave from near the Recolettenbrug, behind the Recollettenlei (Law Courts), at the west end of Zonnestraat. They include day-trips to **Bruges** (July & Aug 4 monthly, 9am–8pm; €13), though these aren't quite as good as they sound: food and drink are expensive, and long sections of the canal are too deep to see over the banks. Further details can be obtained from the tourist office or from Benelux Rederij, the boat operators, at Recollettenlei 32 (☎09 225 15 05).

Accommodation

Ghent has around twenty **hotels**, ranging from the delightful to the mundanely modern, with several of the most stylish and enjoyable – but not necessarily the most expensive – located in the centre, which is where you want to be. The city also has a good supply of inexpensive accommodation. There's a bright, cheerful and centrally located **youth hostel**; several hundred student rooms are available for visitors during the summer recess; a large suburban **campsite**; and a modest range of **B&Bs**, a list of which can be obtained from the tourist office – reckon on €40–60 per double. The places to stay we've reviewed are marked on the map of Ghent on pp.192–93 or on the central Ghent map on p.198.

The tourist office will make **hotel and B&B reservations** on your behalf at no charge, though they do require a small deposit, which is deducted from the final bill. They also publish a free and comprehensive brochure detailing local accommodation, including hotels and hostels along with prices.

Hotels

Over €80

Boatel Voorhuitkaai 29A ☎09 267 10 30, ℱ09 267 10 39, ⓦwww.theboatel.com. Certainly the most distinctive of the city's hotels, the *Boatel* is, as its name implies, a converted boat, an imaginatively and immaculately refurbished canal barge to be precise. It's moored in one of the city's outer canals, a 10–15min walk east from the centre. The seven bedrooms are decked out in crisp, modern style, and breakfasts, taken on the poop deck, are first rate. Two star. Recommended. ⑤

Erasmus Poel 25 ☎09 224 21 95, ℱ09 233 42 41, ⓔhotel.erasmus@proximedia.be. Another contender for Ghent's most distinctive hotel, a friendly family-run affair located in a commodious old town house a few metres away from the Korenlei. Each room is thoughtfully decorated and furnished with antiques. The breakfast is excellent. Reservations strongly advised in summer. One star, but this rating does it precious little justice. Closed mid-Dec to mid-Jan. ⑥

Gravensteen Jan Breydelstraat 35 ☎09 225 11 50, ℱ09 225 18 50, ⓦwww.gravensteen.be. Medium-sized, conducive hotel centred in an attractively restored nineteenth-century mansion adorned with Second Empire trimmings. Great location, close to the castle. The rooms in the annexe and in one wing of the original building are smart and relatively spacious with pleasing modern furnishings. Several of the older rooms are, however, poky beyond belief. Three star. ⑦

Novotel Centrum Goudenleeuwplein 5 ☎09 224 22 30, ℱ09 224 32 95, ⓦwww.novotel.com. First-class, modern chain hotel bang in the middle of the town centre. The rooms are neat and trim, decorated in fetching if standard chain style. Has an outdoor swimming pool and offers good breakfasts. Three star. ⑦

Poortackere Monasterium Oude Houtlei 58 ☎09 269 22 10, ℱ09 269 22 30, ⓦwww.poortackere.com. About 5min walk west of Veldstraat. This unusual hotel-cum-guesthouse occupies a rambling and frugal former monastery, whose dusty brickwork dates from the nineteenth century. The complex includes a modest neo-Gothic chapel, but guests don't stay here. Instead they have a choice between spartan, en-suite rooms in the hotel section, or the more authentic monastic-cell experience in the guesthouse, where some rooms have shared facilities. Breakfast is taken in the old chapterhouse. One star. ⑤

St Jorishof-Cour St Georges Botermarkt 2 ☎09 224 24 24, ℱ09 224 26 40, ⓦwww.courtstgeorges.com. Facing the Stadhuis, the main building dates from the thirteenth century and is notable for its sturdy Romanesque facade, equipped with a slender crow-step gable and mullioned windows. The interior is all neo-baronial, with acres of late nineteenth-century panelling. Inside the main building, the rooms are decorated in broadly period style, but most of the 36 rooms are in a nearby annexe and are best described as adequate to plain. One star. ⑥

Sofitel Gent Belfort Hoogpoort 63 ☎09 233 33 31, ℱ09 233 11 02, ⓦwww.sofitel.com. One of the plushest hotels in town, daintily shoehorned behind an ancient facade across from the Stadhuis. Spacious, pastel-shaded rooms and suites as well as all mod cons, including good fitness facilities. Four star. Inquire direct for discounts. ⑨

Under €80

Chamade Blankenbergestraat 2 ☎09 220 15 15, ℱ09 221 97 66, ⓦwww.bestwestern.be.

About 5min walk north of the train station. Standard three-star accommodation is available in bright, modern bedrooms at this chain hotel, though the building itself – a six-storey block – is a bit of an eyesore. Weekend discounts of twenty percent. ❹

Flandria Centrum Barrestraat 3 ☎ 09 223 06 26, ⓕ 09 233 77 89, ⓦ www.flandria-centrum.be. Somewhat dishevelled hotel located in the narrow sidestreets off the Reep, a 5min walk northeast of the cathedral. Apart from the youth hostel, these are the least expensive rooms in the city centre. All sixteen (modest) rooms are en suite. One star. ❸

Ibis Centrum Kathedraal Limburgstraat 2 ☎ 09 233 00 00, ⓕ 09 233 10 00, ⓦ www.ibishotel.com. Handily situated opposite the cathedral, this large hotel – one of the *Ibis* chain – offers comfortable modern rooms, though the noise from the square in front of the hotel can be irritating late at night – ask for a room at the back. Three star. ❹

Ibis Centrum Opera Nederkouter 24–26 ☎ 09 225 07 07, ⓕ 09 223 59 07, ⓦ www.ibishotel.com. Spick-and-span, modern, five-storey block a 5min walk south of the Korenmarkt. The rooms lack character, but they're perfectly functional. Three star. ❹

Trianon I Sint Denijslaan 203 ☎ 09 220 48 40, ⓕ 09 220 49 50, ⓦ www.hoteltrianon.be. Motel-style accommodation on a quiet residential street about 2km south of the centre, just beyond Ghent St Pieters train station. The nineteen rooms are comfortable and spotless, and all are en suite. One star. ❸

Trianon II Voskenslaan 34 ☎ 09 220 48 40, ⓕ 09 220 49 50, ⓦ www.hoteltrianon.be. Similar to *Trianon I*, 50m away, though the rooms are a tad more commodious – and you're beside a much busier road. Nineteen rooms, all en suite. Two star. ❹

Camping, B&B, hostel and student rooms

Camping Blaarmeersen Zuiderlaan 12 ☎ 09 221 53 99, ⓕ 09 222 41 84. Among the woods beside the watersports centre to the west of town (bus #38 from Korenmarkt; 10min), this large campsite is equipped with laundry, shop, cafeteria and various sports facilities. March to mid-Oct. High season rate per person per night is €3 (low season €2.70), cars €1.60 (€1.50), tent or caravan €3.20 (€3).

Brooderie Jan Breydelstraat 8 (☎ 09 225 06 23). Handily located near the Korenmarkt. An appealing café (see p.208) whose owners rent out three neat and trim little rooms above it. Breakfast is excellent. ❹

Jeugdherberg De Draecke St Widostraat 11 ☎ 09 233 70 50, ⓕ 09 233 80 01, ⓔ youthhostel.gent@skynet.be. Excellent, well-equipped youth hostel in the city centre, a 5min walk north of the Korenmarkt. Over a hundred beds, in two-, three-, four-, five- and six-bed rooms. Advance reservations are advised especially in the height of the season. Breakfast is included, and the restaurant offers lunch and dinner too. There are also lockers, a bar, and facilities for bike rental and currency exchange. Dorm beds €13. ❷

Universitaire Homes Several addresses in the south of town, including Stalhof 4 and 6; general information and reservations on ☎ 09 264 71 12, ⓕ 09 264 72 96. The most central complexes are Home Vermeylen, Stalhof 6 and Home Fabiola, Stalhof 4; Stalhof is a good 15min walk south of the centre via Overpoortstraat. Between mid-July and late September, over a thousand student rooms are let to visitors; rate includes breakfast. ❶

The City Centre

The shape and structure of today's **city centre** reflects Ghent's ancient class and linguistic divide. The streets to the south of the **Korenmarkt**, the former Corn Market, tend to be straight and wide, lined with elegant old mansions, the former habitations of the wealthier, French-speaking classes, while, to the north, Flemish Ghent is all narrow alleys and low brick houses. They meet at the somewhat confusing sequence of large squares that surrounds the town's principal buildings, spreading out to the immediate east of the Korenmarkt. Most of Ghent's leading attractions are within easy walking distance of the Korenmarkt.

St Baafskathedraal

The best place to start an exploration of the city centre is the mainly Gothic **St Baafskathedraal** (St Bavo's Cathedral; daily: April–Oct 8.30am–6pm &

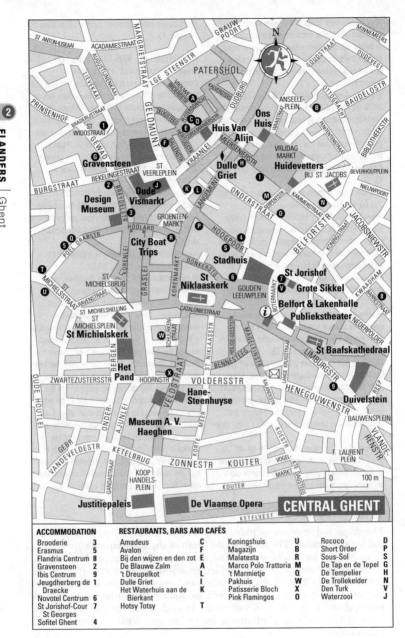

CENTRAL GHENT

ACCOMMODATION

Broderie	3
Erasmus	5
Flandria Centrum	8
Gravensteen	2
Ibis Centrum	9
Jeugdherberg de Draecke	1
Novotel Centrum	6
St Jorishof-Cour St Georges	7
Sofitel Ghent	4

RESTAURANTS, BARS AND CAFÉS

Amadeus	C	Koningshuis	U
Avalon	F	Magazijn	B
Bij den wijzen en den zot	A	Malatesta	R
De Blauwe Zalm	L	Marco Polo Trattoria	M
't Dreupelkot	I	't Marmietje	Q
Dulle Griet	K	Pakhuis	W
Het Waterhuis aan de Bierkant	K	Patisserie Bloch	X
Hotsy Totsy	T	Pink Flamingos	O

Rococo	D
Short Order	P
Sous-Sol	S
De Tap en de Tepel	G
De Tempelier	H
De Trollekelder	N
Den Turk	V
Waterzooi	J

Nov–March 8.30am–5pm; free), squeezed into the eastern corner of St Baafsplein. The third church on this site, and two hundred and fifty years in the making, the cathedral is a tad lop-sided, but there's no gainsaying the imposing beauty of the **west tower**, with its long, elegant windows and perky corner turrets. Some 82m high, the tower was the last major part of the church to be completed, topped off in 1554 – just before the outbreak of the religious wars that were to wrack the country.

The Adoration of the Mystic Lamb

Inside, St Baaf's mighty Gothic **nave** is supported by tall, slender columns that give the whole interior a cheerful sense of lightness, though the seventeenth-century marble screens spoil the effect by darkening the choir. In a small side **chapel** (April–Oct Mon–Sat 9.30am–5pm, Sun 1–5pm & Nov–March Mon–Sat 10.30am–4pm, Sun 2–5pm; €2.50) to the left of the entrance is the cathedral's – and Ghent's – greatest treasure, an **altarpiece** known as the *Adoration of the Mystic Lamb*, by Jan van Eyck. Painted around 1432, it's a seminal work, whose needle-sharp, luminous realism must have stunned van Eyck's contemporaries. The **cover screens** display a beautiful Annunciation scene with the archangel Gabriel's wings reaching up to the timbered ceiling of a Flemish house, the streets of a town visible through the windows. In a brilliant coup of lighting, the darkened recesses around the shadows of the angel dapple the room, emphasizing the reality of the apparition – a technique repeated on the opposite cover panel around the figure of Mary. Below, the donor and his wife kneel piously alongside statues of the saints.

The cover paintings are, however, but a foretaste of what's within – a striking, visionary work of art that was only revealed when the shutters were opened on high days and holidays. On the **upper level** sit God the Father, the Virgin and John the Baptist in gleaming clarity; to the right are musician-angels and a nude, pregnant Eve; and on the left is Adam plus a group of singing angels who strain to read their music. The Lamb stands on an altar whose rim is minutely inscribed with a quotation from the Gospel of St John, "Behold the Lamb of God, which taketh away the sins of the world". The apostles kneel on the right-hand side of the altar, the prophets to the left; in addition four groups converge on the altar from the corners of the central panel – Old Testament patriarchs, bishops carrying palm branches and two groups of saints, one male, the other female. On the **side panels**, approaching the Lamb across symbolically rough and stony ground, are more holy figures – saints to the right and horsemen to the left. The inner group of horsemen symbolize the Warriors of Christ – including St George bearing a shield with a red cross – and the outer the Just Judges, each of whom is dressed in fancy Flemish attire.

The Just Judges panel is not, however, authentic, having been added during the German occupation of World War II to replace the original, which was stolen in 1934 and never recovered. The theft was just one of many dramatic events to befall the painting – indeed it's remarkable that the altarpiece has survived at all. The Calvinists wanted to destroy it; Philip II of Spain tried to acquire it; the Emperor Joseph II disapproved of the painting so violently that he replaced the nude Adam and Eve with a clothed version of 1784 (exhibited today on a column just inside the church entrance); and near the end of World War II the Germans stole the altarpiece and hid it in an Austrian salt mine, where it remained until American soldiers arrived in 1945.

After the altarpiece, the rest of the cathedral can't help but seem something of an anticlimax. The rococo **pulpit**, a whopping oak and marble affair stranded in the nave, is an enjoyable frippery but no more, while the **high altar**, with its tons of marble, features an enthroned St Baaf ascending to heaven on an untidy heap of clouds. Nearby, in the **north transept** – and rather more diverting – is a characteristically energetic painting by Rubens (1577–1640) entitled *St Baaf entering the Abbey of Ghent*. Dating to 1624, it includes a self-portrait – he's the bearded head. Close by is the entrance to the dank and capacious **crypt**, a survivor from the earlier Romanesque church. The crypt is stuffed with religious bric-a-brac of some mild interest, but the highlight is Justus van Gent's superb fifteenth-century triptych, *The Crucifixion of Christ*. This depicts the crucified Christ flanked, on the left, by Moses purifying the waters of Mara with wood, and to the right by Moses and the bronze serpent which cured poisoned Israelites on sight.

The Lakenhalle and the Belfort

On the west side of St Baafsplein lurks the **Lakenhalle**, a gloomy hunk of a building with an unhappy history. Work began on the hall in the early fifteenth century, but the cloth trade slumped before it was finished and it was only in 1903 that it was grudgingly completed. Indeed, the Lakenhalle has never quite sorted itself out, and today it's little more than an empty shell with the city's tourist office tucked away in the basement on the north side. The first-floor entrance on the south side of the Lakenhalle is the only way to reach the adjoining **Belfort** (mid-March to mid-Nov 10am–1pm & 2–6pm, plus free guided tours May–Sept daily at 2pm, 3pm & 4pm; €3), a much-amended medieval edifice whose soaring spire is topped by a comically corpulent, gilded copper dragon. Once a watchtower-cum-storehouse of civic documents, the interior is a real disappointment – an empty shell displaying a few old bells and statues. The belfry is equipped with a glass-sided lift that climbs up to the roof, where consolation is provided in the form of excellent views over the city centre.

The Stadhuis

Just across from the tourist office, the **Stadhuis** (May–Oct Mon–Thurs guided tours only, times from the tourist office; €3) is a sturdy building, whose main facade comprises two distinct sections. Framing the central stairway is the later section, whose austere symmetries are a good example of Italian Renaissance architecture, dating from the 1580s. This part of the facade is, however, in stark contrast to the wild, curling patterns of the section to the immediate north, carved in the Flamboyant Gothic style at the turn of the sixteenth century to a design by one of the most celebrated architects of the day, Rombout Keldermans. The original plan was to have the whole of the Stadhuis built by Keldermans, but the money ran out when the wool trade collapsed and the city couldn't afford to finish it off until much later. Each of Keldermans' ornate niches was intended to hold a statuette, but these were never installed and the present carvings, representing important historical figures in characteristic poses, were inserted at the end of the twentieth century. Look out for **Keldermans**, shown rubbing his chin and holding his plans for the Stadhuis.

Tours of the Stadhuis are mildly enjoyable; of the series of halls open to the public, the most interesting is the old Court of Justice or **Pacificatiezaal** (Pacification Hall), the site of the signing of the Pacification of Ghent in 1576.

A plaque commemorates this agreement, which momentarily bound north and south Flanders together against the Habsburgs. The carrot offered by the dominant Protestants was the promise of religious freedom, but they failed to deliver and much of the south (present-day Belgium) soon returned to the imperial fold. The hall's dark blue and white tiled floor is curiously designed in the form of a maze. No one's quite certain why, but it's supposed that more privileged felons (or sinners) had to struggle round the maze on their knees as a substitute punishment for a pilgrimage to Jerusalem – a good deal if ever there was one.

St Niklaaskerk

The last of this central cluster of buildings is **St Niklaaskerk** (Mon 2–5pm, Tues–Sun 10am–5pm; free), an architectural hybrid dating from the thirteenth century. It's the shape and structure that pleases most, especially the arching buttresses and pencil-thin turrets which, in a classic example of the early Scheldt Gothic style, elegantly attenuate the lines of the nave. Inside, most of the Baroque furnishings and fittings that once cluttered the interior have been removed, but unfortunately this does not apply to a clumsy and clichéd set of statues of the Apostles. Much better is the giant-sized Baroque high altar, with its mammoth representation of God glowering down its back, blowing the hot wind of the Last Judgement from his mouth and surrounded by a flock of cherubic angels.

The Korenmarkt and the Tussen Bruggen

St Niklaaskerk marks the southern end of the **Korenmarkt** (Corn Market), a long and wide cobbled area where the grain which once kept the city alive was traded after it was unloaded from the boats that anchored on the Graslei. The one noteworthy building here is the former **post office**, whose combination of Gothic Revival and neo-Renaissance styles illustrates the eclecticism popular in Belgium at the beginning of the twentieth century. Among the carved heads encircling the building, which represent the rulers who came to the city for the Great Exhibition of 1913, is, bizarrely, a bust of Florence Nightingale. The interior has recently been turned into a sleek shopping mall.

The guildhouses of the Graslei

West of St Niklaaskerk, the neo-Gothic **St Michielsbrug** offers fine views back over the towers and turrets that pierce the Ghent skyline. The bridge also overlooks the city's oldest harbour, the **Tussen Bruggen** (Between the Bridges), from whose quays – the Graslei and the Korenlei – **boats** leave for trips around the city's canals (see p.195).

The **Graslei** holds the late medieval, gabled guildhouses of the town's boatmen and grainweighers. Some of these are of particularly fine design, beginning with – and working your way north from – the **Gildehuis van de Vrije Schippers** (Guildhouse of the Free Boatmen), at no. 14, where the badly weathered sandstone is decorated with scenes of boatmen weighing anchor (there's also a delicate carving of a caravel, the type of Mediterranean sailing ship used by Columbus, located above the door). Medieval Ghent had two boatmen guilds – the Free, who could discharge their cargoes within the city, and the Unfree, who could not, and were thus obliged to unload their goods into the vessels of the Free Boatmen at the edge of the city – an inefficient arrangement by any standard, but typical of the complex regulations governing the guilds.

Close by, at Graslei 12–13, is the late seventeenth-century **Coorenmetershuis** (Corn Measurers' House), where city officials weighed and graded corn behind a facade graced by cartouches and garlands of fruit. Next door, at no. 11, is the quaint **Tolhuisje**, another delightful example of Flemish Renaissance architecture, built to house the customs officers in 1698. Of contrasting appearance, the limestone **Spijker** (Staple House), at no. 10, boasts a surly Romanesque facade and a heavy crow-stepped gable dating to around 1200. It was here that the city stored its grain supply for over five hundred years until a fire gutted the interior. At no. 8, the splendid **Den Enghel** takes its name from the angel bearing a banner that decorates the facade; the building was originally the stonemasons' guildhouse, as evidenced by the effigies of the four Roman martyrs who were the guild's patron saints.

From the north end of Graslei, it's a few metres to the **Groentenmarkt** (Vegetable Market), one of the city's prettier squares, and a couple of minutes more to Het Gravensteen.

Het Gravensteen

Het Gravensteen, the castle of the Counts of Flanders (daily: April–Sept 9am–6pm; Oct–March 9am–5pm; €6.20), looks sinister enough to have been lifted from a Bosch painting. Its cold, dark walls and unyielding turrets were first raised in 1180 as much to intimidate the town's unruly citizens as to protect them. Considering the castle has been used for all sorts of purposes since then (it was even a cotton mill in the nineteenth century), it has survived in remarkably good nick. The imposing gateway is a deep-arched, heavily fortified tunnel that leads to the **courtyard**, which is framed by protective battlements complete with wooden flaps, ancient arrow slits and holes for boiling oil and water. Beside the courtyard stand the castle's two main buildings, the **keep** on the right and, to the left, the **count's residence**, riddled with narrow, interconnected staircases set within the thickness of the walls. A self-guided tour takes you through this labyrinth, and highlights include the cavernous state rooms of the count, a gruesome collection of instruments of torture, and a particularly dank, underground dungeon. It's also possible to walk along most of the castle's encircling wall, from where there are pleasant views over the city centre.

St Veerleplein and the Oude Vismarkt

The counts' public punishments were carried out just across from the castle entrance on **St Veerleplein**, now an attractive cobbled square, but with an ersatz punishment post, plonked here in 1913 and topped off by a lion carrying the banner of Flanders. At the back of the square, beside the junction of the city's two main canals, is the grandiloquent Baroque facade of the **Oude Vismarkt**, which is dominated by a grand relief of Neptune, who stands on a chariot drawn by sea horses. To either side are allegorical figures representing the Leie (Venus) and the Scheldt (Hercules) – the two rivers that spawned the city. The market itself is in a terrible state, scheduled for restoration – or possibly demolition.

The Design Museum

Crossing the bridge immediately to the west of St Veerleplein, turn first left for the **Design Museum**, Jan Breydelstraat 5 (Tues–Sun 10am–6pm; €2.50), one of the city's more enjoyable museums. Focused on Belgian decorative and applied arts, the wide-ranging collection divides into two distinct sections. At the front, squeezed into what was once an eighteenth-century patrician's mansion, lies an attractive sequence of period rooms, culminating in the original dining room, complete with painted ceiling, wood panelling and Chinese porcelain. Linked to the back of the house is the other section, a gleamingly modern display area used both for temporary exhibitions and to showcase the museum's eclectic collection of applied arts dating from 1880 to 1940. There are examples of the work of many leading designers, but pride of place goes to the Art Nouveau material, especially the work of the Belgian **Henry van der Velde**, whose oeuvre is well represented by a furnished room he designed and decorated in 1899.

Huis van Alijn Museum

Back on St Veerleplein, turn down Kraanlei to reach – at no. 65 – one of the city's more popular attractions, the **Huis van Alijn Museum** (Tues–Sun 11am–5pm; €2.50), a rambling folklore museum that occupies a series of exceptionally pretty little almshouses set around a central courtyard. Dating from the fourteenth century, the almshouses were built following a major scandal reminiscent of *Romeo and Juliet*. In 1354, two members of the Rijms family murdered three of the rival Alijns when they were at Mass in St Baafskathedraal. The immediate cause of the affray was that one of each clan were rivals for the same woman, but the dispute went deeper, reflecting the commercial animosity of two guilds, the weavers and the fullers. The murderers fled for their lives and were condemned to death in absentia, but eventually – eight years later – they were pardoned on condition that they paid for the construction of a set of almshouses, which was to be named after the victims. The result was the Huis van Alijn, which became a hospice for elderly women and then a workers' tenement until the city council snapped it up in the 1950s.

The **museum** consists of a long series of period rooms depicting local life and work in the eighteenth and nineteenth centuries, intermingled with rooms that illustrate a particular theme or subject. Frankly, the period rooms are not especially riveting, though the reconstructed pipe-maker's, cobbler's and cooper's workshops are all of some interest, whereas the themed rooms are often intriguing. There are good displays on funerals and death, popular entertainment – from brass bands through to sports and fairs – and on religious beliefs in an age when every ailment had its own allocated saint. The more substantial exhibits are explained in free English-language leaflets that are available in the appropriate room.

The Patershol

Behind the Kraanlei are the lanes and alleys of the **Patershol**, a tight web of brick terraced houses dating from the seventeenth century. Once the heart of the Flemish working-class city, this thriving residential quarter had, by the 1970s, become a slum threatened with demolition. After much toing and fro-ing, the area was ultimately kept from the developers and a process of gentrification begun, the result being today's gaggle of good bars and smashing restaurants (see p.209). The process is still under way – one of the stragglers being the ongoing refurbishment of the grand old Carmelite Monastery on Vrouwebroersstraat – and the fringes of the Patershol remain a ragbag of decay and restoration, but few European cities can boast a more agreeable drinking and eating district.

The Vrijdagmarkt and Bij St Jacobs

Just beyond the Huis van Alijn, an antiquated little bridge leads over to **Dulle Griet** (Mad Meg), a lugubrious fifteenth-century cannon, supposedly the most powerful siege gun ever manufactured. It proved more dangerous to the gunners than the enemy: the barrel cracked the first time it was fired. From the

Huis van Alijn, it's a few seconds' walk to the **Vrijdagmarkt**, a wide, open square that was long the political centre of Ghent, the site of both public meetings and executions (sometimes both at the same time). In the middle of the square stands a nineteenth-century **statue** of the guild leader **Jacob van Artevelde** (1290–1345), portrayed addressing the people in heroic style. Of the buildings flanking the Vrijdagmarkt, the most appealing is the former **Gildehuis van de Huidevetters** (Tanners' Guildhouse), at no. 37, a tall, Gothic structure whose pert dormer windows and stepped gables culminate in a dainty and distinctive corner turret – the **Toreken** – which is crowned by a mermaid weathervane. Also worth a second glance is the old headquarters of the trade unions, the whopping **Ons Huis** (Our House), a sterling edifice built in eclectic style at the turn of the twentieth century.

Adjoining the Vrijdagmarkt, the busy **Bij St Jacobs** is a sprawling square surrounding a sulky medieval church and sprinkled with antique shops. From here, it's a couple of minutes' walk up Belfortstraat back to the Stadhuis and Hoogpoort.

East along the Hoogpoort to Geeraard de Duivelsteen

Facing the Stadhuis, the **St Jorishof** restaurant occupies one of the city's oldest buildings, its sooty, heavy-duty stonework dating from the middle of the fifteenth century. Lining up along the **Hoogpoort**, beyond St Jorishof, are some of the oldest **facades** in Ghent, sturdy Gothic structures that also date from the fifteenth century. The third house along – formerly a heavily protected aristocratic mansion called the **Grote Sikkel** – is now the home of a music school, but the blackened remains of an antique torch-snuffer remain fixed to the wall.

Hoogpoort leads into Nederpolder and a right turn at the end brings you to the forbidding **Geeraard de Duivelsteen** (no admission), a fortified palace of splendid Romanesque design built of grey limestone in the thirteenth century. The stronghold, bordered by what remains of its moat, takes its name from Geeraard Vilain, who earned the soubriquet "duivel" (devil) for his acts of cruelty or, according to some sources, because of his swarthy features and black hair. Vilain was not the only noble to wall himself up within a castle – well into the fourteenth century, Ghent was dotted with fortified houses (*stenen*), such was the fear the privileged few had of the rebellious guildsmen. The last noble moved out of the Duivelsteen in about 1350 and since then the building has been put to a bewildering range of uses, from being an arsenal and a prison through to (dreadfully unsuitable) service as a madhouse and an orphanage; nowadays it houses government offices.

St Baafsabdij

East of the Duivelsteen, Ghent's eighteenth- and nineteenth-century industrial suburbs stretch out toward the **Dampoort train station**. A mishmash of terrace, factory and canal, these suburbs were spawned by the sea canals dug to replace the narrow – and obsolete – waterways of the city centre. Right next to the station, the large (and unappetizing) water-filled hole on **Oktrooiplein** is the link between the old and the new systems.

Visitors to Ghent rarely venture into this part of the city, but there is one really enjoyable diversion, the ivy-clad ruins of **St Baafsabdij** (St Bavo's Abbey; Wed–Sun 9.30am–5pm; free), which ramble over a narrow parcel of land on Gandastraat, beside the River Leie. This was once a strategically important location, and it was here, in 630, that the French missionary St Amand founded an abbey. St Amand was poorly received by the locals, who ultimately drowned him in the Scheldt, but his abbey survived to become a famous place of pilgrimage on account of its guardianship of the remains of the seventh-century **St Bavo**. In the ninth century, the abbey suffered a major disaster when the Vikings decided this was the ideal spot to camp while they raided the surrounding region, but order was eventually restored, another colony of monks moved in and the abbey was rebuilt in 950. The abbey's heyday was during the fourteenth century, when, as a major landowner, its coffers were filled to overflowing with the proceeds of the wool industry.

The monks were loyal to their various rulers, but nevertheless the Emperor Charles V had most of the abbey knocked down to make room for a new castle in the 1540s and the monks were obliged to decamp to St Baafskathedraal. The emperor's fortress was ultimately demolished, but these substantial **abbey ruins** somehow managed to survive and, after extensive repairs, they comprise a fascinating jumble of old stone buildings today.

First up beyond the entrance are the remnants of the Gothic **cloister**, with its long vaulted corridors and a distinctive, octagonal tower, which consisted of a toilet on the bottom floor and the storage room – the sanctuarium – for the St Bavo relic up above. On the far side of the cloister, the lower level was used for workshops and as storage space. It now contains – both on its outside wall and within – an intriguing **lapidary museum**, displaying all sorts of architectural bits and pieces retrieved from the city during renovations and demolitions. There are gargoyles and finely carved Gothic heads, terracotta panels, broken off chunks of columns and capitals, and several delightful mini-tableaux. There's precious little labelling, but it's the skill of the carving that impresses and, if you've already explored the city, one or two pieces are identifiable, principally the original lion from the old punishment post on St Veerleplein. A flight of steps leads up from beside the museum to the Romanesque **refectory**, a splendid chamber whose magnificent, hooped timber roof dates – remarkably enough – from the twelfth century. The **grounds** of the abbey are small, but they are left partly wild on account of several rare plants that flourish here; if your Flemish is up to it, the warden may help to point them out.

South of the centre

Although the majority of Ghent's key attractions are within easy walking distance of the Korenmarkt, two of the city's principal museums are located some 2km south of the centre, the **Museum voor Schone Kunsten** (Fine Art Museum) and the adjacent Museum of Contemporary Art, **S.M.A.K.** Many visitors just hop on a Korenmarkt tram for the quick trip down to the two, but with more time – and energy – a circular walk of around three hours can take in several less well-known parts of the city too. The route suggested below begins by heading south from the Korenmarkt along **Veldstraat**, the main shopping street, and then drops by the historical collections of the **Bijlokemuseum** before proceeding onto the two museums. The return leg to the city centre is via **Overpoortstraat** and **Sint Pietersnieuwstraat**, respectively Ghent's student enclave and the location of the sprawling **St Pietersabdij** (St Peter's Abbey).

South along Veldstraat

Veldstraat cuts south from the Korenmarkt, running parallel to the River Leie. By and large, it's a very ordinary shopping strip, but the eighteenth-century mansion at no. 82 does hold the **Museum Arnold Vander Haeghen** (Mon–Fri

10am–noon & 2–4.30pm; free), with small and temporary exhibitions of art and a Chinese salon, where the original silk wallpaper has survived intact. The Duke of Wellington stayed here in 1815 after the Battle of Waterloo, popping across the street to the **Hôtel d'Hane-Steenhuyse**, at no. 55, to bolster the morale of the refugee King of France, Louis XVIII. Abandoning his throne, Louis had hot-footed it to Ghent soon after Napoleon landed in France after escaping from Elba. While others did his fighting for him, Louis waited around in Ghent gorging himself – his daily dinner lasted all of seven hours and the bloated exile was known to polish off one hundred oysters at a sitting. His fellow exile, François Chateaubriand, the writer and politician, ignored the gluttony and cowardice, writing meekly, "The French alone know how to dine with method". Thanks to Wellington's ministrations, Louis was persuaded to return to his kingdom and his entourage left for Paris on June 26, 1815, one week after Waterloo. The grand **facade** of Louis's hideaway, dating from 1768, has survived in good condition, its elaborate pediment sporting allegorical representations of Time and History, but at present there's no access to the expansive salons beyond.

Pushing on down Veldstraat, it's a couple of minutes more to a matching pair of grand, Neoclassical nineteenth-century buildings. On the left-hand side is the **Justitiepaleis** (Palace of Justice), whose pediment sports a large frieze with the figure of Justice in the middle, the accused to one side and the condemned on the other. Opposite stands the recently restored **opera house**, its facade awash with carved stone panels.

The Bijlokemuseum

From the opera house, it's an easy, if dull, ten-minute stroll to the Bijlokemuseum via the Nederkouter. It's better – and no further – to get there along the banks of the River Leie: turn off Nederkouter at Verlorenkost and then – with the Coupure canal and its dinky swing bridge dead ahead – take the first on the left along the river.

The rambling collection of Ghent-produced applied and decorative art at the **Bijlokemuseum** has been shoehorned into the old Cistercian abbey on Godshuizenlaan (Thurs 10am–6pm, Sun 2–6pm; €2.50). Founded in the thirteenth century, the abbey was savaged by Calvinists on several occasions, but much of the medieval complex has survived, tidy brown-brick buildings that now provide a charming setting for all sorts of (poorly labelled) bygones, from collections of guild pennants and processional banners to Masonic tackle, porcelain, pottery, keys and costumes. Parts of the complex are also used for temporary exhibitions.

At the entrance, the main **gateway** is a handsome Baroque portal decorated by a statue of St Elizabeth with a beggar kneeling gratefully at her feet. Beyond, across the lawn, is the **cloister**, whose lower level is given over to a string of period rooms. A long set of cameo collections occupies the upper level (though this may change), notably an assortment of military hardware featuring the halberds and pikes favoured by the weaver-armies of Flanders. Up above, the **refectory** is a massive affair with a high, vaulted ceiling and a striking, early fourteenth-century fresco of the Last Supper; above this is the former **dormitory**, home to a motley collection of guild mementoes including, in the centre of the room, a splendid model galleon that was carried in processions by the city's boatmen.

In front of the cloister, and reached by a connecting corridor, the **house of the abbess** contains a further sequence of rooms accommodating a miscellany of antique furniture, portrait paintings and several magnificent carved and tiled fireplaces.

S.M.A.K.

Five minutes' brisk walk southeast down the busy boulevard from the Bijlokemuseum is **Citadelpark**, whose network of leafy footpaths circumnavigates a sprawling brick complex that dates from the 1910s. The fortress after which the park is named was demolished long ago and the grounds were prettified during the 1870s, hence today's grottoes and ponds, statues and fountains, waterfall and bandstand.

The park serves as an appealing preamble to the two art museums it encloses, one of which, **S.M.A.K.** (Municipal Museum for Contemporary Art; Tues–Sun 10am–6pm; ⓦwww.smak.be; €5), is housed in a cleverly remodelled 1910s building that previously served as the city's casino. This is one of Belgium's more prestigious – and certainly one of its most adventurous – contemporary art galleries, the museum priding itself on the depth and range of its exhibition programme.

The ground floor is given over to temporary displays of international standing – the works of Rob Birza, Miroslaw Balka and Dirk Braeckman have all been showcased recently. Upstairs, distilled from the museum's wide-ranging permanent collection, is a regularly rotated selection of sculptures, paintings and installations. S.M.A.K. possesses examples of all the major artistic movements since World War II – everything from surrealism, the Dutch CoBrA group and pop art through to minimalism, hyper realism and conceptual art – as well as their forerunners, most notably René Magritte and Paul Delvaux. Perennial favourites include the installations of the influential German **Joseph Beuys** (1921–86), who played a leading role in the European avant-garde art movement of the 1970s, and a characteristically unnerving painting by **Francis Bacon** (1909–92) entitled *A Figure Sitting*. Usually on display also is a healthy selection of the work of the Belgian **Marcel Broodthaers** (1924–76), whose tongue-in-cheek pieces include *Tray of Broken Eggs* and his trademark *Red Mussels Casserole*.

Museum voor Schone Kunsten

The **Museum voor Schone Kunsten** (Fine Art Museum; Tues–Sun 10am–6pm; €2.50) occupies an imposing Neoclassical edifice on the park's edge. Inside, the central atrium and connecting rotunda are flanked by a sequence of rooms, with the older paintings exhibited to the right in Rooms 1–13, the bulk of the nineteenth- and early twentieth-century material mostly on the left in Rooms A–L. There's not enough space to display all the permanent collection at any one time, so there's some rotation, but you can expect to see the paintings mentioned below even if they are not in the room specified. The layout of the collection does not seem to follow much of a scheme, but it's small enough to be easily manageable; free **museum plans** are issued at reception.

The atrium starts the collection in style with a fine head by **Rodin** (1840–1917) and a series of grandiose eighteenth-century tapestries, flowing classical scenes depicting the *Exaltation of the Gods* to a design by Jan van Orley. To the right, in Room 1, is the museum's small but eclectic collection of early Flemish paintings. The highlight here is **Rogier van der Weyden**'s (1399–1464) *Madonna with Carnation*, a charming work where the proffered flower, in all its exquisite detail, serves as a symbol of Christ's passion. Room 2 displays two superb works by **Hieronymus Bosch** (1450–1516), his *Bearing of the Cross* showing Christ mocked by some of the most grotesque and deformed characters Bosch ever painted. Look carefully and you'll see that Christ's head is at the centre of two diagonals, one representing evil, the other good – the latter linking the repentant thief with St Veronica, whose cloak carries the imprint of Christ's face. This struggle between good and evil is also the subject of Bosch's *St Jerome at Prayer*, in the foreground of which the saint prays, surrounded by a menacing landscape. Also in Room 2 is **Adriaen Isenbrandt**'s (d. 1551) *Mary and Child*, a gentle painting showing Mary suckling Jesus on the flight to Egypt, with the artist choosing a rural Flemish landscape as the backdrop rather than the Holy Land.

Among the seventeenth-century Flemish and Dutch paintings, Room 5 weighs in with a powerful *St Francis* by **Rubens** (1577–1640), in which a very sick-looking saint bears the marks of the stigmata. **Jacob Jordaens** (1593–1678) was greatly influenced by his friend Rubens and the robust romanticism of his *Judgement of Midas*, in Room 7, is a case in point. Jordaens was, however, capable of much greater subtlety and his *Studies of the Head of Abraham Grapheus*, also in Room 7, is an example of the high-quality preparatory paintings he completed, which were destined to be recycled within larger compositions. In the same room, **Anthony van Dyck**'s (1599–1641) *Jupiter and Antiope* wins the bad taste award for its portrayal of the lecherous god, with his tongue hanging out in anticipation of sex with Antiope. Next door, Room 8 holds two precise works by **Pieter Bruegel the Younger** (1564–1638), who inherited his father's interest in the landscape and those who worked and lived on it, as evidenced by his *Wedding Breakfast* and *Village Lawyer*.

To the far right of the rotunda, Rooms 16–19 kick off the museum's late eighteenth- and nineteenth-century collection with a handful of romantic historical canvases, plus – and this is a real surprise – a superbly executed portrait of by the Scot **Henry Raeburn** (1756–1823), in Room 17. The assorted canvases of Rooms A–L, to the left of the atrium and rotunda, are a rather skimpy runaround of Belgian peasant scenes, landscapes and seascapes in a variety of styles, but there are several noteworthy canvases, beginning in Room A with a characteristically unsettling work by **René Magritte** (1898–1967). In Room E, the strongest paintings are the dark and broody works of the Expressionist **Constant Permeke** (1886–1952). Room F holds two macabre paintings – *Old Woman and Masks* and the more accomplished *Skeleton looking at Chinoiserie* – by **James Ensor** (1860–1949), one of Belgium's most original modern artists. A small selection of Ensor sketches is exhibited close by in Room J. Rooms M–S here are given over to temporary displays.

North to St Pietersabdij

From behind the Fine Art Museum, **Overpoortstraat** cuts north through the heart of the city's student quarter, a gritty and grimy but vivacious district jam-packed with late-night bars and inexpensive cafés. Overpoortstraat finally emerges onto **St Pietersplein**, a very wide and very long square that is flanked by the sprawling mass of **St Pietersabdij**. The abbey dates back to the earliest days of the city and was probably founded by St Amand (see p.204) in about 640. Protestant iconoclasts destroyed the abbey, a symbol of much that they hated, in 1578, and the present complex – a real Baroque whopper – was erected in the seventeenth and eighteenth centuries. The last monks were ejected during the French occupation in 1796 and since then – as with many other ecclesiastical buildings in Belgium – it's been hard to figure out any suitable use for it. Today, much of the complex serves as municipal offices, but visitors can pop into the domed **church**, which was modelled on St Peter's in Rome, though the interior is no more than a plodding Baroque. To the left of the church, part of the old monastic complex has been turned into an arts exhibition centre, the **Kunsthal St Pietersabdij** (April to mid-Nov Tues–Sun

9am–5pm; free, though some exhibitions do attract an entrance fee).

Much more appealing is **Vooruit**, a brief stroll north of St Pietersplein at St Pietersnieuwstraat 23. To all intents and purposes, this café-cum-performing arts centre is the cultural heart of the city (at least for the under-40s), offering a varied programme of rock and pop through to dance (see p.211). It also occupies a splendid building, a twin-towered and turreted former Festival Hall that was built for Ghent's socialists in an eclectic rendition of Art Nouveau in 1914. The **café**, if that's what you're after, is open from mid-morning till late except on Sunday (Mon–Thurs 11.30am–2am, Fri & Sat 11.30am–3am & Sun 4pm–2am).

Eating, drinking and nightlife

Ghent's numerous **restaurants** and **cafés** offer the very best of Flemish and French cuisines with a sprinkling of Italian, Chinese and Arab places for variety. There's a concentration of deluxe restaurants in and around the narrow lanes of the Patershol quarter and another, of less expensive options, on and around the Korenmarkt.

The city also has a first-rate range of **bars**, from antique drinking dens with nicotine-stained ceilings through to earthy students' pubs and slick, modern places with hi-tech furnishings and fittings. There are good places dotted all over the city, but several of the most distinctive, complete with a beer list long enough to strain any liver, are within a couple of minutes' walk of Het Gravensteen. The **club** and **live music scene** is also first-rate, with several top-ranking, inventive venues. Note that most student bars and clubs don't open at the weekend, when most of the clientele clear off out of town.

Cafés and restaurants

The reviews below give **opening times** along with holiday closures, where these are fixed. Most places close for a week or two over the winter and many shut down for a summer break as well. Telephone numbers are only given where reservations are required or advised. **Prices** run the gamut, but a filling main course in a mid-range restaurant will cost you around €15–20, €7–12 in a café or cheaper restaurant.

Amadeus Plotersgracht 8 ☎09 225 13 85. In the heart of the Patershol, this busy, well-established restaurant specializes in spare ribs. Long tables, oodles of stained glass, low ceilings and an eccentric sprinkling of bygones makes the place relaxed and convivial. Main courses at around €18. Mon–Sat 7pm–midnight, Sun noon–2.30pm & 6pm–midnight.

Avalon Geldmunt 32. This spick-and-span vegetarian restaurant offers a wide range of well-prepared food. The key pull are the daily specials, which cost about €7. Choose from one of the many different rooms or the terrace at the back in the summer. Mon–Sat noon–2pm.

Bij den wijzen en den zot Hertogstraat 42 ☎09 223 42 30. One of the best restaurants in the Patershol, serving up delicious Flemish cuisine with more than a dash of French flair. Soft lighting and classical music set the tone. The premises are charming too – an old brick house of tiny rooms

and narrow stairs with dining on two floors. Prices are moderate, with main courses averaging about €18; house specialities include eel, cooked in several different ways, and *waterzooi*. Tues–Sat noon–2pm & 6.30–10pm.

De Blauwe Zalm Vrouwebroersstraat 2 ☎09 224 08 52. Brilliant seafood restaurant – the best in town – serving up everything from the more usual cod, salmon, monkfish and haddock through to the likes of seawolf, sea bass, turbot and John Dory. Fish tanks keep the crustacea alive and kicking, and the decor has a distinctly maritime feel – though it's all done in impeccable, ultra cool style. Main courses from €20. Reservations pretty much essential. Highly recommended. Tues–Fri noon–1.45pm plus Mon–Sat 7–9.30pm.

Brooderie Jan Breydelstraat 8. Pleasant, informal café with a health-food slant: wholesome breakfasts, lunches, sandwiches and salads from around €7. Central location, near the Gravensteen castle. Tues–Sun 8am–6pm.

Koningshuis St Michielsstraat 31 ☎09 225 86 33. Cosy restaurant, kitted out in style with a stained-wood floor and Flemish bygones decorating the walls. It serves outstanding Flemish cuisine featuring hormone-free meat and the freshest of produce; the imaginative menu includes first-rate vegetarian dishes. Main courses average about €15, but the daily specials are often much less expensive. Tues–Sat 6pm–midnight, Sun 6–11pm; closed the last Tues of the month.

Malatesta Korenmarkt 35. Informally fashionable café-restaurant decorated in strong, modern style and offering tasty pizza and pasta dishes at very affordable prices. Handy location, bang in the centre of the city. Daily except Tues noon–2.30pm & 6–11pm.

Marco Polo Trattoria Serpentstraat 11 ☎09 225 04 20. Part of the Italian "slow food" movement, this simple rustic restaurant serves delicious organic, seasonal food. The menu is small, but all the dishes are freshly prepared – and well worth waiting for. Inexpensive. Tues–Fri noon–2.30pm & 6pm–10pm, Sat–Sun 6pm–10pm.

't Marmietje Drabstraat 30 ☎09 224 30 13. Traditional, family-run restaurant specializing in Flemish cuisine – a good place to try *Gentse waterzooi van kip* and *Gentse stoverij*. Somewhat eclipsed by the newer and more fashionable restaurants of the Patershol, it's still a good bet; the prices are lower than most of its rivals, with daily specials average around €9. Convenient location too, just off Korenlei. Tues–Sat noon–2.30pm & 6–10pm. Usually closed Aug.

Pakhuis Schuurkenstraat 4. One of Ghent's most fashionable spots, the *Pakhuis* is a lively bistro-brasserie offering an extensive menu – Flemish and French and beyond – with main courses averaging around €15. The premises are smashing, an

intelligently remodelled old warehouse with acres of glass and metal down a narrow alley near St Michielsbrug. Good for just drinking too. Mon–Sat noon–2.30pm & 6.30pm–midnight.

Patisserie Bloch Veldstraat 60. Something of a local institution, and a favourite with shoppers for donkey's years, this excellent tearoom offers a lip-smacking variety of cakes and confectioneries, washed down by premium coffees and teas. Snacks are available too – though these are no great shakes – and there's a takeaway service. The decor is really rather ordinary, but if you like cakes you won't give a hoot. On the corner with Voldersstraat. Mon–Sat 8am–7.30pm.

St Jorishof Botermarkt 2 ☎09 224 24 24. Across the street from the Stadhuis, this polished restaurant has a healthy reputation for the quality of its traditional Flemish cuisine. The neo-baronial fixtures and fittings and the (comparatively) formal atmosphere are not to everyone's tastes, but this is certainly a very good place to try eel. Set menus at around €40, plus à la carte. Booking strongly advised. Mon–Fri noon–2.30pm & 7–9.30pm, Sat 7–9.30pm, Sun closed.

Short Order Hoogpoort 11. No-frills veggie café with retro decor serving pasta and Mediterranean dishes, fresh fruit juices and milkshakes, plus sushi on Fridays and Saturdays. You can take out or eat in. Inexpensive. Mon–Sat 11.30am–9pm.

Waterzooi St Veerleplein 2 ☎09 225 05 63. Top-notch, split-level restaurant with pastel-painted walls, a wood-beamed ceiling and dappled lighting. Mixed menu, mostly in the French style, offering the freshest of ingredients from beef and lamb through to lobster and monkfish, plus a good sideline in Flemish favourites – unsurprisingly, including *waterzooi*. Main courses weigh in at about €20. Mon, Tues & Thurs–Sat noon–1.30pm & 7–9.30pm.

Bars and clubs

Bardot Oude Beestenmarkt 8 ☎0478 26 20 44. This hip new venue is one of the top places to be in Ghent. Regular DJs offer funky house, soft-techno and plenty of the newest sounds. Great place to end the night or dance till dawn. Wed–Sat 8pm–5am.

Decadance Overpoortstraat 76. If you fancy a good night out among the city's students this is the place to be: there's a Friday night party feeling on a Tuesday and once inside you wouldn't know what time of day or week it is. Reggae, hip-hop, drum 'n' bass and garage-techno vibes. Mon–Thurs & Sun from 8pm.

't Dreupelkot Groentenmarkt 10. Cosy bar specializing in jenever, of which it stocks more than

one hundred brands, all kept at icy temperatures. Down a little alley, next door to the famous *Het Waterhuis* (see below). Daily from 11am.

Dulle Griet Vrijdagmarkt 50. A long, dark and atmospheric bar with ceiling rugs, all manner of incidental objets d'art – and an especially wide range of beers. Mon from 4.30pm, Tues–Sun from noon.

Hotsy Totsy Hoogstraat 1 ☎09 224 20 12. Singers, comedians, artists, poets – all kinds of entertainment at this venue in the centre of Ghent. Music ranges from traditional Dutch kleinkunst (the Dutch equivalent of chanson) to international jazz. Tues–Sat from 8pm.

Magazijn Penitentenstraat 24 ☎09 234 07 08,

ⓦwww.magazijn.be. Culture temple for exhibitions, concerts and a venue for the Ghent festival. Good food and lots of vegetarian options. Mon–Fri 12–2pm & 6pm–2am, Sat & Sun 6pm–4am.
Pink Flamingos Onderstraat 55. Weird and wonderful – the height of kitsch: film stars, religion, Barbie-dolls, if it's cheesy it's somewhere in the decor. Great place for an aperitif or to sip one of their large selection of cocktails. Recommended. Mon–Wed & Sun noon–midnight, Thurs–Sat noon–3am.
Rococo Corduwaniersstraat 57. Intimate bar attracting a diverse but always cool clientele; a perfect place to be on a cold winter evening. Home-made cakes and amazing hospitality offered by Betty van de Rococo herself. Daily from 9pm.
Sous-Sol Hoogpoort 41. Part of the backbone of hip Ghent, this cellar café-club boasts a moody blue interior and good house/techno sounds. Tues–Sat from 9pm.
De Tap en de Tepel Gewad 7. Charming, candlelit bar with an open fire and a clutter of antique furnishings. Wine is the main deal here, served with a good selection of cheeses. The name translates as "the Tap and Nipple". Wed–Sat from noon.
De Tempelier Meersenierstraat 9. Near the Dulle Griet, off Vrijdagmarkt. Few tourists venture into this small, dark and intriguing old bar which offers a vast range of beers at lower-than-usual prices. Sometimes eccentric clientele, plus occasional live

bands. Mon–Sat from 11am.
De Trollekelder Bij St Jacobs 17. Huge selection of beers in an ancient merchant's house. Dark and atmospheric bar – don't be deterred by the trolls stuffed in the window. Mon, Wed & Thurs 6pm–1.30am & Fri 4pm–2.30am.
Den Turk Botermarkt 3. The oldest bar in the city, a tiny rabbit-warren of a place offering a good range of beers and whiskies and a famous plate of cheese with Ghent mustard. Frequent live music, mainly jazz and blues and a great, moderately highbrow, atmosphere. The beer menu is particularly good on Trappist brews. Daily from 11am, but closed during the Gentse Feesten (see "Festivals", p.212)
Vooruit St Pietersnieuwstraat 23. Part of the city's performing arts centre, this café is a large barn-like affair that gets jam-packed till well in the morning. Mon–Thurs 11.30am–2am, Fri & Sat 11.30am–3am & Sun 4pm–2am.
Het Waterhuis aan de Bierkant Groentenmarkt 9. More than one hundred types of beer are available in this engaging, canal-side bar, just near the castle. Be sure to try Stropken (literally "noose"), a delicious local brew, named after the time in 1453 when Philip the Good, the Duke of Burgundy, compelled the rebellious city burghers to parade outside the town gate with ropes around their necks. Popular with tourists and locals alike. Daily from 11am.

Listings

Banks and exchange The two most central banks are Fortis, Belfortstraat 41 (Mon–Fri 9am–12.30pm & 1.30–4pm, till 6pm on Thurs), and Weghsteen & Driege, St Baafsplein 12 (Mon–Fri 9am–4pm). There are also lots of cash machines in the city centre.
Bike rental Bicycles can be rented at St Pieters station (daily 7am–8pm; €8.80 per day, €6.20 per half day) and also at Biker, Sint Michielsstraat 3 (Tues–Sat 9am–12.30pm & 1.30–6pm; ☏09 224 29 03; same rates).
Books FNAC, Veldstraat 88 (Mon–Sat 10am–6.30pm), close to the junction with Zonnestraat, has several floors of music, books and newspapers, including a good English-language section; it's excellent for maps, stocking a comprehensive range of Belgian hiking maps among others. Atlas & Zanzibar, Kortrijksesteenweg 100, at the junction with Meerssstraat (Mon–Fri 10am–1pm & 2–7pm, Sat 10am–1pm & 2–6pm), is a specialist travel bookshop with a comprehensive collection of Belgian walking maps and many English

guidebooks; it's about 10min walk south of the centre.
Buses and trams City and regional transport enquiries at the kiosks on the Korenmarkt (Mon–Fri 7am–7pm & Sat 10.30am–5.30pm) and beside St Pieters station (Mon–Fri 7am–7pm). Information line ☏09 210 93 11.
Car rental Avis, Kortrijksesteenweg 676 (☏09 222 00 53); Europcar, Brusselsesteenweg 506 (☏09 210 46 62); Hertz, Coupure Links 707 (☏09 224 04 06); Luxauto, Martelaarslaan 4 (☏09 225 30 31).
Chocolates Dulce, Jan Breydelstraat 1 (Tues–Sat 10am–6pm), is an independent chocolatier, the best in Ghent.
Cinema Ghent has two really good cinemas, Sphinx, Sint-Michielshelling 3 (☏09 225 60 86; ⓦwww.weekup.be), which focuses on foreign-language and art-house films (with original soundtrack intact); and Studioskoop, Sint Annaplein 63 (☏09 225 08 45, ⓦwww.studioskoop.be), the cosiest of the city's film venues, but still with five screens.

Festivals Ghent's main festivals are the Gentse Feesten or town fair, held for ten days in mid- to late July (always including July 21); the Patershol feesten, the Patershol knees-up over a weekend in mid-Aug; and the Festival van Vlaanderen (⌚02 548 95 95, ⓦwww.festival-van-vlaanderen.be), the Flanders classical music festival, which runs from May to November. The prestigious Flanders International Film Festival runs in city cinemas for ten days in October.

Gay scene Ghent's gay scene is pretty low-key. Contacts and details from FWH, Kammerstraat 22 (Mon–Fri 9am–4.30pm; ⌚09 223 69 29).

Internet access The handiest place to access the internet and collect emails is the *Coffee Lounge*, across from the tourist office at Botermarkt 6 (daily 10am–10pm; ⓔcoffeelounge@pandora.be). Rates are currently €2.50 for one hour, €0.75 for fifteen minutes. Internet access is also commonplace at the more expensive hotels.

Left luggage Lockers at St Pieters train station: large lockers €3.30 per 24hr, medium-sized €2.80, small €1.50. There's also a left luggage office, charging €2.50 per item.

Mail The main post office is at Lange Kruisstraat 55 (Mon–Fri 8am–6pm, Sat 9am–noon).

Markets and shopping On Saturdays and Sundays, there's a flower market on the Vrijdagmarkt (7am–1pm). There's also a fruit and veg market on Groentenmarkt (Mon–Fri 7am–1pm & Sat 7am–5pm); a flea market (*prondelmarkt*) on Beverhoutplein/Bij St Jacobs (Fri–Sun 8am–1pm); an antique and art market (*kunstmarkt*) on Groentenmarkt (March–Nov Mon–Thurs 10am–5pm); and a bird market on Vrijdagmarkt (Sun 7am–1pm). Superb mustard can be bought from Tierenteyn, an old-fashioned store at Groentenmarkt 3; the smallest pot will set you back about €5. The Flemish tapestry industry sur-

vives, albeit in diminished form, and 't Vlaams Wandtapijt, St Baafsplein 6 (Mon–Sat 9.30am–6pm), specializes in its products. The large tapestries are mostly richly decorated, modern renditions of traditional motifs and styles, but – as you might expect – they are expensive, from around €800. Cushion handbags and other smaller knick-knacks are much more affordable. For a great range of good-quality secondhand clothes, try Alternatief, Baudelostraat 15 (Tues–Sat 2–6.30pm).

Performing arts Ghent has its own opera company, half a dozen theatre troupes, as well as four first-rate venues. Handelsbeurs, on the Kouter, is the city's newest concert hall with two first-rate auditoria, hosting a diverse programme spanning the gamut of the performing arts. Next door is the recently restored Opera House, where the city's opera company, Vlaamse Opera (⌚09 225 24 25, ⓦwww.vlaamseopera.be), perform. A third prime venue is the handsomely restored, nineteenth-century Publiekstheater Groot Huis, the municipal theatre at Sint Baafsplein 17. This is home to the Nederlands Toneel Gent (NTG; ⌚09 225 01 01), the regional repertory company. Almost all of their performances are in Flemish, though they do play occasional host to touring English-language theatre companies. Vooruit Sint-Pietersnieuwstraat 23 is the main venue for rock, pop and jazz concerts (⌚09 267 28 28, ⓦwww.vooruit.be). FNAC (see p.211) sells tickets for most mainstream cultural events.

Pharmacies Two central pharmacies are at 15 St Michielsstraat and 123 Nederkouter. Duty rotas, detailing late night opening pharmacies, are usually displayed in pharmacists' windows.

Taxi V-Tax ⌚09 222 22 22.

Train enquiries ⌚09 222 44 44 (daily 7am–8pm).

Around Ghent

Rivers and canals radiate out from Ghent in all directions, slicing across the flatness of the Flemish plain. By and large there's little here of much interest in what is primarily an industrial area, although – if you have your own transport – you might consider a day-trip southwest to the art museums of **Deurle**, or travel east to the moated castle of **Laarne**.

Deurle and around

A leafy, prosperous village which spreads out among the woods beside the winding course of the River Leie, **DEURLE** lies about 10km southwest of the city. The village was a favourite with two successive schools of early twentieth-century artists who took up residence here and in the adjoining hamlet of **Sint**

Martens–Latem, from which both groups took their name. The first school were Symbolists and their leading light was the sculptor Georges Minne; the second group were Expressionists, and counted among their number Constant Permeke and Gustave de Smet.

To get there with your own transport, take Kortrijksesteenweg out of Ghent, cross over the E40 motorway at junction 14, proceed along the N43, and take the signed turning to Nevele (and Deurle) on the right. After about 1200m, take another right down P de Denterghemlaan, then either turn right again along Dorpstraat, which leads to the old brick cottages that make up the centre of Deurle, or – a little further on – take the first left, Museumlaan, to a trio of signposted art museums. At no. 14, the **Museum Dhondt–Dhaenens** provides an overview of the period and its key players (Tues–Fri 1–5pm, Sat & Sun 11am–5pm; €2.50). The adjacent **Museum Leon de Smet**, Museumlaan 18 (Feb–Easter, Nov & Dec Sat & Sun 2–5pm; Easter–Oct Sat & Sun 2–6pm; free), features the work of the eponymous artist, whose striking blocks of colour and bold lines were clearly influenced by the Fauves. By comparison, Leon's brother Gustave (1877–1943) was much inspired by the Cubists, and some of his canvases and drawings are on display in the nearby **Museum Gustaaf de Smet**, at Gustaaf de Smetlaan 1 (May–Sept Wed–Sat 2–6pm, Sun 10am–noon & 2–6pm; Oct–April Wed–Sun 2–5pm; €1), on the second left turn off P de Denterghemlaan. There are several other art museums in the vicinity of Deurle, the pick of them being the **Museum Gevaert–Minne**, where a few works by Georges Minne are displayed at Kapitteldreef 45, a big old house down a forested track in Sint Martens–Latem (May–Sept Wed–Sat 2–6pm, Sun 10am–noon & 2–6pm; Oct–April Wed–Sun 2–5pm; €1). To get there, carry on down P de Denterghemlaan; take a right along Rode Beukendreef; turn first left onto Warandedreef; and left onto Kapitteldreef at the third crossroads.

Around Deurle: Kasteel Ooidonk

In wooded parkland about 4km from Deurle, the onion domes and crow-stepped gables of the handsome **Kasteel Ooidonk** (April to mid-Sept Sun 2–5.30pm, plus July–Aug Sat 2–5.30pm; €5) mostly date from the 1590s and occupy a scenic spot beside the River Leie. The chateau's interior is, however, disappointing, with heavy-handed nineteenth-century fittings providing an unexciting setting for a large but rather undistinguished collection of antique tapestries, porcelain, silver and furniture. To get here from Deurle, head north toward Nevele from the T-junction at the start of P de Denterghemlaan and then follow the signs. From the chateau, it's around 13km back to Ghent along the north side of the Leie.

Laarne

On the opposite side of Ghent, 15km east of the city, is the moated and turreted chateau of **Laarne** (Easter–Oct Sun 2–5.30pm, plus July & Aug Tues–Thurs, Sat & Sun 2–5.30pm; €5). Most of the present building dates from medieval times, though successive restorations transformed the original castle into a spacious country mansion long ago, enhancing its stately rooms with the addition of a Renaissance entrance hall. Abandoned in the nineteenth century, Laarne was given to the state in 1964, since when a thorough refurbishment has graced the chateau with antique furnishings, including several fine Brussels tapestries. An extensive collection of old silver is exhibited here too. The easiest way to reach Laarne by public transport is to take the train from

Ghent to Wettern (every 20min; 10min), from where bus #688 leaves every hour for the ten-minute trip to Laarne.

The Waasland and Aalst

To the northeast of Ghent lies the agricultural region of the **Waasland**, its sand and clay soils sandwiched between the Dutch border to the north, the Ghent–Terneuzen canal to the west, and the River Scheldt to the east. Once an isolated area of swamp and undrained forest, the lands of the Waasland were first cultivated by pioneering religious communities, who cleared the trees and built the dykes. The soil was poor and conditions were hard, until Ghent's demand for wool encouraged local landowners to introduce the sheep that produced the district's first cash crop, and provided some degree of prosperity. Today, the area is – in a low-key sort of way – popular with day-trippers in search of the quiet of the countryside. It's best explored by bike, with **St Niklaas**, the district's only sizeable settlement, being the obvious place to start, though in itself this modest little town will not detain you long. Rather more enticing as a town – but well to the south of the Waasland – is **Aalst**, a pleasant little place southeast of Ghent, with a splendid belfry and a fine medieval church. There are frequent trains from Ghent to both St Niklaas and Aalst.

St Niklaas

Some 35km northeast of Ghent and 20km west of Antwerp, **ST NIKLAAS** is an unremarkable town whose principal feature is its **Grote Markt**, the largest in Belgium. The square is edged by a motley combination of old and new buildings, including an attractive, bright-white, towered and turreted **Stadhuis** dating from the nineteenth century. Behind lurks the hulking mass of **St Niklaaskerk**, a jumble of architectural styles dominated by a huge tower surmounted by a gilded statue of the Madonna and Child. Subtle it certainly isn't – and neither is the gaudily painted church interior. The only real surprise is the tiny old castle, **Kasteel Walburg**, a couple of minutes' walk from the Grote Markt: it's on the right if you take Apostelstraat from beside the tourist office and continue along Walburgstraat. Built of reddish brick in the middle of the sixteenth century, the castle is in the Flemish Renaissance style and was clearly built for comfort rather than defence. Part of an attractively wooded city park and encircled by a slender moat, it's classically picturesque – and nowadays it accommodates a bar and restaurant.

The **Stedelijk**, Sint Niklaas's municipal museum, consists of several collections displayed at different sites around the city centre. The only one of note is the **Mercator Museum** at Zamanstraat 49 (Thurs–Sat 2–5pm, Sun 10am–5pm; €2.50), about five minutes' walk from the Grote Markt: leave the square via its northeast corner, along Houtbriel, and take the first turning on the left. The museum has an interesting collection of maps, atlases and globes made by the Flemish cartographer **Mercator**, who was born in the neighbouring village of Rupelmonde in 1512. Mercator's projection of the spherical earth onto a two-dimensional map is now accepted as the usual view of the world's surface, and it was originally an invaluable aid to navigation. However, his projection distorts the relative size of the continents at the expense of the southern hemisphere; the other deception is in the layout, which vaingloriously places the colonizing nations of Europe at the centre.

Practicalities

St Niklaas **train station** is situated on the northern edge of the centre, some ten minutes' walk from the Grote Markt – turn right outside the station building, then left down Stationsstraat. There's nowhere very appealing to stay in the centre of town, but the **tourist office**, Grote Markt 45 (Mon–Fri 8am–5pm, mid-May to mid-Sept also Sat & Sun 10am–4pm; ☏03 777 26 81, ⓦwww.sint-niklaas.be), provides a list of **campsites** and **hotels** in the vicinity. They also have a comprehensive selection of **cycling brochures** detailing routes that explore every nook and cranny of the Waasland. One popular option is to make for the quiet villages west of town, such as Sinaai and Eksaarde. You can **rent bikes** at the train station (Mon–Fri 8.30am–noon & 1–4.45pm; €8.80 per day), and leave luggage there too.

Aalst

About 25km southeast of Ghent, the ancient town of **AALST** was first fortified in the eleventh century and became a settlement of some importance as a seat of the counts of Flanders, at the point where the Bruges–Cologne trade route crossed the River Dender. Later on, Aalst became a key industrial centre, producing beer and textiles along with some of the worst slum and factory conditions in the country. Cleaned up in the 1950s, the town has one outstanding building, the fifteenth-century **Belfort**. A slender, balconied turret that rises elegantly from the Grote Markt, the belfry is adorned by the statues of a knight and an armed citizen, symbols of municipal power and individual freedom, and inscribed with the town motto, *Nec spe nec metu* ("Neither by hope nor by fear"). The belfry is attached to the **Schepenhuis** (Aldermen's House), a somewhat incoherent jangle of odds and ends shoved together over the centuries, with a flamboyant Gothic gallery protruding into the square from the main body of the building. Elsewhere on the Grote Markt, there are two more buildings of interest: to the left of the belfry is the ornately gabled and arcaded **Borse van Amsterdam**, which started life as the city meat market but now holds one of the best restaurants in town (see p.216), while along the square to the belfry's right stands the colonnaded, nineteenth-century facade of the **Stadhuis**.

Just to the east of the Grote Markt is the towering sandstone mass of **St Martinuskerk** (daily 8am–noon & 2–7pm), a fine example of late Gothic, though work on the church was interrupted by the Thirty Years' War and only the transept, apse and ambulatory were completed – the brick infills mark the interruption. The church interior boasts a fine vaulted ceiling, rounded pillars with delicately carved capitals, and Aalst's only famous painting, the clumsily named *St Roch Receiving from Christ the Gift of Healing Victims of the Plague* by **Rubens**. Commissioned by the guild of beer brewers and hop growers in 1623, the painting is displayed to the right of the entrance in the transept, still in its original carved wooden frame. The composition flaunts the artist's fluent, exuberant style, with the pallid arms of the sick reaching up to the saint, who shudders at the appearance of a windswept Christ wrapped in a flowing red cloak. Typically, Rubens broke with convention in his chosen arrangement: the saint's dog had always been shown licking a plague blemish on his master's leg, but Rubens' animal simply looks agog at Christ. Nearby, beside the high altar, a wedding-cake **tabernacle** fills out the space between two of the church's pillars, its extravagant mixture of columns and statuettes in several different sorts of marble the work of Jerome du Quesnoy in 1604.

At the back of the church, down the hill, the Oud Hospitaal has been turned into a **museum** (daily except Mon 10am–noon & 2–5pm, Wed until 7pm;

free), whose rambling collection has everything from religious paintings through to ceramic tiles. Although the labelling is only in Flemish, it's worth having a look at the two small display areas near the entrance, one dedicated to the local writer and anarchist Paul Boon (1912–79), the other commemorating the work of a nineteenth-century radical Catholic priest, Adolf Daens, who campaigned to improve the pay and conditions of local workers. It's a modest section, but an engaging one, with sepia photographs illustrating the work of the priest, the organization of a local Catholic-led trade union, and the harsh poverty of the period.

The best time to be in Aalst is during its boisterous **carnival**, known as the **Vastelauved**, held over the four days preceding Ash Wednesday. This is the town's principal festival and, among all sorts of municipal high jinks, there are parades with floats satirizing local and national bigwigs, Broom Dancing by the fancifully dressed Gilles of Aalst, and a (rather dubious) parade of the *Voil Jeannetten* – men in drag – on Shrove Tuesday. The whole thing is rounded off by the burning of the Mardi Gras puppet in front of the Stadhuis on the final night of revelry.

Practicalities

Aalst **train station** is five minutes' walk from the town centre: take Albert Lienartstraat from the square in front of the station building and keep going straight. The **tourist office**, in the belfry (June–Sept daily 10–11.45am & 2–4.45pm; Oct–May Mon–Fri 9.30–11.45am & 1.30–5.45pm; ℡053 73 22 70, ⓦwww.aalst.be), has maps of the town and can help with accommodation. Aalst has several centrally situated **hotels**, among which the four-star *Keizershof*, a standard-issue chain hotel at Korte Nieuwstraat 15 (℡053 77 44 11, ℱ053 78 00 97, ⓦwww.keizershof-hotel.com; ❺), is the most appealing. The two-star *Hotel de la Gare*, Stationsplein 11 (℡053 21 39 11, ℱ053 77 12 89; ❷), with twenty frugal rooms – fifteen en suite – is a bargain alternative. As for **food**, the smart *Borse van Amsterdam*, on the Grote Markt, specializes in Flemish cuisine – try the eels – or, for something lighter and less expensive, try the snacks of the *Graaf van Egmont* café, next to the belfry.

Travel details

Trains

Bruges to: Brussels (every 20min; 60min); Ghent (every 20min; 20min); Knokke (every 15min; 20min); Ostend (every 20min; 15min); Zeebrugge (hourly; 15min).

Ghent to: Aalst (every 30min; 25min); Antwerp Centraal (every 30min; 50min); De Panne (1 hourly; 70min); Kortrijk (every 30min; 20min); Mechelen (every 30min; 40min or 60min); Ostend (every 20min; 40min); Oudenaarde (1 hourly; 30min); St Niklaas (every 30min; 25min); Veurne (1 hourly; 60min).

Ieper to: Kortrijk (1 hourly; 30min).

Kortrijk to: Ghent (every 30min; 20min); Ieper (1 hourly; 30min); Lille, France (1 hourly; 30min); Oudenaarde (hourly; 20min).

Ostend to: Bruges (every 20min; 15min); Brussels (every 20min; 80min); Ghent (every 20min; 40min).

Veurne to: De Panne (1 hourly; 10min); Diksmuide (1hourly; 10min); Ghent (hourly; 60min).

Buses

Ieper to: Diksmuide (2–7 daily; 25min); Lo (2–7 daily; 35min); Veurne (2–7 daily; 60min).

Ostend to: Veurne (Mon–Sat 8 daily, Sun 3 daily; 75min).

Veurne to: Ieper (2–7 daily; 60min); Ostend (Mon–Sat 8 daily, Sun 3 daily; 75min).

Coastal train

Ostend to: De Panne (every 10min or 15min in summer, every 30min in winter; 65min); Knokke (same frequency; 60min).

Antwerp and the northeast

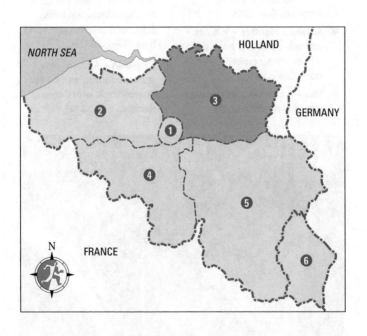

CHAPTER 3 **Highlights**

* **Antwerp's cathedral** – One of the most stunning Gothic buildings in Belgium. See p.229

* **The works of Rubens** – Viewing his magnificent paintings, especially those in the Schone Kunsten, is a must-do on any trip to Antwerp. See p.244

* **Antwerp nightlife** – With its intimate cafés and bars, the city positively grooves after dark. See p.248

* **Lier** – A charming little place with a clutch of fine old buildings, including St Gummaruskerk, which boasts a superb set of stained glass windows. See p.251

* **Leuven** – Besides a couple of outstanding Gothic monuments, this lively university city boasts one of the country's most mouthwatering selections of restaurants and bars. See p.262

* **Tongeren** – A lovely, old-fashioned town, well off the beaten track, with Roman remains. See p.271

3

Antwerp and the northeast

The **provinces** of Antwerp and Limburg, together with a chunk of Brabant, constitute the Flemish-speaking northeastern rim of Belgium, stretching as far as the border with the Netherlands. The countryside is dull and flat on the whole, its most distinctive feature being the rivers and canals that cut across it. Easily the main attraction hereabouts is **Antwerp**, a sprawling, intriguing city with many reminders of its sixteenth-century golden age – before it was upstaged by Amsterdam as the prime commercial centre of the Low Countries – including splendid medieval churches and handsome guildhouses. There's also as fine a set of museums as you'll find anywhere in Belgium, featuring in particular the enormous legacy of **Rubens**, who spent most of his career in the city and produced many of his finest works here. On a more contemporary note, Antwerp is the international centre of the diamond trade and one of Europe's biggest ports, though these roles by no means define its character – for one thing its centre has a range of classy bars and restaurants to rival any city in Northern Europe.

That part of the province of Antwerp lying to the south of the city isn't of much immediate appeal – it's too industrial for that – but there's compensation in a string of old Flemish towns that make ideal day-trips. The first two obvious targets are small-town **Lier**, whose centre is particularly quaint and diverting, and **Mechelen**, the ecclesiastical capital of Belgium, which weighs in with its handsome Gothic churches, most memorably a magnificent cathedral. Southeast from here, just beyond the reaches of Brussels' sprawling suburbs, stands the lively university town of **Leuven** which, boasting its own clutch of fine medieval buildings, is the principal attraction of this corner of Flemish Brabant, although **Diest**, most noteworthy for its well-preserved Begijnhof, comes a reasonable second.

Further to the east, the province of **Limburg** is, unlike Antwerp, seldom visited by tourists, its low-key mixture of small towns and tranquil farmland having limited appeal. Nevertheless, the workaday capital, **Hasselt**, does have an amenable air, and the nearby **Bokrijk** estate holds one of the best open-air museums in the country, primarily dedicated to the rural traditions of Flemish Belgium. Of Limburg's smaller towns, **Tongeren**, on the edge of the linguistic divide, is most worthy of a visit, a pretty and likeable market town dominated by its giant basilica. Just to the west is **Sint Truiden**, from where buses

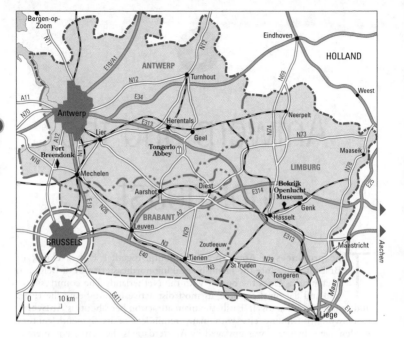

run to the village of **Zoutleeuw**, distinguished by its spectacular fourteenth-century church – the only one in Belgium that managed to avoid the depredations of Protestants, iconoclasts and invading armies.

Hopping from town to town by **public transport** is very easy – there's an excellent network of trains and, where these fizzle out, buses pick up the slack.

Antwerp

About 50km north of Brussels, **ANTWERP**, Belgium's second city, lays claim to be the effective capital of Flemish Belgium, an animated cultural centre with a spirited nightlife. The city fans out carelessly from the east bank of the Scheldt, its centre a rough polygon formed and framed by its enclosing boulevards and the river. Recent efforts to clean and smarten the centre have been tremendously successful, revealing scores of beautiful buildings previously sooted by the accumulated grime. On the surface it's not a wealthy city – the area around the docks is especially run down and seedy – and it's rarely neat and tidy, but it is a hectic and immediately likeable place, with a dense concentration of things to see, not least some fine churches and a varied selection of excellent museums.

East of the centre lies the main shopping street, Meir, whose hotchpotch of old and new buildings rolls past the **Rubenshuis** – one time home and studio of Rubens – en route to the cathedral-like **Centraal Station** and the diamond district – the city has long been at the heart of the international diamond industry. **South** of the centre, Het Zuid, a residential district whose wide boulevards, with their long vistas and central roundabouts, were laid out at the end of the nineteenth century, is a fashionable neighbourhood once again – after years of neglect. The highlight here is the substantial collection of Belgian **art** in the Museum voor Schone Kunsten (the Fine Art Museum), with the invigorating Middelheim Open-Air Sculpture Museum beckoning beyond. Added to this historical and cultural stew is an excellent café, restaurant and bar scene – enough to keep anyone busy for a few days, if not more.

Some history

In the beginning **Antwerp** wasn't much desired: although it occupied a prime river site, it was too far east to be important in the cloth trade and too far west to be on the major trade routes connecting Germany and Holland. However, in the late fifteenth century it benefited from a general movement of trade to the west, a process that was accelerated by the decline of the cloth trade – and the Flemish cloth towns. Within the space of just 25 years, many of the great trading families of western Europe had relocated here, and the tiny old fortified settlement of yesteryear was transformed by a deluge of splendid new mansions and churches, docks and harbours. In addition, the new masters of the region, the Habsburgs, had become frustrated with the turbulent burghers of Flanders and both the emperor Maximilian and his successor **Charles V** patronized the city at the expense of its rivals, underwriting its success as the leading port of their expanding empire.

Antwerp's golden age lasted for less than a hundred years, prematurely stifled by Charles V's son **Philip II**, who inherited the Spanish part of the empire and the Low Countries in 1555. Fanatically Catholic, Philip viewed the Reformist stirrings of his Flemish-speaking subjects with horror, encouraging the Inquisition to send thousands to the gallows – Protestant Antwerp seethed with discontent. The spark was the Ommegang of August 18, 1566, when priests carting the image of the Virgin through the city's streets insisted that all should bend the knee as it passed. The parade itself was peaceful enough, but afterwards, with the battle cry of "Long live the beggars", the city's Protestant guildsmen and their apprentices smashed the inside of the cathedral to pieces – the most extreme example of the **"iconoclastic fury"** that then swept the region. Philip responded by sending in an army of occupation, intended to overawe and intimidate from a brand new citadel he ordered to be built on the south side of town. Nine years later, it was this same garrison that sat unpaid and underfed in its fortress, surrounded by the wealth of what they regarded as a "heretical" city. Philip's mercenaries mutinied, and at dawn on November 4 1576, they stormed Antwerp, running riot for three long days, plundering public buildings and private mansions, and slaughtering some eight thousand of its citizens in the **"Spanish fury"**, a catastrophe that finished the city's commercial supremacy. More disasters were to follow. Philip's soldiers were driven out after the massacre, but they were back in 1585 laying siege outside the city walls for seven months, their success leading to Antwerp's ultimate incorporation within the **Spanish Netherlands**. Under the terms of the capitulation, Protestants had two years to leave town, and a flood of skilled workers poured north to the relative safety of Holland, further weakening the city's economy.

In the early seventeenth century there was a modest recovery, but the Dutch, who were now free of Spain, controlled the waterways of the Scheldt and were determined that no neighbouring Catholic port would threaten their trade. Consequently, in 1648, under the **Peace of Westphalia**, which finally wrapped up the Thirty Years' War, they forced the closure of the river to all

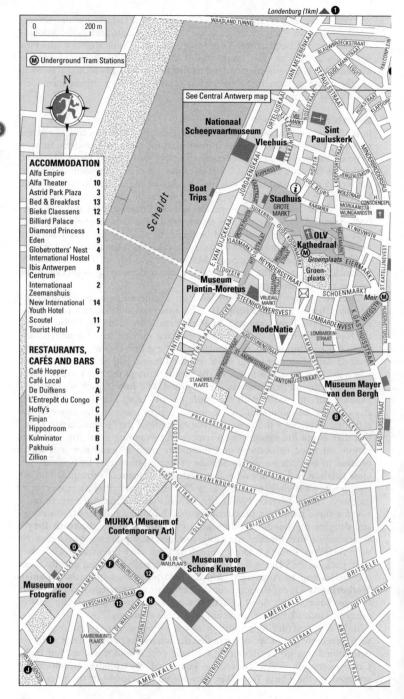

Londenburg (1km)

WAASLAND TUNNEL

0   200 m

(M) Underground Tram Stations

N

See Central Antwerp map

Nationaal
Scheepvaartmuseum

Vleehuis

Sint
Pauluskerk

Boat
Trips

Stadhuis
GROTE
MARKT

Scheldt

OLV
Kathedraal

Groenplaats

Museum
Plantin-Moretus

Groen-
plaats

Meir

M

Schoenmarkt

ModeNatie

LOMBARDENVEST

LOMBARDEN-
STRAAT

Museum Mayer
van den Bergh

PREKERSTRAAT

STROCHUSSTRAAT

KRONENBURGSTRAAT

MUHKA (Museum of
Contemporary Art)

L DE
WAELPLAATS

Museum voor
Schone Kunsten

Museum voor
Fotografie

LAMBERMONTS
PLAATS

AMERIKALEI

ACCOMMODATION

Alfa Empire	6
Alfa Theater	10
Astrid Park Plaza	3
Bed & Breakfast	13
Bieke Claessens	12
Billiard Palace	5
Diamond Princess	1
Eden	9
Globetrotters' Nest	4
International Hostel	
Ibis Antwerpen	8
Centrum	
Internationaal	2
Zeemanshuis	
New International	14
Youth Hotel	
Scoutel	11
Tourist Hotel	7

RESTAURANTS,
CAFÉS AND BARS

Café Hopper	G
Café Local	D
De Duifkens	A
L'Entrepôt du Congo	F
Hoffy's	C
Finjan	H
Hippodroom	E
Kulminator	B
Pakhuis	I
Zillion	J

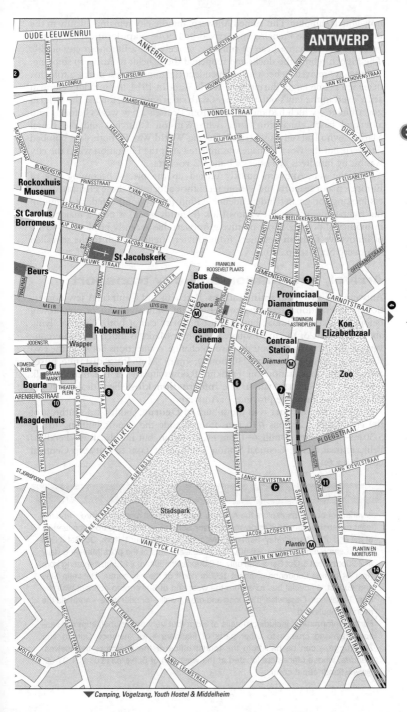

ANTWERP

OUDE LEEUWENRUI
ANKERRUI
CASSIERSSTRAAT
GEN. BELLIARDSTR
FALCONRUI
STIJFSELRUI
HOUWERSTRAAT
VAN KERCKHOVENSTRAAT
OUDE STEENWEG
PAARDENMARKT
VONDELSTRAAT
VAN STRAALENSTR
DIEPESTRAAT
OLIJFTAKSTR
ROTTERDAMSTR
HOLLANDSTR
VEEMSTRAAT
VENUSSTRAAT
ROODESTRAAT
ITALIELIE
MUTSAERDSTR
BLINDERSTR
PRINSSTRAAT
P VAN HOBOKENSTR
ST ELISABETHSTR
LANGE BEELDEKENSSTRAAT
DAMBRUGGESTRAAT

Rockoxhuis
Museum
KEIZERSTRAAT
OSTSTRAAT
VAN ARTEVELDESTR
VAN WESENBEKESTRAAT
VAN SCHOONHOVENSTRAAT

St Carolus
Borromeus
KIP DORP
ST JACOBS MARKT
St Jacobskerk
FRANKLIN
ROOSEVELT PLAATS
GEMEENTESTRAAT
CARNOTSTRAAT
OFFERANDESTRAAT

Beurs
LANGE NIEUWE STRAAT
Bus
Station
Provinciaal
Diamantmuseum
Kon.
Elizabethzaal

MEIR
MEIR
LEYS STR
Opera
Koningin
Astridplein

Rubenshuis
Gaumont
Cinema
Centraal
Station

Wapper
JODENSTR.
Diamant
Zoo

Komedie
Plein
GRAAN
MARKT
Stadsschouwburg

Bourla
THEATER-
PLEIN
PLOEGSTRAAT

Maagdenhuis
ARENBERGSTRAAT
LANG KIEVILSTRAAT
VAN IMMERSEELSTR

ST-JORISPOORT
LANGE KIEVITSTRAAT

Stadspark
JACOB JACOBSSTR

VAN EYCK LEI
Plantin
PLANTIN EN
MORETUSLEI

PLANTIN EN MORETUSLEI

MECHELSE STEENWEG
LANGE LEEMSTRAAT
CHARLOTTALEI

MOLENSTR
ST JOZEFSTR
LANGE LEEMSTRAAT
BELGIE LEI
MERCATORSTRAAT
PROVINCIESTRAAT

▼ Camping, Vogelzang, Youth Hostel & Middelheim

non-Dutch shipping. This ruined Antwerp, and the city remained firmly in the doldrums until the French army arrived in 1797 – **Napoleon** declaring it to be "little better than a heap of ruins . . . scarcely like a European city at all". The French rebuilt the docks and reopened the Scheldt to Antwerp shipping, and the city revived to become independent Belgium's largest port – a role that made it a prime target during both World Wars. In 1914, the invading German army overran the city's outer defences with surprising ease, forcing the Belgian government – which had moved here from Brussels a few weeks before – into a second hasty evacuation along with Winston Churchill and the Royal Marines, who had only just arrived. During **World War II**, both sides bombed Antwerp, but the worst damage was inflicted after the Liberation when the city was hit by hundreds of Hitler's V1 and V2 **rockets**.

After the war, Antwerp quickly picked up the pieces, becoming one of Europe's major seaports and – more recently – a focus for those Flemish-speakers looking for greater independence within (or without) a federal Belgium: the right-wing, nationalist Vlaams Blok (Flemish block) is now a major force in municipal politics. More positively, Antwerp has recently produced a string of innovative **fashion** designers, from Olivier Strelli through to the so-called "Antwerp Six" (see p.240).

Arrival, information and city transport

Antwerp has two main **train stations**, Berchem and Centraal. A few domestic and international trains pause at Berchem, 4km southeast of downtown, before bypassing Centraal, but the vast majority call at both. Centraal, lying about 2km east of the main square, the Grote Markt, is much the more convenient for the centre. If you do have to change, connections between the two stations are frequent and fast (10 hourly; 4min). Most **long-distance buses** arrive at the bus station on Franklin Rooseveltplaats, a five-minute walk northwest of Centraal Station. The **information kiosk** here deals with bus services throughout the province of Antwerp.

Antwerp's tiny **airport** is in the suburb of **Deurne**, about 6km southeast of the city centre. City bus #16 runs from outside the airport building (daily: 5.30am–6pm every 20min, 6–11pm every 30min, but hourly all weekend) to Pelikaanstraat, beside Centraal Station. Failing that, taxis to Antwerp Centraal cost about €15.

Boat trips

A variety of boat trips explore the Antwerp area. The most straightforward – and the least expensive – are cruises down the **River Scheldt**, which leave from the landing at the end of Suikerrui (May–Sept daily every hour on the hour 1–4pm, Oct Sat & Sun only at same times; 50min; €6.50). There are also tours of the **port** (May–Aug daily at 2.30pm; Sept & Oct Sat & Sun only at 2.30pm; 2hr 30min; €11.50), departing from Kaai 14 beside Londenbrug, about 1500m north of the city centre. Between May and August, a special bus runs from the west end of Suikerrui to connect with the Kaai 14 sailings. Otherwise, it's a long and dreary walk – or brief drive – north via the riverside boulevard.

Further information, including details of extra (but very occasional) summer-season, day-long cruises to other parts of Flanders – for instance Ostend and Zeebrugge – can be had from the tourist office or the operators themselves, *Flandria*, whose offices are located at the west end of Suikerrui (☎03 231 31 00, ⓦwww.flandriaboat.com).

Information

The **tourist office** is in the city centre at Grote Markt 15 (Mon–Sat 9am–6pm, Sun 9am–5pm; ☎03 232 01 03, ℱ03 231 19 37, ⒲www.visitantwerpen.be). They have a comprehensive range of information, most notably a very useful and free booklet detailing the city's sights and accommodation – including B&Bs – alongside all sorts of practical details. They also issue free transit maps and city maps (€0.25), display train timetables and sell a number of specialist leaflets (€1 each) – principally a suggested driving route round the port and walking tours detailing where to see the works of Rubens and his contemporary, Jacob Jordaens. Another useful publication is a *Fashion Walk* booklet (€3) describing several routes that take in the city's best designer clothes shops and stores. Finally, their free, quarterly **Cultural Bulletin** has information on forthcoming events, exhibitions and concerts.

City transport

A useful **tram and bus** system serves the city and its suburbs from a number of points around Centraal Station; bus stops are concentrated along Pelikaanstraat and in Koningin Astridplein. **Trams** from Centraal Station to the city centre go underground (#2 or #15 direction Linkeroever; get off at Groenplaats), departing from the adjacent Diamant underground station. There's also a city transport **information office** (Mon–Fri 8am–12.30pm & 1.30–4pm) in the Diamant underground station. They sell tickets for – and issue free maps of – the city transport system (the *Netplan*). A standard one-way fare costs €1 and a ten-strip Rittenkaart €7.50; a 24-hour unlimited city-wide travel card, a Dagpas, costs €2.90. Single tickets – which are valid for one hour – are also available from tram and bus drivers.

Accommodation

Antwerp has the range of **hotels** you'd expect of Belgium's second city, as well as a number of **hostels** and a reasonable supply of **B&Bs**. Consequently, finding accommodation is rarely difficult, although there are surprisingly few places in the centre, which is by far the best spot to soak up the city's atmosphere. Many medium-priced and budget places are clustered in the scruffy area around Centraal Station, where you should exercise caution at night, particularly if travelling alone.

The tourist office has a comprehensive list of hotels and hostels and will make **hotel bookings** on your behalf at no cost, charging only a modest deposit that is subtracted from your final bill. Their list covers all grades of accommodation, from dormitory-style beds to executive suites, but excludes the seedier establishments and the B&Bs; information on the latter can be obtained from Gilde der Antwerpse Gastenkamers (☎03 232 01 03, ⒲www.gastenkamersantwerpen.be).

Antwerp's closest campsite, **Camping Vogelzang**, Vogelzanglaan (☎03 238 57 17; April–Sept), is situated in a sprawling sports area about 5km south of the city centre, near the R1 ring road (Exit 5). It's reachable on tram #2 from Centraal Station, direction Hoboken; get off – or ask to be put off – at the Bouwcentrum shopping mall, from where it's a short walk to the east.

The places to stay reviewed below are marked either on the Antwerp map on pp.222–23 or the map of central Antwerp on p.228.

Hotels

Over €80

Alfa Empire Appelmansstraat 31 ☎03 203 54 00, ℱ03 233 40 60, ⒲www.alfahotels.com. Large, sumptuous and well-equipped rooms in this three-star hotel close to Centraal Station. Weekend discounts bring the cost of a double down by about €20. ⑥

Alfa Theater Arenbergstraat 30 ☎03 203 54 10,
Ⓕ03 233 88 58, ⓦwww.alfahotels.com.
Luxurious, four-star hotel in a wealthy part of
town, just 5min walk south of the Rubenshuis.
Commodious, appealing rooms. ❼

Astrid Park Plaza Koningin Astridplein 7 ☎03
203 12 34, Ⓕ03 203 12 51, ⓦwww.parkplazaww
.com. Koningin Astridplein, the large square beside
Centraal Station, had become something of an
eyesore until the city council took matters in hand,
launching an ambitious refurbishment programme
that has turned it into one of the more appealing
parts of the city. Part of the package was this
whopping four-star hotel with over two hundred
very comfortable rooms. The hotel has a striking
modern design, but the bright paintwork – ochre
and yellow – is frightening. ❻

Best Western Hotel Villa Mozart
Handschoenmarkt 3 ☎03 231 30 31, Ⓕ03 231
56 85, ⓦwww.wanadoo.be/classic.hotels. Plush,
three-star chain hotel with a great if noisy location
opposite the cathedral. Each of the hotel's 25
rooms is pleasantly decorated. Reductions of up to
thirty percent at the weekend. ❼

De Witte Lelie Keizerstraat 16 ☎03 226 19 66,
Ⓕ03 234 00 19, ⓦwww.dewittelelie.be.
Immaculate four-star hotel – the city's ritziest and
most exclusive. Just ten charming rooms in a
handsomely renovated sixteenth-century merchant's house, a 5min walk from the Grote Markt.
❾

Eden Lange Herentalsestraat 25 ☎03 233 06 08,
Ⓕ03 233 12 28, ⓦwww.diamand-hotels.com.
Standard-issue, medium-sized, three-star hotel in
the diamond district near the station. Perfectly
adequate, the rooms are modern but quite plain –
and in the mosquito season stand by for attack.
The breakfasts, though, are very good. ❺

Hilton Antwerp Groenplaats ☎03 204 12 12,
Ⓕ03 204 12 13, ⓦwww.hilton.com. Big, taste-
lessly flashy hotel right in the city centre. Every
facility, from a sauna and gym through to a hair-
dresser's and piano bar. ❾

Ibis Antwerpen Centrum Meistraat 39 ☎03 231
88 30, Ⓕ03 234 29 21, ⓦwww.ibishotel.com.
Relatively inexpensive chain hotel with routine
modern rooms. It's hidden away behind a particularly ghastly concrete exterior, compensated for by
a decent location, close to the Rubenshuis. ❺

Rubens Grote Markt Oude Beurs 29 ☎03 226
95 82, Ⓕ03 225 19 40, ⒺHotel.rubens@glo.be.
Arguably the most agreeable hotel in town, the
four-star *Rubens* has a relaxing air and occupies a
handy downtown location just a couple of minutes'
walk north of the Grote Markt. There are 36 rooms,
modern, comfortable and attractively furnished. ❼

Under €80

Billard Palace Koningin Astridplein 40 ☎03 233
44 55, Ⓕ03 226 14 26, ⓦwww.billardpalace.be.
Basic, verging on the grim, hotel in the station
area with doubles, triples and quads. ❸

Cammerpoorte Nationalestraat 38 ☎03 231 97
36, Ⓕ03 226 29 68. Modern, two-star hotel with
39 frugal, en-suite rooms in a building that looks a
bit like a car park. It has a mildly forlorn air, but
the location is handy, a 5min walk south of
Groenplaats. ❹

Diamond Princess Sint-Laureiskaai 2
(Bonapartedok) ☎03 227 08 15, Ⓕ03 227 16 77,
ⓦwww.diamondprincess.be. Antwerp's most
unusual hotel, occupying a converted former
Norwegian mail boat dating from the 1950s; it's
moored in the old harbour, about 1km north of the
Grote Markt, 600m north of Sint Pauluskerk. Fifty-
two rooms/cabins, all en suite. Three-star. The
boat is also used for parties and discos. ❹

Internationaal Zeemanshuis (Seamen's House)
Falconrui 21 ☎03 227 54 33, Ⓕ03 234 26 03,
ⓦwww.zeemanshuis.be. Located a 10min walk
north of the Grote Markt in a lively-verging-on-the-
seedy part of town. Accommodation is in neat and
trim doubles and singles, all of which are en suite.
Despite the name, it's open to landlubbers and
women as well as mariners. ❷

New International Youth Hotel Provinciestraat
256 ☎03 230 05 22, Ⓕ03 281 09 33,
ⓦwww.niyh.be. A 10min walk from Centraal
Station. Spick-and-span, medium-sized, family-run
hotel-cum-hostel offering bargain singles and doubles, some en suite. Breakfast is included. ❸

Tourist Hotel Pelikaanstraat 20 ☎03 232 58 70,
Ⓕ03 231 67 07, ⓦwww.demahotels.be. An inexpensive if rather uninspiring option near Centraal
Station – OK for a night or two, though
Pelikaanstraat can be noisy. Straightforward,
modern rooms. ❸

Hostels and B&Bs

Bed & Breakfast Verschansingstraat 55 ☎ &
Ⓕ03 248 09 13,
ⓦwww.bedandbreakfast.webb.be. A short walk
from the Museum voor Schone Kunsten, this informal B&B, in a late nineteenth-century terrace, has
a couple of sparse but perfectly adequate guest
rooms. ❸

Bieke Claessens Leopold de Waelplaats 28 ☎ &
Ⓕ03 216 42 44. In the classy modern block of
flats straight opposite the Museum voor Schone
Kunsten. One en-suite room. Breakfast served on
the roof terrace, weather permitting. ❹

Enich Anders Leeuwenstraat 12 ☎03 231 37 92,
Ⓕ03 213 00 45, Ⓔenich.anders@antwerpen.be.

Above a sculptor's workshop on a weather-beaten old narrow street off the Vrijdagmarkt, this B&B offers a furnished studio with bathroom and kitchen. The breakfast part of the arrangement is served up in a baseket in the room itself. ❸

Globetrotters' Nest International Hostel Vlagstraat 25 ☎ & ℱ 03 236 99 28, ℮ globetrotters@freegates.be. Popular with backpackers, this small but well-established hostel has one double, one eight-bedded and one four-bedded room, plus a kitchen, a reading room and bike rental. No lockout or curfew. About 1500m northeast of Centraal Station – take bus #23 and ask to be put off: the bus travels along Pothoekstraat, and Vlagstraat is a turning on the right. Rate includes breakfast. Dorm beds €10, ❶

Jeugdherberg Op Sinjoorke Youth Hostel Eric Sasselaan 2 ☎ 03 238 02 73, ℱ 03 248 19 32, ⓦ www.vjh.be. HI-affiliated hostel close to the ring road about 5km south of the centre, with around

130 beds in two-, four-, six- and eight-bedded rooms. There's a canteen serving lunch and dinner, and there are also self-catering facilities and a laundry room. Closed 10am–4pm. Tram #2 from Centraal Station, direction Hoboken; get off – or ask to be put off – at the Bouwcentrum stop, from where it's a 100m walk to the west. Breakfast included in the rate. Dorm beds €12.50, ❸

Scoutel Stoomstraat 3 ☎ 03 226 46 06, ℱ 03 232 63 92, ⓦ www.vvksm.be. Neat and trim hostel-cum-hotel offering frugal but perfectly adequate singles, doubles, triples and quadruples with breakfast. It's a 5min walk from Centraal Station: head south down Pelikaanstraat, turn left along Lange Kievitstraat, go through the tunnel and it's the first road on the right. There's no curfew, but be sure to check in before 6pm when reception closes. Reservations are advised in the summer. Under-25s get a fifteen percent discount on the regular rate. ❸

The City Centre

Antwerp's bustling **centre** is the most engaging part of the city, its mazy streets and cobbled lanes studded by fine old churches, mansions and museums. The logical place to start an exploration is the **Grote Markt**, still the centre of activities and flanked by the elegant **Stadhuis**. From here, it's a couple of hundred metres south to the splendid Gothic church of **Onze Lieve Vrouwekathedraal**, home to a quartet of paintings by Rubens, with the intriguing old printing house of Christopher Plantin, now the **Museum Plantin-Moretus**, just beyond. Another short hop, this time west to the waterfront, brings up the **Nationaal Scheepvaartmuseum** – the National Maritime Museum – with its first-rate nautical displays, and then comes the striking medieval **Vleeshuis**, one-time headquarters of the guild of butchers. The city centre finishes off with two other excellent attractions, the sinuous Baroque of **Sint Pauluskerk** and a small but superb collection of paintings in the **Rockoxhuis Museum**.

The Grote Markt

The centre of Antwerp is the **Grote Markt**, at the heart of which stands the **Brabo Fountain**, a haphazard pile of roughly sculpted rocks surmounted by a bronze of Silvius Brabo, depicted flinging the hand of the prostrate giant Antigonus into the Scheldt. Legend asserts that Antigonus extracted tolls from all passing ships, cutting off the hands of those who refused to pay. He was eventually beaten by the valiant Brabo, who tore off his hand and threw it into the river, giving the city its name, which literally means "hand-throw". There are more realistic explanations of the city's name, but this is the most colourful, and it certainly reflects Antwerp's early success at freeing the river from the innumerable taxes levied on shipping by local landowners.

The north side of the Grote Markt is lined with daintily restored **guildhouses**, their sixteenth-century facades decorated with appropriate reliefs and topped by finely cast gilded figures basking in the afterglow of the city's Renaissance lustre. No. 7, the House of the Crossbowmen, with its figures of St George and the dragon, is the tallest and most distinctive; it stands next to the Coopers' House, with its barrel motifs and statue of St Matthew. They are, however, both overshadowed by the Stadhuis.

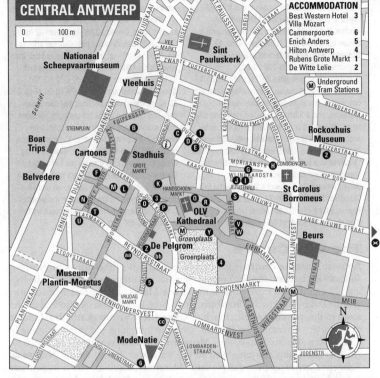

CENTRAL ANTWERP

0   100 m

ACCOMMODATION

Best Western Hotel	3
Villa Mozart	
Cammerpoorte	6
Enich Anders	5
Hilton Antwerp	4
Rubens Grote Markt	1
De Witte Lelie	2

Ⓜ Underground
Tram Stations

RESTAURANTS, CAFÉS, BARS AND CLUBS

Aurelia	I	De Faam	F	Hoorn des Overloeds	S	Pizzeria Da Antonio	K
Café d'Anvers	A	Facade	H	Den Hopsack	N	Popoff	O
Café de Muze	W	De Groote Witte Arend	aa	La Terrazza	C	Satsuma	D
Café Pelikaan	V	Jacqmotte	Y	De Matelote	M	't Stamineeke	T
Den Billekletser	L	De Herk	bb	Oude Beurs	E	De Stoemppot	U
Did's Bistro	X	Het Dagelijks Brood	cc	De Peerdestal	J	De Vagant	Z
Den Engel	B	Het Elfde Gebod	R	Paters' Vaetje	Q	De Volle Maan	P
						't Zolderke	G

The Stadhuis

Presiding over the Grote Markt, the **Stadhuis** was completed in 1566 to an innovative design by Cornelis Floris (guided tours on Mon, Tues, Thurs & Fri at 11am, 2pm & 3pm, Sat 2pm & 3pm; €1) – though there have been several subsequent modifications. The building's pagoda-like roof gives it a faintly oriental appearance, but apart from the central gable it's quite plain, with a long pilastered facade of short and rather shallow Doric and Ionic columns. These, along with the windows, lend a simple elegance, in contrast to the purely decorative gable (there's no roof behind it). The niches at the top contribute to the self-congratulatory aspect of the building, with statues of *Justice* and *Wisdom* proclaiming virtues the city burghers reckoned they had in plenty.

The **main entrance** is on the Suikerrui. Inside, the main staircase climbs up to the lofty main hall, which used to be an open courtyard and was only covered in the late nineteenth century. The monumental gallery flanking the hall is decorated with paintings that took the place of the original windows. They represent aspects of commerce and the arts – a balance of which Antwerp has long been aware, and is now anxious to preserve. Among the other rooms you can see are the **Leyszaal** (Leys Room), named after Baron Hendrik Leys, who painted the frescoes in the 1860s, and the **Trouwzaal** (Wedding Room), which has a chimneypiece from the original interior, decorated with two splendid alabaster caryatids by Floris himself, who doubled as a master sculptor.

The Handschoenmarkt

Leaving the Grote Markt by its southeast corner, you'll come to the triangular **Handschoenmarkt** (the former Glove Market), framed by an attractive ensemble of antique gables. In addition, its tiny **stone well**, adorned by a graceful iron canopy, bears the legend "It was love connubial taught the smith to paint" – a reference to the fifteenth-century painter Quentin Matsys, who learned his craft so he could woo the daughter of a local artist: marriage was then strongly discouraged between families of different guilds. The Handschoenmarkt is the most westerly of a somewhat confusing cobweb of pedestrianized streets and miniature squares that laps the cathedral.

The Onze Lieve Vrouwekathedraal

One of the finest Gothic churches in Belgium, the **Onze Lieve Vrouwekathedraal** (Cathedral of Our Lady; Mon–Fri 10am–5pm, Sat 10am–3pm, Sun 1–4pm; €2, plus €0.25 for a diagrammatic leaflet) is a forceful, self-confident structure that mostly dates from the middle of the fifteenth century. Its graceful spire dominated the skyline of the medieval city and was long a favourite with British travellers. William Beckford, for instance, fresh from spending millions on his own house in Wiltshire in the early 1800s, was particularly impressed, writing that he "longed to ascend it that instant, to stretch myself out upon its summit and calculate, from so sublime an elevation, the influence of the planets". What's more, the church is in better shape than for centuries, after an exemplary 25-year restoration.

The seven-aisled **nave** is breathtaking, if only because of its sense of space, an impression that's reinforced by the bright, light stonework. The religious troubles of the sixteenth century – primarily the Iconoclastic Fury of 1566 – polished off the cathedral's early furnishings and fittings, so what you see today are largely Baroque embellishments, most notably four early paintings by **Pieter Paul Rubens** (1577–1640). Of these, the *Descent from the Cross*, a triptych painted after the artist's return from Italy in 1612, is without doubt the most beautiful, displaying an uncharacteristically moving realism derived from Caravaggio; it's just to the right of the central crossing. Christ languishes in the centre in glowing white, surrounded by mourners or figures tenderly struggling to lower him. As was normal practice at the time, students in Rubens' studio worked on the painting, among them the young **van Dyck**, who completed the face of the Virgin and the arm of Mary Magdalene. His work was so masterful that Rubens is supposed to have declared it an improvement on his own, though this story appears to originate from van Dyck himself. Oddly enough, the painting was commissioned by the guild of arquebusiers, who asked for a picture of St Christopher, their patron saint; Rubens' painting was not at all what they had in mind, and they promptly threatened him with legal action unless he added a picture of the saint to the wings. Rubens obliged, painting in the muscular giant who now dominates the outside of the left panel.

Hanging over the high altar is a second Rubens painting, the *Assumption*, a swirling Baroque scene, full of cherubs and luxuriant drapery, painted in 1625, while, on the left-hand side of the central crossing, Rubens' *The Raising of the Cross* is a grandiloquent canvas full of muscular soldiers and saints; this triptych was painted in 1610, which makes it the earliest of the four.

On the right-hand side of the ambulatory in the second chapel along, there's the cathedral's fourth and final Rubens, the *Resurrection*, painted in 1612 for the tomb of his friend, the printer Jan Moretus, showing a strident, militaristic Christ carrying a red, furled banner. Among the cathedral's many other paintings, the only highlight is **Maarten de Vos'** (1531–1603) *Marriage at Cana*, hung opposite the *Descent from the Cross*, a typically mannered work completed in 1597.

The expansive open square, the **Groenplaats**, behind the cathedral was once the town graveyard; it now holds an uninspired statue of Rubens, as well as the overblown *Hilton Hotel*.

Vrijdagmarkt and the Museum Plantin-Moretus

From the cathedral, it takes a couple of minutes to thread your way west to the **Vrijdagmarkt**, an appealing little square that took a direct hit from a V2 rocket in World War II. The square is in the middle of an old working-class district and hosts a browbeaten open-air **market** of old household effects on Fridays (9am–1pm).

One side of the Vrijdagmarkt is taken up by the **Museum Plantin-Moretus** (Tues–Sun 10am–5pm; €4, but free on Fri), housed in the old mansion of the printer Christopher Plantin, who rose to fame and fortune in the second half of the sixteenth century. Born in Tours in 1520, Plantin moved to Antwerp when he was 34 to set up a small bookbinding business, but in 1555 he was forced to give up all heavy work when, in a case of mistaken identity, he was wounded by revellers returning from carnival. Paid to keep quiet about his injuries, Plantin used the money to start a printing business. He was phenomenally successful, his fortune assured when Philip II granted him the monopoly of printing missals and breviaries for the whole of the Spanish Empire. On Plantin's death, the business passed to his talented son-in-law, Jan Moerentorf, a close friend of Rubens, who Latinized his name, in accordance with the fashion of the day, to Moretus. The family donated their mansion to the city in 1876.

From the **entrance**, a labelled route takes visitors through most of the rooms of the house, which is set around a compact central courtyard. The mansion is worth seeing in itself, its warren of small, dark rooms equipped with mullioned windows and lockable wooden window shutters, plus oodles of leather wallpaper in the Spanish style. As for the museum, it provides a marvellous insight into how Plantin and his offspring conducted their business.

A detailed guidebook is on sale at reception, but **highlights** include several well-preserved pictorial tapestries in Rooms 1 and 6, while Room 4 comprises a delightful seventeenth-century bookshop. Here you'll spot a list of prohibited books – the Habsburg's Librorum Prohibitorum – along with a money-balance to help identify clipped and debased coins. Room 11 has a fine portrait of *Seneca* by Rubens, and Room 14 contains the old print workshop, with seven ancient presses. Upstairs, Room 16 displays examples of the work of Christopher Plantin, notably several finely worked vellum bibles and geographical texts, including one on a French trip to Antarctica dating to 1558.

Throughout the museum there are scores of intriguing, precise **woodcuts** and **copper plates**, representing the best of an enormous number used by several centuries of print workers. In particular, look out for the superbly crafted sample prepared for the publication of a seventeenth-century naturalist book

△ Stadhuis, Antwerp

in Room 18. Concentrated in Room 19 are sketches by Rubens, who occasionally worked for the family as an illustrator, while Room 24 boasts a selection of early printed books from other parts of Europe.

From Vrijdagmarkt north to the waterfront

Across Vrijdagmarkt from the museum is **Leeuwenstraat**, a narrow little street flanked by very old – and very careworn – terrace houses. At the end, turn left and then first right for **Pelgrimstraat**, which provides one of the best views of the Onze Lieve Vrouwekathedraal, with a sliver of sloping, uneven roofs set against the majestic lines of the spire behind. At no. 15, a restored sixteenth-century merchant's house, **De Pelgrom**, has been converted into a tavern; upstairs is a tiny, privately-owned museum decked out with period bric-a-brac (Sat & Sun noon–6pm; €2.50). On the same street, by no. 6, an ancient, cobbled alley called **Vlaaikensgang** (Pie Lane) is a surviving fragment of the honeycomb of narrow lanes that made up medieval Antwerp. It twists a quaint route through to **Oude Koornmarkt**, which itself leads west into **Suikerrui**; this in turn leads to the east bank of the Scheldt, clearly separated from the town since Napoleon razed the riverside slums and constructed proper wharves in the early 1800s. Jutting out into the river at the end of Suikerrui is an overblown, formal **belvedere**, where the Belgian middle classes once took the air, looking out over the river before taking the ferry from the jetty next door. The river ferry is long gone – several roads now run under the Scheldt – and there's precious little to gaze at today except the belvedere, which can't help but seem a little dejected.

Nationaal Scheepvaartmuseum

A few metres north along the riverfront, the sturdy remains of the Steen are approached past a statue of the giant **Lange Wapper**, a somewhat dubious local folklore figure – part practical joker, part Peeping Tom – who, as well as being fond of children, exploited his height by spying into people's bedrooms. The **Steen** marks the site of the ninth-century castle from which the rest of the town spread, later the location of an impressive medieval stronghold, successively reinforced and remodelled to keep the turbulent guildsmen of Antwerp in check.

The stone gatehouse and front section are all that have survived of the medieval stronghold, and today they house the **Nationaal Scheepvaartmuseum** (National Maritime Museum; Tues–Sun 10am–5pm; €4, but free on Fri), whose cramped rooms hold exhibits illustrating a whole range of shipping activity from inland navigation to life on the waterfront and shipbuilding. Clearly laid out and labelled, with multilingual details on all the major displays, the museum is a delight, an appealing mixture of the personal and the public. The high points include a charming British scrimshaw engraved on a whale bone in Room 1, a fascinating fifth-century nautical totem in the form of a snake's head in Room 3, and several fine model ships in Rooms 6 and 9. Look out also for a model of the Italianate barge that was built for Napoleon's second visit to Antwerp, and peek into the old council chamber, decorated by two large paintings of the city's harbour in the seventeenth century. Behind the Steen, the museum has an open-air section (April–Oct) with a long line of tugs and barges parked under a rickety corrugated roof.

The Vleeshuis

Opposite the Steen across Jordaenskaai, filling out the end of narrow Vleeshuisstraat, are the tall, turreted gables of the **Vleeshuis** (Meat Hall; Tues–Sun 10am–5pm; €2.50, but free on Fri), built for the guild of butchers in 1503. This strikingly attractive building, with its alternating layers of red brick and stonework resembling rashers of bacon, was once the suitably grand headquarters of one of the most powerful of the medieval guilds. It was here in 1585, with the Spanish army approaching, that the butchers made the fateful decision to oppose the opening of the dykes along the River Scheldt. William the Silent had strongly recommended this defensive ploy because it would have made it impossible for the Spaniards to mount a blockade of the river from its banks. However, the butchers were more worried about the safety of their sheep, which grazed the threatened meadows, and so they sent a deputation to the city magistrates to object. The magistrates yielded, and the consequences were disastrous – the Spaniards were able to close the Scheldt and force the town to surrender, a defeat that placed Antwerp firmly within the Spanish Netherlands.

Today, the enormous brick halls of the **interior** are used to display a mildly diverting and somewhat incoherent collection of applied arts, though sometimes the whole lot is moved round to make room for temporary exhibitions (which cost extra). The permanent collection is labelled exclusively in Flemish, but it's worth asking at reception to see if they've produced an English guide – one is promised. On the **ground floor**, pride of place in the permanent collection goes to the musical instruments, especially the primly decorated clavichords, which come in all sorts of unwieldy shapes and sizes, and the harpsichords, some of which were produced locally in the Ruckers workshop in the seventeenth century. Among a smattering of medieval woodcarving, the pick is a retable from Averbode Abbey, near Diest, that's stuck right at the back of the hall. This charming triptych features a magnificent high-relief tableau of the Descent from the Cross which escapes religious cliché in the fineness of its detail – one onlooker wipes her eyes, another holds Christ's wrist tenderly in her hand.

It's down to the vaulted **basement** for the Lapidarium, where a motley assortment of old bits of masonry, mostly retrieved from demolished houses and churches, has been amassed. Rather better, and reached via a steep, spiralling staircase, are the **upper floor**'s cameo collections of military gear, coins, clocks and tapestries. Here also are several period rooms, including the relocated Raadzaal (Meeting Room) of the council of the guild of butchers. Next to the coins is a contemporaneous – and anonymous – painting of the *Spanish Fury* of November 1576. It's a gruesome picture of a gruesome event, with bodies piled high in the streets and the city burning in the background as the Spanish mutineers continue to rob, rape and kill. The massacre was a disaster for Antwerp, but although the savagery of the attack was unusual, **mutinies** in the Spanish army were not. The Habsburgs often failed to pay their soldiers for years on end and this failure, combined with harsh conditions and seemingly interminable warfare, provoked at least a couple of mutinies every year. Indeed, the practice became so commonplace that it began to develop its own custom, with the *tercio* (army unit) concerned refusing orders but keeping military discipline and electing representatives to haggle a financial deal with the army authorities. A deal was usually reached and punishments were rare.

To Sint Pauluskerk

The streets around the Vleeshuis and Sint Pauluskerk were badly damaged by wartime bombing, leaving a string of bare, open spaces edged by some of the worst of the city's slums. The whole area is gradually being rebuilt, but progress is slow. Many of the crumbling rows of houses have yet to be restored, though most of the gaps have now been filled by solid modern houses whose pinkish brick facades imitate the style of what went before. Cosy and respectable, these new buildings are in stark contrast to the remaining areas of dilapidation – seedy little streets with sporadic tattoo parlours and bored faces at the windows signifying the start of the red-light area, whose centre of gravity is further north on Sint Paulusplaats.

From the Vleeshuis, it's a couple of minutes' walk north along Vleeshouwersstraat to the **Veemarkt**, where an extravagant Baroque portal leads through to **Sint Pauluskerk** (May–Sept daily 2–5pm; free), one of the city's most delightful churches, an airy, dignified late Gothic structure dating from 1517. Built for the Dominicans, the original church was looted by the Calvinists when they expelled the monks in 1578. Restored to their property after the siege of 1585, the Dominicans refashioned Sint Pauluskerk to illustrate the Catholic Church as the only means of salvation – with the choir symbolizing the Church Glorious, and the nave, aisles and transepts the Church Militant. In addition, the Dominicans commissioned a series of paintings to line the wall of the nave's north aisle depicting the "Fifteen Mysteries of the Rosary". Dating from 1617, the series has survived intact, a remarkable snapshot of Antwerp's artistic talent with works by the likes of Cornelis De Vos (1584–1651) – *Nativity* and *Presentation at the Temple*; David Teniers the Elder (1582–1649) – *Gethsemane*; van Dyck (1599–1641) – *The Bearing of the Cross*; and Jordaens (1593–1678) – the *Crucifixion*. But it is **Rubens'** contribution – the *Scourging at the Pillar* – which stands out, a brilliant, brutal canvas showing Jesus clad in a blood-spattered loin cloth.

There's more Rubens close by – at the far end of the *Mysteries* series – in the *Adoration of the Shepherds*, an early work of 1609, which has a jaunty secular air, with a smartly dressed Mary imperiously lifting the Christ's bedsheet to the wonder of the shepherds. Across the church, in the south transept, there's the same artist's *Disputation on the Nature of the Holy Sacrament*, again completed in 1609, but this time forming part of a grand marble altarpiece sprinkled with frolicking cherubs. The marble was crafted by **Pieter Verbruggen the Elder**, who was also responsible for the extraordinary woodcarving of the confessionals and stalls on either side of the nave, flashy work of arabesque intricacy decorated with fruit, cherubs, eagles and pious saints. Verbruggen takes some responsibility for the huge and ugly high altar too: he didn't fashion the black and white marble – that was the work of a certain Frans Sterbeeck – but he erected it.

Look out also for *Our Lady of the Rosary*, a polychromed wood, early sixteenth-century figure stuck to a pillar next to the nave's north aisle. It's a charming statuette with the Virgin robed in the Spanish manner – it was the Spaniards who introduced dressed figurines to Flemish churches. The two unusual bas-relief medallions to either side of *Our Lady* are just as folksy, telling a Faustian story of a rich woman who is gulled by the devil, shown here as a sort of lion with an extremely long tail. The first panel sees the woman entrapped by the devil's letter, the second shows the good old Dominicans coming to the rescue and the devil being carted off by an angel.

Back outside, in between the Baroque portal and the church, lurks another curiosity in the form of the **Calvarieberg**, an artificial late seventeenth-century grotto; it clings to the buttresses of the south transept, eerily adorned with statues of Christ and other figures of angels, prophets and saints in a tawdry representation of the Crucifixion and Entombment. Writing in the nineteenth century, the traveller Charles Tennant described it as "exhibiting a more striking instance of religious fanaticism than good taste".

Falconplein and Paardenmarkt

Heading east then north from Sint Pauluskerk, it's a five- to ten-minute walk along Zwarte Zusterstraat and Klapdorp to **Falconplein** and **Paardenmarkt**, at the heart of what was, until very recently, a solid working-class district bordering the docks. It was here that Slav and Jewish minorities set up their textile and domestic appliance shops, advertising their goods in Cyrillic script for the benefit of those Russian sailors whose ships bobbed in and out of port. The Cyrillic signs are still here, but the process of gentrification has begun, heralded by the fashion designer Dries van Noten, who moved his offices into an old warehouse on **Godefriduskaai**, just north of Falconplein in 2000: expect more warehouse/loft conversions to follow. Godefriduskaai is on the south side of **Bonapartedok** and **Willemdok**, two large docks dug during the French occupation of the early nineteenth century and part of Napoleon's successful attempt to revive the city's economy.

The Rockoxhuis Museum

Southeast of Sint Pauluskerk, the **Rockoxhuis Museum**, at Keizerstraat 12 (Tues–Sun 10am–5pm; €2.50, but free on Fri), occupies the attractively restored seventeenth-century town house of Nicolaas Rockox, friend and patron of Rubens. Inside, a sequence of rooms has been crammed with period furnishings and art work, based on an inventory taken after the owner's death in 1640. Nevertheless, it's far from a re-creation of Rockox's old home, but rather a museum with a small but highly prized collection. Particular highlights include, in **Room 1**, a gentle *Holy Virgin and Child* by Quentin Matsys (1465–1530) as well as a *Calvary* by one of his sons, Corneliss, and a *St Christopher Bearing the Christ Child*, a typical work by Quentin's collaborator Joachim Patenier (1485–1524). Born in Dinant, Patenier moved to Antwerp, where he became the first Flemish painter to emphasize the landscape of his religious scenes at the expense of its figures – which he reduced to compositional elements within wide, sweeping vistas. Moving on, **Room 2** displays two pictures by Rubens, beginning with the small and romantic *Virgin in Adoration Before the Sleeping Christ Child*, which depicts the Virgin with the features of Rubens' first wife and models Jesus on the artist's son. The second work is his *Christ on the Cross,* a fascinating oil sketch made in preparation for an altarpiece he never had time to paint. Look out also for *Two Studies of a Man's Head* by van Dyck (1599–1641), striking portraits which the artist recycled in several later and larger commissions.

    Room 3 is distinguished by a flashy and fleshy genre painting, *Woman Selling Vegetables* by Joachim Beuckelaer (1533–73), the sixteenth-century Antwerp artist whose work is seen again in **Room 4**, this time in the more restrained *Flight into Egypt*, revealing a bustling river bank where – in true Mannerist style – the Holy Family are hard to spot. There's another good illustration of genre painting in **Room 5**, where the *Antwerp Fish Market* is by Frans Snyders (1579–1657), who sometimes painted in the flowers and fruit on the canvases of his chum Rubens.

    Finally, in **Room 6**, Pieter Bruegel the Younger's (1564–1638) *Proverbs* is an intriguing folksy work, one of several he did in direct imitation of his father, a frenetic mixture of the observed and imagined set in a Flemish village. The meaning of many of the pictured proverbs has been the subject of long debate; unfortunately the museum doesn't provide a caption – see the box on p.236 for some pointers – but there's little doubt about the meaning of the central image depicting an old man dressed in the blue, hooded cape of the cuckold at the behest of his young wife.

Bruegel's proverbs

Pieter Bruegel the Younger's *Proverbs* illustrates over a hundred folk sayings. Some of the more diverting are explained below – to help pick them out we've divided the canvas into four squares.

Upper left

The cakes on the roof represent prosperity.

To fire one arrow after another is to throw good after bad.

The Cross hangs below the orb, which is crapped upon by the fool – it's an upside-down world.

The fool gets the trump card – luck favours the foolish.

The man with toothache behind his ear symbolizes the malingerer.

Lower left

He bangs his head against the wall – stupidity.

She carries water in one hand, fire in the other – a woman of contradictory opinions.

The pig opens the tap of the barrel – gluttony.

The knight, literally armed to the teeth, ties a bell to the cat – cowardice.

One woman holds the distaff, while the other spins – it takes two to gossip.

The hat on the post, as in to keep a secret "under your hat".

The pig shearer is a symbol of foolishness.

Upper right

The opportunist on the tower hangs his cloak according to the wind.

To fall from the ox to the ass is to go from good to bad.

He opens the door with his arse – doesn't know if he is coming or going.

The man with the fan is so miserly he even resents the sun shining on the water.

To have the devil as a confessor – distorted values.

Lower right

The imprudent man fills in the well after the cow has drowned.

The poor man cannot reach from one loaf to another.

The dogs fight over a bone – hence bone of contention.

The monk giving Jesus a false beard symbolizes blasphemy.

The man trapped within the globe suggests you have to stoop low to get through life.

Hendrik Conscienceplein and around

A short stroll from the western end of Keizerstraat, **Hendrik Conscienceplein** takes its name from a local nineteenth-century novelist, who wrote prolifically on all things Flemish. One of the most agreeable places in central Antwerp, the square is flanked by the church of **St Carolus Borromeus** (Mon–Fri 10am–12.30pm & 2–5pm, Sat 10am–6pm; free), whose finely contrived facade is claimed to have been based on designs by Rubens. Much of the interior was destroyed by fire at the beginning of the eighteenth century, but to the right of the entrance, the ornate Onze Lieve Vrouwekapel (Chapel of Our Lady) has survived, its ornate giltwork and luxurious mix of marbles a fancy illustration of the High Baroque. Streaky, coloured marble was a key feature of the original design and here it serves as the background for a series of tiny pictures placed to either side of the high altar.

From Hendrik Conscienceplein, walk west to the end of Wijngaardstraat, where a left and then a right turn takes you into the series of tiny squares that front the northern side of the cathedral. Here, the **Het Elfde Gebod** (The

Eleventh Commandment), on Torfbrug, is one of the most unusual bars in the city, jam-packed with a bizarre assortment of kitsch religious statues – see "Bars", p.247.

East of the centre

Meir, Antwerp's broad and pedestrianized main shopping street, connects the city centre with Centraal Station, some fifteen minutes' walk away to the east. Taken as a whole this part of the city lacks any particular character – it's an indeterminate medley of the old and the new – but there's no disputing the principal sight, the **Rubenshuis**, the cleverly restored former home and studio of Rubens – and the city's most popular tourist attraction. Rubens was buried nearby in **St Jacobskerk**, a good-looking Gothic church that well deserves a visit, but the architectural highlight hereabouts is the neo-Baroque **Centraal Station**, a sterling edifice dating from 1905. The station presides over Koningin Astridplein, an airy square that accommodates both the sleek, new **Provincial Diamond Museum** and the **zoo**.

From the Groenplaats to the Rubenshuis

From the northeast corner of Groenplaats, **Eiermarkt** curves round to **Meir**, Antwerp's main shopping drag. At the beginning of Meir, just beyond its junction with St Katelijnevest, is **Twaalfmaandenstraat,** a truncated street that ends in the **Beurs**, the recently restored late nineteenth-century stock exchange, built as a rough copy of the medieval original which was burned to the ground in 1868. Used for special events but otherwise dusty and deserted, it's still a splendid extravagance, a high, glass-paned roof supported by spindly iron beams displaying the coats of arms of the maritime nations, with walls portraying a giant map of the world.

From the Beurs, it's a five-minute walk east along the Meir to Wapper, a mundane little square, where the **Rubenshuis** at no. 9 (Tues–Sun 10am–5pm; €5) attracts tourists in droves. Not so much a house as a mansion, this was where Rubens lived for most of his adult life, but the building was only acquired by the town in 1937, by which time it was little more than a shell. Skilfully restored, it opened as a museum in 1946. On the right is the classical studio, where Rubens worked and taught; on the left the traditional, gabled Flemish house, to which is attached the art gallery, an Italianate chamber where Rubens entertained the artistic and cultural elite of Europe. He had an enviably successful career, spending the first years of the seventeenth century studying the Renaissance masters in Italy, before settling in this house in 1608. Soon after, he painted the Antwerp Onze Lieve Vrouwekathedraal series and his fame spread, both as a painter and diplomat, working for Charles I in England, and receiving commissions from all over Europe.

Unfortunately, there's only a handful of his less distinguished paintings here, and very little to represent the works of those other artists he collected so avidly throughout his life. The restoration of the rooms is convincing, though, and a clearly arrowed tour begins by twisting its way through the neatly panelled and attractively furnished **domestic interiors** of the Flemish half of the house. Beyond, and in contrast to the cramped living quarters, is the elegant **art gallery**, which, with its pint-sized sculpture gallery, was where Rubens displayed his favourite pieces to a chosen few – and in a scene comparable to that portrayed in Willem van Haecht's *The Gallery of Cornelis van der Geest*, which is displayed here. The arrows direct you on into the **classical studio**, where a narrow gallery overlooks the **great studio**, equipped with a special high door to allow the largest canvases to be brought in and out with ease. Behind the house, the garden is laid out in the formal style of Rubens' day, as it appears in his *Amid Honeysuckle*, now in Munich. The Baroque portico might also be familiar from the artist's Medici series, on display in the Louvre.

St Jacobskerk

Rubens died in 1640 and was buried in **St Jacobskerk**, just to the north of the Wapper – take Eikenstraat off the Meir and it's at the end on Lange Nieuwstraat (April–Oct daily 2–5pm; €2). Very much the church of the Antwerp nobility, who were interred in its vaults and chapels, the church is a Gothic structure begun in 1491, but not finished until 1659. This delay means that much of its Gothic splendour is hidden by an over-decorous Baroque interior, the soaring heights of the nave flattened by heavy marble altars and a huge rood screen.

Seven chapels radiate out from the ambulatory, including the **Rubens chapel**, directly behind the high altar, where the artist and his immediate family are buried beneath the tombstones in the floor with a lengthy Latin inscription giving details of Rubens' life and honours. The chapel's altar was the gift of Helene Fourment, Rubens' second wife, and shows one of his last works, *Our Lady and the Christ Child surrounded by Saints* (1634), in which he painted himself as St George, his wives as Martha and Mary, and his father as St Jerome. It's as if he knew this was to be his epitaph; indeed, he is said to have asked for his burial chapel to be adorned with nothing more than a painting of the Virgin Mary with Jesus in her arms, encircled by various saints.

The rest of the church is crammed with the chapels and tombs of the rich and powerful, who kept the city's artists busy with a string of commissions destined to hang above their earthly remains. Most are only of moderate interest, but the **chapel** next to – and north of – the tomb of Rubens is worth a peek for its clumsily titled *St Charles Borromeo Pleading with the Virgin on Behalf of those Stricken by the Plague*, completed by Jacob Jordaens in 1655. A dark, gaudy canvas, it's not without its ironies: Borromeo, the Archbishop of Milan, was an ardent leader of the Counter Reformation, while the artist was a committed Protestant. In the north aisle of the nave – on the opposite side from the entrance – the third chapel down from the transept holds the remains of members of the **Rockox** family (see p.235). They are pictured on the side panels of a Jan Sanders triptych, their demure modesty in stark contrast to the breezy Neoclassicism of a centrepiece which oozes bare flesh (nudity was permitted in the portrayal of classical figures). In the chapel at the far end of the south aisle, look out also for a flamboyant *St George and the Dragon* by van Dyck (1599–1641).

To Centraal Station

Meir heads east from the Rubenshuis to its junction with Jezusstraat, where the carved figure on the building on the corner honours **Lodewyk van Bercken**, who introduced the skill of diamond-cutting to the city in 1476. From here, Leysstraat, a continuation of Meir, is lined by a sweeping facade ending in a pair of high, turreted gables, whose allegorical figures and gilt cupolas formed the impressive main entrance to the nineteenth-century city. Straight ahead, the magnificent neo-Baroque **Centraal Station** was finished in 1905, a medley of spires and balconies, glass domes and classical pillars designed by Louis Delacenserie, who had made his reputation as a restorer of Gothic buildings in Bruges. Sadly, the station was also the victim of one of the greatest cock-ups in Belgium: the construction of the underground tram tunnels alongside disturbed the water table, causing the oak pillars that support the station to dry out, and threatening it with collapse. The repairs took years and cost millions of francs, but the building has finally been restored to its full glory. It's an extraordinary edifice, a well-considered blend of earlier architectural styles and fashions – particularly the Gothic lines of the main body of the building and the ticket hall, which has all the darkened mystery of a medieval church – yet displaying all the self-confidence of the new age of industrial progress.

Koningin Astridplein and the diamond district

Koningin Astridplein, the large square adjoining Centraal station, has recently been overhauled, its old stone terraces restored and revamped. It is now an appropriately smart setting for the glitzy, new **Provinciaal Diamantmuseum**, at nos. 19–23 (daily: May–Oct 10am–6pm, Nov–April 10am–5pm; €5), dealing with the geology, history, mining and cutting of diamonds in a series of clearly labelled, well-organized displays – and all with the assistance of interactive gadgetry. In the laboratory, visitors can test the specific qualities of diamonds, such as colour, hardness, refraction of light, and thermal and electric conductivity. There are regular diamond-cutting and polishing demonstrations too, but the most popular exhibits are the diamonds themselves, set in all sorts of lavish styles and forms and held in three chambers guarded by heavy steel doors. Footsteps away, also on Koningin Astridplein, is Antwerp's **zoo** (daily 9am–4.30 or 5.30pm; €13), which accommodates around four thousand animals, incorporating an aviary, a reptile house and an aquarium.

The diamond trade

Antwerp's diamond trade is largely run by **Orthodox Jews**, whose ancestors mostly arrived here from Eastern Europe towards the end of the nineteenth century, and whose presence is often the only outward indication that the business exists at all. They make most of their money by acting as middlemen in a chain that starts in South Africa, where eighty percent of the world's diamonds are mined, the rate of production and distribution being controlled by a powerful South African cartel led by the **De Beers** company.

The cartel organizes ten **sights** every year, rotating between London, Lucerne and Johannesburg, the quality of diamonds in each lot being controlled by the producers; guests – the sightholders – are there by invitation only, and if they fail to buy on three consecutive occasions they aren't usually invited again. This system, established in the 1930s when diamonds flooded the market and prices collapsed, has been complemented by a sustained attempt by the cartel to mop up "spare" diamonds mined elsewhere. As a form of price-fixing, it was effective until the 1990s, when both the civil war in Angola and the break-up of the Soviet Union – which had always co-operated with the cartel – brought a veritable mountain of diamonds onto the market. The cartel continued to buy, but by the late 1990s it was sitting on a pile of surplus diamonds to the tune of $5 billion – much too much to be absorbed even by them.

As an interim measure, De Beers abandoned its efforts to control the world supply of rougher diamonds and a more general relaxation is set to follow, with the company concentrating on trying to increase demand instead. To the relief of Antwerp's diamond cutters, polishers and traders, De Beers will, however, stick to providing rough mined diamonds rather than extending vertically into the rest of the industry.

The discreetly shabby streets just to the southwest of Centraal Station along and around **Lange Kievitstraat** are home to the largest **diamond market** in the world. Behind these indifferent facades precious stones pour in from every continent to be cut or re-cut, polished and sold. There's no show of wealth, no grand bazaar – though a rash of little diamond and gold shops does fringe **Pelikaanstraat** – and no tax collector could ever keep track of the myriad deals which make the business hum.

South of the centre

Cutting south from Groenplaats, **Nationalestraat** was once prime real estate, its stately department stores a magnet for the bustles, parasols and top hats of the bourgeoisie. It hit the skids in the 1930s, but now it's on the way back with the construction of **ModeNatie**, a large-scale celebration of the city's fashion designers – and the opening of lots of designer fashion shops nearby. East of here, the **Museum Mayer van den Bergh** boasts an exquisite collection of fine and applied art, while south along Nationalestraat is **Het Zuid** (The South), a residential district that is also reviving/gentrifying after decades in the doldrums. Lined with grand mansions in the French style, Het Zuid's wide avenues and symmetrical squares were laid out at the end of the nineteenth century on the site of the old Spanish citadel, of which nothing now remains. The district came complete with a large **dock**, but this was filled in years ago, becoming the wide and dreary square that now sprawls between Vlaamse and Waalse Kaai. Setting aside the neighbourhood's cafés and bars, the obvious target of a visit is the **Museum voor Schone Kunsten**, which holds an extensive collection of Belgian art from the fourteenth century onwards.

Het Zuid is bounded by the **Amerikalei** and **Britselei** boulevards, which mark part of the course of a circle of city fortifications finished in the early years of the twentieth century. Enormously expensive and supposedly impregnable, the design was a disaster, depending on a series of raised gun emplacements that were sitting targets for the German artillery in September 1914. The Allies had expected Antwerp to hold out for months, but in the event the city surrendered after a two-week siege, forcing Churchill and his party of marines into a hurried evacuation just two days after their arrival. In themselves, the boulevards are without much interest, but just beyond lies the outstanding **Middelheim Open–Air Sculpture Museum**, with three hundred sculptures spread over extensive parkland.

ModeNatie

Heading south from the Groenplaats along Nationalestraat, it takes about five minutes to reach the brand new **ModeNatie** (ⓦ www.modenatie.com), a lavish and extraordinarily ambitious fashion complex. Spread over several floors, the complex showcases the work of local fashion designers and incorporates both the fashion department of the Royal Academy of Fine Arts and the Flanders Fashion Institute. As such, it reflects the international success of local designers, beginning in the 1980s with the so-called "**Antwerp Six**" – including Dries van Noten, Dirk Bikkembergs, Marina Yee and Martin Margiela – and continuing with younger designers like Raf Simons and Veronique Branquinho; all are graduates of the academy. Part of the building contains a fashion museum – **MoMu** (Mode Museum; Tues–Sun 10am–5pm; €5); other sections hold a brasserie and a specialist bookshop. The museum has an extensive historical textile collection, but the contemporary fashion displays are of more immediate interest to the non-specialist.

Fashion shopping in Antwerp

The success of Antwerp's **fashion designers** has left the city with dozens of excellent designer shops and stores. The tourist office produces a booklet entitled **Antwerp Fashion Walk** (€3), which describes five walks in the city that take you past all the best shops and also provides potted biographies of the leading figures of the city's fashion industry. There is, however, a particular concentration of **fashion shops** around the ModeNatie complex. Recommended places include Dries van Noten's Modepaleis, Nationalestraat 16 – at the corner of Kammenstraat – where the women's collection is on the ground floor, the men's up above. Opposite, at Nationalestraat 27, is Alamode, which mostly sells imported designer clothes, while Kammenstraat weighs in with the contemporary jewellery of Anne Zellien, at no. 47, and the secondhand clothes of Naughty-I, at no. 65. Nearby, Sint-Antoniusstraat has Walter, at no. 12, which features the clothes of several domestic designers, as does Louis, Lombardenstraat 2. Also on Lombardenstraat are Chris Janssens, no. 10 and Simple d'Anvers, at no. 17. Arguably the best secondhand clothes shop in town is Francis, at Steenhouwersvest 14, just west of Nationalestraat

The Museum Mayer van den Bergh

A five-minute walk east of ModeNatie, the appealing **Museum Mayer van den Bergh**, at Lange Gasthuisstraat 19 (Tues–Sun 10am–5pm; €4; English guide €2.50), comprises the art collection of the Berghs, a wealthy merchant family who gave their artistic hoard to the city in 1920. Very much a connoisseur's collection, it offers examples of many different branches of applied arts, from tapestries to ceramics, silver, illuminated manuscripts and furniture, all crowded into a reconstruction of a sixteenth-century town house. There are also a number of outstanding paintings, beginning in **Room 2** with a charming portrait of a young brother and sister by the Dutchman Cornelis Ketel (1548–1616). Next door, in **Room 3**, is the earliest panel painting ever to be found in Belgium – a thirteenth-century Italian work entitled the *Virgin and Child Enthroned* by Simeone and Machilone of Spoleto – while pride of place in **Room 4** goes to a *Crucifixion* triptych by Quentin Matsys (1465–1530), with the unidentified donors painted on the wings. Intriguingly, the female donor is pictured alongside one of the family's patron saints, Mary of Egypt – a repentant prostitute who spent her final years in the desert miraculously sustained by three little loaves.

Room 6 holds an early German carving of *St John Resting on the Breast of Jesus*, dating to around 1300, and two tiny panels from a fifteenth-century polyptych that once adorned a travelling altar. The twin panels are beautifully decorated with informal scenes – St Christopher, the patron saint of travellers, crosses a stream full of fish, and Joseph cuts up his socks to use as swaddling clothes for the infant Jesus. St Christopher turns up again in **Room 7**, in Jan Mostaert's (1475–1555) *St Christopher*, the painting's bold tones influenced by the artist's long stay in Italy. **Room 8** is mainly devoted to small-scale medieval sculptures and decorative pieces – including a delightfully intricate *Annunciation* altarpiece – while **Room 9** boasts the museum's best-known work, **Pieter Bruegel the Elder's** (1525–69) *Dulle Griet* or "Mad Meg", one of his most Bosch-like paintings. Experts have written volumes on the painting's iconography, but in broad terms there's no disputing it's a misogynistic allegory in which a woman, weighed down with possessions, stalks the gates of hell in a surrealistic landscape of monsters and pervasive horror. The title refers to the archetypal shrewish woman, who, according to Flemish proverb, "could plunder in front of hell and remain unscathed". Hanging next to it, the same artist's *Twelve Proverbs* is a less intense vision of the world, a sequence of miniatures illustrating popular Flemish aphorisms, including an old favourite – the man in a blue cape symbolizing the cuckold.

To the Bourlaschouwburg

From the Bergh Museum, you can either proceed direct to the Maagdenhuis, just down the street (see below), or make a brief detour east along **Arenbergstraat** to the pleasant pedestrianized streets and squares which flank the **Bourlaschouwburg** (Bourla Theatre), an elegant nineteenth-century rotunda with a handsomely restored interior. Just beyond, at the end of the Graanmarkt, lurks its modern concrete and steel equivalent, the huge and monstrous **Stadsschouwburg** (municipal theatre). From the Graanmarkt, it's the briefest of strolls north to the Rubenshuis (see p.237).

The Maagdenhuis

At Lange Gasthuisstraat 33, the **Maagdenhuis** (Maidens' House; Mon & Wed–Fri 10am–5pm, Sat & Sun 1–5pm; €2.50, including English catalogue) was formerly a foundling hospital for children of the poor, but is now occupied by the city's social security offices and a small museum. Created in the middle of the sixteenth century, the **refuge** was strictly run, its complex rules enforced by draconian punishments. At the same time, those children who were left here were fed and taught a skill, and desperate parents felt that they could at least retrieve their children if their circumstances improved. To make sure their offspring could be identified, they were given **tokens**, usually irregularly cut playing cards or images of saints – one part was left with the child, the other kept by the parent – and there are examples here in the museum. If the city fathers didn't actually encourage this practice, they certainly accepted it, and several municipal buildings even had specially carved alcoves on their facades where foundlings could be left under shelter, certain to be discovered in the morning.

Entrance to the **museum** is through an ornamental archway decorated with figures representing some of the first girls to be admitted to the hospital depicted inside a tidy classroom, so finely chiselled that you can make out the tiny bookshelves. Inside, five ground-floor rooms and a chapel display a varied but modest collection of art. To the right of the entrance, particular highlights in the **chapel** include a cabinet of foundling tokens (labelled C, D, E), an assembly of some fifty colourful, late medieval porridge bowls (no. 46) – the largest collection of its sort in Belgium – and a sealed certificate confirming the election of Charles V as Holy Roman Emperor in 1519 (no. 49). There's also Jan van Scorel's (1495–1562) tiny *Adoration of the Shepherds* (no. 36), in which the finely observed detail so typical of Flemish painting is suffused by Italianate influences, notably the romantic ruin in the background. Scorel, a one-time Vatican employee, was the first Dutch artist of importance to live in Italy and, returning to the Netherlands in 1524, he was largely responsible for introducing the Italian High Renaissance to his fellow artists back home. In the **five rooms** to the left of the entrance, three paintings are also worth seeking out: at the end of the corridor is *Orphan Girl at Work* (no. 1) by Cornelius de Vos (1584–1651), a touching composition showing the young woman cheered by the offer of a red carnation, a symbol of fidelity; and in the end room on the right are both van Dyck's (1599–1641) mournful *St Jerome* (no. 16) and Jordaens' (1593–1678) profound study of Christ in his *Descent from the Cross* (no. 12).

From the Maagdenhuis, it's an uninspiring twenty-minute walk southwest to the Museum voor Schone Kunsten; you're much better off doubling back to ModeNatie to pick up Tram #8, which runs there from the Groenplaats via Nationalestraat.

Museum voor Schone Kunsten

Reached by tram #8 from the Groenplaats, the **Museum voor Schone Kunsten** (Fine Art Museum; Tues–Sun 10am–5pm; €5 including audio guide, but free on Fri) occupies an immense Neoclassical edifice built at the end of the twentieth century. Inside, the **lower level** is mostly devoted to temporary exhibitions – for which there is usually a supplementary charge – while the permanent collection is squeezed into the lettered rooms of the **upper level**. Free plans of the museum are available at reception, and are extremely useful as everything is a little mixed up and the paintings are often rotated. That said, the Flemish Primitives are usually clustered to the left of the top of the main stairway in rooms Q and S, while the rooms to the right – N, O, A, B, C and D – focus on the late nineteenth and early twentieth century. The larger rooms in the middle – I and H – concentrate on Rubens and his cronies; several of the remaining rooms pick through the sixteenth and seventeenth centuries in rather haphazard fashion.

Early Flemish paintings

In Room Q, the early Flemish section isn't as extensive as you might expect in a major Belgian museum, but the collection does include two fine, tiny works by **Jan van Eyck** (1390–1441). These are a florid *Madonna at the Fountain* and a *St Barbara*, where a palm and prayer book, representing her faith and self-sacrifice, has replaced the usual symbol of the saint's imprisonment – a miniature tower held in the palm of her hand. Behind, a full-scale Gothic tower looms over her – a much more powerful indication of her confinement. Also in Room Q is **Rogier van der Weyden**'s (1400–64) *Triptych of the Seven Sacraments*, painted for the Bishop of Tournai in 1445 and graced by an inventive frame, which merges with the lines of the Gothic architecture inside. Weyden's *Portrait of Philippe de Croy* is here too, the artist blending a dark background into the lines of his subject's cloak, a simple technique to emphasize the shape of the nobleman's angular face and his slender hands. **Hans Memling** (1433–94) has two paintings in Room Q, the *Portrait of Giovanni de Candida* and the *Angels Singing and Playing Instruments*. Neither are among his most distinguished works, but they do have that finely textured quality for which he is famous. There are also two pictures by **Gerard David** (1460–1523), each cool and meticulous, though the finer of the two is the evocative *Pilate and the Jews on Golgotha*.

Late medieval paintings

Room S features non-Belgian medieval painters, notably **Jean Fouquet** (1425–80) the most influential French painter of the fifteenth century, who has one canvas on display, a *Madonna and Child* in which remarkable, orange-red latex-like angels surround a chubby Jesus who looks away from a pale, bared breast. **Lucas Cranach the Elder** (1472–1553), the German Protestant and friend of Luther, is here too, but he is poorly represented by a small and patchy *Adam and Eve* – his *Eve*, a sensuous picture displayed in Room L, is much better.

From the early sixteenth century – and exhibited in Room R – look out for **Quentin Matsys**' (1465–1530) triptych of the *Lamentation*. Commissioned for the carpenter's chapel in Antwerp's Onze Lieve Vrouwekathedraal, it's a profound and moving work, portraying the Christ, his forehead flecked with blood, surrounded by grieving followers including Mary Magdalen, who tenderly wipes his feet with her hair as tears roll down her face. The panel on the left shows Salome presenting the head of St John the Baptist to Herod, and on the right is the martyrdom of St John the Evangelist. In the latter, the gargoyle-like faces of the men stoking the fire beneath the cauldron are fine illustrations of one of Matsys' favourite ways of representing evil.

Room L features a modest assortment of sixteenth-century Flemish figures and landscapes. The most diverting works are two miniature landscapes by **Joachim Patenier** (1475–1524), the *Flight from Egypt* and *Lot and the Flight from Sodom and Gomorrah*. Born in Dinant, Patenier moved to Antwerp in his 20s, becoming a member of the local artists' guild in 1515. Although very few of his paintings have survived, he appears to have been an important figure in the development of Flemish art. Here, for the first time, Biblical characters are reduced to small elements in the broad sweep of a highly stylised, pastoral landscape – a style that was to be imitated by scores of later artists.

The sixteenth and seventeenth centuries

In Room G there's a modest sample of work by the Bruegel family, notably the characteristic *Wedding Dance* by **Pieter Bruegel the Elder** (1525–69) and **Jan Bruegel**'s (1568–1625) immaculate *Flowers in a Vase*. Also from the seventeenth century are several earthy, sometimes raucous scenes of peasant life by **Adriaen Brouwer** (1605–38) and **David Teniers the Younger** (1610–90). Born in Flanders, apprenticed to Frans Hals in Haarlem, and very much influenced by Bruegel the Elder, Brouwer bridges the gap between Flemish and Dutch art. When he was imprisoned in 1633, the prison baker, **Joos van Craesbeeck**, became his pupil, and his pictures are in this room too, often outdoing even Brouwer in their violence.

Works by **Rubens** (1577–1640) are grouped together in Room I, including smaller, preparatory paintings – which also spread over into Room J – and a sequence of enormous canvases. Among the latter is an inventive *Last Communion of St Francis* (1619), showing a very sick-looking saint equipped with the marks of the stigmata, a faint halo and a half-smile: despite the sorrowful ministrations of his fellow monks, Francis can't wait for salvation. Also from 1619 is *Christ Crucified Between the Two Thieves*, which, with its muscular thieves and belligerent Romans, possesses all the high drama you might expect, but is almost overwhelmed by its central image – you can virtually hear the tearing of Christ's flesh as the soldier's lance sinks into him. From 1624 comes the outstanding *Adoration of the Magi*, a beautifully free and very human work apparently finished by Rubens in a fortnight. No doubt he was helped by his studio, the major figures of which – van Dyck and Jordaens – are represented in Room H, where you'll spot **Jacob Jordaens**' (1593–1678) striking *Martydom of St Apollonia*. The painting relates the saint's story: during an anti-Christian riot in third-century Alexandria, Apollonia was seized by the mob, who pulled out her teeth in a vain attempt to make her renounce her faith. Frustrated by her steadfastness, the crowd then built a bonfire and threatened to burn her alive, but Apollonia walked into the flames voluntarily – all in all, a grisly martyrdom for which she is honoured as the patron saint of toothache.

Modern Belgian art

The museum has a large collection of modern Belgian art. The paintings are regularly rotated, making it difficult to give particular recommendations, but you can expect to see the work of **James Ensor** (1860–1949), whose subdued, conservative beginnings, such as *Afternoon at Ostend* (1881), contrast with his piercing later works – like *Intrigue* and *Skeletons Fighting for the Body of a Hanged Man*. Also likely to be on show is **Paul Delvaux**'s (1897–1994) much praised *Red Bow*, showing a classical city in the process of disintegration, and several canvases by **René Magritte** (1898–1967), most memorably the macabre *Madame Recamier* and *Storm Cape*. Look out too for **Constant Permeke** (1886–1952), a leading member of the artistic coterie who first congregated at the village of Sint Martens-Latem near Ghent just before World War I. Dark and broody, Permeke's works are mostly Expressionistic studies of rural Flemish life, his style typified by *The Coffee Drinkers*, *Man with the Vest*, and *The Farmer*.

MUHKA and Museum voor Fotografie

Just to the west of the Museum voor Schone Kunsten, the massive – and dreary – square in between Vlaamse Kaai and Waalse Kaai marks the location of one of the city's nineteenth-century **docks**. Near here are two museums. **MUHKA** (Museum of Contemporary Art; Tues–Sun 10am–5pm; €4), in a striking functionalist building at Leuvenstraat 32, specializes in large-scale, ambitious, avant-garde exhibitions – *Anti-art*, *Metalanguage* and the like. A short walk away to the south, the **Provinciaal Museum voor Fotografie**, at Waalse Kaai 47 (Tues–Sun 10am–5pm), mixes displays of all sorts of old photographic equipment with modern exhibitions of different photographic techniques. It is, however, closed until well into 2003 for a major revamp and expansion.

Openluchtmuseum voor Beeldhouwkunst Middelheim

One of Antwerp's most enjoyable attractions is the **Openluchtmuseum voor Beeldhouwkunst Middelheim** (Middelheim Open-Air Sculpture Museum; Tues–Sun: April & Sept 10am–7pm, May & August 10am–8pm, June & July 10am–9pm, Oct–March 10am–5pm; free), comprising over three hundred sculptures spread across the manicured lawns and trees of Middelheim Park, about 6km south of the city centre. The original collection was assembled here in the 1950s at the instigation of an adventurous burgomaster – one Lode Craeybeckx – and has since grown to include examples of all the major modern schools – particularly Realism, Cubism and Surrealism. The open-air collection is supplemented by an indoor section, in which the more delicate pieces – as well as recent acquisitions – are displayed in the pavilion. There is a fair sprinkling of Belgian sculptors, one of the more talented of whom was the painter-sculptor Rik Wouters, plus a handsome sample of the work of leading foreign practitioners like Henry Moore, Auguste Rodin, Panamarenko, Alexander Calder and Ossip Zadkine.

The park is situated just beyond the ring road on Middelheimlaan – take tram #15 there from Centraal Station or tram #7 from beside the Meir tram station; it's a good idea to ask the driver to put you off. By car, take the Berchem-Wilrijk exit off the ring road.

Eating and drinking

Antwerp is an enjoyable and inexpensive place to eat, its busy centre liberally sprinkled with informal **cafés** and **restaurants**, which excel at combining traditional Flemish dishes with Mediterranean, French and vegetarian cuisines. There is a good range of slightly more formal – and expensive – restaurants too, though generally the distinction between the city's cafés and restaurants is blurred. There's a concentration of first-rate places on and around Grote Pieter

Potstraat, off the Suikerrui, and another in the vicinity of Hendrik Conscienceplein. These two areas are a better bet for good food than the gaggle of cafés on the Grote Markt and the Groenplaats, the prime tourist area, but even here you don't pay much of a premium.

As for **opening hours**, most cafés open early-ish in the morning – by about 9am – till late at night, although those geared up for shoppers and office workers mostly close at 5 or 6pm. Restaurants are often open every day of the week from 11am or noon to about 11pm, though some close for a few hours in the afternoon and the smarter establishments sometimes only open in the evening; others have a regular weekly closing day – usually Sunday, Monday or Tuesday.

Antwerp is also a fine place to **drink**. There are lots of bars in the city centre, mostly dark and tiny affairs exuding a cheerful vitality. Some of them regularly feature live music, but most don't, satisfying themselves – and their customers – with everything from taped *chanson* to house. On sunny evenings, the pavement café-bars on the Grote Markt, Handschoenmarkt and Groenplaats are the places to make for – a swirl of jabbering, good-humoured crowds. **Opening hours** are elastic, with many places only closing when the last customers leave – say 2 or 3am – and, unless otherwise stated in our listings below, all are open daily. The favourite local tipple, incidentally, is De Koninck, a light ale drunk in a *bolleke*, or small, stemmed glass.

Cafés

Het Dagelijks Brood Steenhouwersvest 48. Enjoyable and distinctive café where the variety of breads is the main event, served with delicious, wholesome soups and light meals at one long wooden table. No smoking. Daily 7am–7pm.

Did's Bistro St Jacobstraat 21. A few minutes' walk east of the centre, near St Jacobskerk. This student favourite is an unpretentious bistro-café offering tasty and inexpensive light meals and snacks, including vegetarian choices. Mon–Fri 11.30am–2pm & 6–10pm, Sat 6–10.30pm.

L'Entrepôt du Congo De Burburestraat 2. In the fashionable Het Zuid part of town, on the corner of Vlaamse Kaai, near the Museum voor Schone Kunsten. Well-known and justifiably popular café-restaurant serving up fresh salads and pastas at inexpensive prices.

Facade Hendrik Conscienceplein 18. Laid-back, funky café with good music and inexpensive vegetarian, meat and fish dishes. Popular with students.

Finjan Graaf Van Hoornstraat 1. A short walk southwest of the Museum voor Schone Kunsten along Léopold de Waelstraat. Excellent, and inexpensive, falafel and pitta till 4am.

Hoffy's Lange Kievitstraat 52 ☎03 234 35 35. Outstanding, simply decorated traditional Jewish restaurant and takeaway, off Pelikaanstraat, near Centraal Station. Very reasonable prices. Try the *gefillte fisch*. Daily except Sat 11am–9pm.

Jacqmotte Groenplaats 30. Straightforward café with a few modern stools and tables – and the best range of coffees in the city centre. Part of a small Belgian chain. On the northeast corner of the Groenplaats.

Popoff Oude Koornmarkt 18. The best pies, desserts and gateaux in town. Daily except Mon noon–10pm.

Restaurants

Aurelia Wijngaardstraat 22 ☎03 233 62 59. Smart little restaurant, metres from Hendrik Conscienceplein, in an immaculately restored old merchant's house. Serves delicious seafood and meat dishes with main courses costing €15–25.

Hippodroom Leopold de Waelplaats 10 ☎03 248 52 52. Opposite the Museum voor Schone Kunsten. Polished restaurant offering a wide range of Flemish dishes from around €18 per main course. You can eat outside in the garden in summer. Closed Sun.

Hoorn des Overloeds Melkmarkt 5 ☎03 232 83 99. Excellent, unpretentious fish restaurant, good for lunch and dinner; look out for the daily specials. Just east of the cathedral. Noon–2.30pm & 7–10pm.

De Matelote Haarstraat 9 ☎03 231 32 07, off Grote Pieter Potstraat, near the Grote Markt. This modish, pastel-painted fish restaurant serves delicious food, with main courses averaging €20–25. Mon & Sat 7–10pm, Tues–Fri noon–2.30pm & 7–10pm.

Oude Beurs Oude Beurs 46 ☎03 232 16 54. Superb Flemish cuisine from a short but well-chosen menu. The seafood is especially good. Sympathetic, modern decor – all pastel-painted walls and soft lighting. Main courses from around

€18. Daily except Tues 6.30–10.30pm.

De Peerdestal Wijngaardstraat 8 ☎ 03 231 95 03. Just west of Hendrik Conscienceplein. Mid-priced restaurant with a largely uninspiring menu; it is, however, *the* place to try horsemeat.

Pizzeria Da Antonio Grote Markt 6. On the corner of Suikerrui. Tasty, swiftly served pasta and pizza. Very popular and reasonably priced.

Satsuma Wisselstraat 5 ☎ 03 226 24 43. For something completely different, try this Japanese restaurant located just off the north side of the Grote Markt. Main courses from around €15. Evenings only, from 6pm; closed Tues.

De Stoemppot Vlasmarkt 12 ☎ 03 231 36 86. This cosy little restaurant is the best place to eat *stoemp*. Closed Wed.

La Terrazza Wisselstraat 2. High quality, bright and cheerful, moderately priced Italian restaurant down a narrow sidestreet off the north side of Grote Markt. The various spaghetti dishes, costing €9–15, are a house speciality. Closed all day Mon & Sun lunch.

't Zolderke Hoofdkerkstraat 7 ☎ 03 233 84 27. Footsteps from Hendrik Conscienceplein. In an attractively converted old mansion, this appealing restaurant offers a mix of tasty Belgian and Mediterranean dishes, with several good vegetari-an options too. Main courses average out at about €15.

Bars

Den Billekletser Hoogstraat 22. Dog-eared bar with diverse sounds and an offbeat clientele.

De Duifkens Graanmarkt 5. Located on a pedes-trianized square close to the Rubenshuis and behind the Bourla, this old-style Antwerp café-bar is a favourite haunt of the city's actors.

Het Elfde Gebod Torfbrug 10. On one of the tiny squares fronting the north side of the cathedral, this long-established bar has become something of a tourist trap, but it's still worth visiting for the kitsch, nineteenth-century religious statues which cram the interior; don't bother with the food.

Den Engel Grote Markt 3. Handily located, tradi-tional bar with an easy-going atmosphere in a guildhouse on the northwest corner of the main square; attracts a mixture of business people and locals from the residential enclave round the Vleeshuis.

De Faam Grote Pieter Potstraat 12. Cool, groovy bar in small, sparingly lit premises near the Grote Markt. An eclectic soundtrack – from *chanson* to jazz.

De Groote Witte Arend Reyndersstraat 18. Attractive café-bar set around a courtyard in an old mansion; classical music sets the tone. A good range of beers – including authentic gueuze and *kriek* – plus pancakes, waffles and ice cream. Closed Tues & Wed.

De Herk Reyndersstraat 33. Tiny bar in ancient premises – down an alley and set around a court-yard – and a 20-something, modish clientèle. Does a good range of beers and ales – including an excellent Lindemans gueuze.

Den Hopsack Grote Pieter Potstraat 22. Post-modern bar – all wood and spartan fittings – with highbrow conversation, an amenable, low-key atmosphere, and a 30-something clientèle.

Kulminator Vleminckveld 32–34. A 5min walk south of the centre – from the foot of Oude Koornmarkt, follow Kammenstraat, which leads into Vleminckveld. One of the best beer bars in Antwerp, serving over five hundred varieties, with a helpful beer menu. Dark and atmospheric with New Age flourishes. Mon from 8.30pm, Tues–Fri from noon, Sat from 5pm.

Pakhuis Vlaamse Kaai 76. Fashionable café-bar occupying an imaginatively converted two-storey warehouse. Uniformed waiters give the place a brasserie air and the house beers are brewed on the premises.

Paters' Vaetje Blauwmoezelstraat 1. Popular bar – the *Priests' Casket* – in the shadow of the cathedral and offering the widest range of beers and ales in this little area – over a hundred at the last count. Downstairs is the old-fashioned main bar, while upstairs there's a gallery bar.

Café Pelikaan Melkmarkt 14. There's nothing touristy about the *Pelikaan*, a packed and smoky bar where locals get down to some serious drink-ing. On the east side of the cathedral. Closed Sun.

't Stamineeke, Vlasmarkt 23. Vibrant downtown bar, in an old, high-gabled building, playing blues with occasional live bands. Sells over one hundred different sorts of beer. Closed Tues.

De Vagant, Reyndersstraat 21. Specialist gin bar serving an extravagant range of Belgian and Dutch jenevers in comfortable, laid-back surroundings.

De Volle Maan, Oude Koornmarkt 7. Lively, extremely likeable and offbeat bar close to the Stadhuis with a New Age – spot the roll-ups – undertow.

Entertainment and nightlife

Antwerp has a vibrant and diverse cultural scene – and the best way to get a handle on it is to pick up the tourist office's very useful, quarterly **Cultural Bulletin**, a free newssheet which lists all up-and-coming events, exhibitions and concerts alongside practical details of all the venues. The tourist office also issues a free calendar of events, but this provides only the briefest of synopses. The city has its own **orchestra** and **opera** companies as well as several good Flemish **theatre** troupes, and there are occasional appearances by touring English-language theatre companies too. English-language **films** are almost always subtitled – as distinct from dubbed – and the city has a reliable, city-centre art-house cinema.

The *Cultural Bulletin* does not, however, cover the **club scene**, which is in a rude state of health, with a handful of boisterous places dotted round the peripheries of the city centre. They get going at around midnight and admission fees are modest (€6–10) except for big-name DJs. For special club nights and other off-beat events, keep your eyes peeled for fly posters. Antwerp has a flourishing **jazz** scene too – with a couple of good places in the centre.

As regards **festivals**, the city hosts a good portion of the Festival van Vlaanderen (☏03 202 46 60, ⦿www.festival-van-vlaanderen.be), which runs from May to November and features more than 120 classical concerts in cities across the whole of Flemish-speaking Belgium. There's also SFINKS (☏03 455 69 44, ⦿www.sfinks.be), Belgium's best world music festival, held outdoors over the last weekend of July in the suburb of Boechout, about 10km from downtown Antwerp.

Tickets for most events are on sale inside the Cultural Information Centre – Prospekta VZW – across from the tourist office at Grote Markt 40 (Tues–Fri 10am–6pm, Sat noon–5pm; ☏03 220 81 11, ⦿www.ticketantwerpen.be). A comparable service is provided at the Fnac store, Groenplaats 31.

Theatres, cinemas and concert halls

Bourlaschouwburg Komedieplaats 19 ☏03 231 07 50, www.toneelhuis.be. This handsomely restored, nineteenth-century theatre is the city's premier venue for theatrical performances, and the home of the Het Toneelhuis repertory company.

Cartoons Kaasstraat 4, off Suikerrui ☏03 232 96 32. The most distinctive downtown cinema, showing both mainstream and arthouse films in three auditoria.

Gaumont Van Ertbornstraat 17 ☏03 206 70 00. A vast new seventeen-screen complex just west of Centraal Station, off De Keyserlei – though there's an entrance on this street too.

Koningin Elisabethzaal Koningin Astridplein 26 ☏03 203 56 00. the Royal Flemish Philharmonic Orchestra, of international standing, is based here.

deSingel Desguinlei 25 ☏03 248 28 28, ⦿www.desingel.be. Antwerp is on the international circuit for big-name rock/pop artists, who mostly appear here at this modern performance hall. South of the centre near the ring road – Tram #2.

Stadsschouwburg Theaterplein 1 ☏03 227 03 06. A big bruiser of a modern building that mostly hosts musical concerts and theatrical performances. Near the Rubenshuis.

De Vlaamse Opera Frankrijklei 3, on the ring road about halfway between the Grote Markt and Centraal Station; reservations & information on ☏03 233 66 85, ⦿www.vlaamseopera.be. The excellent Flemish Opera company performs here.

Live music and clubs

Café d'Anvers Verversrui 15 ☏03 226 38 70. Youthful, fashionable, energetic club, billed as a "temple to house music", but perhaps a little too well established to be cutting edge. North of the centre in the red-light district. Fri–Sun.

Café Hopper Leopold De Waelstraat 2 ☏03 248 49 33. Laid-back, easy-going bar-café providing an excellent and varied programme of live jazz, sometimes with big international names.

Café Local Waalsekaai 25 ☏03 238 50 04. One-time house and techno haunt, but now drifting into salsa and world sounds. Fri–Sun.

Café de Muze Melkmarkt 15 ☏03 226 01 26. With its bare brick walls and retro film posters, this chic and central little place is lively and popular, and regularly puts on jazz bands.

Zillion Jan Van Gentstraat 4 ☎ 03 248 15 16. In a former sports hall near the south end of Vlaamse Kaai, this giant disco with moving dance floors plays house and more, and has three smaller areas for musical alternatives, as well as a chill-out room. Thurs–Sat and for specials.

Listings

Airport enquiries ☎ 03 285 65 00.

Banks and exchange There are plenty of banks in and around the city centre. KB Kredietbank are at Eiermarkt 20, De Keyserlei 1, and Pelikaanstraat 30; BBL are at Lange Gasthuisstraat 20 and De Keyserlei 11. There are bureaux de change at Centraal Station (daily 9am–9pm), and lots of ATMs in the city centre.

Bike rental De Windroos, Steenplein 1 hires out bikes (☎ 03 480 93 88). Advance booking is recommended.

Beer Belgium Beers, Reyndersstraat 2, sells over two hundred different sorts of Belgian beers along with many of the appropriate/special glasses.

Books English books and a wide range of Belgian road and hiking maps are available from Fnac, in the Grand Bazaar shopping mall on the Groenplaats (Mon–Thurs 10am–6.30pm, Fri 10am–7pm, Sat 10am–6.30pm) – the main entrance is on the left hand side of the *Hilton*. Standaard, at the corner of Huidevettersstraat and Lange Gasthuisstraat, is a weaker alternative (Mon–Sat 9.30am–6pm).

Buses and trams City transport enquiries at the Groenplaats (Mon–Fri 8am–6pm & Sat 9am–noon) and Centraal Station's Diamant (Mon–Fri 8am–12.30pm & 1.30–4pm) underground tram stations. Details of bus services in the province of Antwerp from De Lijn (☎ 03 218 14 06), or the kiosk on Franklin Rooseveltplaats.

Car rental Avis, Plantin en Moretuslei 62 ☎ 03 218 94 96; Europcar, Plantin en Moretuslei 35 ☎ 03 206 74 44; Hertz, at Antwerp airport ☎ 03 239 29 21; National, Mechelsesteenweg 43 ☎ 03 201 00 70.

Consulates New Zealand, Grote Markt 9 ☎ 03 233 16 08; UK, Korte Klarenstraat 7 ☎ 03 232 69 40.

Emergencies Police ☎ 101; ambulance/fire brigade ☎ 100.

Gay scene There's a concentration of gay bars in the seedy area just to the north of Centraal Station along Van Schoonhovenstraat and neighbouring Dambruggestraat. One of the most popular spots here is *Borsalino*, Van Schoonhovenstraat 48. For a bit more politics/social context, head for Café Den Draak, Draakplaats 1 (Mon, Tues, Thurs & Fri 3–11pm, Sat & Sun noon–1am), a café-bar that is part of a larger gay and lesbian project, the Het Roze Huis (🌐 www.hetrozehuis.be). Draakplaats is a 15min walk south from Centraal station via Pelikaanstraat and its continuation, Simonsstraat and Mercatorstraat.

Gin The De Vagant off-licence, opposite the bar of the same name at Reyndersstraat 21, sells a wide range of Dutch and Belgian gins. Mon–Sat 11am–6pm.

Internet easyEverything is on the south side of De Keyserlei, in the ground floor of the Century Shopping Center, a couple of minutes' walk from Centraal Station (daily 8.30am–11.30pm; €2.50 for the first hour).

Left luggage Office and coin-operated lockers at Centraal Station.

Mail Main post office at Groenplaats 43 (Mon–Fri 9am–6pm, Sat 9am–noon).

Markets Theaterplein plays host to a general and bric-a-brac market, along with flowers and plants, on Sat (8am–4pm); and more of the same plus birds on Sunday (8am–1pm). From Easter to Oct, there's also a antique and jumble market on Lijnwaadmarkt (Sat 9am–5pm), immediately to the morth of Onze Lieve Vrouwekathedraal.

Pharmacies There's a pharmacy on the Grote Markt – W. Lotry, at no. 56. Details of 24hr pharmacies are available from the tourist office; duty rotas should also be displayed on all pharmacists' windows or doors.

Taxis There are taxi ranks outside Centraal Station and at the top of Suikerrui, on the edge of the Grote Markt. Antwerp Taxi is on ☎ 03 238 38 38.

Train enquiries Local ☎ 03 204 20 40; nationwide ☎ 02 555 25 55; international ☎ 0900 103 66.

North and east of Antwerp: the Kempen

Filling out the northeast corner of Belgium, just beyond Antwerp, are the flat, sandy moorlands of the **Kempen**. Once a barren wasteland dotted with the poorest of agricultural communities and punctuated by tracts of acid heath, bog and deciduous woodland, its more hospitable parts were first cultivated and planted with pine by pioneering Cistercian monks in the twelfth century. The monks helped develop and sustain a strong regional identity and dialect, and though today the area's towns and villages are drab, modern suburban settlements with little to attract the casual visitor, the small towns of Herentals and Geel are both of limited interest.

Herentals

Some 20km east of Antwerp, dreary **HERENTALS** became the principal town of the Kempen in the fourteenth century and made a living by transporting fresh water by barge along the River Nete to supply Antwerp's brewers. Like many of the area's towns it was partly industrialized in the late nineteenth century, creating the careless, untidy sprawl that fans out into the surrounding countryside today. The only buildings of any real interest are the towered and turreted **Stadhuis**, a handsome, much-modified medieval structure marooned in the middle of the long and narrow Grote Markt, and the nearby Gothic **St Waldetrudiskerk**, on Kerkstraat, home to an intricate altarpiece carved by Pasquier Borremans in the sixteenth century.

Geel

Fourteen kilometres east of Herentals, the equally unappetizing town of **GEEL** has an international reputation for its treatment of the mentally ill, who have been cared for here within the community for hundreds of years, though the system finally came under orthodox medical control in the middle of the nineteenth century. The system has its origins in the tragedy of Saint Dimpna, a thirteenth-century Irish princess who fled her home and went into hiding near Geel as a result of her father's incestuous advances. The king managed to track her down and beheaded her, an act that could only have been committed, it was felt at the time, by a lunatic, and Dimpna's tomb became a centre of pilgrimage for those seeking a cure for madness. The big fourteenth-century church of **St Dimpnakerk**, ten minutes' walk east of the Markt along Nieuwstraat (April–Sept Tues–Fri & Sun 2–5pm; free), supposedly marks the spot where she was interred. Though the huge, striped-brick church itself is much restored and rather lifeless, it's home to several fine examples of medieval craftsmanship, including the alabaster and marble mausoleum of Baron John de Merode III, carved by Cornelis Floris, the architect of Antwerp's town hall, and several fine retables. Unfortunately, the church's one really outstanding treasure, the teemingly realistic **St Dimpna retable** – carved by Jan van Wave in 1515 and illustrating the life of the saint – is roped off behind the high altar, so you'll need binoculars to see it properly.

A ten-minute walk south along Stationsstraat from the **train station** is Geel's **tourist office** (Mon–Fri 9am–noon & 1–3.30pm, Sat 9am–1pm; ☎014 57 09 50, ⊛www.geel.be), in the town centre on the Markt, the large and characterless expanse which does service as Geel's civic heart. There are no hotels in town, but you probably wouldn't want to stay anyway. As far as **eating** goes, there are several perfectly adequate cafés on the Markt – *Taverne van Gogh* at no. 78 has a good choice of snacks and light meals, while the *Flore* brasserie opposite at no. 48 has more upmarket traditional Flemish cuisine.

Tongerlo Abbey

From Geel bus station, it takes just fifteen minutes for a local bus (every 30min) to make the 5km trip south to a bus stop that's a short walk from the low brown buildings of **Tongerlo Abbey**, a large complex on the edge of the village which took its name. Founded in 1130, the abbey played a key role in the district's agricultural development until it was forcibly dissolved by the French in 1796. Re-established in 1840, it has become a flourishing farmstead once again, a hive of activity where the **Da Vincimuseum** (May–Sept Mon–Thurs & Sat–Sun 2–5pm; €1.25) houses a copy of the great man's *Last Supper* by his pupil Andrea del Solario.

Lier

Just 17km southeast of Antwerp, likeable **LIER** has an amenable, small-town air – in contrast to many of its industrial neighbours. It boasts a clutch of handsome medieval buildings, especially St Gummaruskerk, and an enjoyable art museum, but despite its ancient provenance – it was founded in the eighth century – the town has never managed to elude the shadow of its larger neighbour Antwerp. That said, Felix Timmermans, one of Belgium's best-known Flemish writers, did add a certain sparkle when he lived here from 1886 to 1947. The sparkle may have been needed – other Belgians once referred to Lier's citizens as "sheepheads", a reference to their reputation for stubbornness and stupidity.

Lier is an ideal day-trip from Antwerp, from where it is readily reached by train.

The Town

Central Lier spreads out from a large, rectangular **Grote Markt**, encircled and bisected by the waterways that mark the course of its old harbours and moats. At the centre of the Grote Markt is the turreted fourteenth-century **Belfort**, an attractively spikey affair incongruously attached to the classically elegant **Stadhuis**, which was built to replace the medieval cloth hall in 1740. Otherwise, the square is without much architectural distinction, though it's a pleasant enough spot to linger over a beer. Close by, just off its northwest corner, is an enjoyable art gallery, the **Stedelijk Museum Wuyts**, at Florent van Cauwenberghstraat 14 (April–Oct Wed–Sun 10am–noon & 1–5.30pm; €1, combined ticket with Timmermans-Opsomerhuis – see p.253 – €1.50). For a small town, Lier has a surprisingly varied collection of paintings, among them several works by David Teniers the Younger, who made a small fortune from his realistically earthy peasant scenes as represented by *The Jealous Wife* and *The Village of Perk*. There's also a cruelly drawn *Brawling Peasants* by Jan Steen and a pious portrait of *St Theresa* by Rubens, as well as several works by two of the Bruegels – Jan and Pieter the Younger. The most distinguished Bruegel is Pieter's *Flemish Proverbs* (*Vlaamse Spreekworden*), illustrating over eighty proverbs satirizing every vice and foolery imaginable. There are explanations below each picture in Flemish, but many – like the man pissing against the moon – speak for themselves. There's also a laughable, pseudo-religious painting by local artist Isidore Opsomer (see p.253) entitled *Christ Preaches to Lier*.

The Zimmertoren and the Begijnhof

From the southwest corner of the Grote Markt, Eikelstraat leads to the **Gevangenenpoort**, a strongly fortified medieval gate which served as the town's prison for many years. Opposite is the curious **Zimmertoren** (daily: April–Sept 10am–noon & 1–6pm; Oct–March 10am–noon & 2–4pm, March

& Oct until 5pm; €2), an old tower which was formerly part of the city ramparts before being converted into the colourful **Centenary Clock**, whose many dials show the phases of the moon, the zodiac, the tides of Lier and just about everything else you can think of. The clock was the work of one Lodewijk Zimmer (1888–1970), a wealthy city merchant who constructed it in 1931 in an effort to dispel local superstition and show his fellow townspeople how the cosmos worked. However, judging by the woefully inaccurate diagram of the solar system inset into the pavement outside the museum, Lier would benefit from some more of his services. Inside the tower you can see the bevy of rotating dials which makes the clock tick, along with Zimmer's astronomical studio, while in an adjoining pavilion is Zimmer's no-less detailed **Wonder Clock**, which was exhibited at the World Fairs of Brussels and New York in the 1930s. A guide explaining the internal works of the clocks and the meaning of all the dials is available in English for €1.25.

Schapekoppenstraat, in front of the Zimmertoren, leads southwest past a wry modern sculpture of a shepherd and his metal sheep to a side-gate into the **Begijnhof**, whose rather grand terraced streets stretch towards the site of the old city walls. Lier's *begijnhof* was founded in the thirteenth century, but most of the surviving buildings date from the seventeenth century, including the appealing **Begijnhofkerk** (Easter to mid-Oct Sun only 2–5pm; free). For more on *begijnhofs*, see p.407.

The Timmermans-Opsomerhuis

Behind the Zimmertoren, a narrow road crosses over an arm of the River Nete as it gracefully slices Lier into two. To the left, on the far side of the bridge, **Werf** was once the main city dock; to the right, the **Timmermans-Opsomerhuis** (April–Oct Wed–Sun 10am–noon & 1.30–5.30pm; Nov–March Sun 10am–noon & 1–4.30pm; €1) celebrates the town's two most famous inhabitants, the writer Felix Timmermans and the painter Isidore Opsomer (1878–1967). Timmermans and Opsomer were good friends and thought of themselves as leading artistic custodians of Flemish culture, the one writing of traditional village life, most memorably in the earthy humour of his *Pallieter*; the other proud of his sea- and townscapes, and of his influence on contemporary Belgian painters. Inside, the spacious rooms of the first floor contain a comprehensive selection of Opsomer's work, including a whole batch of heavy, pretentious portraits along with a number of more immediately appealing rural scenes, such as the Expressionistic *Middelburg*. An adjoining room is devoted to the work of their friend, the sculptor Lodewijk van Boeckel, whose old forge is surrounded by examples of his intricate, profoundly black ironwork. Upstairs, there's a collection of writings by Timmermans, supplemented by several first editions, together with general details of his life and times, all in Flemish.

St Gummaruskerk

North along the Werf, the third turn on the right, Rechtestraat, leads to **St Gummaruskerk** (daily: April–Oct 10am–noon & 2–5pm; Nov–March 10am–noon & 2–4pm; €1.25), which takes its name from a courtier of King Pepin of France, who settled in Lier as a hermit in the middle of the eighth century. Built in Flamboyant Gothic style in the fifteenth century, and painstakingly restored in the 1980s, the sturdy buttresses of the church, surmounted by a tiered and parapeted tower, dominate the surrounding streets.

Inside, chunky pillars rise up to support a vaulted roof, whose simplicity contrasts with the swirling embellishments of the **rood loft** below, which itself frames a passionate bas-relief of the Calvary and the Resurrection. Behind, the high altar is topped by a second fine carving, a fourteenth-century wooden altarpiece whose inside panels are alive with a mass of finely observed detail, from the folds of the bed linen to the pile of kindling underneath Abraham's son. The church's **stained glass windows** are reckoned to be some of the finest in Belgium. They include five stately, elongated windows above the high altar, which were presented to the town by the Emperor Maximilian in 1516, along with a more intimate sequence by Rombout Keldermans from 1475, overlooking the first section of the left-hand side of the choir.

Practicalities

It's just fifteen minutes by train from Antwerp Centraal to Lier. Lier **train station** adjoins the **bus station** on the north side of the town, from where it's a ten-minute walk to the Grote Markt: veer left out of the train station, turn right at the main road, Antwerpsestraat, and carry straight on. The **tourist office**, in the basement of the Stadhuis on the Grote Markt (April–Oct daily 9am–12.30pm & 1.30–5pm; Nov–March Mon–Fri 9am–12.30pm & 1.30–5pm; ☎03 491 13 93, ⊛www.lier.be), can provide a glossy town brochure with a map (€0.25) and make **accommodation** bookings for free, although the options are limited to just two hotels and a couple of inconveniently located **B&Bs** (❸). Of the **hotels**, the better option is the *Hof van Aragon*, Aragonstraat 6 (☎03 491 08 00, ⑤03 491 08 10, ⊛www.hofvanaragon .be; ❺), a small, unpretentious place occupying a pleasantly renovated old building in the town centre: take Kerkstraat from beside St Gummaruskerk and it's the first turn on the right, just beyond the canal. The other, less attractive possibility is the *Handelshof*, a run-of-the-mill modern hotel in front of the train station at Leopoldplein 39 (☎03 480 03 10, ⑤03 489 01 11; ❻).

For **food**, most day-trippers head for the row of terraced cafés edging the Grote Markt and the Zimmerplein, in front of the Zimmertoren. Prices are generally reasonable, with the *Delfin*, Zimmerplein 6, and the popular *Den Engel*, on the west side of the Grote Markt, serving snacks and light meals as good as any of their rivals. There's a much better option in the laid-back *Oude Komeet*, next to the Stedelijk Museum at Florent van Cauwenberghstraat 18, an attractive café-restaurant (closed Mon) offering wholesome food with the emphasis on vegetarian dishes. For something a little more formal, the pricey but first-rate *De Werf*, Werf 17 (closed Wed & Thurs), specializes in traditional Flemish cuisine. The two liveliest **bars** in town are on tiny Felix Timmermansplein, beside the river just off Rechtestraat – between the Grote Markt and St Gummaruskerk. Here you'll find the fashionable *St Gummarus* along with *De Fortuin*, a charming bar with a riverside terrace and a wide range of ales. Both are also good for a quick bite to eat.

Mechelen and around

Midway between Antwerp and Brussels, **MECHELEN** is the home of the Primate of Belgium and the country's ecclesiastical capital, its Christian past dating back to **St Rombout**, an Irish evangelist who converted the locals in the seventh century. Little is known for sure about Rombout, but legend asserts he was the son of a powerful chieftain, who gave up his worldly possessions to preach to the heathen – not that it did him much good: after publicly criticising a stonemason for adultery, the ungrateful wretch chopped him up with his axe and chucked the body into the river. In the way of such things, Rombout's remains were retrieved and showed no signs of decay, easily enough justification for the construction of a shrine in his honour. Rombout proved a popular saint and pilgrims flocked here, ensuring Mechelen a steady revenue. Indeed, by the thirteenth century Mechelen had become one of the more powerful cities of medieval Flanders and entered a brief golden age when, in 1473, the Burgundian prince, **Charles the Bold**, decided to base his administration here. Impetuous and intemperate, Charles used the wealth of the Flemish towns to fund a series of campaigns that ended with his death on the battlefield in 1477. His widow, Margaret of York, and his son's regent, the redoubtable Margaret of Austria, stayed in Mechelen and formed one of the most famous courts of the day. Artists and scholars were drawn here from all over Flanders, attracted by the Renaissance pomp and ceremony, with enormous feasts in fancy clothes in fancy buildings. For the men two particular peccadilloes were pointed shoes (whose length – up to about 60cm – reflected social status) and bright, two-colour hoses. This glamorous facade camouflaged a serious political motive. Surrounded by wealthy, independent merchants and powerful, well-organized guilds, the dukes and duchesses of Burgundy realized they had to impress and overawe as a condition of their survival.

Margaret of Austria died in 1530, the capital moved to Brussels and Mechelen was never quite the same. The *Baedeker* of 1900 described the town as a "dull place . . . totally destitute of the brisk traffic which enlivens most of the principal Belgian towns". Things aren't nearly so bad today, but considering Mechelen's proximity to Antwerp and Brussels, it has a surprisingly provincial atmosphere – possibly no bad thing. The town's attractions – primarily a cache of **medieval churches**, including a splendid cathedral, and a pair of superb Rubens' paintings – are easily seen on a day-trip from either of its neighbours, but overnight you'll have the time to give the place the attention it really deserves. One blot on the town's history was its use by the Germans as a transit camp for Jews in World War II: there's a **Deportation Museum** in town and a short train ride away is **Fort Breendonk**, a one-time Gestapo interrogation centre.

Arrival, information and accommodation

From Mechelen's **train** and adjoining **bus station**, it's a fifteen-minute walk north to the town centre, straight ahead down Hendrik Consciencestraat and its continuation Graaf von Egmontstraat. The **tourist office** is in the Stadhuis on the east side of the Grote Markt (Mon–Fri 8am–6pm, plus March–Oct Sat & Sun 9.30am–12.30pm & 1.30–5pm, Nov–Feb Sat & Sun 10am–noon & 1–4.30pm; ☏015 29 76 55, ⊛www.mechelen.be/toerisme). They have all the usual municipal information as well as details of a couple of **B&Bs** (❸–❹), which they will book on your behalf at no extra charge. Alternatively, the town has just three recommendable, centrally located **hotels**. The pick is the four-star *Golden Tulip Alfa Alba*, Korenmarkt 22 (☏015 42 03 03, ℗015 42 37 88; ❻), a smart, modern if somewhat bland chain hotel a brief walk south of the Grote Markt via the Ijzerenleen. Second up is the neat, trim and modern *Express by Holiday Inn*, on the Veemarkt (☏ & ℗015 44 84 20, ⊛www.hiexpress.com; ❻), which has seventy comfortable rooms equipped in standard chain style. Less expensive and occupying an older building midway between the station and the Grote Markt is the modest *Hotel Egmont*, metres from Kardinal Mercierplein at Oude Brusselsestraat 50 (☏015 42 13 99, ℗015 41 34 98; ❺).

The Town

The centre of town is, as ever, the **Grote Markt**, a handsome expansive affair marked by a mundane statue of Margaret of Austria and flanked on the eastern side by the **Stadhuis**, whose bizarre and incoherent appearance was partly her responsibility. In 1526, she had the left-hand side of the original building demolished and replaced by what you see today, an ornate arcaded loggia fronting a fluted, angular edifice, to a design by Rombout Keldermans. The plan was to demolish and rebuild the rest of the building in stages, but after her death in 1530 the work was simply abandoned, leaving Keldermans' extravagance firmly glued to the plain stonework and the simple gables of the fourteenth-century section on the right. The **interior** of the later section (occasional guided tours – ask at the tourist office) is just as garbled as the exterior,

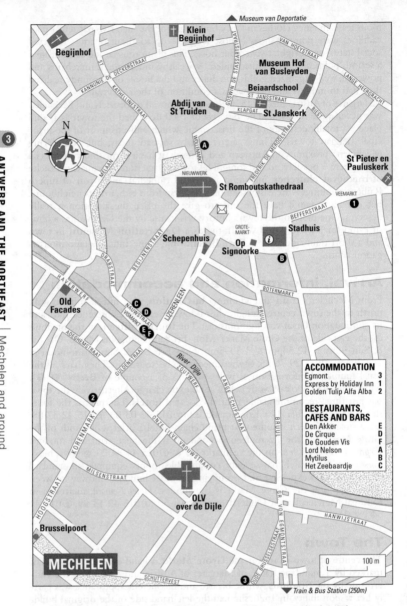

▲ *Museum van Deportatie*

Begijnhof

Klein Begijnhof

VAN HOEYSTRAAT

KANNUNIE DE DECKERSTRAAT

GOSWIN DE STASSARTSTRAAT

Museum Hof van Busleyden

LANGE HEERGRACHT

Beiaardschool

ST JANSSTRAAT

Abdij van St Truiden

KLAPGAT

St Janskerk

BIEST

N

WOLLMARKT

Ⓐ

St Pieter en Pauluskerk

FREDERIK DE MERODESTRAAT

NIEUWWERK

St Romboutskathedraal

VEEMARKT

❶

BEFFERSTRAAT

GROTE-MARKT

ℹ️

Stadhuis

BEGIJNENSTRAAT

Schepenhuis

Op Signoorke

Ⓑ

DRABSTRAAT

LIZEKENLEEN

HAVERWERF

BOTERMARKT

Old Facades

Ⓒ

NAUWSTRAAT

Ⓓ

VISMARKT

ADEGHEMSTRAAT

BRUUL

Ⓔ Ⓕ

GULDENSTRAAT

River Dijle

ZOUTWERF

LANGE SCHIPSTRAAT

KORENMARKT

❷

ONZE LIEVE VROUWSTRAAT

ACCOMMODATION
Egmont	3
Express by Holiday Inn	1
Golden Tulip Alfa Alba	2

RESTAURANTS, CAFES AND BARS
Den Akker	E
De Cirque	D
De Gouden Vis	F
Lord Nelson	A
Mytilus	B
Het Zeebaardje	C

MILSENSTRAAT

HOOGSTRAAT

OLV over de Dijle

BRUUL

GR. VON ESMONTSTRAAT

HANWIJSTRAAT

Brusselpoort

OUDE BRUSSELSESTRAAT

SCHUTTERVEST

❸

0   100 m

MECHELEN

▼ *Train & Bus Station (250m)*

though there are a couple of interesting paintings on display. These are Coussaert's *A Sitting of the Parliament of Charles the Bold* and a fine sixteenth-century tapestry of the *Battle of Tunis*, glorifying an attack on that city by Emperor Charles V in 1535.

In front of the Stadhuis, just outside the tourist office, is a modern **sculpture of Op Signoorke**, the town's mascot, being tossed in a blanket. Once a generalized symbol of male irresponsibility, the doll and its forebears enjoyed a variety of names – *vuilen bras* (unfaithful drunkard), *sotscop* (fool) and *vuilen bruidegom* (disloyal bridegroom) – until the events of 1775 redefined its identity. Every year it was customary for the dummy to be paraded through the streets and tossed up and down in a sheet. In 1775, however, a young man from Antwerp attempted to steal it and was badly beaten for his pains: the people of Mechelen were convinced he was part of an Antwerp plot to rob them of their cherished mascot. The two cities were already fierce commercial rivals, and the incident soured relations even further. Indeed, when news of the beating reached Antwerp, there was sporadic rioting and calls for the city burghers to take some sort of revenge. Refusing to be intimidated, the people of Mechelen derisively renamed the doll after their old nickname for the people of Antwerp – "Op Signoorke", from "Signor", a reference to that city's favoured status under earlier Spanish kings. It was sweet revenge for an incident of 1687 that had made Mechelen a laughing stock: staggering home, a drunk had roused the town when he thought he saw a fire in the cathedral. In fact, the "fire" was moonlight, earning the Mechelaars the insulting soubriquet "Maneblussers" (Moondousers).

St Romboutskathedraal

A little way west of the Grote Markt, **St Romboutskathedraal** (April–Oct daily 9.30am–5.30pm, Nov–March until 4.30pm; free) dominates the town centre just as it was supposed to. It's the cathedral's mighty square tower that takes the breath away, a wonderful, almost imperial Gothic structure with soaring, canopied pinnacles and extraordinarily long and slender windows. Down below, the church's heavy-duty buttressing supports a superb sequence of high-arched pointed windows that encircle the nave and the choir, rising up to the delicate fluting of a stone balustrade.

The construction of the church has not been without its problems. Work began with the draining of the marshes on which it was to be built in 1217, but the money ran out before the tower was erected, and the initial design had

The carillon

It was during the fourteenth century that **bells** were first used in Flemish cities as a means of regulating the working day, reflecting the development of a wage economy – employers were keen to keep tabs on their employees. Bells also served as a sort of public-address system: pealing bells, for example, announced good news, tolling bells summoned the city to the main square, and a rapid sequence of bells warned of danger. By the early fifteenth century, a short peal of bells marked the hour, and from this developed the **carillon** (*beiaard*), in which the ringing of a set of bells is triggered by the rotation of a large drum with metal pegs; the pegs pull wires attached to the clappers in the bells – just like a giant music box. Later, the mechanics were developed so that the carillon could be played by means of a keyboard, giving the player (*beiaardier*) the chance to improvise.

Carillon playing almost died out in the nineteenth century, when it was dismissed as being too folksy for words, but now it's on the rebound, and several Flemish cities – including Bruges and Mechelen – have their own municipal carillon player. Belgium's finest carillon, a fifteenth-century affair of 49 bells, is housed in Mechelen's cathedral tower and resounds over the town on high days and holidays. There are also regular, hour-long **performances** in Mechelen on Saturdays (11.30am), Sundays (3pm), and from June through to mid-September on Monday evenings (8.30pm).

ANTWERP AND THE NORTHEAST | Mechelen and around

to be put on hold until the fifteenth century. In 1451, the Pope obligingly provided the extra funds when he put St Rombout on a list of specified churches where pilgrims could seek absolution for their sins without visiting Rome. The money rolled in and the tower was completed by 1546 – just before the outbreak of the religious wars that would surely have stymied the whole project. More recently, the cathedral literally started to break up as it sunk unevenly into its foundations, prompting an enormously expensive – and long-winded – effort to stabilize it. The works have finally finished, but it remains to be seen if the job was properly done.

The nave and the transepts

The main entrance to the cathedral is just off Grote Markt. Inside, the thirteenth-century **nave** has all the cloistered elegance of the Brabantine Gothic style, although the original lines are spoiled by an unfortunate series of seventeenth-century statues of the apostles. Between the arches lurks an extraordinary Baroque **pulpit**, a playful mass of twisted and curled oak dotted with carefully camouflaged animal carvings – squirrels, frogs and snails, a salamander and a pelican. The main scene shows **St Norbert** being thrown from his horse, a narrow escape which convinced this twelfth-century German prince to give his possessions to the poor and dedicate his life to the church.

Moving on, the chapel next to the **north transept** contains the tomb of Mechelen's **Cardinal Mercier** plus a plaque, presented by the Church of England, commemorating his part in co-ordinating the Mechelen Conversations: investigating the possibility of reuniting the two churches, these ran from 1921 up to the time of Mercier's death in 1926. Nonetheless, in Belgium Mercier is more often remembered for his staunch opposition to the German occupation of World War I. His pastoral letters, notably "Patriotism and Endurance", proclaimed loyalty to the Belgian king, paid tribute to the soldiers at the front and condemned the invasion as illegal and un-Christian. Across the church in the **south transept** is the cathedral's most distinguished painting, **Anthony van Dyck**'s dramatic *Crucifixion*, which portrays the writhing, muscular bodies of the two thieves in the shadows to either side of the Christ, who is bathed in a white light of wonderful clarity. The painting now forms part of a heavy, marble Baroque altarpiece carved for the Guild of Masons, but it was only installed here after the French revolutionary army razed the church where it was originally displayed. Take a look also at the elaborate doors of the **high altar**, which hide the gilt casket containing the remains of St Rombout. They are only opened on major religious festivals, when the reliquary is paraded through the town centre.

The ambulatory

Exhibited in the **aisle of the ambulatory** are twenty-five **panel paintings** relating the legend of St Rombout. Such devotional series were comparatively common in medieval Flanders, but this is one of the few to have survived, painted by several unknown artists between 1480 and 1510. As individual works of art, the panel paintings are not perhaps of the highest order, but the cumulative attention to detail – in the true Flemish tradition – is quite remarkable, with all manner of folksy minutiae illuminating what would otherwise be a predictable tale of sacrifice and sanctity. The panels are exhibited in chronological order, but they aren't labelled in English at present and neither is their meaning always obvious, hence the explanatory box opposite. Many of the panels carry a sombre-looking, kneeling man and woman – these were the donors.

The legend of St Rombout

Panel 1 Bishops and priests pray beside the tomb of the newly-deceased Bishop of Dublin. Up above, an angel instructs them to select Rombout as his successor.

Panel 2 Rombout preaches to his Irish congregation. In the building in the background, an angel summons him to be a missionary.

Panel 3 Rombout crosses by boat to France, where he restores the sight of a blind man.

Panel 4 Rombout arranges an audience with the Pope so that he can surrender his bishop's ring of office.

Panel 5 Rome. Rombout receives the Pope's blessing for his mission to the heathens.

Panel 6 Back in France, Rombout exorcises the devil from a madman.

Panel 7 Arriving in Mechelen, Rombout ticks off the locals for dancing on Good Friday – note the bagpipe player. A messenger arrives from the local lord, Count Ado, inviting him to his castle.

Panel 8 The count and countess receive Rombout. In the background, Rombout promises them a son, despite the countess's advanced years.

Panel 9 The countess's baby is christened.

Panel 10 In the foreground, St Rombout meets St Gommarus of Lier; in the background a messenger announces the death of Gommarus.

Panel 11 St Rombout's prayers revive Gommarus; Count Ado presents Rombout with a parcel of land; work begins on the construction of Rombout's first chapel.

Panel 12 Rombout admonishes the adulterous stonemason, whose face is a picture of guilt.

Panel 13 The mason kills Rombout, his work-mate picks his pockets, and then they throw the body into the river.

Panel 14 Local Christians recover the body, guided by a celestial light.

Panel 15 St Rombout protects his chapel from Viking attack.

Panel 16 The Vikings are about to sail off, with Gerlindis, a devout nun, among their captives; St Rombout's prayers save her.

Panel 17 At Gerlindis's nunnery, a rooster crows the time for prayer, but one day a fox takes it. Rombout says a prayer and the fox returns the bird unharmed.

Panel 18 In St Rombout's chapel, a priest successfully prays for the return of his sight.

Panel 19 A knight wounded in a hunting-party is carried to St Rombout's chapel, where his health is restored.

Panel 20 As in Panel 19, but this time a knight has been attacked by devils.

Panel 21 Same again, though on this occasion healing comes to three possessed men and a woman with a lame hand.

Panel 22 A Flemish lord gives land to the chapel of St Rombout.

Panel 23 & 24 Battle scenes in which reliquaries of St Rombout bring victory to the Mechelaars.

Panel 25 The Brotherhood of St Rombout honour their patron saint.

As for the ambulatory itself, it's not quite all that it seems: many of the columns are made of wood painted as marble, a trompe l'oeil technique for which Mechelen was once famous. Although most of the ambulatory's nine **side-chapels** are really rather dreary, the **Chapel of the Relics** – the eighth one along from the entrance on the ambulatory's north side – is an exception. The chapel is dedicated to a group of monks and priests who the Protestants slaughtered near Dordrecht in Holland in 1572, their supposed remains stored in the silver and gilt casket that occupies central stage. Here also are the coats of arms of the Knights of the Golden Fleece, a chivalric – or at least aristocratic

– order invented by Philip the Good, the Duke of Burgundy and ruler of Flanders, in 1430.

To St Janskerk

From the side of the cathedral, Wollemarkt leads north past the refuge of the **Abdij van St Truiden** (not open to the public), which sits prettily beside an old weed-choked canal, its picturesque gables once home to the destitute. Almost opposite, now on Goswin de Stassartstraat, an alley called Klapgat threads through to **St Janskerk** (April–Oct Tues–Sun 1.30–5.30pm, Nov–March till 4.30pm; free), whose decaying sandstone exterior belies its richly decorated, immaculately maintained interior. Almost everything is on the grand scale here, from the massive pulpit and the whopping organ through to two large and unusual canons' pews, but it's the Baroque high altarpiece that grabs the attention, a suitably flashy setting for a flashy but wonderful painting – Rubens' *Adoration of the Magi*. Painted in 1619, the central panel, after which the triptych is named, is a fine example of the artist's use of variegated lighting – and also has his first wife portrayed as the Virgin. The side panels are occasionally rotated, so on the left hand side you'll see either Jesus baptised by John the Baptist or John the Baptist's head on a platter; to the right it's St John on Patmos or the same saint being dipped in boiling oil.

The Beiaardschool and Museum Hof van Busleyden

A few metres further east, at the far end of St Jansstraat, Mechelen's **Beiaardschool** (Carillon School; no public admission) has become one of the most prestigious institutions of its sort in the world, attracting students from as far away as Japan. Playing the carillon is, by all accounts, extremely difficult and the diploma course offered here in Mechelen takes six years to complete. Next door to the school, the **Museum Hof van Busleyden** (Tues–Sun 10am–5pm; €2) occupies a splendid early sixteenth-century mansion, built in high Gothic style with Renaissance touches for Hieronymus Busleyden, a prominent member of Margaret's court. Highlights of the rambling collection include an interesting assortment of mostly unattributed paintings. Notable among them is a seventeenth-century picture of Mechelen's Groot Begijnhof supplemented by 46 miniatures of the *beguines* at work, along with a graphic series of sixteen panels portraying the multiple sufferings of St Victor, painted for a local convent in around 1510. There's also a display of miscellaneous bells, a variety of guild knick-knacks and a collection of Gallo-Roman artefacts – hardly enough to set the pulse racing, but an agreeable way to spend an hour or so.

Museum van Deportatie en Verzet

Doubling back to Goswin de Stassartstraat, turn right for the five-minute walk to the **Museum van Deportatie en Verzet**, at no. 153 (Museum of Deportation and Resistance; Mon–Thurs & Sun 10am–5pm, Fri 10am–1pm; closed Sat & mid-Aug for two weeks; free). During the German occupation, Nazi officials chose Mechelen as a staging point for Belgian Jews destined for the concentration camps of eastern Europe. Their reasoning was quite straightforward: most of Belgium's Jews were in either Antwerp or Brussels and Mechelen was halfway between the two.

Today's Museum of Deportation occupies the old barracks that were adapted by the Gestapo for use as the principal internment centre. Between 1942 and 1944 over 25,000 Jews passed through its doors; most ended up in Auschwitz and only 1,200 survived the war. In a series of well-conceived, multilingual displays, the museum tracks through this dreadful episode, beginning with Jewish life in Belgium before the war and continuing with sections on the rise of anti-Semitism, the occupation, the deportations, the concentration camps and liberation. It's designed with older Belgian school children in mind, so you may share the museum with one or more school parties, but it's still harrowing stuff and some of the photographs bring a deep chill to the soul. The final section, entitled "Personal Testimonies," is particularly affecting – one of its exhibits is a postcard thrown from a deportation train.

The Veemarkt and St Pieter en Pauluskerk

From the Deportation Museum, the quickest way back to the Grote Markt is along Goswin de Stassartstraat, but instead you might consider detouring south to the **Veemarkt**, a wide square overlooked by the ornately Baroque **St Pieter en Pauluskerk** (April–Oct Tues–Sun 1.30–5.30pm, Nov–March till 4.30pm; free). Built for the Jesuits in the seventeenth century, the interior has a huge oak pulpit honouring the order's missionary work, with a globe attached to representations of the four continents that were known when it was carved by Hendrik Verbruggen in 1701.

South of the Grote Markt

It's a short walk from the Veemarkt back to the Grote Markt, where you can extend your tour by strolling south, past the Gothic **Schepenhuis** (Aldermen's House), home to a workaday historical museum, and onto the **Ijzerenleen**, site of one of the region's best Saturday food **markets** (8am–1pm). At the far end of the Ijzerenleen, just before the bridge, turn right down Nauwstraat and keep going until you spy a quaint little pontoon bridge spanning the River Dilje over to the **Haverwerf** (Oats Wharf), which is graced by three old and contrasting **facades**, each of which has been meticulously restored. On the right is Het Paradijske (The Little Paradise), a slender structure with fancy tracery and mullioned windows that takes its name from the Garden of Eden reliefs above the first-floor windows. Next door, the all-timber De Duiveltjes (The Little Devils), a rare survivor from the sixteenth century, is also named after its decoration, this time for the carved satyrs above the entrance. Finally, on the left and dating to 1669, is Sint-Jozef, a graceful example of the Baroque merchant's house. Its fluent scrollwork swirls over the top of the gable and camouflages the utilitarian, upper-storey door: trade goods were once pulled up the front of the house by pulley and shoved in here for safekeeping.

Kerk van Onze Lieve Vrouw over de Dijle

From Haverwerf, it's a five-minute walk southeast to Onze Lieve Vrouwstraat and the **Kerk van Onze Lieve Vrouw over de Dijle** (Church of Our Lady across the River Dijle; April–Oct Tues–Sun 1.30–5.30pm, Nov–March till 4.30pm; free), a massive, pinnacled and turreted affair that was begun in the fifteenth century and finally completed two hundred years later. It took a direct hit from a V1 rocket in World War II, but has now been restored to its previous appearance – not entirely to its advantage as the interior is a plodding mix of the Gothic and the Baroque. The south transept displays Rubens' *Miraculous Draught of Fishes*, an exquisite triptych painted for the Fishmongers' Guild in 1618. The central panel has all the usual hallmarks of Rubens in his pomp – note the thick, muscular arms of the fishermen – but its glistening and wriggling fish that inspire.

Five minutes' walk away, on the southern edge of the centre, the **Brusselpoort** is the only survivor of Mechelen's twelve fourteenth-century gates, its striped brickwork and twin onion domes striking quite a pose.

Eating and drinking

Mechelen is a tad short on good – or at least distinctive – **cafés** and **restaurants**, though there is lots of choice on and around the Grote Markt. The best bet here is the *Mytilus* (Closed Mon lunch and all day Sun), a more than competent, family-run restaurant offering all the standard Flemish dishes, with main courses averaging about €14; it's next door to the tourist office at Grote Markt 23. Otherwise, head off to Nauwstraat, a short sidestreet by the river at the south end of Ijzerenleen: here at no. 16 is a smart little place, *Het Zeebaardje*, with an excellent line in seafood, main courses starting at €15. Just along the street is *De Cirque*, an appealing café-bar and restaurant with modish decor and a menu that is both a little less expensive and a bit wider than its neighbour.

As for **bars**, the laid-back *De Gouden Vis*, also on Nauwstraat, has more than a little of New-Age-meets-hippie; the adjacent *Den Akker* is much the same. In addition, there's a cluster of bars beside the cathedral on Wollemarkt – nothing special, though the *Lord Nelson* does muster up a neat package of ersatz nautical decoration plus several fine beers: the dark and malty Corsendonk Pater is recommended. Among local brews, be sure to try Gouden Carolus (Golden Charles), a delicious dark-brown brew once tippled by – or so they say – the Emperor Charles V.

Around Mechelen: Fort Breendonk

About 12km west of Mechelen, **Fort Breendonk** (daily: April–Sept 9.30am–6pm; Oct–March until 5pm; €3), built as part of the circle of fortifications that ringed early-twentieth-century Antwerp, was a Gestapo interrogation centre during World War II. The fort's low concrete buildings were originally encased in a thick layer of sand until the Germans had this carted away by their prisoners in 1940. After the war, Breendonk was preserved as a national memorial in honour of the four thousand men and women who suffered or perished in its dark, dank tunnels and cells. As you might expect, it's a powerful, disturbing place to visit, with a clearly marked tour taking you through the SS tribunal room, poignantly graffitied cells, the prisoners' barrack room and the bunker, which was used as a torture chamber. There's also a museum dealing with the German occupation of Belgium, prison life and the post-war trial of Breendonk SS criminals and their collaborators. Other displays explore the origins of Fascism and the development of the Nazi concentration camps.

By car, Fort Breendonk is a stone's throw from the A12 highway linking Antwerp and Brussels – just follow the signs. To get there from Mechelen **by public transport**, take the train to **Willebroek** (hourly; 10min); the fort is on the edge of town, a 1500-metre walk west from the station along Dermondesestenweg. The modern *Breendonck Taverne*, next door to the fort, serves snacks and meals at reasonable prices.

Leuven

Less than half an hour by train from both Mechelen and Brussels, **LEUVEN** offers an easy and enjoyable day-trip from either. The town is the seat of Belgium's oldest university, whose students give the place a lively, informal air – and sustain lots of inexpensive bars and cafés. There are also a couple of notable medieval buildings here, the splendid **Stadhuis** and **St Pieterskerk**, home to three wonderful early Flemish paintings, and the appealing **Oude**

Markt, one of the region's most personable squares. Otherwise, the centre is not much more than an undistinguished tangle of streets with a lot of the new and few remnants of the old. Then again, it's something of a miracle that any of Leuven's ancient buildings have survived at all, since the town suffered badly in both World Wars. Some 1500 houses were destroyed in World War I, and the university library and main church were gutted, only to suffer further damage in World War II. If you stay a while, you may also pick up on the division between town and gown; some of the students see themselves as champions of the Flemish cause, but the locals seem largely unconvinced.

The history of the **university**, founded in 1425, isn't a particularly happy one. By the early sixteenth century it rated among Europe's most prestigious educational establishments: the cartographer Mercator was a student, and Erasmus worked here, founding the *Collegium Trilingue* for the study of Hebrew, Latin and Greek, as the basis of a liberal (rather than Catholic) education. However, in response to the rise of Lutheranism, the authorities insisted on strict Catholic orthodoxy, and drove Erasmus into exile. In 1797 the French suppressed the university, and then, after the defeat of Napoleon, when Belgium fell under Dutch rule, William I replaced it with a Philosophical College – one of many blatantly anti-Catholic measures which fuelled the Belgian revolution. Re-established after independence as a bilingual Catholic institution, the university became a hotbed of Flemish Catholicism, and for much of this century French and Flemish speakers here were locked in a bitter nationalist dispute. In 1970 a separate, French-speaking university was founded at Louvain-la-Neuve, just south of Brussels – a decision that propelled Leuven into its present role as a bastion of Flemish thinking, wielding considerable influence over the region's political and economic elite.

Arrival, information and accommodation

It's a gentle ten- to fifteen-minute walk west along Bondgenotenlaan from the **train** and adjacent **bus station** to the Grote Markt, where you'll find Leuven's **tourist office**, in the Stadhuis (Mon–Fri 9am–5pm & Sat 10am–1pm & 1.30–5pm; March–Oct also Sun 10am–1pm & 1.30–5pm; ☎016 21 15 39, ℻016 21 15 49, ⓦ www.leuven.be). They have a comprehensive town brochure detailing the town's hotels, sights and museums, and also offer a limited supply of **B&Bs** (❷–❸), though most of these are on the outskirts. There's **internet** access at *Spacebar*, Namsestraat 66 (Tues–Sat noon–2am; €0.50 per 15min).

Leuven possesses a handful of central **hotels**, the least expensive of which are the three on Martelarenplein, the square in front of the train station. None of these is particularly enticing, but the recently renovated *Industrie*, a one-star hotel at no. 7 (☎016 22 13 49, ℻016 20 82 85; ❸), has plain and perfectly adequate rooms. Other options, this time right in the centre, include the basic *Professor*, Naamsestraat 20 (☎016 20 14 14, ℻016 29 14 16; ❸), a small, one-star hotel above a bar; the standard-issue, two-star *Ibis Leuven Centrum*, Brusselsestraat 52 (☎016 29 31 11, ℻016 23 87 92; ❹); and the modern *Holiday Inn Garden Court*, a better than average three-star hotel off Tiensestraat at Alfons Smetsplein 7 (☎016 31 76 00, ℻016 31 76 01, ⓦ www.holiday-inn.com; ❾) – don't pay too much attention to the ugly entrance.

The Town

The centre of town is marked by two adjacent squares, the more easterly of which is the **Fochplein**, basically just a road junction whose one noteworthy feature is the modern **Font Sapienza**, a wittily cynical fountain of a student literally being brainwashed by the book he is reading. Next door, the wedge-shaped **Grote Markt** is Leuven's architectural high spot, dominated by two notable late Gothic buildings – St Pieterskerk and the Stadhuis. The **Stadhuis** is the more flamboyant of the two, an extraordinarily light and lacy confection, crowned by soaring pinnacles and a dainty, high-pitched roof studded with dormer windows. It's a beautiful building, but it is slightly spoiled by the clumsiness of its statues, which were inserted in the nineteenth century, representing everything from important citizens, artists and nobles, to virtues, vices and municipal institutions. Until then, the lavishly carved niches stood empty for lack of money. In contrast, the niche bases are exuberantly medieval, depicting biblical subjects in a free, colloquial style and adorned by a panoply of grotesques. After the slender beauty of the exterior, the **inside** of the Stadhuis is something of an anticlimax, with guided tours (April–Sept Mon–Fri at 11am & 3pm; Oct–March daily at 3pm; €1.25) taking you through just four rooms, including overblown salons in high French style and the neo-Gothic council chamber.

St Pieterskerk

Across the square, **St Pieterskerk** (Tues–Sat 10am–5pm, Sun 2–5pm; mid-March to mid-Oct also Mon 10am–5pm; free) is a rambling, heavily buttressed late Gothic pile whose stumpy western facade defeated its architects. Work began on the present church in the 1420s and continued until the start of the sixteenth century when the Romanesque towers of the west facade, the last remaining part of the earlier church, were pulled down to make way for a grand design by Joos Matsys, the brother of Quentin. It didn't work out – the foundations proved too weak – and finally, another hundred years on, the unfinished second-attempt towers were capped, creating the truncated, asymmetrical versions that rise above the entrance today.

Inside, the church is distinguished by its soaring nave whose enormous pillars frame a fabulous **rood screen**, an intricately carved piece of stonework surmounted by a wooden Christ. The nave's Baroque **pulpit** is also striking, a weighty wooden extravagance which shows **St Norbert** being thrown off his horse by lightning, a dramatic scene set beneath spiky palm trees. It was this brush with death that persuaded Norbert, a twelfth-century German noble, to abandon his worldly ways and dedicate himself to the church, on whose behalf he founded a devout religious order, the Premonstratensian Canons, in 1120.

The ambulatory

The ambulatory accommodates the **Museum voor Religieuze Kunst** (Museum of Religious Art; same times as church; €5), whose three key paintings date from the fifteenth century. There's a copy of Rogier van der Weyden's marvellous triptych, the *Descent from the Cross*, the original of which is now at the Prado in Madrid, and two of the few surviving paintings by Weyden's apprentice **Dieric Bouts** (c1415–75), who worked for most of his life in Leuven, ultimately becoming the city's official painter and an influential artist in his own right. Bouts' carefully contrived paintings are inhabited by stiff and slender figures in religious scenes that are almost totally devoid of action – a frozen narrative designed to stir contemplation rather than strong emotion. His use of colour and attention to detail are quite superb, especially in the exquisite landscapes that act as a backdrop to much of his work. Of the two triptychs on display here, the gruesome *Martyrdom of St Erasmus*, which has the executioner extracting the saint's entrails with a winch, is less interesting than the *Last Supper*, showing Christ and his disciples in a Flemish dining room,

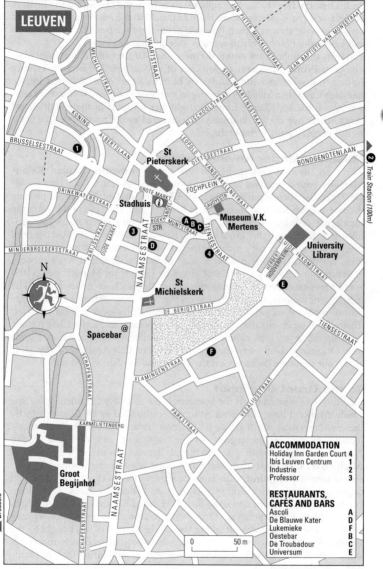

ACCOMMODATION

Holiday Inn Garden Court	4
Ibis Leuven Centrum	1
Industrie	2
Professor	3

RESTAURANTS, CAFÉS AND BARS

Ascoli	A
De Blauwe Kater	D
Lukemieke	F
Oestebar	B
De Troubadour	C
Universum	E

with the (half-built) Stadhuis just visible through the left-hand window; the two men standing up and the couple peeping through the service hatch are the rectors of the fraternity who commissioned the work. Dressed in a purple robe, the colour reserved for royalty, Jesus is depicted as taller than his disciples. It was customary for Judas to be portrayed in a yellow robe, the colour of hate and cowardice, but Bouts broke with tradition and made him almost indistinguishable from the others – he's the one with his face in shadow and his hand on his left hip. The change of emphasis, away from the betrayal to the mystery of the Eucharist, is continued on the side panels: to the left Abraham is offered bread and wine above a Jewish Passover; to the right the Israelites gather manna and below the Prophet Elijah receives angelic succour.

Also in the ambulatory is the **shrine** of St Margaret of Leuven, otherwise known as **Proud Margaret**, patron saint of serving girls. A thirteenth-century servant, she witnessed the murder of her employers, was abducted by the murderers, and then killed for refusing to marry one of them. If you work your way round the ambulatory from the right, her shrine is in the eighth chapel along, where her story is illustrated in grim detail by the paintings of the eighteenth-century artist Pieter Verhagen.

Museum Vander Kelen-Mertens

There are more paintings in the underrated **Museum Vander Kelen-Mertens**, which occupies an old mansion at Savoyestraat 6 (mid-Jan to mid-Dec Tues–Sat 10am–5pm, Sun 2–5pm; €5). The labelling is poor, so pick up the free English leaflet at reception. In keeping with the taste of their day, the nineteenth-century owners had a sequence of rooms kitted out in pseudo-historical style, and the ground-floor Baroque, Renaissance, Rococo and Neoclassical salons survive today. In them is an appealing assortment of stained glass, ceramics, Oriental porcelain and medieval sculpture. There's modern sculpture too – notably a couple of pieces by Constantin Meunier (see p.107) – and a modest sample of nineteenth-century Belgian land- and seascapes. The highlight of the museum, however, is on the floor above, where a small collection of medieval religious sculptures and paintings includes an exquisite *Holy Trinity* by Rogier van der Weyden. At some point, the painting has actually been altered: if you look closely at Christ's shoulder, you'll spot a pair of bird's feet. Originally, these were the feet of the dove that represented the Holy Spirit, but someone decided God the Father and the Son would suffice.

To the Groot Begijnhof

South of the Grote Markt is the boisterous core of Leuven's student scene, the **Oude Markt**, a large cobblestoned square surrounded by an almost perfectly preserved ensemble of tall gabled houses, now home to one of the liveliest collections of bars in the region. To the immediate east of Oude Markt, Naamsestraat leads south past the florid Baroque facade of the Jesuit **St Michielskerk**, restored after wartime damage, towards the wonderfully preserved **Groot Begijnhof**, a labyrinthine sixteenth-century enclave of tall and rather austere red-brick houses tucked away beside the River Dijle: from Naamsestraat, turn right down the little lane called Karmelietenberg and then take the first left, Schapenstraat. Once home to around three hundred *begijns* – women living as nuns without taking vows – the Begijnhof was bought by the university in 1962, since when its buildings have been painstakingly restored as student residences. Even now, when the students are out during the day, a tranquil atmosphere prevails.

Eating, drinking and entertainment

Leuven takes its eating and drinking very seriously, with a baffling range of establishments in which to exercise your stomach and liver. For **cafés and restaurants**, the first place to head for is **Muntstraat**, just southeast of the Grote Markt, a narrow pedestrianized street packed full of fairly formal restaurants, like an untouristed version of Brussels' rue des Bouchers. Walking eastwards along here you'll pass (to name just three of the many options) the *Ascoli*, at no. 17 (closed Wed), which serves up a big range of tasty local cuisine, plus Italian dishes; the gourmet *Oesterbar*, at no. 23 (closed Sun & Mon), probably the best seafood place in town; and *De Troubadour*, at no. 27, a large, smart place that's good for mussels, fish, pasta and pizza. If you want food that's not Flemish or Italian, the place to go is **Parijistraat**, just behind the Oude Markt, which has heaps of ethnic choices, ranging from Thai and Mexican to Moroccan and Portuguese. For something cheap but nourishing, the pub-like *Universum,* on the corner of Tiensestraat and Hooverplein, has a good range of snacks and inexpensive meals (along with a very respectable beer list), while *Lukemieke* at Vlamingenstraat 55 is a good vegetarian café (Mon–Fri noon–2pm & 6–8.30pm).

As a university town, Leuven is chock-a-block with lively student **bars**. The best selection (and setting) is in the **Oude Markt**, almost all of whose old gabled houses have now been turned into drinking holes, with a sea of people sitting out in the square itself in warm weather. The bars around **Grote Markt** attract an older clientele; again, there's plenty of outdoor seating under the imposing shadow of the Stadhuis.

There's regular live music at *De Blauwe Kater*, Hallengang 1, a nice courtyard **jazz and blues** bar with a good beer list. Just outside Leuven, the small town of Werchter plays host to Belgium's most famous open-air rock event, **Rock Werchter** (Ⓦ www.rockwerchter.be/index2.htm), featuring international stars such as Massive Attack, Pulp, Tricky, Beastie Boys and Travis; it's held over the last weekend of June or the first weekend of July. Special festival buses will take you from Leuven train station to the site.

Diest

In a quiet corner of Brabant about 30km northeast of Leuven, the small and ancient town of **DIEST** lies just south of the River Demer, its cramped but leafy centre still partly surrounded by the remnants of the town's once-mighty fortifications, built to guard the eastern approaches to Brussels. Militarily obsolete for many decades, Diest has seen more prosperous days, but it's still worth a brief visit.

The obvious place to start is the **Grote Markt**, an irregularly shaped area edged by trim seventeenth- and eighteenth-century facades and the hulking Gothic stonework of **St Sulpitiuskerk** (May to mid-Sept daily 2–5pm; free), whose interior is remarkable only for the wry, folksy carving of the choir stalls. A few steps from the church, the stately Stadhuis accommodates the **Stedelijk Museum** hidden away in the old vaulted cellars (Mon–Sat 10am–noon & 1–5pm; March–Sept also Sun 10am–noon & 1–5pm; €2), where the prime exhibits are some seventeenth-century suits of armour and a fearful, anonymous *Last Judgement* from about 1430.

More interesting is the **Begijnhof**, a five-minute walk northeast along Koning Albertstraat, one of the best preserved in this part of Belgium. Founded in the thirteenth century, the Begijnhof retains much of its medieval shape and atmosphere, with quiet cobbled streets and simple cottages decorated with statues of saints over the doorways. The main entrance at the far end of Begijnenstraat – a continuation of Koning Albertstraat – is marked by an extravagant Baroque portal with a niche framing a statue of the Virgin above a text that reads "Come into my garden, my sister and bride". Beyond the gateway, the weathered fourteenth-century **Begijnhofkerk** (May to mid-Sept 1.30–5pm; free), with its attractive Rococo interior, nestles among the rows of red-brick and whitewashed cottages that once housed the beguines. Many of the houses are now inhabited by local artists, some of whom open up their workshops at the weekend.

For devotees of nineteenth-century municipal fortifications, the **Schaffensepoort**, a ten-minute stroll northwest from the Begijnhof – back to the beginning of Begijnenstraat and turn right down Schaffensestraat – comprises a dramatic passage through concentric lines of ramparts and across the River Demer. Heavy, studded oak gates indicate an enthusiasm for defence that was superseded by the development of more effective artillery.

Practicalities

It's a fifteen-minute walk south from Diest **train station** to the Grote Markt: turn left out of the station building, take the first right over the river and keep going more or less straight ahead down Weerstandsplein, Statiestraat and Demerstraat. On the Grote Markt, in the basement of the Stadhuis adjoining the museum, the **tourist office** (Mon–Sat 10am–noon & 1–5pm; March–Sept also Sun 10am–noon & 1–5pm; ☏013 35 32 71), has free town maps and a list of local accommodation. There are two recommendable **hotels** in town. The classier option is *The Lodge*, at Refugiestraat 23 (☏013 35 09 35, ℱ013 35 09 34, ⓌÂwww.lodge-hotels.be; ❻), with eighteen comfortable rooms in an attractive old red-brick building – it's on a quiet but central side street off Statiestraat, between the town centre and the train station. Alternatively, there's the modern, three-star *De Fransche Croon* at Leuvensestraat 26 (☏013 31 45 40, ℱ013 33 31 59, Ⓦwww.defranschecroon.be; ❺), a five-minute walk south of the Grote Markt – take Berchmansstraat from the square and then the first right turn. There's also a **youth hostel** at St Jansstraat 2 (☏013 31 37 21, ℱ013 32 23 69; €12.50 per person; closed mid-Nov to mid-Feb), in a pleasant old house overlooking the city park, ten minutes' walk east of the Grote Markt: again take Berchmansstraat, but this time continue onto Botermarkt and take the first left along Wolvenstraat; keep dead ahead as far as the T-junction in front of the fancy park gateway, and then turn right.

Most of the town's **places to eat** are clustered around the Grote Markt. *Pergolesi*, at no. 28, has a good range of cheap and cheerful snacks and meals, while *Casino*, next door, serves well-priced, tasty local cuisine. The most atmospheric place in town, however, is *Gasthof 1618*, on Kerkstraat in the Begijnhof, adorned with all sorts of bric-a-brac ranging from pikes and swords to holy statues, though the main event is the excellent and inexpensive traditional Flemish food; wash it down with the locally brewed Gildenbier. For **nightlife**, *Café Leffe*, a convivial but sedate bar at Grote Markt 24, is about as lively as it gets.

Hasselt and around

The capital of the province of Limburg, **HASSELT** is a busy, modern town that acts as the administrative centre for the surrounding industrial region. A pleasant but unremarkable place, the roughly circular city centre fans out from a series of small interlocking squares, with surprisingly few old buildings as evidence of its medieval foundation. To compensate for this lack of obvious appeal, the local authority has spent millions of francs on lavish and imaginative prestige projects, from an excellent range of indoor and outdoor sports facilities to a massive cultural complex that aims to attract some of the world's finest performers. But perhaps more than anything else, Hasselt is associated with the open-air museum of **Bokrijk**, some 8km northeast of town, an extraordinarily comprehensive evocation of traditional village life featuring buildings brought here from every corner of Flemish Belgium.

The Town

There's nothing special to look at in Hasselt itself, although the **Gerechtshof** (Court of Justice) on Havermarkt, just off Grote Markt, is housed in the town's one surprise – a handsome Art Deco building, whose elegant interior of brown tiles, statuettes and lamps is in pristine condition. In addition, there are no fewer than seven **museums** in town, though ordinary mortals should settle – at most – for the best three, the Jenevermuseum, the Stedelijk Modemuseum and the Museum Stellingwerff-Waerdenhof. A combined museum ticket from the tourist office costs €5.95.

The most interesting museum is the **Nationaal Jenevermuseum**, at Witte Nonnenstraat 19 (Feb, March, Nov & Dec Tues–Fri 10am–5pm, Sat & Sun 1–5pm; April–Oct Tues–Sun 10am–5pm, also open July & Aug Mon 10am–5pm; €3). Sited in a restored nineteenth-century distillery, it shows how jenever – a type of gin – is made and details the history of local production, with a free drink thrown in. To get there, head north from the Grote Markt down Hoogstraat/Demerstraat and watch for the turning on the right. A left turn off Demerstraat opposite Witte Nonnenstraat brings you instead to the **Stedelijk Modemuseum**, Gasthuisstraat 11 (Feb, March, Nov & Dec Tues–Fri 10am–5pm, Sat & Sun 1–5pm; April–Oct Tues–Sun 10am–5pm; €3), with displays on the history of fashion from 1830 to the present. The **Museum Stellingwerff-Waerdenhof**, five minutes' walk east of the Grote Markt at Maastrichterstraat 85 (April–Oct Tues–Sun 10am–5pm; Nov–March Tues–Fri 10am–5pm, Sat & Sun 1–5pm; €3), features some lovely Art Nouveau ceramics and the world's oldest surviving monstrance. Dating from the end of the thirteenth century, this ornamental receptacle held the much-venerated Miraculous Host of Herkenrode, which was reputed to bleed if subjected to sacrilege.

About 1km out of town, the lovely **Jardin Japonais** (April–Oct Tues–Fri 10am–5pm, Sat & Sun 2–6pm; €3, though the combined museum ticket gives a discount) at Kapermolenpark is a joint venture between Hasselt and the Japanese town of Itami. The centrepiece is an impressive Japanese-style wooden structure known as the "house of ceremonies". To get there take the free bus, #H3, which runs every half an hour from the Hasselt train station.

Practicalities

The town centre is a ten-minute walk east of the adjoining **train** and **bus stations**. To get there, turn right out of either station and walk down Bampslaan to the ring road; turn right again for a few metres then left down Ridder Portmansstraat, and continue straight ahead down Havermarkt to reach the Grote Markt. Hasselt's **tourist office** is about 150m north of the Grote Markt, located down an alley off Hoogstraat at Lombaardstraat 3 (Mon–Fri 9am–5pm, Sat 10am–1pm & 2–5pm; April–Oct also Sun 11am–3pm; ☎011 23 95 40, ℗011 22 50 23, ⓦwww.hasselt.be). They provide free maps, information on Hasselt and its surroundings, and sell the combined museum ticket.

The cheapest **hotel** is the *De Nieuwe Schoofs*, opposite the train station at Stationsplein 7 (☎011 22 31 88, ℗011 22 31 66; ❷), but it's very basic and there are several more agreeable choices. Among them, the *Hotel Pax*, in a modern building at Grote Markt 16 (☎011 22 38 75, ℱ011 24 21 37; ❹), occupies a prime location and has reasonably comfortable rooms, while the *Hassotel*, Sint Jozefsstraat 10 (☎011 23 06 55, ℱ011 22 94 77; ❺), is a well-equipped modern hotel with Art Deco flourishes about five minutes' walk south from the Grote Markt – take Maastrichterstraat and turn first right. A few minutes from the Grote Markt, *Century*, at Leopoldplein 1 (☎011 22 47 99, ℱ011 23 18 24; ❹), is somewhat cheaper, and has a reasonable terrace restaurant as well as a good bar. Note that several of the town's hotels lower their prices at weekends.

Finding somewhere to eat isn't a hassle: there are numerous inexpensive **bars** and **restaurants** on the Grote Markt, and yet more on Botermarkt – off Hoogstraat opposite the tourist office – and the adjoining Zuivelmarkt. On the Grote Markt, the popular *Drugstore* brasserie, its facade bizarrely plastered with neon beer signs, is a good place for a snack. Alternatively, the *Martenshuys*, Zuivelmarkt 18, serves both light meals and more substantial dishes, while the cosy *De Karakol*, next door at Zuivelmarkt 16 (closed Mon), offers a varied, more upmarket menu including vegetarian dishes. A five-minute walk south of the Grote Markt, via Havermarkt and left along Cellebroedersstraat, *De Levensboom* serves exclusively vegetarian fare at bargain prices (closed Mon & Tues); it's at Leopoldplein 44 on the right-hand side of the square over the far side of the road.

Hasselt hosts one of Belgium's biggest rock festivals, **Pukkelpop**, in late August (ⓦ www.pukkelpop.be).

The Bokrijk Museum and estate

The **Bokrijk Openluchtmuseum** (April–Oct daily 10am–6pm, Oct until 5pm; €5.60) is one of the best of its type in the country, a series of reconstructed buildings and villages from various parts of Flemish Belgium spread out within a substantial chunk of rolling fields and forest. Each village has been meticulously re-created, each building thoroughly researched, and although the emphasis is still largely on rural life, it's a bias partly addressed by the reconstruction of a small medieval cityscape in its southwest corner. Perhaps inevitably, it gives a rather idealized picture, and certainly the assembled artefacts sometimes feel out of context and rather antiseptic, but the museum is tremendously popular and some of the individual displays are outstanding. An excellent English guidebook (€7.50) provides a wealth of detail about every exhibit, and the whole museum is clearly labelled and directions well marked.

The museum's collection is divided into five sections, each representing a particular geographical area and assigned its own colour code. The most extensive range of buildings is in the **yellow** sector, *The Poor Heathlands*, where there are a number of Kempen farmhouses, from the long gables of a building from Helchteren to a series of compound farms that come from every quarter of the provinces of Antwerp and Limburg. Other highlights include a lovely half-timbered blacksmith's workshop from the village of Neeroeteren, a bakehouse from Oostmalle, a fully operational oil-press from Ellikom, an entire eleventh-century church from Erpekom and a peat-storage barn from Kalmthout. In the same section – inside the wagon shed from Bergeyk – one particular curiosity is the skittle-alley and pall-mall. Throughout the Middle Ages, skittles was a popular pastime among all social classes, played in tavern and monastery alike. The original game had nine targets arranged in a diamond pattern, but this version was banned in the sixteenth century – because of the association of the diamond shape with gambling – and replaced by the more familiar ten-skittle game. Pall-mall, where heavy balls are driven through an iron ring with a mallet, was popular throughout Europe in the seventeenth and eighteenth centuries, but is now confined to some of the more remote villages of Limburg.

The open-air museum occupies most of the western half of the 1440-acre **Bokrijk estate**, whose eastern portion comprises parkland, woods and lakes as well as several marked attractions, principally a fine arboretum, with over three thousand shrubs and trees, and a marshland nature reserve (Het Wiek Natuurreservat). Crisscrossed by footpaths, this part of the parkland is open daily during daylight hours throughout the year and entrance is free.

Practicalities

There are two easy ways to reach Bokrijk from Hasselt: **bus** #46 leaves from the bus station every thirty minutes and halts beside the museum entrance; **trains** leave Hasselt hourly, take ten minutes and cost much the same, but drop you a five-minute walk away to the south. Right by the museum entrance are the nineteenth-century Kasteel Bokrijk – home to the estate's administration and an **information centre** – and the starting point for the toy-town autotrein that shuttles round the estate (but not the museum).

The museum's popular *St Gummarus* **restaurant**, straight ahead of the entrance, serves reasonable meals at affordable prices. There's nowhere to **stay** actually on the estate, and camping is not allowed, but accommodation is fairly near at hand in the Bokrijk **youth hostel**, Boekrakelaan 30 (☎089 35 62 20, ℉089 30 39 80, ℮bokrijk@vjh.be; closed mid-Nov to mid-Feb; dorm beds €12.50), reachable through the park and some 6km north of the train station – pick up a map at the information centre.

South of Hasselt

The **Haspengouw**, an expanse of gently undulating land that fills out the southern part of the province of **Limburg**, begins south of Hasselt, its fertile soils especially suited to fruit growing. Frankly, the scenery is rather dreary, though cherry blossom time shows it at its best, and the area's tiny towns and villages spread carelessly alongside the roads are without much charm or style. Even so, **St Truiden** and more especially **Tongeren** are well worth a visit for their small-town flavour and enjoyable range of historic monuments, while St Leonarduskerk, in the village of **Zoutleeuw**, possesses a splendid interior decked out with furnishings and fittings that survived the Reformation almost untouched.

Tongeren

Twenty kilometres southeast of Hasselt, **TONGEREN** is the oldest town in Belgium, built on the site of a Roman camp that guarded the important road to Cologne. Its early history was plagued by misfortune – it was destroyed by the Franks and razed by the Vikings – though it prospered during the Middle Ages as a dependency of the bishops of Liège. Nowadays, it's a small and amiable market town on the border of Belgium's language divide, quiet for most of week except on Sunday mornings, when the area around Leopoldwal and the Veemark is taken over by the stalls of Belgium's largest **antiques market**.

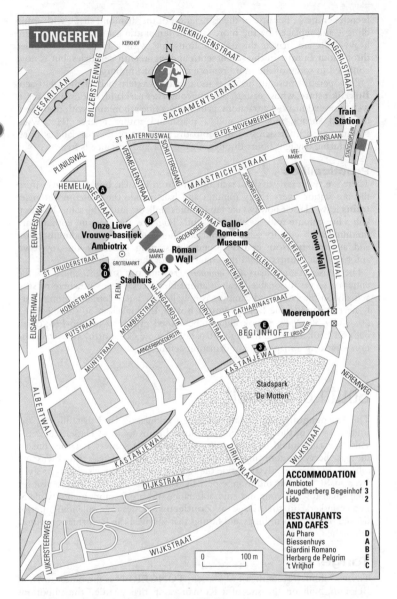

The Onze Lieve Vrouwebasiliek

In the Grote Markt, the mainly Gothic **Onze Lieve Vrouwebasiliek** (Basilica of Our Lady; daily 8am–noon & 1.30–4pm, Sun until 3pm; free) towers over the city centre, with an impressive, symmetrical elegance that belies its piece-meal construction: it's the eleventh- to sixteenth-century outcome of an orig-inal fourth-century foundation that was the first church north of the Alps to be dedicated to the Virgin. Still very much in use, the dark tomb-like interior, with its cavernous, vaulted nave, has preserved an element of Catholic mystery, its holiest object a bedecked, medieval, walnut statue of Our Lady of Tongeren – "**Mariabeeld**" – which stands surrounded by candles and overhung by a gaudy canopy in the north transept. Nearby, in the choir, an intricately carved retable depicts scenes from the life of the Virgin, and just outside are the well-preserved columns of the medieval cloister. The church's **schatkamer** (treasury; April–Sept Mon 10am–noon, Tues–Sun 10am–noon & 1.30–5pm; €2) is full of reliquaries, monstrances and reliquary shrines from as early as the tenth century. Bones and bits of body poke out at you from every corner, the best of which are a beautiful sixth-century Merovingian buckle, a pious *Head of Christ* and an eleventh-century *Reliquary Shrine of the Martyrs of Trier.*

The rest of town

Directly opposite the basilica, the haughty **statue of Ambiorix** is supposed to commemorate a local chieftain who defeated the Romans here in 54 BC, although in fact this "noble savage" owes more to mid-nineteenth-century Belgian nationalism than historical accuracy. A short distance away on the southern side of the Grote Markt, the graceful lines of the eighteenth-century **Stadhuis** are nicely balanced by an external staircase, the whole caboodle imitative of the town hall in Liège. Also close by, in the middle of Graanmarkt on the right-hand side of the church, a small section of the second **Roman city wall** has been carefully excavated. Dating from the fourth century AD, the masonry you can see actually covers the remains of a luxurious third-century villa, evidence that the city was shrinking – and its inhabitants becoming fearful – as the Roman Empire declined.

From here, it's a couple of minutes' walk east round the Onze Lieve Vrouwebasiliek and along Groendreef to the **Gallo-Romeins Museum**, at Kielenstraat 15 (Mon noon–5pm, Tues–Fri 9am–5pm, Sat & Sun 10am–6pm; €5). A flashy affair, the museum makes the most of the town's ancient history in its extensive and well-labelled collection of Roman, Gallo-Roman and Merovingian archeological finds. Finally, you could also take a peek at the angular **Moerenpoort**, one of Tongeren's six medieval gates, which dominates the southern end of Kielenstraat and doubles as the eastern entrance to the pretty little **Begijnhof**.

Practicalities

From Tongeren's **train** and adjoining **bus stations**, it's a five-minute walk west to the Grote Markt, along Stationslaan and Maastrichterstraat. The town's **tourist office**, in the Stadhuis (Easter–Oct Mon–Fri 8.30am–noon & 1–4.30pm, Sat & Sun 9.30am–5pm; Oct–Easter Sat & Sun 10am–4pm; ☎012 39 02 55, ℱ012 39 11 43, ⓦwww.tongeren.be), has details of a handful of **B&Bs** in the ❹ bracket, and will call ahead to make a booking. Another budget option is the *Jeugdherberg Begeinhof* **youth hostel**, St Ursulastraat 1 (☎012 39 13 70, ℱ012 39 13 48, ℮eddymanet@yahoo.com), a smart, modern place in the Begijnhof near the Moerenpoort. It charges just €10 for a bed, with family-, four- and six-bedded rooms as well as dormitory accommodation; reservations are advised. There are also a couple of central **hotels**, the two-star *Lido*, a basic affair with four rooms above its café-bar at Grote Markt 19 (☎012 23 19 48, ℱ012 39 27 27; ❹); and the rather more comfortable *Ambiotel*, beside the east end of Maastrichterstraat at Veemarkt 2 (☎012 26 29 50, ℱ012 26 15 42; ❺), a straightforward modern hotel with spacious rooms. For **camping**, the *De Pliniusbron* complex is in the municipal park at Fonteindreef 3 (☎012 23 16 07), a twenty-minute walk away: take St Truiderstraat west from the Grote

Markt, turn right down Beukenbergweg, the third road along, and head straight down past the eighteenth-century castle of Betho.

Places to **eat** include *'t Vrijthof*, by the Onze Lieve Vrouwekerk at Graanmarkt 5, which serves excellent French-style fish and meat dishes; and the popular *Giardini Romano*, Maastrichterstraat 17 (closed Thurs), which offers first-rate and inexpensive Italian dishes made with the freshest of pastas. Just off Grote Markt at Hemelingestraat 23, the upmarket *Biessenhuys* serves excellent French cuisine – fortunately the food isn't as tasteless as the cherub-encrusted orange facade. For something simpler, the old-fashioned, wood-panelled café *Au Phare*, Grote Markt 21, is good for cheap and simple snacks, including a big range of *gaufres* and crepes. The town's most atmospheric option, however, is the *Herberg de Pelgrim*, beautifully located in an old pilgrim's hostel of 1632 next to the Begijnhofkerk; this establishment has a menu of reasonably priced salads, pastas and meat dishes, plus a couple of vegetarian options.

Sint Truiden

Around 20km west of Tongeren, the small market town of **SINT TRUIDEN** grew up around an abbey founded by St Trudo in the seventh century and is today surrounded by the orchards of the Haspengouw. Known for the variety, if not the excellence, of its ancient churches, St Truiden is a pleasant, easy-going sort of town, with a good-looking centre. It's also the best place to catch a bus to the spectacular village church of Zoutleeuw.

The town's spacious Grote Markt – now turned into an enormous car park – is edged by an elegant eighteenth-century **Stadhuis**, whose flowing lines have remained discordantly attached to an older **Belfort** – the middle of three imposing towers that puncture the skyline on the east side of the square. On the right, the spire of the **Onze Lieve Vrouwekerk** has had a particularly chequered history: built in the eleventh century, it's been dogged by misfortune and ravaged by fire on several occasions. In 1668 the spire gave everyone a shock when it simply dropped off; it wasn't replaced for two hundred years. On the left, the untidy, truncated **Abdijtoren** also dates from the eleventh century, a massive remnant of the original religious complex that once dominated the medieval town, though it's now ignominiously topped by a fat radio mast. The abbey has been replaced by a dull and forbidding seminary that spreads out from the tower, though the grimy, ornate **gateway** does break the monotony, its carved relief showing the misogynistic legend attached to the abbey's foundation. The story goes that every time St Trudo tried to build a church, an interfering woman pulled it down; not to be thwarted, Trudo prayed fervently and the woman was stricken with paralysis.

The pick of Sint Truiden's many other churches are the yellow **St Gangulfus**, northwest of the Grote Markt down Diesterstraat (daily 9am–5pm), with a strikingly bare and unadorned Romanesque interior, and the similar but slightly grander **St Pieters** (same times), a ten-minute walk south of the centre along Naamsesteenweg, also dating from the twelfth century. For its period, the ribless cross-vaulting of St Pieters was experimental; the architect balanced the risk by deciding not to put windows in the upper walls.

Practicalities

St Truiden's **train** and adjacent **bus station** are on the south side of the centre. Buses run regularly to Tongeren (Mon–Sat hourly, Sun every 2hr) and Zoutleeuw (Mon–Fri hourly, Sat & Sun 3–4 daily; 10min). From the stations, it's a five-minute walk along Stationsstraat – or Tiensestraat – to the Grote Markt, where the **tourist office** is in the Stadhuis (April–Oct daily 9am–5pm; Nov–March Mon–Fri 9am–4pm, Sat 9am–1pm; ☎011 70 18 18, ⓕ011 70 18 20, ⓌWww.sint-truiden.be). They have free town maps and brochures with details of cycle routes in the surrounding countryside. There's just one central **hotel**, the spick-and-span, ultra-modern *Cicindria* (☎011 68 13 44, ⓕ011 67 41 38; ❺), part of a shopping mall at Abdijstraat 6 – take Diesterstraat north-west from the Grote Markt and it's the first turn on the right. For a **drink** or a **snack**, the *Bistroke* café-bar, on an alley behind the Stadhuis, is a lively and enjoyable spot, or there's the *Théâtre*, a more formal bistro-type affair on the south side of the Grote Markt, offering cheap pastas and more expensive salads and meat dishes.

Zoutleeuw

In a sleepy corner of Brabant, the hamlet of **ZOUTLEEUW**, some 7km west of St Truiden, was a busy and prosperous cloth town from the thirteenth to the fifteenth centuries. Thereafter, its economy slipped into a long, slow decline whose final act came three hundred years later when it was bypassed by the main Brussels–Liège road. The village has one claim to fame, the rambling, irregularly towered and turreted **St Leonarduskerk** (Easter–Sept Tues–Sun 2–5pm; Oct Sat & Sun 2–5pm; €1.25) has a magnificently intact Gothic interior and is still crammed with the accumulated treasures of several hundred years, being the only major church in the country to have escaped the attentions of both the Calvinist iconoclasts and the revolutionary French. The church is devoted to the French hermit St Leonard, whose medieval popularity was based upon the enthusiasm of returning Crusaders, who regarded him as the patron saint of prisoners.

The church's tall, light-filled **nave** is dominated by a wrought-iron, sixteenth-century double-sided image of the Virgin, suspended from the ceiling, and by the huge fifteenth-century wooden cross hanging in the choir arch behind it. The side chapels are packed with works of religious art, including an intricate altar and retable of St Anna to the right of the entrance in the second chapel of the south side aisle, and a fearsome St George and the Dragon in the Chapel of Our Lady on the opposite side of the nave. The **north transept** is dominated by the huge stone sacramental tower, nine tiers of elaborate stonework stuffed with some two hundred statues, which was carved by Cornelis Floris, architect of Antwerp's town hall, between 1550 and 1552. The **ambulatory**, much darker and more intimate than the nave, is lined with an engaging series of medieval wooden sculptures, most notably a captive St Leonard with his hands chained. There's also a figure of St Florentius, the patron saint of tailors, holding an enormous pair of scissors; and a thirteenth-century statue of St Catherine of Alexandria, shown merrily stomping on the Roman Emperor Maxentius, who had her put to death.

Buses run from outside the church to both Sint Truiden and **Tienen**, 15km to the west (Mon–Fri hourly, Sat & Sun 3–4 daily; 10min & 35min respectively). Opposite the church, the attractive sixteenth-century **Stadhuis** was designed by Rombout Keldermans and adjoins the handsome brick Lakenhalle, home to the **tourist office** (April–Oct Mon–Fri 10am–noon & 1–4pm, Sat & Sun 10am till 5pm; Nov–March Mon–Fri 10am–noon & 2–4pm; ☎011 78 12 88, ⓕ011 78 44 84, ⓌWww.zoutleeuw.be). For something **to eat**, the *Restaurant Pannehuis*, just behind the church, has decent, moderately priced French cuisine. There's nowhere to stay in Zoutleeuw.

Travel details

Trains

Antwerp to: Amsterdam (hourly; 2hr 15min); Bruges (hourly; 1hr 10min); Brussels (every 20 min; 40min); Geel (from Berchem Station only, hourly; 40min); Diest (hourly; 50min); Hasselt (hourly; 60min); Lier (hourly; 15min); Mechelen (every 20 min; 20min).

Diest to: Antwerp (hourly; 50min); Hasselt (every 30min; 15min); Leuven (hourly; 25min).

Geel to: Antwerp (Berchem station only, hourly; 40min); Herentals (hourly; 10min); Lier (hourly; 25min); Mechelen (hourly; 45min).

Hasselt to: Antwerp (hourly; 60min); Bokrijk (hourly; 15min); Diest (every 30min; 15min); Leuven (every 30min; 40min); Liège (hourly; 50min); Lier (hourly; 50min); St Truiden (hourly; 15min); Tongeren (hourly; 25min).

Herentals to: Geel (hourly; 10min); Lier (every 30min; 15min); Mechelen (hourly; 30min).

Leuven to: Brussels (every 30min; 20min); Diest (hourly; 25min); Hasselt (every 30min; 40min); Mechelen (every 20–30min; 20min); Tienen (every 30min; 15min).

Lier to: Antwerp (hourly; 15min); Geel (hourly; 25min); Hasselt (hourly; 50min); Herentals (every 30min; 15min); Mechelen (every 30min; 15min).

Mechelen to: Antwerp (every 20 min; 20min); Brussels (every 20min; 20min); Geel (hourly; 45min); Herentals (hourly; 30min); Leuven (every 20–30min; 20min); Lier (every 30min; 15min).

Tienen to: Brussels (every 30min; 45min); Leuven (every 30min; 15min).

Tongeren to: Hasselt (hourly; 25min); Liège (hourly; 30min).

Buses

St Truiden to: Tongeren (Mon–Sat hourly, Sun every 2hr); Zoutleeuw (Mon–Fri hourly, Sat & Sun 3–4 daily; 10min).

Tienen to: Zoutleeuw (Mon–Fri hourly, Sat & Sun 3–4 daily; 35min).

Hainaut and
Wallonian Brabant

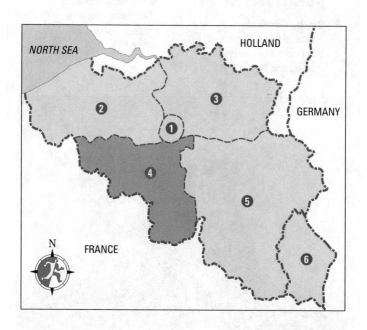

CHAPTER 4

Highlights

✳ **Cathédrale Notre-Dame, Tournai** – One of the most stunning cathedrals in the whole of Belgium. See p.284

✳ **The Château d'Attre** – An especially handsome country house with lovely gardens. See p.294

✳ **Binche Carnival** – Probably the liveliest, most colourful carnival in the country. See p.296

✳ **Villers-la-Ville** – The ruins of a Cistercian abbey here comprise one of the region's most evocative sights. See p.300

✳ **Chimay** – A charming country town with a picture-postcard Grand-Place and enjoyable country walks. See p.307

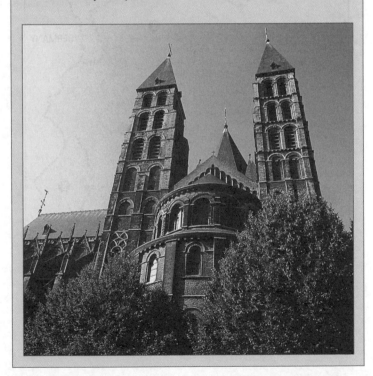

Hainaut and
Wallonian Brabant

S outh of Brussels, the western reaches of Wallonia comprise the province of Hainaut and the French-speaking portion of Brabant, Brabant Wallon. By and large, it's an uninspiring landscape with rolling farmland interspersed by pockets of industrialization, which coalesce between Mons and Charleroi to form one of Belgium's most concentrated belts of industry, but tucked away here and there are a clutch of fascinating old towns, the beautiful ruins of a medieval abbey and a smattering of country houses.

The highlight of Hainaut is **Tournai** in the western part of the province, close to the French border. Once part of France, it's a vibrant, unpretentious town, with a number of decent museums and a fine cathedral. East of Tournai, the agreeable if rather less impressive town of **Mons** is home to a fine Gothic church and a couple of interesting museums covering the town's role in both World Wars. Perched on a hill just to the east of the coal-mining area of the Borinage, Mons is also a useful base for seeing some of the region's more scattered attractions, especially if you're travelling by public transport. Within fairly easy striking distance of Mons and Tournai are several castles – of which **Beloeil** is the grandest and **Attre** the most elegant – and **Soignies**, a workaday town with an imposing Romanesque church. East of here, **Nivelles**, the principal town of Brabant Wallon, boasts an even more impressive example of religious Romanesque architecture in its church of Ste Gertrude, while the elegaic ruins of the abbey of **Villers-la-Ville** lie in a wooded valley just a few kilometres further east again.

To the south, the industrial and engineering centre of **Charleroi** is the biggest city in Hainaut by a long chalk, but it's an unappetizing sprawl with little to recommend it. South of Charleroi, the rural **Botte du Hainaut** is actually an extension of the Ardennes and is named for its position jutting into France; most of the "boot" is part of Hainaut, but it also incorporates a narrow slice of Namur province, which for touring purposes we've included in this chapter. Largely bypassed by the industrial revolution, the area is a quiet corner of the country, its undulating farmland and forests dotted with the smallest of country towns. Among them, Namur's **Walcourt** is the most diverting, a quaint old place that culminates in an imposing medieval church, with **Chimay**, which merits a visit for its castle and pretty old centre, running a close second. Just to the east, **Couvin** is also quite picturesque, and is well

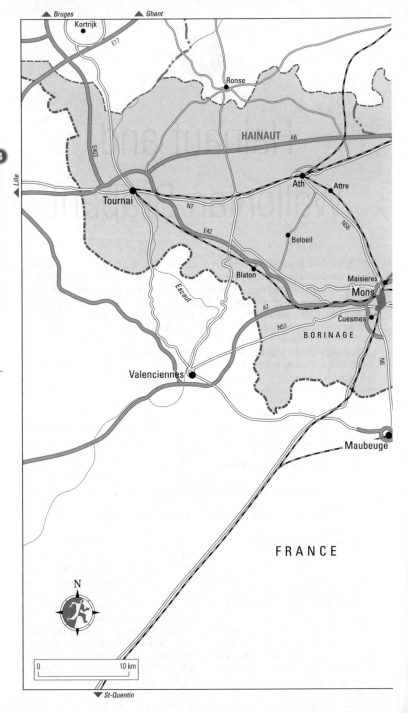

Bruges

Ghent

Kortrijk

E17

Ronse

HAINAUT A8

Lille

E403

Ath

Attre

Tournai

N7

N56

E42

Beloeil

Blaton

Maisieres

Mons

Escaut

Cuesmes

A7

N51

BORINAGE

N6

Valenciennes

Maubeuge

FRANCE

N

0   10 km

St-Quentin

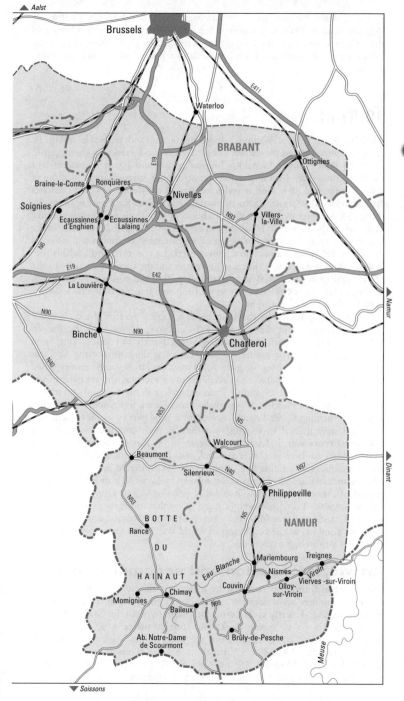

▲ Aalst

Brussels

Waterloo

BRABANT

Ottignies

E411

E19

Braine-le-Comte
Ronquières

Soignies

Nivelles

Ecaussinnes
d'Enghien
Ecaussinnes
Lalaing

Villers-
la-Ville

N93

N6

E19

E42

La Louvière

▶ Namur

N90

Binche

N90

Charleroi

N40

N53

N5

▶ Dinant

Walcourt

Beaumont

Silenrieux

N40

N97

Philippeville

N53

BOTTE

NAMUR

Rance

DU

Eau Blanche

Mariembourg
Treignes

N5

HAINAUT

Nismes

Viroin

Vierves-sur-Viroin

Momignies

Chimay

Couvin

Olloy-
sur-Viroin

Baileux

N99

Ab. Notre-Dame
de Scourmont

Brûly-de-Pesche

Meuse

281

▼ Soissons

endowed with facilities for holidaymakers, since hundreds of vacationing Belgians hunker down in cottages in the surrounding countryside. Outside of these three towns, each of which is readily reached by public transport and has a small supply of hotels and B&Bs, you'll definitely need a car – and sometimes a tent.

Tournai

TOURNAI is one of Wallonia's most interesting and enjoyable towns, its antique centre latticed by narrow cobbled streets and straddling the sluggish, canalized River Escaut (Scheldt). Tournai's pride and joy is its magnificent medieval cathedral, a seminal construction whose stirring amalgamation of Romanesque and early Gothic styles influenced the design of other churches far and wide. Most visitors zero in on the cathedral to the expense of everything else, but the town centre also holds lots of handsome eighteenth-century mansions in the French style – stately structures with double doors, stone lower and brick upper storeys, overhanging eaves, elongated chimneys and, often as not, fancy balconies and a central (horse-carriage) courtyard. Add to this several excellent restaurants, a clutch of lively bars and the town's proximity to the extravagant château **Beloeil** and **Attre** (see p.294), and you've reason enough to stay a night or two – especially as tourism here remains distinctly low-key, with barely a tour bus in sight.

The city was founded by the Romans as a staging post on the trade route between Cologne and the coast of France. Later, it produced the French monarchy in the form of the **Merovingians**, a dynasty of Frankish kings who chose the place as their capital – Clovis, the most illustrious of the line, was born here in 465. The Merovingians ruled until the late seventh century when they were deposed by a palace official, Pepin of Heristal, the ancestor of the Carolingians, but in the meantime Tournai had lost its capital status and reverted to the counts of Flanders. It was finally handed back to France in the twelfth century, remaining under French control for a large part of its subsequent history, and staying loyal to its king – despite English overtures – during the **Hundred Years War**. Indeed, the constancy of its citizens was legendary: Joan of Arc addressed them in a letter as "kind, loyal Frenchmen", and they returned the compliment by sending her a bag of gold. Incorporated into the Habsburg Netherlands in the 1520s, Tournai was retaken by Louis XIV in 1667. This next period of French control only lasted fifty years or so, but Louis left his mark on the town with the heavyweight stone quays that still flank the river, and in scores of handsome mansions. Sadly, much of central Tournai was damaged by German bombing at the beginning of World War II, but enough has survived to reward a thorough exploration.

Arrival, information and accommodation

Tournai's **train and bus stations** are located on the northern edge of town, about ten minutes' walk from the centre: head straight down rue Royale and, with the cathedral clearly visible, cross the Escaut to reach the Grand-Place and the major sites on the south bank. The **tourist office** is at rue du Vieux Marché-aux-Poteries 14, metres from the cathedral and just off the Grand-Place (April–June Mon–Fri 8.30am–6pm, Sat 10am–noon & 3–6pm, Sun 2–6pm; July–Sept Mon–Fri 8.30am–6pm, Sat & Sun 10am–1pm & 3–6pm; Oct–March Mon–Fri 8.30am–5.30pm, Sat 10am–noon & 2–4pm, Sun

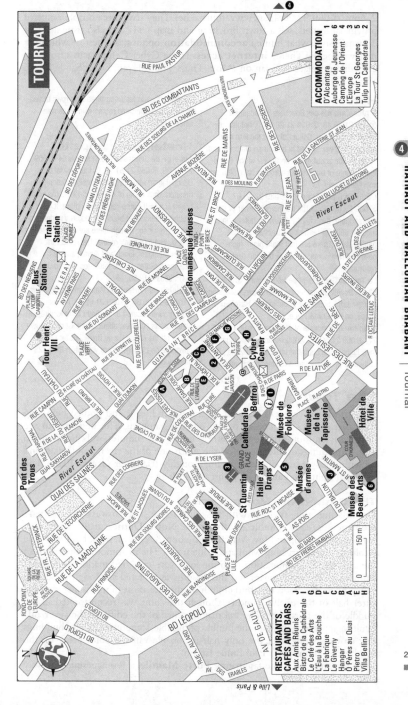

TOURNAI

RUE PAUL PASTUR

BD DES COMBATTANTS

RUE DES SŒURS DE LA CHARITÉ

ALL DES GRISELGELIERS

RUE DES CROISIERS

RUE DE MARVIS

AVENUE BOZIÈRE

RUE NEUVE

RUE ST BRICE

R DES MOULINS

RUE SIX-SILLES

RUE DE LA GALÉTIE ST JEAN

RUE ST JEAN

RUE RIFFÉE

QUAI DU LUCHET D'ANTOING

BD DES DÉPORTÉS

RUE DES NERVIENS

AV VAN CUTSEM

AV DES FRÈRES HAGHE

RUE MOREL

RUE DU QUESNOY

GATIENNES

RUE DE L'ATHÉNÉE

Train
Station
(PLACE
CROMBEZ)

RUE CHILDÉRIC

Romanesque Houses
ROND-
POINT
ST BRICE

RUE CLERCAMPS

River Escaut

Bus
Station

PLACE
CLOVIS

PL. GABRIELLE
PETIT

RUE DU
RIVET

RUE CATHERINE

RSTE CATHERINE

RUE DES RÉCOLLETS

R DE LA DESSUS

QUAI DONAT CASTERMAN

CARBONELLE

PLACE
VICTOR

AV LERAY

AV HENRI PARIS

RUE BEYAERT

RUE ROYALE

PLACE
DE MONNEL

RUE DE BRASSE

DES CORGES

RUE DE PONT

RUE DE MONNEL

RUE CAMBRON

RUE MADAME

RUE DES POISSONSCEAUX

R DES CARLIERS

PUITS L'EAU

RUE SAINT PIAT

RUE DE BÊVE

Tour Henri
VIII

PLACE
VERTE

RUE DE L'ÉPINETTE

QUAI SAINT BRICE

RUE DU BECQUERELLE

RUE ST BRICE & ST BRICE

DES CAMPEAUX

F
C
D
G
@ PL. ST
PIERRE
H

Cyber
Center

RUE DE CLARISSE

R DE CLAIRISSES

R OCTAVE LEDUC

RUE DU CHÂTEAU

R DU CURÉ DU CHÂTEAU

RUE J. HOXIDE

RUE ST BRUNO

QUAI DU MARCHÉ POISSONS

2
E

RUE DE LA LANTERNE
RUE DE L'HÔPITAL N D

B
A

RUE DE L'ABBAYE

P.P.E.
JANSON

R DES CHAPELIERS

FÊTE D'OR

R DES
PARIS

RUE DE PARIS

RUE DE LA TURE

RUE DES JÉSUITES

R OCTAVE LEDUC

Pont des
Trous

River Escaut

QUAI DES SALINES

RUE CAMPIN

R DE L'ARSENAL

RUE DU DISSUS

RUE DU CYGNE

RUE DE CORRIERS

RUE DES CHORAUX

RUE DES CHORAUX

RUE DE COURTRAI

RUE NOTRE DAME

RUE CURÉ

Cathédrale

Beffroi

PLACE
GARNIER

R ASTRID

Musée de
Folklore

Musée de
la Tapisserie

R ASTRID

Hôtel de
Ville

QUAI DU LOUVRE

RUE DU LOUVRE

R DU MARCHÉ
AUX POTERIES

GRAND
PLACE

RUE DE L'YSER

i

RUE DES PARIS

COUR
D'HONNEUR

R ST MARTIN

RUE MARCHÉ

RUE MUCHE

RUE DES VACHES

R DES JACQUES

RUE CARMES NOIRES

RUE D'ORREZ

3
St Quentin

Halle aux
Draps

5
Musée
d'armes

R DU BALLON

J

Musée des
Beaux Arts

6

Musée
d'Archéologie

1

RUE DES SŒURS NOIRES

RUE DES CARMES

PLACE DE
LILLE

RUE ROC ST NICAISE

RUE ST NICAISE

AS-POIS

BD BARA

BD DES FRÈRES RIMBAUT

RUE DE L'ÉCORCHERIE

RUE FR. J. PETRINCK

RUE DE LA MADELEINE

RUE FRINOISE

RUE BLANDINOISE

RUE DES AUGUSTINS

SQUARE
DE LA
REINE

RUE DE
TRÊTES

ROND-POINT
DE
L'EUROPE

BD LÉOPOLD

BD LÉOPOLD

BD DES ERABLES

AV DE GAULLE

AV DES ERABLES

RUE A. ALLARD

N

0   150 m

▲ Lille & Paris

▲ Lille & Paris

ACCOMMODATION

D'Alcantara	1
Auberge de Jeunesse	6
Camping de l'Orient	4
L'Europe	3
La Tour St Georges	5
Tulip Inn Cathédrale	2

RESTAURANTS, CAFÉS AND BARS

Aux Amis Réunis	J
Bistro de la Cathédrale	I
Le Café des Arts	G
L'Eau à la Bouche	D
La Fabrique	F
Le Giverny	C
Hangar	B
Ô Pères au Quai	A
Pietro	E
Villa Bellini	H

2–6pm; ☎069 22 20 45, Ⓦwww.tournai.be). They have a reasonable range of provincial leaflets, sell a town brochure and map (€1) and also issue a list of Tournai's somewhat limited **accommodation** options, the best of which are reviewed below. There's **internet access** at the Cyber Centre, across from the cathedral on place P E Janson (Mon–Thurs 11am–11pm, Fri & Sat 1–11pm, Sun 2–10pm).

Hotels

D'Alcantara rue des Bouchers St Jacques 2 ☎069 21 26 48, Ⓕ069 21 28 24, Ⓔhotelalcantara@hotmail.com. Delightful, chic modern hotel, the best in town, slotted in behind an old brick and stone facade about 400m northwest of the Grand-Place. Some of the fifteen bedrooms have pleasant courtyard views. ❺

L'Europe Grand-Place 36 ☎069 22 40 67, Ⓕ069 23 52 38. At the northwest corner of the main square, this slightly careworn hotel is in a modern building featuring a traditional high-gabled style. There are just eight plain, high-ceilinged bedrooms, all above the bar-cum-restaurant. ❸

La Tour St Georges pl de Nédonchel 2 ☎069 22 53 00. Dowdy, frugal rooms in an unprepossessing modern brick building just behind the Halle aux Draps, on the Grand-Place. ❷

Tulip Inn Cathédrale pl St Pierre 2 ☎069 21 50 77, Ⓕ069 21 50 78, Ⓔtulipinn.tournai@belgacom .net. Right in the centre of town, close by the cathedral. Spick-and-span modern hotel with an attractive facade featuring three long rows of windows, and comfortable rooms with all conveniences. ❺

Hostel and campsite

Auberge de Jeunesse rue St Martin 64 ☎069 21 61 36, Ⓕ069 21 61 40, Ⓔtournai@laj.be. Occupying an attractive old mansion a couple of minutes' walk south of the Grand-Place, the youth hostel is a well-cared-for, friendly place. It has around one hundred beds, the majority in dormitories of five or six, though there are also a handful of two- and four-bunk rooms. The restaurant serves breakfast, lunch and dinner, and self-catering facilities are available too. Closed Jan. Dorm beds €12.50, ❶

Camping de l'Orient rue Vieux Chemin de Mons 8 ☎069 22 26 35, Ⓕ069 21 62 21. All-year campground situated in the Aqua Terra leisure and water sports complex, about 3km east of the town centre off the chaussée de Bruxelles: turn south down rue de L'Orient before you reach the E42 motorway.

The Town

Tournai's town centre is bisected by the River Escaut and girdled by a ring road that follows the course of the old city ramparts. The best way to see Tournai is on foot – the town centre is only a few minutes' walk from end to end. Most things of interest are on the south side of the river, grouped around or within easy reach of the sprawling, roughly triangular **Grand-Place**. The principal sight, the **cathedral**, is just east of here.

The Cathédrale Notre-Dame

Dominating the skyline with its distinctive five towers is Tournai's Romanesque/early Gothic **Cathédrale Notre-Dame** (daily: April–Oct 9am–noon & 2–6pm; Nov–March 9am–noon & 2–4pm; free), built with the wealth of the flourishing wool and stone trades. The mammoth proportions of the cathedral in combination with the local slate-coloured marble were much admired by contemporaries and the design was imitated all along the Scheldt valley. The cathedral is the third church on this site, most of it completed in the latter half of the twelfth century, though the choir was reconstructed in the middle of the thirteenth. The full magnificence of the edifice is, however, difficult to appreciate through the jumble of humble, sometimes ancient buildings that crowd its precincts, the only half-reasonable vantage point being on the north side – from place Paul Emile Janson.

On this side too is the fascinating **Porte Mantile**, a Romanesque doorway adorned with badly weathered carvings of the Virtues and Vices. The scenes are hard to make out, but the animated, elemental force of the carvings is unmistakable. That said, you can spot Avarice, the man impeded by the money-bag round his neck, being carried off by a centaur-like Satan, and discern two knights engaged in brutal conflict, one soldier sticking his spear in the face of the other below. The **west facade**, on place de l'Evêché, also has some interesting carvings, with three tiers of sculptures filling out the back of the medieval portico. Dating from the fourteenth to the seventeenth centuries, the oldest effigies, along the bottom, are mainly drawn from the Old Testament and include Moses with the Sinai tablets and scenes from the story of Adam and Eve. The next tier up has reliefs illustrating the history of the local church, and finally come figures representing various apostles and saints. Adam and Eve appear again on the column between the double doors, this time almost life-size and separated by the Tree of Knowledge.

The interior

Today's **main entrance** is on the south side. Inside, the choir and nave are unexpectedly almost the same length, the stern simplicity of the design modulated by the tunnel-like communication galleries. The **nave** is part of the original cathedral structure, erected in 1171, as are the intricately carved capitals that distinguish the lowest set of columns, but the vaulted roof is eighteenth-century. The capitals were originally painted in bright colours, their fanciful designs inspired by illuminated manuscripts, imported tapestries and popular images of fearsome, mythological animals. The **choir** was the first manifestation of the Gothic style in Belgium, and its too-slender pillars had to be reinforced later at the base: the whole choir still leans slightly to one side due to the unstable soil beneath. In front of the choir, the Renaissance **rood screen** is a flamboyant marble extravaganza by Cornelis Floris embellished by Biblical events, such as Jonah being swallowed by the whale.

The ample and majestic late twelfth-century **transepts** are the most impressive – and most beautiful – feature of the cathedral. Apsed and aisled to a very unusual plan, they impart a lovely diffuse light through their many windows, some of which (in the south transept) hold superb sixteenth-century **stained glass** by Arnoult de Nimegue, depicting semi-mythical scenes from far back in Tournai's history. Opposite, in the north transept, is an intriguing twelfth-century mural, a pock-marked cartoon strip relating the story of St Margaret, a shepherdess martyred on the orders of the Emperor Diocletian. Its characters are set against an exquisite blue background reminiscent of – and clearly influenced by – Byzantine church paintings. Take a look, too, at Rubens' characteristically bold *The Deliverance of Souls from Purgatory*, which hangs, newly restored, beside the adjacent chapel.

Be sure also to see the **trésor** (Mon–Sat 10.15–11.45am & 2–5.30pm, Sun 2–4.30pm, except Nov–March closes 3.30pm throughout week; €0.75), whose three rooms kick off with a splendid wood-panelled, eighteenth-century meeting room and a chapel hung with a rare example of a medieval Arras tapestry. The tapestry consists of fourteen panels depicting the lives of St Piat and St Eleuthère, the first bishop of Tournai. The third room is crammed with religious bric-a-brac – reliquaries, liturgical vestments and so forth.

Among this assorted ecclesiastical tackle are two especially fine **reliquary shrines**. The earlier piece is the silver and gilded copper *châsse de Notre-Dame*, completed in 1205 by Nicolas de Verdun; it's festooned with relief figures clothed in fluidly carved robes, and the medallions depict scenes from the life of Christ. The second shrine, the *châsse de St Eleuthère*, is slightly later and more ostentatious, but doesn't quite have the elegant craftsmanship of its neighbour. There's also an early sixteenth-century *Ecce Homo* by **Quentin Matsys**, showing Christ surrounded by monstrous faces, and a wonderful Byzantine Cross, a classic example of seventh-century Constantinople artistry, its squat arms studded with precious stones.

The Grand-Place

A short stroll from the cathedral's main entrance, virtually on the corner of the Grand-Place, **Le Beffroi** (belfry) is the oldest such structure in Belgium, its lower portion dating from 1200. The bottom level once held a prison cell and the minuscule balcony immediately above was where public proclamations were announced. On top, the carillon tower has been subjected to all sorts of architectural tinkering from the sixteenth through to the nineteenth century – hence its ungainly appearance.

A few steps west of the belfry, the **Grand-Place** is an open and airy piazza equipped with a modern water feature, whose automated jets do very nicely. The middle of the square is occupied by a **statue** of Christine de Lalaing, in heroic "to the ramparts" pose, clad in armour and holding a hatchet. A local aristocrat, Lalaing led the locals in a last-ditch stand against the Spanish Habsburg army in 1581, but to no avail. The south side of the Grand-Place holds the seventeenth-century **Halle aux Draps** (Cloth Hall), a crisply symmetrical edifice, whose facade is graced by slender Renaissance pilasters and a row of miniature lions on the balustrade. The decoration has recently been picked in gold paint, but the interior, completely rebuilt after wartime bombing, is unremarkable. A few metres away, back towards the belfry, an alley – the reduit des Sions – leads through to the amiably old-fashioned **Musée de Folklore** (daily except Tues 10am–noon & 2–5.30pm; €2.50), housed in an antique high-gabled brick mansion known as the Maison Tournaisienne. Here, several floors detail old Tournai trades and daily life in the nineteenth century, but the reconstructions of various workshops and domestic rooms that form the bulk of the collection are not terribly spectacular. The highlight is the replica cloister on the second floor, where one of the cells exhibits the pathetic tokens left by those impoverished parents forced to leave their children with the nuns. Particularly affecting are the letters and playing cards torn in half in the vain hope that they could be rejoined (and the child reclaimed) at a later date – something which rarely happened.

The Tapestry Museum

Just southeast of the Grand-Place on place Reine Astrid, the **Musée de la Tapisserie** (daily except Tues 10am–noon & 2–5.30pm; €2.50) features a small selection of old tapestries alongside modern work, temporary exhibitions and a restoration workshop. Tournai was among the most important pictorial tapestry centres in Belgium in the fifteenth and sixteenth centuries, producing characteristically huge works, juxtaposing many characters and several episodes of history, and leaving no empty space – usually there aren't even any borders. Major themes included history, heraldry and mythology, and although several of the best surviving Tournai tapestries are in Brussels, there are a handful of good examples here on the ground floor. The pick are the three tapestries recounting Homer's tale of **Hercules** and his dealings with Laomedon, the shifty king of Troy. Hercules, dressed here in medieval attire, saved the king's daughter from a sea-monster, but then the Trojan refused to pay him the promised reward. Hercules had to sail away empty-handed, but swore vengeance, returning ten years later to capture Troy and slaughter the king. The tapestries are excellent and still richly coloured instances of the tendency to cram the picture with life and wry observation.

The Fine Art Museum

Just along the street, you can cut up through the gardens to the eighteenth-century **Hôtel de Ville**, the grandest of several municipal buildings that share the same compound. Behind the town hall, the **Musée des Beaux Arts** (Fine Art Museum; daily except Tues 10am–noon & 2–5.30pm; €3) occupies an elegant, Art Nouveau edifice, designed by Victor Horta (see p.105) and surmounted by a rather overblown bronze entitled *Truth, Empress of the Arts*. Inside, its pillars, grilles and low, soft angles provide a suitably attractive setting for a small but enjoyable collection of mainly Belgian painting, from the Flemish primitives to the twentieth century. The paintings, displayed in a series of interconnected rooms that radiate out from a central hall, are sometimes rotated, but in general the earlier works are concentrated on the left-hand side, so you may want to work round the museum in a clockwise direction.

The first room on the left is usually devoted to the nineteenth-century medievalist Louis Gallait, two of whose vast and graphic historical canvases – of the *Plague of 1092* and the *Abdication of Charles V* – cover virtually a whole wall each. Subsequently, Room E accommodates an exquisite *St Donatius* by Jan Gossaert; *The Fowlers*, by Pieter Bruegel the Younger; and a couple of big, fleshy pieces by Jordaens. Here also is a *Holy Family* and a *Virgin and Child* by Rogier van der Weyden, a native of Tournai known around here as Roger de la Pasture. Weyden's artistic output is further celebrated by a separate section containing photographs of all the paintings attributed to him and now exhibited round the world. The idea is to show what would be exhibited in the ideal Weyden gallery, a pleasant little conceit that works very well.

Among the more **modern** paintings are a number of works by French Impressionists. Manet's romantic *Argenteuil* and the swirling colours of Monet's *The Headland* – both in Room J – stand out, though they share the room with a couple of early, slightly tentative canvases by James Ensor, including *The Marsh*.

To the Archeological Museum

From the front of the Musée des Beaux Arts, a cobbled lane leads through to rue St Martin. Turn right (towards the Grand-Place) and then first left and you soon reach **rue Roc St Nicaise**, one of the town's best-looking streets, flanked by lovely old mansions of French inspiration with two lower levels of finely dressed stone beneath a third of brick. One of these old buildings, no. 59, now accommodates the **Musée d'Armes et d'Histoire Militaire** (daily except Tues 10am–noon and 2–5pm; €2.50), but the museum's miscellaneous military hardware is of limited interest. Neighbouring rue des Carmes is of similar appearance, if not quite as· polished, and here, at no. 8, the **Musée d'Archéologie** inhabits a rambling, rather forlorn old brick building (daily except Tues 10am–noon & 2–5.30pm; €2), part of which used to be a pawnshop. On display is a hotchpotch of local archeological finds, the ground floor being where you'll find the best of these – a heavy-duty, Gallo-Roman lead sarcophagus and a smattering of rare Merovingian artefacts, from weapons and the skeleton of a horse through to brooches and bee-shaped jewellery. The latter are thought to have come from the tomb of the Merovingian king Childeric, which was accidentally unearthed in 1653 – on place Clovis, just north of the river. Interestingly, Napoleon adopted the Merovingian bee as his symbol in preference to the fleur-de-lys.

The rest of the town centre

From the Archeological Museum, it's a five- to ten-minute stroll north to the thirteenth-century **Pont des Trous**, spanning the Escaut and the only part of the town's medieval ramparts to have survived. Also of some interest, northeast of the cathedral, is the riverside **quai Notre-Dame**, where many of the buildings were built during the Louis XIV occupation. Curiously enough Tournai was also English for five years from 1513 to 1518 when, having captured the town, Henry VIII promptly built himself a new citadel. Most of it disappeared centuries ago, but one of the towers lingers on, located in a tiny park near the train station. Known, logically enough, as the **Tour Henri VIII**, it's a cylindrical keep, with walls over 6m thick and a conical brick-vaulted roof. Nowadays it's home to the military hardware of the **Musée d'Armes et d'Histoire militaire** (daily except Tues 10am–noon and 2–5pm; €2.50). Also on the north side of the river are two restored **Romanesque houses** on rue Barre St Brice – dating from the late twelfth century, they're said to be the oldest examples of bourgeois dwellings in western Europe. You can't go inside, but their precarious, leaning appearance is convincing enough.

Eating and drinking

Tournai's **cafés** and **restaurants** throng the town centre, offering plenty of choices for an affordable snack or meal. The more predictable places tend to be on the Grand-Place, while the more interesting congregate down towards the river, on and around rue de l'Hôpital Notre-Dame and quai du Marché Poisson. As you would expect in Wallonia, the general standard is extremely high and the best restaurants offer truly superb food. The city's liveliest **bars** are down by the river, too.

Cafés and restaurants

Bistro de la Cathédrale rue Vieux Marché aux Poteries 15. Next to the tourist office. Staid decor, but excellent daily specials for around €11. This is *the* place to try the local speciality *lapin à la Tournaisienne* (rabbit cooked in beer). Family-run and with a good range of Walloon beers – try the Bush. Highly recommended.

L'Eau à la Bouche quai du Marché Poissons 8 ☏069 22 77 20. Trim little restaurant serving mouth-watering seafood, salmon and cheese dishes as well as vegetarian options. Set menus from €25. Closed Mon all day & Thurs eve.

Le Giverny quai du Marché Poisson 6 ☏069 22 44 64. Small, intimate and tastefully furnished restaurant serving exquisite French cuisine. Seafood is the house speciality. Set menus €20–30.

Ô Pères au Quai quai Notre-Dame 18 ☏069 23 29 22. Youthful café-restaurant whose speciality is grilled meat. Daily specials, including wine, average out at about €20.

Pietro rue de l'Hôpital Notre-Dame 15. Extremely popular Italian place, serving an excellent range of tasty pasta and pizza dishes at inexpensive prices. One of the best deals in town. Closed Mon & Tues eve.

Villa Bellini pl St Pierre 15. Quality Italian food in the enjoyable surroundings of a tastefully converted apothecary's – all porcelain drug jars and wooden shelving. It's reasonably priced, with pizzas hovering at around €9, other main courses – seafood and so forth just a few euros more.

Bars

Aux Amis Réunis rue St Martin 89. Dating back to 1911, this traditional Belgian bar has a good range of domestic beers, and its wood-panelled walls and intimate atmosphere make it one of the town's most agreeable watering holes. It also has a table for *jeu de fer* – a traditional game that is rather like a cross between billiards and boules.

Le Café des Arts quai du Marché Poisson 23. Offbeat café-bar with an animated crowd till early in the morning.

La Fabrique quai du Marché Poisson 13b. Busy, boisterous bar attracting a wayward, mostly 20-something clientèle.

Hangar rue de l'Arbalète 6. Post-modernistic decor and thumping sounds – a rare spectacle here in Tournai. Down a narrow sidestreet halfway along rue de l'Hôpital Notre-Dame. Closed Sun.

Mons

About half an hour by train from Tournai, the name of **MONS** may be familiar for its military associations. It was the site of battles that for Britain marked the beginning and end of World War I, and in 1944 it was the location of the first big American victory on Belgian soil in the liberation campaign. It has also been a key military base since 1967, when Charles de Gaulle expelled NATO – including SHAPE (Supreme Headquarters Allied Powers in Europe) – from Paris, SHAPE subsequently moving headquarters to Maisières, just outside Mons. Both continue to provide employment for hundreds of Americans and other NATO nationals – something which gives the town a bustling, cosmopolitan feel for somewhere so small. It's a pleasant town, too, with a smattering of attractions spread over the hill which gave it its name, and makes a useful base for exploring the surrounding countryside – despite the limited number of hotels.

Arrival, information and accommodation

Mons **train station** and the adjacent **bus station** are on the western edge of the town centre, on place Léopold. From here, there's a free bus shuttle to the Grand-Place, or it's a ten-minute walk up the hill: take rue de la Houssière and its continuation rue du Châpitre, which rounds the massive church of Ste Waudru, and then continue along rue des Clercs. The **tourist office**, at Grand-Place 22 (daily: April–Sept 9am–7pm; Oct–March 9.30am–6.30pm; ℡065 33 55 80, ℻065 35 63 36), has information on the town as well as a brochure describing the battlefield sites on its outskirts.

Mons is short of decent **hotels**. Of the six dotted round the centre, only three are of much appeal, beginning with the oddly named but very friendly *Infotel*, which occupies a straightforward modern block, just 100m off the Grand-Place at rue d'Havré 32 (℡065 40 18 30, ℻065 35 62 24, ✉syc@infonie.be; ❹). They have nineteen pleasantly appointed, modern rooms with TV and tele-

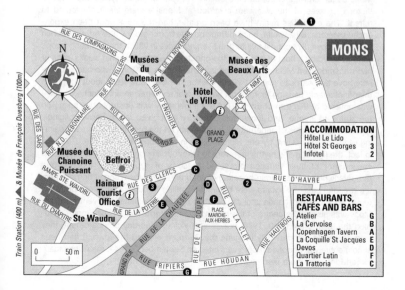

phone. Alternatively, head for the smart modernity of the *Hôtel Le Lido*, rue de Arbalestriers 112, at the top of rue de Nimy, a ten-minute walk north of the Grand-Place (☎065 32 78 00, ℱ065 84 37 22, ⓦwww.lido.be; ❻); here, the rooms have all mod cons and there's a gym and sauna. A third, less expensive choice is the *Hôtel St Georges*, rue des Clercs 15 (☎065 31 16 29, ℱ065 31 86 71; ❸), a well-kept if somewhat dowdy two-star hotel in nineteenth-century premises and with large, high-ceilinged rooms. The tourist office also has details of a handful of **private rooms** and **studios** (❷) for rent, though these are all on the outskirts of town and several are only available in July and August.

The Town

Mons zeroes in on its **Grand-Place**, a long and wide square which is flanked by terrace cafés and framed by a pleasing medley of substantial stone merchants' houses and narrower brick buildings, both old and new. Presiding over the square is the fifteenth-century **Hôtel de Ville**, a considerably altered building whose over-large tower was stuck on top in 1718. The tiny cast-iron **monkey** on the front wall is reputed to bring good luck to all who stroke him – hence his bald, polished crown – which is rather odd considering it was once part of the municipal pillory. Inside, some of the rooms are open for guided tours in July and August (1 daily; €2.50), though the odd fancy chimneypiece, tapestries and paintings are hardly essential viewing.

The porch of the double-doored gateway on the front of the Hôtel de Ville carries several commemorative plaques. One is for the food sent to the town by the Americans at the end of World War II, another recalls the Canadian

The Angels of Mons

Mons has figured prominently in both World Wars. During **World War I**, in the latter part of August 1914, the British forces here found themselves outnumbered by the advancing Germans to the tune of about twenty to one. The subsequent Battle of Mons began on August 26, and the British – in spite of great heroics (the first two Victoria Crosses of the war were awarded at Mons) – were inevitably forced to retreat. The casualties might have been greater, had the troops not been experienced veterans. Meanwhile, back in England, the horror-story writer Arthur Machen wrote an avowedly fictional tale for the *Evening News* in which the retreating troops were assisted by a host of bowmen, the ghosts of Agincourt. Within weeks, rumour had transmogrified Machen's bowmen into the **Angels of Mons**, who had supposedly hovered overhead just at the point when the Germans were about to launch their final attack, causing them to fall back in fear and amazement. Machen himself was amazed at this turn of events, but the angel story was unstoppable, taking on the status of legend, and those soldiers lucky enough to return home obligingly reported similar tales of supernatural happenings on the battlefield. There's a painting of the angelic event, by one Marcel Gillis, in the Mons Hôtel de Ville. This was, in fact, the first of many myths that were to take root among World War I troops: the sheer terror of their situation prompted all sorts of superstitions, legends and rumours, which had a morale-boosting effect both among them and at home, where the dreadful casualty figures were beginning to filter through. Angels or not, Mons remained in German hands until its liberation by the Canadians in November 1918. Mons was also at the centre of the fighting during **World War II**. The French occupied the town on May 10, 1940, but, after a vicious nine-day bombardment, they were forced to withdraw. By the time the Germans entered the town, it had been almost entirely abandoned. Four years later, on September 2, 1944, the Allies recaptured Mons after more fierce fighting.

brigade who liberated Mons in 1918 and yet another – the most finely executed – honours the bravery of the Irish Lancers, who defended the town in 1914. Cross the courtyard beyond and walk through the tunnel to reach the largest of the town's several museums, the **Musées du Centenaire**, which occupies a rambling brick building dating from the sixteenth century. The museum is currently being revamped, but its wide-ranging collection includes ceramics, coins and archeological finds, though the emphasis is on the town's involvement in the two World Wars. The invasion of 1940 was particularly traumatic for Mons: after the French withdrawal, the town was left virtually abandoned, with just 2000 remaining out of a population of 28,000.

The Fine Art Museum

Around the corner from the Hôtel de Ville, on rue Neuve, is the second of the town's recommendable museums, the **Musée des Beaux Arts** (Tues–Sat noon–6pm, Sun 10am–noon & 2–6pm; €2.50), whose mainly Belgian paintings range from the sixteenth century to the present day. Frankly, it's not an especially fulfilling gallery and its permanent collection is in any case only shown in rotation, but some of the (regular) temporary exhibitions are very good indeed and there are, in addition, a handful of superb paintings. Highlights include a striking *Ecce Homo* by the fifteenth-century artist Dieric Bouts, a mischievous *Soup Eater* by Frans Hals, and a ghoulish *The Entombment* by Paul Delvaux. There's also a good sample of the work of modern Hainaut artists, among whom the Expressionist **Pierre Paulus** (1881–1959) stands out – his *La Sambre* of 1912 is especially powerful, the figure of a desperate woman and child set by the eponymous river with a charred industrial landscape beyond. Trained as an architect, Paulus followed in the artistic footsteps of Constantin Meunier (see p.107), painting the coal mines and factories, spoil heaps and furnaces of Hainaut's industrial region with political intent. He was also a leading light of the Nervia Group, a school of artists who came together in Mons in 1928 determined to develop a distinctively Wallonian aesthetic, but unlike Paulus most of them preferred religious and allegorical themes and a classical style.

The belfry and park

To the southwest of the Grand-Place, **rue des Clercs** is one of the prettiest streets in town, shadowed by old mansions as it weaves around the hill that was once occupied by the medieval castle. On top of the hill today, at the end of a steep lane, stands the Baroque **beffroi** (belfry; no admission) and its miniature **park** (May to mid-Sept Tues–Sun 10am–8pm; mid-Sept to April Tues–Sun 10am–6pm; free), from where there are fine views over the town and its surroundings. The park incorporates a small tower that is pretty much all that remains of the medieval castle, as well as a British and Canadian **War Memorial** designed by Lutyens, and the **Chapelle St Calixte**, whose crypt was used as a bomb shelter in World War II.

The Collegiate Church of Ste Waudru

From the hilltop, it's a brief walk down to the late Gothic **Collégiale Ste Waudru** (daily 9am–6pm, 5pm on Sun; free), a massive and majestic church which displays a striking uniformity in its architecture, most memorably in the long, sweeping lines of the windows. The church is named after a seventh-century aristocrat, who did everything by the book: given away by her parents to a local bigwig, she was faithful in marriage and obligingly bore her husband four children, raising them to be singularly virtuous. One sort of duty successfully accomplished, she then had an amicable separation so that she could dedicate the rest of her life to the church, founding a small religious community here in Mons.

There is much to see inside the church, most importantly the work of the local sculptor, architect, builder and general factotum **Jacques du Broeucq**, whose alabaster rood loft (1535–39) was broken up by French Revolutionary soldiers in 1797, and is now spread around different parts of the church. Broeucq's high-relief carvings are simply wonderful, designed to explain the story of Christ to a largely illiterate congregation. To make deciphering easy, Broeucq stuck to certain clear conventions, dressing his soldiers in a rough approximation of Roman uniform and giving the disciples beards and gowns, but it's the detail that delights – from the gentle kiss at Gethsemane to the two incredulous fingers placed in Christ's wound after the Resurrection. The north transept holds the reliefs of the *Resurrection*, the *Ascension* and the *Descent of the Holy Ghost*, while the south transept has the *Flagellation of Christ* and the *Bearing of the Cross*, as well as Broeucq's memorial plaque. The *Last Supper* is displayed in the fourth ambulatory chapel on the north side of the church and is perhaps the finest piece of them all. The carving is so precise that you can spot the bread rolls and the chicken legs plus the face of Judas, turned away from the food as was the artistic convention.

The church **trésor** (March to mid-May & June–Nov Tues–Sat 9am–6pm, Sun 1.30–5pm; €2.50) is also of some interest for its assorted reliquaries and statuettes. Highlights include a thirteenth-century reliquary studded with no less than ten pieces from the Cross and several miniature tableaux by Jacques du Broeucq – King David playing the lyre and Moses with God's Tablets of Stone and so forth.

Incidentally, the over-elaborate, eighteenth-century **Car d'Or**, with its flock of fat cherubs, deposited by the north aisle, is the carriage that is used to transport the shrine of Ste Waudru around town on Trinity Sunday. The procession is followed by a mock-fight between St George and his 38 helpers, all good men and true, and the Dragon, who has his own entourage – devils, the Wild Men of the Woods and the Men in White. They slug it out on the Grand-Place and the crowd helps St George by pulling ribbons off the dragon's tail as it whips through the air just above their heads – no guessing who wins.

The Musées de François Duesberg and Chanoine Puissant

With time to spare, you might consider taking in two more museums of some mild interest, beginning with the **Musée de François Duesberg**, behind Ste Waudru at square Franklin Roosevelt 12 (Tues–Sun 1.30–6pm; €4). Housed in a solid nineteenth-century building, this offers a wide collection of decorative arts dating from 1775 to 1825 – porcelain, engravings, French gilded bronzes, bindings – as well as an eccentric collection of clocks. Nearby also, metres from Ste Waudru at rue Notre-Dame Debonnaire 22, the **Musée Chanoine Puissant** occupies a sixteenth-century house known as the Vieux Logis (Tues–Sat noon–6pm, Sun 10am–noon & 2–6pm; €2.50), and overflows into the adjacent Ste Marguerite's chapel on rue des Sars. The museum holds the private collection of the eponymous canon, who died in 1934 bequeathing an eclectic mix of chimneypieces, furniture, wrought-iron wares, and drawings to the city, the result of a lifetime's compulsive collecting.

Eating and drinking

Mons doesn't perhaps have the range of **restaurants** you might expect of a town of its size, but there's quite enough to be going on with. Pick of the less expensive places is *La Trattoria*, Grand-Place 31, a traditional, even old-fashioned Italian restaurant with red check curtains, decorative wine racks and, more importantly, a wood-fired oven churning out delicious pizzas from around €10. Quality French cuisine is on offer at two excellent restaurants, one of which is *La Coquille St Jacques*, in between the main square and Ste Waudru at rue de la Poterie 27 (℡065 84 36 53; closed all day Mon & Sun eve); the set menu here will cost you about €20, à la carte main courses a very affordable €13. The other is *Devos*, on rue de la Coupe 7 (℡065 35 13 35; closed all day Wed & Sun eve).

As for **bars**, *La Cervoise*, on the Grand-Place just along from the Hôtel de Ville, offers no less than 170 beers in workaday premises, while the *Copenhagen Tavern*, Grand-Place 11, has more atmosphere and a large enough beer menu for ordinary mortals. More youthful/studenty bars are clustered just south of the Grand-Place on and around place Marché-Aux-Herbes. Here you'll find the lively *Quartier Latin*, place Marché-Aux-Herbes 27, as well as the very fashionable-in-a-New-Age-way *Atelier*, at the junction of rue de la Coupe and rue des Fripiers. Both have substantial beer menus.

Around Mons

Railways and roads radiate out from Mons in all directions, putting central Hainaut's key attractions within easy reach and making for enjoyable day-trips; what's more, using Mons as a base avoids the difficulty of finding somewhere to stay – accommodation is thin on the ground hereabouts. The nearest and most obvious of these sights is the **Vincent van Gogh house**, southwest of the city in the suburb of Cuesmes, but this is disappointing and there are other much more worthwhile destinations. To the northwest, well on the way to Tournai, lie two very visitable châteaux – **Beloeil**, an imposing affair with extensive grounds, and the rather more enticing **Château d'Attre**; to the east is the quaint little town of **Binche**, which boasts one of Belgium's most famous carnivals; and it's northeast for **Soignies**, with its splendid Romanesque church.

Vincent van Gogh and the Borinage

The region immediately west of Mons is known as the **Borinage**, a poor, densely populated working-class area that in the latter half of the nineteenth century was one of Belgium's three main coalfields, an ugly jigsaw of slag heaps and mining villages. The mining is finished, but the cramped terraced housing remains, a post-industrial sprawl that extends toward the French frontier. In 1878, after a period in a Protestant school in Brussels, **Vincent van Gogh** was sent to the area as a missionary, living in acute poverty and helping the villagers in their fight for social justice – behaviour which so appalled the church authorities that he was forced to leave. He came back the following year and lived in **Cuesmes**, on the southern outskirts of Mons, until his return to the Netherlands in 1881. It was in the Borinage that van Gogh first started drawing seriously, taking his inspiration from the hard life of the miners: "I dearly love this sad countryside of the Borinage and it will always live with me."

Although the connection was instrumental in the development of the painter's career, there's actually very little to see. In Cuesmes itself, the two-storey brick **house** (Tues–Sun 10am–6pm; €2.50) where van Gogh lodged has been tidily restored, but inside there's merely a couple of rooms containing no original work and not even a reconstruction of how he lived. If you're determined to make a thankless pilgrimage, take bus #20 from outside Mons train station (every 30min) and ask the driver to put you off – the bus stop is 200m from the house.

Beloeil

Roughly halfway between Mons and Tournai, the château of **BELOEIL** (April & May Sat & Sun 10am–6pm; June–Sept daily 10am–6pm; €5) broods over the village that bears its name with its long brick and stone facades redolent of the enormous wealth and power of the Ligne family, regional bigwigs since the fourteenth century. This aristocratic clan began by strengthening the medieval fortress built here by their predecessors, subsequently turning it into a commodious moated castle that was later remodelled and refined on several occasions. The wings of the present structure date from the late seventeenth century, while the main body, though broadly compatible, was in fact rebuilt after a fire in 1900. Without question a stately building, it has a gloomy, rather despondent air – and the interior, though lavish enough, oozing with tapestries, paintings and furniture, is simply the collected indulgences – and endless portraits – of various generations of Lignes. Despite all this grandeur, only one member of the family cuts much historical ice. This is **Charles Joseph** (1735–1814), a diplomat, author and field marshal in the Austrian army, whose pithy comments were much admired by his fellow aristocrats: most famously, he suggested that the Congress of Vienna of 1814 "danse mais ne marche pas". Several of Beloeil's rooms contain paintings of Charles' life and times and there's also a small selection of his personal effects, including the malachite clock given to him by the Tsar of Russia. Otherwise, the best parts are the library, which contains twenty thousand volumes, many ancient and beautifully bound, and the eighteenth-century formal **gardens**, the largest in the country, whose lakes and flower beds stretch away from the house to a symmetrical design by Parisian architect and decorator Jean-Michel Chevotet – though even these are unkempt around the edges.

To reach Beloeil by **public transport**, take the train from Mons or Tournai to **Blaton** (Mon–Fri every 30min, Sat & Sun hourly; 20min) and then local buses from there; check bus times and routings at Tournai tourist office before you set out.

Attre and Ath

Completed in 1752, the elegant, Neoclassical **Château d'Attre** (April–June & Sept–Oct Sat & Sun 10am–noon & 2–6pm; July & Aug Thurs–Tues 10am–noon & 2–6pm; park and castle €4.50; park only €2.50) was built on the site of a distinctly less comfortable medieval fortress for the count of Gomegnies, chamberlain to the emperor Joseph II. It soon became a favourite haunt of the ruling Habsburg elite – especially the Archduchess Marie-Christine of Saxony, the governor of the Southern Netherlands. The original, carefully selected furnishings and decoration have survived pretty much intact, providing an insight into the tastes of the time – from the sphinxes framing the doorway and the silk wrappings of the Chinese room through to the extravagant parquet floors, the ornate moulded plasterwork and the archducal room hung with the first handpainted wallpaper ever to be imported into the country, in about 1760. There are also first-rate silver, ivory and porcelain pieces, as well as paintings by Frans Snyders, a friend of Rubens, and the Frenchman Jean-Antoine Watteau, whose romantic, idealized canvases epitomized early eighteenth-century aristocratic predilections. Neither is the castle simply a display case: it's well cared for and has a lived-in, human feel, in part created by the arrangements of freshly picked flowers chosen to enhance the character of each room.

The surrounding **park** straddles the River Dender and holds several curiosities, notably a 25-metre-high artificial rock with subterranean corridors and a chalet-cum-hunting lodge on top – all to tickle the fancy of the archduchess. The ruins of a tenth-century tower, also in the park, must have pleased her risqué sensibilities too; it was reputed to have been the hideaway of a local villain, a certain Vignon who, disguised as a monk, robbed and ravished passing travellers.

From the **Mévergnies-Attre train station**, on the Mons–Ath line, it's just over 1km to the château – just follow the road downhill from beside the station. Note that although the Mons–Ath train runs hourly every day of the week, it only stops at Mévergnies-Attre from Monday to Friday. The journey time from Mons is twenty minutes, five from Ath, which is also on the main Tournai–Brussels line.

From Attre, it takes the train just five minutes to pull into **ATH**, a run-of-the-mill industrial town whose main claim to fame is its festival, the **Ducasse**, held on the fourth weekend in August and featuring the "Parade of the Giants", in which massive models, representing both folkloric and biblical figures, waggle their way round the town. If you're in the area around this time, don't miss it; otherwise, you'll probably want to change trains pretty promptly – both Tournai and Brussels are but a short ride away.

Binche

Halfway between Mons and Charleroi, **BINCHE**, a sleepy little town at the southern end of Hainaut's most decayed industrial region, comes to life in February with one of the best, and most renowned, of the country's **carnivals**. Pretty much everything of any interest here is clustered round the **Grand-Place** – a spacious square edged by the onion-domed **Hôtel de Ville**, built in 1555 by Jacques du Broeucq to replace a version destroyed by the French the previous year. At the far end of the Grand-Place stands a statue of a Gille – one of the figures that dance through the city streets during carnival – sandwiched between the big but undistinguished **Collégiale St Ursmer** and the modern **Musée International du Carnaval et du Masque** (Mon–Thurs & Sun 9.30am–12.30pm & 1.30–5pm, Sat 1.30–6pm; €5), which claims to have the largest assortment of carnival artefacts in the world. Whether or not this is an exaggeration, its collection of masks and fancy dress from carnivals throughout Europe, Africa, Asia and Latin America is certainly impressive, and it's complemented by an audiovisual presentation on the Binche carnival and temporary exhibitions on the same theme.

Behind the Gille – and in between the church and the museum – a small **park** marks the site of the town's medieval citadel and contains what little remains of the former palace of Mary of Hungary. The park is buttressed by the original **ramparts**, which date from the twelfth to the fourteenth centuries and curve impressively around most of the town centre, complete with 27 towers.

Carnival in Binche

Carnival has been celebrated in Binche since the fourteenth century. The festivities last for several weeks, getting started in earnest on the Sunday before Shrove Tuesday, when thousands turn out in costume. During the main events on **Shrove Tuesday** itself, the traditional **Gilles** – males born and raised in Binche – appear in clogs and embroidered costumes from dawn onwards. In the morning they wear "green-eyed" masks, dancing in the Grand-Place carrying bunches of sticks to ward off bad spirits. In the afternoon they don their plumes – a mammoth piece of head-gear made of ostrich feathers – and throw oranges to the crowd as they pass through town in procession.

The rituals of the carnival date back to pagan times, but the Gilles were probably inspired by the fancy dress worn by Mary of Hungary's court at a banquet held in honour of Charles V in 1549; Peru had recently been added to the Habsburg Empire, and the courtiers celebrated the conquest by dressing up in (their version of) Inca gear.

Practicalities

To get to Binche, take the hourly **train** from Mons to Charleroi and change at La Louvière-Sud – allow forty to fifty minutes for the whole journey. Binche **tourist office** is located in the Hôtel de Ville on the Grand-Place (Tues–Fri 10am–12.30 & 1.30–6pm, Sat & Sun 10–6pm, May–Sept also Mon 1.30–6pm; ☏064 33 67 27), a ten-minute walk from the train station: take rue Gilles Binchois from the square in front of the station building and keep straight ahead until you reach the end of rue de la Gaieté, where you turn left.

Hotel **accommodation** is limited to the two-star *Hotel des Remparts*, rue St Paul 28 (☏ & ☏064 33 55 71; ❸), a cosy little place in a nicely revamped 1880s house with just six rooms, and a garden. It's situated about five minutes' walk from the church/park end of the Grand-Place. For **food**, the unfussy, family-run *Restaurant Industrie*, tucked away in a corner of the Grand-Place near the tourist office, serves hearty Walloon dishes at very reasonable prices – main courses average €12, *plats de jour* €7. The town has a couple of good **bars**, namely the *Taverne Chamade*, Grand-Place 44 (closed Mon, Tues eve & Wed), which offers a good range of beers in plain surroundings, and the Cote de Chez Boule, rue St Paul 13, a cosy little place with eye-catching Art Nouveau flourishes.

Soignies and around

About 15km northeast of Mons and on the Mons–Brussels train line, **SOIGNIES** is easy to reach, although there's nothing much to bring you here apart from the town's sterling Romanesque church, the **Collégiale St Vincent** (daily 8am–5pm; free), bang in the centre on Grand-Place, a ten-minute walk from the train station via rue de la Station. The church is dedicated to one St Vincent Madelgar, a seventh-century noble who was both the husband of Ste Waudru of Mons and the founder of an abbey here in 650. Work began on the church in 965 and continued over the ensuing three centuries, the result being a squat and severe edifice with two heavy towers. Inside, the church's pastel-painted, twelfth-century nave, with its chunky Lombardic arches and plain arcades, is similar to that of Tournai, while the transepts are eleventh-century, their present vaulting added six centuries later. The oldest section is the huge choir, dating from 960 and containing one of the church's

△ Gilles at carnival

most outstanding features, a set of Renaissance choir stalls from 1576. Look out also for the finely crafted fifteenth-century terracotta entombment on the south side of the choir, and the fourteenth-century polychrome Virgin beneath the rood screen. If all this has given you a thirst, wet your whistle at *Les Armoiries*, an old-fashioned brown **bar** near the church at Grand-Place 7.

Ronquières and Ecaussinnes

To the east of Soignies lies one of the quietest corners of Hainaut, a pocket-sized district where drowsy little villages and antique, whitewashed farmhouses are scattered over a bumpy landscape patterned by a maze of narrow country lanes. If you're travelling by car – and especially if you're heading for Nivelles (see p.298) – the district makes for a pleasant detour, but is ill-served by public transport.

The most obvious starting point is **RONQUIÈRES**, about 15km east of Soignies. Here, on the edge of the village – just follow the signs – is a massive transporter lock that's part of the Charleroi–Brussels canal. When it was completed in 1968, this gargantuan contraption cut the journey time between Charleroi and Brussels by around seven hours, a saving of around 25 percent. The lock consists of two huge water tanks, each 91m long, and a ramp, which together shift barges up or down 70m over a distance of 1500m. The main **tower** houses the winch room, runs a video explaining how the whole thing works and, best of all, gives a bird's-eye view of proceedings (April–Oct daily 10am–7pm; €7). There are also hour-long boat trips through the lock (May–Aug Tues & Thurs–Sun 4 daily; €2.50, combined ticket with tower €8), though the tower should be quite sufficient for all but the most enthusiastic.

South of here, it's just 5km to the twin villages of **Ecaussinnes** – industrial d'Enghien to the west and prettier Lalaing to the east – though be warned that the signposted route, along a baffling series of lanes, is easy to lose and hard to rediscover; then again the scenery is delightful. There's just one specific sight, Ecaussinnes Lalaing's frumpy **castle** (April–June, Sept & Oct Sat & Sun 10am–noon & 2–6pm; July & Aug Thurs–Mon 10am–noon & 2–6pm; €5), an imposing towered and turreted edifice stuck on a rocky knoll. The earliest parts of the structure date from the twelfth century, though most of it is the result of much later modifications. Inside, the big and sparsely furnished rooms are hardly essential viewing, but highlights include two fine early sixteenth-century chimneypieces in the hall and armoury, an extremely well-preserved fifteenth-century kitchen and small but high-quality examples of glassware and Tournai porcelain.

Into Brabant: Nivelles and Villers-la-Ville

Travel any distance north or east of Soignies and you cross the border into **Brabant**, whose southern French-speaking districts – known as Brabant Wallon – form a band of countryside that rolls up to and around Waterloo (see p.123), which is now pretty much a suburb of Brussels. **Nivelles** is the obvious distraction en route, an amiable, workaday town worth a visit for its interesting church as well as its proximity to the beguiling ruins of the Cistercian abbey at **Villers-la-Ville**, a short car ride away (train travellers have to make the trip via Charleroi).

Nivelles

NIVELLES grew up around its abbey, which was founded in the seventh century and became one of the most powerful religious houses in Brabant until its suppression by the French Revolutionary Army in 1798. Nowadays, the abbey is recalled by the town's one and only significant sight, the **Collégiale Ste Gertrude** (daily 9am–6pm, mid-Oct to mid-April till 5pm; free), a sprawling edifice erected as the abbey church in the tenth century and distinguished by a huge and strikingly handsome chancel. The church was founded by a Frankish queen, Itta, but is named after her daughter, who she appointed as the first abbess. Little is known of Gertrude, though she certainly imported Irish priests to convert the locals, but her cult was very popular on account of her supposed gentleness – her symbol is a pastoral staff with a mouse running along it. The church has fared badly over the centuries, suffering fire damage on no less than nineteen occasions, most recently during World War II, and inevitably has become something of an architectural hotchpotch, though it's in better shape now than it has been for years following a long-winded restoration. The design is a rare example of an abbey church in the **Ottonian** style, the forerunner of Romanesque; the style was created when Byzantine, early Christian and Carolingian influences were brought together during the reign of the tenth-century Holy Roman Emperor Otto the Great, and his successors.

In terms of the Collégiale Ste Gertrude, Ottonian precepts are reflected by the presence of a transept and a chancel at each end of the nave. The west chancel represents imperial authority, the east papal – an architectural illustration of the tension between the pope and the emperor that defined much of Otto's reign. The **interior** is extremely simple, its long and lofty nave equipped with a flat concrete roof painted in imitation of the wooden original. Between the pillars of the nave is a flashy oak and marble **pulpit** by the eighteenth-century Belgian artist Laurent Delvaux, while the heavily restored, fifteenth-century **wooden wagon**, in the west chancel to the left of the entrance, was used to carry the shrine of St Gertrude in procession through the fields once a year. Unfortunately, the original thirteenth-century shrine was destroyed in 1940, but a modern replacement has been made and the traditional autumn procession has recently been revived.

The **guided tours** are worth considering even if you don't understand French, as they explore parts of the church that are otherwise out of bounds (Mon–Fri at 2pm, Sat & Sun 2pm & 3.30pm; 1hr 30min; €5; reservations on ☏067 21 93 58). They begin by heading upstairs to the large Salle Impériale over the west choir. The function of the room is unknown, but today it's used to house a few ecclesiastical bits and pieces, including the copy of Ste Gertrude's shrine alongside the remains of the original. The tour continues to the large Romanesque crypt, where the foundations of a Merovingian chapel and church (seventh-century) and three Carolingian churches (ninth- and tenth-century) have been discovered, as well as the tombs of Ste Gertrude and some of her relations.

With time to spare after visiting the church, you could drop by the **Musée Communal d'Archéologie**, in the old ivy-clad house a couple of minutes' walk north off the main square at rue de Bruxelles 27 (daily 9.30am–5pm; €1). The ground floor features assorted displays of fine and applied art – everything from locks, keys and weapons through to tapestries, sculptures and paintings. Much of the material on display has actually come from the church, notably four Brabantine Gothic statues of the Apostles from the former rood screen and the splendid terracotta sculptures by Delvaux. Upstairs is a ragbag of local archeological finds, beginning with prehistoric times and ploughing on through the Gallo-Roman period to the Merovingians.

Practicalities

It's a ten-minute walk west down from Nivelles' **train station** to the L-shaped Grand-Place – and the Collégiale Ste Gertrude – along rue de Namur. The tourist office is just off the Grand-Place, near the entrance to the church on place Albert 1er (Mon–Fri 8.30am–1pm & 2–4.30pm, April–Sept also Sat & Sun 9am–4pm; ☏067 84 08 64).

With Brussels so near (30min by train), there's no real reason to hang around after you've visited the church, but there is one central **hotel**, the unexceptional *Commerce*, at Grand-Place 7 (☏067 21 12 41; ❸). The **cafés** edging the Grand-Place are fine for a coffee and a snack, but if you're after anything more substantial, head for the *Restaurant Le 1er Avril*, rue Ste Anne 5, where they serve quality French cuisine at affordable prices: a set three-course lunch costs in the region of €20, main courses €15. Rue Ste Anne leads off the railway-station side of the Grand-Place, to the right of the church.

Villers-la-Ville

The ruined Cistercian abbey of **VILLERS-LA-VILLE** (April–Oct daily 10am–6pm; Nov–March daily except Tues 10am–5pm; €3.80) nestles in a lovely wooded dell just off the N93 some 16km east of Nivelles – and 35km south of Brussels – and is altogether one of the most haunting and evocative sights in the whole of Belgium. The first monastic community settled here in 1146, consisting of just one abbot and twelve monks. Subsequently the abbey became a wealthy local landowner, managing a domain of several thousand acres, with numbers that rose to about a hundred monks and three hundred lay brothers. A healthy annual income funded the construction of an extensive monastic complex, most of which was erected in the thirteenth century, though the less austere structures, such as the Abbot's Palace, went up in a second spurt of activity some four hundred years later. In 1794 French revolutionaries ransacked the monastery, and later a railway was ploughed through the grounds, but more than enough survives – albeit in various states of decay – to pick out Romanesque, Gothic and Renaissance features and to make some kind of mental reconstruction of abbey life possible.

From the entrance a path crosses the courtyard in front of the Abbot's Palace to reach the **warming room** (*chauffoir*), the only place in the monastery where a fire would have been kept going all winter, and which still has its original chimney. The fire provided a little heat to the adjacent rooms: on one side the monks' **workroom** (*salle des moines*), used for reading and studying; on the other the large Romanesque-Gothic **refectory** (*réfectoire*), lit by ribbed twin windows topped with chunky rose windows. Next door is the **kitchen** (*cuisine*), which contains a few remnants of the drainage system, which once piped waste to the river, and of a central hearth, whose chimney helped air the room. Just behind this lies the **pantry** (*salle des convers*), where a segment of the original vaulting has survived, supported by a single column, and beyond, on the northwestern edge of the complex, is the **brewery** (*brasserie*), one of the biggest and oldest buildings in the abbey.

The most spectacular building, however, is the **church** (*église*), which fills out the north corner of the complex. With pure lines and elegant proportions, it displays the change from Romanesque to Gothic – the transept and choir are the first known examples of Gothic in the Brabant area. The building has the dimensions of a cathedral, 90m long and 40m wide, with a majestic nave whose roof was supported on strong cylindrical columns. An unusual feature is the series of bull's-eye windows which light the transepts. Of the original twelfth-century **cloister** (*cloître*) adjoining the church, a pair of twin windows is pretty much all that remains, flanked by a two-storey section of the old monks' quarters. Around the edge of the cloister are tombstones and the solitary sarcophagus of the crusader Gobert d'Aspremont.

Practicalities

There is no public transport direct from Nivelles to Villers-la-Ville, but you can still make the trip by **train**. Every half-hour (hourly at the weekend) a service links Nivelles with Charleroi, where an hourly train (every 2hr at the weekend) goes to Villers-la-Ville; allow about an hour for the whole journey, twenty minutes more on the weekend. To get here from Brussels, catch a Namur train and change at Ottignies – reckon on an hour to an hour and a half depending on connections. The abbey is 1600m from Villers-la-Ville **train station**, which consists of just two platforms. Near the platforms you'll spot a small, faded sign to Monticelli; follow the sign and you'll head up and over a little slope until, after about 100m, you reach a T-junction; turn right and follow the road round.

At the abbey entrance, they sell both an in-depth English guide to the ruins and a French booklet detailing local walks. They also have details of the theatrical productions that are sometimes staged here in the summer. There's also a **tourist office** (May–Sept Tues–Thurs 11.30am–1.30pm & 2–5pm; ☎071 87 98 98), across from the abbey entrance (to the left) in the building that once served as the main abbey gateway. There's no accommodation.

Charleroi

The approaches to **CHARLEROI** are hardly inviting. Decaying factories and grass-covered slag heaps litter the outskirts, while the centre is pressed hard by a whopping steel plant. Glassworks, coal mines and iron foundries made the town the centre of one of Belgium's main industrial areas at the beginning of the nineteenth century, and, although you can reach it from just about anywhere in Belgium, frankly there's little reason to do so. You might, however, find yourself passing through in the course of travelling south to the Botte du Hainaut (see p.304) or east to Namur (see p.316), perhaps via the abbey at Floreffe (see p.322), in which case you'll find Charleroi offers a couple of decent museums to investigate – and a trio of comfortable hotels too.

The Town

Charleroi's large and untidy centre begins promisingly enough down by the **River Sambre** with newly revamped **place Buisset**, an attractive modern square which is just about as near as the town gets to being pretty – the adjacent bridge sports two statues of workers by Constantin Meunier. Place Buisset also marks the start of the **lower town**, which piles up a steep ridge on its way to the **upper town**. The latter was once the site of a substantial fortress, built on the top of the hill in the 1660s – hence today's gridiron street plan – and is now the social and administrative centre. In the middle of the upper town, a brisk ten- to fifteen-minute walk from the river, is **place Charles II**, a care-worn, traffic-choked square, whose western edge is overlooked by the **Hôtel de Ville** of 1936. This is home to Charleroi's best museum, the **Musée des Beaux Arts** (Tues–Sat 9am–5pm; €1.50) – though note that the entrance is round the back at the far end of rue du Dauphin, and at the top of a handsome Art Deco staircase. The museum has a very good collection of Hainaut artists, supplemented by the work of other Belgian painters who lived or worked here. Highlights include the romantic Neoclassical paintings of Charleroi artist François Joseph Navez as well as the contrasting naturalism of Constantin Meunier, whose grim vision of industrial life was balanced by the heroism he saw in the working class. There are also a number of canvases by the talented Pierre Paulus (see p.291), whose oeuvre takes up where Meunier leaves off – and arguably with greater panache, as in *Jeunesse* and *La Berceuse*, in which a mother soothes her child. There are also six paintings by one-time Charleroi resident René Magritte, most notably the whimsical *La Liberté de l'Esprit*, and an indifferent *Annunciation* by Delvaux. Finally, a metal staircase leads up to the attic, where there's a display on the life and times of one Jules Destrée, a local poet, lawyer and socialist politician who campaigned hard for improvements in working conditions in Wallonia during the early years of the twentieth century. He also had little truck with the idea of a united, centralized Belgian state,

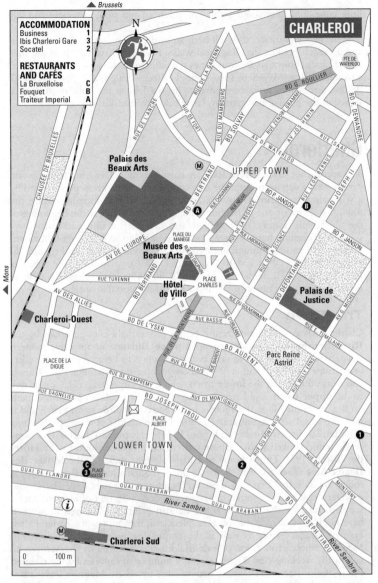

famously writing to King Albert that "the word 'Belgian' has lost all meaning".
Charleroi's other good museum is the inventive **Musée de la Photographie**
(Tue–Sun 10am–6pm; €3.75), housed in the imaginatively renovated neo-
Gothic Carmelite monastery of Mont-sur-Marchienne. Unfortunately, it's a
good 5km southwest from the centre, at avenue Paul Pastur 11, though it's
reachable from Charleroi-Sud train station on buses #70, #71 and #170; ask
the driver to put you off. The museum holds a thought-provoking

Founded by the Spanish in 1666, Charleroi was named after **Charles II** (1661–1700), the last Habsburg king of Spain. He was the son of Philip IV, who sired no less than fourteen children, though only one of his sons – Charles – reached his 20s. With women banned from the succession, the hapless, sickly Charles became king at the tender age of 4 and, much to everyone's surprise, survived to adulthood. After his first marriage in 1679, there were great hopes that he would be able to beget an **heir**, but none arrived, probably because Charles suffered from premature ejaculation. A second marriage, twenty years later, was equally fruitless and, as it became increasingly clear Charles was unable to procreate, Europe focused on what was to happen when Charles died and the Spanish Habsburg line died out. Every ambassador to the Spanish court wrote long missives home about the health of Charles, no one more so than the English representative, **Stanhope**, who painted an especially gloomy picture: "He (Charles) has a ravenous stomach and swallows all he eats whole, for his nether jaw stands out so much that his two rows of teeth cannot meet…His weak stomach not being able to digest the food, he voids it in the same (whole) manner."

In the autumn of 1700, it was clear that Charles was dying and his doctors went to work in earnest, replacing his pillows with freshly killed pigeons and covering his chest with animal entrails. Surprise, surprise, this didn't work and Charles **died** on the first of November, his death leading directly to the **War of the Spanish Succession** (1701–14).

collection of nearly sixty thousand creative and documentary-style photographs, which are displayed in rotation. There's also a well-organized and reasonably interesting permanent exhibition, which takes you through the history of photography to the present day. Temporary exhibitions are held regularly too.

Practicalities

Charleroi has two **train stations**, Charleroi-Sud by the River Sambre, where you're likely to arrive, and less important Charleroi-Ouest, a short walk west of the upper town. The town's **airport** – rather sharply called Brussels-Charleroi – is 6km north of town; Ryanair fly here from England, Scotland and Ireland (see p.12). The **tourist office** occupies a kiosk in front of Charleroi-Sud station (Mon–Fri 9am–12.30pm & 1–5.30pm, Sat 10am–4pm & Sun 9am–1pm; ☏071 86 61 52, ⓦwww.charleroi.be) and hands out free city maps and leaflets. Charleroi-Sud station also acts as the hub for local **buses**, most usefully a shuttle service to the upper town's place du Manège – a route that is followed by the town's pocket-sized **métro**.

The most comfortable **hotel** in town is the three-star *Business*, which occupies a straightforward modern block to the east of the lower town at boulevard Mayence 1A (☏071 30 24 24, ⓕ071 30 49 49; ⓦwww.businesshotel.be; ❺); it has just over fifty pleasantly appointed modern rooms and those on the upper floors have views over town. Very similar is the four-star *Socatel*, boulevard Tirou 96 (☏071 31 98 11, ⓕ071 30 15 96; ⓦwww.hotelsocatel.be; ❺). A third option is the three-star *Ibis Charleroi Gare*, in an older, thoroughly restored block overlooking the river and across from Charleroi-Sud station at quai de Flandre 12 (☏071 20 60 60, ⓕ071 70 21 91, ⓦwww.ibishotel.com; ❹). The rooms here are decorated in modern, chain style – hardly fuel for the imagination but perfectly adequate.

Charleroi has scores of **cafés** and **restaurants**, with several recommendable places either on or around place du Manège in the upper town. The *Traiteur Imperial*, place du Manège 20, is a case in point, a pleasantly old-fashioned restaurant, panelled and beamed and offering a tasty range of Italian dishes. Other options include *Fouquet*, boulevard Paul Janson 70, a cosy café serving up snacks and light meals in brisk modern surroundings, and *La Bruxelloise*, a smart new café-restaurant down near the station on place Buisset, serving up a reasonable range of Belgian standbys.

For **entertainment**, it's worth checking out what's happening at the Palais des Beaux Arts (information & reservations ☎071 31 12 12), behind the Hôtel de Ville, on place du Manège. It's Charleroi's – and the region's – cultural and entertainment centre, attracting some of the bigger names in rock music.

The Botte de Hainaut

A tongue of land jutting south into France, the **Botte de Hainaut** (Boot of Hainaut) is a natural extension of the Ardennes range further east, if a little flatter and less wooded. It's mostly visited for its gentle scenery and country towns, among which **Walcourt** and **Chimay** are the most appealing – the first graced by a handsome basilica, the second by a charming château and perhaps the prettiest main square in the whole of Wallonia. Very much the runner-up is **Couvin**, a modest little town near to a couple of visitable cave systems as well as the tiny villages of the **River Viroin** valley, of which **Vierves-sur-Viroin** is the most appealing.

The Boot's one and only **train** line runs south from Charleroi to Walcourt, Philippeville and ultimately Couvin; local **buses** fill in most of the gaps – with a good service between Charleroi, Couvin and Chimay – but to tour beyond the towns you'll need a car. The other complication is that, apart from campsites, **accommodation** is extremely thin on the ground. Chimay and Couvin have a couple of places each and Walcourt and Vierves-sur-Viroin one apiece – consequently advance reservations are advised.

Walcourt

The straggling hillside settlement of **WALCOURT**, about 20km – and half an hour by train – from Charleroi, is a pleasant old town whose pride and joy is its medieval, onion-domed **Basilique St Materne** (daily 9am–5pm; free). Dominating the town from its hilltop location at the top of the Grand-Place, it's imperious from the outside, while its interior is distinguished by its rood screen, a marvellous piece of work in which the Gothic structure is adorned by a flurry of Renaissance decoration. It was presented to the church by Charles V on the occasion of a pilgrimage he made to the **Virgin of Walcourt**, a silver-plated wooden statue that now stands in the north transept. An object of considerable veneration even today, the statue is believed to have been crafted in the tenth century, making it one of the oldest such figures in Belgium. Equally fascinating are the late medieval **choir stalls**, whose misericords sport a folkloric fantasy of centaurs and griffins, rams locking horns and acrobats alongside Biblical scenes – Jonah and the Whale, David and Goliath and so on. Intricately carved, they are quite simply delightful; a booklet on sale at the back of the church (€2.50) gives the low-down to decipher them all. The **treasury** (€2.50) has, among its assorted monstrances and reliquaries, a thirteenth-century reliquary cross in the style of Hugo d'Oignies (see p.318), a native of Walcourt. That's it as far as sights are concerned, but the town has an easy-going, old-fashioned charm and you may well decide to hang around one of the bars on the square – *La Croix Blanche* is pleasant enough.

From Walcourt **train station** it's a steep 1200-metre walk to the church – turn right outside the station building, hang a left down the short access road, turn right at the T-junction and then follow the road as it curves upwards. The **tourist office** is at the bottom of the wedge-shaped Grand-Place (daily except Wed 10am–noon & 1–5pm; ☎071 61 25 26), just down from the church. There's only one recommendable **hotel**, the *Hôstellerie Dispa*, down a narrow sidestreet near the station at rue du Jardinet 7 (☎071 61 14 23, ℉071 61 11 04; closed late Feb & early March; ❺). A tidy, well-cared-for place in a pretty old house with modern furnishings, the hotel also has the best **restaurant** in town, offering delicious seafood at commendably reasonable prices.

Philippeville and Mariembourg

From Walcourt, it's another short hop south to unexciting **PHILIPPEVILLE**, whose gridiron street plan reflects its origins as a fortress town. Built to the latest star-shaped design by Charles V in 1555, the stronghold has all but disappeared – except for a couple of subterranean artillery galleries, the *souterrains*. Charles didn't actually intend to build the fort at all, but irritatingly the French had captured the emperor's neighbouring fastness of **MARIEMBOURG**, just 12km to the south, and Charles was obliged to respond. Mariembourg is about as interesting as Philippeville – and here the fortress has sunk without trace. However, the town is the terminus of the **Chemin de fer à vapeur des Trois Vallées**, a refurbished steam engine that chugs its way east across the surrounding countryside to Treignes, near the French border (April–Oct 2–7 weekly; call ☎060 31 24 40 for times & tickets; €7). The terminus is 800m from Mariembourg train station, which is on the Charleroi-Sud to Couvin line. Be warned that matters are further confused by an uninspiring *autorail*, which plies the same route and is run by the same company.

Couvin

Just 5km south from Mariembourg, **COUVIN** was one of the first settlements in Hainaut to be industrialized, its narrow streets choked by forges and smelting works as early as the eighteenth century. In the event, Couvin was soon to be marginalized by the big cities further north, but it battled on as a pint-sized manufacturing centre. Tourism has also had an impact as the town lies at the heart of a popular holiday area, a quiet rural district whose forests and farmland are liberally sprinkled with country cottages and second homes. The prettiest scenery hereabouts is to be found east of Couvin along the **valley of the River Viroin**, which extends to Treignes and beyond across the French frontier.

Long and slim, and bisected by the River Eau Noire, Couvin is short on specific sights, but it does possess a good-looking old quarter, set on top of a rocky hill high above the river and the boringly modern main square, place Général Piron. The other noteworthy feature is the **Cavernes de l'Abîme** on rue de la Falaise (April–June & mid-Sept to Oct Sat & Sun 10am–noon & 1.30–6pm; July to mid-Sept daily 10am–noon & 1.30–6pm; €4.50 or €9.80 including admission to Grottes de Neptune), by the river on the east side of the town centre. Inhabited in prehistory and used as a bomb shelter in 1940, these two caves drill into a jagged limestone cliff; the upper cave features an exhibition on prehistoric times, the lower a sound and light show. In addition, there's a rather more impressive limestone cave complex, the **Grottes de Neptune**

(April–Sept daily 10am–noon & 1.30–6pm; Oct–March Sat & Sun 10.30am–4pm; €6.80), about 5km northeast of Couvin on the road between the hamlets of Petigny and Frasnes. The guided tour includes a twenty-minute boat ride on a subterranean river, and (yet another) sound and light show. These caves are easy to reach by car or bike, but there's no public transport.

Practicalities

From Couvin **bus** and **train station** it's a ten-minute walk east to the main square, along rue de la Gare and its continuation, Faubourg St Germain. The **tourist office** is on the way to the Cavernes de l'Abîme, at rue de la Falaise 3 (Mon–Sat 9am–5pm, Sun 10am–4pm; ☎060 34 01 40).

Accommodation is thin on the ground, but there is an inexpensive and well-run B&B, *Le Petit Chef*, in a modern red brick building at rue Dessus de la Ville 6 (☎060 34 79 40; ❸); it's on the edge of the old town not far from the tourist office. Another B&B option is the *Auberge St Roch*, in a tastefully revamped old house at rue de la Gare 34 (☎060 34 67 96; ❸). There are several busy **restaurants** on and around the main square: try *Brasserie Jeanne*, with simple, reasonably priced pasta dishes as well as more substantial choices – but don't expect too much gastronomic pleasure.

The valley of the River Viroin

East from Couvin along the N99, it's just 4km to **NISMES**, a pretty hamlet whose old stone houses are neatly tucked in between the River Viroin and a cluster of wooded hills. Nothing much happens here, but you can spend time pleasantly enough picnicking down by the river, nosing round the ruins of a medieval castle and hiking out into the surrounding countryside. Nismes has two **hotels**, the pricier of which is the two-star, smart and comfortable *Le Melrose*, in an attractive little old house with its own grounds on the southern edge of the village at rue Albert Grégoire 33 (☎060 31 23 39, ℉ 060 31 10 13, ✉melrose@swing.be; ❸). The other is the plainer, one-star *La Calestienne*, also on the edge of the village and occupying a substantial brick villa at rue St Roch 111 (☎060 31 32 00; ❷; no cards; closed March & late Aug). There are several **campsites** in the vicinity; one good one is the all-year *Camping Try des Baudets*, rue de la Champagne 1 (☎ & ℉060 39 01 08, ✉trydesbaudets@hotmail.com), around 5km to the east of Nismes in tiny **Olloy-sur-Viroin**.

Pushing on from Nismes, it's a further 7km east along the N99 to **VIERVES-SUR-VIROIN**, in handsome, hilly countryside near the border with France. This is the prettiest village in the valley, its narrow streets sloping up from the river flanked by crumbly stone houses. Presiding over the scene and the minuscule main square is an antique watchtower, which comes complete with a dinky onion dome – though people come here for the peace and quiet rather than the sights. There's one **hotel**, *Le Petit Mesnil*, in the centre at rue de la Chapelle 7 (☎060 39 55 90, ℉060 39 00 03; ❸), but you're better off in a gîte than in this unprepossessing, albeit well-tended, modern little place near the river – Couvin tourist office will advise.

Brûly-de-Pesche

South out of Couvin on the N5, it's a couple of kilometres to the five-kilometre-long turning that weaves its way up into the wooded hills to **BRÛLY-DE-PESCHE**. Now no more than a handful of log chalets and cabins scattered around an old stone church, Brûly was the site of Hitler's advance headquarters during the invasion of 1940. At the beginning of the war, both the French and the British were convinced that Hitler would attack through northern Belgium. They concluded that the wooded hills of the Ardennes – and the Botte de Hainaut – would be impassable to the Germans, or at least they would take so much time to cross that the Allies would have plenty of time to prepare their response. It was a disastrous miscalculation: the Germans smashed through the light French defences in just a few days and thereafter the fall of France was inevitable. On the edge of the village, the decrepit concrete bunker – the **Abri d'Hitler** (April–Sept daily 10.30am–5.30pm; €3) – where Hitler reviewed progress has survived and is now one part of a larger museum, which occupies a couple of small timber buildings. In one is a very competent explanation of the 1940 campaign, in the other a display on the Resistance.

Incidentally, Hitler went straight from Brûly to Compiègne, in France, to accept the French surrender in the same clearing in the woods – and in the same railway carriage – where the Germans had capitulated in 1918. The war correspondent William Shirer observed proceedings, commenting that "Hitler's face was grave, solemn, yet brimming with revenge." After the ceremony, Hitler had his engineers blow the carriage up.

Chimay

Best known for the beer brewed by local Trappists, the small and ancient town of **CHIMAY**, 14km west of Couvin, is a charming old place, governed for several centuries by the de Croy family, a clan of local bigwigs enlivened by a certain **Madame Tallien**, born Jeanne Cabarrus, the daughter of a Spanish banker. Her credentials were impeccably aristocratic until the French Revolution when, imprisoned and awaiting the guillotine, she wooed a revolutionary leader, Jean Tallien. He saved her, they got married, and she became an important figure in revolutionary circles, playing a leading role in the overthrow of Robespierre that earnt her the soubriquet Notre-Dame de Thermidor. Later, seeing which way the political wind was blowing, she divorced Tallien and hung about for another aristocrat – this time getting a de Croy, whom she married in 1805. Living out the rest of her life in the tranquil environment of Chimay, she died in 1835 and was interred inside the **Collégiale des Sts Pierre et Paul** (Mon–Fri 9am–noon & 2–4.30pm, Sat 9am–5pm, Sun 11am–5pm; free), a mostly sixteenth-century limestone pile with a high and austere vaulted nave. The church is dotted with the graves of Madame Tallien's adoptive family, most notably the splendid mausoleum of Charles de Croy, a recumbent alabaster figure, clad in armour and dating from the 1520s, that reposes in the choir. The church is bang in the middle of town and its walls crowd the slender **Grand-Place**, an eminently bourgeois and exceedingly pretty little square surrounding the dinky **Monument des Princes**, a water fountain erected in 1852 in honour of the de Croys.

From the Grand-Place, an elegant sandstone arch leads through to the **Château des Princes de Chimay**, the old home of the de Croy family (March–Oct daily guided tours at 10.30am, 3pm & 4pm; €6). A considerably altered structure, it was originally built in the fifteenth century, but was reconstructed in the seventeenth, then badly damaged by fire and partly rebuilt to earlier plans in the 1930s. Today the main body of the building is fronted by a long series of rectangular windows, edged by a squat turreted tower. Inside there are mainly old family portraits and a hotchpotch of period furniture, although the carefully restored, gaudy **theatre** (modelled on the Louis XV theatre at Fontainebleau) is worth a look, and there are good views over the river valley and encompassing woods from the gardens.

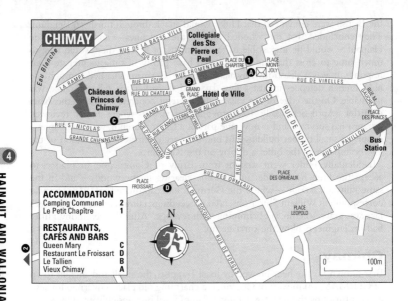

The other sights are to do with the local, beer-brewing Trappist monks – to be precise the monks of the Cistercian Order of the Strict Observance. The modern **Chimay brewery**, some 5km east of Chimay in **Baileux**, offers tours and tastings (mid-June to mid-Sept guided tours at 10am & 2pm; reservations ℡060 21 03 11) and visitors are also allowed in the church and gardens of **Scourmont Abbey**, where the monks actually live. Neither excursion sets the pulse racing, not least because the abbey, which is located 10km to the south of Chimay close to France, is architecturally dull, a mostly modern complex dating from the 1850s.

Practicalities

With regular connections from Charleroi and Couvin, Chimay's **bus station** sits on the edge of the town centre, a five-minute walk from the Grand-Place. The **tourist office** is a few paces east of the Grand-Place at rue de Noailles 4 (April–Sept Mon–Fri 9am–6pm, Sat & Sun 10am–6pm; Oct–March Mon–Sat 9am–noon & 1–4.30pm; ℡060 21 18 46, ⓦwww.coeureurope.org). Apart from the usual gubbins, they issue a comprehensive town guide for free and sell a useful French-language booklet, *Promenades Pédestres Bois*, detailing **local walks** in the woods and along the River Eau Blanche.

There are no hotels in town, but *Le Petit Chapître* is an absolutely delightful **B&B** comprising a handful of period rooms in attractive old premises, metres from the Grand-Place at place du Chapître 5 (℡060 21 10 42 or 0477 76 70 60, ⓔbrim@skynet.be; ❹). Alternatively, there's the almost equally enticing, six-room, two-star *Hostellerie du Gahy*, rue de Gahy 2 (℡060 51 10 93, ⓕ060 51 28 79; ❺), in an imaginatively converted farmhouse, about 12km west of Chimay in Momignies. Chimay also has a rudimentary **campsite**, the *Camping Communal,* just west of the centre on the allée des Princes (April–Oct; ℡060 21 18 43).

Among several **cafés** and **restaurants**, easily the best is *Restaurant Le Froissart*, place Froissart 8 (℡060 21 26 19; closed all day Mon & Sun eve), which serves up traditional French cuisine at reasonable prices – fish dishes weigh in at about €15, other main courses a little less. More informal is *Le Tallien*, a first-floor café-restaurant offering tasty Belgian food at Grand-Place 20. The two best **bars** are the *Queen Mary*, a cosy and popular place at rue St Nicolas 22, and the rather more original *Vieux Chimay*, Grand-Place 22 (closed Tues), whose interior doubles as a tobacconist's; the beer menu here clocks up over forty brews and there's an outside terrace.

Rance and Beaumont

Straggles along the main road 11km north of Chimay, **Rance** is an uninviting town famous for its red marble quarries, which have spawned buildings world-wide, from Versailles to St Peter's in Rome. There's nothing to stop for, and any-way it's only 12km more to **BEAUMONT**, marginally more interesting as an old if somewhat dilapidated town crouched on a hill close to the French bor-der. An important regional stronghold from as early as the eleventh century, Beaumont's fortifications are still partly intact, most notably the **Tour Salamandre** (May, June & Sept daily 9am–5pm; July & Aug daily 10am–7pm; Oct Sun 10am–5pm; €1.50), a thick-walled rectangular structure whose van-tage point, a brief, signposted walk away from the main square, overlooks the river valley. Inside, there's a small museum of regional history, but really you climb the 136 steps for the view. From Beaumont, it's 20km northeast to Charleroi (see p.301) and 30km northwest to Mons (see p.289)

Travel details

Trains

Charleroi-Sud to: Brussels (every 30min; 50min); Couvin (hourly; 1hr); La Louvière-Sud (every 30min; 20min); Mariembourg (hourly; 55min); Mons (every 30min; 40min); Namur (every 30min; 30min); Nivelles (every 30min; 20min); Ottignies (hourly; 40min); Tournai (hourly; 1hr); Villers-la-Ville (hourly; 30min); Walcourt (hourly; 30min).
La Louvière-Sud to: Binche (hourly; 15min); Charleroi (every 30min; 20min).
Mons to: Ath (hourly; 30min); Charleroi (every 30min; 40min); La Louvière-Sud (hourly; 20min); Tournai (every 30min; 40min); Brussels (every

30min; 1hr); Soignies (every 30min; 20min)
Tournai to: Ath (hourly; 20min); Brussels (every 30min; 1hr); Charleroi-Sud (hourly; 1hr); Mons (every 30min; 40min).

Buses

Charleroi to: Beaumont (hourly; 30min); Binche (hourly; 40min); Chimay (hourly; 1hr 10min).
Chimay to: Binche (hourly; 30min); Charleroi (hourly; 1hr 10min); Couvin (every 2hr; 35min).
Couvin to: Chimay (every 2hr; 50min); Namur (hourly; 1hr 15min); Nismes (hourly; 10min).

The Ardennes

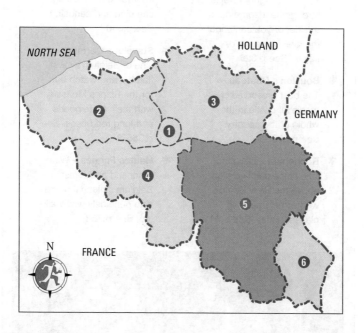

CHAPTER 5

Highlights

✳ **Trésor du Prieuré d'Oignies, Namur** – Exquisitely crafted, jewel-encrusted metalwork from the thirteenth century is on show here. See p.318

✳ **The River Lesse valley** – Offers delightful walks through handsome countryside, or you can shoot the river by canoe or kayak. See p.326

✳ **Bouillon's Château** – The best preserved medieval castle in the whole of the country. See p.338

✳ **Rochehaut** – Delightful little place perched high above the River Semois, with some smashing places to stay. See p.341

✳ **Bastogne Historical Centre** – Learn how the Battle of the Bulge, sealed Hitler's fate. See p.345

✳ **La Roche-en-Ardenne** – Picture-postcard Ardennes resort; an ideal spot for some walking, camping and canoeing. See p.346

✳ **Stavelot's Carnival** – One of Belgium's most flamboyant; watch out for the Blancs Moussis, with their white hoods and long red noses. See p.365

✳ **Hautes Fagnes** – Windy moorland and forest, Belgium's highest terrain, with genuinely wild walking. See p.368

5

The Ardennes

elgium's southern reaches are in striking contrast to the crowded, industrial north, for it's here in the south that the cities give way to the rugged, wilderness landscapes of the Ardennes. Beginning in France, the Ardennes stretches east across Luxembourg and Belgium before continuing on into Germany, covering three Belgian provinces en route – Namur in the west, Luxembourg in the south and Liège in the east. The highest part, lying in the German-speaking east of the country, is the Hautes Fagnes (the High Fens), an expanse of windswept heathland that extends from Eupen to Malmédy. But this is not the Ardennes' most attractive or popular corner, which lies farther west, its limits roughly marked by Dinant, La Roche-en-Ardenne and Bouillon. This region is given character and variety by its river valleys: deep, wooded, winding canyons, at times sublimely and inspiringly beautiful, reaching up to high green peaks. The Ardennes' cave systems are also a major attraction, especially those in the Meuse, Ourthe and Lesse valleys, carved out by underground rivers that over the centuries have cut through and dissolved the limestone of the hills, leaving stalagmites and stalactites in their wake.

The obvious gateway to the most scenic portion of the Ardennes is **Namur**, strategically sited at the junction of the Sambre and Meuse rivers, and well worth a visit in its own right. The town's pride and joy is its massive, mostly nineteenth-century citadel – once one of the mightiest fortresses in Europe – but it also musters a handful of decent museums, great restaurants and (for the Ardennes) a lively bar scene. From Namur you can follow the Meuse by train down to **Dinant**, a pleasant – and very popular – journey, going on to explore the **Meuse Valley** south of Dinant by boat or taking a canoe up the narrower and wilder **River Lesse**. From Dinant, routes lead east into the heart of the Ardennes – to workaday **Han-sur-Lesse**, surrounded by undulating hills riddled with caves, to prettier **Rochefort**, and to **St Hubert**, with its splendid Italianate basilica. The most charming of all the towns hereabouts, however, is **Bouillon**, a delightfully picturesque little place whose narrow streets trail alongside the River Semois beneath an ancient castle. Bouillon is situated close to the French frontier, on the southern periphery of the Belgian Ardennes and within easy striking distance of some of the region's most dramatic scenery, along the valley of the Semois. In terms of good looks, its closest rival is **La Roche-en-Ardenne** to the northeast, a rustic, hardy kind of town, pushed in tight against the River Ourthe beneath wooded hills, and renowned for its smoked ham and game.

If you're visiting the eastern Ardennes, the handiest starting point is big and grimy **Liège**, an industrial sprawl from where it's a short hop south to the his-

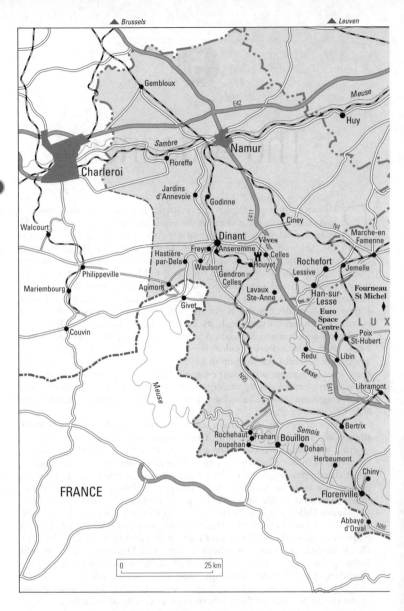

toric – though now engagingly faded – resort of **Spa**, and the picturesque town of **Stavelot**, with its marvellous carnival. You can use Stavelot as a base for hiking or canoeing into the surrounding countryside and to venture into the **Hautes Fagnes**, though the pleasant town of Malmédy is nearer.

Getting around the Ardennes is difficult – or at least time-consuming – without your own transport. The region is crossed by three main rail lines, but

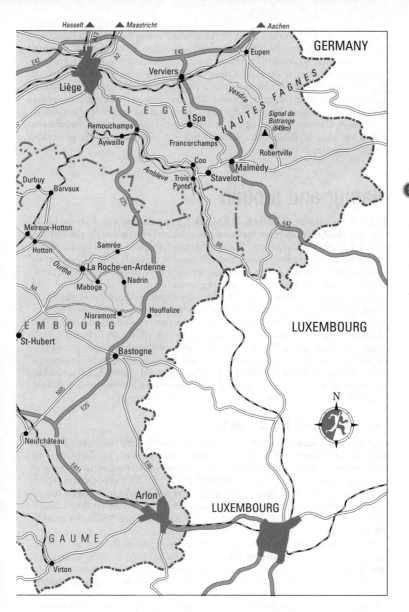

by and large they miss the more appealing places and to get to them you'll be reliant on connecting buses, which can involve a long wait; indeed, a route that looks short and easy on the map may involve several time-consuming changes. Information about bus services can also be difficult to come by as bus stations are thin on the ground – though local tourist offices usually have a good set of timetables. Neither is **accommodation** entirely straightforward. **Hotels** are fairly thin on the ground – most of the region's towns only have a handful – and rooms are often in short supply in high season (late July & Aug). **Camping** is one good way to avoid the problem, but there again many campsites are hard to reach without a car (or bike). Given all this, it's perhaps best to find a place you like and stay put, which gives you a chance to get stuck into the outdoor pursuits which attract so many visitors. Wherever you are, **walking** is the obvious pastime, rarely strenuous and often getting you out into some genuinely wild areas. **Canoes** can be rented at most river settlements, and **mountain bikes** are often available. Cross-country and – in some places – on-piste **skiing** are popular in winter.

Namur and around

Just 60km southeast of Brussels, **NAMUR** is a logical first stop if you're heading into the Ardennes from the north or west, and is refreshingly clear of the industrial belts of Hainaut and Brabant. Many of Belgium's cities have suffered at the hands of invading armies and the same is certainly true of Namur, so much so that from the sixteenth century up until 1978, when the Belgian army finally moved out, Namur remained the quintessential military town, its sole purpose being the control of the strategically important junction of the rivers Sambre and Meuse. Generations of military engineers have pondered how to make Namur's hilltop **citadel** impregnable – no one more so than Louis XIV's Vauban – and the substantial remains of these past efforts are now the town's main tourist attraction. Down below, the **town centre** crowds the north bank of the River Sambre, its cramped squares and streets lined by big old mansions in the French style and sprinkled with several fine old churches and a handful of decent museums. There are top-flight **restaurants** here too and a vibrant nightlife, lent vigour by the presence of the city's university.

Arrival and information

Namur's **train station** is on the northern fringe of the city centre, beside place de la Station. Here you'll also find local bus stops and, at no. 28, La Maison du Tec, the information office for **Tec**, who run bus services across all of French-speaking Belgium (daily 7am–7pm; ℡081 25 35 55). It's also possible to reach Namur from Dinant by **boat** on Saturdays and Sundays from early July to late August, a three-hour trip costing €13 one-way (more details on ℡081 24 64 49); boats arrive from – and depart for – Dinant from Quai #5 on the quai de Meuse.

Two minutes' walk away from the train station – just to the east of place de la Station – is the main **tourist office**, on square Léopold (daily 9.30am–6pm; ℡081 24 64 49; @www.ville.namur.be). They can help with accommodation, issue free town maps and brochures, have details of guided tours and provide information on what's on in town.

From the train station, it takes about ten minutes to walk to the River Sambre via the **main street**, variously rue de Fer and rue de l'Ange. East of the foot of rue de l'Ange, the Pont de France spans the river to reach the tip of the "V" made by the confluence of the two rivers (the *grognon* or "pig's snout"). The **information chalet** on the *grognon* (April–Sept daily 9.30am–6pm; ℡081 24 64 48) offers the same services as the main tourist office and is also the starting point for most guided tours of the citadel (see p.321).

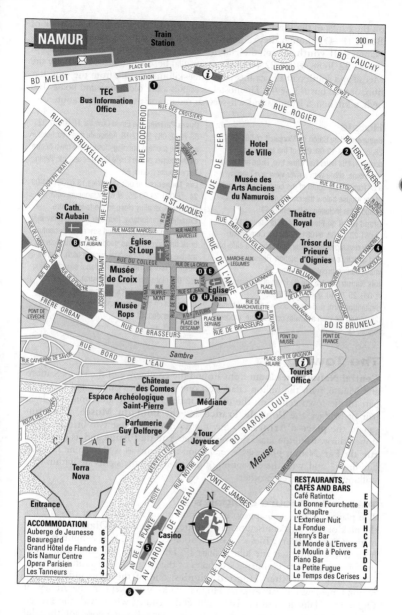

RESTAURANTS, CAFÉS AND BARS

Café Ratintot	E
La Bonne Fourchette	K
Le Chapître	B
L'Exterieur Nuit	I
La Fondue	H
Henry's Bar	C
Le Monde à L'Envers	A
Le Moulin à Poivre	F
Piano Bar	D
La Petite Fugue	G
Le Temps des Cerises	J

ACCOMMODATION

Auberge de Jeunesse	6
Beauregard	5
Grand Hôtel de Flandre	1
Ibis Namur Centre	2
Opera Parisien	3
Les Tanneurs	4

Accommodation

Namur has relatively few hotels, and finding **accommodation** in high season can be a problem if you haven't booked in advance. The cheapest **hotels** are close by the train station, but there are two much more appetizing (and expensive) places – one right in the town centre, the other a short walk to the south on the banks of the River Meuse. Alternatively, the tourist office has a stock of **B&Bs** (❷–❸), though they're mostly a good way from the town centre, as is Namur's HI **youth hostel**, the *Auberge de Jeunesse*, at avenue Félicien Rops 8 (Ⓣ081 22 36 88, Ⓕ081 22 44 12, Ⓔnamur@laj.be; dorm beds €12.50). By the Meuse and south past the casino, it's a three-kilometre walk from the train station, or take bus #3 or #4. The hostel occupies a big old house and boasts 100 beds, a kitchen, a laundry and self-service restaurant; there's no lock-out.

Hotels

Beauregard av Baron de Moreau 1 Ⓣ081 23 00 28, Ⓕ081 24 12 09. Part of the town's casino complex, this hotel has attractive, large and modern rooms, some with a river view and balcony. It's a 5–10min walk south of the centre, on the banks of the Meuse below the citadel. An excellent breakfast is included in the price. ❺

Grand Hôtel de Flandre pl de la Station 14 Ⓣ081 23 18 68, Ⓕ081 22 80 60. Competent, newly revamped three-star hotel above a café-bar and directly opposite the station. Reasonable value, though breakfast is extra. ❸

Ibis Namur Centre rue du Premier Lanciers 10 Ⓣ081 25 75 40, Ⓕ081 25 75 50. Straightforward, mid-range chain hotel in a handy downtown location and with comfortable, modern rooms. ❹

Opera Parisien rue Emile Cuvelier 16 Ⓣ081 22 63 79, Ⓕ081 23 27 18. Adequate one-star hotel in a routine modern building close to the town centre on the corner of rue Emile Cuvelier and rue Pépin. Ten en-suite rooms. ❸

Les Tanneurs rue des Tanneries 13 Ⓣ081 24 00 24 , Ⓕ081 24 00 25, Ⓦwww.tanneurs.com. Down a quiet alley close to the town centre. Extremely comfortable four-star hotel in a lavishly and imaginatively renovated seventeenth-century brick building with two good restaurants, lots of marble and the occasional sunken bath. There's a range of rooms, right up to palatial suites costing €210 a night (breakfast €8 extra). Off-season and at the weekend, it's worth asking about discounts on the more expensive rooms. Highly recommended. ❸

The Town

Central Namur spreads out from around the confluence of the rivers Sambre and Meuse, with the hilltop citadel on one side of the Sambre and the main part of the town centre on the other. Citadel and centre are connected by a pair of bridges, the **Pont de France** and the **Pont du Musée**. The main square, the **place d'Armes**, is a few metres north of these two bridges and a stone's throw from the main shopping streets, **rue de l'Ange** and its extension **rue de Fer**. Namur possesses several good museums as well as some fine old buildings – and, with the exception of the citadel, all the sights are within easy walking distance of each other.

Trésor du Prieuré d'Oignies

The place d'Armes is disappointingly modern and mundane, but close by lies the pick of the town's museums, the **Trésor du Prieuré d'Oignies** (Treasury of the Oignies Priory; Tues–Sat 10am–noon & 2–5pm, Sun 2–5pm; €1.25), housed in a convent at rue Julie Billiart 17. This unique collection, which fills just one small room, comprises examples of the exquisitely beautiful gold and silver work of **Brother Hugo d'Oignies**, one of the most gifted of the region's medieval metalworkers. Hugo's works were kept at the Abbey of Oignies in Hainaut until the late eighteenth century, when, with the French revolutionary army closing in, the monks hid them. It was a good job they did – the soldiers trashed the abbey and subsequently the monks smuggled their treasures to Namur for safekeeping, where they've remained ever since. The nuns provide a guided tour and their enthusiasm is infectious; most of them speak excellent English.

From the eleventh to the thirteenth century, the River Meuse valley was famous for the skill of its craftsmen, especially those working in that part of the valley which is now in Belgium. The **Mosan style** they developed was essentially Romanesque, but its practitioners evolved a more naturalistic and dynamic approach to their subject matter, a characteristic of early Gothic; Hugo's work, dating from the early thirteenth century, demonstrates this transition quite superbly. Hugo was also an innovator in the art of filigree, raising the decoration from the background so that the tiny human figures and animals seem to be suspended in space, giving depth to the narrative. Another technique of which he was fond is **niello**, in which a black mixture of sulphur or lead is used to incise lines into the gold.

Whatever his chosen technique, they're wonderful devotional pieces, elaborately studded with precious and semiprecious stones and displaying an exquisite balance between ornament and form. Most of the figures hold sacred relics that were brought back from the Holy Land by one Jacques de Vitry, a Parisian ecclesiastic who met Hugo in 1208. The filigrees themselves are lively and realistic, often depicting minute hunting scenes, with animals leaping convincingly through delicate foliage, and sometimes engraved with a Christian dedication, or embossed with a tiny picture of the artist offering up his art to God in worship. In particular, look out for the intricately worked double-crosses, the dazzling reliquary cover for St Peter's rib, the charming songbird and a magnificent Book of the Gospels cover, with Christ crucified on one side, God the Father in majesty on the other.

The Musée des Arts Anciens du Namurois

From the convent, it takes about five minutes to walk northwest along rue Emile Cuvelier to rue de Fer where, at no. 24, the **Musée des Arts Anciens du Namurois** occupies one of the finest of Namur's eighteenth-century mansions (Tues–Sun 10am–6pm; €1.30), an elegant structure set back from the street behind a formal gateway and courtyard. The collection begins with an enjoyable sample of Mosan metalwork, religious pieces among which the dinky geometrics of the brass enamels (*cuivre émaillé*) stand out. The craftsmanship is not, perhaps, as fine as that of Hugo d'Oignies, but it's still excellent and it's put into artistic context by the museum's (modest) collection of medieval sculptures and painted wooden panels. Of the museum's many paintings, the most distinguished are by Henri met de Bles, an early-sixteenth-century, Antwerp-based artist who favoured panoramic landscapes populated by tiny figures. Look out also for the temporary exhibitions, most of which are displayed in the gatehouse.

West to the Cathédrale St Aubain

Leaving the museum, it's a short stroll southwest to the finest of Namur's churches, the **Église Saint Loup**, a Baroque extravagance that overshadows the narrow pedestrianized rue du Collège. Built for the Jesuits between 1621 and 1645, the church boasts a fluently carved facade and a sumptuous interior of marble walls and sandstone vaulting. The high altar is actually wood painted to look like marble – the ship carrying the last instalment of Italian marble sank and the Jesuits were obliged to finish the church off with this imitation.

At the west end of rue du Collège, on place St Aubain, the **Cathédrale St Aubain** might well be the ugliest church in Belgium, a monstrous Neoclassical pile remarkably devoid of any charm. The interior isn't much better, with acres of creamy white paint and a choir decorated with melodramatic paintings by Jacques Nicolai, one of Rubens' less talented pupils. The attached **Musée Diocésain et Trésor de la Cathédrale** (Easter–Oct Tues–Sat 10am–noon &

2.30–6pm, Sun 2.30–6pm; Nov–Easter Tues–Sun 2.30–4.30pm; €1.25) displays objects gathered from diocesan churches across Namur and Luxembourg provinces. Highlights include a golden crown reliquary with thorns supposedly from Christ's crown of thorns, a twelfth-century portable altar with eleventh-century ivory carvings, and a silver statuette of St Blaise.

The Musée Felicien Rops

Heading south from the cathedral towards the river, turn left along rue des Brasseurs and then first left for the **Musée Felicien Rops**, rue Fumal 12 (July & Aug daily 10am–6pm; rest of year closed Mon; €2.50), devoted to the life and work of the eponymous painter, graphic artist and illustrator. Born in Namur, **Felicien Rops** (1833–98) settled in Paris in the 1870s, acquiring a reputation for delving into the occult and for his "debauched" lifestyle. He also dabbled in art and illustrated the works of Mallarmé and Baudelaire. Rops was, apparently, greatly admired by the latter, but he is better known for his erotic drawings, which reveal an obsession with the macabre and perverse – skeletons, nuns and priests are depicted in oddly compromising poses, and old men are serviced by young, partly-clad women. He also drew many satirical cartoons, savagely criticizing the art establishment with which he never had much of a rapport, partly because his Impressionistic paintings were (justifiably) considered dull and derivative. The museum possesses a large collection of his works and has recently been extended to provide enough space to display it all.

The citadel

The result of centuries of military endeavour, Namur's **citadel** is an immense complex, which crawls all over the steep and craggy hill that rises high above the confluence of the rivers Sambre and Meuse. Understanding quite what was built, when and why is well-nigh impossible, though salient features are easy enough to decipher.

The first people to be attracted by Namur's defensive capabilities were the Aduatuci, a Gallic tribe who named the place Nam, after one of their gods. Later, in medieval times, a succession of local counts elaborated each other's fortifications and by the fourteenth century the town was protected by four sets of walls, which guarded the riverfront and climbed steeply up the hill behind. By the early sixteenth century, it was clear that improved artillery had rendered stone walls obsolete and every major European city set about redesigning its defences. Here in Namur the riverside fortifications were gradually abandoned while the section near the top of the hill – now loosely known as the **Château des Comtes** – was incorporated into a partly subterranean fortress, the **Médiane**, whose ramifications occupy the eastern portion of the present citadel. This part of the fortress was always the most vulnerable to attack and for the next two hundred years successive generations of military engineers, including Vauban and the Dutchman Coheoorn, tried to figure out the best way to protect it. The surviving structure reflects this preoccupation, with the lines of defence becoming more complex and extensive the further up you go. To further strengthen the fortress, in the 1640s the Spanish completed the **Terra Nova** bastion at the west end of the citadel, the two separated by a wide moat. Altogether, this made Namur one of the strongest fortresses in Europe, but its importance guaranteed the attentions of Louis XIV, who besieged the town in 1692, and of William of Orange just three years later. The Dutch rebuilt the citadel between 1816 and 1825, and much of today's remains date to this period.

Visiting the site

The plateau which comprises the top of the citadel can be reached by car and bike as well as on foot. Furthermore, a **minibus** cruises the town centre and then travels up to the citadel at regular intervals every day during the summer months; one of its stops is at the tip of the *grognon*.

The tourist office produces a glossy, easy-to-use leaflet entitled "Storming the Citadel," which suggests five colour-coded **walking routes**; the shortest takes forty minutes, the longest nearly three hours. Well-signed and featuring interpretative plaques along the way, each focuses on a different theme, but the two most interesting are the yellow "1000 years of time", which takes in parts of both the Médiane and the Terra Nova, and the purple "History of the Siege of 1692", concentrating on the Terra Nova. Both start on the plateau at the top of the citadel, whereas the red, green and blue walks begin at the tip of the *grognon* and thus involve a dull and mildly exerting walk up the flanks of the fortress.

There's no admission fee, though certain additional attractions do attract charges. The most popular of these is the electric train **guided tour** of the citadel, which includes a visit to the underground casements of the Terra Nova and an audiovisual display on Namur's history (early April & June–Sept daily 11am–7pm; late April & May Sat & Sun 11am–7pm; €6). Also inside the citadel, and free to visit, are the **Espace Archéologique Saint-Pierre** on the east edge of the Terra Nova (March–Dec Tues–Sun noon–5pm), which has temporary displays on local archeological digs and discoveries; and a perfume shop and mini-factory, the **Atelier de Parfumerie Guy Delforge**, in the old casements (July & Aug daily 9.15am–5.30pm, Sun 2.15–5.30pm; rest of year closed Mon).

Eating and drinking

Namur has an excellent selection of **restaurants** and a good supply of lively **bars**, many of them clustered in the quaint, pedestrianized squares just west of rue de l'Ange – on and around place Marché-aux-Legumes and neighbouring place Chanoine Descamps.

Restaurants

La Bonne Fourchette rue Notre Dame 112 ☏081 23 15 36. Pint-sized, informal and family-run restaurant down below the citadel on the way to the casino. Prices are very reasonable and the food, in true Franco-Belgian style, is delicious. Evenings only.

La Fondue rue St Jean 19, just off place Marché-aux-Legumes. Medium-sized restaurant serving excellent fondues and steaks for around €16 a head.

Le Grill des Tanneurs rue des Tanneries 13 ☏081 24 00 24. Situated on the 1st floor of the *Hôtel Les Tanneurs*, this excellent restaurant features French-style cuisine in smooth (and convincing) repro-antique surroundings. Main courses start at a very reasonable €12.

Le Moulin à Poivre rue Bas de la Place 19 ☏081 23 11 20. Cosy little restaurant offering tasty French food. Main courses hover around €16. Closed Mon & Sun.

La Petite Fugue pl Chanoine Descamps 5 ☏081 23 13 20. Outstanding, chic restaurant with mouth-watering Franco-Belgian dishes – €35 for a three-course feast, worth every cent.

Le Temps des Cerises rue des Brasseurs 22 ☏081 22 53 26. Pocket-sized, intimate restaurant offering a quality menu of dishes prepared in the French manner. Main courses average around €20. Open Wed–Sat.

Bars

Le Chapitre rue du Séminaire 4. Unassuming, sedate little bar with an extensive beer list.

L'Exterieur Nuit pl Chanoine Descamps. Bustling brasserie-cum-bar with occasional live music.

Henry's Bar pl St Aubain 3. Right by the cathedral, this is a big loud brasserie in the best tradition.

Le Monde à L'Envers rue Lelièvre 28. Lively, fashionable bar just up from the cathedral. A favourite spot for university students.

Piano Bar pl Marché-aux-Legumes. One of Namur's more popular bars, with live jazz Fri and Sat evenings from about 10pm.

Café Ratintot pl Marché-aux-Legumes. With its attractive antique decor, including an old French cockerel or two, this is one of central Namur's most appealing bars.

Around Namur

Namur is a pleasant place to spend two or three days, which gives you time to visit the area's two main attractions: the splendid hilltop **L'Abbaye de Floreffe**, to the west of town, and the classically landscaped **Jardins d'Annevoie**, set beside the Meuse halfway to Dinant. A visit to the gardens is readily incorporated into a longer day-trip (by car or train) along this stretch of the **Meuse**. The river is too wide to be all that dramatic, but it's still an enjoyable journey as it passes through a varied landscape of gentle wooded slopes interrupted by steep escarpments capped by ruined castles. The area draws rock-climbers in their droves, and it was a few miles to the northeast of Namur that King Albert I fell to his death in a climbing accident in 1934.

L'Abbaye de Floreffe

Founded in 1121, **L'Abbaye de Floreffe** lies some 10km west of Namur (℡081 44 53 03; guided tours April–Sept daily at 1.30pm, 2.30pm, 3.30pm & 4.30pm, plus July & Aug at 10.30am & 11.30am; €2), towards Charleroi. The town of **Floreffe** itself is drab and dreary, but the abbey, with its well-kept grounds populated by a flock of peacocks, occupies a splendid hilltop location above the town with wide views over the River Sambre. Little remains of the original complex and the imposing brick buildings of today are mainly eighteenth-century. The main exception is the **abbey church**, a hotchpotch of architectural styles with Romanesque, Gothic and Baroque features.

The interior is best known for its remarkable carved oak **choir stalls**, the work of one man, Pierre Enderlin, who took sixteen years (1632–48) over them. In a superb state of preservation and displaying a marvellous inventiveness and intricacy, the stalls are carved with a stunning variety of figures, including biblical characters, eminent and holy persons, and some 220 angels – each one of them different. Many of the faces are obviously portraits, humorous, sometimes satirical in tone, and there's a self-portrait of the artist hidden among them. Also in the church is a very graceful wooden **Virgin**, carved in 1692, the sculpting of her robes being extremely adept. Tours, which are conducted in French, finish with a video on the history of the abbey and the choir stalls.

Below the main complex, the **Moulin Brasserie** (all year, Mon–Fri 11am–6pm, Sat & Sun 11am–8pm), comprising the creatively refurbished old mill and brewery, showcases the abbey's products, principally beer and cheese. Amongst the abbey's several brews, the most distinctive is Floreffe La Meilleure (9 percent), a strong, dark and tangy brew.

The abbey makes a comfortable half-day excursion by car from Namur or Charleroi, but getting there by **public transport** is a bit of a pain. There are buses (#28) but they run infrequently – every two hours or so. The Namur–Charleroi train is more frequent (hourly; 10min), but it's a boring 1500-metre walk from Floreffe train station on one side of the town to the abbey on the other: turn right outside the station and keep going along the main street.

Les Jardins d'Annevoie

Extremely popular with day-trippers, **Les Jardins d'Annevoie** (April–Oct daily 9.30am–6.30pm; €6.20), in the wooded hills above the River Meuse about 18km south of Namur, are generally reckoned to be among the most appealing gardens in the whole of the country. The estate – gardens and manor house – has been in the hands of the Montpelliers since 1675 and one of the clan – a certain Charles Alexis – turned his hand (or rather those of his gardeners) to garden design in the 1770s. Charles was inspired by his travels in France, Italy and England, picking up gardening tips which he then rolled into one homogeneous creation. From the French came formal borders, from the Italians the romance of mossy banks and arbours, while the English influence is most obvious in the grotto of Neptune. The common denominator is water – everywhere you look there are fountains, jets and mini-waterfalls, all worked from natural pressure with the tree-lined Grand Canal, immediately above the gardens, acting as a reservoir.

Bus #21 between Dinant and Namur bus station runs to the stop outside the gardens, but it's a patchy service (1–4 daily; 40min). The nearest **train station** is Godinne, 2km from the gardens and served by hourly trains on the Namur–Dinant line; to reach the gardens, walk up the ramp of the flyover from the station, turn right at the top and then hang a left to cross the bridge over the Meuse. It isn't a pleasant walk though – there's too much traffic.

Dinant

Slung along the River Meuse beneath craggy green cliffs, **DINANT**, 30km from Namur, has a picture-postcard setting, its distinctive, onion-domed church lording it over the comings and goings of the barges and cruise boats. The Romans were the first to put the place on the map, occupying the town and naming it after Diana, the goddess of the hunt, but Dinant's heyday was the fourteenth century when it boomed from the profits of the metalworking industry, turning copper, brass and bronze into ornate jewellery known as *dinanderie*. Dinant's prosperity turned rival cities, especially Namur, green with envy, and they watched with some satisfaction as local counts slugged it out for possession of the town. They may have been even happier when, in 1466, Charles the Bold decided to settle his Dinant account by simply razing the place to the ground. One result of all this medieval blood and thunder was the construction of an imposing **citadel** on the cliff immediately above the town and, although Dinant was sacked on several subsequent occasions and damaged in both World Wars, the fortress has survived to become the town's principal attraction.

Nowadays, Dinant makes a healthy living both as a base for visiting Les Jardins d'Annevoie (see above) and as the centre of the tourist industry on the rivers **Meuse** and **Lesse** (see p.326), its cruise boats, canoes and kayaks providing watery fun and games for thousands of visitors – though frankly the scenery is not nearly as wild as you'll find deeper in the Ardennes. The other quibble is that Dinant gets much too crowded for comfort in the height of the season, when its long main street – **rue Grande** – chokes with traffic. Nevertheless, Dinant has enough going for it – including several good restaurants and a couple of comfortable hotels – to justify a stay of a night or two, especially if you intend to go canoeing or kayaking.

Arrival, information and accommodation

Dinant **train station** is about 300m from the bridge that spans the Meuse over to the church of Notre-dame and the town centre. **Buses** arrive and leave from outside the train station. The **tourist office** is beside the west (train-station) end of the bridge at avenue Cadoux 8 (Easter–Oct Mon–Fri 8.30am–6pm, Sat 9.30am–5pm, Sun 10am–4.30pm; Nov–Easter Mon–Fri 8.30am–6pm, Sat 9.30am–4pm, Sun 10.30am–2pm; ☎082 22 90 38, ⓦwww.dinant.be). They will make hotel reservations on your behalf and have an excellent range of local information, including walking and cycling maps, principally the Institut Géographique National's *Dinant et ses anciennes communes* (see p.22). On the other side of the bridge, the church of Notre-Dame is next to what passes for the main square, the inconsequential **place Reine Astrid**. The square is the starting point for the **téléférique** (cable car) up to the citadel and also marks the end of the narrow main street, **rue Grande**, which trails south, one block in from the riverside, from where you can travel the Meuse by **boat** (see p.327).

Dinant's small supply of **hotels** is supplemented by a handful of **B&Bs** (❸–❹), whose details are kept by the tourist office. There is no hostel, but there are plenty of **campsites** in the locality, one of the better ones being the well-appointed *Camping de Villatoile* (☎082 22 22 85; March–Oct), in a wooded setting beside the River Lesse in Anseremme, about 4km south of Dinant.

Hotels

Hôtel La Couronne rue A. Sax 1 ☎082 22 24 41, ⓕ081 22 70 31. This hotel is about as central as it's possible to get – metres from the church. There are 22 plain but perfectly adequate rooms in a modern block and above a bar. ❸

Hostellerie Le Freyr chaussée des Alpinistes 22 ☎082 22 25 75, ⓕ082 22 70 42. Smooth and polished four-star hotel, with just six reasonably comfortable rooms, plus a first-rate restaurant. Occupies a good-looking older building close to the Meuse, about 4km south of Dinant proper in Anseremme. Closed Feb & March. ❹

Hôtel Ibis Dinant Rempart d'Albeau 16 ☎082 21 15 00, ⓕ082 21 15 79. In a newly constructed brick block metres from the south end of rue Grand, 1km or so from the bridge. No points for originality, but this chain hotel does what it does proficiently enough, with most of its neat and trim, modern rooms looking out over the river. ❹

Taverne Le Rouge et Noir rue Grande 26 ☎082 22 69 44. Right in the centre of Dinant, on the main street, this tavern offers a few spartan rooms above its bar. Light sleepers beware. ❷.

The Town

Dinant's most distinctive landmark is the originally Gothic **church of Notre-Dame** (daily 10.30am–6pm; free), topped with the bulbous spire that features on all the brochures. Rebuilt on several occasions, it doesn't feature a huge amount to see inside, but it's worth a quick look for its cavernous, high-vaulted nave and a couple of paintings by Antoine Wiertz, who was born here (and has his own museum in Brussels; see p.101). Neither painting is especially inspiring, one a desultory black and white affair, the other, *The Assumption*, a typically crude and harsh vision, even without any of the ghoulish tricks for which Wiertz was famous. If you want to see the birthplace of another native, **Adolphe Sax** (1814–94), the inventor of the saxophone, walk north down rue A. Sax from just in front of the church. Sax lived at no. 35, a modest dwelling marked by a commemorative plaque and a neat stained-glass mural of a man blowing his horn.

From place Reine Astrid, head south down rue Grande and take the third turning on the left for place du Palais de Justice, home to the big and blousy, château-style **Palais de Justice**, which dates from the 1880s. From here, it's

△ Citadel, Dinant

another short walk south to **square Lion**, which is – oddly enough – flanked by mock-Tudor, half-timbered houses in the English style. Wiertz makes an appearance here too in the form of a badly weathered **statue**, *The Triumph of the Light*, a melodramatic piece that comes close to being absurd. From the square, a *télésiège* (chairlift) climbs up the cliff to the **Parc Familial de Mont-Fat** (April–Oct daily 10.30am–7pm; €5), a sort of low-key children's theme park with caves and playground.

Rather more appealing is the **Grotte La Merveilleuse** (April–June, Sept & Oct daily 10am–5pm; July & Aug daily 10am–6pm; Nov–March Sat & Sun 1–4pm; guided visits on the hour, in French and Flemish only; €5), across the bridge from the church and a fairly stiff 800m up along route de Philippeville. The unique feature of these caves is the whiteness of their rock formations, although again there are better caves to explore in the Ardennes proper (principally at Han-sur-Lesse – see p.332).

The citadel

Visible from just about anywhere in town, the austere stone walls of Dinant's **citadel** (April–Sept daily 10am–6pm; Oct to mid-Dec & mid-Feb to March daily except Fri 10am–4pm; €5.20) roll along the clifftop high above the church of Notre Dame. There are three ways to get there: you can drive out of town and approach the citadel from the east, climb the four hundred or so steps that lead up the cliff from beside the church, or save yourself the sweat by catching the adjacent cable car – the *téléférique* – whose cost is included in the price of admission. From the top, the views out over the Meuse valley are extensive, but the citadel is itself only mildly diverting. The French destroyed the medieval castle in 1703 and the present structure, mostly dating from the Dutch occupation of the early nineteenth century, largely consists of a series of stone-faced earthen bastions.

The citadel saw heavy **fighting** in both World Wars. In 1914, the Germans struggled to dislodge the French soldiers, who had occupied the stronghold just before they could get here. Peeved, the Germans took a bitter revenge on the townsfolk, whom they alleged had fired on them, executing over six hundred and deporting several hundred more before torching the town. The Germans took the citadel again in 1940, and it was the scene of more bitter fighting when the Allies captured Dinant in 1944. There's a memorial to those who gave their lives here and part of the interior has been turned into what is essentially a historical museum, with models recreating particular battles and the Dutch occupation, plus a modest military section with weapons from the Napoleonic era to the last war. You can also see the wooden beams which supported the first bridge in Dinant, built nine hundred years ago by monks and found again by accident in 1952, as well as prison cells and the kitchen and bakery of the Dutch stronghold.

Eating and drinking

Catering for Dinant's passing tourist trade is big business, which means that run-of-the-mill **cafés and restaurants** are ten-a-penny, whereas quality places are much thinner on the ground. That said, there are more than enough good choices for a short stay and several enjoyable neighbourhood **bars** too.

Cafés and restaurants

La Broche rue Grande 24 ☏ 082 22 82 81. Smart restaurant with an inventive menu mixing Asian Indian and French cuisines. Main courses average about €15. Closed Tues.

Chez Leon pl Reine Astrid 15. There was a time when Brussels' original Chez Leon was *the* place for mussels and fries. Those days are long gone and today its many branches – including this one – offer pretty routine fare, including the mussels. At least the service is speedy.

Patisserie Jacobs rue Grande 147. The best patisserie in town – with fruit tarts to cry for. Small café section too. Footsteps from the church.

Le Thermidor rue de la Station 3 ☏ 082 22 31 35. Excellent, if slightly old-fashioned, restaurant with a good line in local specialities and lobsters. Main courses hover around €20. Closed Mon eve & Tues.

Villa Casanova av Churchill 9, just south along the river from the bridge. Mid-range Italian restaurant with substantial pasta and pizza dishes from around €8.

Bars

Café Leffe rue A Sax 2. Café-bar serving very average food, the compensation being the first-floor terrace overlooking the river and the bridge.

Le Sax pl Reine Astrid 13. Unpretentious bar with a good beer selection – sit outside and peer up at the floodlit citadel.

Le Themis rue de Palais de Justice 26. Relaxed and easy-going neighbourhood joint with a better-than-average beer menu. A short walk south of the church along rue Grande – the third turning on the left.

South of Dinant: the Meuse and the Lesse

Beyond Dinant, the **River Meuse** loops its way south to Givet, across the border in France. This stretch of the river is pleasant enough, but certainly not exciting – it's too wide and sluggish for that – and neither is the scenery more than mildly inviting, its best feature being the steep, wooded cliffs framing portions of the river bank. The tiny settlements lining up along the river are pretty bland too, the only real exception being **Hastière-Par-Delà**, which boasts a superb Romanesque-Gothic church. This part of the river can be explored by cruise boat from Dinant and, at a pinch, by local bus: the Givet bus, departing from outside Dinant station, calls at all the riverside villages, but operates no more than twice daily.

Wilder and prettier than the Meuse, the **River Lesse** spears off the Meuse in **Anseremme**, an inconsequential town some 3.5km south of Dinant along the N96. The basic drill here is to head upstream by catching the train from Dinant – or one of the special minibuses run by canoe and kayak rental outlets in Anseremme – and then paddle back. There are, however, no cruises along the River Lesse.

The **Dinant tourist office** sells the Institut Géographique National's **map** *Dinant et ses anciennes communes* (1:25,000; €7), which shows fifteen numbered **circular walks** in the Dinant area. Each of the walks has a designated starting point at one of the district's hotels. Also shown on the map are one cycling circuit and five **mountain-bike routes**, the latter ranging from five to forty kilometres in length; to see the most attractive scenery you need to get out on the longer routes 19 and 20. You can rent mountain-bikes from Kayaks Ansiaux in Anseremme (see p.329).

The Meuse

From Anseremme, it's 2.5km southwest to the solitary **Château de Freÿr**, a crisply symmetrical, largely eighteenth-century brick mansion pushed up against the main road and the river (☏082 22 22 00). The compulsory guided tour (March & Oct–Dec Sun at 3pm; April–June & Sept Sat & Sun at 11am, 2.30pm & 4pm; July & Aug Tues–Fri at 11am, 2.30pm & 4pm; €6; 1hr 30min) traipses through a series of opulent rooms, distinguished by their period furniture and thundering fireplaces. Running parallel to the river are the adjoining **gardens**, laid out in the formal French style, spreading over three terraces and including a maze. A pavilion at the highest point provides a lovely view over the château and river.

Further downriver, about 15km from Dinant, tiny Hastière-Lavaux is unremarkable, but neighbouring **HASTIÈRE-PAR-DELÀ**, just across the bridge, holds the fascinating **Église Notre Dame** (April–Oct daily 1–5pm; free). A finely proportioned edifice, the church was built at the behest of a colony of Irish monks in the 1030s, though the Gothic choir was added two hundred years later. Subsequent architectural tinkering followed two attacks – one by Protestants in 1568, the other by the French revolutionary army in the 1790s – but most of the medieval church has survived intact, with a flat wooden roof, plain square pillars and heavy round arches. The **triumphal arch** bears a faded painting dating from the original construction and is underpinned by gallows (wooden scaffolding), which in their turn support an unusual German fifteenth-

By boat from Dinant

Despite its serpentine profile, the **River Meuse** south of Dinant is not especially scenic, though the town's boat tour operators still drum up lots of business for their **river cruises**. There are several different companies located on avenue Winston Churchill, one block from the main street, rue Grande, but prices and itineraries are pretty standard whichever company you choose. Two good bets are the cruises to Anseremme (mid-March to Oct every 30min; €4.80; 45min return trip), where you can hike off into the surrounding countryside (see p.328); and Hastière (June & early July 1 daily on Sun only, mid-July to late Aug 1 daily; €11; 3hr 15min return trip). There are also boats north along the Meuse to Namur (see p.316) on Saturdays and Sundays from early July to late August (€13 one-way; 3hr).

century Calvary, depicting Christ, Mary and St John standing on a dragon. Close by, the wooden thirteenth-century **choir stalls** are among the oldest in Belgium, with unique misericord carvings – some allegorical, some satirical and some purely decorative. Curiously, a number of them were replaced with a plain triangle in 1443 on the grounds that they were blasphemous – or at least disrespectful. Finally, next to the baptismal font are two **statues** of the Virgin, one of which – the one on the left in the glass case – is an exquisite sixteenth-century carving, whose graceful posture has earned it a place in several national exhibitions.

After you've explored the church, you can pop across the road to *Le Côté Meuse*, a pleasant **café** with a good line in crepes. As for moving on, the N915 cuts southeast across country from Hastière to the N95, which has turnings to Houyet (see below).

The Lesse valley

Unlike the Meuse, there isn't a road along the Lesse valley and although a network of country lanes reaches most of its nooks and crannies, driving and cycling here can be very confusing. Fortunately, an hourly **train** runs south from Dinant, stopping at Anseremme before proceeding up the Lesse to Gendron-Celles and Houyet. Trains take five minutes from Dinant to Anseremme, with Houyet another fifteen minutes away. **Beyond Houyet** the train leaves the Lesse valley bound for the rail junction of Bertrix, where you can change for either Libramont (for Arlon & Luxembourg), or Florenville (see p.342) and Virton (see p.344). The River Lesse continues to worm its way southeast, largely inaccessible until it reaches **Rochefort** (see opposite), a short drive from Dinant, and best reached via Namur if you're travelling on from Dinant by train.

Walking and biking along the Lesse

Among the walks detailed in the specialist map sold by the Dinant tourist office, the five-kilometre-long **Walk 5** takes in much of the locality's most pleasant scenery, weaving its way along and around the River Lesse between the hamlets of Anseremme and Pont à Lesse. Walk 5 involves some reasonably testing ascents, whereas **GR route 126** offers about three hours of gentle walking along the Lesse between Houyet and Gendron-Celles. Take the timetable along with your picnic and you can plan to arrive at Gendron-Celles in time for the return train to Dinant.

The eight-kilometre-long **Walk 8** is not one of the more spectacular routes – much of it is over tarmac road – but it does allow you to visit a couple of places of some interest. From **Gendron-Celles train station**, the route leads about 2km northeast along a country road – and beside a small tributary of the Lesse – to **Vêves**, whose fifteenth-century **château** is perched on a grassy mound overlooking the surrounding countryside (April & Oct Tues–Sun 10am–5pm; May, June & Sept Tues–Sun 10am–6pm; July & Aug daily 10am–6pm; €4.70). With its spiky turrets and dinky towers, the château is inordinately picturesque, but the interior is disappointingly mundane – mostly eighteenth-century period rooms. A couple of kilometres further on, **Celles** is one of the prettier villages hereabouts, gently filing up the slope of a wooded hill, underneath the huge tower and Lombard arches of the Romanesque **Église St Hadelin** (daily 9am–5pm, till 7pm in July & Aug; free). There's a sporadic bus service from here to Dinant or you can return to Gendron-Celles train station via the Bois de Hubermont. If you're driving, note that Celles is on the N94, about 8km east of Dinant.

There's precious little point in hanging around in **ANSEREMME**, though its **train station** is a good starting point for local hikes and is also just a couple of minutes' walk from the river – and two thoroughly reputable **canoe and kayak** rental outlets. Operating from April to October, Kayaks Ansiaux (☎082 21 35 35, ⓦwww.ansiaux.be) and Lesse Kayaks (☎082 22 43 97) both rent out a variety of boats, principally one- and two-seater kayaks, three-person canoes and large piloted boats for up to twenty passengers; advance reservations are required. Reckon on paying €17 for a single canoe for a day, €20 for a double.

The standard itinerary for drivers and cyclists begins at Anseremme, where they take the train (or special minibus) to either **Gendron–Celles** (for the 12km, 3hr paddle back) or **Houyet** (21km, 5hr). If you're travelling by train to begin with, you can go straight to Gendron-Celles or Houyet from Dinant and pick up a boat there – but remember that advance reservations are well-nigh essential. The Lesse itself is wild and winding, with great scenery, though be warned that sometimes it gets so packed that there's a veritable canoe log-jam. Consequently, it's a good idea to set out as early as possible to avoid some of the crush – though if you're paddling back from Houyet you really have to get going early anyway. Both Gendron-Celles and Houyet train stations are metres from the river – and the boats – and also make good starting points for hiking the surrounding countryside.

Rochefort, Han and around

A few kilometres upstream from Houyet, to the southeast, lies one of the Ardennes' most beautiful regions, centring on the tourist resorts of **Han-sur-Lesse** and **Rochefort**. The district offers one or two specific sights, most notably the Han-sur-Lesse caves as well as a scattering of castles, but the real magnet is the splendid countryside, a thickly wooded terrain of plateaux, gentle hills and valleys, and with good roads perfect for cycling. The best base for these rural wanderings is Rochefort, a middling sort of place with a good range of accommodation – and few of the crowds that swamp Han-sur-Lesse.

As for **public transport**, access is difficult from Dinant (and Houyet), from where the best bet is to backtrack to Namur and take the train from there to **Jemelle**, east of Rochefort and on the Brussels–Namur–Luxembourg line; regular trains also go to Jemelle from Liège. From Jemelle station, it's about 3km west to Rochefort, 6km more to Han, and there is an hourly **bus** service linking all three.

Rochefort

Situated in the midst of some lovely scenery, the small town of **ROCHEFORT** is a very good base for exploring the Ardennes. It's not an especially attractive place in itself, but it has none of the crass commercialism of neighbouring Han, and does have a good range of cheap accommodation, as well as other facilities like bike rental. Rochefort also has the dubious benefit of a brightly-coloured, motorized **tourist train**, which shuttles round the town from April to mid-October, with twice weekly excursions to the château Lavaux Ste Anne, near Han, from mid-May to mid-September.

Rochefort follows the contours of an irregularly shaped hill, its long and pleasant main street, **rue de Behogne**, slicing through the centre from north to south, although the only things of tangible interest are actually outside the town centre. The big deal is the **Grotte de Lorette** (Feb–April & Sept–Nov daily except Wed 10am–4.30pm; May & June daily except Wed 10am–5pm; July & Aug daily 10.30am–5.30pm; hour-long guided tours May–Aug every 45min, rest of year every 2hr; €6), a ten-minute walk from the central cross-roads, where rue de Behogne intersects with place Albert 1er: walk down rue Jacquet and follow the signs. The caves are at the top of rue de Lorette. First discovered in 1865 by a man walking his dog (the dog disappeared suddenly through a hole in the ground), the caves are cold and eerie, their most impressive feature the huge Salle du Sabbat (Hall of the Sabbath) – no less than 85m high. Renovations have recently been made to improve access and lighting – the most spectacular innovation being an underground sound-and-light show. Close by the entrance, the small and still-in-use **Lorette Chapel** dates from the 1620s. Built for a local countess, it's a reproduction of the Santa Casa chapel in Loreto, Italy; according to local legend, a monkey stole the countess's child and she promised to build the chapel if the child was returned unharmed.

Château Comtal

Doubling back from the caves, turn left along rue Jacquet for Rochefort's other main attraction – the ruins of the medieval **Château Comtal** (April–Oct daily 10am–6pm; €1.50), which offers fine views from its rocky outcrop. The original castle dates from 1155, although there was almost certainly some sort of fortification here a lot earlier. In the 1740s the local count decided to convert it into a more informal, less forbidding place, demolishing the keep and incorporating the old walls into a new palace. Within a century, however, the owners had run into financial trouble and the château was gradually demolished; some of the massive stones were used in the adjoining Maison Carré (square house), built in 1840, and in the new neo-Gothic castle of 1906 which now houses the ticket office. Other fragments of the old castle were sold off to local builders and the distinctive, irregular limestone stones are now incorporated in buildings all over town.

Unsurprisingly, there's not an awful lot left of the old castle now, but it's a pleasant enough place to wander for an hour or so. Alongside the remains of the old walls there are a couple of wells that were dug out of the bare rock while, in the small park just below the entrance, you can see the eighteenth-century arcades added to prop up the fashionable formal gardens. A tiny museum in the castle has objects from down the centuries: old cannonballs, ceramics, oyster shells and wine bottles.

Abbaye de St Remy

The town's surroundings also reward exploration (see box opposite for suggested routes). Thirty minutes' walk through the woods to the north, the **Abbaye de St Remy** is a Cistercian monastery founded in 1230, best known today for producing the Rochefort Trappist beer (see p.435). The monastery buildings are closed to the public, but you are welcome to attend the daily services in the church (times from the tourist office – see below). The church is down the slope to the right and then on your left after you enter the monastery grounds.

Practicalities

Buses to Rochefort pull in along the main street, the rue de Behogne. The town's friendly and well-organized **tourist office** is at rue de Behogne 5 (Mon–Fri 9am–12.30pm & 1–5pm, Sat 9.30am–12.30pm & 1–5pm; ☎084 21 25 37, ⓔrochefort.tourisme@skynet.be). They have oodles of local information and will make accommodation bookings at no charge.

Walking, cycling and canoeing around Rochefort and Han

Criss-crossed by rivers, the handsome countryside around Rochefort provides lots of opportunities for walking, canoeing and mountain-biking. **Walkers** need the Institut Géographique National's map, *Rochefort et ses villages* (€7 from the tourist offices in Rochefort and Han), which lists 27 numbered walks, as well as eight routes for **mountain-bikers** and three for **cyclists**. Kayaks Lesse et Lomme in Han rents out **mountain bikes** for €20 per day and regular bikes for €10 per day, and organizes excursions involving a combination of canoeing and cycling (see below); mountain bikes can also be rented from the tourist office in Rochefort at comparable rates.

Walks from Rochefort

The Résurgence d'Eprave – **Walk 12** – is one of the most scenically varied, a twelve-kilometre circular route. Take rue Jacquet out of town past the château and the route is signposted to the right, through **Hamerenne** with its tiny Romanesque chapel of St Odile, and across fields full of wildflowers, to the River Lomme. Follow the river-bank to the spot where the River Wamme emerges from underground to join the Lomme; don't try to cross the river but double back and turn right for the stiff climb uphill past the Eprave Grotto for grand views over the cornfields. Fifteen minutes' walk further on, the village of **Eprave** has a restored mill with a working waterwheel and, opposite, the rusticated *Auberge du Vieux Moulin*, on rue de l'Aujoule, makes a delightful place to stay or eat (☎084 37 73 18, ✉auberge@eprave.com; ⑤). The walk back to Rochefort from here is rather dull, following the road, and you may want to retrace your steps, or join **Walk 4**, Grotte d'Eprave, to Han for the hourly bus back to Rochefort.

A couple of good shorter walks around Rochefort include **Walk 7**, Lorette, a thirty-minute climb up through the woods above town, taking in the Lorette chapel and some decent views over the castle. Head up rue de Lorette towards the caves and turn left, keeping to the left, where the track is signposted. The six-kilometre **Walk 10**, Abbaye Saint Rémy, goes the other way out of town, across the bridge and cutting north off the main road through some thickly wooded scenery as far as Abbaye de St Remy, before looping back to Rochefort.

Walks around Han

The walks around Han are less interesting than those from Rochefort, though you can create a very pleasant half-day itinerary by following **Walk 2**, Turmont, through the Lesse and Lomme Nature Reserve to Auffe, where **Walk 20**, Les Etouneaux, climbs up through the dense woods of Serivau – good hunting territory in the past and still with a touch of the "Hansel and Gretel" feel to it. Returning past Auffe, take **Walk 24**, Les Pics Epeiches, across the fields as far as Lessive, where you can get a decent lunch at *Le Vieux Lessive* (closed Mon Oct–May) before returning to Han.

Canoeing and kayaking on the Lesse

To mess about on the river, **canoes and kayaks** can be rented from Kayaks Lesse et Lomme, near the bridge in Han (☎082 22 43 97; May to mid-Sept daily 9.30am–6pm, April, late Sept & Oct Sat & Sun 9.30am–6pm). They have a few canoes and pedal boats for splashing around town, but it's much more scenic and fun to join one of their **excursions**; on offer are several different types of trip and a choice of transport – bus or mountain-bike and kayak. The shortest (and least expensive) trip is the two-hour jaunt to Lessive, 6km away on the river and 4km back by bike (€17 per person, €23 for two, all inclusive). The longest is to Wanlin, 19km by kayak and 13km return by bike or bus (€45, €60). You can start the shortest trip anytime between 10am and 4pm, 10am to noon for Wanlin. Incidentally, in high summer the water level on the Lesse can drop far enough to make canoeing impossible; call ahead to confirm.

Accommodation

Of the seven central **hotels**, easily the pick of them is *Le Vieux Logis*, rue Jacquet 71 (☎084 21 10 24; ❸), housed in a lovely old building with an immaculate, antique interior and attractive gardens. Rue Jacquet is a southerly continuation of rue de Behogne and is also home to *La Fayette*, at no. 87 (☎084 21 42 73, ☎084 22 11 63, ✉hotel.lafayette@swing.be; ❸), a one-star establishment with just eight plain and simple rooms, half of which are en suite; it's housed in an old, whitewashed brick building. Rue de Behogne chips in too, with *La Malle Poste*, no. 46 (☎084 21 09 86, ☎084 22 11 13; ❹), a pleasant if spookily old-fashioned three-star hotel in a well-kept building that comes complete with a cobbled courtyard. Finally, there are two workaday three-star hotels on place Albert 1er – *Le Central*, at no. 30 (☎084 21 10 44, ☎084 21 22 19; ❸), and *Le Limbourg*, at no. 21 (☎084 21 10 36, ☎084 21 44 23; closed late Jan; ❸).

The tourist office has the details of local **B&Bs** – there are half a dozen in town and more on the outskirts. There's a convenient **campsite**, *Camping Communal* (☎084 21 19 00; April–Oct) a ten-minute walk east of rue de Behogne via rue de Marche – take the first left after the river along rue du Hableau.

Eating and drinking

Besides boasting the best restaurant in town, the *Hôtel La Malle Poste* has a convivial **bar** – *La Coterie* – which dates back to the sixteenth century and is fully stocked with a fine selection of Belgian beers.

Bella Italia rue de Behogne 44. A good choice, offering substantial pizzas, pasta dishes, and truly splendid calzone from €8, as well as an extensive menu of good-value Belgian cuisine.

La Gourmandise rue de Behogne 24, opposite the tourist office. Superb crepes and simple, good-value meals – pasta, salads – from around €7.

Hôtel La Malle Poste rue de Behogne 46. The restaurant here features an imaginative menu with an excellent range of Ardennes dishes. Closed Wed out of season.

Le Limbourg pl Albert 1er 21. Does a good line in local specialities, with main courses averaging about €15. Closed Wed out of season.

Le Luxembourg Brasserie pl Albert 1er 2. Serves very tasty snacks and meals in brisk, modern surroundings and at very reasonable prices. Closed Mon out of season.

Han-sur-Lesse and around

Just 6km southwest of Rochefort, tiny **HAN-SUR-LESSE** is well known for its caves, which are the most impressive in the Ardennes – with the result that in summer at least the village is jam-packed. There are masses of hotels and eating places to absorb the invasion, most in the immediate vicinity of the centre, but the frantic atmosphere will probably make you want to curtail your visit.

In fact there's not much to actually see in Han apart from the **Grottes de Han**, located outside the village a little way downriver (April–Oct daily 10am–noon & 1.30–4.30pm, closes 5.30pm July & Aug; also occasional holiday opening Nov–March; €10.30; ⓦwww.grotte-de-han.be). The caves were discovered at the beginning of the nineteenth century and measure about 8km in length, a series of limestone galleries carved out of the hills by the River Lesse millions of years ago. Access is only possible by special **tram** (no extra charge), dinky little things which leave from the centre of the village, beside the ticket office, on the corner of rue Joseph Lamotte and rue d'Hamptay. The **tours** only visit a small part of the cave system (April, Sept & Oct hourly, May–Aug every 30min), taking in the so-called Salle du Trophée, the site of the largest stalagmite; the Salle d'Armes, where the Lesse reappears after travelling underground for 1km; and the massive Salle du Dôme – 129m high – which contains a small lake. After the tour, you make your own way back to the village on foot – a five- to ten-minute walk.

For an insight into how the caves were formed, head to the **Musée du Monde Souterrain**, place Théo Lannoy 3 (daily: April–Aug noon–6pm, Sept & Oct 2–5pm; €3); it's behind the tourist office and across the street and behind the church from the caves' ticket office. A section of the museum explains the process, while other sections display the prehistoric artefacts unearthed during a series of archeological digs in and around the caves. Most were found where the Lesse surfaces again after travelling through the grottoes – among them flints, tools and bone ornaments from the Neolithic period, as well as weapons and jewellery from the Bronze Age.

Han's other attractions are dreary in the extreme. The most conspicuous is the **Réserve Animalier** (wild-animal reserve; guided tours as for the caves; €7.80), just south of the town and covering an area of 2.5 square kilometres. A special bus trawls around the reserve for about an hour and a half, seeking out the assorted boars, stags, deer and bison. The other well-trailed attraction is the **Expothème** (daily: April–Oct noon to 6 or 7pm; €5), devoted to exhibitions with an international flavour – recently on, of all things, the Masai. It's on the first-floor of a former farmhouse, which is itself part of a recreation area with playground and petting animals, just east of the tram station along rue des Grottes. A **combined ticket** covering the caves, Expothème, the Réserve Animalier and the Musée du Monde Souterrain costs €16.10.

Lavaux Ste Anne

About 10km west of Han, on the road to Dinant, the hamlet of **LAVAUX STE ANNE** is dominated by its **château** (daily 9am–6pm, July & Aug until 7pm; €4.70), parts of which – principally the keep and its trio of onion-domed towers – are of medieval provenance. The moat dates back to the same period, but most of the rest of the complex is eighteenth century, from the main building, with its high-pitched gables and dormer windows, through to the quadrangular former stables and farm buildings. The interior holds a sleep-inducing museum of nature and hunting. Without your own transport, you can get here on the tourist train from Rochefort (see p.329).

Practicalities

Buses to Han pull in close to the main crossroads, where rue Joseph Lamotte meets both rue d'Hamptay and rue des Grottes. Metres from the crossroads is the **tourist office** (May–Sept daily 10am–4.30pm; ℡084 37 75 96, ℅han.tourisme@euronet.be), which occupies a chalet opposite the caves' ticket office. They will make hotel bookings on your behalf for free and also have a substantial list of local **B&Bs** (❶–❷).

There are four central **hotels**, all with three stars. Among them, the *Hôtel des Ardennes*, footsteps from the crossroads at rue des Grottes 2 (℡084 37 72 20, ℻084 37 80 62; ❸), is competent enough, with twenty neat and trim – if unexceptional – rooms in a large, old stone building. The *Hôtel des Ardennes 2*, next door (same phone and fax numbers; ❹), has fifteen modern rooms and is somewhat smarter, though more expensive. Ten minutes' walk north of the crossroads, the *Hostellerie Henry IV*, at rue des Chasseurs Ardennais 59 (℡084 37 72 21, ℻084 37 81 78; ❸), the road to Rochefort, occupies a modern, three-storey building with a terrace. The rooms are hardly inspiring, but the *hostellerie* does have the advantage of being removed from Han's summer hubbub. There are also two **campsites**, both by the river's edge and open all year:

Camping du Pirot, rue de Charleville (☏084 37 72 90), which is near the bridge, about 200m west of the tourist office at the end of rue Joseph Lamotte; and the equally convenient *Camping de la Lesse*, about 300m from the tourist office along rue d'Hamptay and its continuation, rue du Grand Hy (☏084 37 72 90).

The day-tripping hordes keep prices up and quality down in many of Han's **cafés** and **restaurants**. An exception is *La Stradella*, rue d'Hamptay 59, a proficient Italian place serving pizzas and pastas from €7. The *Hôtel des Ardennes* has a popular restaurant, with main (standard–Belgian) courses coming in at around €17, but the *Belle Vue Café*, rue Lamotte 1 (closed Mon out of season), has a more imaginative menu, offering good-quality, traditional Belgian cuisine at affordable prices – main courses from around €15.

St Hubert and around

About 20km southeast of Rochefort, **ST HUBERT** is another popular Ardennes resort, albeit one with an entirely different feel from its neighbours, partly on account of its solitary location, up on a plateau and surrounded by forest. A small town with just six thousand inhabitants, it's well worth a visit, though its **basilica** apart, St Hubert is otherwise distinctly short of sights. It takes only about an hour to wander round the **town centre**, which is too dishevelled to be particularly endearing, and the lack of really good accommodation may make you think twice about staying; you're better off heading out to a couple of nearby attractions or **hiking** in the surrounding countryside.

Basilique St Hubert

The **Basilique St Hubert** (daily 9am–6pm, Nov–Easter till 5pm; free) is easily the grandest edifice in the Ardennes and has been an important place of pilgrimage since the relics of the eponymous saint were moved here in the ninth century. A well-respected though shadowy figure, **St Hubert** (c.656–727) spent years in the Ardennes preaching against the prevailing animism. He seems to have died as result of a fishing accident, but this wasn't didactic enough for the church, who concocted a much fancier tale. In this, Hubert becomes Count Hubert, a Frankish noble whose hedonistic lifestyle comes to an abrupt end on a hunting trip he irreligiously organized on Good Friday. Just when Hubert's hounds corner a stag, the beast turns to reveal, between his antlers, a luminous vision of Christ on the Cross. Shocked to his cotton socks, Hubert promptly abandons the hunt, gives his money away and dedicates his life to the church, becoming a (Belgian) bishop. This was all copybook stuff and sufficient justification for Hubert's canonization – as patron saint of hunters and trappers.

The first abbey here predated the cult of St Hubert, but things really got going after the saint's relics arrived and the abbey – as well as the village that grew up in its shadow – was named in his honour. In medieval times, the abbey became one of the region's richest and a major landowner. The French suppressed the abbey in the 1790s, but the abbey church – now the basilica – plus several of the old abbey buildings survived; the latter flank the grand rectangular **piazza** that leads to the basilica's main entrance.

From the outside, the basilica's outstanding feature is the Baroque **west facade** of 1702, made of limestone and equipped with twin pepper-pot towers, a clock and a carving on the pediment depicting the miracle of St Hubert. Inside, the clear lines of the Gothic nave and aisles have taken an aesthetic hammering from both an extensive Baroque refurbishment and a heavy-handed neo-Gothic make-over of the 1840s. The result doesn't sit easily on the eye, but there are one or two redeeming features, most notably the fetching pink and black stripes on the columns in the nave. Also of interest are the whopping **choir stalls**, typically Baroque and retelling the legend of St Hubert (on the right-hand side) and St Benedict (on the left), as well as the elaborate **mausoleum** of St Hubert, at the beginning of the ambulatory, on the left. The mausoleum was carved in the 1840s, with King Léopold I, a keen huntsman, picking up the bill. Beside the mausoleum is the only stained-glass **window** to have survived from the sixteenth century, a richly coloured, wonderfully executed work of art, down to the folds of the table cloth.

Practicalities

The nearest **train station** to St Hubert is Poix St Hubert, 7km away to the west on the Namur–Libramont line. From here, there are regular **buses** into St Hubert (Mon–Fri 12 daily, Sat & Sun 4 daily; 20min), which stop at place du Marché, metres from the basilica. The **tourist office**, rue St Gilles 12 (daily 9am–6pm; ☎061 61 30 10, ⓦwww.sthubert.be), is just across the street from the beginning of the piazza that leads to the basilica entrance. They sell **maps** of the area's marked walks, including the functional *Carte des Promenades Pedestre*, which details eleven circular routes (**Walk 5** is perhaps the best of the bunch, a two- to three-hour jaunt through the woods and onto the edge of open moorland), as well as stocking plenty of other Ardennes literature.

Of the four **hotels** in the town centre, the *Hôtel de l'Abbaye*, opposite the basilica at place du Marché 18, (☎061 61 10 23, ⓕ061 61 34 22, ⓦwww.hotelabbaye.be; ❶), has a real claim to fame as the place where Hemingway hunkered down in 1944 as he advanced across Europe with the US army. Perhaps surprisingly, the hotel doesn't make much of the connection and, although it occupies an attractive old building and the public rooms are pleasantly old-fashioned, its twenty rooms – of which fourteen are en suite – are very plain and frugal. Somewhat more enticing is the *Hôtel du Luxembourg*, place du Marché 7 (☎061 61 10 93, ⓕ061 61 32 20; ❷), an unassuming two-star hotel with eighteen modest rooms, most of which are en suite. Finally, the three-star *Le Cor de Chasse*, avenue Nestor Martin 3 (☎061 61 16 44, ⓕ061 61 33 15; ❸), occupies a modest, inter-war terraced house, but its eleven rooms are a bit more commodious than those of its rivals, though not by much. To get there, walk down rue St Gilles, past the tourist office, and it's at the end of the street, 300m or so from the basilica. The nearest **campsite** is the large, family-oriented *Europacamp* on route de Martelange, 2km southwest of town (☎061 61 12 69).

The **restaurants** of both the *Hôtel de l'Abbaye* and the *Hôtel du Luxembourg* specialize in Ardennes dishes. Of the two, the *Luxembourg* does things slightly better and their *plat du jour* works out at a very reasonable €10. The premises are enjoyable too – decorated in a sort of neo-baronial style with acres of wood panelling and stuffed animal heads on the walls. Alternatively, *L'Entracte*, rue St Gilles 9, is a chic(ish) bistro that offers a good line in Ardennes specialities, plus excellent crepes, all at very affordable prices.

Around St Hubert

Apart from the scenery, nothing in the vicinity of St Hubert sets the pulse racing, but there are a couple of mildly enjoyable attractions within easy striking distance by car or bike. First up, in the green and fertile Masblette valley some 8km **north** of St Hubert, is **Fourneau St Michel** (March–Dec daily

9am–5pm, July & Aug till 6pm; €2.50), in part a reconstruction of the iron-works built here by the last abbot of St Hubert in the late eighteenth century. The complex includes an old blast furnace, casting bay, bellows and forge, plus a barn packed with firebacks and a museum showing old tools and the like. Here also is the **Musée Redouté** (same details), which chronicles the life and work of Pierre-Joseph Redouté (1759–1840). A native of St Hubert, Redouté spent most of his working life in France, where he established himself as a much-sought-after illustrator of botanical works and a painter of flowers. The adjacent **Musée de la Vie Rurale en Wallonie** (March to mid-Nov daily 9am–5pm, July & Aug till 6pm; €2.50) spreads out over a large area, an open-air museum made up of about fifty relocated buildings typical of rural Wallonia. There are farmhouses and stables, a sawmill, cottages and a chapel, along with the usual cafés and restaurants.

Some 12km **west** of St Hubert, right by the E411 (Exit 24), the **Euro Space Centre** is a hugely popular attraction (☎061 65 01 33; April–Sept daily 10am–5pm, with some variations during school terms & limited opening Oct–March; €10). Easily identified by the space rocket parked outside, its hangar-like premises house a hi-tech museum telling you everything you ever wanted to know about space travel and the applications of space and satellite technology. There are lots of buttons for kids to press in the many interactive displays, as well as full-scale models of the space shuttles and of the Mir space station. From the Space Centre, it's a further 6km west, across the E411, to **Redu**, a small village that has reinvented itself – à la Hay-on-Wye – as a bibliophile's paradise at the instigation of a local antiquarian bookseller, one Noel Anselot. The village now heaves with bookstores, selling new and used books, prints and pictures (Mon–Sat), and offers a programme of literary events to match. Obviously most of the books are in French or Flemish, but several bookstores have a reasonable selection of English titles – try De Boekenwurm, Voie d'Hurleau 51, for starters.

Bouillon and around

Forty-odd kilometres southwest of St Hubert, close to the French border, beguiling **BOUILLON** is a well-known and extraordinarily handsome resort on the edge of the Ardennes, enclosed in a loop of the River Semois and crowned by an outstanding castle. It's a relaxed and amiable place, with a healthy supply of hotels and restaurants, and, what's more, it's an excellent base for exploring – by foot, cycle or car – the wildly dramatic scenery of the **Semois river valley**.

Bouillon isn't on the train network, but there are regular **buses** from the nearest train station at **Libramont**, 30km northeast (Mon–Fri 6 daily, Sat & Sun 3 daily; 50min). There's also an infrequent service from Bertrix station, at the end of the branch line from Dinant; **Bertrix** is 20km away, again to the northeast.

Arrival and information

Though Bouillon is a small town, getting your bearings can be a little difficult at first. The thing to remember is that the **quai du Rempart**, the main street, is below and to the east of the castle; its north end is marked by the Pont de Liège, the south by the Pont de France. The quickest way to get from one side of the castle to the other is via the tunnel beside the Pont de France.

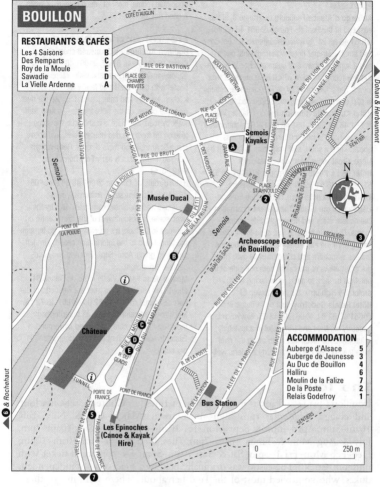

BOUILLON

RESTAURANTS & CAFÉS

Les 4 Saisons	**B**
Des Remparts	**C**
Roy de la Moule	**E**
Sawadie	**D**
La Vielle Ardenne	**A**

ACCOMMODATION

Auberge d'Alsace	**5**
Auberge de Jeunesse	**3**
Au Duc de Bouillon	**4**
Halliru	**6**
Moulin de la Falize	**7**
De la Poste	**2**
Relais Godefroy	**1**

0   250 m

Buses pull in on the quai du Rempart and beside the river; they then proceed south to the **bus station**, just across the Pont de France. The **tourist
office** (☏061 46 62 57, ⑩ www.bouillon-sedan.org) is based in the castle, and
shares its complex opening times (see p.338); there's also an **information
chalet** beside the Pont de France (Easter–June & Sept Sat & Sun 10am–1pm
& 2–6pm; July–Aug daily 10am–1pm & 2–7pm; ☏061 46 42 02). Both have
oodles of local information, book accommodation at no extra cost and sell
local hiking maps (see p.340).

Accommodation

Bouillon has a good range of **accommodation**, with around a dozen hotels,
a hostel, and a couple of campsites. In addition, the tourist office has the details
of a handful **B&Bs** (⑤), both in town and on the outskirts.

337

Hotels

Auberge d'Alsace Faubourg de France 3, at the east end of the Pont de France ☎061 46 65 88, ⓕ061 46 83 21, ⓦwww.aubergedalsace.be. Cosy and smart four-star hotel with traditional decor and a sombre brown and beige exterior. Very comfortable rooms, most of which have pleasant river views. The adjacent *Hôtel de France* (same details) is part of the same complex. Closed Jan. **❹**

Hôtel Au Duc de Bouillon rue des Hautes Voies 2 ☎061 46 63 20, ⓕ061 46 83 17. Straightforward two-star hotel in newly refurbished premises above – and a short, stiff walk from – the Pont de Liège. Great views over to the castle. **❸**

Hôtel de La Poste pl St Arnould 1 ☎061 46 51 51, ⓕ061 46 51 65, ⓦwww.hotelposte.be. There's been a hotel here, right by the Pont de Liège, since the 1730s. The present incarnation claims four stars and 66 sprightly decorated rooms. The main building is a good-looking affair dating from the early twentieth century, but the annexe is modern and comparatively dull. There are great views of the castle from one side of the hotel, so be sure to get a room facing west, and preferably high up in the hotel tower. **❹**

Hôtel Relais Godefroy quai de la Tannerie 5 ☎061 46 62 04, ⓕ061 46 42 05, ⓦwww.relais-godefroy.be. Neat and trim hotel in a tastefully refurbished old block just north along the river from the Pont de Liège, with thirty modern, well-appointed rooms, most of which have river views. A good bet. **❸**

Hostel and campsites

Bouillon Auberge de Jeunesse chemin du Christ 16 ☎061 46 81 37, ⓕ061 46 78 18, ⓔbouillon@laj.be. Large and well-equipped HI hostel with dorm beds and family rooms, plus kitchen, laundry and café. It's east across the river from the castle, on the hill opposite – a long, stiff walk by road, but there is a shortcut: the steps leading up from rue des Hautes Voies, just above place St Arnould, go there directly. Reservations advised. Closed Jan & early Feb. Dorm beds €12.50, **❶**

Halliru route de Corbion ☎061 46 60 09 or 061 46 74 11. Medium-sized, reasonably well-equipped and appointed campsite down by the river, some 2km southwest of the town centre on the road to Corbion. It's an easy walk – go through the tunnel next to the information chalet, turn left and keep going. April–Sept. Tent and two occupants €9 per night.

Moulin de la Falize Vieille route de France 64, about 1km south of town from the west end of the Port de France ☎061 46 62 00, ⓕ061 46 72 75. Medium-sized campsite with all the trimmings, including laundry, café, sauna and playground. Easter to early Nov. Tent and two occupants €11 per night.

The Town

Bouillon's pride and joy is its impossibly picturesque **Château**, set on a long and craggy ridge that runs high above town (March, Oct & Nov daily 10am–5pm; April–June & Sept Mon–Fri 10am–6pm, Sat & Sun 10am–7pm; July & Aug Mon & Thurs 10am–7pm, Tues, Wed & Fri–Sun 10am–10pm; Dec–Feb Mon–Fri 1–5pm, Sat & Sun 10am–5pm; €4, combined ticket with museum €6.30). The castle was originally held by a succession of independent dukes, who controlled most of the land hereabouts. There were five of these, all called **Godfrey de Bouillon**, the fifth and last of whom left on the First Crusade in 1096, selling his dominions (partly to raise the cash for his trip) to the prince-bishop of Liège. Later, Louis XIV got his hands on the old dukedom and promptly had the castle re-fortified to the design of his military architect **Vauban**, whose handiwork defines most of the fortress today.

The castle is an intriguing old place, and paths wind through most of its courtyards, along the battlements and towers, and through dungeons filled with weaponry and instruments of torture. Most visitors drive to the entrance, but walking there is easy enough too – either via rue du Château or, more strenuously, by a set of steep steps that climbs up from rue de Moulin, one street back from the river. A brochure in English, on sale at the entrance, describes the various parts of the stronghold and is well worth picking up. Among the highlights, the **Salle de Godfrey**, hewn out of the rock, contains a large wooden cross sunk into the floor and sports carvings illustrating the castle's history; there's also the **Tour d'Autriche** (Austrian Tower) at the top of the castle, enjoying fabulous views over the Semois valley.

Le Musée Ducal

Downhill from the castle, just to the north on rue du Petit, is **Le Musée Ducal**, which exhibits a wide-ranging collection in an attractive eighteenth-century mansion (Easter to mid-Nov daily 10am to 5 or 6pm; €3.30, combined ticket with castle €6.30). Of particular interest are the artefacts relating to the fifth Godfrey, most notably a replica of his tomb in Jerusalem, where he died in 1100. The Crusaders had captured Jerusalem the year before and speedily elected Godfrey their king. However, he barely had time to settle himself before he became sick – either from disease or, as was suggested at the time, because his Muslim enemies poisoned him. The museum also has some gruesome, medieval paraphernalia, including assorted weaponry and several vicious, spiked dog collars for wolf-hunting, while another section concentrates on the folklore and history of the town and region. Downstairs, there's a large-scale model of the town in 1690, various shooting and hunting accessories, and a room devoted to the printing activities of local author Pierre Rousseau, who printed the work of some of the authors of the Enlightenment in Bouillon after they were banned in France. Upstairs, a series of period rooms showcases local industries from weaving to clog-making.

Archeoscope Godefroid de Bouillon

For yet more on old Godfrey, head for the **Archeoscope Godefroid de Bouillon** (Feb Tues–Fri 1–4pm, Sat & Sun 10am–4pm; March–Sept daily 10am–5pm; Oct & Nov Tues–Sun 10am–4pm; Dec Tues–Sun 1–4pm; €6, combined ticket with castle & museum €10.70), occupying an old convent near the Pont de France at quai des Saulx 14. A new historical centre, its exhibitions – on the Crusades, Arab culture, castle-building and so forth – kick off with a multimedia show on the duke himself.

Eating and drinking

Bouillon heaves with **cafés** and **restaurants**, nowhere more so than on the quai du Rempart. Quite a few are geared up for the day-trippers, serving some pretty innocuous stuff, but there are lots of good places too. Note also that many places close down fairly early, especially out of season, and after 10pm, or even 9pm in winter, you'll be struggling to get yourself fed.

Les 4 Saisons quai du Rempart 12. Smart little bistro with a lively, imaginative menu, featuring fish and meat dishes – and local ingredients. Recommended.

Des Remparts quai du Rempart 31. This cosy restaurant offers delicious Walloon cuisine, both set meals and à la carte. Main courses hover around €15. Closed Thurs.

Roy de la Moule quai du Rempart 42. Mussels-every-which-way restaurant with a good choice of beers.

Sawadie quai du Rempart 33. Competent, straightforward and inexpensive Thai restaurant, which often stays open till late.

La Vieille Ardenne Grand-rue 9, near the Pont de Liège. Slightly old-fashioned restaurant specializing in regional dishes, main courses averaging around €15. Also has a long beer menu.

Around Bouillon: the Semois valley

To the west of Bouillon, quiet roads negotiate the **Semois river valley**, repeatedly climbing up into the wooded hills before careering down to the riverside. Holidaying Belgians descend on this beautiful area in their hundreds, and today the hardy farmers who once tilled the land, grazed their flocks and

The **River Semois** snakes its way across much of southern Belgium, rising near Arlon and then meandering west until it finally flows into the Meuse in France. The most impressive part of the Semois river valley lies just to the west of Bouillon, the river wriggling and worming beneath steep wooded hills and ridges – altogether some of the most sumptuous scenery in the whole of the Ardennes.

Before setting out, **walkers** should get hold of the *Cartes des Promenades du Grand Bouillon* map (€7 from the tourist office), with nine "*grandes promenades*" marked and a further ninety circular walks that begin and end in Bouillon or one of the nearby villages. The routes are well marked, but you need to study the map carefully if you want to avoid having to walk on major or minor roads; the map also gives (pretty generous) suggested times for completing the walks. Note that the marked river crossings are not bridges, so you can may well end up with wet feet. The tourist office also sells a map detailing suggested **cycling** routes, while **mountain-bikes** can be rented from Semois Kayaks (see below) – reckon on around €15 for half a day, €20 for a day.

Walks

From Bouillon's Pont de France, **Walk 11** (7km; 2hr) heads south to the French border, a pretty walk through woods, although the return is mostly along a main road. A better option is to take **Walk 12** (4km; 1hr 30min) through the arboretum and down to the *Halliru* campsite by the river, joining **Walk 13** along the riverbank up to the Rocher du Pendu and as far as Moulin de l'Épine, where you can wade across the river to a superb restaurant-bar – with great local food at around €16 for a main course – and the minor road that leads back to town above the Semois. More serious walkers can pick up **Walk 37** (7km; 3hr) or **72** (16km; 6hr) at Moulin de l'Épine for some fabulous views either side of the river, Walk 72 being particularly glorious as it heads around Le Tombeau du Géant. If you just want a brief walk around Bouillon, **Walk 16** (5km; 1hr 30min) is a good choice – a brief walk that climbs up out of town, with great views of the castle and surrounding countryside, and back through the outskirts of the Ferme de Buhan.

In the other direction from Bouillon, the Semois twists its way to the resort-village of **Dohan**. The mammoth **Walk 19** (23km; 7hr) runs direct to Dohan from Bouillon, although it's more attractive to follow the river via **Walk 17** (11km; 3hr) as far as **Saty**, from where you can either canoe back to Bouillon (see below), or join Walk 19 towards Dohan. Finally, for an ambitious and varied day's walking, you can take **Walk 7** (21km; 6hr) from the Pont de France in Bouillon across the Ferme du Buhan and through Saty and Dohan as far as **La Maka**. Here you can pick up **Walk 45** (3.5km; 2hr), which incorporates the **waterfalls** at Saut de Sorcières and the lovely views over the river valley from Mont de Katron. From Les Hayons, **Walk 6** (23km; 7hr) runs directly back to Bouillon through Moulin Hideux.

Canoeing

As regards canoeing, the riverscape is gentle and sleepy, the Semois slow-moving and meandering – and the whole shebang is less oversubscribed than, say, Dinant. Bouillon has two main canoe **rental** companies: Les Epinoches, by the Pont de France (☏061 25 68 78); and Semois Kayaks (☏0475 24 74 23, ⊛www.semois-kayaks.be), whose shorter trips depart from beside the Pont de Liège. Both companies offer a similar range of excursions at comparable prices and provide transport either to the departure point or from the destination. Advance reservations are strongly advised. The most popular options are the trips downriver from Bouillon to Poupehan (15km; 3hr; €25 for a two-seater) or from Poupehan to Frahan (5km; 1hr; €15). For an active day out, you can canoe to Poupehan and either pick up walking routes back to Bouillon or walk one of the circular routes around the village – if you do the latter, check when the last of the canoe company's minibuses return to Bouillon.

harvested the forests are well-nigh invisible, their old cottages turned into gîtes. Of all the villages hereabouts, the most appealing is **Rochehaut**, a simply delightful little place perched high above the river and with a couple of great places to stay; the runner-up is **Frahan**, a secluded hamlet with a charming, bucolic setting. To the east of Bouillon, the Semois valley is pleasantly rural, but no more; the most worthwhile target here is **Herbeumont**, an attractive little place with a ruined medieval castle.

There are local **buses** along the Semois valley, but these are few and far between, and realistically you're going to need a car or bike to get around.

Poupehan and Frahan

Heading west from Bouillon along the N810, it's just 12km to **POUPEHAN**, an inconsequential village that straggles along the banks of the River Semois. The target of one of the most popular canoe trips from Bouillon, Poupehan makes a healthy living from its many visitors, most of whom are here to enjoy the peace and quiet and to mess around in the river. The village has two **hotels**, the more appealing of which is the *Hôtel Chaire à Precher* (☎061 46 61 54; ❸), a modest two-star establishment with an attractive riverside location. There are also three **campsites** in the village, including the well-equipped and well-appointed *Île de Faigneul*, on the river at rue de la Chérizelle 54 (☎061 46 68 94, ⓦwww.camping-iledefaigneul.com; April–Oct).

West along the N810 from Poupehan, it's just 1km or so to the two-kilometre-long turning that leads to the hamlet of **FRAHAN**, a huddle of stone houses draped over a steep hillock, tucked away in a tight bend in the river and surrounded by meadows. A footbridge crosses the Semois here and there are footpaths on both sides of the river – walking being the obvious activity. Most of the houses here have been turned into chi-chi gîtes, but there is also a delightful **hotel** – the four-star Aux Roches Fleuries (☎061 46 65 14, ⓕ061 46 72 09, ⓦwww.aux-rochers-fleuries.com; ❸; closed Jan), with fourteen stylish and comfortable rooms in both the old building and the modern annexe. Most of them have views over the river.

Rochehaut

Back at Poupehan, cross the bridge and it's a steep four-kilometre drive up through the woods to **ROCHEHAUT**, an especially beguiling hilltop village whose rustic stone cottages amble across a gentle dip between two sloping ridges. Gîtes rule the roost here, but the old stone **church**, with its stocky tower, is a reminder of more agricultural days, when this isolated community eked out a living from the land. Nowadays, most visitors come here to **hike**, exploring the locality's steep forested hills and the valley down below by means of a network of marked trails. Local hiking maps are available at all the local **hotels**. Among them, the pick is the three-star *Auberge de la Fermette* (☎061 46 10 00, ⓕ061 46 10 01, ⓦwww.aubergedelaferme.be; ❹; closed most of Jan), which offers lodgings in a tastefully modernized old stone inn, an immaculately renovated barn, a new annexe and a converted farmhouse. The **restaurant** is excellent too, but you can also eat more informally – and just as well – in the bar. A first-rate alternative is the *Auberge de L'An* (☎061 46 40 60, ⓕ061 46 83 82, ⓦwww.an1600.be; ❹; closed Jan & late June to early July), whose ten rooms – and top-quality restaurant – occupy a charming whitewashed cottage. There are superb views over the Semois from the edge of the village, and it's here you'll also find the aptly named *Le Pointe de Vue*, a plain and simple café-bar with a terrace.

Herbeumont

In the opposite direction from Bouillon, some 15km to the east, is **HER-BEUMONT**, a pleasant village distinguished by the ruins of its medieval **château** (free), perched on a bluff above the Semois, five minutes' walk from the centre of the village. The castle is little more than a shell now, but worth the scramble up the hill for the panoramic views. The other specific sight is the splendid early-twentieth-century **viaduct**, just outside the village off the main road towards Florenville, but the main activity hereabouts is **walking**. The **tourist office**, at rue des Combattants 7 (Mon–Fri 9am–5pm; ☎061 41 24 12), has a brochure detailing fifteen routes along the Semois and through the Forêt d'Herbeumont just to the east.

Herbeumont has three **hotels**, all on the main square, the Grand-Place. The most recommendable is *La Renaissance*, at no. 3 (☎ & ⓕ061 41 10 83; ❹), a friendly, well-kept and unassuming hotel with ten en-suite rooms, behind a modern half-timbered facade. The other good bet is *La Chatelaine*, at no. 8 (☎061 41 14 22, ⓕ061 41 22 04; ❹), a compact three-star affair, also with modest but perfectly adequate rooms. Note, however, that *La Chatelaine* is closed from January to mid-March, in June and early July as well as in late August and early September. There are several **campsites**, the handiest being the *Bains et Garenne*, rue de la Garenne 8 (☎061 41 25 93; April–Nov), by the river about 300m from the village. As for **food**, the restaurant of *La Renaissance* offers smashing Ardennes specialities at affordable prices, as does *L'Herbeumont*, Grand-Place 4. There's also a very good creperie, *L'Abri*, just off the Grand-Place at rue des Ponts 4.

The Gaume and Arlon

Stretching south from the River Semois to the French frontier, the **Gaume** is a compact, very rural district comprised of tiny villages amid thickly wooded hills. It is thought to be named after the Gaumains, porters who once carried locally mined iron ore north to Liège, but no one knows for sure. More certainly, the locals did develop a distinctive dialect, an amalgamation of Walloon and Luxembourgish, but in the last decades a tide of incomers has diluted this considerably. Nowadays, the Gaume is dotted with second homes and gîtes, leaving slim pickings for the passing tourist, with accommodation especially thin on the ground. Neither is there anywhere special you'll want to head for – the most likely exception the beer-producing **Abbaye d'Orval** – though, on a positive note, the countryside is very attractive. The Gaume ends just to the southwest of **Arlon**, the capital of Luxembourg province, though otherwise a bit of a disappointment considering its long history.

The **train** network here does extend as far as Florenville and Virton, but otherwise you'll be reliant on local **buses** and services are patchy; to get around the Gaume therefore, you really need a car (or bike). No such problems affect Arlon, which is on the main Brussels–Luxembourg train line.

Florenville

Close to the French border, on a branch rail line and an important crossroads, unassuming **FLORENVILLE** straggles up and over a sandstone ridge beside the River Semois. The town took a pasting in 1940, and thus much of it is modern, but it's an attractive little town nonetheless, set around a large and pleasant square and with a bustling main street. There are panoramic views over the river valley from the terrace behind the **church**, a conspicuous structure rebuilt in 1950, but that's pretty much it as far as specific sights go – and most visitors use the town merely as a base for exploring the surrounding countryside. In this regard, the **tourist office**, right on the main square (Mon–Sat 9am–noon & 2–6pm; ☎061 27 18 59), sells **walking** maps detailing several circular hiking routes, the pick of which explores the forests around Les Epioux to the north of town.

With regard to **accommodation**, the three-star *Hôtel de France*, on the main street at rue Généraux Cuvelier 26 (☎061 31 10 32, ⓕ061 32 02 83; ❹; closed Jan to early March), occupies a substantial stone building in fin-de-siècle style and has thirty comfortable, en-suite rooms, an excellent restaurant, and a lovely garden. If you're **camping**, head for the well-equipped and appointed *La Rosière* (☎061 31 19 37, ⓕ061 31 48 73; April–Oct), 500m from the main street and down by the riverbank.

The *Hôtel de France* has the best **restaurant** in town, but there are several good alternatives on and around the main square. First port of call should be *L'Étoile du Sud*, a tearoom which sells excellent-value breakfasts – tea or coffee, cheese, bread rolls, preserves and honey – for only €5, plus a wide range of tasty snacks and pastries. For a **drink**, *Brasserie Albert 1er*, on the main square, has a substantial beer menu and a relaxed atmosphere.

Abbaye d'Orval

Some 9km south of Florenville, beside the main road, the **Abbaye d'Orval** (daily: March–May & Oct 9.30am–12.30pm & 1.30–6pm; June–Sept 9.30am–6.30pm; Nov–Feb 10.30am–12.30pm & 1.30–5.30pm; €3.50) is a place of legendary beginnings. It was founded, so the story goes, when Countess Mathilda of Tuscany lost a gold ring in a lake and a fish recovered it for her, prompting the countess to donate the surrounding land to God for the construction of a monastery. A fish with a golden ring is still the emblem of the monastery, and can be seen gracing the bottles of **beer** for which the abbey is most famous these days – the abbey is itself of only moderate architectural interest.

Originally a Benedictine foundation, then Cistercian, the abbey has always been first and foremost a working community, making beer, cheese and bread (samples of which are on sale in the abbey shop). Indeed, of the original twelfth- and thirteenth-century buildings, only the ruins of the Romanesque-Gothic **church of Notre-Dame** are left, with the frame of the original rose window and Romanesque capitals in the nave and transept. Most of the medieval abbey disappeared during an eighteenth-century revamp, but much of this was, in its turn, destroyed by the French Revolutionary army in 1793. Thereafter, the abbey lay abandoned until 1926, when the **Trappist** order acquired the property and built on the site to the eighteenth-century plans, creating an imposing new complex, complete with a monumental statue of the Virgin. You can wander around the ruins, and they are picturesque enough, but many of the new buildings are closed to the public. The only parts you can visit are the eighteenth-century **cellars**, which come complete with a small museum and a model of how the abbey looked in 1760.

Driving to the abbey is quick and easy, but getting there by **public transport** is difficult – there's an infrequent bus from Florenville, the nearest town on the train network. Not far from the abbey, back on the main road, **accommodation** is available at the rusticated, half-timbered *Nouvelle Hostellerie d'Orval* (☎061 31 43 65, ⓕ061 32 00 92; ❷; closed Mon). Besides six simple but comfortable rooms, it has a **restaurant** serving good-value Belgian fare – three-course lunch menus from €12 – as well as bar snacks, including large platters of Orval cheese.

Virton

Heading southeast through the wooded hills from the Abbaye d'Orval along the N88, it's about 20km to **VIRTON**, a lively town whose compact centre retains the circular shape of its medieval walls. Nevertheless, despite the town's long history, there's nothing much to hold you here for more than an hour or two beyond exploring its one real attraction, the **Musée Gaumais**, situated on the way out of the centre at rue d'Arlon 38–40 (April–Nov daily except Tues 9.30am–noon & 2–6pm; June–Aug daily same hours; €3). The museum's collection of period rooms and prehistoric finds is saved from mediocrity by an outstanding array of iron fireplaces, a local speciality dating from as early as the fifteenth century, some of which are superbly decorated, illustrating Biblical themes and the like.

Virton is the last stop on the Libramont–Bertrix–Florenville branch line. The town's **train station** is 1km from the centre, straight down avenue Bouvier. The **tourist office** is in the centre at rue des Grasses Oies 2b (July & Aug daily 10am–noon & 1.30–5.30pm; Sept–June Mon–Fri 9am–noon & 1.30–5pm; ☎063 57 89 04). The town has a couple of reasonably priced **hotels**, the more agreeable of which is the three-star *Hôtel de La Tour d'Harival* at rue d'Arlon 1 (☎063 58 88 00, ℉063 58 88 11; ❹), with nine en-suite rooms. There are a few **restaurants**, the most recommendable being the pretty *La Maison Verte*, serving inexpensive Belgian specialities and located close by the church on the square, and the larger *Brasserie du Chalet*, rue Dr Jeanty 7, which has a wide menu of inexpensive snacks such as croque-monsieurs, salads and soups.

Arlon

The capital of Luxembourg province, **ARLON** is one of the oldest towns in Belgium, a trading centre for the Romans as far back as the second century AD. These days it's an amiable country town, perhaps a little down on its luck, but with a relaxed and genial atmosphere that makes it a pleasant pit-stop – although there's not a lot to see. The modern centre of the town is **place Léopold**, with the clumping Palais de Justice at one end and a World War II tank in the middle, commemorating the American liberation of Arlon in September 1944. Behind the Palais de Justice, to the left, the **Musée Luxembourgeois**, rue des Martyrs 13 (Tues–Sat 9am–noon & 1.30–5pm, mid-April to mid-Sept also Sun 2–5pm; €4), has a good collection of Roman finds from the surrounding area, many of which are evocative of daily life in Roman times. There are pieces from the Merovingian era, too, as well as a marvellously realistic sixteenth-century retable. A couple of minutes' walk from place Léopold, up a flight of steps, is Arlon's diminutive **Grand-Place**, where there are more fragments from Roman times, namely the **Tour Romaine** (no public access), in the corner and formerly part of the third-century ramparts.

Arlon **train station** is five minutes' walk away from the south side of the town centre. The **tourist office** is just off the main square on rue des Faubourgs (Mon–Fri 8.30am–5pm, Sat 8.30am–1pm; ☎063 21 63 60). There's nowhere good to **stay** in the centre – the best you'll do is *À L'Écu de Bourgogne*, place Léopold 10 (☎063 22 02 22; ❸), a two-star hotel right in the middle of town and with nineteen plain and frugal rooms above its very old-fashioned bar.

For **food**, the *Maison Knopes* on the Grand-Place serves tasty crepes as well as more substantial meals, and does a great line in coffee. For a cheaper meal, head to place Léopold, where *Gathay*, at no. 7, and *Les Arcades*, at no. 5, are both popular local haunts for traditional Belgian food. Note that Arlon in general **closes early** – after 8 or 9pm you'll be struggling to find anywhere to eat.

Bastogne

BASTOGNE, forty-odd kilometres north of Arlon, is a brisk modern town and important road junction, whose strategic position has long attracted the attentions of just about every invading army. Indeed, the town is probably best known for its role in World War II, when the Americans held it against a much larger German force in December 1944 – a key engagement of the Battle of the Bulge. The American commander's response to the German demand for surrender – "Nuts!" – is one of the more quotable, if apocryphal, of martial rallying cries. Nowadays, there's no strong reason to overnight here, but there are several sights, the more interesting of which are connected with the events of 1944.

As a token of its appreciation, the town renamed its main square **place McAuliffe**, after the American commander, and plonked an American **tank** here just to emphasize the point. Wide and breezy, the square is the most agreeable part of town and very much the social focus, flanked by a string of busy cafés. From the northeast corner of the square, **Grand-rue** – the long main street – trails off to place St Pierre, a ten-minute walk away, where the **Église St Pierre** sports a sturdy Romanesque tower topped by a timber gallery.

The Battle of the Bulge

Though there's not a lot to see now beyond parked tanks, cemeteries and the odd war memorial, the Ardennes was the site of some of World War II's fiercest fighting during the **Battle of the Bulge**. The Allied campaign of autumn 1944 had concentrated on striking into Germany from Maastricht in the north and Alsace in the south, leaving a lightly defended central section, whose front line extended across the Ardennes from Malmédy to Luxembourg's Echternach. In December 1944, Hitler embarked on a desperate plan to change the course of the war by breaking through this part of the front, the intention being to sweep north behind the Allies, capture Antwerp and force them to retreat. To all intents and purposes, it was the same plan Hitler had applied with such great success in 1940, but this time he had fewer resources – especially fuel oil – and the Allied airforce ruled the skies.

Von Rundstedt, the veteran German general who Hitler placed in command, was acutely aware of these weaknesses – indeed he was against the operation from the start – but he hoped to benefit from the wintry weather conditions which would limit Allied aircraft activity. Carefully prepared, Von Rundstedt's offensive began on December 16, 1944, and one week later had created a "bulge" in the Allied line that reached the outskirts of Dinant – though the American 101st Airborne Division held firm around Bastogne. The success of the operation depended on rapid results, however, and Von Rundstedt's inability to reach Antwerp meant failure. Montgomery's forces from the north and Patton's from the south launched a counterattack, and by the end of January the Germans had been forced back to their original position. The loss of life was colossal – 75,000 Americans and over 100,000 Germans died in the battle.

Inside, and more unusually, the vaulting of the well-proportioned Gothic nave is decorated with splendid, brightly-coloured frescoes, painted in the 1530s and depicting biblical scenes, saints, prophets and angels. Of note also are a finely carved Romanesque baptismal font and a flashy Baroque pulpit.

Close by, the chunky **Porte de Trèves** is the last vestige of the town's medieval walls – as illustrated in the nearby **Maison Mathelin**, rue G. Delperdange 1 (July & Aug Tues–Sun 10am–noon & 1–5pm; €1.50), which has a model of the medieval town among a series of rooms tracking through Bastogne's history. Several rooms are devoted to the Battle of the Bulge, but the story is more fully told at the **American Memorial** (open access; free), situated 2km north of town on Mardasson hill – from place St Pierre, take rue G. Delperdange and keep going. This large, star-shaped memorial, inscribed with the names of all the American states, probably looks a great deal better from the air than it does from the ground, but the panels around the side do an excellent job of recounting different episodes from the battle, and the crypt, with its three altars, is suitably sombre. It's possible to climb up onto the roof for a windswept look back at Bastogne and the slag heaps and quarries of the surrounding countryside. Next door to the memorial, the **Bastogne Historical Centre** (daily: Feb–April & Oct–Dec 10am–4.30pm; May–June & Sept 9.30am–5pm; July & Aug 9.30am–6pm; €7.50) collects together all manner of war-related artefacts – uniforms, vehicles, etc – in an impressive and imaginative series of displays, and shows a film of the battle compiled from live footage.

Practicalities

Bastogne is not on the train network, but there are connecting **buses** from the nearest train station, at Libramont. The journey takes about forty minutes and buses pull into the main square, place McAuliffe, which is where you'll find the **tourist office** (mid-June to mid-Sept daily 8.30am–6.30pm; mid-Sept to mid-June daily 9.30am–12.30pm & 1–5.30pm; ☎061 21 27 11, www .bastogne-tourisme.be). They supply free town maps, have a variety of brochures on the Battle of the Bulge and will book accommodation on your behalf for free.

Bastogne has five **hotels**, two handily located on place McAuliffe. These are *Le Caprice*, a routine, modern three-star at no. 25 (☎061 21 81 40, ℱ061 21 82 01; ❹), and the much more agreeable *Collin* (☎061 21 43 58, ℱ061 21 80 83, www.hotel-collin.com; ❹), a smart and tasteful conversion of an older building, complete with Art Deco flourishes, at no. 8. For **food**, head for the cafés and restaurants on and around place McAuliffe. Among them, the Hotel Collin's *Le Circo* is a smart and well-turned-out café that's good for snacks and light meals, while the bright and cheerful *Le Grill*, at no. 21, does a tasty line in mussels, plus delicious meat and fish dishes from around €15. Last but not least, *Le Bistro Leo*, housed in a 1930s railway carriage just off the main square at rue du Vivier 8, also serves light meals and has an excellent range of Belgian **beers**.

La Roche-en-Ardenne and around

About 30km northwest of Bastogne and 25km northeast of St Hubert, **LA ROCHE-EN-ARDENNE** is amazingly picturesque, hidden by hills until you're right on top of it, and crowned by romantic castle ruins. It's a strange mixture: a hidden place, geographically cut off from the rest of the world and surrounded by some of the wildest scenery in the Ardennes, yet it teems with people during the summer (most of whom come to get out into the countryside on foot or by canoe) and – by Ardennes standards – has a relatively animated nightlife, with plenty of bars and late-night restaurants. Near here too, to the north, is **Durbuy**, a pretty little place with excellent accommodation and great walking.

The Town

The greying stone **centre** of La Roche squeezes into one small bend of the River L'Ourthe, its main street winding between the two bridges, an unashamedly exploitative stretch of shops flogging Ardennes ham, knickknacks and camping gear. That, however, is about it as far as development goes, and the streets around are unspoiled and quiet. The only tangible "sight" is the **château** (April–June, Sept & Oct daily 10am–noon & 2–5pm; July & Aug daily 10am–7pm; Nov–March Mon–Fri 1.30–4.30pm, Sat & Sun 10am–noon & 2–4pm; €2.50), construction of which began in the ninth century and continued over four hundred years. It was destroyed in the late eighteenth century on the orders of the Habsburgs – to stop it falling into the hands of the French – and today its ruins still command sweeping views over the valley and of the surviving fragments of the curtain wall that once enclosed the town. There is also a tiny museum with archeological finds and a pictorial history of La Roche. To get to the castle, take the steps that lead up from place du Marché, at the south end of the high street.

On the high street itself, the **Musée Bataille des Ardennes** (daily 10am–6pm; €5.50) holds a small collection of military artefacts dedicated to the Battle of the Bulge (see p.345), but frankly it's eminently missable, especially if you've been to the superior museum at Bastogne. Curiously enough, the corner of the high street and rue de la Gare, a few metres to the north, is the spot where US and British soldiers met on January 11, 1945, as their respective armies converged on La Roche; a commemorative **plaque** depicts the wintry scene.

That's pretty much it as far as sights go, but you might consider taking the electric miniature train out to the **Parc à Gibier** (Wildlife Park; daily: Easter–June & Sept to mid-Nov 10am–5pm; July & Aug 10am–8pm; €3), which is situated on the Deister plateau, and is home to various creatures including red deer, pheasants and wild boar.

Practicalities

La Roche is not on the rail network; the nearest **train station** is Melreux-Hotton, about 15km to the northwest and on the Jemelle–Liège line. From here, there are nine **buses** a day on a weekday (4 on Sat & Sun) to La Roche. Buses pull in along the town's high street before proceeding to the **bus station**, over the bridge on the northern edge of town.

The **tourist office** is located at the south end of the high street, at place du Marché 15 (daily: July & Aug 9.30am–6pm; Sept–June 9.30am–noon & 1.30–5pm; ☎084 41 13 42, ⓦwww.mid.be/infolr). They have maps and booklets on the town and bus timetables, and sell a combined walking and cycling map (*Carte des Promenades Pedestres et Circuits Cyclotouristes*). **Canoes**, **kayaks** and **mountain bikes** – as well as skis in winter – can be rented from Ardennes-Aventures by the north bridge (☎084 41 19 00, ⓔkayak@ardenne-aventures.be).

Accommodation

The tourist office has details of accommodation possibilities, including plenty of **B&Bs** (❷–❹). Despite the abundance of **hotels**, booking is advisable in season. One good and inexpensive choice is the pleasant *Le Luxembourg*, avenue du Hadja 1a (☎084 41 14 15, ⓕ084 41 19 71; ❸), with eight simple rooms – four en suite – in a pleasant, three-storey building just beyond the bridge on the north side of the centre. The nearby *Hôtel de Liège*, rue de la Gare 16 (☎ & ⓕ 084 41 11 64; ❶), is even more affordable, but don't expect any frills. Moving upmarket, there's the delightful, three-star *Les Genets* (☎084 41 18 77, ⓕ084 41 18 93; ❹), with seven cosy rooms in an immaculate lodge-like stone building that also provides superb views over the town from its perch at corniche de Deister 2. It's a steep, ten-minute climb up from the high street: walk south from place du Marché towards the bridge, turn left out of town up rue Clerue and veer left again up along rue St Quoilin. Not quite as appealing, but still first-rate, is *La Claire Fontaine*, about 2km out of town on the road to Marche-en-Famenne (☎084 41 24 70, ⓕ084 41 21 11, ⓦwww.clairefontaine.be; ❻). With expansive gardens and on the edge of the forest, the hotel consists of a lovely old lodge, strewn with antiques – including a giant bellows – and an architecturally harsh 1970s extension, though in fairness the rooms are large and extremely well appointed.

There are no fewer than nine **campsites** in the vicinity, most of them packed with trailers. Among the closest is a group along rue de Harzé by the River Ourthe, north of town. Here you'll find *Le Benelux*, about 800m out along rue de la Gare from the north bridge (☎084 41 15 59, ⓕ084 41 23 59; April–Sept); *Camping de l'Ourthe* (☎084 41 14 59; mid-March to mid-Oct) and *Le Grillon* (☎084 41 20 62; April–Oct) are just beyond.

Eating and drinking

La Roche boasts lots of **cafés** and **restaurants**, though – given the number of day-trippers – it's hardly surprising that standards are very variable. There's a cluster of excellent places on and around place du Bronze, next to the south bridge. These include *La Sapinière*, rue Nulay 4, which serves good-value Belgian country food, as does *Restaurant L'Apero*, just across the bridge from place du Bronze at rue Clerue 5, a small, family-run restaurant with fine local cooking. Alternatives include the cheap pizzas of the brash *Mezzogiorno*, place du Bronze 1, while gastronomes can head for the *Hôtel Clairefontaine*, whose wonderful set menus start at €25. They feature regional specialities – try the wild boar – and also do à la carte. If you just want to **drink**, try the *Vénetien*, a popular local bar halfway down the main street, next to the church.

Around La Roche: Durbuy

Inordinately pretty, tiny **DURBUY**, a circuitous 25km northwest of La Roche, is tucked into a narrow ravine beside the River L'Ourthe and below bulging wooded hills. Perhaps inevitably, the town (it's been a town since the fourteenth century) attracts far too many day-trippers for its own good, but out of season and late in the evening it remains a delightful spot. Its special appeal is its immaculately maintained huddle of seventeenth- and eighteenth-century **stone houses**, set around a cobweb of cobbled lanes, and you can always escape the crush by hiking up into the surrounding hills. Also firmly set against all the razzmatazz is Durbuy's **château** (no access), whose turrets and towers are locked away on a knoll and behind iron gates.

The tourist office in **La Roche** sells a (rather rudimentary) walking map (*Carte de Promenades*; €4), with a dozen circular walks marked in the vicinity. The longest and most attractive of these routes is the thirteen-kilometre-long **Walk 5**, which takes about six hours and is mildly strenuous. It starts on rue Bon Dieu du Maka, near place du Bronze, and rises steeply before levelling out through the woods above town and across fields of wildflowers. The walk follows GR route 57, dropping sharply to the river at **Maboge**, where several cafés offer lunch, then rejoining the main road for 500m until it turns left alongside a tributary of the Ourthe as far as the farm at Borzee. From here the route is easy to find, again heading through the woods with fabulous views, but when it descends towards the town keep your eyes peeled for a right and then an immediate left down an unpromising footpath that drops you onto the main road by the river. From here, take the second right for a final gentle stretch above the road, with good views over the town. Allow around three hours' walking time for the 13km; to extend the route by an hour or so, pick up **Walk 12** at Borzee, joining **Walk 11** as far as the small town of Samree and returning through the forest to La Roche.

If you're after a shorter hike, follow **Walk 4**, a six-kilometre route that takes about two hours. From the tourist office, head for place du Bronze and before you cross the bridge turn left on rue Clerue and sharp left again up rue St Quolin. Then turn left at the top to **St Margaret's Chapel**, built in 1600 and once connected to the castle by an underground passage. Just left of the chapel, a scramble up the steep slope leads up to a look-out point with views over La Roche, while continuing up the footpath brings you to the attractive but rather twee and often crowded **Parc Forestier du Deister**. The tourist office has a map of the park, including descriptions of where various types of tree have been planted. If you continue through the park you'll rejoin Walk 4, looping briefly north and then dropping back to town, all along the roadway.

Alternatively, **GR route 57** provides a full half-day's walking between La Roche and the hamlet of **Nadrin**, a distance of around 15km. Nadrin is home to a belvedere – actually a high tower with a restaurant attached – from which you can see the Ourthe at six different points on its meandering course in and out of the tightly packed hills. The return journey can be completed by bus, but this only runs twice daily, so be sure to check times with the tourist office before you leave.

Cycling, canoeing and other activities

Obviously enough, renting a **mountain-bike** allows you to see more of the surrounding forests: eight circular routes are set out in the *Carte des Circuits Cyclotouristes*, on sale at the tourist office. Bikes can be rented for €22 per day from Ardennes Aventures, at a chalet sited below the bridge at the northern end of town on rue du Hadja (☎084 41 19 00, @kayak@ardenne-aventures.be). Ardennes Aventures also organize **canoeing** trips on the Ourthe, bussing you (or letting you mountain-bike) to Maboge for the 10km paddle downstream to La Roche (€15 per person, €28 with the bike ride), or to Nisramont for the strenuous 25-kilometre river trip (€20). They also organize **river rafting** and **cross-country skiing** in the winter.

Practicalities

Getting to Durbuy by **public transport** is awkward. From La Roche, nine **buses** a day on a weekday (4 on Sat & Sun) travel northwest the 15km to Melreux-Hotton train station, where you change for the onward train (every 2hr; 7min) to Barvaux (and Liège). From Barvaux station, it's about 4km to Durbuy; there is a local bus, but it's infrequent, so you may well have to walk in.

The **tourist office** (Mon–Fri 9am–12.30pm & 1–5pm, Sat & Sun 10am–6pm; ℡086 21 24 28), on the large and modern main square, place aux Foires, has a long list of suggested activities – from canoeing and fishing through to catching the electric train that shuttles round town. They also sell local **hiking maps** – there are nine, mostly short trails in the hills around town – and will also book accommodation on your behalf for free.

There are several top-ranking **hotels** here, most memorably the four-star *Clos des Récollets*, in a charmingly kept, partly whitewashed and half-timbered house right in the centre on place des Récollets (℡086 21 29 69, ℻086 21 36 85; ❹). Two other, equally splendid hotels are close by: the *Château Cardinal*, rue des Récollectines 1 (℡086 21 32 62, ℻086 21 24 65; ❼), where the rooms are larger and (even) more comfortable; and the ivy-clad *Du Prevot*, rue des Récollectines 4 (℡086 21 23 00, ℻086 21 27 84; ❹).

As for **food**, the restaurants at both the *Hôtel des Récollets* (closed Wed) and the *Hôtel Du Prevot* are excellent, with main courses, featuring French and Walloon specialities, costing in the region of €20. Several less expensive places flank place aux Foires – *La Brasserie Ardennaise* is as good as any, offering a wide range of meat and fish dishes plus snacks.

Huy and around

Midway between Namur and Liège, and easily accessible by train from either, the bustling town of **HUY** – aside from Liège, the major centre of the northern Ardennes – spreads across both sides of the Meuse. One of the oldest towns in Belgium and for a long time a flourishing market centre, the place was badly damaged by the armies of Louis XIV in the late seventeenth century. Little remains of the old town, but Huy is certainly worth a brief look, mainly for its splendid church – even if you're only passing through.

The Town and around

Huy's compact old centre is dominated by the **Collégiale Notre-Dame** (daily 10am–noon & 2–5pm), an imposing Gothic church that towers majestically over the banks of the River Meuse, backed by high cliffs and the walls of the citadel. Built between 1311 and 1536, the church's interior is decked out with fine stained glass, especially the magnificent rose window, a dazzling conglomeration of reds and blues. On the right side of the nave as you enter, stairs lead down to a Romanesque crypt, where the relics of Huy's patron saint, St Domitian, were once venerated. His original twelfth-century shrine stands upstairs in the **trésor** (€1.25) under the rose window, along with three other large shrines from the twelfth and thirteenth centuries, crafted by the Mosan gold- and silversmiths for which Huy was once famous. They're somewhat faded, but the beauty and skill of their execution still shines through. Outside, on the side of the church facing the town centre, look out for the **Porte de Bethléem**, topped by a mid-fourteenth-century arch decorated with scenes of the nativity.

It's a short walk from here across busy avenue des Ardennes to the centre of town at the **Grand-Place**, its bronze fountain of 1406 decorated with a representation of the town walls interspersed with tiny statues of the same saints commemorated in the church. The wrought-iron and stone vats were added in the eighteenth century. The square is flanked on the far side by the solid-looking, eighteenth-century **Hôtel de Ville**, behind which is the quiet place

Verte – follow rue St Mengold, which leads off its southeast corner and curves round to meet the tiny rue des Frères Mineurs. On the corner here stands the oldest house in Huy, the late twelfth-century **Maison de la Tour**, a tall, almost windowless structure which looks more like a fortress than a home.

Beyond, cobbled rue des Frères Mineurs runs picturesquely between high stone walls to the late seventeenth-century former friary of the same name. This now houses the varied exhibits of the **Musée Communal**, including old wine-making equipment alongside items of daily life, reconstructions of period rooms, ceramics, coins and religious paintings and an oak carving of Christ on the Cross, called the *Beau Dieu de Huy*, a typical Mosan thirteenth-century sculpture. The museum has been closed for restoration, and is not likely to reopen until at least 2003.

The citadel

The last sight worth taking in is Huy's **citadel** (April–June & Sept Mon–Fri 9am–12.30pm & 1–4.30pm, Sat & Sun 11am–6pm; July & Aug daily 11am–7pm; €3). It's accessible on foot from the quai de Namur by taking the path up to the left just beyond the tourist office, or via the weekend **cable car** (Easter, May, June & Sept Sat 1–6pm, Sun 10am–12.15pm & 1–6; July & Aug daily 11am–7pm; one-way €3.10, round trip €4.40) from avenue Batta on the other side of the river: cross over the Pont Roi Baudouin and turn left down the riverside quai du Halage. Although it occupies a vantage point that has been fortified for over a thousand years, Huy's present citadel was only built in the early nineteenth century by the Dutch. It was used as a prison by the Nazis during World War II, and is now a museum of that period, preserving prisoners' cells and the Gestapo interrogation room. It's a massive complex, and the marked tour of the seemingly endless galleries is eerie and disorientating.

Château de Modave

A rewarding side trip from Huy is to the mostly seventeenth-century **Château de Modave** (April to mid-Nov daily 9am–6pm; €5), dramatically situated on a forest-covered cliff above the River Hoyoux 14km south of Huy, and with great views over the valley. The château was the home of a string of lesser members of the aristocracy after its completion in 1673, and twenty of the rooms are now open to the public, all crammed with period furniture, Brussels tapestries and some impressive stucco ceilings by one Jean-Christian Hansche. An hourly bus, #126a (direction Ciney), runs from Huy's train station past the château.

Practicalities

Huy's **train station** is on the opposite side of the river from the town centre, a fifteen-minute walk: head straight out of the station down to the river, then turn right along the river and cross the Pont Roi Baudouin to reach the Collégiale Notre-Dame. The **tourist office** (℡085 21 29 15, ℻085 23 29 44, Ⓦwww.huy.be) is right by the entrance to the church, though due to funding problems it's impossible to say exactly when it will be open, if at all. There are just two central **hotels**: the cheap and central *Hôtel du Fort*, chaussée Napoléon 5–6 (℡085 23 04 04, ℻085 23 18 42; ❸), five minutes' walk along the river past the tourist office, with a range of variously sized and equipped rooms; and the more upmarket *Sirius*, quai de Compiègne 47 (℡085 21 24 00, ℻085 21 24 01; ❺), by the church. However, you might just as well stay in Liège or in a pleasanter spot further south.

The old town centre has plenty of convivial **cafés and restaurants**. Just past the tourist office on the riverfront, *Le Jupy*, quai de Namur 12 (not to be confused with the bar of the same name a couple of doors down), serves mussels in many guises, while *San Martino*, slightly further down the river at Chaussée Napoleon 2, does good French and Italian food. *Le Central* in the Grand-Place has reasonably priced *plats du jour*, while nearby, at rue Griange 14, *Caffé e Cucina* offers upmarket Italian cuisine in an exquisite ivy-covered courtyard. Most people do their **drinking** around the Grand-Place too – try *Aux Caves d'Artois* or the flash *La Brasserie*, which has a good selection of beers; alternatively, the *XIXième*, by the Porte de Bethléem, is a cheaper, easy-going alternative. If you're hankering after a pint of Watney's ale, try the painfully authentic *Big Ben* pub on the corner of Grand-Place.

Liège

Though the effective capital of the Ardennes, and of its own province, **LIÈGE** isn't the most obvious stop on most travellers' itineraries. It's a large, grimy, industrial city, with few notable sights and little immediate appeal. However, it's hard to avoid if you're heading on down this way to Luxembourg, and once you've got to grips with the place, Liège even has a few surprises. Certainly, if you're overnighting here, give yourself at least half a day to nose around.

Liège was actually independent for much of its history; from the tenth century onwards it was the seat of a line of **prince-bishops**, who ruled over bodies as well as souls for around eight hundred years. The last prince-bishop was expelled in 1794 by soldiers of revolutionary France, who added salt to the wound by torching the cathedral. Later, Liège was incorporated into the Belgian state, rising to prominence as an industrial city. The coal and steel industries here date back to the twelfth century, but it was only in the nineteenth century that real development of the city's position and natural resources took place – not least under one Charles Cockerill, a British entrepreneur whose name you still see around town. However, the heavy industry Cockerill bequeathed is in decline and today the city is ringed by post-industrial sprawl.

Arrival, information and transport

Liège has three **train stations**. All trains stop at the main terminal, **Guillemins**, about 2km south of the city centre, while most services (with the exception of express trains to Brussels, Maastricht and Luxembourg City) also call at Liège's other two stations – **Jonfosse**, not far from boulevard de la Sauvenière just to the west of the centre, and **Palais**, near place St Lambert in the city centre. To get to the centre of town from Guillemins Station, take bus #1 or #4 to place St Lambert; the journey by taxi will cost you around €8.

There's a small **information** office at Guillemins station (Mon–Sat 9.30am–12.30pm & 1–5pm, Sun 10am–noon & 1–4pm; ☎04 252 44 19), but for more comprehensive bumph, head for the main **tourist office** at Feronstrée 92 (Mon–Fri 9am–6pm, Sat 10am–4pm & Sun 10am–2pm; ☎04 221 92 21, ⓦwww.liege.be). For €1.25 they'll sell you a useful information pack, including a town map and leaflets giving basic details of the city's sights and of the "Simenon Route" walking tour through the Outremeuse district, where author Georges Simenon spent his childhood. There's also a **provincial tourist office** in the centre of town at boulevard de la Sauvenière 77

(Mon–Fri 8.30am–5pm, Sat 9am–1pm; ☎04 232 65 10) for information on the surrounding region.

Liège is a big, rambling place, and to get from one side of town to the other you'll need to take a **bus**. Tickets cost €1 for a journey in the city centre, either from the driver or from one of the ticket booths located at major bus stops such as place St Lambert, place de la Cathédrale or the train station. If you're staying for a couple of days, it's worth investing in a book of eight tickets for €5.40.

Accommodation

Liège suffers from a paucity of **hotels**, and most are also inconveniently located. In addition, room rates can almost double during the annual Formula 1 Belgium Grand Prix (late Aug), which is held at the nearby Spa-Francorchamps circuit, or if the Tour de France (July) happens to be passing through the area. On the plus side, the city's low ranking as a tourist destination also means hotels are rarely full, especially at weekends, when you may be able to wangle a discount. As usual, the most economical choices are around the train station.

There's one **youth hostel**, the *Georges Simenon*, rue Georges Simenon 2 (☎04 344 56 89, ℻04 344 56 87, ✉liege@laj.be; ❷; closed from around Jan 10 till Feb 10), a modern affair in the heart of Outremeuse, with pleasant four- to seven-bed dorms (dorm beds €14.50), plus a few singles and doubles.

Hotels

Bedford quai St Léonard 36 ☎04 228 81 11, ℻04 227 45 75, ✉hotelbedfordlg@pophost.eunet.be. Liège's most luxurious hotel, with large and well-appointed rooms boasting all mod-cons – though despite the hefty price-tag it's in a disappointingly run-down and inconvenient location, on the riverfront 500m east of the tourist office. The rack rate is €236, though weekend discounts can cut this price by half. Breakfast included. ❾

Comfort Inn L'Univers rue des Guillemins 116 ☎04 254 55 55, ℻04 254 55 00, ✉comfort.inn.liege@skynet.be. Comfortable, newly renovated hotel opposite Guillemins train station; all rooms come with TV and phone. Breakfast €7.50. ❹

Cygne d'Argent rue Beeckman 49 ☎04 223 70 01, ℻04 222 49 66, ⊛www.cygnedargent.be. Small and friendly place occupying a town house in a quiet side street, with comfortable old-fashioned rooms. It's a 10min walk from Guillemins station: head straight ahead out of the station down rue Guillemins and its continuation, bd d'Avroy, until you reach the small rue du Jardin Botanique on your right; rue Beeckman is just up

here to the left. ❹

Hotel des Nations rue des Guillemins 139 ☎04 252 44 14, ℻04 252 44 15. Basic but friendly hotel opposite Guillemins Station, attracting a backpackerish clientele. All the recently refurbished rooms come with shower, and there's a café. ❸

Ibis pl de la République Française 41 ☎04 230 33 33, ℻04 223 04 81, ⊛www.ibis.com. Functional modern hotel – nothing special but quite modestly priced and excellently located bang in the centre of town. Room rates can fall by fifteen percent at weekends depending on availability. Breakfast €7.50. ❹

Mercure bd de la Sauvenière 100 ☎04 221 77 11, ℻04 221 77 01. Faceless concrete block in a good location on a main road skirting the city centre. Rooms are plush but expensive, and geared mainly to business travellers. Breakfast included in the rate. ❽

Metropole rue des Guillemins 141 ☎04 252 42 93, ℻04 252 70 29. Pleasantly old-fashioned hotel, the cheapest in the city, with a wide range of variously appointed and excellent-value rooms, including cheap singles and triples with and without bath and TV. ❷

The City

Situated on the west bank of the Meuse, Liège's centre divides into two parts: the so-called **new town**, girdled by the traffic artery of boulevard de la Sauvenière, which curls around to the centre of town at place St Lambert; and the **old town**, east of here, with Feronstrée as its spine, right below the steep

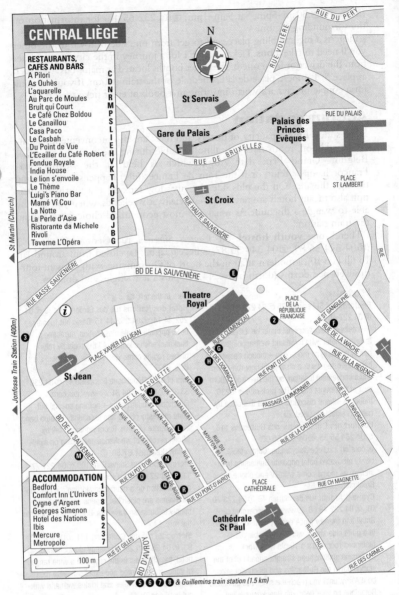

CENTRAL LIÈGE

RESTAURANTS, CAFES AND BARS

A Pilori	C
As Ouhès	D
L'aquarelle	N
Au Parc de Moules	R
Bruit qui Court	M
Le Café Chez Boldou	P
Le Canaillou	S
Casa Paco	L
Le Casbah	I
Du Point de Vue	E
L'Ecailler du Café Robert	H
Fondue Royale	V
India House	K
Le lion s'envoile	T
Le Thème	A
Luigi's Piano Bar	U
Mamé Vi Cou	F
La Notte	Q
La Perle d'Asie	O
Ristorante da Michele	J
Rivoli	B
Taverne L'Opéra	G

ACCOMMODATION

Bedford	1
Comfort Inn L'Univers	5
Cygne d'Argent	8
Georges Simenon	4
Hotel des Nations	6
Ibis	2
Mercure	3
Metropole	7

0   100 m

▼ ❺❻❼❽ & Guillemins train station (1.5 km)

heights that ascend to the former citadel. In addition, the district of **Outremeuse**, across the river on what is in effect an island in the Meuse, harbours a cluster of fine bars and restaurants.

Place St Lambert and around

The nominal centre of the city is **place St Lambert**, a vast and rather cheerless gravel expanse which was formerly the site of the great Gothic cathedral

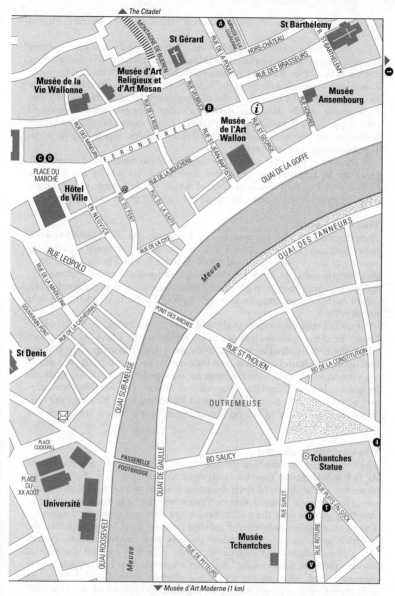

The Citadel

MONTAGNE DE BUEREN

St Gérard

IMPASSE DE LA COURONNE

RUE DE LA POULE

HORS-CHÂTEAU

St Barthélemy

R. ST-BARTHÉLEMY

RUE DES BRASSEURS

Musée de la Vie Wallonne

Musée d'Art Religieux et d'Art Mosan

RUE VELBRUCK

RUE DE LA ROSE

FERONSTRÉE

RUE DES MINEURS

RUE HONGRÉE

Musée Ansembourg

Musée de l'Art Wallon

RUE ST-GEORGE

RUE ST-JEAN-BAPTISTE

RUE DE LA BOUCHERIE

QUAI DE LA GOFFE

PLACE DU MARCHÉ

Hôtel de Ville

RUE DU PONT

RUE DE LA GAFFE

EN NEUVICE

RUE DE LA CITÉ

QUAI DES TANNEURS

Meuse

RUE LEOPOLD

RUE DE LA MADELEINE

RUE DE LA CATHÉDRALE

SOUVERAIN-PONT

PONT DES ARCHES

RUE ST PHOLIEN

BD DE LA CONSTITUTION

St Denis

OUTREMEUSE

QUAI SUR-MEUSE

4

Tchantches Statue

PLACE COCKERILL

PASSERELLE FOOTBRIDGE

BD SAUCY

QUAI DE GAULLE

RUE SURLET

RUE PUITS-EN-SOCK

PLACE DU XX AOÛT

Université

S
U

T

RUE ROTURE

QUAI ROOSEVELT

Meuse

Musée Tchantches

RUE DE PITTEURS

V

THE ARDENNES | Liège

5

▼ Musée d'Art Moderne (1 km)

of St Lambert, destroyed by the French in 1794. The modern-day square's only touch of distinction is provided by the long frontage of the **Palais des Princes Evêques** (Palace of the Prince-Bishops). The present building dates largely from 1737 and was further restored and expanded in the eighteenth century – from when dates the rather incongruous neo-Gothic facade facing the Palais train station. You can usually wander into the palace's two courtyards during office hours: each of the pillars in the first is carved with a different selection of grotesques, while the second harbours a smaller and prettier space, planted with greenery.

The eastern edge of the place St Lambert narrows into the smaller, tree-lined and much more attractive **place du Marché**, its northern side flanked by a row of atmospheric bars and restaurants, behind which looms the curiously Russian-looking onion dome of the Église Saint-André. The south side of the square is occupied by the run-of-the-mill eighteenth-century **Hôtel de Ville**, while in the middle stands **Le Perron**, a rather unprepossessing fountain of 1697, topped by a statue of the Three Graces, which came to symbolize Liège's hard-won independence under the last prince-bishops, and still serves as an important marker of civic pride.

To the west of place St Lambert lies the third of the main central squares, the **place de la République Française**, flanked on one side by the shed-like Neoclassical Théâtre Royale, in front of which stands a statue of the Liège-born composer André Grétry (his heart is contained in the urn just below).

The old town

From place du Marché, **Feronstrée** heads east into the so-called **old town**, a rather optimistic description for a district now largely occupied by a rag-tag assortment of cut-price shops and 1960s concrete blocks. The area does, however, contain the city's densest concentration of museums and a smattering of historic buildings, though in general the streets here are strangely devoid of life, except on Sunday mornings, when the vigorous **La Batte market** takes over the river bank.

For an impressive overview of the old town – and indeed of the whole of Liège – head to rue Hors-Château, on the northern edge of the old town, from where the four hundred or so steps of the very steep **Montagne de Bueren** lead up to the **citadel**, which is now little more than a set of ramparts enclosing a modern hospital. The views, however, are superlative, worth the genuinely lung-wrenching trek, looking right out over the city and the rolling countryside beyond. Afterwards you can follow an interesting route back into the centre of the city by way of rue du Pery and rue Volière, which brings you out behind Gare de Palais.

The Walloon museums

The first turn off Feronstrée to the left, rue des Mineurs, leads up to the **Musée de la Vie Wallonne** (Tues–Sat 10am–5pm & Sun 10am–4pm; €2), the most impressive of the three old town museums devoted to aspects of Walloon culture. Housed in a restored former Franciscan friary, the museum offers an absorbing glimpse into the past traditions and superstitions of the Liège area. There's an extensive collection of exhibits covering local trades, including the recreated workshops of candlemakers, coopers, pipe makers and slate cutters, plus a large collection of entertaining shops signs and a quaint selection of wooden **puppets** from various Liège marionette theatres. The puppets feature personages both religious and secular – a diminutive Napoleon shares a case with Herod – and among them are an engaging selection of rakish Tchantchès puppets, depicting the town's folkloric hero (see p.358). The museum periodically arranges puppet shows in which you can see the marionettes in action. In addition, a couple of rooms are devoted to the region's quirky folk traditions, with cases packed full of tarot cards, horoscopes, horseshoes and other, more outlandish, exhibits including a piece of waffle in the form of a crucifix, a bone necklace to protect against jaundice, and a piece of fetal membrane carefully preserved in a small bag, which was thought to confer luck on its owner.

Almost next door, along rue Hors–Château, the rather less interesting **Musée d'Art Religieux et d'Art Mosan** holds a roughly chronological assortment of local carvings and paintings from the Middle Ages onwards (Tues–Sat 11am–6pm & Sun 11am–4pm; €2.50). Highlights include some sixteenth-century wood carvings of St Lambert and St Hubert – the latter, patron saint of hunting in the Ardennes, pictured with his symbol, a stag. Other exhibits include a seated Christ from 1240, and the wooden *Virgin of Berselius*, an exquisite sculpture from 1530. Among the paintings is a *Virgin with St Donatrice and Mary Magdalen* by the Master of St Gudule, as well as some lush landscapes by the early sixteenth-century Antwerp painter Joachim Patenier. There's also a large assortment of gilded ecclesiastical gewgaws – chalices, reliquaries, ciboria – whose opulence witnesses the former wealth of the Liège church.

On the opposite side of Feronstrée, 150m to the east, the third of the city's Walloon museums, the **Musée de l'Art Wallon** at Feronstreé 86 (Tues–Sat 1–6pm, Sun 11am–4.30pm; €2.50), comprises an attractive selection of works by French-speaking Belgian artists. Again, the collection is arranged chronologically, starting at the top and leading down in a descending spiral. The collection begins with the wonderfully varied sixteenth-century paintings of Henri Blès, plus a few canvases by Liège's greatest artist, Lambert Lombard (1505–66), including the wonderfully irascible self-portrait which formerly adorned the nation's 100-franc note. It's the nineteenth- and early twentieth-century sections which are the strongest, however, ranging from the Manet-inspired portraits of Léon Philippet to the Seurat-like landscapes of Albert Lemaître, punctuated by moments of high pretension, such as Antoine Wiertz's immense and wonderfully overblown *Greeks and Trojans in Dispute over the Body of Patrocles*, a wall-full of splendidly superfluous male flesh. Look out too for the small group of works by Delvaux and Magritte, notably the former's wacky *L'Homme de la Rue*, showing a bowler-hatted businessman imperviously reading his newspaper amid a landscape of classical ruins and cavorting nymphs.

The Musée d'Ansembourg and St Barthélemy

Further along Feronstrée, a little way past the tourist office, the **Musée d'Ansembourg** (Tues–Sun 1–6pm; €2.5) occupies a grand, eighteenth-century mansion, whose interior is distinguished by its sweeping wooden staircase, stucco ceilings and leather wallpaper. This provides a suitably lavish setting for a sumptuous collection of period furniture, Delftware, a selection of clocks (including an unique six-faced specimen by Hubert Sarton from 1795), and portraits of various local bigwigs – including several of Liège's prince-bishops – in various stages of self-importance.

A few metres further down Feronstrée is the Romanesque church of **St Barthélemy** (daily Mon–Sat 10am–noon & 2–5pm, Sun 2–5pm; €1.25), whose late twelfth-century exterior is currently under wraps as part of an extensive restoration project. That said, you can still go in to see its magnificent bronze baptismal font of 1118. The work of a certain Renier de Huy, the font is decorated with a graceful, naturalistic relief depicting various baptisms in progress, and rests on ten oxen, who bend their heads and necks as if under the weight of the great bowl.

The new town

Stretching south of the place de la République Française, Liège's **new town** is an altogether livelier and more engaging quarter than the old town – though with fewer specific sights – and home to the bulk of the city's shops, bars, restaurants and nightlife. Just south of the place de la République Française is the unprepossessing church of **St Denis** (Mon–Sat 9am–noon & 1.30–5pm, Sun 9–10am), whose gloomy and formless exterior conceals a striking early sixteenth-century wooden retable, standing a good 5m high. The top – and principal – section has six panels showing the Passion of Christ, very Gothic in tone, full of drama and assertively carved. The bottom set of panels is later and gentler in style, with smaller figures telling the story of St Denis from baptism to decapitation.

From St Denis, rue de la Cathédrale leads down to **place Cathédrale**, a tree-lined square whose pavement cafés supply a welcome touch of elegance. Looming over the southern side of the square is the spartan **Cathédrale St Paul** (daily 8am–noon & 2–5pm), its imposing grey steeple making a useful city landmark. Begun in the fourteenth century, the cathedral wasn't completely finished until the nineteenth, after it had been elevated to cathedral status following the destruction of St Lambert. Inside are some swirling roof paintings of 1570 and a late-thirteenth-century polychrome Madonna and Child at the base of the choir. Of most interest, however, is the **trésor** (Tues–Sun 2–5pm; €4), entered via the attractive cloisters, whose small collection includes a massive 90kg bust reliquary of St Lambert, the work of a goldsmith from Aachen, and dating from 1512. It contains the skull of the saint and depicts scenes from his life – the miracles he performed as a boy, his burial in Maastricht and the translation of his body from Maastricht to Liège by St Hubert, who succeeded him as bishop of the area. There are also some lovely examples of ivory work from the eleventh century, and a similarly dated missal, stained by the waters of a 1920s flood that inundated the church.

Outremeuse

The district across the river from the centre of Liège is the working-class quarter of **Outremeuse**, a neighbourhood that's said to be the home of the true Liègeois – it's sometimes known as the "free republic of Outremeuse", in part due to the traditional radicalism of the city's workers. This is epitomized by the folkloric figure known as **Tchantchès** (Liège slang for "Francis"), the so-called "Prince of Outremeuse", an earthy, independent-minded, brave but drunken fellow, who is said to have been born between two Outremeuse paving stones on August 25, 760. In later life, legend claims, he was instrumental in the campaigns of Charlemagne, thanks to the use of his enormous nose. Nowadays, Tchantchès can be seen in action in traditional Liège puppet shows such as those arranged by the Musée de la Vie Wallonne; he's also represented in a **statue** on place l'Yser, the traditional place of his death, carried as a symbol of freedom by a woman dressed as a coal miner. There's a **museum** devoted to Tchantchès nearby at rue Surlet 56 (Aug–June Tues & Thurs 2–4pm; €1), displaying various bygones, costumes and incidental paraphernalia relating to him – and his life as a puppet character.

If your appetite for museums still isn't sated, there's the **Maison de la Métallurgie** (Mon–Fri 9am–5pm, Sat & Sun 2–6pm; €5), a fifteen-minute walk south (beyond Outremeuse proper) at boulevard R. Poincaré 17, devoted to the coal and iron industries which formed the basis of Liège's nineteenth-century prosperity. Exhibits include displays of metalwork and a reconstructed forge from the eighteenth century. Five minutes' walk from here, at the western end of Outremeuse, the **Musée d'Art Moderne** (Tues–Sat 1–6pm, Sun 11am–4.30pm; €2.50) occupies the southern part of the leafy Parc de Boverie, five minutes' walk from the Palais de Congrès. The museum is something of a curate's egg, giving a whistle-stop tour of art since 1850. Many major artists are represented – Picasso in blue mood with *La Famille Soler*, Gauguin's Tahitian *Le Sorcier d'Hiva-Oa* and Signac's *Le Château de Comblat* – but these are relatively minor works, and it's the work of lesser-known artists who catch the eye: Alfred Steven's wistful *La Parisienne Japonaise*, Emile Claus's truculent *Le Vieux Jardinier* and the coastal scenes of Eugène Boudin.

Eating

Liège can be an excellent and often inexpensive place **to eat** – a quick trawl round the main streets of the new town reveals a wide range of cuisines, everything from Chinese, Vietnamese and Indian to Spanish, Latin American, Middle Eastern and Thai, not to mention plenty of places dishing up classy French and Walloon cooking. The best options are concentrated in the rectangle of streets northeast of the cathedral. It's also worth a trip across the river to Outremeuse's **rue Roture**, a narrow (and easy-to-miss) alleyway which spears right off the main shopping thoroughfare of rue Puits-en-Sock, and which is thick with restaurants and bars.

The new town

Au Parc de Moules rue Tête de Boeuf 19. Functional café serving up mussels of every conceivable variety (from €15) along with moderately priced French meat and fish dishes.

Bruit qui Court bd de la Sauvenière. Trendy eatery serving simple and reasonably priced meals – crepes, salads, lasagne; there's also a cool bar in an old converted bank vault downstairs.

Le Casbah rue Bergerue. Atmospherically gloomy restaurant decked out with kitsch Moroccan lanterns and dishing up all sorts of couscous from €12.

Du Point de Vue pl de la République Française. Claims to be the oldest tavern in Liège, and still pulls in the punters with its homely bar atmosphere and cheap lunchtime and evening meals.

L'Ecailler du Café Robert rue des Dominicains 26. Behind the Théâtre Royale, this popular restaurant is a good place for fish and seafood, with main courses from €16.50 and set three-course menus from €24.

India House rue St Jean en Isle 5. Refreshingly naff decor and a standard menu of well-prepared north Indian favourites from €11.

Mamé Vî Cou rue de la Wache 9. Just off the main squares, this is the last word in traditional Liègeoise cooking, where you can sample all manner of local specialities such as *Rognon de veau à Liège* and *Rable de lapin aux juneaux* – though at rather hefty prices, with full meals starting at around €25.

La Perle d'Asie rue du Pot d'Or 49. Excellent and authentic Vietnamese food, including good seafood choices, with set lunch menus from €7 (Tues–Fri only) and dinner menus from €10. It also has an excellent-value plat du jour for €4.75 and a four-course vegetarian meal for a very modest €10 (weekdays only, except Fri evening). Closed Mon.

Ristorante da Michele rue de la Casquette 25. Big, sloppy pizzas from €5.50, plus pasta dishes and three-course set menus from €10.

Taverne L'Opéra On the corner of rue des Dominicans. Unexciting but cheap eating, with many dishes for under €6.50.

The old town and Outremeuse

As Ouhès pl du Marché 19. Traditional Walloon cooking, with lots of meat, game and sausages along with *boulets sauce lapin* – a variation on the local delicacy *boulettes de Liège* (meatballs filled with a sweet black filling made of apples and pears).

Le Canaillou rue Roture 18, Outremeuse. French–Belgian cuisine, with excellent three-course menus for €25 and à la carte dishes from €15.

La Fondue Royale rue Roture 68, Outremeuse. Every imaginable kind of fondue, including meat and cheese (from €11.25) and chocolate (€6.25).

Rivoli Feronstrée 83, on the corner of rue St Jean Baptiste. A good lunch option in the museum area, with daily specials for €4.50.

Le Thème Impasse de la Couronne 9 ☎04 222 02 02. Excellent and quite reasonably priced French cuisine in an intimate setting on a tiny alleyway in the old town, with three-course (€20) and five-course (€30) menus. Closed Sun.

Drinking and nightlife

The grid of streets in the new town running north from rue Pont d'Avroy up to rue de la Casquette is the hub of the city's **nightlife**, with heaps of good **bars**, largely student-oriented. Rue Pont d'Avroy itself has lots of drinking haunts, but most of the best establishments are on the narrower streets behind, especially in the tiny alleyways of rue Tête du Boeuf and the parallel rue d'Amay. There's also a clutch of more sedate venues on the place du Marché and a couple more over in **Outremeuse**, on rue Roture.

A Pilori pl du Marché 7. Tiny, historic tavern popular with locals, with wooden beams and a cosy feel. Good range of beers and outdoor seating if it's packed inside – which it often is.

L'Aquarelle Corner of rue Pot d'Or and rue Tête de Boeuf. Dim student hangout pumping out mainstream rock and pop.

Le Café Chez Boldou rue Tête de Boeuf 15. Entertainingly decorated bar full of eclectic bric-a-brac. It's popular with students and there's live music at weekends (no cover charge), as well as a nightclub – *En Bas* (Fri & Sat 11pm–8am; free) – downstairs.

Casa Paco Corner of rue Pot d'Or and rue St Jean en l'Isle. Attractively tiled tapas bar with Iberian tipples, Latin music and cheap snacks, salads and tapas.

Le Lion S'Envoile rue Roture 13, Outremeuse. Hip club and music venue, with cool live jazz acts.

Luigi's Piano Bar rue Roture 22, Outremeuse. Nice bar with a live pianist most nights.

La Notte rue Tête de Boeuf 10. Popular music venue with live jazz on Tues (€6.25 cover charge).

Listings

Books Pax, place Cockerill 4, has a small stock of English paperbacks.
Bureaux de change There's a 24hr office at Guillemins Station.
Buses Timetable information on ☏ 04 361 91 49.
Car rental Avis, bd d'Avroy 238b ☏ 04 252 55 00; Europcar, bd de la Sauvenière 37 ☏ 04 222 40 07; Hertz, bd d'Avroy 60 ☏ 04 222 42 73.

Internet access There's a (nameless) Internet centre at the corner of rue du Pont and rue de la Boucherie (daily 10am–10.30pm; €2 per hour).
Laundry Ipsomat, Feronstrée 146 (daily 7am–10pm).
Mail The main post office is at rue de la Régence 61 (Mon–Fri 8.30am–7pm, Sat 8.30am–12.30pm).
Train enquiries ☏ 04 229 26 10.

Verviers, Spa and Eupen

East of Liège, the River Vesdre winds through attractive wooded countryside, with sharp hills plunging down into deep wooded valleys, before it reaches **Verviers**, a humdrum textile town whose limited attractions should not detain you long. Much more enticing is nearby **Spa**, famous for its thermal waters and nowadays retaining an appealing air of faded gentility. Nearby also, surrounded by undulating pastureland, is **Eupen**, a modest little town on the edge of open moorland – the Hautes Fagnes (see p.368). There are frequent **trains** from Liège-Guillemins station to Verviers-Central and Eupen; change at Verviers-Central for the hourly service to Spa.

Verviers

Some 30km east of Liège, **VERVIERS** is a thriving town of around fifty thousand souls which grew to prosperity during the nineteenth century on the back of the wool and textile industry. Though Verviers' industrial heyday is long past, the town is still home to a couple of textile factories, while a new museum celebrates its days as a centre of the international wool industry.

The centre of town is **place Verte** and – a block away – **place des Martyrs**. Five minutes' walk from the latter, down rue de Collège and left onto rue Renier, is the **Musée des Beaux Arts** (Mon, Wed & Sat 2–5pm, Sun 3–6pm; €1.75 combined ticket with the Musée d'Archéologie, Sat & Sun free), with a small but eclectic collection of paintings. Among them are landscapes and portraits by Dutch artists – including a fine *Adoration of the Magi* by Gerrit Dou – as well as later nineteenth-century works by Johan Barthold Jongkind, such as *The Skaters*. Look out, too, for the room entirely decorated with murals by an unknown eighteenth-century artist depicting views of the Vesdre valley (which runs alongside the museum) and parts of Malmédy. In addition, there's a small collection of more modern paintings on the first floor, including works by Magritte and Delvaux. Verviers' other museum, the **Musée d'Archéologie** (Tues & Thurs 2–5pm, Sat 9am–noon, Sun 10am–1pm), is of less interest, but it's nearby at rue des Raines 42 and can be entered with the same ticket, so you may as well have a look. Expect a handful of rooms furnished in period style, some weaponry, artefacts pertaining to the nineteenth-century violin virtuoso and composer Henri Vieuxtemps – who was a native of Verviers – and a small collection of Roman coins and other local historical finds.

Verviersima

Verviers' principal attraction, however, is the new **Verviersima** (April–Oct daily 10am–6pm, Nov–March Tues–Sun 10am–5pm; €5), which celebrates the town's once flourishing cloth and wool industry with exhibits spread over three floors of a restored nineteenth-century wool factory on rue de la Chapelle. The museum starts on the second floor, where a sequence of rooms takes you through the cloth-making process from sheep to garment, complete with interesting documentary footage and some impressive, antiquated machines. An English-language audioguide supplies a garrulous and occasionally entertaining commentary, including nuggets such as the fact that the factory's wool was formerly bleached in human urine purchased from the town's needier inhabitants. Even worse, factory employees were obliged to taste consignments of the stuff prior to purchase to check it hadn't been diluted. The centre's altogether less interesting lower two floors are devoted to fashion, with a threadbare collection of film clips, cartoons and replica costumes purporting to offer a history of clothing. The centre is in a rather out-of-the-way location ten minutes' walk from the train station: head left down rue de la Concorde to the river and look for the signs.

Practicalities

Twenty minutes by train from Liège, Verviers' **Central station** is ten minutes' walk from place Verte. The main **tourist office** is halfway between place Verte and the station at rue Vieille-Xhavée 61 (Mon–Fri 10am–4pm; ☎087 33 57 03, ⑩www.verviersima.be) – head downhill along the left side of the small park in front of the station. There's also a tourist office in Verviersama (April–Oct daily 8.30am–6.30pm; Nov–March until 5.30pm; ☎087 30 79 26). Both issue maps of town, co-ordinate walking tours and will make hotel bookings on your behalf for free.

There are three reasonable **hotels**: *Des Ardennes*, opposite the Central station at place de la Victoire 15 (☎087 22 39 25; ❷); the more comfortable eighteen-room *Park*, opposite the tourist office at rue Vielle-Xhavée 90 (☎087 33 09 72, ⑰087 31 60 91; ❹); and, best of the lot, the four-star *Amigo* just south of place du Général Jacques at rue Herla 1 (☎087 22 11 21, ⑰087 23 03 69; ❺). There are any number of **cafés** and **restaurants** on place Verte and place des Martyrs

– those on the latter tend to be slightly cheaper but less atmospheric. Try *La Bourse*, on the corner of place Verte, a pleasant brick-and-beamed bar with outdoor seating and an inexpensive lunch menu, or *Au Vieux Bourg*, also on place Verte, for a drink and a snack.

Spa

SPA, about 20km south of Verviers, was the world's first health resort, established way back in the sixteenth century: Pliny the Elder knew of the healing properties of the waters here, and Henry VIII was an early visitor. Since then the town has given its name to thermal resorts worldwide, reaching a height of popularity in the eighteenth and nineteenth centuries, when it was known as the "Café of Europe" and graced by monarchs, statesmen, intellectuals and aristocrats from all over the continent. Later the town went into slow decline – when the poet Matthew Arnold visited in 1860, he claimed it "astonished us by its insignificance". The years since have been no kinder, but present-day Spa preserves an endearing sense of faded distinction and continues to draw a loyal clientele of elderly locals; it also makes a good base for excursions into the Hautes Fagnes (see p.368), a short drive to the east.

The Town

Despite the eclipse of its reputation, the **town centre** preserves a striking cluster of grand Neoclassical buildings, presided over by the three towering steeples

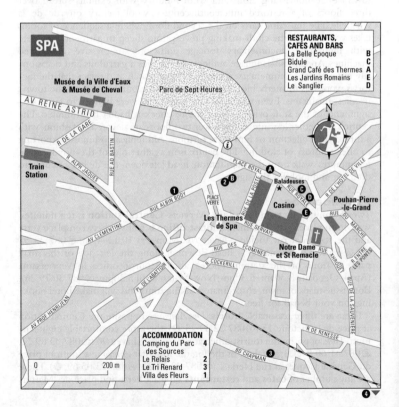

SPA

RESTAURANTS, CAFÉS AND BARS
La Belle Époque   B
Bidule   C
Grand Café des Thermes   A
Les Jardins Romains   E
Le Sanglier   D

Musée de la Ville d'Eaux & Musée de Cheval

Parc de Sept Heures

AV REINE ASTRID

R DE LA GARE

Train Station

RUE AD BASTIN

RUE ALPH JAQUES

RUE ALBIN BODY

PLACE VERTE

PLACE ROYAL

RUE DE LA POSTE

Baladeuses

RUE ROYALE

Casino

RUE DE L'HÔTEL DE VILLE

Pouhan-Pierre -le-Grand

RUE DU MARCHÉ

Les Thermes de Spa

RUE SERVAIS

Notre Dame et St Remacle

RUE XHROUET

RUE ENTRE LES PONTS

RUE DE LA SAUVENIÈRE

AV CLEMENTINE

RUE DES ECOMINES

C. COCKERILL

PL. DE L'ABATTOIR

AV PROF HENRIJEAN

R DE RENESSE

BD CHAPMAN

ACCOMMODATION
Camping du Parc des Sources   4
Le Relais   2
Le Tri Renard   3
Villa des Fleurs   1

0   200 m

of the church of Notre Dame et St Remacle. Chief among these are the main thermal baths, the fancy neo-Baroque **Les Thermes de Spa** (℡087 77 25 60; Mon–Fri 9am–noon & 1–5pm, Sat 9am–5pm; prices start from €80 per day, or from €15 for individual baths and treatments). Right in the centre on the main place Royale, these provide a very grand setting for the arthritis- and hypertension-curing mud and water treatments – which, if you're feeling flush, you'll need to book a couple of weeks in advance. For €0.12 you can also sample a glass of pleasantly fizzy water from the Marie-Henriette Spring – it's more palatable, but allegedly less efficacious, than the waters served up at Pouhan-Pierre-le-Grand (see below). The opulent **Casino** next door is the oldest in the world, originally founded in 1763 under the improbable auspices of the prince-bishop of Liège, though the current building dates only from 1919.

A little further along down rue Royale is **Pouhan-Pierre-le-Grand**, the town's main mineral spring (daily: April–Oct 10am–noon & 1.30–5pm; Nov–March Mon–Fri 1.30–5pm, Sat & Sun 10am–noon & 1.30–5pm). It's housed in a barn-like Neoclassical pavilion and named after Peter the Great, who appreciated the therapeutic effects of its waters and visited often; for €0.20 you can try a cup of the cloudy water, which contains iron and bicarbonate of soda, allegedly beneficial for lung and heart ailments as well as rheumatism. A number of Spa's **other springs** – notably Tonnelet, Barisart, Géronstère and Sauvenière – can be visited on the *baladeuse*, a kind of toy-train on wheels, which plies around the outskirts of town, but they don't normally let you get off to take the waters and there's precious little to see. The *baladeuses* leave from a stop on the main square; trips (there's a variety of itineraries) cost about €4.

Five minutes' walk west of the town centre, situated in the former mansion of Queen Marie-Henriette, the **Musée de la Ville d'Eaux** displays posters and objects relating to the resort and its waters (mid-March to June & Oct–Dec Sat & Sun 1.30–5.30pm; July–Sept daily 2.30–5.30pm; €2.5, or €3.75 combined ticket with the Musée du Cheval). The stables next door have been turned into the **Musée du Cheval** (same times; €2), exhibiting all things equine. A ten-minute walk south of the tourist office on route de la Géronstère 10 is the almost frighteningly surreal **Musée de la Lessive**, the last resting place of dozens of antiquated washing machines (Easter, July & Aug daily 2–6pm; rest of year Sun 2–6pm; €2).

Practicalities

With an hourly service from Verviers, Spa's **train station** is five minutes' walk from the town centre, which can be reached by going straight ahead out of the station down rue de la Gare and turning right at the bottom. The **tourist office** is in a pavilion near the baths at place Royale 41 (April–Sept Mon–Fri 9am–6pm, Sat & Sun 10am–6pm; Oct–March Mon–Fri 9am–6pm, Sat 10am–5pm, Sun 1–5pm; ℡087 79 53 53, ⓦwww.spa-info.be). It is extremely well stocked with books, maps and leaflets describing walking routes and cycle circuits. **Guided walks** in the area (€1.25) are organized three or four times a week in July and August and on Sundays throughout the year – both half- (6–8km) and full-day (10–12km) excursions.

There are plenty of reasonably priced places **to stay**. One good choice is the centrally located *Le Relais*, a well-cared-for small hotel at place du Monument 22 (℡087 77 11 08, ℻087 77 25 93, ✉fr.viteux@skynet.be; ❸). Moving slightly upmarket, there's the homely and very tranquil *Hostellerie Le Tri Renard*, a six-roomed establishment in a quiet residental street just south of town at boulevard Chapman 5 (℡ & ℉087 77 22 40; ❹), while for a real touch of nineteenth-century splendour, head for the *Hôtel Villa des Fleurs*, rue Albin Body 31 (℡087 79 50 50, ℉087 79 50 60, ⓦwww.hotel-villadesfleurs.be; ❹), located in a grand town house with handsome rooms and a nice private garden. Spa's only **campsite**, *Camping du Parc des Sources*, is farther along on rue de la Sauvenière itself, at no. 141 (℡087 77 23 11; April–Oct).

Among Spa's many **restaurants**, the hotel restaurant *Le Relais* has good, reasonably priced food, including very fresh seafood, served in convivial surroundings; a few doors along at no. 15, the elegant *La Belle Époque* also has excellent food, with fish dishes from €12.50 and three-course menus from around €23. The *Grand Café des Thermes*, opposite the baths on rue Royale, does snacks and meals from €9 – cheap if not terribly atmospheric, but with nice outdoor seating opposite the baths. *Les Jardins Romains*, in a wing of the Casino building, has a big range of inexpensive pizzas and pastas. Given the advanced age of most visitors to Spa, the town is never going to win any awards for nightlife, but if you fancy an after-hours **drink**, *Bidule* and *Le Sanglier*, close to one another opposite the Casino, are both good, popular local bars.

Eupen

Pleasant but unexceptional is the best way to describe the little town of **EUPEN**, some 15km east of Verviers. It is, however, the capital of the German-speaking region of Belgium, a pint-sized area pushed tight against the German border. Once part of Prussia, the area was ceded to Belgium by the Treaty of Versailles in 1919, but German remains the main language. Eupen certainly has a distinctive Teutonic feel, not least in the curvy twin towers of the eighteenth-century church of **St Nicholas** on the main Marktplatz, which sports some ornate Baroque altarpieces and an extravagant pulpit that could be straight out of rural Bavaria. Sweet-toothed visitors might also fancy a visit to the **Musée du Chocolat** (Mon–Fri 9am–5pm, Sat 11am–5pm; €1), on the northern outskirts of town at Industriestrasse 16. Part of the Chocolaterie Jacques factory, the museum has exhibits and videos on the history and production of the sweet brown stuff; you're also given a bird's-eye view of the factory floor, while a resident chocolatier dishes out free samples in a room upstairs.

Practicalities

Eupen's **train station** is ten minutes' walk from the main square, the Marktplatz, where the **tourist office** is at no. 7 (Mon–Fri 9am–5pm, Sat 10am–2pm; ℡087 55 34 50, ⓦwww.eupen.be). There are three **places to stay** in town: the comfortable if pricey four-star *Ambassador Hôtel Botsen*, Haasstrasse 81 (℡087 74 08 00, ℉087 74 48 41; ❺); the mid-range *Rathaus*, Rathausplatz 13 (℡087 74 28 12, ℉087 74 46 64; ❹); and the budget *Zum Goldenen Anker* pension, Marktplatz 13 (℡087 74 39 97, ℉087 55 73 69; ❷). There's good regional **food** at the *Delcoeur* brasserie and restaurant, Gospertstrasse 22, with main courses from €15, and decent Italian cuisine at the *San Marco*, Aachener Strasse 90.

An interesting way to arrive in – or leave – Eupen is on the **Vennbahn** from Trois Ponts (see p.365) via Malmédy (see p.367), a scenic three-hour train ride (€22.50 one way) around the fringes of the Hautes Fagnes (see p.368); some services are pulled by a restored steam engine. Unfortunately, the Vennbahn currently only runs two or three times a month between May and October – contact the tourist office in Eupen for schedules.

Stavelot, Malmédy and the Hautes Fagnes

South of Liège, the character of the landscape changes as you slip into the Ardennes, with rearing wooded hills rising high above winding rivers. The first obvious port-of-call is **Remouchamps**, whose main appeal is its cave complex, and from here it's another short hop to **Stavelot**, easily the most interesting town hereabouts, with the substantial remains of its abbey and an attractive upland setting. Nearby, **Malmédy** and **Robertville** are two fairly inconsequential tourist resorts, but either – as well as Stavelot – is a good base for hiking the high moorland of the Hautes Fagnes.

There are regular **trains** from Liège-Guillemins station to Aywaille (for Remouchamps), Coo and Trois Ponts (for Stavelot and Malmédy). The connecting services are by **bus**. Other bus services network the region, but they are characteristically infrequent.

Remouchamps

About 20km south of Liège, **REMOUCHAMPS** is a small resort on the River Amblève, visited mainly for the **Grottes de Remouchamps**, in the centre of town (daily: mid-Feb to mid-Nov daily 9am–6pm; mid-Nov to mid-Feb 9.30am–5pm; last departure 1hr before closing; €8.30). You can see the caves by way of what is claimed to be the longest subterranean boat trip in Europe, through beautiful coloured galleries of stalagmites and stalactites. The nearby **Monde Sauvage safari park** (mid-March to mid-Nov daily 10am–7pm; €10, or €14 for a combined ticket with the Grottes) might appeal if you've got kids in tow.

Regular **trains** from Liège-Guillemins stop at **Aywaille station**, around 3km west of Remouchamps and linked by a reasonably frequent shuttle **bus** to the Grottes and the safari park (€3.75 round trip). There's little reason to stay in Remouchamps, though the rather grand *Royal Hôtel Bonhomme*, rue de la Reffe 26 (✆04 384 40 06, ℻04 384 37 19, ⊛www.hotelbonhomme.com; ❹), is reasonably priced and has a good restaurant.

Stavelot

A couple of stops further down the railway line from Aywaille, **Trois Ponts** station is the starting point for hourly buses to the small and tranquil town of **STAVELOT**, a ten-minute trip. Stavelot's abbey was – with that of nearby Malmédy – home to a line of powerful abbot-bishops, who ran the area as an independent principality from the seventh right up to the end of the eighteenth century. The town was also the scene of fierce fighting during the Ardennes campaign of the last war, and some of the Nazis' worst atrocities in Belgium were committed here. These days Stavelot is a pleasant old place, falling away down the hillside from its attractively cobbled main square, **place St Remacle**, with pretty streets lined by half-timbered eighteenth-century houses. The best time to be in Stavelot is for its renowned annual carnival, the **Laetare**, first celebrated here in 1502 and held on the third weekend before Easter, from Saturday to Monday evening; the main protagonists are the **Blancs Moussis**, figures with white hoods and long red noses. There are also festivals of theatre and music in July and August respectively, with performances in the abbey buildings. For more information, consult the tourist office.

The lower part of the town is largely occupied by the former **Abbey**, a sprawling complex of mainly eighteenth-century buildings, though the soaring archway, the abbey's dominant feature, dates back two centuries more. The buildings now house a new cultural and tourist complex including three museums, all recently refurbished, plus a restaurant and souvenir shop. The most notable of the museums is the **Musée d'histoire de l'ancienne principauté de Stavelot-Malmédy** (Tues–Sun 10am–6pm; €5.5, or €9 for a combined ticket for all three museums), which traces the history of the principality from the seventh century to the present day by means of religious artefacts, town crafts and folkloric exhibits alongside multimedia displays. In another wing of the abbey, the **Musée du Circuit de Spa-Francorchamps** (same times; €4) contains a collection of racing cars and motorcycles from the nearby race track, home of the Belgium Formula 1 Grand Prix. Just over the courtyard, on the second floor of the Hôtel de Ville, the **Musée Guillaume Apollinaire** (same times; €3) was set up to commemorate the eponymous French writer, who spent the summer of 1899 in the town and wrote many poems about Stavelot and the Ardennes. The museum contains newspaper articles, letters, poems, sketches and photos relating to the man who – despite his early death – was one of the most influential of early twentieth-century poets.

Back in the upper part of the town, around the corner from place St Remacle, the church of **St Sebastien** (Mon–Sat 10am–12.30pm & 2–5pm; free) has an enormous thirteenth-century shrine of Saint Remacle, the founder of Stavelot abbey in the seventh century. You'll see him elsewhere too, most notably on the town's coat of arms, building the abbey with the aid of a wolf he supposedly tamed for the purpose. Mosan in style, the shrine is of gilt and enamelled copper with filigree and silver statuettes, though you can normally view it only from a distance. A short walk downhill, the little **chapel of St Laurent** was founded in 1030 by Saint Poppon, Abbot of Stavelot, and contains the sarcophagus that originally held his remains. To get there, turn left out of the abbey gateway, walk downhill across the bridge, and take the first left.

Practicalities

Stavelot's **tourist office** is located in the abbey (daily: 10am–12.30pm & 2–5.30pm; ℡ & ℱ 080 86 27 06). **Accommodation** can be difficult to find during carnival time, but shouldn't be a problem otherwise, although there are no budget options. The charming *Hôtel d'Orange*, a couple of minutes east of place St Remacle at rue Devant les Capucins 8 (℡080 86 20 05, ℱ080 86 42 92, ⓦwww.hotel-orange.be; ❹), has a range of variously sized rooms with either shower or bath, while the comfortable *La Maison* is located in a fine old building at place St Remacle 19 (℡080 86 41 65, ℱ080 88 02 75; ❹). The town's plushest option is the four-star *Le Val d'Amblève*, in a large country house ten minutes' walk out of town at route de Malmédy 7 (℡080 86 23 53, ℱ080 86 41 21, ⓔleval.dambleve@gate71.be; ❺).

For **food**, the intimate *Restaurant à l'Abbaye*, on place St Remacle, has good French meat and fish dishes from €10, while *Figaros*, also on the square, has tasty pizzas and pasta from €6. The *Hôtel d'Orange* and *La Maison* both have three-course menus from €17. If you're just after a **drink**, try *Aux Vieilles Caves d'Artois*, with outdoor seating overlooking the abbey buildings at avenue Ferdinand Nicolay 7, or the arty *Mal Aimé* bar at rue Neuve 12 – Apollinaire once stayed here and his poems are scrawled over the walls.

Around Stavelot: Coo

The Stavelot tourist office has a **walking map** (*Carte des Promenades de Stavelot*), which details fourteen circular routes starting in Stavelot or one of the nearby villages, with the most attractive walks heading east along the Amblève towards Warche or west through Ster to the waterfalls at **COO**, 7km away. Coo – with its own **train station**, one stop down from Aywaille and on the Liège–Luxembourg line – can get jam-packed with tourists in the summer, but a little walking soon gets you away from the crowd. There's a riot of amusements – go-carts, a deer park and a cable car up the mountain (€3.75 round trip) – just off the main street, and Coo is also the starting-point for **canoe trips** on the Amblève (March to mid-Nov), organized by Cookayak in Stavelot (☎080 68 42 65, ℻080 68 44 43, ⊛www.telecoo.be). Options include the nine-kilometre paddle to Cheneux (€15 for a one-seat kayak; €20 for a two-seater) or the 23-kilometre excursion to Lorce (€20/€27.50); advance reservations are recommended. In addition, Coo Bike Adventure (☎080 68 91 33, ⊛www.coobike.be), at Coo Cascade, rent out **mountain-bikes** (€18.75 per day) and can suggest biking circuits, and there is an excellent open-air **swimming pool** (July & Aug 10am–1pm & 2–7pm; €2.25), five minutes' walk from the tourist office at plaine des Bressais.

Malmédy and around

About 8km east from Stavelot, and connected to it (and Trois Ponts) by regular buses, the bustling resort of **MALMÉDY** is a popular destination for Belgian tourists, its attractive streets flanked by lively restaurants, smart shops and cheap hotels. There's not much to the town, but it's a pleasant place to spend a night or two and makes a relatively inexpensive base for the Hautes Fagnes. Malmédy is also home to the **Cwarmê**, one of Belgium's most famous festivals, held over the four days leading up to Shrove Tuesday. The festival's main day is the Sunday, during which roving groups of masked figures in red robes and plumed hats, the so-called **Haguètes**, wander around town seizing people with long wooden pincers – derived, it's thought, from the devices that were once used to give food to lepers.

The compact centre runs between **place de Rome** and the town's main square, **place Albert 1er**, with the imposing but rather plain eighteenth-century **Cathedral** (guided visits July & Aug; 10am–noon & 2–5pm) halfway between the two, surrounded by a clutch of fancy Germanic buildings. In terms of specific attractions, you're limited to the **Musée du Cwarmê** (Tues–Sun 2–5pm; €2.50), on place de Rome, which is devoted to Malmédy's annual carnival, and the **Musée National du Papier** in the same building (same times and ticket), which is about as interesting as its name suggests.

Practicalities

The superbly equipped **tourist office**, on place Albert 1er (daily except Thurs 10am–6pm, Sun until 5pm; ☎080 33 02 50, ℻080 77 05 88, ⊛www .eastbelgium.be), has truckloads of free information. **Accommodation** is notable for its quantity rather than quality, with a long list of hotels in and around town: all are comfortable and inexpensive, though there's little to distinguish one hotel from another. Options include *La Forge* (☎080 79 95 95, ℻080 79 95 98, ✉laforge@skynet.be; ❸), at rue Devant-les-Religeuses 31, which runs south off place de Rome; *Saint-Géreon*, place St Géreon 7–9 (☎080 33 06 77, ℻080 33 97 46; ❸), on a square just off place Albert 1er; and the slightly more expensive *Le Chambertin*, at Chemin-rue 46 (☎080 33 03 14, ℻080 77 03 38; ❸), which runs west off place Albert 1er. The closest campsite is *Mon Repos*, avenue de la Libération 3 (☎080 33 86 21; open all year), about 2km out of town.

Malmédy's popularity with holidaymakers means that there are plenty of good places **to eat**: *A Vî Mâm'di*, place Albert 1er 41, serves good regional food, while *Au Petit Chef*, on place de Rome, is good for snacks and cheaper meals, including mussels. There are also a couple of good places on Chemin-rue, which connects place Albert 1er and place de Rome: try *Au Petit Louvain*, at no. 47, which has game and fish dishes, or the more informal *L'ange gourmand*, at no. 21, which has regional cooking and salads, plus a range of snacks.

Around Malmédy: Robertville and Reinhardstein Castle

ROBERTVILLE, 8km northeast of Malmédy, is a bland resort that has grown up around the lake created by the **barrage** of the same name. There's little to do in the town itself, but it makes an excellent base for the surrounding area. The **tourist office** is at rue Centrale 53 (Mon–Sat 9am–noon & 1–6pm, Sun 11am–noon & 1–3pm; ☎080 44 64 75).

There are several good **hotels** on rue du Barrage, most notably the pretty, three-star *La Chaumière du Lac*, at no. 23 (☎080 44 63 39, ℗080 44 46 01, Ⓦwww. east-belgium.com/chaumiere.htm; ❹), and, close by at no. 5, the cheaper, two-star *Résidence du Lac* (☎080 44 46 94, ℗080 44 77 52; ❸). Finally, the three-star *Auberge du Lac*, rue de Lac 24 (☎080 44 41 59, ℗080 44 58 20; ❸), is a friendly old place, if a tad mundane.

The lake itself is the start of a lovely one-kilometre walk to the **Château de Reinhardstein** (mid-June to mid-Sept Sun tours every hour 2.15–5.15pm; July & Aug also Tues, Thurs & Sat 3.30pm; €5.50) – which is also reachable by road from the village of Orvifat, though you still have to leave your vehicle half a kilometre from the castle and walk the rest of the way. A squat stone structure nestled in the valley, and still privately owned, the castle was originally built in the fourteenth century and restored earlier last century; it now houses the usual array of weaponry and old paintings – a mildly enjoyable insight into the life of your average Belgian aristocrat.

The Hautes Fagnes

The high plateau that stretches north of Malmédy up as far as Eupen is known as the **Hautes Fagnes** (in German, Hohes Venn, or High Fens), nowadays protected as a national park. This area marks the end of the Ardennes proper and has been twinned with the Eifel hills, which stretch east from the German border, to form the sprawling Deutsch-Belgischer Naturpark. The Hautes Fagnes accommodates Belgium's highest peak, the Signal de Botrange (694m), but the rest of the area is boggy heath and woods, windswept and rather wild – excellent hiking country, though often fiercesome in winter.

Some 10km north of Robertville, on the road to Eupen, the **Centre Nature Botrange** (☎ 080 44 03 00, ℗080 44 44 29; €2.50; daily 10am–6pm) provides a focus for explorations of the Hautes Fagnes national park. A **bus** runs to the centre from Eupen (7 daily; 20min), but otherwise you'll need your own car to get there. Multilingual headphones guide you around a permanent exhibition that describes the flora and fauna of the area and explains how the *fagnes* were created and how they've been exploited. There's a coffee shop, a bookstore and, most importantly, a roaring log fire when the weather turns cold. The centre also rents out skis in winter (€10 per day) and runs organized hikes (see box opposite).

Walking around the Hautes Fagnes

Large parts of the Hautes Fagnes are protected zones and are only open to walkers with a registered guide. Three- and six-hour walks in these areas are arranged by the **Centre Nature Botrange** at weekends and by other groups during the week (℡080 44 03 00; €3–4). Each walk is organized around a feature of the local ecology, from medicinal plants to the endangered tetras lyre bird. In summer the walks can feel a bit crowded, and the guide's patter is normally in French or German, but they're a good way to see some genuinely wild country that would otherwise be off-limits.

To see some of the moorland on your own, ask staff at the centre for their free **map** (*Ronde de Botrange*) showing footpaths in the area. Many of them run along the edges of the protected areas, giving you a chance to see something of the *fagnes* even if you can't get on a guided walk. Dozens more local routes are marked on the map *Promenades Malmédy*, also available from the centre or from any local tourist office, though most are south of the Hautes Fagnes around Robertville, Xhoffraix and Malmédy. The varied eleven-kilometre route **M6** can be picked up in Botrange, crossing the heath as far as the main road before dropping down through the woods and along the river to Bayhon, returning through some attractive, almost Alpine scenery. From M6 you can take a detour north to incorporate the Fagne de la Poleur, or cross the main road and join route **M9**, which winds through the woods to Baraque Michel and then cuts south across the moors on the edge of the protected Grande Fagne.

A kilometre or so further up the main road is the **Signal de Botrange**, although the high-plateau nature of the Hautes Fagnes means it actually does not feel very high at all. A tower marks the summit, offering a good panorama over the *fagnes*, and there's a restaurant that's ultra-popular with coach parties and walkers.

Travel details

Trains

Arlon to: Jemelle (6 daily; 50min); Libramont (6 daily; 30min); Luxembourg (hourly; 20min); Namur (6 daily; 1hr 40min).

Dinant to: Anseremme (hourly; 5min); Bertrix (every 2hr; 1hr 20min); Gendron-Celles (hourly; 10min); Houyet (hourly; 20min); Libramont (every 2hr; 1hr 30min).

Jemelle to: Brussels (hourly; 1hr 40min); Libramont (hourly; 20 min); Luxembourg (hourly; 1hr 10min); Namur (hourly; 40 mins).

Libramont to: Bertrix (hourly; 10min); Florenville (hourly; 30min); Poix St Hubert (hourly; 10min); Virton (hourly; 50min).

Liège to: Aywaille (every 2hr; 30min); Barvaux (every 2hr; 50min); Brussels (every 30min; 1hr 20min); Coo (every 2hr; 50min); Huy (every 20min; 20min); Jemelle (every 2hr; 1hr 10min); Leuven (every 30min; 50min); Luxembourg (every 2hr; 2hr 30min); Melreux-Hotton (every 2 hours; 1hr); Namur (every 20min; 40min); Trois Ponts (every 2hr; 50min); Verviers (hourly; 20min). Change at Verviers-Central for Eupen (every 2hr; 15min) and Spa (hourly; 25min).

Namur to: Arlon (hourly; 1hr 20min); Charleroi (1–2 an hour; 50min); Dinant (every 30min; 30min); Floreffe (1–2 an hour; 10min); Godinne (every 30min; 20min); Huy (every 20min; 20min); Jemelle (hourly; 40min); Libramont (hourly; 1hr); Liège (every 30min; 45min); Luxembourg (hourly; 1hr 40min).

Buses

Bertrix train station to: Bouillon (Mon–Fri 5 daily, Sat & Sun 2 daily; 1hr); Herbeumont (Mon–Fri 6 daily, no weekend service; 40min).

Dinant to: Hastière (6 daily; 35min).

Jemelle train station to: Han-sur-Lesse

(June–Aug Mon–Fri 5 daily, Sat & Sun 10 daily; Sept–May Mon–Fri 4 daily, Sat 3 daily, no Sun service; 15min); Rochefort (as for Han-sur-Lesse; 7 min).

Libramont train station to: Bastogne (hourly; 50min); Bouillon (Mon–Fri 7 daily, Sat & Sun 4 daily; 50min).

Melreux-Hotton train station to: La Roche-en-Ardenne (Mon–Fri 8 daily, Sat & Sun 4 daily; 30min).

Namur to: Annevoie (1-4 daily; 40min); Floreffe (7 daily; 30min).

Poix St Hubert train station to: St Hubert (Mon–Fri 12 daily, Sat & Sun 4 daily; 15min).

Trois Ponts train station to: Malmédy (hourly; 25min); Stavelot (hourly; 10min).

Luxembourg

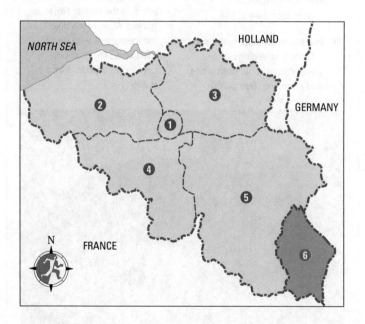

✳ **Chemin de la Corniche** – Fabulous views over the capital's bastions and bulwarks from the elevated walkway. See p.384

✳ **The Schueberfouer** – Luxembourg City's big annual funfair, held over the first three weeks of September. See p.388

✳ **The River Moselle wine trail** – Tours and tastings of Luxembourg wine, both white and sparkling. See p.390

✳ **Echternach** – A lovely little town with a splendid abbey and haughty basilica, and some excellent hiking in the surrounding wooded hills and valleys. See p.392

✳ **Vianden** – Featuring an inordinately picturesque castle, crowning a steep, forested hill; and the *Heintz Hotel*, a perfect Alpine-lookalike establishment with great food and extraordinarily comfortable beds. See p.395

6

Luxembourg

A cross the border from the Belgian province of Luxembourg (with which it has a closely entwined history), the **Grand Duchy of Luxembourg** is one of Europe's smallest sovereign states, a mere 85km from tip to toe. As a country it's relatively neglected by travellers, which is surprising considering its varied charms, not least its marvellous scenery: the rearing green hills and deep forested valleys that stretch along much of its eastern edge make for glorious hiking, and there's more of the same further to the west. The sharp, craggy hills that punctuate this dramatic landscape are crowned with often stunningly handsome **châteaux** – around 130 altogether, some austere, fortified castles, others lavish country mansions.

The obvious place to start a visit is **Luxembourg City**, once the Habsburg's strongest fortress, and now one of the best-looking capital cities in Europe home to a fifth of Luxembourg's population. Portions of its massive bastions and zigzag walls have survived in good order, while the broken terrain, with its deep winding valleys and steep hills, has restricted development, making the city feel more like a grouping of disparate villages than an administrative focus for the EU and a world financial centre. It's true that the city is not overly endowed with sights, but there's compensation in the excellence of its restaurants and the liveliness of its bar and club scene.

Within easy striking distance of the capital, in the southeast corner of the country, are the **vineyards** that string along the west bank of the **River Moselle**, the border with Germany. Tours and tastings of the wine cellars (*caves*) are the big deal here and, among a scattering of small riverside towns, the most appealing – in a low-key sort of way – are **Remich** and **Ehnen**. To the southwest of the capital is an industrial belt of little attraction – though you might consider a day-trip to the Duchy's second city, **Esch-sur-Alzette**; a much better bet is to head north into the **Gutland**, whose rolling farmland is intercepted by gentle river valleys, the most diverting of which is the **Vallée de l'Eisch**.

Further afield, beyond the Gutland, the northeastern corner of the Duchy boasts spectacular scenery with rugged gorges gashing a high, partly wooded plateau. This beautiful district is commonly known as **La Petite Suisse Luxembourgeoise** – less fancifully Das Mullerthal in Luxembourgish – and the inviting town of **Echternach**, which boasts a fine old abbey, is easily the best base. Similarly delightful, and just a few kilometres further to the north in the **Luxembourg Ardennes**, is **Vianden**, an extremely popular resort, surrounded by craggy green hills and topped by a glistening and glowering castle. Nothing in the Duchy quite matches Echternach and Vianden – both are outstanding – but **Diekirch**, a much more humdrum town in between the two,

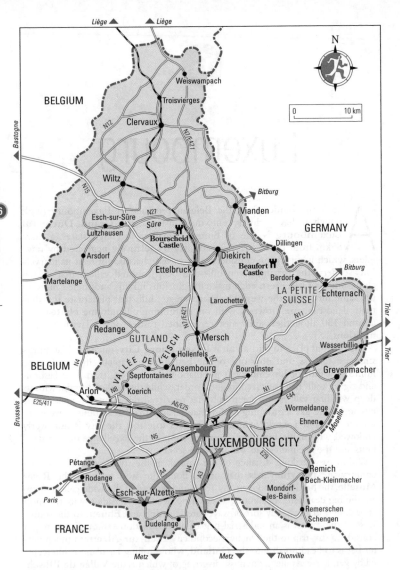

does hold a couple of decent museums, one of which details the Battle of the Bulge, much of which was fought in northern part of the country. Diekirch is also a handy base for venturing north into another beguiling part of the Luxembourg Ardennes, tracking along the valley of the **River Sûre** from the imposing castle of **Bourscheid** to the village of **Esch-sur-Sûre**, clasped in the horseshoe bend of its river.

Luxembourg has a very good public-transport system. With Luxembourg City as its hub, the **rail network** has three main lines. One reaches up through the centre of the country, connecting the capital with Ettelbruck, Clervaux and ultimately Liège; a second runs west bound for Arlon, Namur and Brussels; and a third heads east passing through Wasserbillig on the Moselle before proceeding on into Germany. Two branch lines respectively link the capital with Esch-sur-Alzette and Ettelbruck with Diekirch. **Buses** supplement the trains with regular and reliable services to and from all the larger towns and villages not on the rail network, including Echternach and Vianden. The smaller villages can, however, be much more difficult to reach, especially as some local services are geared to the needs of commuters and schoolchildren rather than the tourist. Free timetables are available at train and bus stations, and at all but the smallest tourist office.

Some history

Before Napoleon rationalized much of western Europe, Luxembourg was but one of several hundred petty kingdoms dating back to medieval times, and perhaps the most surprising thing about the modern state is that it exists at all. You'd think that Luxembourg, sandwiched between France and Germany, would have been gobbled up by one or the other of its neighbours – which is precisely what they would have done but for some strange quirks of history. The Romans had incorporated the region into their empire, colonizing Luxembourg City, which lay at the intersection of two of their military roads, and it was this same settlement which was fortified in 963 by **Count Siegfried of Lorraine**, who in so doing laid the foundations of the independent state. Siegfried and his successors ensured that Luxembourg City remained – as it had been under the Romans – a major staging point on the trade route between German Trier and Paris, its strategic importance enhanced by its defensibility, perched high above the sheer gorges of the Pétrusse and Alzette rivers. These counts ruled the area first as independent princes and then as (nominal) vassals of the Holy Roman Emperor, but, in the early fourteenth century, dynastic politics united Luxembourg with Bohemia. In 1354 Luxembourg was independent again, this time as a **duchy**, and its first dukes – John the Blind and his son Wenceslas – extended their lands up to Limburg in the north and down to Metz in the south. This state of affairs was also short-lived; in 1443, Luxembourg passed to the dukes of Burgundy and then, forty years later, to the **Habsburgs**. Thereafter its history mirrors that of Belgium, successively becoming part of the Spanish and Austrian Netherlands before occupation by Napoleon.

Luxembourg has three **official languages**: French, German and **Luxembourgish** (Lëtzebuergesch), a Germanic language derived from the Rhineland and Salian Franks, who migrated into the area in the fifth century AD. Most education is in **French** and **German**. French is the official language of the government and judiciary, but all Luxembourgers speak German with equal ease. **English** is very widely understood and spoken well too, especially by the younger generation, many of whom also speak **Italian** and **Portuguese**, a reflection of several decades of southern European immigration. The industrial districts of the south as well as Luxembourg City are noticeably cosmopolitan, the more rural districts less so. Nonetheless, there is a palpable sense of national identity, with one indication being the duchy's motto, which can be seen engraved or painted on buildings around the country: *Mir Wöelle Bleiwe Wat Mir Sin* (We want to remain what we are). Attempts by visitors to speak Lëtzebuergesch are well received – though sometimes locals are too surprised to seem exactly pleased.

Moien	Good morning/hello
Äddi or *a'voir*	Goodbye
Merci (villmols)	Thank you (very much)
Pardon	Sorry
Entschëllegt	Excuse me
Wann-ech-glift (pronounced as one word)	Please
Ech verstin Iech nët	I don't understand you
Ech versti kee Lëtzebuergesch	I don't understand any Luxembourgish

Things got really complicated in the early nineteenth century. In 1814, the Congress of Vienna decided to create the **Grand Duchy of Luxembourg**, nominally independent but ruled by **William I** of Orange-Nassau, who doubled as the newly appointed king of the newly created united Kingdom of The Netherlands (including Belgium). This arrangement proved deeply unpopular in Luxembourg and when the Belgians rebelled in 1830, the Luxembourgers joined in. It didn't do them much good. The Great Powers recognized an independent Belgium, but declined to do the same for Luxembourg, which remained in the clutches of William. Even worse, the Great Powers were irritated by William's inability to keep his kingdom in good nick, so they punished him by giving a chunk of Luxembourg's Ardennes to Belgium – now that country's *province* of Luxembourg. By these means, however, Luxembourg's survival was assured: neither France nor Germany could bear to let the Duchy pass to its rival and London made sure the Duchy was declared neutral. The city was demilitarized in 1867, when most of its fortifications were torn down, and the Duchy remained the property of the Dutch monarchy until 1890 when the ducal crown passed to another (separate) branch of the Orange-Nassaus.

In the **twentieth century**, the Germans overran Luxembourg in 1914 and again in 1940, when the royal family and government fled to Britain and the USA via Lisbon. The second occupation was predictably traumatic. At first, the Germans were comparatively benign, but as the tide of war turned against them, so the occupation grew harsher. They banned the Luxembourgish language, dispatched local conscripts to the Russian front, and took savage reprisals against any acts of resistance. **Liberation** by US forces led by General Patton came in September 1944, but the suffering didn't end there. In December of that year, the Germans launched an offensive through the Ardennes between Malmédy in Belgium and Luxembourg's Echternach. The ensuing **Battle of the Bulge** (see p.345) engulfed northern Luxembourg: hundreds of civilians were killed and a great swathe of the country was devastated – events recalled today by several museums and many roadside monuments.

In the **postwar period**, Luxembourg's shrewd policy of industrial diversification has made it one of the most prosperous parts of Europe. It has also discarded its prior habit of neutrality, joining NATO and becoming a founder member of the EEC, now the EU. It remains a **constitutional monarchy**, ruled by Grand Duke Henri, who succeeded his long-serving father, Jean, in 2000. The grand duke has a twelve-member cabinet of ministers, selected from a directly elected chamber of deputies that meets in the Parliament building in the capital. Luxembourg **politics** have a relaxed feel, with a number of green and special-interest parties vying with the more established centre-left and conservative parties – and the telephone directory lists direct lines for all ministers.

Luxembourg City

LUXEMBOURG CITY is one of the most spectacularly sited capitals in Europe. The valleys of the rivers Alzette and Pétrusse, which meet here, cut a green swath through the city, their deep canyons once key to the city's defences, but now providing a beautiful setting. These gorges have curtailed expansion and parcel the city up into clearly defined sections. There are four main districts (*quartiers*), beginning with the pint-sized **Old Town**, the location of almost all the sights and most of the best restaurants, high up on a tiny plateau on the northern side of the Pétrusse valley. Today's old town dates from the late seventeenth century, by which time it had been rebuilt after a huge gunpowder explosion in 1554, though wholesale modifications were made a couple of hundred years later. Furthermore, over half of its encircling **bastions and ramparts** were knocked down when the city was demilitarized in 1867 – boulevards Royal and Roosevelt are built on their foundations – though the more easterly fortifications have survived pretty much intact. These give a clear sense of the city's once formidable defensive capabilities, and were sufficient to persuade UNESCO to designate the city a World Heritage Site in 1994.

Below the old town and its ramparts are the **river valleys**, a curious – and curiously engaging – mixture of huddles of old stone houses, vegetable plots, medieval fortifications and parkland. They are well worth a leisurely exploration – allow an hour or two – unlike the mundane, early-twentieth-century **modern quarter**, which trails south from the Pétrusse valley to the train station and beyond. It's here you'll find the majority of the city's hotels plus some rather unsavoury bars and strip joints. Similarly unexciting is the fourth part of the city, the **Kirchberg plateau**, to the northeast of the old town, on the far side of the Alzette valley and reached by the imposing modern span of the Pont Grand-Duchesse Charlotte, usually known as the "Red Bridge" for reasons that will be immediately apparent. Kirchberg accommodates the **Centre Européen**, which is home to – among several EU institutions – the European Investment Bank and the Court of Justice, but frankly there's no reason to go there unless, of course, you're on business.

Arrival and information

Findel, Luxembourg's **airport**, is situated 6km east of the city on the road to Grevenmacher. There are a number of ways of getting into town from here. **Bus** #9 (Mon–Sat every 15–20min, Sun every 30min) runs to the **bus station** in the old town on place E. Hamilius, and then proceeds onto the train station. The whole journey takes about half an hour and costs a flat-rate €1.10, plus a small extra charge for any large items of luggage. There are also **Luxair buses** to the same places (€3.70), which are a little faster (20min) but more irregular – about a dozen services a day connect with major flight arrivals and departures. Travelling by **taxi**, expect to pay €18 to get to the city centre.

The **train station** is in the city's modern quarter, a ten- to fifteen-minute walk from the old town. The station has a left-luggage office and coin-operated luggage lockers and many of the city's cheaper hotels are located nearby. Most **long-distance buses** stop beside the train station. Almost all of the city's buses are routed via the train station, and the vast majority go on to (or come from) the bus station.

Information

Luxembourg National Tourist Office is inside the train-station concourse (June–Sept Mon–Sat 9am–7pm, Sun 9am–12.30pm & 2–6pm; Oct–May daily 9.15am–12.30pm & 1.45–6pm; ☎42 82 82 20, ⓦwww.ont.lu). They supply free city maps, transit maps, all manner of glossy leaflets, details of guided tours and can advise on – and book – accommodation right across the Grand Duchy. There's also a busy **Luxembourg City tourist office**, in the middle of the Old Town on place d'Armes (Jan–March & Oct–Dec Mon–Sat 9am–6pm, Sun 10am–6pm; April–Sept Mon–Sat 9am–7pm, Sun 10am–6pm; ☎22 28 09, ⓦwww.luxembourg -city.lu/touristinfo). They offer a similar service, though – as the name suggests – they deal only with the city. The city office also dishes out free copies of two monthly French-language **listings magazines**, *Rendez-Vous* and *Nightlife.lu*.

These services are supplemented by a network of **interactive computer terminals** in a variety of locations, including the airport and several motorway service areas. Besides giving tourist information of a general nature, these allow hotel bookings to be made with a credit card.

City transport and tours

Luxembourg City has an excellent public-transport system, with **buses** from every part of the city and its surroundings converging on the **bus station** on place E Hamilius. Usefully, most services are also routed via the train station. The Old Town itself, where you are likely to spend time most, is very small and is most readily explored on foot. **Tickets** on the city's buses cost a flat-rate €1.10 and are valid for an hour, while a block of ten tickets costs €8.80; alternatively, you can buy day-tickets for the whole of the Duchy's public transport system (see p.375). Before collapsing into a **taxi**, bear in mind that Luxembourg's are expensive – the fixed rate during the day is €0.80 per kilometre, with a ten percent surcharge at night, and a whopping 25 percent supplement on Sunday.

To take advantage of the **cycle trail** which encircles the city, you can **rent a bike** from an outlet at rue Bisserwe 8, Grund (☎47 96 23 83; Mon–Fri 2–8pm, Sat–Sun 10am–noon & 1–8pm; advance booking is advised), charging €2.50 an hour, €6.15 for a half-day, €10 a day, and €50 for a week, with twenty-percent discounts available for groups and under-26s. They'll provide you with details of the cycle route (also available from the tourist office) and offer a repair service as well.

Tours

To orient yourself, you may want to take a **guided tour**, though the multi-lingual commentary that accompanies most of them is wearying. **Bus tours**, operated by Voyages Sales Lentz (☎65 11 65; €12; 2hr), whisk around the main

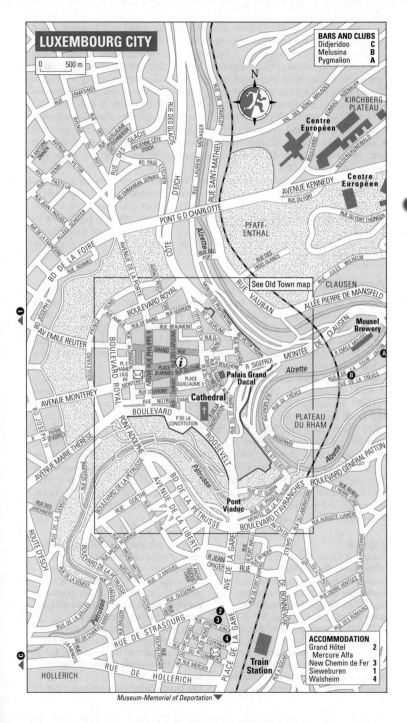

LUXEMBOURG CITY

0 — 500 m

BARS AND CLUBS
Didjeridoo **C**
Melusina **B**
Pygmalion **A**

N

KIRCHBERG PLATEAU

Centre Européen

Centre Européen

AVENUE KENNEDY
RUE DU FORT

RUE DES GLACIS
ANCIENNE CÔTE D'EICH
BD PAUL EYSCHEN
RUE ERMESINDE
AVENUE DES GLACIS
RUE GUILLAUME SCHNEIDER
RUE LAURENT MÉNAGER
RUE SAINT-MATHIEU
RUE DE STAVELOT
VAL DES BONS MALADES
KONRAD ADENAUER
BOULEVARD KONRAD ADENAUER
BOULEVARD NIEDERGRUNEWALD

AV ANTOINE PINARD
AVENUE VICTOR HUGO
AVE HENRI
AV PASTEUR
RUE JEAN L'AVEUGLE
ALLÉE SCHEFER
AVE DE LA FAIENCERIE
BD EMMANUEL SERVAIS
DEICH
CÔTE D'EICH

PONT G D CHARLOTTE

PFAFF- ENTHAL

RUE VAUBAN

See Old Town map

RUE DE LA TOUR JACOB
RUE JULES WILHELM
RUE DES TROIS GLANDS
ALLÉE PIERRE DE MANSFELD
CLAUSEN

Mousel Brewery

BD DE LA FOIRE
RUE ADAMES
AVENUE DE LA PORTE NEUVE
BOULEVARD ROYAL
BOULEVARD ROYAL
BD JOSEPH II
AV EMILE REUTER
AVENUE EMILE REUTER
PRINCE HENRI
AVE AMÉLIE
ALDRINGEN
RUE ALDRINGEN
RUE NEUVE
RUE PHILIPPE II
RUE DE BAINS
RUE GOERGEN
RUE BEAUMONT
GRAND RUE
RUE DES CAPUCINS
RUE
MONTÉE DE PFAFFENTHAL
CÔTE D'EICH
BD PICTOR THORN
RUE W WETTER
RUE SIGEFROI
R SIGEFROI
MONTÉE DE CLAUSEN
R EMILE MOUSEL
RUE DE TRÈVES

Palais Grand Ducal
i
PLACE D'ARMES
PLACE GUILLAUME II
RUE DU CURÉ
RUE LOUVIGNY
CHIMAY
PL DE L'HAMÉLIUS AV MONTEREY

AVENUE MONTEREY
RUE NOTRE DAME
BD JOSEPH II
R PIERRE D'ASPELT
BOULEVARD
Cathedral ✝
P DE LA CONSTITUTION
RUE DU ST ESPRIT
AVENUE MARIE THÉRÈSE
PONT ADOLPHE
BOULEVARD ROOSEVELT
RUE SOSTHÈNE WEIS
BISSERWEE
Alzette
MONTÉE DE CLAUSEN
MONTÉE DE TRÈVES
RUE DE TRÈVES

PLATEAU DU RHAM

BOULEVARD DE LA PÉTRUSSE
RUE SÉJOURNÉE
RUE GOETHE
BD DE LA PÉTRUSSE
AVENUE DE LA PÉTRUSSE
Pétrusse
RUE ST ULRIC
RUE ST QUIRIN
Pont Viaduc
RUE DE PRAGUE
MONTÉE DE LA PÉTRUSSE
BOULEVARD D'AVRANCHES
BOULEVARD GÉNÉRAL PATTON
RUE MARIE ET PIERRE CURIE
RUE DU LABORATOIRE
RUE AUGUSTE LUMIÈRE

RUE DES JARDINIERS
ROUTE D'ESCH
BOULEVARD DE LA PÉTRUSSE
RUE MICHEL RODANGE
RUE MICHEL WELTER
RUE GOETHE
RUE STE ZITHE
AV DE LA LIBERTÉ
R JEAN ORIGER
RUE DE LA GARE
RUE DE FORT NEIPPERG
RUE BENDER
BOULEVARD DE LA FRATERNITÉ
RUE PIERRE HENTGES
RUE DU CHICAGO
BOULEVARD DE BONNEVOIE
RUE DES ROMAINS

RUE DE LA SEMOIS
Pétrusse
RUE DE LA VALLÉE
J-B ARNEDS
RUE DR CHARLES MARX
BOULEVARD DE LA PÉTRUSSE
RUE DE ANVERS
RUE DE ANVERS
FISCHER
RUE GLESENER
RUE DOLPHE FISCHER
RUE JOSEPH JUNCK
RUE DE STRASBOURG
RUE D'EPERNAY
RUE DE COMMERCE
RUE MERCIER
RUE DU DEMY
RUE MICHEL WELTER
PLACE DE LA GARE
AV CH DE GAULLE
RUE DE FORT WALLIS
RUE DE FORT BOURBON
RUE DU PLÉBISCITE

Train Station

HOLLERICH
RUE DE HOLLERICH

➋ Grand Hôtel
➌ New Chemin de Fer
➍ Walsheim

ACCOMMODATION
Grand Hôtel **2**
Mercure Alfa
New Chemin de Fer **3**
Sieweburen **1**
Walsheim **4**

379

Museum-Memorial of Deportation ▼

city and suburban sites every afternoon between April and mid-November and on Saturdays from mid-November to March. These tours leave from place de la Constitution and work on a first-come, first-served basis. Rather more enjoyably, the tourist office organizes an excellent programme of **guided walks**, with the basic two-hour version (€6) taking place every afternoon from Easter to October and four times weekly the rest of the year. The main options are a City Promenade (Easter–Oct 1 daily, Nov–Easter 4 weekly; 2hr; €6) and the excellent Wenzel Walk (Easter–Oct 1 weekly; 2hr; €7), which is touted as "a thousand years in a hundred minutes". The latter starts from the Casemates du Bock, and takes you right around the fortifications on the east side of the Old Town. Reservations are advised either in person at the city tourist office or on ☎47 96 27 09.

Alternatively, a **miniature train** – the Pétrusse Express – travels along the floor of the Pétrusse valley from Pont Adolphe to Grund and up to the plateau du Rham immediately to the east. This hour-long tour gives a good idea of the full extent of the city's fortifications and takes in some pleasant parkland too. The train leaves at regular intervals from place de la Constitution (mid-March to early Nov daily 10am–6pm), where you buy tickets – €6.20 per person or €17.50 per family.

Accommodation

Most of the city's **hotels** are clustered near the train station, which is disappointing as this is the least interesting part of town – indeed the sidestreets opposite the station (rue d'Epernay etc) are a little seedy. You're much better off staying in the Old Town (places to stay listed here are marked on the map on p.382) and won't necessarily pay much more, though you are limited to just a handful of places.

For **budget accommodation**, there's *Auberge de Jeunesse*, rue du Fort Olisy 2 (☎22 68 89, ☎22 33 60, ✉luxembourg@youthhostels.lu; ❸, dorm beds €15.50, including breakfast), a barracks-like HI **hostel** located down below the Bock fortifications in the Alzette valley. With a laundry, cooking facilities and cycle rental, it's reachable from the train and bus stations as well as the airport on bus #9 – ask the driver put you off as otherwise you risk whistling by on the main road, about 300m from the hostel; on foot it takes about thirty minutes to cover the 3km from the train station. The nearest **campsite** is *Camping Bon Accueil*, rue du Camping 2 (☎36 70 69; April–Oct), just 5km south of the city on the banks of the River Alzette, in the village of Alzingen. It charges €3 per person per night, plus supplementary fees for everything from electrical hook-ups to tents and cars.

Hotels

Français pl d'Armes 14 ☎47 45 34, ☎46 42 74, ✉hfinfo@pt.lu. This attractive three-star hotel has smart and spotless rooms furnished in a crisp modern style. Great location too, on the main square in the Old Town. Recommended. ❻

Grand Hôtel Cravat bd Roosevelt 29 ☎22 19 75, ☎22 67 11, 🖥www.hotelcravat.lu. Charming, medium-sized, four-star hotel in the heart of the Old Town. The exterior is a little sombre, but the inside has oodles of atmosphere: instead of a designer make-over, the hotel has accumulated its furnishings and fittings, from the antique lift, fresco and chandelier to the signed sepia photographs of distant celebrities and heroes, including the American General Omar Bradley. The rooms are in similar style – lovely varnished wood trimmings for a start – and the best have appealing views over place de la Constitution. You won't do better – but it doesn't come cheap. ❾

Grand Hôtel Mercure Alfa pl de la Gare 16 ☎49 00 11, ☎49 00 09. Occupying an attractive and recently refurbished Art Deco building, this flashy, four-star hotel has every convenience. Opposite the train station. ❾

New Chemin de Fer rue Joseph Junck 4 ☎49 35

28, ⓕ 40 30 69. Rather unkempt, bargain-basement hotel in what passes for the city's red-light area. ❸

Rix bd Royal 20 ⓣ 47 16 66, ⓕ 22 75 35, ⓔ rix-hotel@cmd.net.lu. Smart, four-star hotel conveniently situated a couple of minutes' walk west of place d'Armes, just outside the Old Town in a road that's home to many of the city's offshore banking businesses – hence the high-rise office blocks. The public rooms are in plush antique style, all gilt mirrors, chandeliers and big fireplaces. There are just twenty rooms, each tastefully decorated and most with balconies. ❽

Schintgen rue Notre Dame 6 ⓣ 22 28 44, ⓕ 46 57 19, ⓔ schintgen@pt.lu. Bang in the middle of the Old Town, this simple, rather glum-looking hotel is short on accessories, but it is reasonably priced and the rooms are perfectly adequate. ❺

Sieweburen rue des Septfontaines 36 ⓣ 44 23 56, ⓕ 44 23 53, ⓔ siewebur@pt.lu. Alpine-lodge-style accommodation in the countryside just 2km northwest of the Old Town in the district of Rollingergrund. Three-star hotel plus a popular restaurant. Bus #2. ❻

Walsheim pl de la Gare 28 ⓣ 48 47 98, ⓕ 29 01 56, ⓔ hotel.walsheim@internet.lu. No great shakes, but this modest two-star hotel, with 24 en-suite rooms in a well-kept building opposite the station, is more than competent. The cheerful flower boxes set the tone. ❹

The City

No more than a few hundred metres across, the **Old Town** – La Vieille Ville – is not actually very old, its tight grid of streets maintaining much of the medieval layout, though the buildings which flank them are mostly eighteenth- and nineteenth-century. The rambling collection of the **Musée National d'Histoire et d'Art** here comes second best to the old **fortifications**, the earliest surviving examples of which flank the Montée de Clausen, linking the Old Town with Clausen in the valley below. These medieval bits and pieces are, however, insignificant when compared with the mighty bastions and ramparts that are seen to best advantage on the east side of the Old Town along the superbly scenic **chemin de la Corniche** walkway. These later works reflect the combined endeavours of generations of military engineers from the seventeenth to the nineteenth century, as does the honeycomb of subterranean artillery **casemates**, portions of which can be entered on both the Montée de Clausen and the place de la Constitution.

In the **river valley** to the east of the Old Town – directly below the chemin de la Corniche – lies the cluster of antique houses that constitute **Grund**, an attractive village-like enclave that once housed the city's working class, but is now partly gentrified. From Grund, it's a few minutes' walk round to the long and verdant **park** that stretches along the valley to the south of the Old Town and beneath the Pont Adolphe and Pont Viaduc bridges. Incidentally, note that you can reach the Pétrusse and Alzette river valleys from the Old Town by road, steps or **elevator**. The main elevator runs from place St Esprit to the Grund (daily 6.30am–3.30am).

Place d'Armes and place Guillaume II

At the centre of the Old Town is **place d'Armes**, a shady oblong fringed with pavement cafés and the sturdy Palais Municipal of 1907. It's a delightful spot and throughout the summer there are frequent free concerts – everything from jazz to brass bands – as well as a small (and expensive) flea market most Saturdays. Near the square are the city's principal shops, concentrated along **Grand Rue** and rue des Capucins to the north, rue du Fossé to the east, and rue Philippe II running south. Just off the southeast corner of the square, on rue du Curé, a side entrance into the Palais Municipal accesses the **Maquette de la Forteresse** (July–Sept daily 10am–5pm; €1.50). This is a scale model of the old city equipped with a multilingual commentary and spotlights illustrating how and when the city developed. It's not a bad introduction, but it's hardly riveting.

The passage from the southeast corner of place d'Armes leads through to the expansive **place Guillaume II**, in the middle of which is a jaunty-looking equestrian statue of William II. The square, the site of Luxembourg's main fresh-food market on Wednesday and Saturday mornings, is flanked by pleasant old townhouses as well as the solid Neoclassical **Hôtel de Ville**, adorned by a pair of gormless copper lions. There's also a modest stone water fountain bearing a cameo of the nineteenth-century Luxembourg poet Mighel Rodange.

The cathedral

From place Guillaume II, it's a brief stroll south down the steps beside the Rodange fountain to rue Notre Dame, where an ornate Baroque portico leads into the back of the **Cathédrale Notre Dame** (daily 10am–noon & 2–5.30pm; free), whose slender black spires dominate the city's puckered skyline. It is, however, a real mess of a building: the transepts and truncated choir,

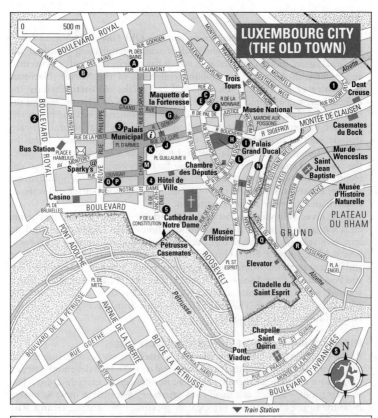

ACCOMMODATION		RESTAURANTS, CAFÉS AND BARS					
Auberge de Jeunesse	1	Brasserie Chimay	L	Le Bouquet Garni	K	Scotts	Q
Français	3	Bredewee	M	Giorgio's Pizzeria	E	Soda2 Café	G
Grand Hôtel Cravat	5	Café des Artistes	P	Kirin	B	The Tube	H
Rix	2	Chiggeri	C	L'Ocean	O	Via Sud	I
Schintgen	4	Conquest	F	Maison des Brasseurs	D	Vis-à-vis	A
		Brasserie Guillaume	J	Pulp	R	Wengé	N

dating to the 1930s, are in a clumping Art Deco style and have been glued onto the (much more appealing) seventeenth-century nave. Items of interest are few and far between, but there is a **plaque** in the nave honouring those priests killed in World War II, and the Baroque **gallery** at the back of the nave is a likeable affair – graced by alabaster angels and garlands of flowers, it was carved by a certain Daniel Muller in 1622. In the apse is the country's most venerated **icon**, *The Comforter of the Afflicted*, a seventeenth-century lime-wood effigy of the Madonna and Child which is frequently dressed up in all manner of lavish gear with crowns and sceptres, lace frills and gold brocade.

A door on the south side of the chancel leads through to the front entrance of the cathedral. On the way, you'll pass the stairs down to the **crypt**, more sterling Art Deco architecture among which is a barred chapel containing ducal tombs. Here also is the Baroque **tomb** of John the Blind – Jean l'Aveugle – which depicts the Entombment of Christ in a mass of mawkish detail. John was one of the most successful of Luxembourg's medieval rulers, until he came a cropper at the battle of Crécy in 1346.

Pétrusse Casemates and the Casino

Across from the main entrance to the cathedral, **place de la Constitution** sits on top of one of the old bastions, whose subterranean depths – the **Casemates de la Pétrusse** (Easter, Whitsun & July–Sept guided tours daily 11am–4pm; €1.75) – are entered via a stone stairway. The Spaniards dug these artillery chambers in the 1640s and they make for a dark and dank visit. Place de la Constitution also acts as the starting point for the Pétrusse Express (see p.380).

A couple of hundred metres away to the west, at rue Notre Dame 41, is the **Casino**: it's not a "Casino" in the sense of gaming at all, but an old bourgeois salon that has been turned into a gallery for contemporary art (Mon, Wed & Fri–Sun 11am–6pm, Thurs 11am–8pm; €4), featuring exhibitions that are often challenging.

The ducal palace and the Chambre des Députés

From place de la Constitution, pleasant **rue Chimay**, lined by shops and cafés, leads back towards place Guillaume II. Just to the east of the square, on rue du Marché aux Herbes, stands the **Palais Grand-Ducal** (guided tours mid-July to Aug Mon–Fri pm & Sat am; 1 daily in English; 45min; €5.50), originally built as the town hall, but adopted by the Luxembourg royals as their winter residence in the nineteenth century. Remodelled on several occasions, the exterior, with its dinky dormer windows and spiky little spires reveals a Moorish influence – though the end result looks more Ruritanian than anything else. The interior is, as you might expect, lavish in the extreme, with dazzling chandeliers, Brussels tapestries, frescoes and acres of richly carved wood panelling. Tours are very popular, so book at least a day in advance at the tourist office. To the right of the palace, an extension of 1859 houses the Luxembourg Parliament, the **Chambre des Députés**, in plainer but similarly opulent surroundings.

The museums

Walk round the corner – left along rue de l'Eau – and you'll soon reach **Marché aux Poissons**, an attractive little plaza flanked by immaculately restored, antique buildings, all turrets and towers, arcaded galleries, pastel paintwork and stone balconies. South of here, rue du St Esprit offers the **Musée d'Histoire de la Ville de Luxembourg** (Tues–Sun 10am–6pm, Thurs till 8pm; €5). Converted from four historic houses, this hi-tech museum tells the story of the city, taking full advantage of interactive displays and models to enliven the exhibits, which include wooden models of the city through the ages. Even the glass lift is used to highlight the geology of the area as it moves through various layers of rock.

Musée National d'Histoire et d'Art

Very much the key attraction here, however, is on Marché aux Poissons itself – the group of patrician mansions that comprises the **Musée National d'Histoire et d'Art** (Tues–Sun 10am–5pm; €5). Recently revamped and extended in lavish modern style, including the addition of a glassy atrium, this is the country's largest museum by a long chalk, and besides its permanent collections, it mounts an ambitious programme of temporary exhibitions, with one focus being contemporary art.

Among its several sections, the extensive **Gallo–Roman** collection is the special highlight. Containing the many archeological artefacts unearthed in the south of the country, it includes bronzes and terracottas, glassware, various funerary objects, a fine if weathered marble bust of a certain Septimius Severus and, best of the lot, a magnificent mosaic from Vichten. A second section is devoted to Decorative Art, Folk Art and Popular Traditions, with all sorts of bygones from traditional costumes and ornate firebacks through to a series of period rooms. Particularly fascinating is the sub-section on **black magic**, which has inverted crosses, strange and eerie statuettes and so forth.

The **Fine Art** section holds an enjoyable sample of fifteenth- and sixteenth-century paintings, notably a bold and brassy *Actuality* by Lucas Cranach the Younger; an exquisite *Pietà* by Adriaen Isenbrandt; an expressive *Presentation in the Temple* by Quentin Matsys; and a madly romantic *Bacchus, Venus and Love* by Rosso Fiorentino. Later Dutch works include a soft *Young Girl on the Balcony* by Ferdinand Bol, a portrait by Hals, genre scenes by Jan Steen and Adrien van Ostade, Brouwer's *Mussel Eater* and a Turner. It's a surprise to learn that Turner spent a lot of time in Luxembourg and painted some evocative landscapes during his stays. The museum's modern art is less revealing, but you might look out for the forceful Expressionism of Luxembourg's own Joseph Kutter (1894–1941).

From the museum, the obvious option is to head east to the Bock and then proceed down to Clausen. There are, however, three other worthwhile **routes**. One leads south along rue Large and its continuation Montée du Grund, which passes through some of the city's medieval fortifications on its way down to Grund; the other two begin by heading north round the side of the museum along cobbled rue Wiltheim. Where the road forks, one alley, the rue du Palais de Justice, weaves uphill through one of the most attractive parts of the Old Town, while the other tunnels down to the medieval Porte des Trois Tours gateway, beyond which there are wide views over the Alzette valley.

The Bock and the chemin de la Corniche

In 963 Count Siegfried of Lorraine decided to build a castle on the **Rocher du Bock**, a sandstone outcrop rising high above the Alzette just to the east of today's Marché aux Poissons. The city of Luxembourg originated with this stronghold, but precious little survives of Siegfried's construction – it was incorporated into the much more impressive fortifications that were built round the city from the seventeenth century onwards. The only significant piece of masonry to survive is the so-called **Dent Creuse** (Hollow Tooth) stone tower on the north side of the rue Sigefroi/Montée de Clausen. This same road, linking the Old Town with the suburb of Clausen, makes it doubly difficult to appreciate the layout of the original castle, which was – in medieval times – linked to the Marché aux Poissons by a drawbridge. That said, the views looking out over the spires, outer fortifications and aqueducts of the Alzette valley are superb.

In 1745, the Spaniards began digging beneath the site of Siegfried's castle. Eventually, they honeycombed the Bock with around 20km of tunnels and galleries, within which they placed bakeries, kitchens, stables and all the other amenities necessary to support a garrison. Today a tiny portion of the tunnels can be visited on a guided tour of the **Casemates du Bock** (March–Oct daily 10am–5pm; €1.75). It's a rather damp and drafty way to spend half an hour, and there's nothing much to see beyond a few rusty old cannons, but it's good fun all the same, an audiovisual presentation filling in the historical background.

From just above the Casemates du Bock on rue Sigefroi, you can follow the pedestrianized **chemin de la Corniche** along the ramparts marking the eastern perimeter of the main fortress. The views are absolutely spectacular and there's no better way to get a sense of the strength of the city's fortifications, which several major European powers struggled to improve, no one more than the French who, after 1684, made Luxembourg into one of the continent's most strongly defended cities – the so-called "Gibraltar of the north". After a few minutes you emerge at place St Esprit and more fortifications in the form of the **Citadelle du St Esprit**, a colossal, stone-faced bastion built in 1685. Its flattened top is where you'll find the main elevator down to Grund and, beyond in a grassy little park that's also above the bastion, there are views over the Pétrusse Valley and of the Pont Viaduc, which leads south toward the train station.

The Alzette and Pétrusse river valleys

Below and to the east of the Old Town, the **Alzette river valley** is dotted with ancient, pastel-painted houses and the battered remains of the outer fortifications – with the walls of the fortress rising steeply above. The best approach, down Montée de Clausen, brings you to the somewhat dishevelled district of **Clausen**. From here, rue de la Tour Jacob tracks along the riverside, passing the rickety Mousel brewery before reaching the medieval curtain wall – the **Mur de Wenceslas** – which both spans the Alzette and serves as a fortified footbridge leading back towards the Old Town. Dead ahead, through the gate, is **Grund**, once a thriving working-class quarter but now an uneven mixture of fine old houses and dilapidation that strings along the river for a few hundred metres. The most striking building here is the church of **St Jean Baptiste**, down near the river on rue Münster (daily 10am–noon & 2–6pm), an imposing structure with a massive spire and a flashy Baroque entrance way. Inside, the most conspicuous feature is the whopping – and inordinately gaudy – high altar; a side chapel holds a much venerated black Madonna. Also on rue Münster, before you get to the church, the **Musée National d'Histoire Naturelle** (mid-May to mid-Sept Tues–Sun 10am–6pm, mid-Sept to mid-May Tues–Fri 2–6pm, Sat & Sun 10am–6pm; €4.50) occupies a medieval hospital that has seen service as a prison, asylum and orphanage. It's popular with school groups for its displays on the workings of the human body, the natural environment and the creation of the solar system. The stuffed animals are less sought after.

At the centre of Grund, a chunky little **bridge** spans the Alzette. On the far side, you can regain the Old Town either by taking the elevator up to place St Esprit or by hoofing it up Montée du Grund. Alternatively, a left turn leads along **rue St Ulric**, where the markers at no. 14 show how high the river has risen in flood years – the worst inundation was in 1756. Continuing, rue St

Ulric cuts beneath the massive walls of the Citadelle du St Esprit before meeting **rue St Quirin**, a pathway which threads its way west through the wooded parkland of the **Pétrusse river valley**. There's one specific sight here, the mostly fourteenth-century **Chapelle St Quirin,** a tiny chapel chiselled out of – and projecting into – the rock-face and equipped with a dinky little spire. Further along the Pétrusse valley, paths clamber up to both ends of the **Pont Adolphe**, from where it's the briefest of walks back into the Old Town, or half an hour's walk south to Hollerich.

The Museum-Memorial of Deportation

Hollerich's modest **Museum–Memorial of Deportation** (May–Sept Tues–Fri 2–5.30pm, Oct–April Thurs 2–5.30pm; free) remembers those unfortunate enough to have been forcibly deported from Luxembourg City by the Germans in World War II. It's in the old train station, on rue de la Déportation: to get there take rue d'Alsace south from the junction of place de la Gare and rue de Hollerich and subsequently turn right onto rue de la Déportation – a walk of about twenty minutes from today's train station.

Eating and drinking

Luxembourg City's Old Town is crowded with **cafés** and **restaurants**, from inexpensive places where a filling plat du jour can cost as little as €9, through to lavish establishments with main courses costing twice as much and more. French cuisine is popular and traditional Luxembourgish dishes are found on many menus too, mostly meaty affairs such as neck of pork with broad beans (*judd mat gaardebounen*), black sausage (*blutwurst*) and chicken in Riesling (*hahnchen im Riesling*), not to mention freshwater fish from the River Moselle. Keep an eye out also for *gromperenkichelchen* – potato cakes usually served with apple sauce – and in winter, stalls and cafés selling *glühwein*, hot wine mulled with cloves. One of the great Luxembourg traditions is **coffee and cakes** in a salon or one of the city's numerous patisseries; here, as in Belgium, pavement cafés are thronged in the summertime, place d'Armes being the centre of the café scene. Multilingual menus are the norm and the only fly in the gastronomic ointment is that many places close on Sunday. Note also that most of the smarter restaurants close from around 2pm to 7pm.

Most visitors to the city are content to drink where they eat, but there is a lively **bar** and **club** scene spread around the various parts of town. Opening hours are fairly elastic, but bars usually stay open till around 1am, clubs till 3am. While you're out on the tiles, try one of the local Pilsner ales – Mousel and the tasty Bofferding are the most widely available.

Restaurants and cafés

Le Bouquet Garni rue de l'Eau 32 ☎26 20 06 20. Polished restaurant with beamed ceilings and starched tablecloths. They serve up French and Luxembourgish cuisine featuring local ingredients and supplemented by an excellent wine cellar. Main courses from around €20. Closed Sat lunch & Sun. **Brasserie Chimay** rue Chimay 15. Small, pleasantly old-fashioned café-restaurant near place d'Armes. Traditional, straightforward dishes – including a few Luxembourg favourites – at reasonable prices. Also a good place to sample its namesake Trappist beer. Closed Sun.

Brasserie Guillaume pl Guillaume II 12. Bright, modern brasserie specializing in Luxembourgish dishes, and also boasting a fine line in mussels and carpaccio. A popular, fashionable spot and very affordable too – main courses from as little as €10.
Bredewee rue Large 9 ☎22 26 96. Excellent little restaurant at the expensive end of the market offering gourmet, mostly French-style cuisine. The (summer) terrace on the chemin de la Corniche has superb views over the Alzette valley. Reservations advised. Closed Sun Oct–March.
Français pl d'Armes 14. The pavement café of the

Hôtel Français offers tasty salads and a wide-ranging menu including several Luxembourgish standbys. The daily specials are a real snip at around €8.

Giorgio's Pizzeria rue du Nord 11. A sociable and eminently fashionable place that serves until about 11pm, although pizzas – which start at €9 – often run out before then. Closed Sun.

Kirin rue des Bains 17. Decorated like Aladdin's cave, this reasonably priced and popular restaurant serves Chinese, Thai and Vietnamese dishes, with main courses averaging about €10, less for the plat du jour. In the Old Town.

Maison des Brasseurs Grand rue 48 ☏ 47 13 71. Modern Grand rue, the city's main shopping strip, Is also home to this long-established and smartly decorated restaurant, which serves up delicious Luxembourgish dishes. Sauerkraut is the house speciality. Highly recommended. Mon–Sat 11am–10pm.

Oberweis Grand rue 19. Classic coffee and cake salon that has been magnetizing the sweet of tooth for decades. Closed Sun.

L'Ocean rue Louvigny 7 ☏ 22 88 66. Smart, expensive seafood restaurant in the Old Town.

La Taverne Brasserie *Grand Hôtel Cravat*, bd Roosevelt 29. Waiters in bow ties and waistcoats set the scene for this smart bistro on the ground floor of the *Hôtel Cravat*. An older clientele tuck into classy French-inspired cuisine from a wide-ranging menu – including the best steaks in town – with main courses averaging a more-than-reasonable €15. It's open Sundays, something of a rarity here. There's also a much smarter, more formal and more expensive restaurant on the hotel's first floor.

Via Sud rue du Curé, off place d'Armes 22 ☏ 22 82 50. Intimate, tastefully furnished restaurant serving first-class, thoughtfully prepared food from a Franco-Mediterranean menu. Main courses average around €20. Closed Sun.

Wengé rue Louvigny 15. Mouth-watering patisseries and chocolates are on sale in the front part of *Wengé*, smashing salads and light meals – costing between €10 and €13 – at the back.

Bars and clubs

Café des Artistes Montée du Grund 22. Charming café-bar close to the bridge in Grund. Piano accompaniment and *chanson* most nights. Tues–Sun eve.

Chiggeri rue du Nord 15. Groovy ground-floor bar in the Old Town, with a great atmosphere, funky decor and a mixed clientèle.

Conquest rue du Palais de Justice 7 ☏ 22 21 41. Old Town gay club, playing house music. Ring for hours of opening.

Didjeridoo rue de Bouillon 31 ☏ 29 67 78. Everything from jungle to techno at this boisterous club in the Hollerich district west of the train station. Fri & Sat, sometimes more.

Melusina rue de la Tour Jacob 145, Clausen. Varied sounds Fri and Sat plus live jazz and folk music nights, as well as occasional theatrical performances. Expat favourite. Has a restaurant (open daily) and outside terrace too.

Pulp bd d'Avranches 36, on the south side of the Pétrusse valley ☏ 49 69 40. Established club with house and techno sounds, themed nights and occasional live acts. Fri & Sat, sometimes other nights too – ring for schedule.

Pygmalion rue de la Tour Jacob 19, Clausen. Busy Irish bar down in the depths of Clausen. Open till 1am weekdays and 3am weekends.

Scott's By the bridge in Grund. Pubby English bar where expats congregate for draught Guinness and bitter.

Sodaz Café Bar rue de la Boucherie 16, Old Town. Small, crowded bar featuring cocktails plus varied sounds. Closed Sun.

The Tube rue Sigefroi 8, Old Town. Lively, earthy nitespot named after London's Underground – hence the tube memorabilia. One of the city's more fashionable places; varied sounds from techno through to soul.

Vis à Vis At the junction of rue des Capucins and rue Beaumont. Laid-back, comfortable brasserie-bar with old posters and antique woodwork. Closed Sun.

Listings

Airlines Air Canada, av de la Gare 63 ☏ 48 81 36; British Airways, at the airport ☏ 0800 2000; Luxair, at the airport ☏ 47 98 42 42.

Bookshops Papeterie Ernster, rue du Fossé 27, has a reasonable range of English-language books and newspapers. Footsteps from place Guillaume II.

Banks and exchange You can change money at virtually any bank. Cash machines are dotted round the centre – there's a Caisse d'Epargne

cash machine at the east end of pl Guillaume II on rue du Fossé.

Car parks There are four underground car parks in the Old Town, though spaces can still be hard to find. One is off bd Royale beside the bus station; another beneath pl du Théâtre; a third under pl Guillaume; and a fourth is at the east end of bd Roosevelt, near the Viaduc bridge. All charge around €1.20/hr during the day, with cheaper rates in the evening and on the weekend. There's some especially handy on-street parking on pl de la Constitution, though there aren't many parking spaces here and they fill up fast, but it's always worth trying – particularly early in the morning and at night.

Car rental Autolux, bd Prince Henri 33 ☏22 11 81; Avis, at the train station ☏48 95 95; Europcar, route de Thionville 84 ☏40 42 28; Hertz, at the airport ☏43 46 45.

Cinemas Cinemas show films in their original language, subtitled (rarely dubbed) as appropriate in French. A varied programme of art-house and classic films is screened in the Old Town at Cinémathèque Municipale, on place du Théâtre (☏47 96 26 44). Mainstream films are on offer at, among a dozen other cinemas, the five-screen Ciné Utopia, north of the Old Town at avenue de la Faiencerie 16 (☏47 21 09) and the ten-screen Utopolis, avenue Kennedy 45, in Kirchberg (☏42 95 95).

Embassies Belgium, rue des Girondins 4 (☏44 27 46); Ireland, rte d'Arlon 28 (☏45 06 10); Netherlands, rue C.M. Spoo 5 (☏22 75 70); UK, bd Roosevelt 14 (☏22 98 64); USA, bd E. Servais 22 (☏46 01 23).

Emergencies Fire & ambulance ☏112; police ☏113.

Festivals The Schueberfouer, held over the first three weeks of September, is the city's main knees-up, featuring one of the biggest mobile fairs in Europe. It started out as a medieval sheep market, as recalled by the Hammelsmarsch, on the middle Sunday, in which shepherds bring their sheep to town, accompanied by a band, and work their way round the bars. The city also puts on an annual Summer in the City programme of free music concerts, fashion shows and parades, beginning in late June and ending in the middle of September.

Internet access Two Old Town internet centres are Sparky's, where place d'Armes meets ave Monterey (☏26 20 12 23; Mon–Sat 7.30am–8pm); and Chiggeri, rue du Nord 15 (☏22 82 36; daily 9am–1am).

Laundry Quick-Wash, near the train station at rue de Strasbourg 31 (☏48 78 33). Dry cleaners are dotted around the city – look out for branches of 5 à sec. There's one south of the Old Town, not far from the train station at rue de Bonnevoie 106 (☏48 06 60).

Left luggage There are coin-operated lockers and a luggage office at the train station.

Mail The main post office adjoins the bus station on pl E. Hamilius (Mon–Fri 7am–7pm, Sat 7am–5pm).

Newspapers English-language newspapers are available from most newsagents from about 11am on the day of publication.

Pharmacies Central pharmacies include Goedert, place d'Armes 5, and Mortier, avenue de la Gare 11. Duty rotas are displayed in pharmacy windows.

Police Main station is at rue Glesener 58–60.

Spa waters City folk often pop over to the spa town of Mondorf-les-Bains, on the French border 20km southeast of Luxembourg City, to take the mineral waters, which emerge from the ground at a steady 24°C. There's a sauna pavilion, with indoor and outdoor swimming pools, massage, solariums, Turkish baths, whirlpools plus medicinal treatments.

Telephones International calls can be made from all public telephones and booths have multilingual instructions. Buy phone cards from post offices or newsagents.

Train enquiries The CFL office in the station is open daily 6am–9pm (☏49 90 49 90).

Around Luxembourg City

Luxembourg City is fringed by three very different parts of the country. Easily the most appealing is the **Gutland** – literally Good Land – which fills out much of the middle of the Duchy, rolling north to workaday **Mersch** and west to the Belgian border, its green and fertile farmland intercepted by long and gentle river valleys. The Gutland is dotted with prosperous, good-looking villages, but specific targets are hard to pin down, two exceptions being the pretty little hamlet of **Bourglinster** and the **Vallée de l'Eisch**, the most scenic part of which weaves its way west from **Hollenfels** to **Koerich**.

In the other direction, east of Luxembourg City, the landscape is flatter and duller, and there's nothing much to detain you until you reach the gentle, sweeping scenery of the **River Moselle**, which, for 50km or so, forms the border with Germany. The river's west bank is lined with small towns and vineyards, whose grapes sustain the Duchy's thriving wine industry. Almost all of the wine is white, perked up with a little rosé, and most is good quality, varying from fruity Rieslings to delicate Pinot Blancs and flowery Gewurztraminers, plus some excellent, often underrated *méthode champenoise* sparkling wines. A number of wine producers run tours and tastings of their **wine cellars** (*caves*) – a popular day-trip for Germans and Luxembourgers alike. In themselves, however, the Moselle towns are really rather mundane – the most agreeable targets being the pleasant town of **Remich** and the pretty village of **Ehnen**.

To the southwest of Luxembourg City lies the most crowded part of the country, an industrial district whose red rock produced the iron that transformed the Duchy from a rural backwater into a modern, urban state. That said, industrial districts are rarely appealing to the passing tourist and this is no exception – though brisk and modern **Esch-sur-Alzette**, the Duchy's second largest town, does have its moments.

Getting from Luxembourg City to any of the towns and larger villages that surround it by **public transport** presents few difficulties, though you'll really need your own transport to make much of a tour of either the Gutland or the Moselle valley. Distances are predictably small: it's 30km from Luxembourg City to the Moselle, half that to Mersch.

Bourglinster and Mersch

Running parallel to the Liège train line, the main road north out of Luxembourg City – the N7 – seems to take ages to clear the trailing suburbs of the city, but eventually it reaches the five-kilometre-long turning that leads east to **BOURGLINSTER**, a pretty little place set in a wooded valley. Overlooking the village are the turrets and towers of the state-owned **château**, which is now used for art exhibitions and chamber music concerts. The château is also home to two **restaurants** – the formal *La Distillerie* (☎78 78 78), which serves French cuisine, and *La Taverne*, a much less expensive brasserie with both French and Luxembourgish dishes. It only takes half-an-hour or so to look round Bourglinster, but there is an HI **hostel** here – at rue de Gonderange 2 (☎26 78 07; ✉bourglinster@youthhostels.lu; dorm beds €15.50).

Back on the N7, it's just 6km more to **MERSCH**, a rather unexciting crossroads town with little to recommend it beyond the rather thin remains of a **Gallo-Roman villa**, southwest of the centre on rue des Romains (daily 8am–5.30pm; free). The villa is a little tricky to find: approaching the town from the south on the N7, cross the bridge over the Alzette and take the first left along rue G. D. Charlotte; follow this round – ignoring the N8/N7 turning on the right – until you reach place d'Église, where you turn right. Rue des Romains begins at the other end of place d'Église.

The Vallée de l'Eisch

From Mersch, the CR105 – a minor road – snakes its way south along the **Vallée de l'Eisch**, one of the Gutland's most attractive river valleys. The problem is actually finding the right road: the CR105 begins to the west of the centre of Mersch. To get there, take the N8 out of town, go underneath the motorway and then look for the turning on the left – but not the road to Saeul. The CR105 threads its way through pretty countryside before reaching, after about 10km, minuscule **Hollenfels**, above the river, where the old château, which mostly dates from the eighteenth century, has been turned into one of the country's most beautifully sited **hostels** (☎30 70 37; dorm beds €13.60). It's a few kilometres more to **Ansembourg**, a sliver of town that possesses two castles (no public access) – one up on the hillside dating from the twelfth century and a later one down below, which was built for a local iron-smelting baron. It's a pretty spot and so is the next village along, **Septfontaines**, 8km to the west on the CR105. There's another privately owned castle here, up on the hill, as well as a fine old **church**, whose grave-yard holds several unusual and elaborate Stations of the Cross. Four kilometres further and you reach the two-kilometre-long turning along the C110 that leads to the final valley village, **Koerich**, not as picturesque a spot as its neigh-bours, but with the valley's most interesting **church**, whose interior boasts splendid Baroque furnishings and fittings. From Koerich, it's just 12km west over the Belgian border to Arlon (see p.344).

Remich to Grevenmacher

Heading east from Luxembourg City along the E29, it's about 30km to **REMICH**, whose humdrum modern streets slope steeply up from the River Moselle. **Buses** from Luxembourg City to Remich drop passengers in the town centre. The town is the headquarters of the Duchy's wine industry – with its own Appellation Contrôlée – and thus a suitable home for the **Caves St Martin** (April–Oct daily tours & tastings 10am–noon & 1.30–6pm; €2.25), where the house speciality is sparkling wine. This is one of the region's most interesting cellar tours, taking in the minutiae of the *méthode champenoise* process, which is still carried out in a fairly traditional way here – the bottles are, for example, still turned by hand. The *caves* are located fifteen minutes' walk north along the river from the centre of town, on the left of the main road (the N10), at route de Stadtbredimus 53. Remich is also a major stop for the **cruise boats** that ply up and down the Moselle from Easter to October, connecting Remich with Schengen to the south and Wormeldange, Grevenmacher and Wasserbillig to the north. These cruises are operated by Entente Touristique de la Moselle Luxembourgeoise about once a day (☎75 82 75); as a sample fare, a single from Remich to Grevenmacher costs €6.50, €10 return. In addition, Remich's Navitours (☎75 84 89) offers one- and two-hour excursions on the Moselle from March to October for around €6, €10 respectively.

There's no strong reason to stay in Remich, but the town does have several **hotels**, one of the most agreeable of which is the two-star *Auberge des Cygnes*, in a comfortable 1950s building on the riverfront at rue Esplanade 11 (☎69 88 52, ℱ69 75 29, ✉hpcygnes@pt.lu; ❸). Also on the riverfront is the smart, four-star *Hôtel St Nicolas*, Esplanade 31 (☎26 66 30, ⓦwww.saint-nicolas.com; ❻), which occupies a distinguished old building dating back to the 1880s. Both the *Auberge des Cygnes* and the *Hôtel St Nicolas* have first-class **restaurants** – the first concentrating on Luxembourg dishes, the second French. That said, on a hot evening the terrace at the *Hôtel d'Esplanade*, rue Esplanade 5, is *the* place to eat.

Ehnen

North of Remich along the Moselle, vineyards furrow the hillsides, intermit-tently interrupted by craggy bluffs – pretty scenery that heralds the hamlet of **EHNEN**, whose huddle of old and very quaint stone buildings is tucked away in a wooded dell just off the main road. There's a **Musée du Vin** here (April–Oct Tues–Sun 9.30–11.30am & 2–5pm; €3) – nothing very exciting, but with informative exhibits in the old fermenting cellar detailing various aspects of the wine-making process, past and present – and a couple of invit-ing **hotels**. These are the neat and trim, three-star *Simmer* (☎76 00 30, ℱ76

03 06, @www.hotel-simmer.lu; ❹), in a rambling, turreted brick mansion that
dates back to the late nineteenth century; and the three-star *Bamberg*, in more
modern premises just along the street at route du Vin 131 (☎76 00 22, ⓕ76
00 56, ⓔbamberg@pt.lu; ❺; closed Dec). The Bamberg has an excellent
restaurant too. **Bus** #450 runs north from Remich to Ehnen and
Grevenmacher five times daily.

Grevenmacher

With a population of just over three thousand, **GREVENMACHER**, about
20km upriver from Remich, is the pint-sized capital of the Luxembourg
Moselle. It has a pleasant old town, complete with a comely set of stone houses, and also offers guided tours and tastings of its wineries. The most prominent among them is the **Caves Bernard Massard** (April–Oct daily
9.30am–6pm; €2.50), on the southern side of the town centre, right next to
the main street and river. To get there, follow rue de Trèves from the bus stop
and turn left as if to go over the bridge. Like the St Martin *caves* in Remich,
Bernard Massard is known for its sparkling, *méthode champenoise* wine, though
it is a much bigger concern, producing around four million bottles a year to
St Martin's eight hundred thousand or so. It shows in the production methods, which are far more automated, making it a less interesting – and shorter
– tour (though it is preceded by a short slide show and a tasting in the slick
hospitality suite afterwards).

An hour or two is all you'll need in Grevenmacher, but there is an HI **hostel** here, a short walk from the main bus stop at Gruewereck 15 (☎75 02 22,
ⓔgrevenmacher@youthhostels.lu; dorm beds €13.60). From Grevenmacher,
there is a regular bus service (12 daily; 10min) north along the river to
Wasserbillig, where you can pick up the train back to Luxembourg City.
Another (less frequent) bus links Grevenmacher with Echternach (see p.392),
further to the north and one of the Duchy's most appealing towns.

Esch-sur-Alzette and the southwest

The area immediately southwest of Luxembourg City used to be pretty dire,
an iron-ore mining and steel-making region whose heavy industry and urban
sprawls were best glimpsed from a train window on the way to somewhere
else. Nowadays, with much of the steel-making closed down, the towns are
being greened and cleaned, nowhere more so than **ESCH-SUR-ALZETTE**,
whose population of around 27,000 includes a large number of Italians, who
migrated here to work the steel. Esch is at its most agreeable among the shops
and cafés of its pedestrianized main street, **rue de l'Alzette**. It also possesses
one worthwhile sight, the **Musée de Résistance Nationale**, at the west end
of rue de l'Alzette in place de la Résistance (Thurs, Sat & Sun 3–6pm; free),
which tracks through the history of the Resistance in thorough detail.

Just 17km from Luxembourg City, Esch's **train station** is on the south side
of the town centre, about 300m from rue de l'Alzette along avenue de la Gare.
The **tourist office** is in the Hôtel de Ville at the east end of rue de l'Alzette
on place de l'Hôtel de Ville (Mon 1.30-6pm, Tues–Fri 10am–12.30pm &
1.30–6pm, Sat 10am–2pm; ☎54 16 37, @www.esch-city.lu). The best **hotel** in
town is the *Mercure-Renaissance*, a smart, four-star chain hotel at place Boltgen
2 (☎54 19 91, ⓕ54 19 90; ❺). The hotel **restaurant** is top-notch and prides
itself on its use of local ingredients; their plat du jour comes in at a very reasonable €9. Place Boltgen is just off rue de l'Alzette, near its junction with
avenue de la Gare.

Echternach and around

Some 35km northeast of Luxembourg City, the delightful little town of **Echternach** cuddles up to a bend in the River Sûre on the German border. The town is one of the Duchy's most beguiling, not least because of its splendid abbey, and has the added advantage of being at the heart of some wonderful scenery, comprising a parcel of land commonly – if rather oddly – called **La Petite Suisse Luxembourgeoise**. Despite the name, there are no Alpine peaks here, but the area is beautiful all the same, with steep and rocky wooded gorges gashing a rolling mountain plateau of open farmland and forest. The most enjoyable way to explore La Petite Suisse Luxembourgeoise is on its excellent network of **hiking trails**, with Echternach as a base. In addition, there are a couple of castles you might wish to visit – one each in the villages of **Larochette** and **Beaufort**.

Getting to Echternach from other parts of the Duchy by **bus** – including Luxembourg City, Diekirch and Viandem – is straightforward, but bus services to the surrounding villages are patchy.

Echternach

A town of just four thousand souls, **ECHTERNACH** grew up around an abbey that was founded here in 698 by **St Willibrord**, a Yorkshire missionary-monk who, according to legend, cured epilepsy and cattle. Such finely balanced skills went down a treat among the locals, most of whom had been converted to Christianity long before his death here in 739 at the grand old age of 81. Nowadays, Willibrord is commemorated by a renowned day-long **dancing procession** in which the dancers cross the town centre in leaps and jumps – signifying epilepsy – to the accompaniment of the polka and holding white handkerchiefs. The procession, which first took place in 1533, is held annually on Whit Tuesday – nine days after Easter Sunday – and begins at 9am, though you have to get here much earlier to get a decent view.

At the centre of Echternach is **place du Marché**, an airy, broadly rectangular piazza, which is flanked by an elegant conglomeration of old buildings. The most notable among them is the fifteenth-century **Palais de Justice** – or Denzelt (Law Courts) – a striking, turreted structure of roughly dressed stone held together by pinkish mortar and given poise by its Gothic arcade. The statues on the facade – of local, ecclesiastical and Biblical figures – were, however, added in the 1890s. The Denzelt is now part of the **Hôtel de Ville**, the bulk of which was completed in a pleasing version of French Empire style, again in the nineteenth century.

The Basilique St Willibrord

From place du Marché, it's a short stroll north to the **Basilique St Willibrord** (daily 9.30am–6.30pm; free), a brooding, forceful edifice equipped with two sets of slender, turreted towers. The church has had a long and chequered history. The first structure was a relatively modest affair, but as the Benedictine monastery grew richer, so the monks had it extended, filling it with all sorts of holy treasures. This made it a tempting target for the French Revolutionary army, who sacked the abbey and expelled the monks in 1797. Thereafter the monastery was turned into a pottery factory, but the Benedictines returned a few years later and promptly restored the abbey to an approximation of its medieval layout. There was yet more trouble during the Battle of the Bulge, when the abbey was heavily bombed, but the monks persevered, rebuilding the whole abbey – again to the medieval plan – and re-consecrating the church in

1952. The postwar reconstruction was skilfully executed and today's basilica has all the feel of a medieval church, most notably in its yawning, dimly-lit nave. That said, the church's furnishings are pretty pedestrian, and the only significant piece to have survived the bombing is the exquisite **crucifix** on the nave's left-hand wall. Downstairs, the **crypt** is also a survivor, dating back to the original eighth-century foundation. The crypt's whitewashed walls are decorated by several faded frescoes and accommodate the primitive **coffin** of Saint Willibrord, though this is enclosed within a hideously sentimental marble canopy of 1906.

The abbey

The huge **abbey complex** spreads out beyond the church, its crisply symmetrical, mainly eighteenth-century buildings now used as a school and for offices – including the tourist office. Next door to the church, the vaulted cellars of the former Abbot's Palace contain the **Musée de l'Abbaye** (Easter–June, Sept & Oct daily 10am–noon & 2–5pm, July & Aug daily 10am–6pm; €2), which has an excellent display on the medieval illuminated manuscripts for which Echternach once had an international reputation. Organized chronologically, the display explores the artistic development of these manuscripts, beginning in the eighth century, when Celtic and Anglo-Saxon influences are clearly discernible, and continuing through to the scriptorium's eleventh century, German-influenced heyday. Among the exhibits, two of the finest are the tenth-century *Codex Caesareus Upsaliensis* and the book of pericopes (a selection of Biblical texts) made for the Holy Roman Emperor Henry III (1017–56). Many of the manuscripts are illustrated and explained at some length (in French and Luxembourgish), though most are actually reproductions. The rest of the museum holds a few incidental bits and pieces, including a couple of eighth-century sarcophagi, a piece of mosaic flooring from a Roman villa discovered just outside town, and a modest display on St Willibrord's life and times. The formal beds of the old abbey gardens, by the river to the rear of the complex, have been turned into the very strollable **parc municipal**.

Practicalities

With regular services from Luxembourg City, Diekirch and Ettelbruck, Echternach's **bus station** is 500m from place du Marché, straight down rue de la Gare. Opposite the entrance to the basilica, the **tourist office** (Mon–Fri 9am–noon & 2–5pm, also July & Aug Sat & Sun 9am–noon & 2–5pm; ☎72 02 30) supplies free town maps, has lots of local information, sells hiking maps of the surrounding region and will book accommodation on your behalf at no extra cost.

Accommodation

There are plenty of **hotels** in Echternach, with several of the cheapest dotted along rue de la Gare. Options here include *Le Pavillon*, an unassuming hotel in an older building metres from place du Marché at no. 2 (☎72 98 09, Ⓕ72 86 23, ⓦwww.lepavillon.lu; ❸), and the similarly simple *Aigle Noir*, at no. 54 (☎72 03 83, Ⓕ72 05 44; ❸; closed Jan & Feb). Other budget hotels include *Le Petit Poète*, again with plain but perfectly adequate rooms and plum in the middle of town at place du Marché 13 (☎72 00 72, Ⓕ72 74 83, closed Jan; ❸); and the brightly-painted, neat and trim *Regine*, rue de la Gare 53 (☎72 00 77, Ⓕ72 87 11, Ⓔhotelregine@internet.lu; ❸). The smartest hotel in the centre is the four-star *Hostellerie de La Basilique*, place du Marché 7 (☎72 94 83, Ⓕ72 88 90, ⓦwww.hotel-basilique.lu; ❺), with thirty or so well-appointed, modern rooms, some of which overlook the main square.

The tourist office sells a **hiking map** for the Echternach district entitled *La Petite Suisse Luxembourgeoise et Basse-Sûre*. This details around fifty potential hikes, anywhere between 2km and 25km in length, and the majority are clearly marked. One popular route, taking in some fine rugged scenery, is the six-kilometre walk west from Echternach to the plateau hamlet of **Berdorf**, up the dramatic **Gorge du Loup**. At the top of the gorge are an open-air theatre and grottoes, which may have been where the Romans cut mill stones. There's a fairly frequent bus service between Berdorf and Echternach, or you can extend the hike by returning down the next valley to the south, with the path weaving through the woods across the valley from the main road into Echternach, the N11.

It's also possible to **kayak** down the River Sûre to Echternach from Dillingen, Wallendorf or Diekirch, the starting point depending on the time of year. The Outdoor Freizeit, rue de la Sûre 10, Dillingen (☎86 91 39), offers lots of advice – though the route is not especially difficult – and rents out both single and double kayaks; advance booking is essential.

Echternach also has a **hostel** – *L'Auberge de Jeunesse* – in a solid-looking older building at rue André Duchscher 9 (☎72 01 58, ℮echternach@youthhostels .lu; dorm beds €13.60; closed Nov to mid-Dec & Jan to mid-Feb); rue André Duchscher runs south from the corner of place du Marché and rue de la Gare. The nearest **campsite**, *Camping Officiel* (☎72 02 72; open mid-March to Oct), occupies a shaded site some 800m beyond the bus station, following the river out of town on route de Diekirch.

Eating and drinking

Most of the hotels have competent, occasionally very good **café-restaurants** that are done out in a sort of semi-Alpine style with oodles of wood. Many offer competitively priced **plats du jour**, others focus on Luxembourgish specialities – and some do both. Two of the better places are at the hotels *Regine* and *Le Pavillon*. Alternatively, *Giorgio's Pizzeria*, rue André Duchscher 4, serves excellent pizzas from €7 – it has the same owner as its namesake in Luxembourg City – and *Le Petit Palais*, next door to the *Hôtel Aigle Noir*, has delicious crepes. One other recommendation is the smart *Restaurant La Coppa*, rue de la Gare 22 (☎72 73 24; closed Mon & Tues), where an imaginative menu features the best of French and Luxembourgish cuisine; main courses average around €20. As for **drinking**, there's a lively scene among the pavement cafés fringing the place du Marché, or you could head off to *Bit Beim Dokter*, a cosy café-bar up by the tourist office.

Larochette and Beaufort

Among the villages that dot the forested valleys and open uplands of La Petite Suisse, **LAROCHETTE**, a scenic 25km west of Echternach, is one of the most interesting, largely on account of its **château** (Easter–Oct daily 10am–6pm; €1.50), whose imposing ruins sprawl along a rocky ridge. There's been a fortress here since the tenth century, but the most significant remains date from the fourteenth century, when the local lords controlled a whole swath of Luxembourg. Allow a good thirty minutes to explore the fortress and then pop down to the village, which strings along the valley below, its attractive medley of old houses harbouring a fine old church and three **hotels**. The pick of the three is the *Hôtel Residence*, a comfortable three-star establishment in the centre at rue de Medernach 14 (☎83 73 91, ⓕ87 94 42; ❹). A little less expensive – but more routine – is the *Grand Hôtel de la Poste*, at place Bleech 11 (☎87 81 78, ⓕ83 70 07, ⓦwww.grhopola.lu; ❹). The village also possesses a **hostel** – *Auberge de Jeunesse* – at Osterbour 45 (☎83 70 81, ⓔlarochette@youthhostels.lu; dorm beds €15.50; closed Jan, Feb & Nov to mid-Dec), in a well-kept older building on the edge of the village; and a **campsite** – *Camping Birkelt* – at rue de la Piscine 1 (☎87 90 40; March–Oct). As for eating, the *Hôtel Residence* has a first-rate **restaurant**, where the emphasis is on local dishes and ingredients.

Beaufort

From Larochette, it's about 15km northeast along pretty country roads to **BEAUFORT**, a humdrum agricultural village that straggles across a narrow, open plateau. In the wooded valley below is Beaufort's one and only claim to fame, its **château** (July & Aug daily 8am–7pm; Sept–June Mon–Fri 8am–noon & 2–5pm, €2), a rambling, mostly medieval stronghold whose stern walls and bleak towers roll down a steep escarpment. The most impressive part of a visit is the climb up the stone stairway into the fortress, past a series of well-preserved gateways. There's not too much to look at inside, though the old torture chamber is suitably grim and the stinky old well is a reminder that, by the fourteenth century, castles were as likely to surrender because of the stench of the sanitation as they were from enemy action.

Once you've seen the castle, there's no strong reason to hang around, but the village does have a pleasant, modern **hostel**, at rue de l'Auberge 6 (☎83 60 75; ⓔbeaufort@youthhostels.lu; dorm beds €13.60; closed Nov–Jan) and a couple of reasonable **hotels**. The best is the well-appointed *Hôtel Meyer*, in a sprightly modern building with an indoor pool and sauna at Grand rue 120 (☎83 62 62, ⓕ86 90 85, ⓔhomeyer@pt.lu; ❺). The *Meyer* has the village's best **restaurant** too.

Vianden

Hidden away in a deep fold in the landscape, beneath bulging forested hills and its mighty hilltop castle, tiny **VIANDEN**, about 30km northwest of Echternach, is undoubtedly the most strikingly sited of all Luxembourg's provincial towns. The setting, the castle and the magnificent scenery have long made it a popular tourist destination – and the town has the range of hotels and restaurants to prove it. Wherever else you go in Luxembourg, don't miss the place.

The Town

Some 500m from top to bottom, Vianden's main street – the **Grand rue** – sweeps down a steep, wooded hill to the pint-sized **bridge** that both spans the River Our and serves as the centre of town. On the bridge there's a **statue** of St John Nepomuk, a fourteenth-century Bohemian priest, who was thrown into the River Vltava for refusing to divulge the confessional secrets of his queen – an untimely end that was to make him the patron saint of bridges. Also on the bridge is a fine bust of **Victor Hugo** by Rodin. Expelled from France for supporting the French revolutionaries of 1848, Hugo spent almost twenty years in exile, becoming a regular visitor to Vianden and living here in the summer of 1871. Hugo's former house, at the east end of the bridge, has been turned into a modest **museum** (currently closed for long-term renovation) commemorating his stay here, with many letters and copies of poems and manuscripts, including his *Discourse on Vianden*. There are also photographs of the town during the nineteenth century, and sketches by the great man of local places of interest – the castles at Beaufort and Larochette, for example. Sadly, though, there's not much left from Hugo's stay, apart from the bedroom furniture, complete with original bed.

Strolling up Grand rue from the bridge, look out for the Gothic **Église des Trinitaires** on the left (daily 9am–6pm; free). The church's twin naves date back to the thirteenth century, as does the subtle, sinuous tracery of the adjoining **cloître** (cloister). Further up the street, the town's other museum, the **Musée d'Art Rustique**, occupies an old and distinguished-looking house at Grand rue 96 (Easter–May, Sept & Oct Tues–Sun 11am–5pm; June–Aug daily 11am–5pm; €2.50). This holds an enjoyable hotchpotch of rural furniture, fancy firebacks and old clothes, plus a sprawling display of toys and, on the top floor, a small room devoted to some fascinating historical documents and photographs of the town and castle.

The castle

Vianden's major sight is inevitably its inordinately picturesque **château** (daily: March & Oct 10am–5pm; April–Sept 10am–6pm; Nov–Feb 10am–4pm; €4.50), perched high above the town. Originally a fifth-century structure, the castle you see today dates mostly from the eleventh century and shows features from the Romanesque and Gothic through to the Renaissance. It was the home of the counts of Vianden, who ruled the town and much of the area during the twelfth and thirteenth centuries – until they fell under the sway of the House of Luxembourg in 1264. Later, in 1417, the Luxembourg family took over the building, and it remained the property of the grand dukes until 1977 when it was handed over to the state.

A very large complex, the castle is now open in its entirety following a very thorough and sensitive restoration (previously much of it was in ruins), though the crowds trooping through the pristine halls and galleries on the self-guided

△ Château, Vianden

tour can't help but spoil the atmosphere. Some rooms have been furnished in an approximation of period style – the **Banqueting Hall** being a case in point – while others display suits of armour and suchlike, but much has just been left pleasingly empty. Of particular architectural merit are the long **Byzantine Room**, with its high trefoil windows, and the octagonal **Upper Chapel** next door, surrounded by a narrow defensive walkway. There are, furthermore, exhibits on the development of the building, detailing its restoration, and on the history of the town. For a bit of authentic mustiness, peek down the **well** just off the Grand Kitchen – its murky darkness lit to reveal profound depths (in which, locals maintain, a former count can be heard frantically playing dice to hold the Devil at bay, his soul at stake).

The obvious approach to the castle is along the short access road at the top of Vianden's main street. More interestingly, a fairly easy footpath leads round to the castle from one of the hills immediately to the north. Even better, it's possible to reach this hilltop, 450m above the river, without breaking sweat by means of a **télésiège** (chairlift; Easter–May & Sept to mid-Oct daily except Fri 10am–5pm, June–Aug daily 10am–6.30pm; €4.50 return). This departs from rue du Sanatorium, a five- to ten-minute walk north from the east end of the town bridge – just follow the signs. The upper terminal of the télésiège also has a café and offers extravagant views over Vianden.

Practicalities

With regular services from Diekirch and Ettelbruck, Vianden's tiny **bus station** is about five minutes' walk east of the town bridge along rue de la Gare and its continuation rue de la Frontière. When you're **moving on** from Vianden, the most obvious choice is to head southwest for Diekirch and the valley of the River Sûre (see p.398). Equally enticing, however, is the scenic drive or cycle ride north along the River Our and the short onward journey west to Clervaux (see p.401), northern Luxembourg's most interesting town.

The **tourist office** is at the west end of the bridge, on rue du Vieux Marché (June–Aug Mon–Fri 8am–6pm, Sat & Sun 10am–4pm; Sept–May Mon–Fri 9am–noon & 1–5pm; ☏83 42 57, ⓦwww.vianden.lu). They have copious local information and sell hiking maps as well as a small booklet describing around thirty **walks** in the vicinity of Vianden, ranging from a short ramble along the river to more energetic hauls up into the surrounding hills. **Cycling tracks** link Vianden with both Diekirch and Echternach; **mountain-bikes** can be rented from the Pavillon de la Gare (☏84 92 48; advance booking recommended), beside the bus station, for €15 per day, €40 for three days.

Accommodation

Accommodation isn't usually a problem in Vianden – virtually every other building seems to be a hotel – but you'd still be well advised to reserve in advance during the high season. Pick of the hotels – indeed one of the most charming hotels in the whole of Belgium and Luxembourg – is the *Hôtel Heintz*, Grand rue 55 (☏83 41 55, Ⓕ83 45 59, ⓦwww.hotel-heintz.lu; April to mid-Nov; ❸). The hotel's modest façade does no more than hint at what lies behind, the public areas sporting oodles of wood panelling and sprinkled with local bygones in thoroughly Alpine style. The rooms are very comfortable and well-appointed, and again there's lots of wood, while the rooms in the annexe behind the main building have balconies offering views down to the river. If the Heintz is full, another good bet, also on the castle side of the river but with plainer rooms, is the *Hôtel Collette*, in a large nineteenth-century building at Grand rue 68 (☏83 40 04, Ⓕ83 47 05, Ⓔhotelcollette@pt.lu; ❸; April to early Nov). A third recommendation is the *Auberge du Château/Hostellerie des Remparts*, in expansive older premises at Grand rue 74-89 (℡83 45 74, 🖷83 47 20, 🌐www.auberge-du-chateau.lu; ❸). There's also a **hostel** nicely placed – but difficult to find – in a imaginatively revamped stone building at the top of Grand rue, near the castle at montée du Château 3 (℡83 41 77, ✉vianden@youthhostels.lu; dorm beds €13.60; closed mid-Jan to mid-Feb, March, Nov & early Dec).

The nearest **campsite** is *Op dem Deich* (℡83 43 75; April to early Oct) by the river behind – and just along from – the bus station. In addition, there are two other campsites further on down the road to Echternach. First up, about 1km from the bridge, is *De l'Our* (℡83 45 05; April to late Oct) and then, after another 400m or so, comes *Du Moulin* (℡83 45 01; May–Sept). All three are well equipped.

Eating and drinking

Almost all of the town's hotels have **restaurants** – in fact there's barely a restaurant in town which isn't part of a hotel. The restaurant of the *Hôtel Heintz* is especially good, serving an excellent line in Luxembourgish dishes at reasonable prices, a description which applies in equal measure to the restaurant of the *Auberge du Château*. Another – more casual – alternative is the café-restaurant of the *Hôtel Auberge de l'Our*, by the bridge, where they serves both Luxembourgish and French dishes. The riverside terrace **bar** here is one of the most convivial places in town, though it gets jam-packed on summer weekends; there's also a cosy, wood-panelled bar in the *Hôtel Heintz*.

Diekirch and around

Southwest of Vianden, it's just 12km to **Diekirch**, a busy little town, which – along with neighbouring **Ettelbruck** – has long been a major staging point on the highway north from Luxembourg City to Belgium's Liège. Both towns were badly mauled during the Battle of the Bulge (see p.345), but Diekirch – unlike its neighbour – has retained a modicum of charm and also has a couple of good museums and a reasonable supply of hotels. Furthermore, Diekirch is a handy base for venturing out along the upper reaches of the **River Sûre**, attractive scenery that accommodates both the impressive castle of **Bourscheid** and the picture-postcard hamlet of **Esch-sur-Sûre.**

As for **public transport**, Ettelbruck is on the main rail line between Luxembourg City and Liège, with a branch line linking it to Diekirch. There are local buses from both Ettelbruck and Diekirch to the villages along and around the River Sûre, but services are generally infrequent.

Diekirch

The compact centre of **DIEKIRCH** hugs the north bank of the River Sûre, its encircling boulevard marking the path of the long-demolished medieval walls. The town took a pounding in 1944 – hence the modern buildings that characterize the centre – but bits and pieces of the old have survived. Most notable amongst them is the **Église St Laurentius** (Easter–Oct Tues–Sun 10am–noon & 2–6pm; free), partly dating from the ninth century and located about 100m east of the top of the pedestrianized main shopping street, Grand rue. The church is equipped with a dinky little spire and a pair of comely towers, while the interior is noteworthy for its spooky Roman and medieval sarcophagi, discovered when the floor was re-laid.

Immediately to the west of the old centre, across the retaining boulevard, is **place Guillaume**, a breezy, open square that marks the centre of the nineteenth-century town. From here, it's about 250m north along the boulevard – and across place des Recollets – to the **Musée National d'Histoire Militaire**, at rue Bamertal 10 (daily: April–Oct 10am–6pm, Nov–March 2–6pm; €5). This provides an excellent historical survey of the Battle of the Bulge, with special emphasis on US forces. The photographs are the real testimony, showing both sets of troops in action and at leisure, some recording the appalling freezing conditions of December 1944, others the horrific state of affairs inside the medics' tents. There's a variety of dioramas, many modelled diligently on actual photographs (which are often displayed alongside), along with a hoard of military paraphernalia – explosives, shells, weapons, and personal effects of both American and German soldiers (prayer books, rations, novellas, etc). There's also a display entitled "**Veiner Miliz**", detailing the activities of the Luxembourg resistance movement based in Vianden, and a room devoted to **Tambow**, the camp to which all the Luxembourgers captured by the Germans were sent. Ask here also for the free *Battleground Luxembourg* brochure, which outlines a car tour of the major Battle of the Bulge sites, monuments and remains.

Diekirch's other, lesser museum, the **Musée Mosaïques Romaines** (Easter–Oct daily except Thurs 10am–noon & 2–6pm; €1.30), is on place Guillaume. It comprises two rooms, each featuring a reasonably well-preserved Roman floor mosaic, one from the middle of the first century, the other from around the third century, found in the centre of Diekirch, just off rue Esplanade, and displayed with a handful of other artefacts. The best mosaic is the one in the right-hand room, its design centring on a two-faced depiction of Medusa. Alongside it are a couple of skeletons, one still in its original wooden coffin, which were also found nearby.

Practicalities

Readily accessible by train from Ettelbruck and Luxembourg City, and by bus from Echternach and Vianden, Diekirch's combined **bus** and **train station** is a five- to ten-minute walk southwest of the centre on avenue de la Gare; many buses also stop on or near place Guillaume. The **tourist office** is in the old centre, on place de la Libération, at the north – or top – end of Grand rue (mid-July to mid-Aug Mon–Fri 9am–5pm, Sat & Sun 10am–noon & 2–4pm; late Aug to early July Mon–Fri 9am–noon & 2–5pm; ☏80 30 23, ⓦwww.diekirch.lu). They issue free town maps, have lots of local leaflets and will book accommodation on your behalf for free.

Of the town's five **hotels**, the pick is the three-star *Hôtel Du Parc*, a spick-and-span, modern hotel facing the River Sûre at avenue de la Gare 28 (☏80 34 72, Ⓕ80 98 61, ⓦwww.hotel-du-parc.lu; ❹). A reasonably good alternative is the three-star *Hotel Hiertz*, in a plain older building at rue Clairefontaine 1 (☏80 35 62, Ⓕ80 88 69; ❹), the boulevard girdling the north side of the old centre; note that the traffic can be irksome. The town's two **campsites** – *de la Sûre* (☏80 94 25; April–Sept) and *Op de Sauer* (☏80 85 90; Jan–Sept) – are handily placed a few minutes' walk from the old centre by the river on route de Gilsdorf. To get there, cross the town's principal bridge and take the riverside path.

For **food**, the excellent *Brasserie du Commerce*, on place de la Libération, serves tasty, traditional Luxembourgish dishes at reasonable prices, or you could head for the cheap and cheerful *City Restaurant*, Grand rue 46, which offers good-value tortellini, soups, and salads. Alternatively, the restaurant of the *Hotel Hiertz* is renowned as one of the best restaurants in the region – and has the Michelin stars to prove it; the cuisine is very French and advance booking is essential.

West along the Sûre

Just 30km north of Luxembourg City and 5km from Diekirch is **ETTEL-BRUCK**, a workaday crossroads town at the confluence of the rivers Alzette and Sûre. Badly damaged in the fighting of 1944, the town is mostly resolutely modern, the only significant sight being the **Musée Général Patton**, rue Dr Klein 5 (July to mid-Sept daily 10am–5pm; mid-Sept to June Sun 2–5pm; €2.50), which focuses on the eponymous general's involvement in the Battle of the Bulge (see p.345). The museum is located a short walk north of the **train station**, just off avenue J F Kennedy. Free town maps are available at the **tourist office**, inside the train station (Mon–Fri 9am–noon & 1.30–5pm, plus July & Aug Sat 10am–noon & 2–4pm; ☎81 20 68, ⓦwww.ettelbruck.lu). Otherwise, there's precious little reason to hang around, though the town does have a **hostel**, a short walk south of the train station on rue Grande-Duchesse Josephine-Charlotte (☎81 22 69, ⓔettelbruck@youthhostels.lu; dorm beds €13.60; closed Dec–March).

Bourscheid

North of Ettelbruck, two equally appealing country roads – the CR348 and the CR349 – slip along the valley of the River Sûre to **BOURSCHEID**, a ten-kilometre journey. This particular village rambles along a bony ridge, down below which, on the steep and heavily wooded valley slopes, lurks its massive **château** (daily: April 11am–5pm; May–June & Sept 10am–6pm, July & Aug 10am–7pm, Oct 11am–4pm; Nov–March Sat & Sun 11am–4pm; €3). The first proper fortifications were erected here around 1000, when a stone wall was substituted for a previous wooden structure. Predictably, little of this original stronghold has survived and most of what you see today – most memorably its mighty turrets and thick towers – dates from the fourteenth century. By comparison, the interior is something of a disappointment, with precious little to see, though the gabled **Stolzembourg house** gamely displays a ragbag of artefacts unearthed during several archeological digs, alongside temporary exhibitions featuring the work of local artists.

Pushing on down from the castle, the road plunges into the woods before emerging – after about 1500m – beside the River Sûre. Here, by the bridge in pocket-sized **BOURSCHEID-MOULIN**, is the four-star *Hôtel du Moulin* (☎99 00 15, ☎99 07 40, ⓦwww.moulin.lu; ❹; closed mid-Nov to Feb), which occupies a large and expansive lodge-like mansion with lovely views along the valley. If your wallet can't stand the strain, Bourscheid-Moulin has two riverside **campsites**, both open from mid-April to mid-October – *Um Gritt* (☎99 04 49) and *Du Moulin* (☎99 03 31).

Esch-sur-Sûre

From Bourscheid-Moulin, you can follow the River Sûre along the N27 to reach, after about 20km, **ESCH-SUR-SÛRE**, a small village with a reputation out of all proportion to its size, mainly on account of its gorgeous situation, draped over a hill within an ox-bow loop in the river. Esch also lies close to the N15, just 16km from Ettelbruck and 30km from Belgium's Bastogne (see p.345).

The village is short on specific sights, but wandering its old cobbled streets, lined with good-looking stone houses, is very enjoyable and you can scramble round the hilltop ruins of its medieval **château** (free). Afterwards, stroll along to the **watchtower** for views over the town and valley. **Accommodation** includes the first-rate, four-star *Hôtel de la Sûre*, at rue du Pont 1 (☎83 91 10,

Ⓕ89 91 01, Ⓦ www.hotel-de-la-sure.lu; ❹; closed Jan); and the equally inviting *Hôtel Beau-Site*, down by the main town bridge at rue de Kaundorf 2 (Ⓣ83 91 34, Ⓕ89 90 24; ❺). There's also a large riverside **campsite**, *Im Ahl* (Ⓣ83 95 14; closed Jan & Feb).

Clervaux

Beyond Ettelbruck lies the narrowing neck of northern Luxembourg, where rolling forest sweeps over an undulating plateau. This is the **Luxembourg Ardennes** (D'Éisléck in Luxembourgish), to all intents and purposes indistinguishable from much of its Belgian namesake. Scenically, it's at its most appealing around Vianden (see p.395), but the rest of the region is pleasant enough.

The most interesting town hereabouts is **CLERVAUX**, an ancient place with a great setting and an attractive castle. Some 30km from Ettelbruck, the town boasts a fine setting, its jumble of slate roofs and whitewashed walls tumbling over a hill in a tight loop of the River Clerve. At the centre of things is Clervaux's **château**, dating from the twelfth century, but rebuilt in the seventeenth century and again after considerable damage in the last war, as is recounted in the **Battle of the Bulge Museum** beside the central courtyard (June daily 1–5pm; July to mid-Sept daily 11am–6pm; mid-Sept to May Sun 1–5pm; €1.25). Another part of the castle holds a **museum of models** (same times and price), with dioramas incorporating several of the castles of Luxembourg. The crowning glory of the castle's exhibitions though, is the **Family of Man**, a remarkable collection of photographs compiled by Edward Steichen (March & Oct–Dec Tues–Sun 10am–6pm; April–Sept daily 10am–6pm; €3.70).

A one-kilometre hike uphill from the castle, the nineteenth-century **Abbaye Bénédictine St Maurice** has exhibitions on monastic life (daily 9am–7pm) as well as Gregorian masses and vespers (daily 10.30am & 6pm, 5pm on the weekend; free).

Practicalities

Clervaux is on the Luxembourg City–Liège **train line**, which bisects northern Luxembourg. From the **train station**, it's a good ten-minute walk into town. The **tourist office**, in the castle (April–June Mon–Sat 2–5pm; July & Aug daily 9.45–11.45am & 2–6pm; Sept Mon–Sat 9.45–11.45am & 1.30–5.30pm; Oct Mon–Sat 9.45–11.45am & 1–5pm; Ⓣ92 00 72, Ⓦ www.clervaux-city.lu), has details of local accommodation and free town maps.

There are plenty of **hotels**, including the modern, central, cosy and well-kept *Hôtel du Commerce*, rue de Marnach 2 (Ⓣ92 10 32, Ⓕ92 91 08, Ⓦ www .hotelcommerce-clervaux.lu; ❹). Another recommendation is the *Hôtel du Parc*, rue du Parc 2 (Ⓣ92 06 50, Ⓕ92 10 68, Ⓦ www.hotelduparc.lu; ❹), occupying a large nineteenth-century mansion which clings to a wooded hill overlooking the town. There are also a couple of **campsites**, the better one being *Camping* Reilerweier (Ⓣ92 01 60; April–Oct), about 2km out of town on the Vianden road, beside the river.

An inexpensive place to **eat** is the canteen-like café *Splendid* at Grande rue 32. Much better is *Vieux Château*, inside the castle precincts, near the entrance, at rue du Château 4. It's a popular, rustic place serving good-value and tasty fish, beef and chicken main courses, as well as mussels served every which way.

Travel details

Trains

Luxembourg City to: Arlon (hourly; 20min); Brussels (hourly; 3hr); Clervaux (hourly; 1hr 5min); Diekirch (change at Ettelbruck; hourly; 40min); Ettelbruck (hourly; 35min); Liège (every 2hr; 2hr 30min); Namur (hourly; 2hr); Wasserbillig (hourly; 30min).

Buses

Diekirch to: Echternach (hourly; 35min); Vianden (hourly; 20min).
Echternach to: Beaufort (10 daily; 20min); Diekirch (hourly; 35min); Ettelbruck (15 daily; 45min); Grevenmacher (hourly; 40min);

Larochette (Mon–Fri every 1 or 2 hr; 1hr); Luxembourg City (hourly; 1hr 10min); Wasserbillig (hourly; 30min).
Ettelbruck to: Diekirch (every 30min; 10min); Echternach (15 daily; 45min); Esch-sur-Sûre (6 daily; 40min); Vianden (12 daily; 30min).
Grevenmacher to: Echternach (hourly; 40min); Wasserbillig (hourly; 10min).
Luxembourg City to: Diekirch (every 2hr; 1hr 20min); Echternach (hourly; 1hr); Mondorf-les-Bains (hourly; 30min); Remich (hourly; 45min).
Remich to: Ehnen (every 2hr; 15min). Grevenmacher (every 2hr; 30min); Wasserbillig (every 2hr; 40min).
Wasserbillig to: Echternach (hourly; 30min); Grevenmacher (hourly; 10min).

Contexts

Contexts

The historical framework

Jumbled together throughout most of their history, the countries now known as Belgium, Luxembourg and the Netherlands didn't reach their present delimitations until 1830. Before then, their borders were continually being redrawn following battles, treaties and alliances, a shifting pattern that makes it impossible to provide a history of one without frequent reference to the others. To make matters more involved, these same three countries were – and still are – commonly lumped together as the "Low Countries" on account of their topography, though, given the valleys and hills of southern Belgium and Luxembourg, this is more than a little unfair. Even more confusing is the fact that the Netherlands is frequently called "Holland", when "Holland" is actually a province in the Netherlands. In the account that follows we've used "Low Countries" to cover all three countries and "Holland" to refer to the province. In addition, we've termed the language of the northern part of Belgium "Flemish" to save confusion, though "Dutch" or even "Netherlandish" are sometimes the preferred options among Belgians themselves.

Beginnings

Little is known of the prehistoric settlers of the **Low Countries**, their visible remains largely confined to the far north of the Netherlands, where mounds known as *terpen* were built to keep the sea at bay. By the fifth century BC, the **Celts** are believed to have established an Iron Age culture across much of the region, though these tribes only begin to emerge from the prehistoric soup after Julius Caesar's conquest of Gaul (broadly France) in 57–50 BC. The **Romans** found three tribal groupings living in the region: the mainly Celtic **Belgae** (hence the nineteenth-century term "Belgium") settled by the rivers Rhine, Meuse and Waal to the south; the Germanic **Frisians** living on the marshy coastal strip north of the Scheldt; and the **Batavi**, another Germanic people, inhabiting the swampy river banks of what is now the southern Netherlands. The Belgae were conquered and their lands incorporated into the imperial province of **Gallia Belgica**, but the territory of the Batavi and Frisians was not considered worthy of colonization. Instead, these tribes were granted the status of allies, a source of recruitment for the Roman legions and curiosity for imperial travellers. In 50 AD Pliny observed, "Here a wretched race is found, inhabiting either the more elevated spots or artificial mounds . . . When the waves cover the surrounding area they are like so many mariners on board a ship, and when again the tide recedes their condition is that of so many shipwrecked men."

The **Roman occupation** continued for nigh on five hundred years until the legions were pulled back to protect the heartland of the crumbling empire. But despite the length of their stay, there's a notable lack of material evidence to indicate their presence, an important exception being the odd stretch of city wall in Tongeren, one of the principal Roman settlements. As the empire collapsed in chaos and confusion, the Germanic **Franks**, who had been settling within Gallia Belgica from the third century, filled the power vacuum to the south, and, along with their allies the Belgae, established a **Merovingian** kingdom based around their capital in Tournai. A great swath of forest extending from the Scheldt to the Ardennes separated this predominantly Frankish kingdom from the more confused situation to the north and east, where other tribes of Franks settled along the Scheldt and Leie – a separation which came to delineate the ethnic and linguistic division that survives in Belgium to this day. North of the Franks of the Scheldt were the Saxons and finally the north coast of the Netherlands was settled by the Frisians.

Towards the end of the fifth century, the Merovingians extended their control over much of what is now north and central France. In 496 their king, **Clovis**, was converted to Christianity, a faith which slowly filtered north, spread by energetic missionaries like St Willibrord, first bishop of Utrecht from about 710, and St Boniface, who was killed by the Frisians in 754 in a final act of pagan resistance before they too were converted. Meanwhile, after the death of the last distinguished Merovingian king, Dagobert, in 638, power passed increasingly to the so-called "mayors of the palace", a hereditary position whose most outstanding occupant was **Charles Martel** (c.690–741). Martel dominated a large but all too obviously shambolic kingdom whose military weakness he determined to remedy. Traditionally, the Merovingian (Frankish) army was comprised of a body of infantry led by a small group of cavalry. Martel replaced this with a largely mounted force of trained knights, who bore their own military expenses in return for land, the beginnings of the **feudal** system. Actually, these reforms came just in time to save Christendom: in 711 that extraordinary Arab advance which had begun at the beginning of the seventh century reached the Pyrenees and a massive Muslim army occupied southern France in preparation for further conquests. In the event, Martel defeated the invaders outside Tours in 732, one of Europe's most crucial engagements and one that saved France from Arab conquest for good.

Ten years after Martel's death, his son, Pepin the Short, formally usurped the Merovingian throne with the blessing of the pope, becoming the first of the **Carolingian** dynasty, whose most famous member was **Charlemagne**, king of the west Franks from 768. In a dazzling series of campaigns, Charlemagne extended his empire south into Italy, west to the Pyrenees, north to Denmark and east to the Oder, his secular authority bolstered by his coronation as the first **Holy Roman Emperor** in 800. The pope bestowed this title on him to legitimize the king's claim to be the successor of the emperors of imperial Rome – and it worked a treat. Based in Aachen, Charlemagne stabilized his kingdom and the Low Countries benefited from a trading boom that utilized the region's principal rivers. However, unlike his Roman predecessors, Charlemagne was subject to the divisive inheritance laws of the Salian tribe of Franks, and after his death in 814, his kingdom was divided between his grandsons into three roughly parallel strips of territory, the precursors of France, the Low Countries and Germany.

The growth of the towns

The **tripartite division** of Charlemagne's empire placed the Low Countries between the emergent French- and German-speaking nations, a dangerous location, which was subsequently to decide much of its history. This was not, however, apparent in the cobweb of local alliances that made up early feudal

The béguinages

One corollary of the urbanization of the Low Countries from the twelfth century on was the establishment of **béguinages** (*begijnhoven* in Flemish) in almost every city and town. These were semi-secluded communities, where widows and unmarried women – the **béguines** (*begijns*) – lived together, the better to do pious acts, especially caring for the sick. In **construction**, béguinages follow the same general plan with several streets of whitewashed, brick terraced cottages hidden away behind walls and gates and surrounding a central garden and chapel.

The origins of the *béguine* movement are somewhat obscure, but it would seem that the initial impetus came from a twelfth-century Liège priest, a certain Lambert le Bègue (the Stammerer). The main period of growth came a little later when several important female nobles established new *béguinages*, like the ones in Kortrijk and Ghent (by Joanna of Constantinople, the Countess of Flanders), and, shortly afterwards, the one in Bruges (at the behest of Margaret, also Countess of Flanders).

Béguine communities were different from convents in so far as the inhabitants did not have to take vows and had the right to return to the secular world if they wished. At a time when hundreds of women were forcibly shut away in convents for all sorts of reasons (primarily financial), this element of choice was crucial.

Western Europe in the ninth and tenth centuries. During this period, French kings and German emperors exercised a general authority over the Low Countries, but power was effectively in the hands of local lords who, remote from central control, brought a degree of local stability. From the twelfth century, feudalism slipped into a gradual decline, the intricate pattern of localized allegiances undermined by the increasing strength of certain lords, whose power and wealth often exceeded that of their nominal sovereign. Preoccupied by territorial squabbles, this streamlined nobility was usually willing to assist the growth of towns by granting charters, which permitted a certain amount of autonomy in exchange for tax revenues, and military and labour services. The first major cities were the **cloth towns** of Flanders, particularly Ghent, Bruges and Ieper, which grew rich from the manufacture of cloth, their garments exported far and wide and their economies dependent on a continuous supply of good-quality wool from England. Meanwhile, the smaller towns north of the Scheldt concentrated on trade, exploiting their strategic position at the junction of several of the major waterways and trade routes of the day.

Predictably, the **economic interests** of the urbanized merchants and guildsmen soon conflicted with those of the local lord. This was especially true in Flanders, where the towns were anxious to preserve a good relationship with the king of England, who controlled the wool supply, whereas their count was a vassal of the king of France, whose dynastic aspirations clashed with those of his English rival. As a result, the history of thirteenth- and fourteenth-century Flanders is punctuated by sporadic fighting, as the two kings and the guildsmen slugged it out, the fortunes of war oscillating between the parties but the underlying class conflict never resolved.

Burgundian rule

By the late fourteenth century the political situation in the Low Countries was fairly clear: five lords controlled most of the region, paying only nominal homage to their French or German overlords. Yet things began to change when, in 1419, **Philip the Good**, Duke of Burgundy, succeeded to the countship of Flanders and by a series of adroit political moves gained control over the southern Netherlands, Brabant and Limburg to the north, and Antwerp, Namur and Luxembourg to the south. He consolidated his power by establishing a strong central administration based in Bruges and by curtailing the privileges granted in the towns' charters. Less independent it may have been, but **Bruges** benefited greatly from the duke's presence, becoming an emporium for the **Hanseatic League**, a mainly German association of towns which acted as a trading group and protected their interests by an exclusive system of trading tariffs. The wealth of Bruges was legendary, and the Burgundian court patronized the early and seminal Nederlandish painters like Jan van Eyck and Hans Memling, whose works are displayed in Ghent and Bruges today.

Philip died in 1467 to be succeeded by his son, **Charles the Bold**, who was killed in battle ten years later, plunging his father's carefully crafted domain into turmoil. The French seized the opportunity to take back Arras and Burgundy and before the people of Flanders would agree to fight the French they kidnapped Charles's successor, his daughter Mary, and forced her to sign a charter that restored the civic privileges removed by her grandfather.

The Habsburgs

After her release, Mary married the **Habsburg Maximilian of Austria**, who assumed sole authority when Mary was killed in a riding accident in 1482. Today, her tomb stands beside that of her father in the Onze Lieve Vrouwekerk in Bruges. A sharp operator, Maximilian continued where the Burgundians had left off, whittling away at the power of the cities with considerable success. When Maximilian became Holy Roman Emperor in 1494, he transferred control of the Low Countries to his son, Philip the Handsome, and then – after Philip's early death – to his grandson **Charles V**, who in turn became king of Spain and Holy Roman Emperor in 1516 and 1519 respectively. Charles ruled his vast kingdom with skill and energy, but, born in Ghent, he was very suspicious of the turbulent Flemish burghers. Consequently, he favoured **Antwerp** at their expense and this city now became the greatest port in the Habsburg empire, part of a general movement of trade and prosperity away from Flanders to the cities further north. In addition, the Flemish cloth industry had, by the 1480s, begun its long decline, undermined by England's new-found cloth-manufacturing success.

By sheer might, Charles systematically bent the merchant cities of the Low Countries to his will, but regardless of this display of force, a spiritual trend was emerging that would soon not only question the rights of the emperor but also rock the power of the Catholic Church itself.

The Reformation

An alliance of church and state had dominated the medieval world: pope and bishops, kings and counts were supposedly the representatives of God on earth, and they worked together to crush religious dissent wherever it appeared.

Much of their authority depended on the ignorance of the population, who were entirely dependent on their priests for the interpretation of the scriptures, their view of the world carefully controlled.

The **Reformation** was a religious revolt that stood sixteenth-century Europe on its head. There were many complex reasons for it, but certainly the development of **typography** was a crucial element. For the first time, printers were able to produce relatively cheap Bibles in quantity, and the religious texts were no longer the exclusive property of the priesthood. The first stirrings of the Reformation were in the welter of debate that spread across much of Western Europe under the auspices of theologians like **Erasmus of Rotterdam** (1465–1536), who wished to cleanse the Catholic church of its corruptions, superstitions and extravagant ceremony; only later did many of these same thinkers – principally **Martin Luther** – decide to support a breakaway church. In 1517, Luther produced his 95 theses against indulgences, rejecting – among other things – Christ's presence in the sacrament of the Eucharist, and denying the Church's monopoly on the interpretation of the Bible. There was no way back and when Luther's works were disseminated his ideas gained a European following among reforming groups branded as **Lutheran** by the Church, whilst other reformers were drawn to the doctrines of **John Calvin** (1509–64). Luther asserted that the Church's political power was subservient to that of the state; Calvin emphasized the importance of individual conscience and the need for redemption through the grace of Christ rather than the confessional.

These seeds of **Protestantism** fell on fertile ground among the merchants of the cities of the Low Countries, whose wealth and independence had never been easy to accommodate within a rigid caste society. Similarly, their employees, the guildsmen and their apprentices, had a long history of opposing arbitrary authority, and were easily convinced of the need to reform an autocratic, venal church. In 1555, **Charles V abdicated**, transferring his German lands to his brother Ferdinand, and his Italian, Spanish and Low Countries territories to his son, the fanatically Catholic **Philip II**. In the short term, the scene was set for a bitter confrontation, while the dynastic ramifications of the division of the Habsburg empire were to complicate European affairs for centuries.

The revolt of the Netherlands

After his father's abdication, Philip decided to teach his heretical subjects a lesson. He garrisoned the towns of the Low Countries with Spanish mercenaries, imported the **Inquisition** and passed a series of anti-Protestant edicts. However, other pressures on the Habsburg Empire forced him into a tactical withdrawal and he transferred control to his sister **Margaret of Parma** in 1559. Based in Brussels, the equally resolute Margaret implemented the policies of her brother with gusto. In 1561 she reorganized the church and created fourteen new bishoprics, a move that was construed as a wresting of power from civil authority, and an attempt to destroy the local aristocracy's powers of religious patronage. Protestantism – and Protestant sympathies – spread to the nobility, who now formed the "League of the Nobility" to counter Habsburg policy. The League petitioned Philip for moderation but were dismissed out of hand by one of Margaret's Walloon advisers, who called them "*ces geux*" (those beggars), an epithet that was to be enthusiastically adopted by the rebels. In 1565 a harvest failure caused a winter famine among the urban workers and, after years of repression, they struck back. The following year, a Protestant sermon in the tiny Flemish textile town of Steenvoorde incited the congregation to purge the local church of its papist idolatry. The crowd smashed up the church's reliquaries and shrines, broke the stained-glass windows and terrorized the priests, thereby launching the **Iconoclastic Fury**. The rioting spread like wildfire and within ten days churches had been ransacked from one end of the Low Countries to the other, nowhere more so than in Antwerp.

The ferocity of this outbreak shocked the upper classes into renewed support for Spain, and Margaret regained the allegiance of most nobles – with the principal exception of the country's greatest landowner, Prince William of Orange-Nassau, known as **William the Silent**. Of Germanic descent, he was raised a Catholic but the excesses and rigidity of Philip had caused him to side with the Protestant movement. A firm believer in individual freedom and religious tolerance, William became for many a symbol of liberty; but after the Fury had revitalized the pro-Spanish party, he prudently slipped away to his estates in Germany. Meanwhile, Philip II was keen to capitalize on the increase in support for Margaret and, in 1567, he dispatched the **Duke of Albe**, with an army of ten thousand men, to the Low Countries to suppress his religious opponents absolutely. Margaret was not at all pleased by Philip's decision and, when Albe arrived in Brussels, she resigned in a huff, initiating what was, in effect, military rule. One of Albe's first acts was to set up the Commission of Civil Unrest, which was soon nicknamed the "**Council of Blood**", after its habit of executing those it examined. No fewer than 12,000 citizens were polished off, mostly for taking part in the Fury. Initially the repression worked: in 1568, when William attempted an invasion from Germany, the towns, garrisoned by the Spanish, offered no support. William waited and conceived other means of defeating Albe. In April 1572 a band of privateers entered Brielle on the Meuse and captured it from the Spanish. This was one of several commando-style attacks by the so-called **Waterguezen** or sea-beggars, who were at first obliged to operate from England, although it was soon possible for them to secure bases in the Netherlands, whose citizens had grown to loathe Albe and his Spaniards.

After the success at Brielle, the revolt spread rapidly: by June the rebels controlled the province of Holland and William was able to take command of his troops in Delft. Albe and his son Frederick fought back, but William's superior naval power frustrated him and a mightily irritated Philip replaced Albe with **Luis de Resquesens**. Initially, Resquesens had some success in the south, where the Catholic majority were more willing to compromise with Spanish rule than their northern neighbours, but the tide of war was against him – most pointedly in William's triumphant relief of Leiden in 1574. Two years later, Resquesens died and the (unpaid) Habsburg garrison in Antwerp mutinied and attacked the town, slaughtering some eight thousand of its people in what was known as the **Spanish Fury**. Though the Habsburgs still held several towns, the massacre alienated the south and pushed its peoples into the arms of William, whose troops now swept into Brussels, the heart of imperial power. Momentarily, it seemed possible for the whole region to unite behind William and all signed the **Union of Brussels**, which demanded the departure of foreign troops as a condition for accepting a diluted Habsburg sovereignty. This was followed, in 1576, by the **Pacification of Ghent**, a regional agreement that guaranteed freedom of religious belief, a necessary precondition for any union between the largely Protestant north (the Netherlands) and Catholic south (Belgium and Luxembourg).

Philip was, however, not inclined to compromise, especially when he realized that William's Calvinist sympathies were giving his newly-found Walloon and

Flemish allies the jitters. The king bided his time until 1578, when, with his enemies arguing among themselves, he sent another army from Spain to the Low Countries under the command of Alessandro Farnese, the **Duke of Parma**. Events played into Parma's hands. In 1579, tiring of all the wrangling, seven northern provinces agreed to sign the **Union of Utrecht**, an alliance against Spain that was to be the first unification of the Netherlands as an identifiable country – the **United Provinces**. The agreement stipulated freedom of belief, an important step since the struggle against Spain wasn't simply a religious one: many Catholics disliked the Spanish occupation and William did not wish to alienate this possible source of support. The assembly of these United Provinces was known as the **States General**, and met at The Hague; it had no domestic legislative authority, and could only carry out foreign policy by unanimous decision, a formula designed to make potential waverers feel more secure. The role of **Stadholder** was the most important in each province, roughly equivalent to that of governor, though the same person could occupy this position in any number of provinces. Meanwhile, in the south – and also in 1579 – representatives of the southern provinces signed the **Union of Arras**, a Catholic-led agreement that declared loyalty to Philip II and counterbalanced the Union of Utrecht in the north. Parma used this area as a base to recapture Flanders and Antwerp, which fell after a long and cruel siege in 1585. But Parma was unable to advance any further north and the Low Countries were, de facto, divided into two – the Spanish Netherlands and the United Provinces – beginning a separation that would lead, after many changes, to the creation of three modern countries.

The Spanish Netherlands (1579–1713)

With his army firmly entrenched in the south, Philip was now prepared to permit some degree of economic and political autonomy, exercising control over the **Spanish Netherlands** through a governor in Brussels, but he was not inclined to tolerate his newly recovered Protestant subjects. As a result, thousands of weavers, apprentices and skilled workers – the bedrock of Calvinism – fled north to escape the new Catholic regime, thereby fuelling an economic boom in Holland. It took a while for this migration to take effect, and for several years the Spanish Netherlands had all the trappings – if not the substance – of success, a mini-economy sustained by the conspicuous consumption of the Habsburg elite. Silk weaving, diamond processing and tapestry- and lace-making were particular beneficiaries and a new canal was cut linking Ghent and Bruges to the sea at Ostend. This commercial restructuring underpinned a brief flourishing of artistic life centred on **Rubens** and his circle of friends – including Anthony Van Dyck and Jacob Jordaens – in Antwerp during the first decades of the seventeenth century.

Months before his death in 1598, Philip II had granted control of the Spanish Netherlands to his daughter and her husband, appointing them the **Archdukes Isabella and Albert**. Failing to learn from experience, the ducal couple continued to prosecute the war against the Protestant north, but with so little success that they were obliged to make peace – the **Twelve-Year Truce** – in 1609. When the truce ended, the new Spanish king, Philip IV, bypassed Isabella

– Albert was dead – to launch his own campaign against the Protestant Dutch. This was part of a general and even more devastating dispute, the **Thirty Years' War** (1618–48), a largely religious-based conflict between Catholic and Protestant countries that involved most of Western Europe. The Spanish were initially successful, but they were weakened by war with France and Dutch seapower. Thereafter, from 1625 onwards, the Spaniards suffered a series of defeats on land and sea that forced them out of what is today the southern part of the Netherlands, and in 1648 they were compelled to accept the humiliating terms of the **Peace of Westphalia**. This was a general treaty that ended the Thirty Years' War, and its terms both recognized the independence of the United Provinces and closed the Scheldt estuary, an action designed to destroy the trade and prosperity of Antwerp. By these means, the commercial preeminence of Amsterdam was assured.

The only major fly in the United Provinces' ointment was the conflict between central authority and provincial autonomy. Although the **House of Orange** had established something like royal credentials, many of Holland's leading citizens were reluctant to accept its right to power. The republicans held the upper hand for most of the seventeenth century until an attack on the country by Louis XIV in 1672 forced the States General to seek the help of **William of Orange**, whose success in dealing with the crisis resulted in his appointment to the office of Stadholder (which had actually been abolished in 1650). It was this same William who was to become the king of England (and his wife Mary the queen) in 1689.

In stark contrast, the Spanish Netherlands paid dearly for its adherence to the Habsburg cause. In the course of the Thirty Years' War, it had teetered on the edge of chaos – highwaymen infested the roads, trade had almost disappeared, the population had been halved in Brabant, and acres of fertile farmland lay uncultivated – but the peace was perhaps as bad. Denied access to the sea, Antwerp was ruined and simply withered away, while the southern provinces as a whole spiralled into an economic decline that pauperized its population. Yet the ruling families seemed proud to appear to the world as the defenders and martyrs of the Catholic faith; those who disagreed left.

The Counter-Reformation

Politically dependent on a decaying Spain, economically ruined and deprived of most of its more independent-minded citizens, the country turned in on itself, sustained by the fanatical Catholicism of the **Counter-Reformation**. Religious worship became strict and magnificent, medieval carnivals were transformed into exercises in piety, and penitential flagellation became popular, all under the approving eyes of the **Jesuits**. Indeed, the number of Jesuits was quite extraordinary: in the whole of France, there were only 2000, but the Spanish Netherlands had no less than 1600. It was here that they wrote their most important works, exercised their greatest influence and owned vast tracts of land. Supported by draconian laws that barred known Protestants from public appointments, declared their marriages illegal and forbade them municipal assistance, the Jesuits and their fellow Catholic priests simply overwhelmed the religious opposition; in the space of fifty years, they transformed this part of the Low Countries into an introverted world shaped by a mystical faith, where Christians were redeemed by the ecstasy of suffering.

The visible signs of the change were all around, from extravagant Baroque churches to Crosses, Calvaries and shrines scattered across the countryside. Literature disappeared, the sciences vegetated and religious orders multiplied.

In **painting**, artists – principally Rubens – were used to confirm the ecclesiastical orthodoxies, their canvases full of muscular saints and angels, reflecting a religious faith of mystery and hierarchy; others, such as David Teniers and the later Bruegels, retreated into minutely observed realism.

French interference

In 1648, the **Peace of Westphalia** freed the king of France from fear of Germany, and the political and military history of the Spanish Netherlands thereafter was dominated by the efforts of **Louis XIV** to add the country to his territories. Fearful of an over-powerful France, the United Provinces, England and Sweden, among others, determinedly resisted French designs and, to preserve the balance of power, fought a long series of campaigns beginning with the **War of Devolution** in 1667 and ending in the **War of the Spanish Succession**. The latter was sparked by the death in 1700 of **Charles II**, the last of the Spanish Habsburgs, who had willed his territories to the grandson of Louis XIV of France. An anti-French coalition refused to accept the settlement and there ensued a haphazard series of campaigns that dragged on for eleven years, marked by the spectacular victories of the Duke of Marlborough – Blenheim, Ramillies, Malplaquet. Many of the region's cities were besieged and badly damaged during these wars, and only with the **Treaty of Utrecht** of 1713 did the French abandon their attempt to conquer the Spanish Netherlands. The latter were now passed to the Austrian Habsburgs in the figure of the emperor Charles VI.

The Austrian Netherlands (1713–94)

The transfer of the country from Spanish to **Austrian control** made little appreciable difference: there were more wars and more invasions and a remote central authority continued to operate through Brussels. In particular, the **War of the Austrian Succession**, fought over the right of Maria Theresa to assume the Austrian Habsburg throne, prompted the French to invade and occupy much of the country in 1744, though imperial control was restored four years later by the **Treaty of Aix-la-Chapelle**. Perhaps surprisingly, these dynastic shenanigans had little effect on the country's agriculture, which survived the various campaigns and actually became more productive, leading to a marked increase in the rural population, especially after the introduction of potato cultivation. But intellectually the country remained vitrified and stagnant – only three percent of the population were literate, workers were forbidden to change towns or jobs without obtaining permission from the municipal authorities, and skills and crafts were tied to particular families.

This sorry state of affairs began to change in the middle of the eighteenth century as the Austrian oligarchy came under the influence of the **Enlightenment**, that belief in reason and progress – as against authority and tradition – that had first been proselytized by French philosophers. In 1753, the arrival of a progressive governor, the **Count of Cobenzl**, signified a transformation of Habsburg policy. Eager to shake the country from its torpor, Cobenzl initiated an ambitious programme of public works. New canals were dug, old canals deepened, new industries were encouraged and public health was at least discussed, the main result being regulations forbidding burial inside churches and the creation of new cemeteries outside the city walls. Cobenzl also took a firm line with his clerical opponents, who took a dim view of all this modernizing and tried to encourage the population to thwart him in his aims.

In 1780, the **Emperor Joseph II** came to the throne, determined, as he put it, to "root out silly old prejudices" by imperial decree. His reforming zeal was not, however, matched by any political nous and the deluge of edicts that he promulgated managed to offend all of the country's major groups – from peasants, clerics and merchants right through to the nobility. Opposition crystallized around two groups – the liberal-minded **Vonckists**, who demanded a radical, republican constitution, and the conservative **Statists**, whose prime aim was the maintenance of the Catholic status quo. Pandemonium ensued and, in 1789, the Habsburgs dispatched an army to restore order. Against all expectations, the two political groups swallowed their differences to combine and then defeat the Austrians near Antwerp in what became known as the **Brabant Revolution**. The rebels promptly announced the formation of the United States of Belgium, but the uneasy alliance between the Vonckists and Statists soon broke down, not least because the latter were terrified by the course of the revolution which had erupted across the border in France. Determined to keep the radicals at bay, the Statists raised the peasantry to arms and, with the assistance of the priests, encouraged them to attack the Vonckists, who were killed in their hundreds. The Statists now had the upper hand, but the country remained in turmoil and when Emperor Joseph died in 1790, his successor, **Léopold**, was quick to withdraw many of the reforming acts and send in his troops to restore imperial authority.

French rule and its aftermath (1794–1830)

The new and repressive Habsburg regime was short-lived. French Republican armies brushed the imperial forces aside in 1794, and the Austrian Netherlands were annexed the following year, an annexation that was to last until 1814. The **French** imposed radical reforms: the Catholic Church was stripped of much of its worldly wealth, feudal privileges and the guilds were abolished, and a consistent legal system was formulated. **Napoleon**, in control from 1799, carried on the work of modernization, rebuilding the docks of Antwerp and forcing the Netherlanders, whose country the French had also occupied in 1795, to accept the re-opening of the Scheldt. Unrestricted access to French markets boosted the local economy, kick-starting the mechanization of the textile industry in Ghent and Verviers and encouraging the growth of the coal and metal industries in Hainaut, but, with the exception of a radical minority, the French occupation remained unpopular with most of the populace. Looting by French soldiers was commonplace, especially in the early years, and the French introduced conscription, most hated of all, provoking a series of (brutally repressed) peasant insurrections.

The Republican regime was generally disliked in the Netherlands too. The French had begun by dissolving the United Provinces, setting up the "**Batavian Republic**" in its stead. In this, they were aided and abetted by a group of local sympathizers, pro-French merchants who called themselves "**Patriots**" in opposition to their bitter rivals, the "**Orangists**" (after the House of Orange) – factional squabbling had dogged the country throughout the second half of the eighteenth century. The Netherlanders were, however, unenthusiastic about helping the French in their war against England and paid the price in 1806 when Napoleon appointed his brother Louis as their king. In the event, this didn't satisfy Bonaparte either and just four years later he incorporated the country into the French Empire.

The United Kingdom of the Netherlands

French rule in both countries began to evaporate after Napoleon's disastrous retreat from Moscow in 1812 and had all but disappeared long before Napoleon's final defeat just outside Brussels at the Battle of Waterloo in June 1815. At the **Congress of Vienna**, called to settle Europe at the end of the Napoleonic Wars, the main concern of the great powers was to create a buffer state against any possible future plans the French might have to expand to the north. With scant regard to the feelings of those affected, they therefore decided to establish the **United Kingdom of the Netherlands**, which incorporated both the old United Provinces and the Spanish (Austrian) Netherlands. On the throne they placed Frederick William of Orange, crowned **King William I**. The great powers also decided to give Frederick William's German estates to Prussia and in return presented him with the newly independent **Grand Duchy of Luxembourg**. This was a somewhat confused arrangement. The duchy had previously been part of both the Spanish and Austrian Netherlands, but now it was detached from the rest of the Low Countries constitutionally and pushed into the German Confederation at the same time as it shared the same king with the old United Provinces and Austrian Netherlands.

Given the imperious way the new Kingdom of the Netherlands had been established, it required considerable royal tact to make things work. William lacked this in abundance and indeed some of his measures seemed designed to inflame his French-speaking (Belgian) subjects. He made Dutch the official language of the whole kingdom and, in a move against the Catholics, he tried to secularize all Church-controlled schools. Furthermore, each of the two former countries had the same number of representatives at the States General despite the fact that the population of the old United Provinces was half that of its neighbour. There were competing economic interests too. The north was reliant on commerce and sought free trade without international tariffs; the industrialized south wanted a degree of protectionism. William's refusal to address any of these concerns united his opponents in the south, where both industrialists and clerics now clamoured for change.

Independent Belgium: 1830–1900

The **revolution** against William began in the Brussels opera house on August 25, 1830, when the singing of a duet, *Amour Sacré de la Patrie*, hit a nationalist nerve and the audience poured out onto the streets to raise the flag of Brabant in defiance of the king. At first the revolutionaries only demanded a scaling down of royal power and a separate "Belgian" administration, but negotiations soon broke down and in late September the insurrectionists proclaimed the **Kingdom of Belgium**. William prepared for war, but the liberal governments of Great Britain and France intervened to stop hostilities and, in January of the following year, they recognized an independent Belgian state at the

Léopold I (reigned 1830–65). Foisted on Belgium by the great powers, Léopold, the first king of the Belgians, was imported from Germany, where he was the prince of Saxe-Coburg. Also the uncle of Queen Victoria, Léopold lacked a popular mandate, but made a fairly good fist of things, keeping the country neutral as the great powers had ordained.

Léopold II (1865–1909). The son of Léopold I, Léopold II was energetic and forceful, encouraging the urbanization of his country and promoting its importance as a major industrial power. He was also the man responsible for landing Brussels with such pompous monuments as the Palais de Justice and for the imposition of a particularly barbaric colonial regime on the peoples of the Belgian Congo (now the Republic of Congo).

Albert I (1909–34). Easily the most popular of the dynasty, Albert became a national hero thanks to his bravery in World War I, when the Germans occupied almost all of the country. His untimely death, in a climbing accident, traumatized the nation. He was the nephew of Léopold II and the father of Léopold III.

Léopold III (1934–51). In contrast to his father, Léopold III had the dubious honour of becoming one of Europe's least popular monarchs. His first wife died in a suspicious car crash; he nearly lost his kingdom by remarrying (then anathema in a Catholic country); and he was badly compromised during the German occupation of World War II. Many felt his surrender to the Germans was cowardly and his subsequent willingness to work with them treacherous; others pointed out his efforts to increase the country's food rations and his negotiations to secure the release of Belgian prisoners. HIs remaining in Belgium during the war fuelled rumours that he was a Nazi collaborator – though his supporters maintained that he prevented thousands of Belgians from being deported. After several years of heated postwar debate, during which the king remained in exile, the issue of Léopold's return was put to a referendum in 1950. Just over half the population voted in his favour, with opposition to the king concentrated in Wallonia. Fortunately for Belgium, Léopold abdicated in 1951 in favour of his son.

Baudouin I (1951–93). A softly spoken family man, Baudouin did much to restore the popularity of the monarchy, not least because he was generally thought to be even-handed in his treatment of the French- and Flemish-speaking communities. He also hit the headlines in April 1990 by standing down for a day so that an abortion bill (which he as a Catholic had refused to sign) could be passed. Childless, he was succeeded by his brother.

Albert II (1993–). The present king will have his work cut out if he wants to become the national figurehead that his father was. The Belgian royal family is one of the few unifying forces in a country divided by French–Flemish antagonisms; one major slip off the linguistic tightrope could have untold consequences. So far Albert has acquitted himself competently – or at least impartially – enough.

Conference of London. The caveat – and this was crucial to the great powers given the trouble the region had caused for centuries – was that Belgium be classified a "neutral" state, that is one outside any other's sphere of influence. To bolster this new nation, they ceded to it the western segments of the Grand Duchy of Luxembourg and dug out Prince Léopold of Saxe-Coburg to present with the crown. William retained the northern part of his kingdom and even received the remainder of Luxembourg as his personal possession, but he still hated the settlement and there was a further bout of sabre-rattling before he finally caved in and accepted the new arrangements in 1839.

Shrewd and capable, **Léopold I** (1830–65) was careful to maintain his country's neutrality and encouraged an industrial boom that saw coal mines developed, iron-making factories established and the rapid expansion of the railway system. One casualty, however, was the traditional linen-making industry of rural Flanders. The cottagers who spun and wove the linen could not compete with the mechanized mills, and their pauperization was compounded by the poor grain harvests and potato blight of 1844–46. But their sufferings were of only limited concern to the country's political representatives, who were elected on a strictly limited franchise, which ensured the domination of the middle classes. The latter divided into two loose groups, the one attempting to undermine Catholic influence and control over such areas as education, the other profoundly conservative in its desire to maintain the status quo. Progressive elements within the bourgeoisie coalesced in the **Liberal party**, which was free trade and urban in outlook, whereas their opponents, the **Catholic party**, promised to protect Belgian agriculture with tariffs. The political twist was that the Catholic party, in its retreat from the industrialized and radicalized cities, began to identify with the plight of rural Dutch-speaking Belgians – as against the French-speaking ruling and managerial classes.

Léopold II's long reign (1865–1909) was dominated by similar themes, and saw the emergence of Belgium as a major industrial power. However, the 1860s and 1870s also witnessed the first significant stirrings of a type of **Flemish nationalism** which felt little enthusiasm for the unitary status of Belgium, divided as it was between a French-speaking majority in the south – the Walloons – and the minority Dutch-speakers of the north. There was also industrial unrest towards the end of the century, the end results being a body of legislation improving working conditions and, in 1893, the extension of the **franchise** to all men over the age of 25. The Catholic party also ensured that, under the Equality Law of 1898, Dutch was ratified as an official language, equal in status to French – the forerunner of many long and difficult debates. Another matter of concern was the **Belgian Congo**. Determined to cut an international figure, Léopold II had decided to build up a colonial empire. The unfortunate recipients of his ambition were the Africans of the Congo River basin, who were effectively given to him by a conference of European powers in 1885. Ruling the Congo as a personal fiefdom, Léopold established an extraordinarily cruel colonial regime – so cruel in fact that even the other colonial powers were appalled and the Belgian state was obliged to end the embarrassment by taking over the region – as the Belgian Congo – in 1908.

The first half of the twentieth century

At the beginning of the twentieth century, Belgium was an industrial powerhouse with a booming economy and a rapidly increasing workforce – 934,000 in 1896, 1,176,000 in 1910. It was also determined to keep on good terms with all the great powers, but could not prevent getting caught up in **World War I**. Indifferent to Belgium's proclaimed neutrality, the Germans had decided as early as 1908 that the best way to attack France was via Belgium, and this is precisely what they did in 1914. They captured almost all of the country, the exception being a narrow strip of territory around De Panne. Undaunted, **King Albert I** (1909–34) and the Belgian army bravely manned the northern part of the Allied line, and it made the king a national hero. The trenches ran through western Flanders and all the towns and villages lying close to them – principally

Ieper (Ypres) – were simply obliterated by artillery fire. Belgium also witnessed some of the worst of the slaughter in and around a bulge in the line, which became known as the **Ypres Salient** (see p.152). The destruction was, however, confined to a narrow strip of Flanders and most of Belgium was practically untouched, though the local population did suffer during the occupation from lack of food and hundreds of men were forced to work in German factories.

After the war, under the terms of the **Treaty of Versailles**, Belgium was granted extensive reparations from Germany as well as some German territory – the slice of land around Eupen and Malmédy and, in Africa, Rwanda and Burundi. Domestically, the Belgian government extended the franchise to all men over the age of 21, a measure which, in the event, ended several decades of **political control** by the Catholic party. The latter were now only able to keep power in coalition with the Liberals – usually with the Socialists, the third major party, forming the backbone of the opposition. The political lines were, however, increasingly fudged as the Catholic party moved left, becoming a Christian Democrat movement that was keen to co-operate with the Socialists on such matters as social legislation. The political parties may have been partly reconciled, but the **economy** staggered from crisis to crisis even before the effects of the Great Depression hit Belgium in 1929. The political class also failed to placate those Flemings who felt discriminated against. There had been a widespread feeling among the Flemish soldiers of World War I that they had borne the brunt of the fighting and now an increasing number of Flemings came to believe – not without justification – that the Belgian government was overly Walloon in its sympathies. Only reluctantly did the government make Flanders and Wallonia legally unilingual regions in 1930, and even then the linguistic boundary was left unspecified in the hope that French-speakers would come to dominate central Belgium. Furthermore, these communal tensions were fuelled by changing expectations. The Flemings had accepted the domination of the French-speakers without much protest for several centuries, but as their region became more prosperous and as their numbers increased in relation to the Walloons, so they grew in self-confidence, becoming increasingly unhappy with their social and political subordination. Inevitably, some of this discontent was sucked into **Fascist** movements, which drew some ten percent of the vote in both the Walloon and Flemish communities, though for very different reasons: the former for its appeal to a nationalist bourgeoisie, the latter for its assertion of "racial" pride among an oppressed group.

World War II and the immediate postwar period

The Germans invaded again in May 1940, launching a blitzkrieg that overwhelmed both Belgium and the Netherlands in short order. This time there was no heroic resistance by the Belgian king, now **Léopold III** (1934–51), who ignored the advice of his government and surrendered unconditionally and in such great haste that the British and French armies were, as their Commander-in-Chief put it, "suddenly faced with an open gap of twenty miles between Ypres and the sea through which enemy forces might reach the beaches". It is true that the Belgian army had been badly mauled and that a German victory was inevitable, but the manner of the surrender infuriated many Belgians, as did the king's refusal to form a government in exile. At first the occupation was relatively benign and most of the population waited apprehensively to see just what would happen. The main exception – setting aside the king, who at best played an ambivalent role – was the right-wing edge of the Flemish Nationalist movement, which cooperated with the Germans and (unsuccessfully) sought to negotiate the creation of a separate

Flemish state. Popular opinion hardened against the Germans in 1942 as the occupation became more oppressive. The Germans stepped up the requisitioning of Belgian equipment, expanded its forced labour schemes, obliging thousands of Belgians to work in Germany, and cracked down hard on any sign of opposition. By the end of the year, a **Resistance** movement was mounting acts of sabotage against the occupying forces and this, in turn, prompted more summary executions – of both Resistance fighters and hostages.

The summer of 1942 witnessed the first round-ups of the country's **Jews**. In 1940, there were approximately 50,000 Jews in Belgium, mostly newly arrived refugees from Hitler's Germany. Much to their credit, many Belgians did their best to frustrate German efforts to transport the Jews out of the country – usually to Auschwitz; the Belgian police did not cooperate, Belgian railway workers left carriages unlocked and/or sidelined trains, and many other Belgians hid Jews in their homes for the duration. The result was that the Germans had, by 1944, killed about half the country's Jewish population, a much lower proportion than in other parts of occupied Europe.

With the occupation hardening, the vast majority of Belgians were delighted to hear of the D-Day landings in June 1944. The **liberation** of Belgium began in September with the American troops in the south and the British and Canadian divisions sweeping across Flanders in the north.

After the war, the Belgians set about the task of economic **reconstruction**, helped by aid from the United States, but hindered by a divisive controversy over the wartime activities of King Léopold. Inevitably, the complex shadings of collaboration and forced cooperation were hard to disentangle, and the debate continued until 1950 when a referendum narrowly recommended his return as king from exile. Léopold's return was, however, marked by rioting across Wallonia, where the king's opponents were concentrated, and Léopold **abdicated** in favour of his son, **Baudouin** (1951–93).

To the present

The development of the postwar Belgian economy follows the pattern of most of Western Europe – reconstruction in the 1950s; boom in the 1960s; recession in the 1970s; and retrenchment in the 1980s and 1990s. Significant events have included the belated extension of the franchise to women in 1948; an ugly, disorganized and hasty evacuation of the Belgian Congo in 1960 and of Rwanda and Burundi in 1962; and the transformation of Brussels from one of the more insignificant European capitals into the home of the EU and NATO. There was also acute labour unrest in the Limburg coalfield in the early 1980s, following plans to close most of the remaining pits, and a right royal pantomime, when Catholic King Baudouin abdicated for the day while the law legalizing abortion was ratified in 1990.

But, above all, the postwar period has been dominated by the increasing **tension** between the Walloon and Flemish communities, a state of affairs that has been entangled with the relative economic decline of Wallonia, formerly the home of most of the country's heavy industry, as compared with burgeoning Flanders. Every **national institution** is now dogged by the prerequisites of **bilingualism** – speeches in parliament have to be delivered in both languages – and all the main political parties – conservative, liberal and socialist – have separate Flemish- and French-speaking sections. Add this to an already complex

The Flemish–French **language divide** has troubled the country for decades, its significance rooted in deep class and economic divisions. When the Belgian state was founded in 1830, its ruling and middle classes were predominantly French-speaking and they created the new state in their linguistic image: French was the official language and Flemish was banned in schools. This Francophone domination was subsequently reinforced by the way the economy developed, with Wallonia becoming a major coal mining and steel-producing area, while Flanders remained a predominantly agricultural, rural backwater. There were nationalist stirrings among the Flemings from the 1880s onwards, but it was only after World War II – when Flanders became the country's industrial powerhouse as Wallonia declined – that the demand for linguistic and cultural parity became irresistible. In the way of such things, the Walloons read Flemish "parity" as "domination", setting the scene for all sorts of inter-communal hassle.

As a response to this burgeoning animosity, the **Language Frontier** was drawn across the country in 1962, cutting the country in half, from west to east. The aim was to distinguish between the French- and Flemish-speaking communities and thereby defuse tensions, but it didn't work. In 1980, this failure prompted another attempt to rectify matters with the redrafting of the constitution and the creation of a federal system, with three separate **communities** – the Flemish North, the Walloon South and the German-speaking east – responsible for their own cultural and social affairs and education. At the same time, Belgium was divided into three **regions** – the Flemish North, the Walloon South and bilingual Brussels, with each regional authority dealing with matters like economic development, the environment and employment.

The niceties of this **partition** have undoubtedly calmed troubled waters, but in bilingual Brussels and at national-government level the division between Flemish and French speakers still influences many aspects of working and social life. Schools, political parties, literature and culture are all segregated along linguistic lines, and mutual stereotypes are deeply ingrained, leading to a set of complex, face-saving rules and regulations which can verge on the absurd. Governmental press conferences, for example, must have questions and answers repeated in both languages, one after the other. Across Belgium as a whole, bitterness about the economy, unemployment and the government smoulders within (or seeks an outlet through) the framework of this linguistic division, and individual neighbourhoods can be paralysed by language disputes. The communities of **Voeren/Fourons**, for instance, a largely French-speaking collection of villages in Flemish Limburg, almost brought down the government in the mid-1980s when the Francophone mayor, Jose Happart, refused to take the Flemish language exam required of all Limburg officials. Barred from office, he stood again and was re-elected, prompting the prime minister at the time, Wilfred Martens, to offer his own resignation. The Fourons affair was symptomatic of the obstinacy that besets the country to this day. This, of course, fuelled the conflict and gave succour to the political extremists on both sides – namely the **Vlaams Blok** on the Flemish side and, for the French-speakers, the **Front des Francophones**.

All this said, it would be wrong to assume that Belgium's language differences have gone beyond the level of personal animosity and institutionalized mutual suspicion. Belgian **language extremists** have been imprisoned over the years, but very few, if any, have died in the fight for supremacy. Indeed, some might see a bilingual nation as a positive thing in a Europe where trading – and national – barriers are being increasingly broken down. Suggesting this to a Belgian, however, is normally useless, but there again the casual visitor will rarely get a sniff of these tensions. It's probably better to speak English rather than Flemish or French in the "wrong" part of Belgium, but if you make a mistake, the worst you'll get is a look of glazed indifference.

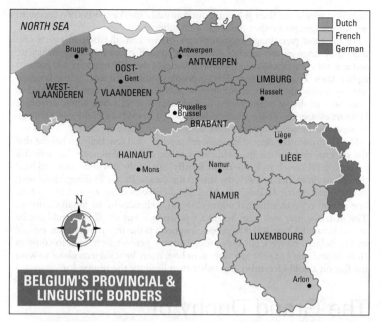

BELGIUM'S PROVINCIAL & LINGUISTIC BORDERS

NORTH SEA

Dutch
French
German

Brugge
WEST-VLAANDEREN
OOST-VLAANDEREN
Gent
Antwerpen
ANTWERPEN
LIMBURG
Hasselt
Bruxelles
Brussel
BRABANT
Liège
HAINAUT
Mons
Namur
LIÈGE
NAMUR
LUXEMBOURG
Arlon

system of proportional representation and it's hardly surprising that national government often appears extraordinarily cumbersome and bafflingly complicated. **Regional government** has also been transformed by this communal tension. The country has long been divided into provinces, but superimposed on this, in 1962, was the **Linguistic Divide** (or Language Frontier; see box opposite), which recognized three linguistic communities – French-, Flemish- and German-speaking. This was supplemented, in 1980, by the division of the country into three regions, one each for the French and Flemish, with Brussels, the third, designated a bilingual region. The transfer of major areas of administration from the centre to the regions followed.

In many ways, therefore, Belgium is a divided society, the two linguistic groups viewing each other with suspicion punctuated by hostility. In essence, the **Walloons** fear that the wealthier and more numerous Flemings will come to dominate the state, and indeed they may make this a self-fulfilling prophecy with their reluctance to learn Flemish – bilingualism being a prerequisite for any national job. The **Flemings**, on the other hand, want political and cultural recognition, and many bristle at what they perceive as Wallonian cultural and linguistic arrogance. Such nebulous but pervasive fears are hard to combat, and it's sometimes difficult to see what will hold the country together. That said, the political class did manage to overcome a crisis in the mid-1980s, when it looked as if the whole governmental system was about to founder, and up until now, coalitions of right- and left-wing politicians have always managed, with some energetic horse-trading, to keep the national government going. In this regard, the example of Antwerp is instructive: in local elections, the right-wing, nationalist Fleming **Vlaams Blok** regularly polls more votes than any of its rivals, but has been kept from power by all sorts of unlikely alliances – with Greens and Christian Democrats, for instance, working together to shut them out. What's more, much of the political class is at least partly reliant on the linguistic divide for their jobs and, institutionally speaking, has little reason to see the antagonisms either resolved or embittered.

For the most part, things just rumble on, but in 1996 the Belgian police, also dogged by language and regional divides, proved itself at best hopelessly inefficient, and at worst complicit in, the gruesome activities of the child murderer and pornographer **Marc Dutroux**. Over 350,000 people – from both sides of the language divide – took to the streets, demanding the police and justice system be overhauled. This rare outburst of public protest peaked again two years later when, amazingly, Dutroux escaped his police guards, stole a car and headed out of the city. Although he was subsequently recaptured, most Belgians were simply appalled.

The Dutroux affair dented the national psyche – and few Belgians believe that the reforms imposed on the police have made much difference – but into this psychological breach rode the **royal family**, one of the few institutions to bind the country together. In 1999, the heir to the throne, Prince Philippe, broke with tradition and married a Belgian – Mathilde d'Udekem d'Acoz – and, to top that, one of non-royal descent and with family on both sides of the linguistic divide. The marriage may well have healed a few wounds, but its effects should not be over-estimated. Over 400,000 people snapped up the free travel tickets offered by the Belgian railways, but only around twenty percent were used to come to Brussels, and one can only speculate as to how many loyal subjects chose to wave the flag on a cold December day rather than head for the nearest bar.

The Grand Duchy of Luxembourg from 1830

At the Congress of Vienna in 1815, Luxembourg had been designated a **Grand Duchy** by the great powers and given (as personal property) to King William I of Orange-Nassau, the ruler of the United Kingdom of the Netherlands (including Belgium). After Belgium broke away from William's kingdom in 1830, Luxembourg remained the property of the Dutch monarchy until 1890 when the ducal crown passed to another (independent) branch of the Nassau family, who have ruled ever since. In 1867, the great powers made further decisions about Luxembourg: the **Treaty of London** reaffirmed the duchy's territorial integrity and declared it neutral in perpetuity, thereby – it was hoped – protecting it from the clutches of both Germany and France. Following this declaration, Luxembourg City's fortifications were largely destroyed.

The second half of the nineteenth century saw Luxembourg's poor, agricultural economy transformed by the discovery and mining of **iron ore deposits**, which led to the foundation of what was soon one of Europe's largest steel industries. In 1914, the Grand Duchy confirmed its neutrality, but was still occupied by the Germans as it was again in **World War II** when the Luxembourgers put up a stubborn resistance, leading to many brave acts of defiance and considerable loss of life. In particular, the Battle of the Bulge was a major disaster and, as the war ended in 1945, one third of the country's farmland lay uncultivated, the public transportation system was in ruins, and some sixty thousand people were homeless.

In the **postwar years**, reconstruction was rapid and the government wisely pursued a policy of industrial diversification that has made the country one of the most prosperous parts of Europe. Disappointed by the results of neutrality, Luxembourg also joined the EC and NATO and is now home to many major Community departments.

An introduction to Belgian art

Designed to serve only as a quick reference, the following **outline** is the very briefest of introductions to a subject that has rightly filled volumes. Inevitably, it covers artists that lived and worked in both the Netherlands and Belgium, as these two countries have for most of their history been bound together as the so-called Low Countries. For in-depth and academic studies, see the recommendations in the "Books" listings on p.442.

The Early Flemish Masters

Throughout the medieval period, Flanders was one of the most artistically productive parts of Europe with each of the cloth towns, especially Bruges and Ghent, trying to out-do its rivals with the quality of its religious art. Today, the works of these early Flemish painters, known as the **Flemish Primitives**, are highly prized and an excellent sample is displayed in both Ghent and Bruges as well as in Brussels.

Jan van Eyck (1385–1441) is generally regarded as the first of the Flemish Primitives, and has even been credited with the invention of oil painting itself – though it seems more likely that he simply perfected a new technique by thinning his paint with (the newly discovered) turpentine, thus making it more flexible. His fame partially stems from the fact that he was one of the first artists to sign his work – an indication of how highly his talent was regarded by his contemporaries. Van Eyck's most celebrated work is the *Adoration of the Mystic Lamb*, a stunningly beautiful altarpiece displayed in St Baafskathedraal in Ghent. The painting was revolutionary in its realism, for the first time using elements of native landscape in depicting Biblical themes, and was underpinned by a complex symbolism which has generated analysis and discussion. Van Eyck's style and technique were to influence several generations of Low Countries artists.

Hugo van der Goes (d.1482) was the next Ghent master after van Eyck, most famous for the Portinari Altarpiece in Florence's Uffizi. After a short painting career, he died insane, and his late works have strong hints of his impending madness in their subversive use of space and implicit acceptance of the viewer's presence.

Firmly in the Eyckian tradition was **Rogier van der Weyden** (1400–64), one-time official painter to the city of Brussels. Weyden's religious paintings do, however, show a greater degree of emotional intensity than those of van Eyck, while his serene portraits of the bigwigs of his day were much admired across a large swath of western Europe. Van der Weyden influenced many painters, but one of the most talented of these was **Dieric Bouts** (1415–75). Born in Haarlem in what is now The Netherlands but active in Leuven, Bouts is recognizable by his stiff, rather elongated figures and horrific subject matter, all set against carefully drawn landscapes. **Hans Memling** (1440–94), whom few doubt was a pupil of van der Weyden, is best remembered for the pastoral charm of his landscapes and the quality of his portraiture, much of which survives on the rescued side panels of triptychs. The Memling Museum in Bruges, the city where he was active throughout his life, has a wonderful sample of his work.

Both **Gerard David** (1460–1523) and **Jan Provoost** (1465–1529) moved to Bruges at the back end of the fifteenth century. Mostly they painted religious scenes, but their secular works are much more memorable, especially David's *Judgement of Cambyses*, exhibited in the Groeninge in Bruges. David's best-known apprentice was **Adriaen Isenbrant** (d.1551), whose speciality was small, precisely executed panels – his *Madonna of the Seven Sorrows* in Bruges' Onze Lieve Vrouwekerk is quite superb. Isenbrant was the last of the great painters to work in that city before it was superseded by Antwerp – which itself became the focus of a more Italianate school of art in the sixteenth century.

Hieronymus Bosch (1450–1516) lived for most of his life in Holland, though his style is linked to that of his Flemish contemporaries. His frequently reprinted religious allegories are filled with macabre visions of tortured people and grotesque beasts, and appear at first faintly unhinged, though it's now thought that these are visual representations of contemporary sayings, idioms and parables. While their interpretation is far from resolved, Bosch's paintings draw strongly on subconscious fears and archetypes, giving them a lasting, haunting fascination.

The sixteenth century

At the end of the fifteenth century, the Flemish cloth towns were in decline and the leading artists of the day were drawn instead to the booming port of Antwerp. The artists who worked here soon began to integrate the finely observed detail that characterized the Flemish tradition with the style of the Italian painters of the Renaissance. **Quentin Matsys** (1464–1530) introduced florid classical architectural details and intricate landscapes to his works, influenced perhaps by the work of Leonardo da Vinci. As well as religious works, he painted portraits and genre scenes, all of which have recognizably Italian facets, and paved the way for the Dutch genre painters of later years. **Jan Gossart** (1478–1532) made the pilgrimage to Italy too, and his dynamic works are packed with detail, especially finely drawn classical architectural backdrops. He was the first Low Countries artist to introduce the subjects of classical mythology into his works, part of a steady trend through the period towards secular subject matter, which can also be seen in the work of **Joachim Patenier** (d.1524), who painted small landscapes of fantastical scenery.

The latter part of the sixteenth century was dominated by the work of **Pieter Bruegel the Elder** (c.1525–69), whose gruesome allegories and innovative interpretations of religious subjects are firmly placed in Low Countries settings. Pieter also painted finely observed peasant scenes, though he himself was well connected in court circles in Antwerp and, later, Brussels. **Pieter Aertsen** (1508–75) also worked in the peasant genre, adding aspects of still life: his paintings often show a detailed kitchen scene in the foreground, with a religious episode going on behind. Bruegel's two sons, **Pieter Bruegel the Younger** (1564–1638) and **Jan Bruegel** (1568–1625) were lesser painters: the former produced fairly insipid copies of his father's work, while Jan developed a style of his own – delicately rendered flower paintings and genre pieces that earned him the nickname "Velvet".

Towards the latter half of the sixteenth century highly stylized Italianate portraits became the dominant fashion, **Frans Pourbus the Younger** (1569–1622) being the leading practitioner. Frans worked for the likes of the Habsburgs and the Médicis, his itinerant life in contrast to that of his grandfather, the Bruges-based **Pieter Pourbus** (1523–84), the founder of this artistic dynasty.

The seventeenth century

Belgian painting of the early seventeenth century is dominated by **Pieter Paul Rubens** (1577–1640), who was easily the most important exponent of the Baroque in northern Europe. Born in Siegen, Westphalia, Rubens was raised in Antwerp, where he entered the painters' guild in 1598. He became court painter to the Duke of Mantua in 1600, and until 1608 travelled extensively in Italy, absorbing the art of the High Renaissance and classical architecture. By the time of his return to Antwerp in 1608 he had acquired an enormous artistic vocabulary: the paintings of Caravaggio in particular were to influence his work strongly. His first major success was *The Raising of the Cross*, painted in 1610 and displayed today in Antwerp cathedral. A large, dynamic work, it caused a sensation at the time, establishing Rubens' reputation and leading to a string of commissions. *The Descent from the Cross*, his next major work (also in the cathedral), consolidated this success; equally Baroque, it is nevertheless quieter and more restrained. Thereafter, he was able to set up his own studio, where he gathered a team of talented artists, thus ensuring a high rate of productivity and a degree of personality flexibility; the degree to which Rubens personally worked on a canvas would vary – and would determine its price.

From the early 1620s onwards Rubens turned his hand to a plethora of themes and subjects – religious works, portraits, tapestry designs, landscapes, mythological scenes, ceiling paintings – each of which was handled with supreme vitality and virtuosity. From his Flemish antecedents he inherited an acute sense of light, and used it not to dramatize his subjects (a technique favoured by Caravaggio and other Italian artists), but in association with colour and form. The drama in his works comes from the vigorous animation of his characters. His large-scale allegorical works, especially, are packed with heaving, writhing figures that appear to tumble out from the canvas.

The energy of Rubens' paintings was reflected in his **private life**. In addition to his career as an artist, he also undertook diplomatic missions to Spain and England, and used these opportunities to study the works of other artists and – as in the case of Velázquez – to meet them personally. In the 1630s, gout began to hamper his activities, and from this time his painting became more domestic and meditative. Hélène Fourment, his second wife, was the subject of many portraits and served as a model for characters in his allegorical paintings, her figure epitomizing the buxom, well-rounded women found throughout his work.

The followers of Rubens

Rubens' **influence** on the artists of the period was enormous. The huge output of his studio meant that his works were universally seen, and widely disseminated by the engravers he employed to copy his work. Chief among his followers was the portraitist **Anthony van Dyck** (1599–1641), who worked in Rubens' studio from 1618, often taking on the depiction of religious figures in his master's works that required particular sensitivity and pathos. Like Rubens, van Dyck was born in Antwerp and travelled widely in Italy, though his initial work was influenced less by the Italian artists than by Rubens himself. Eventually van Dyck developed his own distinct style and technique, establishing himself as court painter to Charles I in England, and creating portraits of a nervous elegance that would influence the genre there for the next hundred and fifty years. Most of his great portraiture remains in England, but his best religious works – such as the *Crucifixion* in Mechelen's Cathedral – can be found in Belgium.

Jacob Jordaens (1593–1678) was also an Antwerp native who studied under Rubens. Although he was commissioned to complete several works left unfinished by Rubens at the time of his death, his robustly naturalistic works have an earthy – and sensuous – realism that is quite distinct in style and technique.

Genre painting

As well as the Baroque creations of Rubens and his acolytes, another style emerged in the seventeenth century, that of **genre painting**. Often misunderstood, the term was initially applied to everything from animal paintings and still lifes through to historical works and landscapes, but later came to be applied only to scenes of everyday life. One of its early practitioners was **Frans Snijders** (1579–1657), who took up still-life painting where Aertsen left off, amplifying his subject – food and drink – to even larger, more sumptuous canvases, while doubling up as a member of the Rubens art machine, painting animals and still-life sections for the master's works. In the southern Netherlands the most skilful practitioner was Oudenaarde's **Adriaen Brouwer** (1605–38), whose peasant figures rivalled those of the painters Jan Steen and Adriaen van Ostade to the north. Brouwer's output was unsurprisingly small given his short life, but his riotous tavern scenes and tableaux of everyday life are deftly done, and were well received in their day, collected by, among others, Rubens and Rembrandt. Brouwer studied in Haarlem for a while under Frans Hals (and may have picked up much of his painterly technique from him), before returning to his native Flanders to influence **David Teniers the Younger** (1610–90), who worked in Antwerp and later in Brussels. Teniers' early paintings are Brouwer-like peasant scenes, although his later work is more delicate and diverse, including *kortegaardje* – guardroom scenes that show soldiers carousing.

The eighteenth and nineteenth centuries

By the end of the seventeenth century, French influences had overwhelmed Belgium's native artistic tradition with painters like **Jan Joseph Horemans I** and **Balthasar van den Bossche** modifying the Flemish genre painting of the previous century to suit Parisian tastes. Neoclassicism was also coming into vogue at this time, a French-led movement whose leading light was **Jacques Louis David** (1748–1825), the creator of the *Death of Marat*, an iconic work displayed in Brussels' Musées Royaux des Beaux Arts. **Laurent Delvaux** (1696–1778) was another important figure during this period, a Flemish sculptor who produced a large number of works for Belgian churches, including the pulpit of Ghent's cathedral.

French artistic fashions continued to rule the Belgian roost well into the **nineteenth century**, and among them Neoclassicism remained the most popular. Of the followers of Jacques Louis David, **François Joseph Navez** (1787–1869) was the most important to work in Belgium, furthering the influence of the movement via his position as director of the Brussels academy. With Belgian independence from the Netherlands in 1830 came, as might be expected, a new interest in nationalism, and artists such as **Louis Galliat** (1810–87) and **Henri Dobbelaere** (1829–85) spearheaded a romantic interpretation of historical events, idealizing Belgium's recent and medieval history.

Antoine Wiertz (1806–65) was celebrated for his grandiose amalgamation of romantic and Neoclassical themes in his sculptures and paintings, while **Henri de Braekeleer** (1840–88) was highly regarded for his Dutch-inspired interiors and landscapes. Indeed, landscape painting underwent a resurgence of popularity in France in the mid-nineteenth century, and once again Belgian artists flocked to reflect that country's tastes. More positively, **Émile Claus** (1849–1924) adapted French Impressionist ideas to create an individual style known as Luminism, and **Théo Rysselberghe** (1862–1926) followed suit. The talented **Fernand Khnopff** (1858–1921) developed his own style too, in his case inspired by the English Pre-Raphaelites.

One artist who stands out during this period is **Constantin Meunier** (1831–1905), a painter and sculptor whose naturalistic work depicting brawny workers and mining scenes was the perfect mirror of a fast-industrializing Belgium. But the most original Belgian artist of the late nineteenth century was **James Ensor** (1860–1949). Ensor, who lived in Ostend for most of his life, painted macabre, disturbing works, whose haunted style can be traced back to Bosch and Bruegel and which was itself a precursor of Expressionism. He was active in a group known as **Les XX**, which organized exhibitions of new styles of art from abroad, and greatly influenced contemporary Belgian painters.

Les XX

Founded in 1883, **Les XX** (Les Vingt) was an influential group of twenty Belgian painters, designers and sculptors, who were keen to bring together all the different strands of their respective crafts. For ten years, they staged an annual exhibition showcasing both domestic and international talent, and it was here that Cézanne, Manet and Gauguin were all exhibited at the very beginning of their careers. With members as diverse as Ensor and the architect-designer Henri van de Velde, Les XX never professed to be united by the same artistic principles, but several of its members, including Rysselberghe, were inordinately impressed by the Post-Impressionism of Seurat, whose pointillist *The Big Bowl* created a sensation when it was exhibited by Les XX in 1887.

Les XX – and the other literary-artistic groupings that succeeded it – were part of a general **avant-garde** movement which flourished in Brussels at the end of the nineteenth century. This avant-garde was deeply disenchanted with Brussels' traditional salon culture, not only for artistic reasons but also because of its indifference to the plight of the Belgian working class. Such political views nourished close links with the fledgling **socialist movement**, and Les XX even ran the slogan "art and the people have the same enemy – the reactionary Bourgeoisie". Indeed, the Belgian avant-garde came to see art (in all its forms) as a vehicle for liberating the Belgian worker, a project regularly proclaimed in *L'Art Moderne*, its most authoritative mouthpiece.

The twentieth century

Each of the major modern art movements had its followers in Belgium, and each was diluted or altered according to local taste. **Expressionism** was manifest in a local group of artists established in a village near Ghent, with the most eye-catching paintings produced by **Constant Permeke** (1886–1952), whose bold, deeply coloured canvases can be found in many Belgian galleries. There was also **Jean Delville** (1867–1953), not as talented as Permeke perhaps, but an artist who certainly set about his religious preoccupations with gigantic gusto. **Surrealism** also caught on in a big way, perhaps because of the Belgian penchant for the bizarre and grotesque. **René Magritte** (1898–1967), one of the leading lights of the movement, was born and trained in Belgium and returned there after being involved in the movement's birth in 1927. His Surrealism is gentle compared to the work of Dalí or de Chirico: ordinary images are used in a dreamlike way, often playing on the distinction between a word and its meaning. His most famous motif was the man in the bowler hat, whose face was always hidden from view. **Paul Delvaux** (1897–1994) adopted his own rather salacious interpretation of the movement – a sort of "what-the-butler-saw" Surrealism.

Most of the interwar artists were influenced by van Doesburg and de Stijl in Holland, though none figured highly in the movement. The abstract geometrical works of **Victor Severanckx** (1897–1965) owed much to de Stijl, and he in turn inspired the postwar group known as **La Jeune Peinture**, which gathered together some of the most notable artists working in Belgium, the antecedents of the Abstract Expressionists of the 1950s. A similar collective function was served by **CoBrA**, founded in 1948 and taking its name from the first letters of Copenhagen, Brussels and Amsterdam. While none of the Belgian participants in CoBrA achieved the fame of one of its Dutch members, Karel Appel, the name of **Pierre Alechinsky** (1927–) is certainly well known in his hometown, Brussels.

Probably the most famous recent Belgian artist is **Marcel Broodthaers** (1924–76). He initially worked in the Surrealist manner, but soon branched out, quickly graduating from cut-paper geometric shapes into both the plastic arts and most famously, sharp and brightly coloured paintings of everyday artefacts, especially casseroles brimming with mussels.

Belgium's great beers

Belgian beers have recently become fashionable, yet the pleasures they offer have been truly explored by only a discerning minority of drinkers. The rule "Never ask for 'a beer'" applies especially in Belgium. Such a request will bring forth a perfectly acceptable lager, but of a type that could just as easily be found in many other countries. The great beers of Belgium are not its lagers. Its native brews are in other styles, and they offer an extraordinary variety, some so different from more conventional brews that at the initial encounter they are scarcely recognizable as beers. Yet they represent some of the oldest traditions of brewing in the Western world. No other country (even those with far more breweries) has among its native styles of beer such diversity, individuality, idiosyncrasy and colour. Nor does any other country present beers so beautifully. Belgian brewers often use wired and corked champagne bottles, and serve each beer in its own shape of glass, ranging from flutes to snifters and chalices. It is something of a Belgian speciality to bottle beers with a sediment of live yeast, so that they can be laid down to mature. This technique is usually indicated on the label by the phrase "re-fermented in the bottle" (*refermentée en bouteille/hergist in de fles*).

The following introduction includes all the major types of Belgium beers: from winey-tasting Lambics, some with whole fruit added; "white" wheat beers in the vein of the popular Hoegaarden; sour-ish red and brown beers; strong ales from Trappist monasteries; powerful golden brews like the famous Duvel; plus endless local and seasonal specialities.

The Lambic family of beers

The **Lambic family of beers** is the winiest of all the world's beers, and specific to the Brussels area. There are several possible explanations for the odd name (which is spelled in a variety of ways), but its most likely origin is the small town of Lembeek ("Lime Creek"), to the immediate southwest of Brussels, in the heart of the producing area. A handful of breweries around Lembeek, Beersel and Schepdaal, all in the valley of the River Zenne, have persisted with techniques that pre-date the culturing of yeasts. Their brews are of the type seen in Bruegel's paintings, and represent the oldest style of beer readily found in the developed world. Lambic beers gain their tartness from a content of at least thirty percent raw **wheat** in addition to the more usual malted **barley**, but their defining characteristic is the use of **wild yeast**. This "wild", or "spontaneous", fermentation imparts the distinctive acidity. The yeasts of the atmosphere descend into open vessels in the attics of the breweries, and the fermentation and maturation continue in wooden casks, some more than one hundred years old, many previously used to transport wine. The casks, and the walls of the breweries, play host to a menagerie of wild yeasts. Elsewhere in the world of brewing, wood is today scarcely used in fermentation or maturation. While conventional ales ferment and mature for a week or two, and lagers for a month or two, Lambics may have two or three years of fermentation. Most of these beers have a conventional alcohol content, in the range of 4.0 to 6.0 percent alcohol by volume (**abv**).

Straight Lambic

In its most natural form a draught beer, almost still, unsweetened and unblended, **straight Lambic** can seem less like a beer than some hybrid of hard cider and fino sherry. Some of the yeasts that develop during its fermentation are, indeed, very similar to those at work in sherry bodegas. Straight Lambic is hard to find. It is served in only one or two cafés in Brussels and a handful in the area of production. Typically, it is tapped directly from the cask, and decanted from a pitcher into tumblers. In much the way that fino sherry is served in Andalusia with tapas, so Lambic is sometimes offered with snacks of sharp, soft cheeses like the fresh-curd Plattekaas and the acidic Pottekaas, with silverskin onions, radishes, brown bread, and sometimes sausages similar to English saveloys or black pudding.

The most central Lambic café, albeit offering sweetened interpretations, is *A la Bécasse*, near the lower end of Brussels' Grand-Place, down an alley off rue Tabora (see p.116). It has "Dutch" tiled walls and scrubbed tables, and serves the beer with snacks. In Brussels too is *Le Vieux Château d'Or*, at rue Ste Catherine 26, which can, on occasion, also have straight Lambic.

A rare bottled version, very dry and lemony, is sometimes available to visitors at the renowned small brewery Cantillon, at the **Musée Bruxellois de la Gueuze** in Brussels' Anderlecht neighbourhood (see p.110). The brewery, near Bruxelles-Midi train station, is an essential visit for anyone with even the slightest interest in beer. Cantillon is one of the most traditional Lambic producers, along with the brewery of Frank Boon (pronounced as in "bone" – or "Beaune"), in Lembeek itself (☎02 356 66 44). Boon has tours (July–Sept Wed 3pm) starting at *Café Kring*, next to the main church. A third traditionalist is Girardin, a brewery that grows its own wheat, but unfortunately does not have tours. Other well-known Lambic breweries include Timmermans, Lindemans, De Troch, Mort Subite and Belle-Vue. The last two are genuine Lambic brewers owned by national groups, respectively better known for Kronenbourg and Stella Artois lagers. Belle-Vue has a tasting room at its brewery in the Brussels neighbourhood of Molenbeek, at quai du Hainaut 43 (☎02 512 28 21). It offers a sweetened blend of Lambics on draught. The Mort Subite beer was originally brewed for the *À La Mort Subite* café-bar, not far from the Grand-Place (see p.116). It was founded in about 1880, refitted in 1926, and was the inspiration for a ballet by Maurice Béjart. Straight Lambic is not usually served, though Gueuze and Kriek (see below) are.

Faro

Faro is also hard to find, but is sometimes available at Lambic cafés. This is a version of Lambic sweetened with rummy-tasting dark candy sugar, and occasionally spices. Some cafés serve a do-it-yourself version, with a pestle or cocktail barman's muddler to crush the sugar. Faro was once the restorative for the working man in Brussels.

Gueuze

A bottled, sparkling style, **gueuze** is much easier to find than its fellow Lambics. It often has the toasty and Chardonnay-like notes found in champagne.

The word gueuze (hard "g", and rhymes with "firs") may have the same etymological origins as the English words *gas* and *ghost*, and the Flemish *gist* (yeast), referring to carbonation and rising bubbles. The carbonation is achieved by blending young Lambic (typically six months old) with more mature vintages (two to three years). The residual sugars in the young Lambic and the yeasts that have developed in the old cause a new fermentation. The most traditional examples may bear on the label the endorsement of the consumerist organization De Objectieve Bierproevers. References to "old" (*oud, vieux/vieille*) on the label indicate a minimum of six months and a genuine Lambic process. Without these legends, a Lambic may have been "diluted" with a more conventional beer. Apart from the producers mentioned above, blenders like Drie Fonteinen and Hanssens produce outstanding examples and the equally outstanding Cam can be found in the village of Gooik, 10km west of Brussels, adjoining a café (next door to the police station).

Fruit Lambic

The acidity of Lambic provides a particularly good base for **fruit beers**. Because these begin with a fermentation of grain, and are primed with fruit later, they are beers and not wines. The use of fruit (like that of spices) almost certainly pre-dates the hop as a flavour modifier in beer. In the traditional method, the fruit is added during the maturation of the beer, causing a further fermentation. The happiest results are arguably with fruits that have **stones**, which can impart a balancing, almondy dryness. The best of Belgian fruit beers have the dryness of a pink champagne, rather than the sweetness of a soda-pop. Like champagnes, they are often served in flute-style glasses. In the Brussels area, the home of Lambic, a typical local fruit is a small, dark variety of **cherry**, known in Flemish as the *kriek*. Lambic-based kriek beers are the most traditional fruit brews. **Raspberries**, known in Flemish as *frambozen*, and French as *framboises,* are also widely used. The Cantillon brewery has in recent years experimented to interesting effect with Muscat **grapes**, which are grown under glass in Belgium as dessert fruit. More exotic fruits, added as syrups, are used in novelty beers by the more commercially minded breweries. The term Lambic is used only when that style of beer is used as the base. Contrary to misunderstandings in some other countries, there is no connection between the term Lambic and the use of fruit. Equally, many good fruit beers in Belgium are not based on Lambic. For example, several of the brown brews made in Oudenaarde are used as the base for *kriek* or *frambozen* beers.

White beers

The best-known Belgian **white beer** (*witbier* or *bière blanche*) is the principal product from **Hoegaarden**, a small town in a wheat-growing region east of Brussels. The Hoegaarden beer, which in the 1960s revived the traditional style of the region, has inspired many other examples throughout Belgium. This style is usually made from equal portions of raw wheat and malted barley, spiced with ground coriander seeds and dried Curaçao orange peels, and fermented with a fairly conventional yeast. The fruitiness imparted by the wheat, sometimes with suggestions of plum, apple or banana, melds well with the orange and coriander. Beers in this style, usually with a conventional alcohol content, are regarded especially as a summertime refresher, though they also make a good accompaniment to fruity desserts. They are typically served in chunky tumblers. Wheat beers are identified as being "white" in several brewing nations. The designation may refer to the pale head formed during fermentation, or to the fact that these beers are often unfiltered, and therefore hazy. Wheat beers can be filtered, but less easily than those made from barley malt.

For good examples of the beer look no further than Hoegaarden itself or the creamy Limburgse Witte, the honeyish-tasting Brugs Tarwebier, the cinnamon-spiced Steendonk, the Lambic-based Witte (two t's), from Timmermans, and Wittekerke Wit, smoothened with oats. The last is named after a Flemish soap opera. Hoegaarden produces a slightly stronger (5.6abv), less wheaty, winter companion called Speciale. It also has several non-wheat beers with the same spicing, including an amber ale with an older spelling, Hougaerdse DAS (the mysterious initials are a revival of an old beer name in Belgium); the strong (8.7abv), golden Hoegaarden Grand Cru; and the strong (9.0abv), dark "Forbidden Fruit", labelled as *Le Fruit Defendu* in French and *De Verboden Vrucht* in Flemish. The last two beers are Belgian classics.

Brown beers

Many distinctive variations of **dark brown ales** are made in Belgium, especially in Flanders. The classic style, with an interplay of caramel-like malty sweetness and a sourness gained in several months of maturation (usually in metal tanks), is sometimes identified as *oud* (old) *bruin* (the pronunciation is almost the same as the English word "brown"). The most complex examples have a secondary fermentation in the bottle. The flavour and acidity render these the perfect base for the Flemish beef stew *carbonnade flamande*. The most famous producing town is **Oudenaarde** (see p.159), in East Flanders. Oudenaarde's water, low in calcium and high in sodium carbonate, gives a particularly textured character to the beers. Its small Felix brewery, owned by a family named Clarysse, the weekend-only brewery of the Cnudde family and the larger brewery of the Roman family all make examples of the style. Roman, which dates from 1545, has magnificent 1930s buildings, and a brewhouse from the same period. It makes a "single" version at 5.5abv and a "double" at 8.0abv. These are labelled Special Roman and Dobbelen Bruinen respectively. The most typical example of browns, in three ages and strengths, are fermented and matured at Liefmans, in Oudenaarde, from brews made by Riva of Dentergem, in West Flanders. The classic example, Goudenband (Golden Band), at 8.0-plus, is also the basis for an excellent cherry beer, Liefmans' Kriek.

Liefmans offers tours, a small museum and an art gallery. Their bar-restaurant *Zaal de Baudelot*, Aalststraat 200, Oudenaarde (℡055 31 13 91; Mon–Fri 8am–5pm), is open for breakfast and serves Flemish dishes for lunch.

Red beers

The world-classic beers of the **Rodenbach** brewery, and several similar products from competitors, mainly in West Flanders, are a distinct style without a name but might be described as "red" beers. They are more sharply acidic, leaner, more reddish half-brothers to the brown beers of East Flanders, with the additional difference that they are often filtered and pasteurized. Their sharpness makes them perhaps the most quenching beers in the world, and their acidity renders them very food-friendly. The sharp acidity, and some of the colour, derives from ageing in large, fixed, wooden tuns. Rodenbach, in Roeselare, has ten or eleven halls full of these tuns. There is nothing comparable in any brewery elsewhere in the world, and the whole establishment is a museum of industrial archeology. The brewery's Rodenbach Grand Cru (5.2–5.6abv) is aged for between eighteen months and two years or more. The regular Rodenbach Bier (4.6–5.0abv) is a blend containing some younger beer. The slightly stronger Rodenbach Alexander (5.2–5.6abv) is sweetened with cherry essence but generally Rodenbach beers have a distinct passion-fruit character. Rivals include the more chocolatey Petrus Oud Bruin, the tart Bellegems Bruin, the smoother Bourgogne des Flandres, the slightly lactic Bios Vlaamse Bourgogne, the fruity Vichtenaar and the rich Duchesse de Bourgogne.

British-style ales

During the two world wars, the beers brought by British troops to Belgium inspired similar British-style brews locally. Several Belgian brewers still produce "Le Pale Ale" and "Le Scotch". The first is usually stronger, hoppier and fruitier than an English pale ale or bitter, and is served as sociable beer. The second is typically more potent, maltier and richer, than a strong dark ale in Scotland, and is served as a digestif or winter warmer, often in a thistle glass. John Martin's is a well-known example of a Belgian-brewed "English Pale Ale". Other British brews include Gordon's Highland Scotch Ale (8.0abv) and a fractionally stronger Christmas version both brewed in Scotland for the Belgian market.

(Amber) Belgian ales

Beers similar to an English pale ale or bitter, but with no direct allusion to Britain, are often made by Belgian brewers. Some are labelled with the English word **"Ale"**, others as **"Special"** (various spellings), as a simple distinction from standard lager beers. Some of these are spiced (eg Petrus Speciale, with coriander), and others simply derive a spicy taste from the yeasts used. Typical examples, all at around 5.0abv, include the fruity Palm Special, the spicy Horse Ale, the hoppy Op-Ale, dry Ginder Ale (after a brewer named van Ginderachter) and the sherbety Vieux Temps. The most famous example of all is made by the De Koninck brewery of Antwerp. This is identified as neither ale nor special, but simply as **De Koninck**. In the Antwerp area, where it is very much the local brew, it is colloquially ordered in a *bolleke*, a reference to its curved goblet. The beer has a dense head, a toasty palate, and a spicy, delicate hop in the finish. Its subtlety is much more evident on draught than in the bottle. De Koninck is widely available and outlets include *Den Engel*, on the Grote Markt (see p.247) and *Quinten Matsijs*, Moriaanstraat 17, near Hendrik Conscience-plein, the city's oldest pub, dating from 1565.

Saisons

Saisons are nominally seasonal beers for the summer, but are available all year round. Only in a country with so many strong beers would brews of 5.0–6.5 percent be regarded as "light" summer specialities. Despite their typical strengths, saisons usually have a citric, peppery, quenching quality, due variously to hard water, heavy hopping, spicing or deliberate souring. They are usually amber to orange in colour, and often quite dry. Saisons are largely confined to the French-speaking part of the country, especially the western part of the province of **Hainaut**, in old, small, farm-like breweries close to the Borinage coalfield, near Mons (see p.289). Examples include the crisp Saison 1900, from the brewery Lefèbvre, in Quenast, south of Brussels; the tart Saison Silly (named after its home village); and the spiced Saison de Pipaix. The last is made at Brasserie à Vapeur, a steam-powered brewery dating from the 1780s, at rue de Maréchal 1, Pipaix (details of tours and tastings on ☏069 66 20 47). The hugely lively **Saison Dupont** is made at a farm brewery, Basse 5, in the village of Tourpes, near Pipaix, that uses its spent grain in bread and also produces a hop-flavoured cheese. There is a café opposite the brewery in which to sample the produce. The perfumy **Saison D'Epeautre** (made with spelt grain) is produced commercially at a private house in the village of Blaugies, near Dour, south of Mons, rue de La Frontière 435 (☏065 65 06 30). The aromatic **Saison Régal** is from a larger independent brewery, in Purnode, in the province of Namur. A variety of beers for different seasons are made by the Fantôme brewery, rue Préal 8, which opens its own café at weekends and school holidays, in the village of Soy, in the province of Luxembourg (☏086 47 70 44). Many small breweries in the French-speaking part of Belgium make similar beers, not necessarily identified as saisons.

The saison style does not exist in the Flemish-speaking part of the country, but a paler, wonderfully flowery, hoppy beer called **Sezoens**, made by the Martens brewery, of Bocholt, in Limburg, is something of a counterpart. This is a house speciality at Brussels' *De Ultieme Hallucinatie* (see p.116).

Trappist beers

This term is properly applied only to a brewery in a **Trappist monastery**. The Trappists are one of the most severe orders of monks, established at La Trappe, in Normandy as a breakaway – with a stricter observance – from the Cistercian rule, which itself broke from the Benedictines. Among the dozen or so surviving abbey breweries in Europe, seven are Trappist, six in Belgium and one just across the Dutch border. The Trappists have the only monastic breweries in Belgium, all making strong ales with re-fermentation in the bottle. Some gain a distinctive rummy character from the use of candy sugar in the brew-kettle. They do not represent a style, but they are very much a **family of beers**. The three in the French-speaking part of the country are all in the forested Ardennes, where hermitages burned charcoal to fuel early craft industries. It is not usually possible to visit the abbeys without prior arrangement by letter and it can be difficult even then. Most offer their beers in a nearby café or *auberge* and several are widely available in many parts of the country.

Orval

Orval is the most singular of the Trappist brewing abbeys, in both its architecture and its beer. It can be found on the French frontier, near Villers-devant-Orval in the Belgian province of Luxembourg, not far from Florenville. The name derives from Vallée d'Or (Golden Valley). Legend has it that Countess Matilda of Tuscany (c.1046–1115) lost a gold ring in the lake and when it was brought to the surface by a trout, she thanked God by endowing a monastery. The monastery was certainly brewing before the French Revolution, when it was sacked (it was only rebuilt in the 1930s). The finest craftsmen of the period worked on the abbey, which was specially refurbished to crown the centenary of the modern kingdom of Belgium. The present abbey, officially called **Notre Dame d'Orval** (see p.343) stands alongside the ruins of the old. Bread and cheese are made for sale here, as well as a startlingly dry, hoppy ale of approximately 6.2abv, with a dark orange colour. This world-classic brew gains some of its astonishing complexity from a secondary fermentation with multiple strains of yeast, including "semi-wild" *brettanomyces* yeast which imparts a "hopsack" or "horse-blanket" character. Devotees like to bottle-age this beer for between six months and three years. It is a powerful aperitif. There is a shop at the abbey, and a bar-restaurant nearby at *A l'Ange Gardien*, rue d'Orval 3 (℡061 31 18 86).

Chimay

Chimay is the best known of the Trappist brewing monasteries. The abbey, also called Notre Dame, stands on a small hill called Scourmont, a few kilometres to the south of the town of Chimay (see p.307). The abbey, in the Romanesque style, was built in 1850. While the early abbeys brewed for their own communities, Chimay was the first to sell its beer commercially. Between the two world wars, it coined the appellation "Trappist Beer". After the Second World War, Chimay's great brewer, Father Théodore, worked with a famous Belgian brewing scientist, Jean De Clerck, to isolate the yeasts that identified Chimay's beers as classic Trappist brews. These yeasts, which work at very high temperatures (up to 30°C), impart a character reminiscent of Zinfandel or port wine, especially to Chimay's 7.0abv and 9.0abv beers, which have a colour to match. Between the two is a drier, paler, hoppier version at 8.0abv. In ascending order of strength, the standard bottlings are identified by **red**, **white** and **blue crown tops**. There are also larger, corked bottles as Première, Cinq Cents and Grande Réserve. The strongest will mature in the bottle for at least five years. It makes an excellent accompaniment to Chimay's Trappist cheese (similar to a Port Salut) and is even better with Roquefort. The beers are widely available in Belgium and abroad.

Rochefort

The least well known of the established Trappist breweries. **Rochefort** is brewed in Notre Dame de St Rémy, near the small town of Rochefort, in the Ardennes (see p.330). The abbey dates from at least 1230, when it was a convent, and brewing started at least as early as 1595. The oldest parts of the buildings date from the 1600s but restoration was required after the Napoleonic period. The beers are tawny to brown in colour, have an earthy honesty, perhaps deriving from a quite simple formulation, in which dark candy sugar is a significant ingredient. They have flavours reminiscent of figs, bananas and chocolate. The range is divided, according to an old Belgian measure of density, into beers of 6.0, 8.0 and 10.0 degrees, with 7.5, 9.2 and 11.3 percent alcohol by volume respectively. The brewery has always quietly gone about its business, but in recent years its 10.0-degree beer has won a growing appreciation. The abbey does not have its own inn, but the beers can be tasted locally at two hotels (see p.332): *Le Limbourg*, which also serves good charcuterie and game, and the slightly more expensive *La Malle Post*.

Westvleteren

The smallest of the Trappist breweries, the abbey of St Sixtus, at **Westvleteren**, near Ieper and Poperinge, dates from the 1830s. Its beers are not filtered or centrifuged at any stage of production, and emerge with firm, long, big, fresh, malty flavours and suggestions of plum brandy. The Belgian degree system is again used to identify the beers. The figures 4.0°, 6.0°, 8.0° and 12.0° on the crown cork roughly reflect the alcohol content in this instance (though that cannot be precise in a strong, bottle-conditioned ale). The strongest might be closer to 11.5 but has on occasion been rated the most potent beer in Belgium. The beers are available next door at the café *In De Vrede*. Otherwise, trade and public alike have to go to a serving hatch at the abbey. A recorded phone message (☎057 42 20 75) tells callers which beer will be available, and when. If the 12° is on sale, cars will begin queuing long before the 10am opening time. Each car is rationed to ten cases and the monks are inflexible on this point, even toward a café-owner who makes a round-trip from Odense, on the Danish island of Fynen. "We make as much beer as we need to support the abbey – and no more," say the monks.

Westmalle

Westmalle is famous for one beer in particular, a world classic, though it also makes two others. The abbey of Our Lady of the Sacred Heart is in flat countryside at Westmalle, between the city of Antwerp and the Dutch border. The monastery was established in 1794, and has brewed since 1836. It is thus the oldest of Belgium's post-Napoleonic Trappist breweries. Its renown, though, derives from the introduction of golden Trappist ales to meet competition from fashionable Pilseners after the Second World War. Its beers include a marvellously subtle, golden "Single" (curiously called Extra), brewed at 4.0 percent for the monks' own consumption, but sometimes also found outside the abbey; a dark-brown, fruity Dubbel (the Flemish spelling), at 6.5 percent; and its most famous beer, its golden-to-bronze, aromatic, orangey-tasting, complex Tripel, at 9.0 percent. These Trappist classics have popularized the notion that an "abbey-style Double" should be strong and dark and a "Triple" yet more potent but pale. Locally, the beers are available in the village at the café *Trappisten*, Antwerpsesteenweg 478.

Abbey beers

The term **abbey beers** is applied to ranges of strong ales in a similar vein to some of the famous Trappist brews, but not made in monasteries. Some have names indicating a business relationship between an abbey (which may have brewed on its own in the past) and a commercial brewery. The Norbertine abbeys of Leffe and Grimbergen, for example, have royalty agreements with Interbrew and Alken-Maes respectively. So does the Benedictine monastery of Maredsous, with the brewery that also makes Duvel. Another Benedictine monastery, Affligem, played a significant role in the history of hop-growing and brewing, and made beer until the First World War. Its excellent beers are now made by the De Smedt brewery. There are several other religious institutions that license breweries, and other beers that are simply named after an abbey ruin or local saint. An excellent newcomer is **Karmeliet**. This beer owes something to a style of beer made by the Carmelite monks of Dendermonde, in East Flanders, in the 1600s. It contains barley, wheat and oats, in both raw and malted forms, and is very heavily spiced. It is made by the Bosteels Brewery, which also produces a pleasant dark ale called Kwak, famously served in a stirrup cup.

Golden ales

In seeking to compete with Pilsner lagers by using very pale malts and Czech, Slovenian or German hops, while retaining ale yeasts, Belgium has created a wide range of aromatic, fruity-tasting, golden ale specialities. Some of these are at a conventional alcohol content, like the Special made by **Anne De Ryck** at her brewery in Herzele, near the hop-growing town of Aalst, in East Flanders. Others are stronger, like the 6.0 percent **Straffe Hendrik** Blonde, brewed in Bruges at De Halve Mann (see p.184). The most famous are the very strong ones like the deceptively drinkable classic **Duvel**, at 8.5 percent. This has a very complex regime of four temperature stages in its fermentation and maturation. The name (pronounced Doov'l) is a corruption of the Flemish for Devil. This beer has many competitors, usually with devilish names. A good example is **Hapkin**, named after an axe-wielding count of Flanders.

Local specialities

Many breweries in Belgium produce characterful beers that defy categorization. Among these **local specialities**, Van Honsebrouck's very strong (11.0 percent) Château/Kasteel Beer, aged in a château at Ingelmunster, East Flanders, is perhaps comparable to a strong old ale or dark-brown barley wine in the English-speaking world. A wide range of strong specialities is made by **De Dolle Brouwers**, at Esen, near Diksmuide, not far from Ostend. These "Mad Brewers" are a family of professional people who stepped in when their local brewer retired due to ill-health. They operate the brewery at weekends, when they also open a sample room and shop (☎051 50 27 81). It is a fine example of a country brewery – and its beers are well worth tasting. So is **Grottenbier Bruin**, partly aged (for one to two months) in limestone caves, and turned weekly like champagne. This project has been a long-term dream of the ever-inventive Belgian brewer Pierre Celis. The beer is made by the De Smedt brewery, noted for its Affligem range. The "Grotto Beer" is a strongish (6.5abv) dark ale, in which small quantities of "exotic" spices are added to create a gentle, balancing dryness and crispness. A lover of pale barley wines would enjoy the powerful but beautifully balanced **Bush Beer**, at 12 percent, a Belgian classic from Dubuisson, of Pipaix, in Hainaut. In the same province, the town of Binche, famous for its pre-Lenten Carnival, also has a brewery, La Binchoise, which makes a range of honeyish, spicy-tasting beers. North of Bastogne, near the small town of Houffalize, the Ardennes hamlet of Achouffe has a well-known speciality brewery. Its emblem is **La Chouffe**, a bearded gnome wearing a red hood. The brewery La Chouffe has a tavern and dining room serving dishes prepared with its beers (☏061 28 81 47) and a shop selling its products. The principal beer, made with soft spring water and coriander, has great complexity and delicacy, and can be laid down to mature.

Golden lagers

The world's first golden lager was made in the town of Pilsen, in Bohemia, in what is now the Czech Republic. The best of the Czech and German **Pilsner-style** beers still have more malt and hop character than most derivatives elsewhere in the world, including Belgium. The Belgian examples, and some of those from just across the Dutch border, are in general slightly more characterful than the better-known labels from the Netherlands and Denmark. In the rest of the world, the best-known Belgian Pilsner is the lightly hoppy, grassy Stella Artois. Within Belgium, the slightly maltier Jupiler is a bigger seller. Both are made by Interbrew. The rival national grouping produces the flowery Maes and the beautifully clean, dry Cristal-Alken. Among the national brews, Cristal-Alken is the truest to the description Pilsner. It is made in the province of Limburg. Other good examples of Pilsner are Pax and Martens' Pils, perhaps the two best from independent brewers.

© Michael Jackson

Books

Most of the following books should be readily available, though some titles listed are currently out of print (denoted o/p) or likely to be available only in certain countries (in which case we've indicated where the book remains in print). Titles marked with the ⋆ symbol are particularly recommended.

Travel and general

Harry Pearson *A Tall Man in a Low Land*. The product of an extended visit to the lesser-known parts of Belgium, this racy book is in the style of (but not as perceptive as) Bill Bryson. Pearson has oodles of comments to make on Belgium and the Belgians – on everything from DIY to architecture – and although he sometimes tries too hard, this is a very enjoyable read.

Luc Sante *The Factory of Facts*. Born in Belgium but raised in the US, Sante returned to his native land for an extended visit in 1989 – at the age of 35. His book is primarily a personal reflection, but he also uses this as a base for a thoughtful exploration of Belgium and the Belgians – from their art to their food and beyond.

Marianne Thys (ed) *Belgian Cinema*. This authoritative volume, 992 pages long, has reviews of just about every Belgian film ever made.

San van de Veire *Belgian Fashion Design*. The staggering success of Flemish fashion designers is chronicled in this well-illustrated book. Particularly interesting on the factors underpinning the burgeoning of Belgian fashion in the early 1980s.

Specialist guides

Alan Castle *Walking in the Ardennes*. The best available general guide to hiking in Belgium's most scenic landscapes.

Chris Craggs *Selected Rock Climbs in Belgium and Luxembourg*. All you could ever wish to know about climbing in these two countries. Scores of route descriptions and loads of helpful advice. In Belgium, most of the climbs are in the Namur-Dinant area while in Luxembourg the focus is around Berdorf.

Major & Mrs Holt *Major & Mrs Holt's Battlefield Guide to Ypres* Everything you could ever want to know about the Ypres Salient and then some. Includes a detailed, fold-out map.

Beers

⋆ **Michael Jackson** *The Great Beers of Belgium*. Belgium produces the best beers in the world. Michael Jackson is one of the best beer writers in the world. The result is cheeky, palatable and sinewy with just a hint of fruitiness. See also his piece on pp.429–438.

⋆ **Tim Webb** *Good Beer Guide to Belgium, Holland & Luxembourg*. Detailed and enthusiastic guide to the best bars, beers and breweries. A good read, and extremely well informed to boot.

Tintin

Michael Farr *Tintin: The Complete Companion*. A Tintinologists' treat, this immaculately illustrated book – written by the world's leading Tintinologist – explores every aspect of Hergé's remarkably popular creation. Particularly strong on the real-life stories that inspired Hergé, but you do have to be seriously interested in Tintin to really enjoy this book.

Hergé *The Calculus Affair; The Making of Tintin: Cigars of the Pharaoh & the Blue Lotus.* Tintin comic strips come in and out of print at a rapid rate and there is a wide selection of audio cassettes too. The two books listed here are as good a place as any to start.

Benoit Peeters *Tintin and the World of Hergé: An Illustrated History.* Examines the life and career of Hergé, particularly the development of Tintin, and the influences on his work. No less than 300 illustrations.

History and politics

Neal Ascherson *The King Incorporated.* Belgium's own King Léopold II was responsible for one of the cruellest of colonial regimes, a savage system of repression and exploitation that devastated the Belgian Congo. Ascherson details it all.

J C H Blom (ed) *History of the Low Countries.* Belgian history books are thin on the round, so this heavy-weight volume, in which a series of historians weigh in with their specialities – from Roman times onwards – fills a few gaps, though it's hardly sun-lounge reading. Taken as a whole, its forte is in picking out those cultural, political and economic themes that give the region its distinctive character.

Paul van Buitenen *Blowing the Whistle.* All your worst fears about the EU confirmed. Buitenen was an assistant auditor in the EU's Financial Control Directorate in Brussels and this book, published in 1998, exposed the fraud and corruption. Needless to say, the EU was far from grateful for his revelations and forced him to resign, but even so the scandal stories became so widespread that the entire Commission was obliged to resign en bloc.

Martin Conway *Collaboration in Belgium.* Authoritative and well-written analysis of wartime collaboration and the development of Fascism in Belgium in the 1930s and 1940s.

Nicholas Crane *Mercator* Arguably the most important map-maker of all time, Gerard Mercator was born in Rupelmonde near Antwerp in 1512. This book details every twist and turn of his life and provides oodles – perhaps too many oodles – of background material on the Flanders of his time.

Galbert of Bruges, *The Murder of Charles the Good.* A contemporaneous chronicle of the tempestuous events that rattled early twelfth-century Bruges, this detailed yarn gives all sorts of insights into medieval Flanders.

⭐ **Pieter Geyl** *The Revolt of The Netherlands* 1555–1609 (US only). Geyl presents a concise account of the Netherlands during its formative years, chronicling the uprising against the Spanish and the formation of the United Provinces. Without doubt the definitive book on the period.

Christopher Hibbert *Waterloo.* Hibbert is one of Britain's leading historians, an astute commentator who writes in a fluent, easily accessible style. This book is divided into three parts – the first examines Napoleon's rise to power, the second looks at Wellington and his allies, the third deals with the battle.

Adam Hochschild *King Leopold's Ghost.* Harrowing account of King Leopold's savage colonial regime in the Congo. A detailed assessment – perhaps a little too long – explains and explores its gruesome workings. Particularly good on Roger Casement, the one-time British consul to the Congo, who publicized the cruelty and helped bring it to an end. Hochschild's last chapter – "The Great Forgetting" – is a stern criticism of the Belgians for their failure to acknowledge their savage colonial history.

E.H. Kossmann *The Low Countries 1780–1940*. Gritty, technically detailed but ultimately rather turgid narrative of the Low Countries from the Austrian era to World War II. Concentrates on the narrow arena of party politics and is therefore something of a specialist work. Only available in hardback, it costs a bomb.

★ **Geoffrey Parker** *The Dutch Revolt* (UK). Compelling account of the struggle between the Netherlands and Spain. Probably the best work of its kind. His *The Army of Flanders and the Spanish Road 1567–1659* may have an academic-sounding title, but gives a fascinating insight into the Habsburg army which occupied "Belgium" for well over a hundred years – how it functioned, was fed and moved from Spain to the Low Countries along the so-called Spanish Road.

Simon Schama *The Embarrassment of Riches: An Interpretation of Dutch Culture in the Golden Age*. Long before his reinvention on British TV, Schama had a reputation as a specialist in Dutch history and this chunky volume draws on a huge variety of archive sources. Also by Schama, *Patriots and Liberators: Revolution in the Netherlands 1780–1813* focuses on one of the less familiar periods of Dutch history and is particularly good on the Batavian Republic set up in the Netherlands under French auspices. Both are heavyweight tomes; leftists might well find Schama too reactionary by half.

Andrew Wheatcroft *The Habsburgs*. Enjoyable and well-researched trawl through the family's history, from eleventh-century beginnings to its eclipse at the end of World War I.

Geoffrey Wootten *Waterloo 1815*. About one third of the length of Hibbert's *Waterloo*, this 96-page book focuses on the battle, providing a clear, thorough and interesting account.

World War I

★ **William Allison & John Fairley** *The Monocled Mutineer*. An antidote to all those tales of soldiers dying for their country in World War I, this little book recounts the story of one Percy Toplis, a Nottinghamshire lad turned soldier, mutineer, racketeer and conman who was finally shot by the police in 1920. Intriguing account of the large-scale mutiny that broke out along the British line in 1917.

Martin Gilbert *First World War*. Highly regarded account of the war focused on the battles and experiences of the British army. Very thorough – at 640 pages.

B.H. Liddell Hart (ed) *The Letters of Private Wheeler*. A veteran of World War I, Liddell Hart writes with panache and clarity, editing up the letters penned by the eponymous private as he fought Napoleon and the French across a fair slice of Europe. Wheeler fought at Waterloo, but the section on the battle is surprisingly brief. As a whole, the letters are a delight, a witty insight into the living conditions and attitudes of Wellington's infantry. Includes an excellent section on the Battle of the Bulge.

★ **A.J.P. Taylor,** *The First World War: An Illustrated History*. First published in 1963, this superbly written and pertinently illustrated history offers a penetrating analysis of how the war started and why it went on for so long, including a penetrating insight into the events at the Ypres Salient. Many of Taylor's deductions were controversial at the time, but such was the power of his arguments that much of what he said is now mainstream history.

Art and architecture

★ **Ulrike Becks-Malorny** *Ensor*.
Eminently readable and extensively illustrated account of James Ensor's life and art. Very competitively priced too.

Kristin Lohse Belkin *Rubens*. Too long for its own good, this book details Rubens' spectacularly successful career both as artist and diplomat. Belkin is particularly thorough in her discussions of technique and the workings of his workshop. Extensive reference is made to Rubens' letters. Excellent illustrations.

Robin Blake *Anthony van Dyck*. Whether or not van Dyck justifies 448 pages is a moot point, but he did have an interesting life and certainly thumped out a fair few paintings. This volume explores every artistic nook and cranny.

David Dernie *Victor Horta*. Perhaps surprisingly, this is the only readily recommendable book dedicated to that pioneer of Art Nouveau, Victor Horta (see p.105). It competently describes his milieu and lingering on his architectural legacy, but it does cost an arm and a leg.

Max J. Friedlander *From Van Eyck to Bruegel* (o/p). Scholarly and thoughtful account of the early Flemish masters, though stylistically and factually (in the light of modern research) beginning to show its age.

R.H. Fuchs *Dutch Painting*. Thoughtful and well-researched title which tracks through the history of its subject from the fifteenth century onwards.

R.H. Fuchs et al. *Flemish and Dutch Painting (from Van Gogh, Ensor, Magritte and Mondrian to Contemporary)*. Excellent, lucid account giving an overview of the development of Flemish and Dutch painting.

Suzi Gablik *Magritte*. Suzi Gablik lived in Magritte's house for six months in the 1960s and this personal contact informs the text, which is lucid and thoughtful. Most of the illustrations are in black and white. At 208 pages, much longer than Hammacher (see below).

Walter S. Gibson *Bosch*. Everything you wanted to know about Bosch, his paintings and his late fifteenth-century milieu. Superbly illustrated. Also, try the beautifully illustrated *Bruegel*, which takes a detailed look at the artist with nine well-argued chapters investigating the components of Pieter Bruegel the Elder's art.

Paul Haesaerts *James Ensor* (o/p). It may weigh a ton, but this excellent volume is an outstanding exploration of the work of this often neglected, Ostend-born painter. The illustrations and photos are well chosen.

★ **A.M. Hammacher** *René Magritte*. Part of Thames & Hudson's outstanding "Masters of Art" series, this is a beautifully illustrated, detailed examination of Magritte's life, times and artistic output. Very competitively priced too.

Craig Harbison *Jan van Eyck: the Play of Realism*. Not much is known about van Eyck, but Harbison has done his best to root out every detail. The text is accompanied by illustrations of all of Eyck's major paintings.

Bruce McCall *Sit!: The Dog Portraits of Thierry Poncelet*. This weird and wonderful book features the work of the Belgian Thierry Poncelet, who raids flea markets and antique shops for ancestral portraits, then restores them and paints dogs' heads over the original faces. Uuummmm.

Melissa McQuillan *Van Gogh*. Another in the Thames & Hudson "Masters of Art" series, this is an extensive, in-depth look at van Gogh's paintings as well as his life and times.

Alastair Smart *The Renaissance and Mannerism outside Italy* (o/p). A very readable survey that includes lengthy chapters on van Eyck and his contemporaries, their successors, Bosch and Bruegel, and the later, more Mannerist-inclined painters of the Low Countries. A fine introduction to an extraordinary period.

Dirk de Vos *Rogier van der Weyden*. One of the most talented and influential of the Flemish Primitives, Weyden was the official city painter to Brussels in the middle of the fifteenth century. This 400-page volume details everything known about him and carries illustrations of all his works – but then no more than you would expect from such an expensive tome.

Peter Weiermair *Eros & Death: Belgian Symbolism*. Great title and an original book exploring the nature of Belgian symbolism, with reference to drawings, prints, paintings and sculptures. Artists featured include James Ensor and Felician Rops.

★ **Mariët Westerman** *The Art of the Dutch Republic 1585–1718* (o/p). Most of Belgium's better art musums have a good healthy sample of Dutch painting. This fascinating, excellently written and well-illustrated book tackles its subject by theme and is absolutely enthralling.

Christopher White *Peter Paul Rubens: Man and Artist* (o/p). A beautifully illustrated introduction to both Rubens' work and social milieu.

Literature

Mark Bles *A Child at War*. This powerful book describes the tribulations of Hortense Daman, a Belgian girl who joined the Resistance at the tender age of fifteen. Betrayed to the Gestapo, Daman was sent to the Ravensbruck concentration camp, where she was used in medical experiments, but remarkably survived. This is her story, though the book would have benefited from some editorial pruning.

Charlotte and Emily Brontë (ed. Sue Lonoff) *The Belgian Essays*. The Brontë sisters left their native Yorkshire for the first time in 1842 to make a trip to Brussels. Charlotte returned to Brussels the following year. This handsome volume reproduces the twenty-eight essays they penned (in French) during their journey and provides the English translation opposite. A delightful read; particular highlights are "The Butterfly", "The Caterpillar" and "The Death of Napoleon".

★ **Hugo Claus** *The Sorrow of Belgium* (US). Born in Bruges in 1929, Claus is generally regarded as Belgium's foremost Flemish-language novelist, and this is generally regarded as his best novel. It charts the growing maturity of a young boy living in Flanders under the Nazi occupation. Claus' style is somewhat dense to say the least, but the book gets to grips with the guilt, bigotry and mistrust of the period, and caused a minor uproar when it was first published in the early 1980s. His *Swordfish* (Dufour) is a story of an isolated village rife with ethnic and religious tensions, the effects of which prove too much for a boy in his spiral down to madness. Another work, *Desire*, is the strange and disconcerting tale of two drinking buddies, who, on an impulse, abandon small-town Belgium for Las Vegas, where both of them start to unravel.

Michael Frayn *Headlong*. Subtle, gripping yarn in which the protagonist, Martin Clay, an English art historian, stumbles across – or thinks he does – a "lost" Flemish medieval painting of immense value. But he doesn't own it and the lies – and moral slide – begin.

⭐ **Robert Graves** *Goodbye To All That*. Written in 1929, this is the classic story of life in the trenches. Bleak and painful memories of First World War army service written by Graves, a wounded survivor.

Alan Hollinghurst *The Folding Star*. Not a Belgian novel, but the British writer Hollinghurst's evocation of a thinly disguised Bruges, in a compelling novel of sex, mystery and obsession. The enthusiastic descriptions of gay male sexual encounters make this a climactic book in more ways than one.

Barbara Kingsolver *The Poisonwood Bible: A Novel*. In 1959, an American Baptist missionary and his family set out to convert souls in the jungly depths of the Belgian Congo. They are unprepared for the multiple disasters that befall them – from great, stinging ants to irregular Congolese soldiers.

Amelie Nothomb *Loving Sabotage*. English language translations of modern Belgian writers are a rarity, but Nothomb, one of Belgium's most popular writers, has made the linguistic leap. This particular novel deals with the daughter of a diplomat stationed in Peking in the 1970s, a rites of passage story with a Maoist backdrop. Her *The Stranger Next Door*, an account of weird and disconcering happenings in the Belgian countryside, is perhaps Nothomb's most successful translated work. *Fear and Trembling* (US only) is a sharply observed tale of the shoddy treatment meted out to a young Western businesswoman in a big corporation in Tokyo.

Jean Ray *Malpertuis* (UK). This spine-chilling Gothic novel was written by a Belgian in 1943. It's set in Belgium, too, where the suffocating Catholicism of the Inquisition provides a perfect backcloth.

⭐ **Georges Rodenbach** *Bruges la Morte*. First published in 1892, this slim and subtly evocative novel is all about love and obsession – or rather a highly stylised, decadent view of it. It's credited with starting the craze for visiting Bruges, the "dead city" where the action unfolds.

⭐ **Siegfried Sassoon** *The Memoirs of an Infantry Officer*. Sassoon's moving and painfully honest account of his experiences in the trenches of the First World War. A classic, and infinitely readable. Also Siegfried Sassoon's *Diaries 1915–1918* (o/p).

Émile Zola *Germinal*. First published in 1885, *Germinal* exposed the harsh conditions of the coal mines of northeast France. It was also a rallying call to action with the protagonist, Étienne Lantier, organizing a strike. A vivid, powerful work, Zola had a detailed knowledge of the mines – how they were run and worked – and makes passing reference to the coal fields of southern Belgium, where conditions and working practices were identical. This novel inspired a whole generation of Belgian radicals.

Language

language

Flemish and French

Throughout the northern part of Belgium, in the provinces of East and West Flanders, Antwerp, Limburg and Flemish Brabant, the principal language is Dutch, which is spoken in a variety of distinctive dialects commonly (if inaccurately) lumped together as Flemish. Flemish-speakers have equal language rights in the capital, Brussels, where the majority of Belgians speak a dialect of French known as Walloon, as they do in the country's southern provinces, known logically enough as Wallonia. Walloon is almost identical to French, and if you've any knowlege of the language, you'll be readily understood. French is also the most widely spoken language in Luxembourg, along with German – although most Luxembourgers also speak a local and distinctive German dialect, Lëtzebuergesch (see p.376).

Flemish

Flemish, or Dutch, is a Germanic language – the word "Dutch" itself is a corruption of Deutsche, a label inaccurately given by English sailors in the seventeenth century. If you know any German you'll spot many similarities with Dutch, though the Dutch – and the Flemish – are at pains to stress the differences.

Most Flemish-speakers, particularly in the main towns and in the tourist industry, speak English to varying degrees of excellence. Indeed, Flemish-speakers have a seemingly natural talent for languages, and your attempts at speaking theirs may be met with bewilderment – though this can have as much to do with your pronunciation (Dutch is very difficult to get right) as their surprise that you're making an effort. The *Rough Guide Dutch Dictionary Phrasebook* has a perfectly adequate dictionary section and a menu reader; it also provides a useful introduction to grammar and pronunciation.

Consonants

Double-consonant combinations generally keep their separate sounds in Flemish – **kn**, for example, is never like the English "knight". Note also the following consonants and consonant combinations:

v like the English *f* in far
w like the *v* in vat
j like the initial sound of yellow
ch and **g** are considerably harder than in English, enunciated much further back in the throat; in Antwerp at least, where the pronunciation is particularly coarse, there's no real English equivalent. They become softer the further south you go, where they're more like the Scottish loch.
ng is as in bri**ng**
nj as in o**nio**n

Doubling the letter lengthens the vowel sound.

a is like the English apple

aa like cart

e like let

ee like late

o as in pop

oo in pope

u is like the French tu if preceded by a consonant; it's like wood if followed by a consonant

uu the French tu

au and ou like how

ei and ij as in fine, though this varies strongly from region to region; sometimes it can sound more like lane.

oe as in soon

eu is like the diphthong in the French leur

ui is the hardest Dutch diphthong of all, pronounced like how but much further forward in the mouth, with lips pursed (as if to say "oo").

French

L

LANGUAGE

French isn't a particularly easy language, despite the number of words shared with English, but learning the bare essentials is not difficult and makes all the difference. Even just saying "Bonjour, Madame/Monsieur" when you go into a shop and then pointing will usually get you a smile and helpful service. People working in hotels, restaurants etc, almost always speak some English and tend to use it if you're struggling – be grateful, not amused.

Differentiating words is the initial problem in understanding spoken French – it's very hard to get people to slow down. If, as a last resort, you get them to write it down, you'll probably find you know half the words anyway. Of the available **phrasebooks**, Rough Guide's own *French Dictionary Phrasebook* should sort you out better than most.

Consonants

Consonants are pronounced much as in English, except:

ch is always **sh**

c is **s**

h is silent

th is the same as **t**

ll is like the y in yes

w is **v**, and

r is growled (or rolled).

Vowels

These are the hardest sounds to get right. Roughly:

a as in hat

e as in get

é between get and gate

è between get and gut

eu like the **u** in hurt

i as in machine

o as in hot

o, au as in over

ou as in food

u as in a pursed-lip version of use

More awkward are the combinations below when they occur at the ends of words, or are followed by consonants other than *n* or *m*:

in/im like the *an* in anxious

an/am, en/em as in don when said with a nasal accent

on/om like don said by someone with a heavy cold

un/um like the *u* in understand.

Useful words and phrases

In the vocabulary lists below, each English phrase is followed by its **Flemish** and **French** equivalent, in that order.

Greetings and civilities

please - **alstublieft** - *s'il vous plaît*
(no) thank you - **(nee) dank u/bedankt** - *(non) merci*
hello - **hallo/dag** - *bonjour*
how are you? - **hoe gaat het met u?** - *comment allez-vous?/ça va?*
good morning - **goedemorgen** - *bonjour*

good afternoon - **goedemiddag** - *bonjour*
good evening - **goedenavond** - *bonsoir*
good night - **goedenacht** - *bonne nuit*
goodbye - **tot ziens** - *au revoir*
see you later - **tot straks** - *à bientôt*
sorry - **sorry** - *pardon, Madame, Monsieur/je m'excuse*

Basics terms and phrases

yes - **ja** - *oui*
no - **nee** - *non*
do you speak English? - **spreekt u Engels?** - *parlez-vous l'anglais?*
I (don't) understand - **ik begrijp het (niet)** - *je (ne) comprends (pas)*
women - **vrouwen** - *femmes*
men - **mannen** - *hommes*
men's/women's toilets - **heren/dames** - *hommes/femmes*
children - **kinderen** - *enfants*
when? - **wanneer?** - *quand?*
I want . . . - **ik wil . . .** - *je veux . . .*
I don't want - **ik wil niet . . . (+verb)** or **ik wil geen . . . (+noun)** - *je ne veux pas*
OK/agreed - **OK** - *d'accord*

good - **goed** - *bon*
bad - **slecht** - *mauvais*
big - **groot** - *grand*
small - **klein** - *petit*
open - **open** - *ouvert*
closed - **gesloten** - *fermé*
push - **duwen** - *pousser*
pull - **trekken** - *tirer*
new - **nieuw** - *nouveau*
old - **oud** - *vieux*
hot - **heet** - *chaud*
cold - **koud** - *froid*
with - **met** - *avec*
without - **zonder** - *sans*
a lot - **veel** - *beaucoup*
a little - **klein** - *peu*

Money

how much is . . . ? - **wat kost . . . ?** - *c'est combien . . . ?*
cheap - **goedkoop** - *bon marché*
expensive - **duur** - *cher*
post office - **postkantoor** - *la poste*

stamp(s) - **postzegel(s)** - *timbre(s)*
money exchange - **wisselkantoor** - *bureau de change*
cashier - **kassa** - *la caisse*
ticket office - **loket** - *le guichet*

Getting around

how do I get to . . .? - **hoe kom ik in. . .?** - *comment est-ce que je peux arriver à . . . ?*
where is . . . ? - **waar is. . . ?** - *où est . . . ?*
how far is it to . . . ? - **hoe ver is het naar . . ?** - *combien y a-t-il jusqu'à . . . ?*
far - **ver** - *loin*
near - **dichtbij** - *près*
left - **links** - *à gauche*

right - **rechts** - *à droite*
straight ahead - **recht uit gaan** - *tout droit*
behind - **achter** - *derrière*
here - **hier** - *ici*
there - **daar** - *là*
platform - **spoor** - *quai*
through traffic only - **doorgang verkeer** - *voie de traversée*

L

LANGUAGE

Days and times

Monday - **Maandag** - *lundi*
Tuesday - **Dinsdag** - *mardi*
Wednesday - **Woensdag** - *mercredi*
Thursday - **Donderdag** - *jeudi*
Friday - **Vrijdag** - *vendredi*
Saturday - **Zaterdag** - *samedi*
Sunday - **Zondag** - *dimanche*
morning - **de morgen** - *le matin*
afternoon - **de middag** - *l'après-midi*
evening - **de avond** - *le soir*
night - **de nacht** - *la nuit*
yesterday - **gisteren** - *hier*

today - **vandaag** - *aujourd'hui*
tomorrow - **morgen** - *demain*
tomorrow morning - **morgenochtend** - *demain matin*
minute - **minuut** - *minute*
hour - **uur** - *heure*
day - **dag** - *jour*
week - **week** - *semaine*
month - **maand** - *mois*
year - **jaar** - *année*
now - **nu** - *maintenant*
later - **later** - *plus tard*

Numbers

0 - **nul** - *zéro*
1 - **een** - *un*
2 - **twee** - *deux*
3 - **drie** - *trois*
4 - **vier** - *quatre*
5 - **vijf** - *cinq*
6 - **zes** - *six*
7 - **zeven** - *sept*
8 - **acht** - *huit*
9 - **negen** - *neuf*
10 - **tien** - *dix*
11 - **elf** - *onze*
12 - **twaalf** - *douze*
13 - **dertien** - *treize*
14 - **veertien** - *quatorze*
15 - **vijftien** - *quinze*
16 - **zestien** - *seize*
17 - **zeventien** - *dix-sept*

18 - **achttien** - *dix-huit*
19 - **negentien** - *dix-neuf*
20 - **twintig** - *vingt*
21 - **een en twintig** - *vingt-et-un*
30 - **dertig** - *trente*
40 - **veertig** - *quarante*
50 - **vijftig** - *cinquante*
60 - **zestig** - *soixante*
70 - **zeventig** - *soixante-dix (local usage is septante)*
80 - **tachtig** - *quatre-vingts*
90 - **negentig** - *quatre-vingt-dix (local usage is nonante)*
100 - **honderd** - *cent*
101 - **honderd een** - *cent-et-un*
200 - **twee honderd** - *deux cents*
500 - **vijf honderd** - *cinq cents*
1000 - **duizend** - *mille*

A Flemish food and drink glossary

Basic terms and ingredients

appelmoes - apple purée
boter - butter
brood - bread
broodje - sandwich/roll
doorbakken - well done
dranken - drinks
droog - dry (of alcoholic drinks)
eieren - eggs
groenten - vegetables
half doorbakken - medium done
Hollandse saus - Hollandaise sauce
honing - honey

hoofdgerechten - entrées
kaas - cheese
koud - cold
nagerechten - desserts
met ijs - with ice
met slagroom - with whipped cream
peper - pepper
pindakaas - peanut butter
proost! - cheers!
sla/salade - salad
smeerkaas - cheese spread
stokbrood - french bread

suiker – sugar
vis – fish
vlees – meat
voorgerechten – appetizers, hors d'oeuvres

vruchten – fruit
warm – hot
zoet – sweet
zout – salt

Cooking methods

gebakken – fried/baked
gebraden – roasted
gekookt – boiled
gegrild – grilled

geraspt – grated
gerookt – smoked
gestoofd – stewed

Meat and poultry

biefstuk (hollandse) – steak
eend – duck
fricandeau – roast pork
fricandel – a frankfurter-like sausage
gehakt – ground meat
ham – ham
hutsepot – beef stew with vegetables
kalkoen – turkey
kalfsvlees – veal

karbonade – chop
kip – chicken
kroket – spiced meat in breadcrumbs
lamsvlees – lamb
lever – liver
rookvlees – smoked beef
spek – bacon
worst – sausages

Fish and seafood

forel – trout
garnalen – shrimp
haring – herring
haringsalade – herring salad
kabeljauw – cod
makreel – mackerel

mosselen – mussels
paling – eel
schol – flounder
schelvis – shellfish
tong – sole
zalm – salmon

Vegetables and grains

aardappelen – potatoes
bloemkool – cauliflower
boerenkool – kale
bonen – beans
champignons – mushrooms
erwten – peas
gerst – semolina
knoflook – garlic

komkommer – cucumber
prei – leek
rijst – rice
sla – salad, lettuce
tomaat – tomato
uien – onions
wortelen – carrots
zuurkool – sauerkraut

Fruit and nuts

aardbei – strawberry
amandel – almond
appel – apple
citroen – lemon
druif – grape
framboos – raspberry
hazelnoot – hazelnut

kers – cherry
kokosnoot – coconut
peer – pear
perzik – peach
pinda – peanut
pruim – plum/prune

Appetizers and snacks

erwtensoep/snert - thick pea soup with bacon or sausage
huzarensalade - egg salad
patats/frites - french fries
soep - soup

uitsmijter - ham or cheese with eggs on bread
koffietafel - a light midday meal of cold meats, cheese, bread and perhaps soup

Flemish specialities

hutsepot - a winter-warmer consisting of various bits of beef and pork (including pigs' trotters and ears) casseroled with turnips, celery, leeks and parsnips
karbonaden - cubes of beef marinated in beer and cooked with herbs and onions
konijn met pruimen - rabbit with prunes
paling in 't groen - eel braised in a green (usually spinach) sauce with herbs

stoemp - mashed potato mixed with vegetable and/or meat purée
stoverij - stewed beef and offal (especially liver and kidneys), slowly tenderized in dark beer and served with a slice of bread covered in mustard
waterzooi - a delicious, filling soup-cum-stew, made with either chicken (van kip) or fish (van riviervis)

Sweets and desserts

appelgebak - apple tart or cake
drop - liquorice, available in sweet or salty varieties
gebak - pastry
ijs - ice cream
koekjes - cookies
oliebollen - doughnuts

pannekoeken - pancakes
poffertjes - small pancakes, fritters
(slag) room - (whipped) cream
speculaas - spice- and honey-flavoured biscuit
stroopwafels - waffles
vla - custard

Drinks

anijsmelk - aniseed-flavoured warm milk
appelsap - apple juice
bessenjenever - blackcurrant gin
chocomel - chocolate milk
citroenjenever - lemon gin
frisdranken - soda
jenever - Dutch gin
karnemelk - buttermilk
koffie - coffee
koffie verkeerd - coffee with warm milk

kopstoot - beer with a jenever chaser
melk - milk
pils - Dutch beer
sinaasappelsap - orange juice
thee - tea
tomatensap - tomato juice
vieux - Dutch brandy
vruchtensap - fruit juice
(wit/rood/rose) wijn - (white/red/rosé) wine

A French food and drink glossary

Basic terms and ingredients

á point - medium done
beurre - butter
bien cuit - well done
chaud - hot
crème fraîche - sour cream

dessert - dessert
escargots - snails
frappé - iced
fromage - cheese
froid - cold

gibiers – game
hors d'oeuvre – starters
légumes – vegetables
oeufs – eggs
pain – bread
poisson – fish
poivre – pepper

saignant – rare
salade – salad
sel – salt
sucre – sugar/sweet (taste)
tourte – tart or pie
tranche – slice
viande – meat

Cooking methods

au four – baked
bouilli – boiled
frit/friture – fried/deep fried
fumé – smoked
grillé – grilled

mijoté – stewed
pané – breaded
rôti – roast
sauté – lightly cooked in butter

Meat and poultry

agneau – lamb
bifteck – steak
boeuf – beef
canard – duck
cheval – horsemeat
cuisson – leg of lamb
côtelettes – cutlets
dindon – turkey

foie – liver
gigot – leg of venison
jambon – ham
lard – bacon
porc – pork
poulet – chicken
saucisse – sausage
veau – veal

Fish and seafood

anchois – anchovies
anguilles – eels
carrelet – plaice
cervettes roses – prawns
hareng – herring
lotte de mer – monkfish

maquereau – mackerel
morue – cod
moules – mussels
saumon – salmon
sole – sole
truite – trout

Vegetables and grains

ail – garlic
asperges – asparagus
carottes – carrots
champignons – mushrooms
choufleur – cauliflower
concombre – cucumber
genièvre – juniper

laitue – lettuce
oignons – onions
petits pois – peas
poireau – leek
pommes (de terre) – potatoes
riz – rice
tomate – tomato

Fruit and nuts

amandes – almonds
ananas – pineapple
cacahouète – peanut
cérises – cherries
citron – lemon

fraises – strawberries
framboises – raspberries
marrons – chestnuts
noisette – hazelnut
pamplemousse – grapefruit

L

LANGUAGE

poire - pear
pomme - apple
prune - plum

pruneau - prune
raisins - grapes

Snacks

un sandwich/une baguette . . . - a sandwich
. . .
  de jambon - with ham
  de fromage - with cheese
  de saucisson - with sausage
  à l'ail - with garlic
  au poivre - with pepper
croque-monsieur - grilled cheese and ham
  sandwich
oeufs . . . - eggs . . .
  au plat - fried eggs
  à la coque - boiled eggs
  durs - hard-boiled eggs

brouillés - scrambled eggs
omelette . . . - omelette . . .
  nature - plain
  au fromage - with cheese
salade de . . . - salad of . . .
  tomates - tomatoes
  concombres - cucumbers
crêpes . . . - pancakes . . .
  au sucre - with sugar
  au citron - with lemon
  au miel - with honey
  à la confiture - with jam

Soups and starters

assiette anglaise - plate of cold meats
bisque - shellfish soup
bouillabaisse - fish soup from Marseilles
bouillon - broth or stock

consommé - clear soup
crudités - raw vegetables with dressing
potage - thick soup, usually vegetable

Walloon and Brussels specialities

carbonnades de porc Bruxelloise - pork
  with a tarragon and tomato sauce
chicorées gratinés au four - chicory with
  ham and cheese
fricadelles à la bière - meatballs in beer
fricassée Liègeois - fried eggs, bacon and
  sausage or blood pudding

le marcassin - young wild boar, served either
  cold and sliced or hot with vegetables
pâté de faisan - pheasant pâté
truite à l'Ardennaise - trout cooked in a wine
  sauce

Sweets and desserts

crêpes - pancakes
crêpes suzettes - thin pancakes with orange
  juice and liqueur
glace - ice cream

madeleine - small, shell-shaped sponge cake
parfait - frozen mousse, sometimes ice cream
petits fours - bite-sized cakes or pastries

Drinks

bière - beer
café - coffee
eaux de vie - spirits distilled from various fruits
jenever - Dutch/Flemish gin
lait - milk
orange/citron - pressé fresh orange/lemon juice
thé - tea

vin . . . - wine . . .
  rouge - red
  blanc - white
  brut - very dry
  sec - dry
  demi-sec - sweet
  doux - very sweet

Glossary

Flemish terms

Abdij Abbey or group of monastic buildings.

Beiaard Carillon (ie a set of tuned church bells, either operated by an automatic mechanism or played by a keyboard).

Begijnhof Convent occupied by beguines (*begijns*), ie members of a sisterhood living as nuns but without vows, retaining the right of return to the secular world.

Belfort Belfry.

Beurs Stock exchange.

Botermarkt Butter market.

Brug Bridge.

Burgher Member of the upper or mercantile classes of a town, usually with certain civic powers.

Fiets Bicycle.

Fietspad Bicycle path.

Gasthof Inn.

Gasthuis Hospital.

Gemeente Municipal; eg *gemeentehuis* – town hall.

Gerechtshof Law Courts.

Gilde Guild.

Gracht Urban canal.

Groentenmarkt Vegetable market.

Grote markt Central town square and the heart of most north Belgian communities, normally still the site of weekly markets.

Hal Hall.

Hof Court(yard).

Huis House.

Ingang Entrance.

Jeugdherberg Youth hostel.

Kaai Quay or wharf.

Kapel Chapel.

Kasteel Castle.

Kerk Church; eg Grote Kerk – the principal church of the town; Onze Lieve Vrouwekerk – church dedicated to the Virgin Mary.

Koning King.

Koningin Queen.

Koninklijk Royal.

Korenmarkt Corn market.

Kunst Art.

Kursaal Casino.

Lakenhalle Cloth hall. The building in medieval weaving towns where cloth would be weighed, graded, stored and sold.

Luchthaven Airport.

Markt Marketplace.

Molen Windmill.

Ommegang Procession.

Paleis Palace.

Polder Low-lying land that has been reclaimed from the sea or a river.

Poort Gate.

Postbus Post-office box.

Plaats A square or open space.

Plein A square or open space.

Rijk State.

Schepenzaal Aldermen's Hall.

Schouwburg Theatre.

Schone Kunsten Fine arts.

Sierkunst Decorative arts.

Spoor Track (as in railway) – trains arrive and depart on track (as distinct from platform) numbers.

Stadhuis The most common word for a town hall.

Station (Railway or bus) station.

Stedelijk Civic, municipal.

Steen Fortress.

Stitching Institute or foundation.

Toren Tower.

Tuin Garden.

Uitgang Exit.

Vleeshuis Meat market.

Volkskunde Folklore.

L

French terms

Abbaye Abbey or group of monastic buildings.
Aéroport Airport.
Auberge de la jeunesse Youth hostel.
Beaux arts Fine arts.
Beffroi Belfry.
Béguinage Convent occupied by beguines, ie members of a sisterhood living as nuns but without vows and with the right of return to the secular world.
Bourse Stock exchange.
Chapelle Chapel.
Château Mansion, country house, or castle.
Cour Court(yard).
Couvent Convent, monastery.
Dégustation Tasting (wine or food).
Donjon Castle keep.
Église Church.
Entrée Entrance.
Étage Floor (of a museum etc).
Fermeture Closing period.
Fouilles Archeological excavations.
Gare Railway station.
Gîte d'étape Dormitory-style lodgings situated in relatively remote parts of the country which can house anywhere between ten and one hundred people per establishment.

Grand-place Central town square and the heart of most French communities, normally still the site of weekly markets.
Halle aux draps Cloth hall. The building in medieval weaving towns where cloth would be weighed, graded, stored and sold.
Halle aux viandes Meat market.
Halles Covered, central food market.
Hôpital Hospital.
Hôtel Hotel or mansion.
Hôtel de ville Town hall.
Jardin Garden.
Jours feriés Public holidays.
Maison House.
Marché Market.
Moulin Windmill.
Municipal Civic, municipal.
Musée Museum.
Notre Dame Our Lady.
Palais Palace.
Place Square, marketplace.
Pont Bridge.
Porte Gateway.
Quai Quay, or station platform.
Quartier District of a town.
Sortie Exit.
Syndicat d'initiative Tourist office.
Tour Tower.
Trésor Treasury.

Art and architectural terms

Ambulatory Covered passage around the outer edge of the choir in the chancel of a church.
Apse Semicircular protrusion at (usually) the east end of a church.
Art Deco Geometrical style of art and architecture popular in the 1930s.
Art Nouveau Style of art, architecture and design based on highly stylized vegetal forms. Popular in the early part of the twentieth century.
Baroque The art and architecture of the Counter-Reformation, dating from around 1600 onwards, and distinguished by extreme ornateness, exuberance and complex but harmonious spatial arrangement of interiors.
Basilica Catholic church with honorific privileges.

Carillon A set of tuned church bells, either operated by an automatic mechanism or played by a keyboard.
Carolingian Dynasty founded by Charlemagne; mid-eighth to early tenth century. Also refers to art, etc, of the time.
Caryatid A sculptured female figure used as a column.
Chancel The eastern part of a church, often separated from the nave by a screen (see "rood screen" below). Contains the choir and ambulatory.
Classical Architectural style incorporating Greek and Roman elements – pillars, domes, colonnades etc – at its height in the seventeenth century and revived, as **Neoclassical**, in the nineteenth century.

L

LANGUAGE

Clerestory Upper storey of a church, incorporating the windows.

Flamboyant Florid form of Gothic.

Fresco Wall painting – durable through application to wet plaster.

Gable The triangular upper portion of a wall – decorative or supporting a roof.

Gallo-Roman Period of Roman occupation of Gaul, from the first to the fourth century AD.

Genre painting In the seventeenth century the term "genre painting" applied to everything from animal paintings and still lifes through to historical works and landscapes. In the eighteenth century, the term came only to be applied to scenes of everyday life.

Gothic Architectural style of the thirteenth to sixteenth centuries, characterized by pointed arches, rib vaulting, flying buttresses and a general emphasis on verticality.

Merovingian Dynasty ruling France and parts of Belgium from sixth to mid-eighth centuries. Refers also to art, etc, of the period.

Misericord Ledge on choir stall on which occupant can be supported while standing; often carved with secular subjects (bottoms were not thought worthy of religious ones).

Mosan Adjective applied to the lands bordering the River Meuse – hence Mosan metalwork.

Nave Main body of a church.

Neoclassical Architectural style derived from Greek and Roman elements – pillars, domes, colonnades etc – popular in the Low Countries during and after French rule in the early nineteenth century.

Renaissance The period of European history marking the end of the medieval period and the rise of the modern world; defined, among many criteria, by an increase in classical scholarship, geographical discovery, the rise of secular values and the growth of individualism. Begins in Italy in the fourteenth century. Also the art and architecture of the period.

Retable Altarpiece.

Rococo Highly florid, light and graceful eighteenth-century style of architecture, painting and interior design, forming the last phase of Baroque.

Rood loft Gallery (or space) on top of a rood screen.

Rood screen Decorative screen separating the nave from the chancel.

Romanesque Early medieval architecture distinguished by squat forms, rounded arches and naive sculpture.

Stucco Marble-based plaster used to embellish ceilings etc.

Transept Arms of a cross-shaped church, placed at ninety degrees to nave and chancel.

Triptych Carved or painted work on three panels. Often used as an altarpiece.

Tympanum Sculpted, usually recessed, panel above a door.

Vauban Seventeenth-century military architect whose fortresses still stand all over Europe and the Low Countries; hence the adjective Vaubanesque.

Vault An arched ceiling or roof.

Index

and small print

Index

Map entries are in colour

I

INDEX

C

D

Twenty years of Rough Guides

In the summer of 1981, Mark Ellingham, Rough Guides' founder, knocked out the first guide on a typewriter, with a group of friends. Mark had been travelling in Greece after university, and couldn't find a guidebook that really answered his needs. There were heavyweight cultural guides on the one hand – good on museums and classical sites but not on beaches and tavernas – and on the other hand student manuals that were so caught up with how to save money that they lost sight of the country's significance beyond its role as a place for a cool vacation. None of the guides began to address Greece as a country, with its natural and human environment, its politics and its contemporary life.

Having no urgent reason to return home, Mark decided to write his own guide. It was a guide to Greece that tried to combine some erudition and insight with a thoroughly practical approach to travellers' needs. Scrupulously researched listings of places to stay, eat and drink were matched by careful attention to detail on everything from Homer to Greek music, from classical sites to national parks and from nude beaches to monasteries. Back in London, Mark and his friends got their Rough Guide accepted by a farsighted commissioning editor at the publisher Routledge and it came out in 1982.

The Rough Guide to Greece was a student scheme that became a publishing phenomenon. The immediate success of the book – shortlisted for the Thomas Cook award – spawned a series that rapidly covered dozens of countries. The Rough Guides found a ready market among backpackers and budget travellers, but soon acquired a much broader readership that included older and less impecunious visitors. Readers relished the guides' wit and inquisitiveness as much as the enthusiastic, critical approach that acknowledges everyone wants value for money – but not at any price.

Rough Guides soon began supplementing the "rougher" information – the hostel and low-budget listings – with the kind of detail that independent-minded travellers on any budget might expect. These days, the guides – distributed worldwide by the Penguin group – include recommendations spanning the range from shoestring to luxury, and cover more than 200 destinations around the globe. Our growing team of authors, many of whom come to Rough Guides initially as outstandingly good letter-writers telling us about their travels, are spread all over the world, particularly in Europe, the USA and Australia. As well as the travel guides, Rough Guides publishes a series of dictionary phrasebooks covering two dozen major languages, an acclaimed series of music guides running the gamut from Classical to World Music, a series of music CDs in association with World Music Network, and a range of reference books on topics as diverse as the internet, pregnancy and unexplained phenomena. Visit **www.roughguides.com** to see what's cooking.

Rough Guide credits

Text editor: Richard Lim
Series editor: Mark Ellingham
Editorial: Martin Dunford, Jonathan Buckley, Kate Berens, Ann-Marie Shaw, Helena Smith, Judith Bamber, Orla Duane, Olivia Swift, Ruth Blackmore, Geoff Howard, Claire Saunders, Gavin Thomas, Alexander Mark Rogers, Polly Thomas, Joe Staines, Duncan Clark, Peter Buckley, Lucy Ratcliffe, Clifton Wilkinson, Alison Murchie, Matthew Teller, Andrew Dickson, Fran Sandham (UK); Andrew Rosenberg, Stephen Timblin, Yuki Takagaki, Richard Koss, Hunter Slaton, Julie Feiner (US)
Production: Susanne Hillen, Andy Hilliard, Link Hall, Helen Prior, Julia Bovis, Michelle Draycott, Katie Pringle, Zoë Nobes,
Rachel Holmes, Andy Turner
Cartography: Melissa Baker, Maxine Repath, Ed Wright, Katie Lloyd-Jones
Cover art direction: Louise Boulton
Picture research: Sharon Martins, Mark Thomas
Online: Kelly Cross, Anja Mutic-Blessing, Jennifer Gold, Audra Epstein, Suzanne Welles, Cree Lawson (US)
Finance: John Fisher, Gary Singh, Edward Downey, Mark Hall, Tim Bill
Marketing & Publicity: Richard Trillo, Niki Smith, David Wearn, Chloë Roberts, Demelza Dallow, Claire Southern (UK); Simon Carloss, David Wechsler, Kathleen Rushforth (US)
Administration: Tania Hummel, Julie Sanderson

Publishing information

This third edition published November 2002 by **Rough Guides Ltd**,
80 Strand, London WC2R ORL
Penguin Putnam, Inc., 375 Hudson Street, NY 10014, USA
Distributed by the Penguin Group
Penguin Books Ltd,
80 Strand, London WC2R ORL
Penguin Putnam, Inc.,
375 Hudson Street, NY 10014, USA
Penguin Books Australia Ltd,
487 Maroondah Highway, PO Box 257, Ringwood, Victoria 3134, Australia
Penguin Books Canada Ltd,
10 Alcorn Avenue, Toronto, Ontario, Canada M4V 1E4
Penguin Books (NZ) Ltd,
182–190 Wairau Road, Auckland 10, New Zealand
Typeset in Bembo and Helvetica to an original design by Henry Iles.

Printed and bound in China

©Martin Dunford and Phil Lee 2002

504pp, includes index
A catalogue record for this book is available from the British Library.

ISBN 1-85828-871-1

3   5   7   9   8   6   4

Help us update

We've gone to a lot of effort to ensure that the first edition of **The Rough Guide to Belgium and Luxembourg** is accurate and up to date. However, things change – places get "discovered", opening hours are notoriously fickle, restaurants and rooms raise prices or lower standards. If you feel we've got it wrong or left something out, we'd like to know, and if you can remember the address, the price, the time, the phone number, so much the better.

We'll credit all contributions, and send a copy of the next edition (or any other Rough Guide if you prefer) for the best letters. Everyone who writes to us and isn't already a subscriber will receive a copy of our full-colour thrice-yearly newsletter. Please mark letters: "**Rough Guide Belgium and Luxembourg Update**" and send to: Rough Guides, 80 Strand, London WC2R ORL, or Rough Guides, 4th Floor, 345 Hudson St, New York, NY 10014. Or send an email to **mail@roughguides.com**

Have your questions answered and tell others about your trip at **www.roughguides.atinfopop.com**

Acknowledgements

Phil and **Martin** would like to extend a special thanks to Sue Heady, of the Belgian Tourist Office – Brussels & Wallonia; Ailsa Uys of Tourism Flanders–Brussels; and Jean Claude Conter of the Luxembourg Tourist Office. Thanks are also due to Suzy Sumner, who helped with Brussels. **Gavin** thanks Clare Jones, Ailsa Uys and Sue Heady for help with travel arrangements; Phil, for introducing him to previously unimagined corners of Flanders and the Ardennes; and Allison, for seeing him through a very wet weekend in Brussels. Collective appreciation goes to our extremely diligent and hard-working editor, Richard Lim; Maxine Repath, Ed Wright, Katie Pringle and Stratigraphics for the maps; Link Hall and Rachel Holmes for typesetting; John Sturges for proofreading; and Zoë Nobes for picture research.

Readers' letters

Thanks to all the following for their letters and emails: Kelley Alexander, Patrick Baughan, Peter Bennett, George Blazyca, Charles Booth, Paul Brierley, John Burton, Nigel Byrne, Sylvia Chen, Paul Cross, Ursula Davey, John & Frances Davies, A. Davis, Barry Dawson, Luc Fossaert, Linda Gibbs, Ivor Grote, John Harris, Luna Hawxwell, Stephen Hayward, Peter Howard, Kevan Hubbard, Georgina Hutber, D.M. Jennings & K.W. Tipping, N.J. King, Christine Minshall, Jacquie Mowbray, Gareth Nortje, Claire O'Donnell, John Parrott, M.I. Readman, Jim Reese, David Rogers, Neil Roland, Alison Ross, M. Rudman, Ana Russell, Dena Seki, Anamaria Crowe Serrano, Keith Spanner, David Stocker, Cathy Tero, Richard Thorpe, Dawn Tilbury Joris Verboomen, Toni Vitanza, John Wall, Cynthia Warden, Mick Welch, and I. Williams.

SMALL PRINT

Photo Credits

SMALL PRINT

around the world

in twenty years

London Mini Guide ★ London Restaurants ★ Los Angeles ★ Madeira ★ Madrid ★ Malaysia, Singapore & Brunei ★ Mallorca ★ Malta & Gozo ★ Maui ★ Maya World ★ Melbourne ★ Menorca ★ Mexico ★ Miami & the Florida Keys ★ Montréal ★ Morocco ★ Moscow ★ Nepal ★ New England ★ New Orleans ★ New York City ★ New York Mini Guide ★ New York Restaurants ★ New Zealand ★ Norway ★ Pacific Northwest ★ Paris ★ Paris Mini Guide ★ Peru ★ Poland ★ Portugal ★ Prague ★ Provence & the Côte d'Azur ★ Pyrenees ★ The Rocky Mountains ★ Romania ★ Rome ★ San Francisco ★ San Francisco Restaurants ★ Sardinia ★ Scandinavia ★ Scotland ★ Scottish Highlands & Islands ★ Seattle ★ Sicily ★ Singapore ★ South Africa, Lesotho & Swaziland ★ South India ★ Southeast Asia ★ Southwest USA ★ Spain ★ St Lucia ★ St Petersburg ★ Sweden ★ Switzerland ★ Sydney ★ Syria ★ Tanzania ★ Tenerife and La Gomera ★ Thailand ★ Thailand's Beaches & Islands ★ Tokyo ★ Toronto ★ Travel Health ★ Trinidad & Tobago ★ Tunisia ★ Turkey ★ Tuscany & Umbria ★ USA ★ Vancouver ★ Venice & the Veneto ★ Vienna ★ Vietnam ★ Wales ★ Washington DC ★ West Africa ★ Women Travel ★ Yosemite ★ Zanzibar ★ Zimbabwe

also look out for our maps, phrasebooks, music guides and reference books

The ideas expressed in this code were developed by and for independent travellers.

Learn About The Country You're Visiting

Start enjoying your travels before you leave by tapping into as many sources of information as you can.

The Cost Of Your Holiday

Think about where your money goes - be fair and realistic about how cheaply you travel. Try and put money into local peoples' hands; drink local beer or fruit juice rather than imported brands and stay in locally owned accommodation. Haggle with humour and not aggressively. Pay what something is worth to you and remember how wealthy you are compared to local people.

Embrace The Local Culture

Open your mind to new cultures and traditions - it will transform your experience. Think carefully about what's appropriate in terms of your clothes and the way you behave. You'll earn respect and be more readily welcomed by local people. Respect local laws and attitudes towards drugs and alcohol that vary in different countries and communities. Think about the impact you could have on them.

Exploring The World – The Travellers' Code

Being sensitive to these ideas means getting more out of your travels - and giving more back to the people you meet and the places you visit.

Minimise Your Environmental Impact

Think about what happens to your rubbish - take biodegradable products and a water filter bottle. Be sensitive to limited resources like water, fuel and electricity. Help preserve local wildlife and habitats by respecting local rules and regulations, such as sticking to footpaths and not standing on coral.

Don't Rely On Guidebooks

Use your guidebook as a starting point, not the only source of information. Talk to local people, then discover your own adventure!

Be Discreet With Photography

Don't treat people as part of the landscape, they may not want their picture taken. Ask first and respect their wishes.

We work with people the world over to promote tourism that benefits their communities, but we can only carry on our work with the support of people like you. For membership details or to find out how to make your travels work for local people and the environment, visit our website.

www.tourismconcern.org.uk

TourismConcern

Campaigning for Ethical and Fairly Traded Tourism